Breaking into
Commercials -11

Terry Berland

New and Revised 11th Gold Edition
Custom collection of resources
Expert Interviews, L. A. Hangouts

D0197571

YES, YOU CAN LIVE YOUR LIFE AS AN ACTOR!

*Acting Is Everything you do, you are,
you have been or hope to be in your life.*

*What you need to know to master acting is
everything you need to know to master your life.*

Welcome to *Acting Is Everything*. In this 11th Gold Classic Edition, I will guide you toward fulfilling your dreams, giving you important information about developing the actor inside you. I share ideas, facts and many special secrets for establishing your career.

If your dream is to live your life as a professional actor, your first tool is your basic acting craft. Good training helps you discover the power, control and confidence to act. Once you have confidence and know how to interpret a script and develop a character, then the business side of acting begins. It takes desire, guts, preparation, discipline, talent and luck to have an acting career.

This advice has helped bring a great deal of success to countless readers and many of my students over the years. I hope it will do the same for you.

Judy Kerr,
Studio City, California

What people are saying about this book and Judy Kerr:

"Practical information and sound advice. I use it myself."
Joel Asher, Acting Coach/Director

"Informative and to the point. She knows the roads that every actor must walk on." Michael Richards, Actor

"If show biz had a good mother, it would be Judy!" Jennifer Grey, Actor

"A great handbook for every actor, beginner or pro!"
Beverly Long, Casting Director

"A must for anyone thinking of getting into show business. It is more than a guidebook. . . it is a bible." Jonathan Silverman, Actor

"A must-read for actors who are serious about a career."
Eric Morris, Acting Coach/Author/Director

"Judy is an inspiration and a love." Maureen McCormick, Actor

"When I first came to Los Angeles, this book could have saved me from getting ripped off many times." Ernest Borgnine, Actor

"For any actor who wants to know the who's, what's and where's of L.A."
Deborah Kurtz, Casting Director

"I wish I'd had this book when I was starting out." Susan Blakely, Actor

"Judy Kerr's book will help you get jobs and grow as an artist."
Joan Darling, Director/Acting Coach

"If you really want to know how to make it in Los Angeles, this book is a must." Bill Macy, Actor

"More real help per page than stacks of other books on the subject!"
Al Burton, Producer

"Excellent. Helpful and direct." Bud Cort, Actor

"Rich with the wisdom of a dedicated professional."
Eve Brandstein, Casting Director/Producer/Director

"Don't make the mistake so many actors make. Read this book."
Dan Gauthier, Actor

"It took me fourteen years to discover the Hollywood secrets that Judy Kerr gives you." Dianne Kay, Actor (Eight Is Enough)

Buckets of gratitude to my husband Ron Gorow—without his love, support and formatting skills you would not be reading this; my daughters, Christina, Cynthia and Catherine for their encouragement and enthusiasm; friends: Robin Gee for her time, inspiration and start-up skills; Steven Nash for his valuable opinions; Samantha Harper for her magic; assistants: Christine Niemi, Tricia Gilfone and Carol Hernandez; proofreaders: Ron Gorow and Bonnie Howard; to the two newest people in my life: my research editor Jim Martyka who has helped me produce this edition with joy and ease, and to my friend Distinguished Professor Charles Rossman, who has awakened me to the world of literature and language—you have made this truly the golden edition. Finally, to my teacher Joan Darling, for her continued guidance and all my students over the years for whom this was written.

Thank you to the many experts who have been so generous with their contributions, especially:

Joan Darling
Lori Frankian
Bonnie Gillespie
Carlyne Grager
Wendy Haines
Bonnie Howard
Kimberly Jentzen
Jim Martyka
Steven Nash
Scott Sedita
Brittani Taylor
Michael Wallach
Caryn West

Cover Design: Thomas Cobb and Greg Hain

Cover Photo: Kevyn Major Howard

ACTING IS EVERYTHING

An Actor's Guidebook for a Successful Career in Los Angeles

by Judy Kerr

11th Gold Edition, Completely Revised

Fall, 2006

September Publishing

Studio City, California, USA

ActingIsEverything.com

Distributed By:
SCB Distributors
15608 South New Century Drive
Gardena, California, 90248, USA
800/729-6423
scbdistributors.com

ACTING IS EVERYTHING

An Actor's Guidebook for a Successful Career in Los Angeles
by Judy Kerr

Published by: **September Publishing**
Studio City, California, USA
actingiseverything.com
Distributed by: **SCB DISTRIBUTORS**
15608 S. New Century Dr., Gardena, CA 90248, USA
800/729-6423
scbdistributors.com

Copyright © 1981, 1989, 1992, 1994, 1997, 2000, 2003, 2006
1st Edition 1981
2nd Edition 1983, updated
3rd Edition 1988, updated
4th Edition 1989, completely revised
5th Edition 1990, updated
6th Edition 1992, completely revised and expanded
7th Edition 1994, completely revised and expanded
8th Edition 1997, revised, updated and expanded
9th Edition 2000, completely revised and expanded, first printing
9th Edition 2000, second printing, updated
10th Edition 2003, completely revised and expanded
10th Edition 2004, second printing, updated
11th Gold Edition 2006, completely revised and expanded

Publisher's Cataloging in Publication Data
Kerr, Judy
Acting Is Everything: An Actor's Guidebook for a Successful Career in Los Angeles by Judy Kerr.
—11th edition, completely revised.
Bibliography: k.
Includes index
1. Acting—Guidebooks, handbooks, manuals, etc.
2. Career—Guidebooks, handbooks, manuals, etc.
Library of Congress Catalog Card Number: 99-60713
ISBN-10: 0-9629496-6-3
ISBN-13: 978-0-9629496-6-1

Table of Contents

SECTION ONE

Developing Your Talent

SECTION TWO

Pictures and Resumes

SECTION THREE

Working As An Actor

Section Four

Professional Tools

SECTION FIVE

Career Team

SECTION SIX

Personal Tools

Creating Your Style and Image

SECTION SEVEN

Acting Is Everything

SECTION EIGHT

Becoming Geographically Desirable

SECTION NINE

Child Actors

SECTION TEN

Cities Outside of Los Angeles

REFERENCE SECTION

BEGINNERS: HOW TO GET STARTED

This book offers advice for actors at all stages of their careers. Here, I am speaking to beginners and actors new to Los Angeles.

To prepare to come to Los Angeles, act where you live. Read about acting, writing, directing, producing, editing; read screenplays and plays. Listen to books at audible.com. Take classes at your local college—English, literature, writing, speech, communications. The reading and writing can lead to writing a short film. Invest in the industry software Final Draft, finaldraft.com. This software contains many scripts from films and television shows. You can use them to learn how scripts are written, and use them for acting scenes. Gather a group together to read and discuss scripts, to write and shoot short scenes. Edit the scenes. In editing, you will learn about acting and the camera.

When you move to Los Angeles you must move into the center of things—the Valley, Hollywood, the West Side. Don't even consider Ventura, Riverside or Orange counties.

"It is in your moments of decision that your destiny is shaped." – Anthony Robbins.

Fear is usually what stops us from trying something new. Learn how to "act as if" you are not afraid. Develop and value your beginner's mind. You can't be good right off the bat. Acting is a craft. If you tried to play a musical instrument or draw a picture you would not expect to be good, you would be willing to not know how to do it. You would jump in and try to play a couple of chords or to draw a tree trunk. Because acting is walking and talking it looks like it should be easy. But you have to learn things, you have to exercise muscles—so to speak—to get some experience to start to sound and look like your real self when you are saying words off a page others have written.

"You gain strength, courage and confidence by every experience in which you really stop to look fear in the face... You must do the thing you think you cannot do." - Eleanor Roosevelt

"If you want to be more successful, double your failure rate." - Bill Gates

There is so much to do, it is overwhelming and demanding. It is action. It always takes more time to accomplish what needs to get done than you think it should. Take action, jump in.

Michelle Danner teaches a monthly Technique Breakdown weekend intensive where she instructs how to build a character from scratch. Scott Sedita teaches a one-day comedy intensive. Todd Rohrbacher teaches improv classes. Actorsite provides classes and seminars for their members. Sign up for the free showbiz email newsletters. These are steps to take to explore the idea of being an actor. This book will guide you on investigating many paths.

Some people try to become actors without making the dollar investment in themselves. One of your most important tasks is to find something you are good at and you enjoy doing to earn a living. It is grand when you have a craft that you can exchange for something like classes and headshots.

ACTORS by David Ackert

Actors are some of the most driven, courageous people on the face of the earth. They deal with more day-to-day rejection in one year than most people do in a lifetime. Every day, actors face the financial challenge of living a freelance lifestyle, the disrespect of people who think they should get "real" jobs, and their own fear that they'll never work again. Every day, they have to ignore the possibility that the vision they have dedicated their lives to is a pipe dream. With every role, they stretch themselves, emotionally and physically, risking criticism and judgment. With every passing year, many of them watch as the other people their age achieve the predictable milestones of normal life—the car, the family, the house, the nest egg.

But they stay true to their dream, in spite of the sacrifices. Why?

Because actors are willing to give their entire lives to a moment— to that line, that laugh, that gesture, or that interpretation that will stir the audience's soul. Actors are beings who have tasted life's nectar in that crystal moment when they poured out their creative spirit and touched another's heart. In that instant, they were as close to magic, God, and perfection as anyone could ever be. And in their own hearts, they know that to dedicate oneself to that moment is worth a thousand lifetimes.

How To Use This Book

• **You are holding a workbook.** It is designed to be studied, highlighted marked in. Using this book as a guide, many actors and potential actors have traveled from all over the country to fulfill their dreams, seeking fame and fortune in Los Angeles. I love to see their well-used copies of *Acting Is Everything*.

• **This book is big**—think of each section as almost a separate book. This is not necessarily a book to be read cover to cover. Study and take the appropriate actions for what is most important to you. I've tried to give you some information on most aspects of the acting/entertainment business. Discover your own favorite people and services.

• **To get the full benefit** from this book, you must have a computer and computer skills, a printer, an email address and be *internet savvy*. My advice is to start or upgrade to a MAC; it is the entertainment industry standard. If you're stuck with a PC, it will also serve you well.

• **Your cell phone should have a Los Angeles prefix**, 310, 323, 213, 818. When you have an out of the area prefix you are considered to be just passing through and are not taken seriously.

• *Acting Is Everything* is protected under copyright law but you have my permission to make copies of pages you need to keep with you and to share with your friends. I think they'll need and want a book of their own.

• **I can't always resolve the he/she pronoun issue,** so I have broken the rules; I use *they* and *their* as singular pronouns meaning *he* or *she.*

• **I love beginnings and helping you make your dreams come true.** Now is the time to turn your dreams into goals and to aim your heart toward them.

• **"Our doubts are traitors,** and make us lose the good we oft might win by fearing to attempt." - William Shakespeare

• **"You can't let doubts get in your way.** Just do it, be bold. Mighty forces will come to your aid." - Anthony Hopkins

• **"Get the knack of getting people to help you** and also pitch in yourself. A little money helps, but what really gets it right is to never... I repeat, never, under any conditions, face facts." - Ruth Gordon

• **Let the fears and doubts be there** and still go for your dreams. You deserve it.

actingiseverything.com.

About the Resources
Listed in _Acting Is Everything_
and
What's available on the Website

• **All of the resources included** have been personally researched by me and Jim Martyka, my research editor. I have used most of the services myself or have had excellent reports from my students and friends who have used them.

• **In this 11ᵗʰ Gold Edition,** many new resources have been added. Others have been reviewed and updated and some deleted. In Los Angeles, phone area codes change fairly often; we do our best to have the latest ones for you.

• **New information and updated resources** are downloadable from the website, actingiseverything.com.

• **Also on the website are many links** to other showbiz sites. Documents available for downloading are: _On The Set Vocabulary, Online Demo Reels_, and the _Showbiz Websites_. There are flyers for past workshops I've taught in cities outside of Los Angeles, pictures of when I worked on _Seinfeld_ and other shows, a reading list, a link for actors based in Los Angeles to sign up for my Email News Group.

• **If you have a problem** with any of the businesses listed, please let me know by email: judy@JudyKerr.com.

• **I provide resources to help you begin your own list** of special people and services. Always research your contacts carefully; prices and integrity have been known to change. This book will point you in the right direction and help you get the maximum value for every dollar spent.

I BELIEVE...

- That we can fulfill our dreams.

- We must accept responsibility for our actions and choices.

- We choose our paths daily and are offered many opportunities.

- It takes extreme focus and clear intentions to fulfill our dreams.

- We need tenacity not to give up and to see adversities as opportunities.

- It takes extreme curiosity.

- We must use time and organizational skills to our advantage and respect them for the power they give us.

- When we operate from poverty thinking, we will always be lacking.

- Without a developed spiritual life and fundamental values/beliefs, we will not experience real joy and are likely to feel empty.

- Having fun can be the most important goal in life.

I've written this book for you.
I want to help you design an artistic
career and to live life as an actor. . .

so the journey begins...

Section One
Developing Your Talent

Preparing For Success
AND
Living Your Dream

- **Making a living as an actor** is a worthy goal and a grand dream. I believe it is attainable for many. However, most actors never achieve this dream. From what I have observed, actors who make a good living, or even become wealthy, always seem surprised and grateful.

- **My goal, my dream is to help you become a working actor**; an actor who is enjoying the process of being an actor, one who understands that the process is the journey. During this process you reset your goals over and over even though the dream may remain the same. Living life as an actor can mean earning a living doing something else. You may have years of working as an actor and also years of acting without having a paying acting job.

- **By following the advice in this book** from the experts I quote and from my experiences, you can create opportunities to make money as an actor and fulfill your personal acting goals.

- **If you have chosen this career** because you want to be rich and famous and you think this book will have the answers, choose another book. You can sacrifice your whole life chasing after those dreams without achieving them. There are many other professions, even in show business, that if done well, can bring wealth. Fame can come in many ways—get on a reality show.

• **Spike Lee,** when interviewed on *Inside The Actors' Studio,* spoke of how difficult an actor's life is when dealing with the many rejections. "It's a very, very tough business, but if this is what you want to do, if it's what you love, then you're not going to let that stop you from doing what you want to do."

• **Steven Nash, personal manager, producer** and president of the Talent Managers Association says, "Actors and creative people who aim to make it in Hollywood have to trust that being true to the journey is the real measure of a successful life."

• **Whatever your acting career dreams and goals are,** creating a successful business to support and propel your career is necessary and exciting. Simply speaking, an acting career consists of three components: the acting (which is the art), the business and your dream. As you begin to develop your career, you are in fact, setting up a small business in which you are both the president and CEO. When setting up your business, you'll be making many decisions and purchasing quality goods and services for, hopefully, the best price. This book will guide you as you make those decisions. The best career choices are made when you follow your instincts and use your own good judgment, based on who you are and your values.

• **To be an actor you must act.** Study, always study, and find places to express your art; act for audiences and for the camera. If you have the business but not the art, you are likely to feel something is missing in your life. Discover the ways to satisfy the artist within your soul.

• **Lucille Ball,** speaking about why she succeeded: "I acted anywhere and everywhere they would let me."

• **Develop the art and the business** so you will have a well-rounded, enduring acting career. Labors of love (usually jobs without financial reward) often lead to life-changing career paths.

• **Lili Taylor,** when asked by *Back Stage West* what she would say to actors trying to break into the business, said: "Have faith and trust. And know that there are no rules. Knock down rules."

- **Joan Darling, Emmy-award winning director, acting coach and actress:**

Q: What does it take to be a success in this business?

- **There are two things** you have to make a delineation between. One is to succeed in the business, which takes one set of skills, and the other is to succeed for yourself as an artist, which is another kettle of fish altogether.

- **To succeed in the business,** you have to come to where the business is happening, which is either New York or Los Angeles. Get yourself into an acting class; that is how you meet people and begin to network. You need a resume, good pictures and an audition scene, three minutes long, that shows you off. Show the scene to anyone who will let you. Go to all the open calls and start to get used to auditioning; work breeds work.

- **If you can't get in the door anywhere,** then get together a little showcase, rent a theater and invite as many people as you can. Start networking, which is why class is very helpful—any kind of class that gets you in touch with other actors, because that's where you begin to get the information about how to do it. Learn everything you don't know; study body movement, voice and speech. The more skills you have, the more chances you have to succeed.

- **Make a list of anyone you or your parents know** who is connected with the business. Contact them all and see if there is anyone they can introduce you to, so you can start making your own connections in the business. Keep performing someplace and get people in to see you. And the rest of it is: pray a lot.

- **Jay Bernstein, manager, writer, publicist, producer, director** and EMMY winner, taught a course called *Stardom, the Management of, the Public Relations for, and the Survival and Maintenance In*. He managed careers for many stars, including Farrah Fawcett, Drew Barrymore, Suzanne Somers, William Shatner, Donald Sutherland, Stacy Keach, Mary Hart and Linda Evans.

Q: What does it take to be a star?

- **To be a star, everything has to be 100%** with your talent, your representation and your presentation. For example, if you're talented and you present yourself well but you don't have an agent, it's going to be pretty hard to get a job—so your representation is failing. If you're very talented and the representation is the best you can get but you dress like a rock star, they're probably not going to hire you to play a nun—so that's your presentation.

- **If your presentation and your representation** are wonderful, maybe you need some work on your talent. If talent is a problem, maybe there won't be stardom. There's nothing you can do with just representation and presentation. I think that talent is 35% of making it. The other 65% is having the right team with you.

- **The team is the right agent who gets you the jobs**, the right personal manager who gives you direction, the right business manager who makes sure your money grows as your career grows, the right entertainment attorney because there's an awful lot of small print in Hollywood, and the right public relations person that will help you maximize what you've done.

Q: What if actors are shy about asking for help?

- **If you don't ask, the answer is already no.** The worst thing that will happen if you ask is, the answer will still be no.

Scott Sedita of the **Scott Sedita Acting Studios** and the acting coach on the E! series *Fight For Fame.* KTLA-TV calls him: "One of the hottest coaches in town." I asked what he thought it takes to make it in Hollywood. Is it luck?

- **During my 20 years in the business** as a talent agent, casting director and acting coach, I've seen many actors become successful working actors, some even big stars. They all had the same three things in common: talent, perseverance and confidence. I believe you can't take one component out of the equation. If you have confidence and perseverance but no talent for acting, you'll never make it, and I don't care who your daddy is. You can't just have talent and confidence without perseverance, because no one is going to knock on your door and hand you a three-picture deal. And equally as important is self-confidence; you have to always believe in yourself. If you let the business regulate your self-esteem, you'll be in big trouble.

- **In class, I talk a lot about the "I want"** (objective) of a character and the obstacles he/she endures in order to get what they want. The same is true for actors. You have to want it. Passionately. If you can enjoy the process and stay on the path, no matter what obstacles come your way, you will make it.

- **Many people believe that luck** should be part of this equation. I believe luck is when opportunity meets preparation. If you study hard, put yourself out there and believe in yourself, you'll be prepared when the opportunity arrives.

- **Antwone Fisher's first screenplay,** based on his life, was made into a movie. The first-time director was Denzel Washington, who also had a starring role in the movie. Another success story is how Derek Luke landed the starring role playing Antwone Fisher.

• **Antwone Fisher was an abused child and homeless teen.** He began his career in show business in 1992 as a security guard on the Sony Pictures lot. His boss became interested in his life story. Several producers were interested too but wouldn't hire Antwone to write the script. He had been taking a screenwriting course. Producer Todd Black said he would hire him and helped him write 41 drafts of the screenplay. The picture was shot in 2002, ten years after Antwone's arrival in Los Angeles.

• **Derek Luke had started working as a clerk** in the gift shop on the Sony Pictures lot in 1997. Antwone was now writing the screenplay and would often stop by the gift shop to visit. They became friends and many times talked about their life stories. When they were doing the first open-call auditions Derek couldn't get an appointment, so he crashed it. He says he was "horrible." But the production of the film was stalled for two years allowing him time to prep himself and again go after the role he felt he "had" to play. When the time came for the next round of auditions he was ready, he got callbacks and finally to read with Denzel. Then he waited to hear.

• **Denzel Washington,** two months later, came into the gift shop to tell Derek he had the part. Denzel said, "Derek was jumping, screaming, crying, laughing." After shooting *Antwone Fisher* and before it was released, Derek landed two more films—an independent film, *Pieces of April,* and an action movie, *Biker Boyz.*

• **Derek encourages actors to continue to pursue their dreams.** "There have been so many dreamers like me. Everyone out here [in Hollywood] has a mission."

• **During the above process** these individuals had to make a living; they had hardships. Derek says, "There was a time when we [he and his wife] were homeless, living out of her car, because all I had was a BMX bicycle." He kept working on his craft so he would be a better artist when the opportunities came along. This is the process, the journey.

• **Personally, I haven't known any overnight successes.** It can take years to get a big break but along the way you work on projects that encourage you. You have fun acting. Many times you have to create the break by writing a part for yourself or finding a project and producing it on your own.

• **You will have your dreams, you will set your goals.** This is what starts your adventure. You will accomplish goals but the mystery, the unexpected, the surprises are what the adventurous path is all about. You never know what the final destination might be.

• **Salma Hayek** was Oscar-nominated for *Frida*. This was a project that took her many years to bring into being. Her next project was as a first time director of *The Maldonado Miracle* staring Peter Fonda, Ruben Blades and Mare Winningham. When Showtime asked her to direct, she said, "You're crazy, I don't know how to do that." Then she found a script she liked and said, "Yes, I'll direct." Salma, when talking about dreams, says, "You do something, you give it your best, and then when it's done you let it go and then you dream a new dream."

• **Choices are where the real talent lies.** If you choose to love the process, life can be so much easier. You can learn and grow through pleasure as well as pain; both are simply choices. Try to choose pleasure whenever you can; it's more fun. You will be able to observe people all around you who choose to take the painful road. Acting, though it takes work, is fun and easy; getting the job is tough, but possible. Lots of actors get roles each and every day.

• **Acting is an art and a craft.** Some people make a living at acting while others act and make their living doing other things. Both ways are valid and artistic. Being an actor takes dedication, desire and ambition beyond reason. Most actors are gamblers—there is something about gambling with your life and your security that is attractive to you. An actor must be a survivor, must persevere.

• **James Gandolfini** (*The Sopranos*) when receiving his Best Actor s tatuette at the SAG Awards said, "To all the actors who are working hard and struggling, things can change very quickly. Hang in there. Enjoy what's happening to you now 'cause things get pretty weird later on if it works."

• **Show business is the most exciting business** in the world and no one can keep you out of it. No matter how big your dreams are, how long it takes or what paths there are to follow, you are willing to do it. Why? For the THRILL of putting yourself on the line, jumping off the cliff, wonderful close-ups and actors you respect telling you they enjoy your acting work. A career break can be a phone call away; don't let anyone convince you differently. Make your choices and commit. You can have everything you *intend* to have.

• **Abraham Lincoln** said, "Always bear in mind that your own resolution to succeed is more important than any other one thing."

What Is Acting?

• **Acting is living your life**, then using those experiences to enable the audience to experience their own lives and emotions.

• **Acting *in the moment*** is always the goal. The *moment* is that instant in time when the actor's imagination and talent create a flash of truth. The audience recognizes and identifies with this truth and is transported and moved.

• **Robert De Niro** said, "Sometimes I get moments I know are right on the head, almost an epiphany, knowing you're exactly there; you're in the moment, in character. Most of the other times it's just a struggle to get through it and hope that it's right."

• **Emmy Award-winning Director Joan Darling** said, "Acting, when it is done at its best, is behaving as if you were alive in a set of given circumstances that are different from your own given circumstances."

• **Richard Dreyfuss** said, "An actor's job is not to feel things, it is to make the audience feel them."

• **Meryl Streep, when asked about spontaneity.** "It's the only thing worth looking at, what nobody expected to happen. In a play, when somebody drops something, forgets a line, suddenly it all becomes electric, alive, it all feels real. The spontaneous is what you dream of, wish for and hope appears."

• **Actors cannot always depend** on this *spontaneous moment* happening by accident or luck. By learning the craft of acting, you can *deliver the goods* on demand, whether you feel like it or not. In acting classes, you can learn the craft of using your own life experiences as your acting tools.

25

• **Acting is a physical, athletic event.** As you are always in a changing, growing process, you need to develop an awareness of what is going on in your life at all times; be aware of every emotional and physical fiber in your body.

• **Your face, body, voice and spirit** are your billboards—what sells you. They are what the casting directors who interview you notice first. You cannot have the right *look* for every role, nor can you figure out what each director, producer or writer has in mind for each role. However, you can make the best of every casting meeting by figuring out who you are and giving of your whole self at each and every meeting.

• **Discovering the *inner you*** takes time spent thinking, reading and soul searching. Finding the *physical you* takes honesty when looking at yourself in the mirror and on camera. Presence, vocal quality, hair, makeup, clothes, weight, height and your spiritual development are all important aspects of the presentation of your unique self. Only you can decide who you are and then make the commitment to perfect and fine-tune your acting instrument—you.

• **The best part** about all this self-discovery is that it makes you an actor every minute of the day. Even though it may have been a long time since a job or interview, you are still working, studying, preparing all the time. Actors usually don't work as much as they would like, so it is very important to enjoy the process, the privilege of living an actor's life. If you become discouraged and unhappy, the great destroyer—negativity—sets in.

• **Tom Hanks, on acting as a profession.** "It requires a knowledge of why you're doing it in the first place. If it's power, well, you'll never be able to hold on to that. It it's money, eventually they are not going to pay your price; it's going to drift away. If it's influence, that's going to shift as well. If your sense of purpose for doing it is because there is no life like it and it's more fun than you can imagine and you'd be doing it anyway, then you might be a little ahead of the game. I think that's why I do it."

• **Michelle Danner of the Larry Moss Studio** is an acting coach as well as a stage and film director. She said: "Acting is to be interested in going deeper into what it's like to be human."

• **Susan Batson,** head of the New York based Black Nexxus Acting Studio, who has coached many Oscar-nominated actors, said in a *Hollywood Reporter* interview: "A great actor can—with great artistic ease—create a walking, talking human being. To make a walking, talking human being, you have to be connected to the need of this character. A great actor can determine the need of the character and is then able to experience internally the need of that character. The actor is then capable of crafting the expression of that need."

• **Dee Wallace,** wonderful, talented actress and acting coach, said: "Acting is being joyful, trusting, committed and willing to share every ounce of your soul with millions of people."

• **Nicholas Cage** said about shooting *The Rock* with Sean Connery, "It's like playing cops and robbers in the backyard." This is the ideal for every actor to reach in each role. The dialogue and movement will be absolutely believable for the audience.

• **Leonardo DiCaprio** said: "I don't really understand the process. The main thing is just getting into the reality of what the character is, finding all the suitable things to go along with it. I often look at a situation from the outside, like I was a camera."

• **John Malkovich** said: "Acting is a job; if it's not fun, why do it?"

• **Kimberly Jentzen,** acting coach and film director, said: "Acting is an art form of compassion. It is an act of courage. Great acting will move the audience from thinking to feeling, from judging to identifying—giving us subtle but sacred permission to feel when we are too proud to release our own fears, laughter and tears, creating a pathway to experience our connection to each other. When this occurs, a performance is truly memorable."

• **Sally Field** said, "Being an actor is both wonderful and horrible—you never know what's next. After my children, acting's the love of my life, my best friend, my lover, my companion."

• **Harrison Ford**—when speaking of why acting is fun—said, "There is a certain foolish pleasure in having these experiences."

• **Richard Gere** said, "This is what we do in acting—we embarrass ourselves all the time. You have to be able to make a fool of yourself regularly to do this; otherwise it is not going to be any good."

• **Warner Loughlin**, acting coach, director and actress said, "Rather than the putting on of masks, acting is the willingness to rip them off and allow the passion of the inner life to be exposed. It is the great unveiling. Choosing to be an actor is brave and courageous. When you choose to be an actor, you have chosen to be a giver of life."

• **Anthony Hopkins** said, "My goal, principally, is to always get into the technical relaxation that Stanislavski talks endlessly about in his books and just listen."

• **Leigh Kilton-Smith**, acting teacher, coach and director said, "For me acting is listening. Actors are storytellers who work very hard to make it look as though they haven't worked at all. They trust their homework is present and listen. If an actor is listening, they are telling the truth."

• **Cherie Franklin**, actress, coach and on-set dialogue coach said, "Acting is creating 'life' from the written word. A successful actor must master the ability to create and sustain this 'life' while respecting the script, director's vision and always taking into consideration the specific medium, i.e. feature film, sit-com, episodic, stage or commercials, wherein this 'life' must live."

• **Steve McQueen** said, "Acting was hard; playing a role was like reaching inside you and pulling out broken glass." He "treated every script like an enemy."

• **Willliam H. Macy** told *Back Stage West,* "I think an actor's task is to read the script, figure out the action—the objective—and do that and let everything else go hang. We can never forget acting is a big fat trick that we play on the audience. You're standing in a set. It's not real, but it's real enough, and the audience is willing enough to suspend disbelief that there you are in the setting and you're wearing somebody else's clothes that have been designed. So it's the actor's job to figure out what his character wants and to do something that's similar to that so that it looks like you're making it up as you go along. The emotions will follow; they will be there as you need them."

Acting Technique

• **This is the most important section of this book.** A solid acting craft or technique is what makes a career possible.

• **You will probably remember your first acting class session.** Mine was at El Camino College in Redondo Beach. I took a basic acting class in my thirties as a fluke, I thought. In my first class, the teacher presented a scene from *Applause* with two experienced actors. One of them, Bob White, remains a close friend. When I saw those actors on stage, my life changed. I knew I had to learn to act so I could *try* to move an audience like I was moved. That moment in time led me on this adventure.

• **In basic acting class, you learn specific acting tools**—how to develop characters and how to interpret a script. You can decide where to study by going to watch different classes or interviewing teachers to discover who might teach the best techniques for you. There are many acting coaches to choose from. I would encourage you to pick a coach who is supportive, not abrasive or negative. There is no reason to be humiliated in order to learn.

• **If you can afford it**, study basic craft, improvisation, voice and scene study at the same time. Four classes a week and all the homework in between for a year or two would give you a solid foundation. If you could also work in the theater and do student films, you would gain actual experience too. I know this isn't possible if you have to make a living at the same time. If you are not one of those actors who are lucky enough to be funded for a year or two, take on as much as your time and money will allow. Think of it as financing an advanced degree in professional acting. Taking professional classes and landing professional acting roles is what makes you a professional actor.

- **There are several different schools of thought for teaching and approaching acting.** The following are some of the masters, whose methods are still taught today. Some methods might work for you and others might not, but it would benefit you to study the theories of all or at least some of these acting greats: Constantin Stanislavsky, Lee Strasberg, Stella Adler, Sanford Meisner, Uta Hagen and Robert Lewis.

- **The most important technique to learn in acting** is how to make the script look truthful; it is not about how to say the lines; it is about being truthful in your behavior. Follow Marc Durso's instructions below to learn what truthful acting behavior looks like.

- **Marc Durso, acttrue.com, is an acting coach** based in Miami and Los Angeles who conducts worldwide workshops. He teaches the Uta Hagen techniques based on her book, *A Challenge For The Actor*.

  - **The simple is the profound.** Without the accumulation of simple truths in the work, how can you be truthful in the "big, dramatic" moments? How? You can't. You will not have engaged the audience along the path of dramatic life, and they will not accept your "great conflict," your tears, your screams, your heroic fight at the end of the movie. The audience will not trust you. Prior to their study of the Hagen Object Exercises, ActTrue students are required to watch the following films:

  - *The Hunchback of Notre Dame, Grapes of Wrath, Jeremiah Johnson, Bridges of Madison County, Castaway.* The Truth of the acting never changes. These films exemplify how Action with Thought creates Behavior.

  - **In the** *Hunchback of Notre Dame*, Charles Laughton, the monster on the flogging wheel, is given water by the beautiful Maureen O'Hara. Watch the battered, beaten Laughton as he decides whether to take the offered drink. You will see a dozen different thoughts, actions, behaviors and changes of self, of persona, all flashing before our eyes. He transforms into new beings before our eyes. And not a word of dialogue. And all this through a prosthetic mask that covers half of his creative tool: his face.

  - **In** *The Grapes of Wrath*, **Henry Fonda** meets a preacher on a dust bowl road of '30s Depression Oklahoma. Watch Fonda as he swigs and throws the bottle away and invites the preacher to walk with him. Thoughts, images of such violence, behaviors of startling power and clarity all underline the simple Oklahoma drawl, the flat, passionless Midwestern accent. He teaches us that it's not what we say, or how we say it, but what we do that truly connects to the audience.

- In *Jeremiah Johnson*, **Robert Redford** as the last of the mountain men, reaches across the valley toward the Native American warrior, with every fiber of his being, his wants, his needs all flowing from his thoughts through his body, through his fingertips to touch time, to feel peace. Not a word in this scene, yet this is the movie encapsulated in images and action.

- In *The Bridges of Madison County*, Meryl Streep expresses character through her reactions to circumstance. Her behaviors, reactions, say far more than the dialogue. Watch the beginning of the film, as she fixes breakfast for her family to the moment she finally sits down at the table: thoughts, expectations, wants, all racing across her face, and then the scene where she gives directions to the bridges to Clint Eastwood. See her seeing every image: it is the image that connects her to the story, to Eastwood, to the audience. See and Say!

- In *Castaway*, **Tom Hanks** is stranded on a speck of land in the endless ocean. He opens FedEx boxes that have washed ashore. Watch as he creates his truthful human behavior in imaginary circumstances. He speaks only when he reads the card. No dialogue, no "how to say the lines." Just actions and reactions. Simplicity and Truth. Count the number of camera angles in this scene, realize the number of setups, then multiply that by the possible number of takes of each one and you'll see how repetitive and mechanical film acting can be, which demands we connect again and again and again to the cause of what we do, the thoughts, images, judgments, expectations to each and every circumstance. We are in reaction.

- **Scene study classes** are often taken after you've honed your basic craft. The actors prepare scenes and present them to the teacher for critique. It takes personal motivation and homework.

- **Jason Alexander** (*Seinfeld*) gives an understandable explanation of what acting technique is.

  - **Technique for me is:** How do I do enough crafting so that I can re-hearse intelligently, and how do I then make choices that will sustain me for a run? That's all it is. It's nothing that a studied actor has not heard before; it's just very clear-cut. You have to answer four questions: Who am I speaking to? What do I want from them? How am I going to get it? What is standing in the way of what I want?

  - **But it's not just answering the questions**—you have to answer them so incredibly specifically that it can take weeks to come up with answers for these things. You not only have to make choices that are smart but fit the material. And ideally you're making choices that, once you get them, they make your instrument do things so that you don't have to manufacture a performance—they're so strong that when you plug in the right thought, or the right word, or whatever it is, your instrument starts to respond. And that's hard.

- **That's the difference between a craftsman and a non-craftsman.** Actors have to take the responsibility that any artist makes in saying, "I choose that color, that stroke, right there. Right or wrong, there it is." Actors have to say, "I'm not winging it, I'm not waiting to see what happens; I'm making this choice right here with my intelligence and with my instrument."

- **It's especially good when you're preparing sides for auditions.** No one's gonna tell you different; no one's gonna direct you out of it. So you have to be able to craft this material so that it shows you in a great light, shows your range, shows your ability, and shows your everything. How do I walk into that room and be undeniably more masterful than anyone that's walked in before me? It can't just be cockiness, it just can't be, "I know I'm good." It has nothing to do with me being good or not. It's that I'm doing things that the average schmo on the street is not doing. They don't know how. I craft, and they hope. That's the difference.

- **Caryn West, well-respected acting coach, actress, director** and teacher speaks of acting technique.

  - **Good acting is good acting,** in any medium. The foundations of good acting are all found organically in thorough training. The beginning actor learns the skills to pursue objectives, moment-to-moment tactics and actions, factoring in internal and external obstacles to those actions. They learn to inhabit an acute sensory world with physical and vocal skills, to be sensitive to text and subtext, to be a keen listener, to glean information from given circumstances and back-story. They learn to create character detail and nuance, to open the channel of one's being to psychological truth, organic impulses and spontaneity. Actors further learn to foster and fan a comic idea in farce or commedia and to serve the story.

- **Director Martha Coolidge** said, "Acting is an art form and is probably one of the toughest. You need to learn as much about it as any musician knows about their instrument. Ironically, it's a career chosen by people who need to be loved, people who will probably receive 98% rejection in their lives. Without a craft to back you up, you're riding for a fall."

• **Brad Pitt** worked as an extra in 1989 on *Cutting Class*. He says, "I am the living testament that you can learn anything, because I was so bad."

• **Jason Alexander** was doing a scene on *Seinfeld* about why he had to postpone his wedding. It wasn't getting the laughs. The writers changed a line to include the name of the hall the reception was to be held in. On the next take Jason got a huge laugh. I asked him how he did that so fast. He said he immediately identified the reception hall with a place he knew that was specific, eventful, truthful and full of history. The audience couldn't help but identify with his wedding dilemma, believe it, and laugh at his performance.

• **Lisa Kudrow** of *Friends* said about her character, Phoebe: "She's operating out of a huge amount of denial; so many horrible things have happened to her that she would not be able to even breathe another breath if she took it all in. She's in search of whatever feels good. I think Phoebe thinks she's a very talented, struggling artist, but she's just not." When you know the truth of the character you are playing, it will make your acting choices specific and identifiable for the audience.

• **Dustin Hoffman said**, "If an actor can find the personal rhythm to a character, he's home free."

• **Director Martin Scorsese says about Harvey Keitel**, with whom he has worked five times, "He pays scrupulous attention to the smallest detail of a role. I've seen him get deeper and deeper into himself. Harvey travels into very forbidding regions of his soul for his work, and he's able to have that experience and put it on the screen in an absolutely genuine way I find very touching."

• **Laurence Fishburne**, Oscar nominee, says about acting, "I want to startle people in a subtle kind of way—the way people are startled when they catch sight of themselves in a mirror. That's the goal of my work: communicating with people on a much deeper level than whatever is obviously going on. It's not so much about finding the truth as *revealing* it. Getting to the truth requires a tremendous amount of patience because things are only revealed to you when you're ready to deal with them."

• **Sally Field** said, "Anyone who isn't terrified of acting is a liar. I'm always terrified when I know I have to be emotional."

• **Dinah Manoff** said: "My process is to use whatever works. I studied method and it is wonderful. And sometimes I have an onion in my purse in case I have to cry."

• **Dustin Hoffman's colleague, Jessica Lange** said, "Dustin has obsessive curiosity." Meryl Streep said, "His mantra is specificity, specificity, specificity."

• **Danny Glover** said, "Listening is the key to acting. Listening and relaxing, because if you're not relaxed you can't listen."

• **Joan Allen** said, "If you lose your focus, regain it by really listening.

• **Billy Wilder**, legendary director, said about an actor's preparation, "You can tell how good an actor is by looking at his script. If he's no good, the script will be neat as a pin. Charles Laughton's script was so filthy it looked like a herring had been wrapped in it."

• **Anthony Hopkins** told Ed Bradley on *60 Minutes* that Katharine Hepburn gave him his most valuable piece of advice on his first movie, *The Lion In Winter*. She said, "Don't do anything; don't act. Just be what you are. Acting is reacting; just listen."

• **Albert Einstein said**, "Imagination is more important than knowledge. Knowledge is limited."

• **Dee Wallace**, actress and acting coach, answered when I asked her how actors act: "Well, five-year-olds do it 50 times a day. They just get up, have fun, jump in and believe. It ain't the cure for cancer, its just play time. Most of us lose our joy and go into fear. Everything shuts down when we ask 'My God, am I good enough?' When you are in fear you can't go to where your instinct takes you because you are always afraid you are going to go the wrong way. Be in the moment!"

• **Jeffrey Marcus, acting coach** and very sensitive, caring human being asks his actors in class to work with an open heart. I asked Jeffery to explain what that meant.

- **Open-hearted means that the fear and defenses are down** so the love and passion can come to the surface. It's when you're more concerned with what you have to give than what you can receive. It's when you're willing to be seen without artifice, raw and vulnerable. When you are in the moment, trusting the moment and trusting that your talent and being are sacred and non-rejectable. Basically, the fear of rejection or judgment or criticism is overruled by the responsibility of bringing more love into being. It's the first mandate of true creativity.

- **Mala Powers, actress, author and acting teacher** in her Discovery-Guide to the audio CD and cassette titled, *Michael Chekhov: On Theatre and the Art of Acting,* said:

  - **The actor should train himself** to notice the *atmospheres* which exist around him in life—a library, cluttered antique shop, a street fair or the waiting room at an audition. Ask yourself what happens to your psychology and feelings when you are open to these atmospheres.

Q: How do you create what you notice?

  - **These *atmospheres* are simple to create** on the stage or for film through the use of your imagination. Imagine the space, the very air around you to be filled with whatever atmosphere you wish—impending doom, the color blue, a cathedral, a graveyard at midnight, ecstatic joy, a street accident, springtime, champagne bubbles; the choices are endless. Once created, these atmospheres then begin to influence the actors, often guiding their character's reactions and behavior. Emotional nuances are added to the performance. In addition, the audience senses the invisible, but very present atmosphere created by the actors, and an additional bond is formed between them.

Q: What is a good exercise to start with?

  - **Most great performances appear to be effortless.** It is important for the actor to practice the *feeling of ease.* Practice walking with the feeling of ease. Lift your arms with the feeling of ease. Pick up an object, even a chair or a table while consciously employing the feeling of ease. Once you have exercised this many times, you will begin to notice when you tighten-up or are pushing. You can then immediately call up the feeling of ease to come to your rescue.

• **Joan Darling, my teacher,** has been nominated for an Emmy, three times as a director and once as an actor. She won for directing. She was the original director of *Mary Hartman, Mary Hartman*—one of the first women to direct film and television in the 1970s. She is a legendary acting teacher in Los Angeles, New York and Sundance.

Q: Can acting be taught?

• **It is possible to teach someone** the techniques of how to wake up different portions of their own personality in order to create a set of given circumstances inside the actor that are similar to what the character is experiencing. That is a craft that can be taught to anybody; everybody knows how to be alive. It is easier for some people to immediately understand and process this craft almost innately without thinking about it and to be able to do it right away.

• **People tend to think that actors** who can do it right away, because it is easy for them, are talented and other people who can't do it right away aren't talented. I've taught long enough to see that if people work hard enough they will learn everything they need to learn to really be wonderful. I think the measure of whether a person can do it or not is totally dictated by how much they want it.

Q: What are some specific acting tools you teach?

• **Acting is a sport** and you have to learn the tools and techniques in your body. Everything that you know and understand is stored in your body through information you got from your five senses. There is an acting technique called "sense memory" which teaches you how to evoke that memory. When you let yourself remember the different sensory stimulus surrounding a particular event, it wakes up the memory of that event and makes it present for you to use in an acting scene. While people know how to do this by just thinking about an event that is similar to the event in the play, "sense memory" is a real craft technique that wakes up the information of the event for you in a much deeper and much more reliable way.

• **Another acting technique** is called "personalizing." If the other actor on stage is your sister in the play and it is a sister your character hates, then you might "personalize" that other actor as someone you hate, meaning you would deal with them as if they were that person you hate.

• **"Relaxation"** is one of the single most important acting techniques. You really need "relaxation" because when you have impulses come into and go out of your body, any physical tension you have will prevent that flow. Just so you don't make a mistake: "Relaxing exercise" in acting is not like yoga or meditating. You are not trying to calm yourself down; you're simply trying to get your body to let go, relax and be curious about what emotionally is going on with you and to not meddle with it. Don't think you are supposed to become calm when you are "relaxing."

Q: What does "being in the moment" mean?

- **Briefly, "being in the moment"** means that not only does the actor deal with all the stuff they have awakened, with whatever acting technique they use that makes them similar to the play, or allows them to function as if they were in the play, but the actor is also relating to themselves at that moment in time on stage. The actor that allows himself or herself to be totally conscious of their experience at a given moment on stage, along with the work they created as an actor, is much more compelling to watch.

Q: What should new actors focus on?

- **I think new actors should read a lot of plays,** get acquainted with what their appetite is, what parts they love, the little child in them that really wants to be the princess or the athlete in the story.

- **If you are really serious about acting** you need to gather information. Try all kinds of acting techniques. I strongly recommend that new actors be insistent that their teachers are not punitive (punishing) and that their teachers have real information for them. If teachers ask you to do something, they have to be able to tell you how to do it. If they can't tell you how, then they are not teaching you.

- **Look around and see the actors you admire.** Make it a quest to find out how they do whatever you can't do and teach yourself how to do it.

Q: Is acting magic?

- **Yes and no.** I believe there is something magical in acting; in the communication between a person standing on a stage and the people sitting in the audience. An actor can stand on stage in a 1500 seat auditorium and have a wave of jealousy go through her and somebody from the back of the audience will say, "Oh, she's jealous," without the actor saying anything or making a face to show it. That is kind of magical.

- **In terms of learning to act,** there are very pragmatic things you can learn to do. If you do them like a recipe, you will be able to act a scene and act it well. So in that regard, I don't think it's magical at all. The magical question relates back to: do some people have talent and others not? I don't believe that's the case: I believe anybody can learn anything about acting that they need to know to be a good actor.

• **Michelle Danner of the Larry Moss Studio** is an actress, coach, stage and film director. She teaches a weekend *Acting Technique Breakdown Workshop* where she thoroughly discusses using back-story and trigger techniques.

Q: Why is it good to have a backstory for your character?

- **A complex, personal and imaginative back story** on stage and on film will ground in a foundation that gives you authenticity and a freedom to play because you know who you are.

- **To have a diary that you know inside out,** ask a zillion questions and let each one bring out an emotional response. That is how you'll find the physical life, the behavior and the emotional river of your character. Having a backstory is what enables you to listen with the thoughts and point of view that your character would have. This is what makes your performance riveting to watch. Everyone is different; you find your own way to write your backstory whether it's using your personal life, your imagination or a combination of both.

Q: What are triggers and how do you find them?

- **Triggers are tools** that you use to create the emotional river of the character.

- **They're sensory realities** such as visuals, smells, sounds, tastes, textures from your life and from your imagination that produce emotionality in you.

- **Every time you read an article,** watch a movie, the news, a homeless person on the street and you're moved, that's your golden box of triggers and no one has the key to that box but you.

- **You have to live your life, be open, be affected,** stay responsive and dare to feel all the time. It takes courage to do that.

• **Kimberly Jentzen,** acting coach and author of *Acting with Impact* answers:.

Q: What goes on "two inches behind the eyes?"

- **We have witnessed actors "phone in" a performance** and have commented, "the lights are on, but no one is home." We have seen actors speak without digesting what they are saying and watch a manufactured, artificial performance.

- **Acting demands that each image and impulse** radiates from behind the eyes. Physiologically speaking, the optical images collected by the brain are not "two inches behind the eyes", but rather, at the very back of the brain. However, all of your thoughts and ideas come into creation in the frontal lobe, which is one to two inches behind the eyes. In our work, the thoughts and ideas radiated are closer and more readable than we have ever imagined. Your eyes are like pools of water in which your very essence, depth and energy communicate.

• To "radiate" means to send feelings, thoughts and desires. Not to "show" us, but rather, to truly send thoughts and feelings. Before you attempt to act, you must experience the subtext of the material. Those thoughts come through the eyes and permit a genuine performance to effortlessly come through.

• There is no "being in your head," for the experience of the emotion is now coming from behind your eyes. Try it yourself; picture a favorite animal right now. Discover that image is alive right there, behind your eyes. And what follows are the feelings that naturally attach to the picture in your mind. That picture was formed from two inches behind your eyes.

• Alan Ball (*American Beauty, Six Feet Under*) tells this story of Annette Bening during the shooting of *American Beauty*: "During one rehearsal, director Sam Mendes asked the actors where they were before the scene begins. Annette didn't lose a beat: 'I was at the dry cleaner's, and I'm *very* upset because they lost my cream-colored blouse and they shouldn't be allowed to get away with that because it's the second blouse they've lost, and I'm going to write a letter! This can't happen anymore!' Our jaws dropped. It was as though she was channeling." As actors we all need to be this thorough in knowing where we are and who we are at every moment of the character's full life.

• Kim Darby, veteran actress, three-time Emmy and two-time Golden Globe nominee.

Q: From your view point, what is most important in acting?

• You must learn a technique that doesn't involve playing the words, the emotions or the feelings. Actors are afraid the audience won't feel or understand that conflict is going on. You have to play the action in the scene and deal with the resistance you are getting from the other character. When you put the action and obstacle on the other person then the drama and conflict come out of trying to change that person. Acting is not self-absorbed; it is the interaction that is important.

- **This technique shouldn't be academic and complicated.** What do I want and what is keeping me from getting it? There is always preparation. How do I feel at the top of the scene, what am I thinking about, what is my rhythm? You do your preparation and when the scene starts you drop the preparation and play the action again. If you play the results it will not be truthful and the audience will not be involved.

• **Larry Moss is the acting teacher Helen Hunt thanked** when she accepted her Golden Globe, SAG, and Academy Award for *As Good As It Gets*. When Karen Kondazian asked him in a *Back Stage West* interview about acting techniques, he replied:

- **The three things that actors need the most** are relaxation, imagination and the ability to analyze a script.

- **I work enormously with intentions.** And to find those, you need to know who the character is. You've got to understand their background. I'm a great believer in building a character's biography, because once you've done that, you walk into the play or screenplay with a full life. Things like the character's education, religion, relationship to parents, past events that were troubling or exciting, politics, dreams, etc. And what you create should be a combination of your own experiences and your imagination. If you just use yourself and not your imagination or you just use your imagination and not yourself, you're going to come off half-baked. I think it's absurd for any teacher to say that an acting student could just walk in and be themselves in any play. It's almost sophomoric and it's very, very destructive to the actor.

- **Film acting is all about containment**, but you have to have something to contain. The problem that some people have is they have nothing to contain and that's when you see bad acting. All good film and television acting has an enormous volcano in it that's being held back.

• **Janice Lynde, prominent Emmy-nominated,** Obie Award-winning actress and acting coach for actors as well as faculty members at the American Film Institute, teaches directors how to work with actors.

Q: How do you create a character that is very different from yourself?

- **Do research; it grounds you in authenticity.** Choose personalizations, where you may have behaved in a similar way as the character, imitation and sense memories to support the imitation. I find animal exercises enormously valuable. Imitate someone you know who is like the character. Dress like them—I always insist on the right shoes. How do they move? What mannerisms are keys to their psychology? Then personalize the other characters and each "event."

- **Example: When I played Marilyn Monroe,** I watched films and newsreels and read everything I could about her life. I began to imitate her physicality. Then I found a sense memory of a feather tickling my lips, which not only made me look "as if" I were her, but gave me an inner glow. My secret "acting work" tickled me which resulted in giving me an incandescent sparkle. I also did an animal exercise of Kitty, the brown skunk who lived next door. She would taunt my dog, brushing her tail in his face and moving in a slow luxurious, sensual way. Then from scene to scene, I personalized the other characters as people with whom I was very sensual, or vulnerable. My "event" was to get them to love me, including the audience.

- **Example: A heroin addict.** I found a drug rehab center, watched someone in withdrawal and talked to people who had been addicted. I chose a sense memory of an itch I couldn't scratch and a migraine headache for when the character was in need of a "fix." For right after a "fix," I chose a smell from a place remembering thunderous applause and a specific smell after orgasm. For the "high" state, I also did an animal exercise of a gorilla after a nap.

- **Once you have the craft to support your ideas,** your artistry guides you in your choices. It's fun. To me, character work takes me to the edges and depth of my own spiritual being. As a result I "own" more of myself, I am more whole. The process of becoming whole is the most fulfilling aspect of acting.

• **Warner Loughlin,** acting coach, director, and actress, teaches classes and coaches privately. Many professionals, award winners and celebrities are in her master class.

Q: Is there a formula for acting?

- **I believe there is no set formula for acting,** but if some essential elements could be described, I would characterize them as: A) the actor's complete suspension of disbelief, wholly immersed in the moment; plus B) total, specific and extremely detailed knowledge of the character through specific analytical and emotional investigation; plus C) a hefty dose of willingness to focus only on the task in front of you; minus D) the fear of negative comment.

- **One universal formula would be difficult to pinpoint.** Because we have all lived our lives with individual experiences and perceptions of the world, each of us possesses a unique inner voice. When we choose to immerse ourselves in the life of a character, our uniqueness of being simmers within that character, allowing that character to be unique as well. The actor therefore constantly births unique gifts into the world. The actor celebrates life.

• **John Kirby, acting coach, director,** teaches classes as well as privately coaches many top industry actors, including international and Broadway personalities.

Q: What are the mistakes you see in actors' work?

• **One of the biggest problems** actors have in their work and especially what they do on auditions is to *suggest* the work! They suggest the character and the events of the script, but never reveal a life—a true living person. They go on automatic and stay in the *event* of the audition. The actor is so caught up on being good or not being bad that they forget these thoughts are of no concern to their character and have nothing to do with what their character wants or is happening in their character's life. The greatest lesson an actor can learn is to own the room and make the place safe to live in!

• **Anita Jesse, acting coach, author** of *Let The Part Play You: A Practical Approach To The Actor's Creative Process* and *The Playing Is The Thing: Learning to Act Through Games and Exercises.*

Q: What would you say is the best method for improving an actor's concentration?

• **It takes time and patience to master concentration.** However, you can learn to choose a mental target, place it at the center of your awareness, and hold it there regardless of distractions. Script exploration, remembering lines, audition pressures, staying in character—all these become manageable only if you master concentration.

• **Sometimes you consciously order your mind** to focus on a particular mental target, then struggle to screen out distractions. Other times it's almost as if the mental target chooses you and everything else seems to automatically fade from awareness. For example, you effortlessly become enthralled by an appealing movie or book, a person you find attractive or your favorite music. It's almost as if you have *unconsciously* hit the switch that focuses attention on a particular object or train of thought.

Q: Would you explain how to do one of the concentration exercises from your book, *Let The Part Play You?*

• **A favorite seems to be,** "Doing My Job." While driving, make that activity the center of your awareness. When your mind wanders, re-focus. When you find yourself thinking about what you will do when you get to your destination or replaying past events, gently redirect your attention to *this* moment—to what is happening right now. Pay attention to the cars around you, the feel of your car, everything happening on the road and exactly how it relates to you. Use variations of this exercise anytime during the day—while reading, eating, talking to a friend or washing dishes.

• **Eric Morris, actor, acting coach** and author, travels the world giving seminars on acting.

Q: What is your approach to teaching technique?

- **I do something that Lee Strasberg** was terrified about, which he would have called "therapy." Psychotherapy it isn't. It's a behavioral-modification therapy. The circle of the work is the instrument, which is the actor—his mind, body, voice, and his emotions. Truth can only come from a place of truth, and unless you accomplish your "being" state, your place of truth, you cannot act from an organic place. So largely the instrumental emphasis of my work is to eliminate obstacles and liberate the actor to be free, to be who he or she is.

- **I ask actors to do the hardest things** for them to do first. To people who are very proper and socially obligated, I give exercises that break down that propriety, antisocial exercises. My work is profoundly life-changing because an actor is liberated to be a free person, to enjoy life on an impressive and expressive level.

- **I teach actors to be professional experiencers.** Your responsibility as an actor is to fulfill the author's intentions, obligations and responsibilities. You have to be able to really experience, from your own frame of reference and inner, organic fabric of emotions, what the character is experiencing. You become, not an actor who acts, but an experiencer who really experiences. You have to be able to discover the next moment of behavior in the next moment, at exactly the same moment the audience does. That's true acting, true experiencing.

• **Joel Asher, well-respected acting coach** and director of film and television, produces training videos for actors.

Q: What acting techniques do you teach?

- **I use many techniques.** Just as a carpenter wouldn't go to a job carrying only one tool, an actor can't do that either. If an actor uses the same technique to audition for a soap opera as a situation comedy, it's not going to work. So I give actors different scenes with different styles, different challenges, so they can constantly be expanding their techniques. I teach weekly technique, professional and master scene study classes. We do exercises and improvisations that grow out of the scene work. These are improvisations that are done to isolate a specific skill and work on that issue.

• **In Don Richardson's book,** *Acting Without Agony: An Alternative to the Method,* he has an extensive list of emotions that may help you when making your acting choices. Here are a few he lists: admiration, amazement, anger, awe, boredom, curiosity, desire, desperation, disbelief, disgust, embarrassment, envy, expectation, fascination, fear, grief, hatred, hope, anger, horror, hysteria, indignation, jealousy, loneliness, lust, panic, pity, pride, relief, remorse, respect, serenity, shame, suspicion and terror. It is absolutely essential to figure out what your character is thinking and feeling. As an exercise, pick any sentence and try using a different emotion each time you say the sentence. This will help you to realize it is the acting that is most important, not the words.

• **On the set of** *Seinfeld* one day, Jerry, Julia and Jason were playing around, thinking of all the ways you can say *"all right"* or *"okay"* and which one should be used in specific circumstances. During the laughter, Jerry said, "Hey, Judy, that would be a great exercise for your actors." It is a great exercise. Try it with your friends.

Acting Training: Coaches and Teachers

• Remember your teachers and give them thanks in your Oscar acceptance speech.

• Besides my husband and children, these are the teachers I want to thank: Bill Kerr, Greg Quandt, Bob White, Rick Davis, Samantha Harper, Joan Darling, Steven Nash; current acting coaches Caryn West, Scott Sedita, Kimberly Jentzen; life coaches Dee Wallace, Wendy Haines and literature tutor, Chuck Rossman.

The mediocre teacher tells. The good teacher explains. The superior teacher demonstrates. The great teacher inspires. - William A. Ward

Great teachers have always been measured by the number of their students who have surpassed them. - Don Robinson

• It takes many teachers in life to develop an actor. Following are teachers, tools, suggestions and recommendations that have helped me and others to develop our lives and careers. There are countless paths, and part of an actor's job is to keep exploring new ones.

• You should always be studying. Your training will be a constant expenditure so don't skimp in this area. Your technique and acting knowledge will make you more employable.

• Choosing an acting coach is an important choice, but it is not a life or death one. Choose one, take a month's classes, give it your all and then evaluate what you have learned. If you've improved and others in class have grown and improved, then stick with it.

- **Jeffrey Marcus, an inspiring acting coach, answers, "Why train?"**

  - **An athlete, musician or doctor** would never ask such a question. If acting were such an easy career, why wouldn't everyone want to do it?

  - **Acting is a discipline that demands such skill,** and yet, can be done without any. Of course, we can all act passionately and emotionally all by ourselves. But when the stakes are high and tension and self-consciousness creep in, we need techniques to fall back on in order to soar.

- **William H. Macy,** when asked in *Back Stage West* about what kind of teachers actors should seek out, said, "I believe that an actor is held in better stead if he doesn't rely on his talent. What you rely on is technique. Talent is given by God and there's no negotiating. Technique is something anybody can learn, and for a technique to be a valid technique, it's got to be scientific. It's got to be repeatable. It's got to be testable. That's what they should look for in a teacher."

- **Eve Brandstein, Casting Director, Producer, Career Coach,** says about choosing an acting coach:

  - **I think you have to see a teacher work.** You could have heard that this is the greatest teacher in the whole world and they've taught some of the biggest names in the business, but if there's no chemistry, forget it. Some actors are better off in a negative situation and others in a positive one. One teacher says, 'Why do you bring that piece of s— into class? You're a terrible actor; who ever said you could act?' And this inspires the actor to greatness. Another teacher says, 'That was beautiful work, but what about this?' And that works for that actor. You have to find out if the teacher and you are magical together.

- **Joan Darling, legendary acting teacher and director:**

Q: Should working actors still go to class?

  - **If you find yourself starting to be disappointed** after you finish a job instead of feeling that you grew and things are wonderful and you can't wait to act again—then you should get into a class where the working on one's art is respected and you have fun. If you don't exercise your acting muscles at top capacity, you'll lose them.

Q: What if an actor can't afford to study?

  - **Find a teacher that you can apprentice yourself to.** Or get other actors with the same desire and meet in your living room once a week. Ask a friend who knows about acting to conduct this workshop for you.

• **Larry Moss, respected acting coach,** when asked about acting teachers in a *Back Stage West* interview, said:

> • **I believe that the aim of a teacher** should be to help the individual students find the tools to realize their greatest potential. When you try to teach from a singular point-of-view or method, you're going to hurt the student.

• **About the expense of acting classes.**

> • **I have actors who hold down two jobs** in order to take class. I think that your education as an actor is something that you pay for because you care about it. It's like therapy. I had a therapist who once said to me, "If you don't think enough of yourself to pay for therapy, how do you think you're going to get well?" I don't think the classes would be as productive for the students if they weren't making some sacrifices. I don't think that life is about getting it easy. I don't think being an artist is easy. I think you get to earn things in life.

• **Cherie Franklin, actress, acting coach and well-known dialogue coach on feature films and television:**

Q: What should an actor gain by working with a coach?

> • **The value of working** with an acting coach on an ongoing basis is this: they can offer a safe environment that can allow you to reveal your fears and bring your work to a place where you can face your truths. This work state will invite you to trust in yourself, creating confidence and steering you clear of self-sabotage throughout your journey as an actor.

Q: Who is your ideal student?

> • **One who is committed to excellence,** to daily homework, to investigating his emotional levels, to understanding his blocks, and understanding what he does and doesn't do well. Someone who wants to be the best actor they can be, who is willing to do all that it takes to get what they want. Homework might include journal work to discover emotional blocks, practicing cold reading, vocalizing, the reading of a play, seeing a TV show or a new director's work and so on. Bottom line, an actor should remember that perfect is an end state. Therefore, as actors, we have the privilege of becoming a better craftsman with each new day, whether working on set or at home. We can continue learning and advancing as the business changes.

Q: How does an actor stay prepared to work between auditions and jobs? Are you an actor when you are not acting?

- **Daily homework and classes** keep an actor prepared. If you are not acting daily on-set, in class or in your bedroom, you are not an actor.

• **Leigh Kilton-Smith, director, teacher** and well-respected on-set coach comments on choosing an acting coach, and what she looks for in a student.

- **Find the acting coach that speaks your language** and addresses the issues you are currently dealing with. No actor should have to compromise, ever. As in all decisions regarding their craft, actors should feel empowered.

- **I look for a student to be committed:** committed to the work beyond their fears and insecurities. Committed to a life of *process*. Actors who are willing to recognize that they are not half-empty vessels waiting to be filled, but are actually artists who seek out teachers, not gurus, as a form of collaboration.

• **Anita Jesse, acting coach and author:**

Q: How can actors make the most of class?

- **Be professional.** Be on time. Be prepared. Be "present." Fully commit all your energies to learning. I'm amazed at how many actors throw away their time and money. If you aren't ready to commit to the training, save your money and wait until you are.

- **Learn to listen.** Learn to take what you can from every comment given you and don't waste time arguing with the teacher. If you disagree with the majority of what a particular coach has to say, you are in the wrong workshop.

- **No one can teach you to be an artist.** Whether or not you become an artist must be left to you and your creative spirit. You hope to find a workshop where you can learn your craft.

• **Dee Wallace, actress, acting and life coach:**

Q: What is important for the actor to learn in class?

- **It is important to know** that everyone is looking for you to bring your own essence, your own idea and your own self to the material.

I think we spend half of our careers trying to figure out what *they* want. *They* want you to come in and bring to the piece *yourself*, totally committed and in the moment.

- **Eric Morris, actor, acting coach and author, says:**

  - **My ideal student** is a person who commits himself to acting on a level of artistry. Somebody who is so committed to the work that it becomes a way of living. Unless you must act, because it's a calling, something you need to do, forget it! It'll break your heart.

- **Joel Asher, well-respected acting coach, describes his ideal actor:**

  - **Someone who is so hungry to grow** constantly that they will be eating, sleeping, and breathing acting 24 hours a day. When an actor is walking down the street, it's a sense memory exercise. You can constantly be training yourself as an actor by being alive in the space that you inhabit. Preparation is the key to spontaneity.

- **John Kirby, popular acting coach,** makes observations regarding actors studying:

  - **It feels like there is a breed of young actors** who want a "quick fix approach" to learning their craft. They run to any cold reading class or gimmick to keep themselves from doing the real kind of work that's going to raise their abilities to greatness. This can be very detrimental to anyone who does not already have a strong foundation in training. Their work becomes automatic, cranked out and extremely technical. They may feel they have given a great audition, what they have produced is slick, and may appear perfect because they did not drop a line or held their sides (script) correctly, but they have revealed nothing in the room that could blow anyone away with their performance. Their audition will lack dimension and effective moments. I love the actors who are in acting for the long run, who invest themselves in the work and take all the time necessary to be truly great.

- **Terrance Hines, acting coach and personal manager,** Hines and Hunt Entertainment, explains why he thinks training is so important:

  - **Whether you are one of the Three Tenors,** a member of the Bolshoi Ballet, an Iron Man in baseball, an Olympic swimmer or a waiter at Denny's, you have a coach and a trainer who warms you up, guides you and prepares you for the physical and emotional struggle that lies ahead that day. For an actor, it is important to be in a class so that your instrument stays flexible and focused.

Unlike a violinist who plays an instrument, you the actor are the instrument you play. It is as wrong to mistreat your body with alcohol and smoke as it is to deny this same instrument the opportunity to be nurtured by exposure to good writing, risk taking and the emotional communion that happens with other artists in a safe landscape. Class offers you the opportunity to share your losses and gains with others who will understand. Compliments or criticism from a fellow artist you trust are the highest form of support and sharing.

• **Scott Sedita,** acting coach on the E! series *Fight For Fame,* featured in a KTLA-TV story titled "Where Young Hollywood Goes and Studies" talks of the kind of training that best helps an actor.

   • **I believe in the development of the well-rounded actor.** Every actor needs to start with a good foundation class to learn the techniques of acting. When you have your foundation take a Scene Study class to work on character development and script analysis. An On Camera class is a must for those actors seeking a career in TV and Film. A Cold Reading class is essential for audition preparation. These types of classes are all offered at my studio. We also offer classes in Sitcom Acting. Every agent and manager in Hollywood wants to find actors who can do half hour comedy. Also important is Comedy Improvisation. I find improvisation really helps actors get out of their heads and be spontaneous in auditions. We also offer Voice and Speech, because an actor should be able to say anything boldly and with confidence. Your voice should be heard and your words should be understood.

• **Kimberly Jentzen,** acting coach and author of *Acting With Impact* answers: How should an actor listen to feedback in class?

   • **Receiving feedback is an actual skill.** Your work must be exciting, electric and captivating. Anything less deserves feedback with insight into how to improve your effect; it should supply you with answers to support your next attempt. Actors sometimes attempt to defend their performance. They are not listening to the feedback as constructive support. Instead they are thinking it is a personal attack. Anytime an actor defends his work, he takes two steps backward. Good acting involves flexibility and adaptability. The actor's performance is enhanced when accepting feedback and incorporating the new direction. A director cannot work with an actor who refuses or rejects feedback.

• **The following list of teachers are experts** and have good reputations. These few are just a small representation of what is available in Los Angeles. Extensive lists of teachers are in the *Working Actor's Guide, The Selective Hollywood Acting Coaches and Teachers Directory* and in special issues of *Back Stage West.* Follow your intuition on choosing a teacher and also when it is time to move on. Some actors change teachers every few months while some keep the same coach for years. Find the way that is best for you to study and grow.

• **If you are reading this outside of Los Angeles,** use these guidelines to pick your teachers in preparation for your move to a bigger market. Good and bad acting coaches teach all over the country. See the teachers in the *Cities Outside of Los Angeles* section.

• **After each acting class, make notes in an acting notebook** on what exercises you did and what the reports were from your teacher and the other actors; put your feelings down too. The exercises you learned in class will be helpful in choosing acting work for your scripts; they are your acting tools. When you are looking for a piece of acting work to help you interpret a script, you can look in your notebook to see if one of the exercises will help you.

• **Keep a copy of all monologues and scenes you do.** They will come in handy when someone asks you to bring in a scene at the last minute or just for practice.

• **Beginners are welcomed by the following teachers:** Judy Kerr, Ron Burrus, Joan Darling, Kimberly Jentzen, Warner Loughlin, Brian Reese, Jamie Rose, Scott Tiler, Michael Bofshever, Bernard Hiller, Jeffrey Marcus, Janice Lynde, Michelle Danner, Dee Wallace Stone, Doug Warhit, John Sudol, Hugh O'Gorman, Cherie Franklin, Joel Asher, Tony Barr, Ivana Chubbuck, Kim Darby, Wayne Dvorak, Laura Gardner, Brad Heller, John Sarno, Laura James, Leigh Kilton-Smith, Ken Lerner, Joanne Linville, Alan Feinstein, Tom Todoroff and Baron/Brown Studio.

• **Almost all of these teachers and coaches** have profiles on IMDB.com so you can look up their credits.

Resources

To download and print an updated version of this and all resource lists, go to actingiseverything.com.

FOUNDATION, BASIC TECHNIQUE AND SCENE STUDY TEACHERS

Judy Kerr's Acting Workshop, 818/505-9373, JudyKerr.com. I'm always available to work with actors privately and on-set. I coach all levels of actors privately and do career counseling. I love beginners. I teach occasional weekend workshops in cities outside of Los Angeles. More about me in the *Private Coach Section*.

Joan Darling's Acting Class, 323/964-3410. $400 for four weekends, once a year in Los Angeles, usually in May. She is a master teacher, director and actress. In North Carolina, 919/928-8088. Don't miss out on the opportunity to have at least one session with her. Very supportive and insightful. Her scene study classes are great even for beginners because she incorporates her very valuable basic exercises. She is also wonderful for working professionals who have been beat up on their jobs; she will help you heal. Lots of homework in this fast paced class. Auditing permitted.

Caryn West Scene Study, 323/876-0394. Los Angeles website: http://groups.yahoo.com/group/CarynWest-ActorsLA. The website for New York actors is: http://groups.yahoo.com/group/CarynWest-ActorsNY. You can subscribe to her very informative, instructional yahoo groups, and receive more information about her classes. $660 for 12 weeks. Four to six scenes an evening. She co-teaches the Scene Study Workshop with director Jessica Kubzansky. Script analysis; actions; character work; comedy dynamics; physicality; pursuing truth; genre/style work; risk taking and acquiring a new skill. A terrific opportunity to hear two different insights. Not designed for the beginner but for those who know the Stanislavsky basics and are looking for growth, especially by working on roles outside your industry typecasting. Caryn also teaches a very well-known and respected six to 11-week Audition Skills Workshop. "There is emphasis on script analysis, breath, presence and spontaneity." Privates are $90 ($75 if a currently enrolled in a class). She regularly teaches in June and December at Michael Howard's Studio in New York.

Kimberly Jentzen, 818/779-7770, kimberlyjentzen.com. Author of *Acting with Impact*. On-going classes as well as the Cold Reading Weekend Intensive, the Essence Weekend Intensive and Singing for Actors-Acting for Singers. Award-winning director and acting coach, creator of audio tapes *Fearless Acting* and *Coming From Love*. She says, "My goal is to create a safe place for actors to take risks, explore and develop skills, stretch their emotional range and learn how to make choices that allow their own individuality, depth and power to emerge." Training covers: scene study, monologues, cold reading, improv, concentration, imagination, audition technique and film acting. Admission by interview/audition. Beginning to master classes. I study with Kimberly in her master class, I look forward to it every week. Auditing available.

Anita Jesse Studio, 323/876-2870, anitajessestudio.com. The author of *Let The Part Play You: A Practical Approach To The Actor's Creative Process* and *The Playing Is The Thing: Learning to Act Through Games and Exercises*. Through her classes and books, Anita Jesse has been providing a practical approach to the actor's creative process since 1978. Anita says, "We offer a technique that prepares you to get work in film and television, yet celebrates and nurtures your creative spirit. It's a delicate balance, and we welcome a limited number of fearless and determined actors who are willing to embrace the challenge." Classes are taught by Anita Jesse and James Ingersoll. Actors work at least twice every week. Placement in classes is by audition and working audit. When members of the classes produce original short films, the studio hosts film festivals to showcase the work. Anita encourages her students to produce a three minute or less short film on their own without her help. There were 16 at the recent festival and the acting was wonderful in each one. The production values were mixed but on an acting reel it is always most important for the acting to be good.

Janice Kent, 818-906-2201, janicekent.com. Small ongoing classes held weekly. $240 per month. Classes are limited in size and very intensive. Audition material is put on camera and critiqued. Emphasis is on understanding the different "forms" as well as your own personal development as an actor in TV/Film. By interview and referral.

Michael Bofshever, 310/281-9580, michaelbofshever.com. Teaches techniques that can be applied to the stage and the camera. Classes meet on Mondays and consist of exercises and scene work. He focuses on you as an individual actor, helping you find the best techniques to unleash your individual creativity. Michael has been a working actor, acting teacher and director for thirty years and knows what he is talking about! Author of *Your Face Looks Familiar: How to Get Ahead as a Working Actor*.

Bernard Hiller, 818/781-8000, bernardhiller.com. On-going classes, held every Thursday 3-7. $385 for six week sessions. Bernard believes that you must first find what is truly unique about you to achieve success. He has been a premier acting and dialect coach for over 30 years. He trains professionals at his studio in Los Angeles and in London, Paris, Rome and Madrid. Actors will learn the latest film acting technique using monologues, scene study, movement and exercises. He will also help you map out a strategy for a long and successful career. The studio offers beginning, intermediate, and professional levels as well as Film/TV casting workshops. An introductory private lesson is required.

Jeffrey Marcus, 323/965-9392, jeffreymarcus.com. $200 for four classes. Jeffrey teaches ongoing basic and advanced technique classes. When I sat in on his workshop I was very impressed with the actors' work and Jeffrey's teaching style. To quote from his website: "My belief is that each actor has talent, wisdom, courage and boldness locked inside him or her. I aim to train the artist to unlock their potential using methods I've gleaned from Stanislavsky to Tantric Yoga and Spiritual Psychology." My favorite quote is, "Wanting to learn to act by taking Cold Reading classes is like wanting to learn to paint by using a 'paint by number' kit." Classes are small so actors can work each week. $15 audit fee may be put towards tuition.

Janice Lynde, 323/650-0515, janicelynde.com. $200 a month on an ongoing basis. She teaches Joan Darling's technique. Working with all levels of actors, she teaches exercises and scene study in a loving, safe environment. Class limited to 15 actors so everyone works every week. She also teaches an audition formula involving three simple acting choices that helps actors book the jobs. She is the author of the book *Ten Minutes to the Audition*. Janice is a working, two-time Emmy nominated actress, winner of an Obie award and director. Also offers private coaching.

Scott Sedita Acting Studios, 323/465-6152, scottseditaacting.com, 526 N. Larchmont Blvd., Los Angeles, 90004. Scott says, "Our goal is to help the actor discover their own unique talent, realize their greatest potential and provide them with knowledge to successfully 'market' themselves in today's competitive industry." Seven staff teachers. Professional Classes: On Camera Television and Film Acting Classes; Situation Comedy Acting Classes; Cold Reading and Audition Techniques; Scene Study; Master Scene Study; On Camera Young Adult Acting Classes; Voice and Speech Classes; Acting Foundation/Technique Courses; Comedy Improv and Commercial Workshop. Industry showcases presented regularly. Public performances presented once a year. Admittance is through the monthly Free Audit Seminar or a one on one interview with a staff member. Speak to Andy for an appointment.

Scott Tiler of the Scott Sedita Acting Studios, 323/465-6152, scottseditaacting.com, 526 N. Larchmont Blvd., Los Angeles, 90004. $330 for six weeks of Nuts and Bolts. Focuses on developing the actor's foundation, technique and the ability to prepare. Incorporates elements of relaxation, repetition, improvisation, imagination and sense memory. Actors work several times each session. Recommended for the new actor and those who need to re-invigorate their technique. Scott also teaches the TV & Film Acting Class focusing on character analysis, emotional depth, living the part and imagery exercises. In this class, students work two or more times per class. Emphasis is on Cold Reading, Scene Study and on camera Audition Technique. This class is $330 for six weeks.

Larry Moss, 310/399-3666, Edgemar.com, 2437 Main Street, Santa Monica, 90405. Professional Scene Study Class. Very famous actting coach from New York, he taught at Juilliard Studio and Circle in the Square. Helen Hunt and Hilary Swank thanked him when they accepted their Academy Awards. Many well-known professionals study scene work with him. Jason Alexander of *Seinfeld* says that classes with Larry Moss are what made his acting career. Highly recommended. No auditing; acceptance is by interview.

Michelle Danner of The Larry Moss Studio, 310/399-3666, Edgemar.com, 2437 Main Street, Santa Monica, 90405. $352 for six weeks in an advanced or intermediate/advanced class. Cold Reading on the big screen exploring all the different genres—horror, period, action/adventure, film/slapstick comedy, sitcom, soap operas, drama, and erotic—is $475 for an eight week tuition. Michelle teaches a weekend $195 Technique Breakdown Workshop that should be taken by all actors who love acting; it's a complete breakdown on how to build a character from scratch. For beginners it brings you to an understanding of what it is to act. For seasoned actors, even those (me) who have been teaching for 25 years, she reminds you what all actors are capable of. Her seminar is required if you are going to study with this organization. **John Cirigliano** is also a very respected teacher at The Larry Moss Studio.

Dee Wallace Acting Studio, 818/876-0386, Ext. 3, dwsactingstudio.com. $250 a month. Put the joy back in acting. Dee is a very special person, actress and teacher. She is interested in the spiritual side of the actor and in helping each actor achieve their best. "A positive approach to fearless acting." Her technique is loosely based on Meisner and Charles Conrad, but she has developed her own way of acting that works under all the pressures you will encounter on the set. The actors are encouraged to treat the class as an on-set working environment. Her required and suggested reading list will be of great value. The class is held in a theater in a church basement. Auditing is required.

Doug Warhit, 310/479-5647, 310/479-5647. $200 for the first month (which includes one private session) $185 a month thereafter. Scene study and cold reading classes, beginning through advanced. All work is geared for television and film and videotaped each week; at the end of each month, an industry guest (casting director, agent, etc.) is invited to observe the actors' work. Casting Director Junie Lowry-Johnson of *Desperate Housewives* says, "I wish I could see actors trained by him at every casting session." My student, David Roth, found the showcasing to be very valuable.

Sal Romeo, 323/665-6360, salromeo.com. $200 a month for one class per week, $275 a month for two classes. A workout for working and intermediate actors. Based in Stanislavski, classes focus on relaxation, self exploration, voice and speech, camera technique, cold reading, improvisation and building the character. Movement, yoga and voice and speech classes are free for actors enrolled in his other classes. Sal has over 25 years of experience in stage, television and film directing, as well as professional teaching. I really like the way Sal thinks and talks about acting. One of his "team teachers" is Michael Nehring, who also teaches at Chapman University. This is definitely a class to check out!

John Sudol, 818/505-1223, johnsudolstudio.com. Teaches acting basics, scene study, audition technique for improving your reading skills and a commercial seminar all about the business. John is a well known and respected acting coach and independent director. Highly recommended from many top industry professionals.

Hugh O'Gorman, 213/840-6729, hughogorman.com. Head of Acting, Department of Theatre Arts California State University, Long Beach. Hugh teaches three eight-week "process" classes a year at his studio in Culver City. The heart of the work is a warm-up based on the technique of Michael Chekhov and the second half of every class focuses on "playing action" in scene work as taught by Earle Gister, formerly of the Yale School of Drama. The classes are small and selective. Admission for intermediate or advanced actors is by audition. Beginners only by interview and audition. Also private audition coaching, workshops in the Michael Chekhov technique and Stanislavski's Event Analysis.

Cherie Franklin, 818/762-4658. $200 to $250 a month, all levels. Cherie is a very inspirational coach. She teaches classes for feature films, comedy, situation comedy, dramady and episodic television. In addition, she teaches privately and on-set, emphasizing confidence, pacing, behavior, developing a character and how to remove fear. Her on-camera awareness classes include audition technique and especially how to identify the emotional arc of the character and how to nail those emotions throughout the filming process of shooting out of sequence. She travels giving seminars and teaching workshops worldwide.

Joel Asher Studio, 818/785-1551, Joel-Asher-Studio.com. $250 a month, one class a week plus unlimited private work at no charge. Takes beginners. Three ongoing, different level, scene study classes. He incorporates as many techniques as possible with an emphasis on film and television work. His six-week on-camera cold reading class is $195. He also offers Jeff Doucette's "Acting on Instinct" improvisation class, $150 a month. Private coaching $100-$125 an hour, but free with Scene Study Class. His informative, instructive video tapes are *Getting the Part, All About Cold Readings*; *Casting Directors "Tell It Like It Is;"* and *Agents "Tell It Like It Is."* The newest is: *Directors on Acting!* He has a great little theater in the valley which he designed and built. Uses video in classes so you can see the details of your performance and monitor your performance. The goal is working in front of the camera, so the scenes are primarily from film and TV scripts; and the approach is to make you as professional and secure as possible.

Tony Barr's Film Actors Workshop, 310/442-9488, filmactorsworkshop.com. $185 per month and first time registration fee of $55 includes copy of *Acting for the Camera* and one free hour of private coaching. Classes are held once a week. Taught by Eric Kline. Held in a three-camera video studio. Students cold read, rehearse and tape scenes from feature films. Emphasis is on the listening technique Barr developed in his book. Ongoing beginning and advanced classes. Actors must interview for the class and no auditing is permitted.

Janet Alhanti Studio, 323/465-2348. She and her associate, Iris Klein, teach two 20-week session professional technique classes a year, one in January and one in July. Students must be recommended by agents, managers, casting directors or actors who have studied with them. Janet also teaches a poetry monologue class and a master class. She is one of the most respected teachers in the business.

Ron Burrus Acting Studio, 323/953-2823, ronburrus.com. Training world-class actors in Los Angeles and NY for thirty-three years. Film Acting Foundation day intensive program is six weeks, M-Th, 10-1, $900. Evening Foundation program is M&W, 7-10pm, for three months at $300 monthly. Tuesday, Character Scenes from Film is $200 monthly and Thursday, Audition Workshop on Camera is $200 monthly. Leonard Salazar, Burrus trained teacher, heads Rehearsal/Performance Workshops for Industry and evening program. Apprenticed under Stella Adler to teach technique, he emphasizes imagination as the actors' primary tool to include and supersede self within the script. "Film needs actors who undertstand how to supply the unspoken life of dialogue—this is your craft." Admittance by interview. Takes beginners.

Anthony Caldarella, 310/828-6898. Director/Writer, Acting Coach, imdb.com. On Camera Film Technique Class, $200 a month.

Ivana Chubbuck, 323/935-2100. Author of *Script Analysis* and *The Power of the Actor*. There are several other instructors who teach at the studio. Scene study, beginning, advanced and master classes. Has taught several of today's stars, including Brad Pitt, Halle Berry and Charlize Theron. Several of my students have studied with her organization and they gave glowing reports.

Kim Darby, 818/985-0666, kimdarby.com. $200 a month. Scene study and cold reading. Actors work in every class on camera. All levels and beginners are very welcome. She is a veteran actress, three-time Emmy and two-time Golden Globe nominee. To keep a "safe atmosphere," she limits the class size and requires auditions for admittance. "My class is based on a listening process, always honoring the author by learning the words but not letting the words tell you how you feel; you learn to listen to full implication."

Joanne Baron, D.W. Brown Studio, 310/451-3311, baronbrown.com. Studio offers intensive long and short-term study to professional working and beginning actors, writers, directors and producers. Includes Meisner, scene study, audition technique, Alexander Technique and more. Admission by interview only. Also offers private and on-set coaching. Lots of big names have worked at the studio.

Wayne Dvorak, 323/462-5328, actingcoachdvorak.com. $145-$155 a month. Ongoing classes for all levels, incorporating techniques from Meisner to marketing. Interview, audition and free audit are required for admittance. Class sizes are limited. The highly selective professional networking class showcases in front of top casting directors and agents on a regular basis. This class offers the next step, once you have done serious training.

Howard Fine Studio, 323/951-1221, howardfine.com. $695 for a 12-week comprehensive technique class taught by Howard. $650 for a 12-week scene study class and ongoing intermediate and advanced classes. Other teachers and classes are available. An audit, referral and audition are required. Class size ranges from 2-35 students.

Laura Gardner, 323/957-4764, Email: lauramaegardner@comcast.net, lauragardner. org. On the faculty of the Howard Fine Studio. Teaches comprehensive technique which gives working and beginning actors the tools to bring themselves to any role and open the way to strong auditions and work choices. Each class will focus on different tools that include physical relaxation, ability to play, take risks, gain creativity, and build self-esteem. Much of the work is based on Uta Hagen's book, *The Challenge For The Actor*, which is required reading. She also teaches advanced scene study and offers private coaching. Laura has taught in NYC at HB Studios, Stella Adler Institute, and the American Academy of Dramatic Arts.

Brad Heller, "The Acting Without Agony School," 323/962-8077, actingwithoutagony.com. Classes held Tuesdays and Thursdays, $195 a month for once a week, and $295 a month for twice a week. Brad was a longtime protege of the late director Don Richardson, who wrote *Acting Without Agony: An Alternative to the Method*. His classes focus on Scene Study, Cold Reading/Audition Technique, and Career Management. He teaches all levels, from beginner to expert. And says, "He especially likes teaching beginners, as there are no habits to break." I don't know Brad but I was a big fan of Don and I'm glad to see his work carried on. Brad is also a professor at UCLA.

John Sarno, 818/761-3003, hollywoodacting.com. Teaches Classes and privately; focus on Method acting and auditioning. Recommended by Agent Bonnie Howard.

Actors Studio, West Coast, 323/654-7125, actors-studio.com, 8341 Delongpre Ave., West Hollywood, 90069. Theatre workshop for professional actors. Anyone over 18 can audition and it takes two auditions to get in; not for beginners. Martin Landau and Mark Rydell are the executive directors in Los Angeles. Al Pacino, Harvey Keitel and Ellen Burstyn are New York co-presidents.

Catlin Adams Acting Lab, 323/851-8811, actinglab.com. Strasberg trained director. All levels, improv, cold reading, sensory work, scene study. Endorsed by Melanie Mayron, Lee Grant, Ellen Burstyn, Dinah Manoff, Joe Bologna and Lily Tomlin. After interview, $25 fee for a working audit.

The Hull Actors Studio, Lorrie Hull, Ph.D. and **Dianne Hull Acting Workshops**, 310/828-0632, actors-studio.com/hull/class. $400 for six weeks, price drops if you take more than one class. Workshops offer intensive training in a broad spectrum of acting tools. Techniques of relaxation, concentration, sense memory, affective memory, emotional recall, improvisation, cold reading, preparing and learning the role, motivating and justifying behavior. Auditing allowed for a fee. Author of *Strasberg's Method: As Taught by Lorrie Hull: A Practical Guide for Actors, Teachers and Directors* and video: *The Method.*

Laura James, 818/562-3075. Ongoing acting workshop, "A safe place for the novice to learn, develop and practice your craft, and the experienced actor to be challenged and grow in your craft." Exercises, improvs, scenes, monologues, cold reading and audition techniques are taught. Small classes with individual nurturing attention. The technique is always geared to freeing you so that your own true voice comes through. Laura studied with Strasberg and Hagen, among others. First class is free. Private coaching available.

Leigh Kilton-Smith Scene Study Class, 323/650-6774. $225 a month. I first met Leigh on the set of *It's Like, You Know...* She was Jennifer Grey's acting coach, working with Jennifer to help her attain the performance she wanted. I respect Leigh's view on acting very much. She is mainly an on-set coach but also teaches acting techniques on Wednesdays. She accepts experienced and inexperienced actors working side by side as is often the case on sets. Current client list includes recognized celebrities. Auditing is permitted.

The John Kirby Studio, 323/467-7877, jkcoaching@sbcglobal.net. $525 for a 12-week commitment, classes ongoing. Intensive scene study classes for the adult professional, as well as newcomer and the Saturday young professional's class. Classes are extremely disciplined and require a strong commitment. No gimmicks, exercises or class member critique. John personally selects all material and scene partners in order to constantly challenge the actor. Homework and rehearsals required. Uta Hagan fundamentals. Auditing, $10.

Ken Lerner Studio, 818/753-7744, kenlerner.com, 14366 Ventura Blvd., Sherman Oaks, 91423. $200 to $250 a month. Scene study and cold reading. Ken uses methods culled from his own acting experiences as well as his own teachers: Stella Adler, Peggy Feury and Roy London, who handpicked Ken as his first student teacher. All classes are ongoing, beginners to advanced. Free audits by appointment. He gives you his insights into script interpretation so that you learn to make the "hottest" choices that will deepen your acting. See website for many celebrity endorsements.

M.K. Lewis Workshops, 310/826-8118, mklewisworkshops.com, 1513 Sixth St., Santa Monica, 90401. $200 a month. Author of *Your Film Acting Career*. Offers a 10-week cold read intensive that also stresses the interview portion. Also teaches an ongoing "Acting for the Camera" class. Also a 10-week film technique for professional and mid-level performers. Auditing is free.

Joanne Linville Studio, 310/248-4825. Teaches technique for all levels of actor; $150 a month. Also offers scene study and private coaching; $100 an hour. Michael Richards credits Joanne for his work on *Seinfeld*.

Warner Loughlin, 310/276-0555, warnerloughlin.com. $260 monthly. She was trained by Michael Kahn, Sonia Moore and Strasberg. Intensive on-going scene study with an emphasis on growth in skills. Focus also includes basics of camera technique, cold reading and performance fear. Her technique melds several schools of thought with her own unique concepts developed through her experience as an actress, teacher and director. Classes are small with a concentration on a safe environment to create. Strong commitment to the craft required. Fast-paced and intensive. Committed beginners; intermediate; advanced and master classes. Many professionals, award winners and celebrities in the master class. Admittance by audition. Auditing is required. Private coaching for $160 an hour.

Allan Miller, 818/907-6262, allanmiller.org. $140 a month. Author of *A Passion for Acting* and instructional DVD *Auditioning*. Ongoing classes in techniques to refresh the creative imagination. A very passionate, experienced teacher and accomplished director. Class limited to 15 people. Private coaching available for $125 an hour, $75 if you're a student.

Eric Morris Actors Workshop, 323/466-9250. $250 for four classes. He offers three ongoing weekly classes focusing on group exercises, instrumental work, craft work, scenes and monologues. Auditing permitted. He has developed his own system and has written some excellent books about how acting works: *No Acting Please, Being & Doing, Irreverent Acting, Acting From The Ultimate Consciousness, Acting & Imaging*. Private coaching.

Mala Powers, 818/364-9644, powerhouse2@comcast.net. Mala holds two eight-week scene study classes each year; she gives an occasional weekend Intensive Workshop and coaches privately. Mala Powers is an actress, Hollywood Walk of Fame honoree and has been directing and teaching the Michael Chekhov Technique of acting for the past twenty years. She studied intensively with Chekhov and is the Executrix of the Chekhov estate. She conducts workshops in her home base of Los Angeles and throughout the United States at various Conferences and Universities. Mala teaches all aspects of Chekhov's techniques including the development of Stage Presence, Imagination, and the creation of interesting and believable Characterizations through the use of Imaginary Center, Imaginary Body, and Psychological Gesture.

Anthony Meindl's Actor's Lab, 323/461-4792, metatheatre.org, 7801 Melrose Ave., West Hollywood, 90046. Teaches his own method of acting that helps keep actors "living moment to moment in the material." A foundation course that breaks down more popular methods and helps actors view scene study and acting work in general in a different, effective way. Introduction course is $450 for eight weeks. More advanced courses are $200 per month. An experienced actor, Anthony also operates the MetaTheare Company. He offers showcases, casting/agent/manager seminars, readings of new plays, a Directing Series, where actors work with established directors and even meditation workshops. When I attended one of his showcases the whole evening was filled with dynamic acting. He cares very much about his actors working in this business. Takes beginners. Auditing permitted.

Brian Reise Acting Studios, 323/874-5593, 7954 Fountain Ave., West Hollywood, 90046. $190 a month. Brian's classes specialize in Acting and Cold Reading for beginners through professional levels. The focus is on the reality of the acting business, teaching actors how to develop their acting skills so they can audition more effectively, book jobs, get agents and guide them in their careers. Ongoing classes are held in the afternoons and evenings. The studio offers free bi-monthly orientations for information about the classes. James Lew, a successful working actor, who is interviewed in the *Action Actor section* has been studying with Brian for five years. He is a big fan of the classes, says he enjoys being able to work in every class.

Stuart K. Robinson, of Robinson Creative, 310/558-4961. $350 for five weeks. Teaches commercial audition technique for five weeks and film and television audition ongoing. Class size is limited to 16 students. Stuart is the kind of teacher who inspires his actors to greatness. As a commercial teacher, he is a genius, His theatrical classes are very special too. Many of my students have taken his class and loved it. He gets to the heart of figuring out why the producers/directors need this character in the script and what is the character's function. He teaches a motivating, positive acting philosophy, very focused on actors landing the jobs. His classes always have waiting lists—good luck.

Jamie Rose Studio, 323/799-1183, jrosestudio.com. Classes $195/month. In over thirty years as a professional actor, Jamie Rose has been employed as everything from a "day player" to the star of a major network television series. Her acting technique tools are not theoretical, but tried and true strategies based on practical situations in the working environment. Her teaching methods draw from her studies with renowned acting coach Roy London and her extensive professional experience. The JRose Studio offers acting technique/scene-study classes and private coaching to all levels. Private coaching $100-$125/hour.

Tom Todoroff, 310/281-8688, tomtodoroff.com. Tom is an expert in all areas of the industry, armed with a unique knowledge and understanding of actors and acting. His classes draw students who are unusually warm, supportive and generous with each other. The environment is safe, encouraging, and growth oriented. Tom's class includes scene study, cold-reading, on-camera technique, and career guidance. Each evening begins with a warm-up class consisting of vocal work, movement, and improvisation. Tom has produced ten films and has acted with Harrison Ford, Tommy Lee Jones and Peter O'Toole among many others. After training at Juilliard, he specialized in voice placement and dialects for many years. Tom says, "It's my belief that whenever the voice is blocked it is always emotional; witness that babies have free voices. Teaching is deeply gratifying as it transforms people's lives; suddenly their work is free because their life is."

UCLA Extension, 310/825-9064, uclaextension.org/entertainmentstudies. Many weekend intensives and weekly evening classes; a typical 12-week course is $465. Classes taught by working professionals. It is good to get on their mailing list just to see the wide array of classes.

The Acting Corps, 818/753-2800, theactingcorps.com, 5508 Cahuenga Blvd., North Hollywood, 91601. I first noticed this group at Back Stage's Actorfest and I am very impressed with their website. I like the idea of going to school all day. They do a four-week Boot Camp in a Meisner based acting program and how it applies to Cold Reading and Scene Study. $550. They have many other general classes including The Advanced and The Professional Programs. The staff has very impressive credentials. This may be a good place to get your feet wet when you are new in town, if you can afford it and you have the stamina to take full advantage of the program.

Actors Creative Workshop, 818/752-1922, trulyacting.com, 10523 Burbank Blvd., Ste. 206, North Hollywood, 91601. Studio offers classes on comedy, drama, stand-up, auditioning, commercials, the business and even acting for non-actors. A number of coaches, including Jeffery Brooks, who worked as a dialogue coach for several years on *Friends.* They also have a production company attached to the studio and offer their students a number of other services, such as headshots and demo reels.

Alan Feinstein and Paul Tuerpe Acting Studio, 323/650-7766, Feinstein-tuerpe.com. Lots of theatre and film experience between the two coaches; teach beginning and advanced level scene study as well as an on-camera intensive. Also offers private coaching.

Marc Durso of ActTrue, 954/647-7569, acttrue.com. Classes in the Hagen Process, Linklater voice and Imagery Tech throughout the USA and Europe. ActTrue clients star in blockbuster films, prime time TV shows, American and Latin soap operas, Teen Sitcoms, Broadway musicals, national commercials and independent films. Proven technique that reveals Truthful Human Behavior: NO TRICKS, NO GIMMICKS, NO SHORTCUTS, NO ATTITUDES. ActTrue clients say, "life changing...epiphanies...rock solid base...passion and energy that surpass all!" Ft. Lauderdale, Miami, and Los Angeles. Acting coach Marc Durso has a wonderful site for all actors. Many monologue and script sites.

For coaches not in Los Angeles, see Cities Outside of Los Angeles.

Audition Techniques
and Teachers

• **Cold reading is an old-fashioned term.** It means you pick up a script and actually read the words off the page for the very first time. It doesn't take an actor to do that; almost anyone can do it. At cold reading workshops you will be doing lukewarm readings; you will get the script and have twenty minutes to work on it before you present it to the casting director, agent, manager or director that is the guest that evening. In order to do an audition in twenty minutes, you will have to make many acting choices plus memorize as much as you can. It doesn't really give the full report of how good you are as an actor. Many actors have been fired from the set because they were good at auditioning but couldn't deliver on the set.

• **You can become excellent at auditioning** but it most likely will be because you have the sides at least the night before, as SAG guarantees in the contract. Where cold reading or quick audition skills will come in handy is at auditions for independent or student films when the script isn't available ahead of time. The students haven't learned yet that they are unable to cast the best actor from that type of audition. If you can't see the script ahead of time, go in early, pick up the sides, take them out to your car, and work on them for twenty minutes.

• **On actual professional auditions,** you should never be asked to cold read. Casting directors' jobs depend on them calling in good actors to read. The exception might be if you come in to audition for one role and they think you would be better in another role. Again, take the script away from their office and prepare it using your quick skills then go back to the office and tell them you are ready.

• **I would suggest studying your basic acting technique first,** then take an audition technique class to enhance your acting skills. You will be able to get the most for your money because you will understand the acting skills your audition teacher is talking about. There are special skills for auditioning. I took Caryn West's Audition Workshop a couple of times and Kimberly Jentzen's Cold Reading Intensive Weekend and learned so much. I've been auditioning for years but it is great to stretch and expand one's skills.

• **Caryn West taught me about "butt breathing."** The name alone tickles me and keeps me thinking about it. Conscious breathing is essential in all acting; in fact it is helpful in many life situations. We use our breath to find our center, to allow the tension to drop from our bodies through the floor. When we hold our breath, it short circuits our acting instincts; we lose power.

• **Caryn gives her explanation:**

  • **Having been an athlete most of my life** and at one time a world class Alpine skier (National Alpine ski team for 4 years), I learned a lot from my years of competition about "peak performance" skills under pressure. My ongoing investigation of that phenomenon has really helped both myself and other actors prepare for auditions and with their acting in general. It has a lot to do with centering and breath.

  • **Auditioning as a process has similarities to acting** in rehearsal, onstage or in actual shooting, but with a big, confusing twist: The actor is necessarily put into a "proving mode," yet the conundrum is the only way he/she will get the job is to "not need the job." The actor can often feel threatened by the authority figures in the room. The "fight or flight syndrome" of the situation can physically and psychologically overwhelm the actor. And the trouble starts when the actor walks in holding their breath. Or starts holding his/her breath the minute they begin their lines. Even the well-trained and talented actor can "choke" and audition badly coming from this place. Basically, the actor in not breathing or, in taking very shallow breaths, has to sprint to get to the end of the material.

  • **I teach actors to use a bigger "uber breath,"** not unlike the large, diaphragmatic ways opera singers train to sustain a legato phrase or produce the big high note. I rather comically refer to good audition breathing as "butt breathing." Because if you consciously breathe very low and deep and pull in a large of volume of air, you will indeed feel it, ever so slightly, in your anal sphincter. So your "butt" essentially clues you in to whether you are really breathing deeply.

- **In fact, when you do breathe deeper in auditions,** it seems easier to center oneself, stay in your body and commit to physical choices, to listen more acutely, to assimilate emotional stimuli, to think a sub-textual thought that we could read on your face, to access your courage and spontaneity. In other words, deep "butt breathing" is the essential lubricant to a well-oiled acting engine. Without it, we choke, we sputter, we get all "gummed up" and awkward, we run out of gas in the room or spin out of control.

- **Deep breathing is the simple key** to correcting many problems that appear to be more complicated.

- **Cherie Franklin**, noted audition and on-set coach, answers: Are there different styles to auditioning for films, soaps, episodics and sitcoms?

  - **For feature films,** the actor must remember the screen is 30 feet high, and tailor his/her movements and expressions accordingly. The old adage "Less is More" is never more true than in acting for the feature film.

  - **Soap Opera** is a very personality-driven medium, and the audition must show a character with a full personality. Knowing your lines for the soap audition is essential.

  - **Episodics** play heavily on the 2 shot/3 shot and single reaction shots. Audition with these shots in mind, not the master. Episodics feature one to three story lines, and knowing to what story line your character belongs is necessary to deliver an audition appropriate to the show as a whole. Some story lines are resolved each week, others are on-going, and still others are set-ups for resolution down the line. Know your spot.

  - **Sitcom** has a specific timing and rhythm and pace, and your audition must include all of these. Recognize what attitudes, emotions and/or behaviors are necessary to support the 22 minute show.

  - **For all mediums, the story is like a puzzle.** It is essential for the actor to recognize exactly where his/her character fits into this puzzle and to provide an audition that delivers the "missing piece" his/her character has to provide. Providing too much or too little will lose the job.

- **Caryn West answers,** Do you audition differently for different types of projects?

  - **Yes! Some elements are essential in all forms,** but styles and genre dictate a lot of your choices. One cannot approach a noir film or an edgy cop drama as you would a broad commedia based sitcom or even a silly Rob Schneider or David Spade farcical comedy. You certainly approach Moliere or neoclassicism differently than Odets or Arthur Miller. So too must an actor adapt and learn the world of a film or TV genre. How a show is shot and the size of frame also dictate much about choices. Many stage-trained actors when auditioning for camera, don't realize they are 'muscling' a part and showing and telling too much about a character when the simplicity of the communication can speak for itself. Trusting subtext and inferences best left to the audience to decipher for themselves are essential camera skills. They are some of the hardest lessons to learn, as I had to suffer through them myself, but once mastered makes the actor even more versatile.

• **Casting director Junie Lowry Johnson** says this about all types of auditions:

  • **Substance in your craft** is ultimately much more important than how smooth you are in the room. Do less, bring it down, be still. Focus, honesty and realness. I am more touched by the actor that comes in the room, does the work and leaves quickly.

• **Anthony Caldarella, talented director/writer/coach,** says when auditioning:

  • **Figure out what the scene is about.** It is best to play the circumstances of the scene using your own essence, instead of trying to play the character. Make a strong personal choice, commit yourself to it, and walk into that casting office like you own it. Confidence is a positive force.

  • **When auditioning on camera**, be aware of the camera but do not pay attention to it. Never try to act in front of a camera, create real emotions. If you're playing an intimate scene you don't need to use much voice, think loud and speak softly. If you're playing a confrontation scene then go for the truth and express your emotions as you would in life. Remember the camera doesn't lie; it demands honesty and sincerity from the actor.

• **Kimberly Jentzen, who teaches a Cold Reading Weekend Intensive** in a truly innovative and jam-packed weekend, talks about the "booking formula."

  • **Your booking formula** is the most captivating, authentic you. Angelina Jolie, Paul Giamatti, Meryl Streep—all have booking formulas. It is a combination of qualities that consistently generates successful callbacks and acting jobs. I am not referring to an actor's *type* or *category*, this is much more specific. It is that "thing" you do in the zone that allows you to shine. Your unique formula can include how you look, how you think, energy, intensity, emotional depth and sense of humor. It is always a combination of elements. Knowing your booking formula supports the building of a booking attitude. And in using your formula you must be willing to be directed and to deliver that unique X Factor which is yours alone!

Resources

To download and print an updated version of this and all resource lists, go to actingiseverything.com.

AUDITION TEACHERS & WORKSHOPS

Judy Kerr, 818/505-9373, JudyKerr.com. $100 an hour. Private coaching for film and television. We study the audition material and decide how to portray your character. We work on camera until you can deliver the performance that could land the job. You keep the tape.

Caryn West's Audition Workshop, 323/876-0394, Los Angeles Web Site: http://groups. yahoo.com/group/CarynWest-actorsLA. For New York: http://groups.yahoo.com/group/ CarynWest-ActorsNY. $660 for 11 weeks. Not designed for the beginner but for those who have their basic technique and are actively auditioning. "There is emphasis on script analysis, breath, presence and spontaneity." Privates are $90 ($75 if a currently enrolled in a class). She regularly teaches in June and December at Michael Howard's Studio in New York. Sign up online to receive her informative, instructive newsletters.

Kimberly Jentzen's Cold Reading Weekend Intensive, 818/779-7770, kimberlyjentzen.com. Author of *Acting with Impact*. $345 for three-day course. This inspiring and extremely helpful Intensive is packed with powerful tools. Class size is small allowing for many breakthroughs! Kimberly helps you find your strong points and guides you to building a powerful audition process. Offered every 4 to 6 weeks. For all levels, from beginning to masters. I took this weekend last year and discovered many empowering, life enhancing tools. Just great!

Doug Warhit, 310/479-5647, 310/479-5647. $200 for the first month (which includes one private session) $185 a month thereafter. Scene study and cold reading classes, beginning through advanced. All work is geared for television and film and videotaped each week; at the end of each month, an industry guest (casting director, agent, etc.) is invited to observe the actors' work.

Kimberly Crandall, 310/463/7136, kimberlycrandallactingcoach.com. Kimberly has been seen coaching on *Access Hollywood, The Today Show, Showbiz Moms & Dads* and *Oprah*. Her well-rounded and comprehensive classes focus on audition technique and acting fundamentals, helping students cultivate the skills needed to have the best chance possible to book the part! Classes include: cold reading, scene study, on-camera technique, script analysis, mock auditions, interview skills, commercial techniques and much more all with a major focus on "audition technique." I've worked with Kimberly and love her classes and approach, she gets results.

Anthony Caldarella's On Camera Film Audition Technique Class, 310-828-6898. Director/Writer, Acting Coach, imdb.com. $200 a month. On going for professionals and beginners, limited to 12 students. My audition technique deals with how to improvise by yourself to find out what the scene is about, and to make a personal connection with the material. Great readings are about knowing how to apply your imagination, personal experience, and being willing to take risks.

Michelle Danner of The Larry Moss Studio, 310/399-3666, Edgemarcenter.org, 2437 Main Street, Santa Monica, 90405. Cold Reading on the big screen explores all the different genres—horror, period, action/adventure, film/slapstick comedy, sitcom, soap operas, drama and erotic—is $475 for an 8-week tuition.

Joel Asher, 818/785-1551. Teaches a 6-week cold reading class for $225, all on camera. The course covers script handling, instant scene breakdown, intuitive auditioning, advanced techniques, as well as how to conduct interviews, photos and resumes, how to create demo reels and web sites. Actors learn how to audition with confidence, use their imagination and create believable auditions within the shortest possible time without self-consciousness.

Cherie Franklin, 818/762-4658, cherolynfranklin@msn.com. $85-$200 an hour private coaching for auditioning. Also teaches a class on audition technique. Cherie is a very inspirational teacher and on-set coach. She teaches seminars, classes and privately, emphasizing confidence, pacing, behavior, developing a character and how to remove fear.

Stuart K. Robinson, of Robinson Creative, 310/558-4961. $350 for five weeks. Teaches commercial audition technique for five weeks and film and television audition ongoing. Class size is limited to 16 students. Stuart is the kind of teacher who inspires his actors to greatness. As a commercial teacher, he is a genius, His theatrical classes are very special too. Many of my students have taken his class and loved it. He gets to the heart of figuring out why the producers/directors need this character in the script and what is the character's function. He teaches a motivating, positive acting philosophy, very focused on actors landing the jobs. His classes always have waiting lists—good luck.

Margie Haber Studio, 310/854-0870, margiehaber.com. Very well-respected audition technique teacher. Author of the book: *How To Get The Part Without Falling Apart.* Several teachers teach her technique at the studio. She also does seminars all over the world, many on auditioning.

Sandy Holt, 310/271-8217. $400 for 8 weeks. She is a *Second City* alumni. She will point out what is working or not working in the characters you create. She teaches how to take care of yourself at auditions, how to switch gears in a second, "how to be interesting and specific, get to the heart of the character, and audition with power." Hones in on what is special about you so you can totally rely on yourself. She says, "80% of the actors who work with me are landing the jobs. They're prepared, open to taking risks and committed to going full out with their characters. They make an impression; they stand out."

Kip King, 818/784-0544, kipking.actorsite.com. One of the original Groundlings. Private coaching $75. Helps you bring yourself to each character you play. Especially helpful with comedy. *See Commercials and Improv sections.*

M. K. Lewis Workshops, 310/826-8118, mklewisworkshops.com, 1513 Sixth St., Santa Monica, 90401. $200 a month. Author of *Your Film Acting Career.* 10-week cold read intensive that also stresses the interview portion. Teaches an ongoing "Acting for the Camera" class and a 10-week film technique for professional and mid-level performers. Free auditing.

Scott Sedita Acting Studios, 323/465-6152, scottseditaacting.com. 526 N. Larchmont Blvd., Los Angeles, 90004. Cold Reading and Audition Techniques tailored for the professional actor who is represented and is currently auditioning. All aspects: working the sides, preparing the character, coaching for the role, the callback, the screen test, group auditions, entrance and exits. Admittance is through the monthly Free Audit Seminar or a one on one interview with a staff member.

Melissa Skoff, CSA, 818/760-2058, alphaquad.net/Melissa, $175 a month. Respected casting director discusses how to make the right choices and how to get the job. Often has industry guests.

Clair Sinnett, head of Clair Sinnett Casting, 310/606-0813, Actorsworking.com $250 for a Weekend Intensive; includes marketing, cover letters, interview techniques, cold reading, script analysis, screen tests, etc. All sessions videotaped, followed by in-depth critique. Author of *Actors Working: Marketing For Success*. Clair is available for audition coaching and career consultations. Private sessions $100 an hour.

Janice Kent, 818-906-2201, janicekent.com. Small ongoing classes held weekly. $240 per month. Classes are limited in size and very intensive. Audition material is put on camera and critiqued. Emphasis is on understanding the different "forms" as well as your own personal development as an actor in TV/Film. By interview and referral.

Janice Lynde, 323/650-0515, janicelynde.com. $200 a month on an ongoing basis. Class limited to 15 actors so everyone works every week. She teaches an audition formula involving three simple acting choices that helps actors book the jobs. She is the author of the book *Ten Minutes to the Audition*. Janice is a working, two-time Emmy nominated actress, winner of an Obie award and director. Also offers private coaching.

John Sudol, 818/505-1223, johnsudolstudio.com. Teaches audition technique for improving your reading skills and a commercial seminar all about the business. John is a well known and respected acting coach and independent director. Highly recommended from many top industry professionals.

Ron Burrus Acting Studio, 323/953-2823, ronburrus.com. Training world-class actors in LA and NY for thirty-three years. Audition Workshop on Camera is $200 monthly. Apprenticed under Stella Adlert. Takes beginners.

John Sarno, 818/761-3003, hollywoodacting.com. Teaches Classes and privately; focus on Method acting and auditioning. Well known; has trained many actors. Recommended by Agent Bonnie Howard.

Ken Lerner Studio, 818/753-7744, kenlerner.com, 14366 Ventura Blvd., Sherman Oaks, 91423. $250 a month for cold reading. Ken uses methods culled from his own acting experiences as well as his own teachers: Stella Adler, Peggy Feury and Roy London, who handpicked Ken as his first student teacher. All classes are ongoing, beginners to advanced. Free audits by appointment. He gives you his insights into script interpretation so that you learn to make the "hottest" choices that will deepen your acting. See his website for many celebrity endorsements.

COMEDY

SITCOM AND STAND-UP

AND

COMEDY COACHES

• **Performing stand-up comedy** is a good way to get noticed. Take a chance; hit all the open mikes at your local comedy clubs. In Los Angeles the clubs are listed in *Back Stage West* and *L.A. Weekly.* Many comedians have been signed to development deals or cast as regulars on sitcoms because of characters they portray in their acts.

• **Buy the DVD of** *Comedian,* **the movie about Jerry Seinfeld** getting his act together. Rent DVDs of stand-ups doing their acts. Watch Comedy Central or, for something edgier, any of the HBO comic specials. Read books the comics have written. *SeinLanguage* by Jerry Seinfeld is one of the best. Figure out why you laugh on each page. His sense of language and vocabulary is extraordinary; he can turn a phrase better and funnier than most. Jerry just walking around is funny; his thought process is funny. One thing I like most about him is his loyalty to all of his stand-up friends. He looked for roles on the show where he could hire them, and then always appreciated their work.

• **Rita Rudner** analyzed the science of comedy by playing all of Woody Allen's albums from his stand-up comedy years, listened to Jack Benny albums and every comedy album she could get at the library. She tried to figure out what was funny. She would try a joke out on her friends and if they laughed, she would use it. "It's hard, yet you do feel a tremendous power."

• **Eve Brandstein, who has managed several comics**, says, "You can develop characters or material in an improv, acting, writing or stand-up workshop. Work your material among your colleagues. Then go to one of the small clubs on their audition night, get up and try it. If it's for you, you'll know it; you'll get bitten by it. Bingo!"

• **Landing a series regular role on a sitcom** is one of the best jobs an actor can have. The hours are usually good for having a life outside of the studio. When you go to work you spend a lot of time laughing. Most of my on-set coaching work has been on sitcoms—of course my favorite job was on *Seinfeld*. The days were filled with very exacting work, loads of pressure and lots of laughs. It is fun to be on a hit show; nothing better.

• **Scott Sedita is one of the most well-respected comedy coaches in Hollywood.** With more than 20 years in the business, as an actor, agent, writer, casting director and renowned acting coach, Scott has worked with many of today's top talent, including Courteney Cox, Matt LeBlanc, Brandon Rough, Josh Duhamel and Jennifer Finnigan. He has appeared on several shows, including the "E!" series *Fight For Fame*, where he starred as the resident acting coach. He is also the author of *The Eight Characters of Comedy: A Guide to Sitcom Acting and Writing*. He is THE coach to see for sitcom work.

Q: What does an actor need to be a successful comedic actor?

• **First, you need an innate ability to act**, to pretend, to perform. What a coach can do is give you techniques to help you access your emotions and personal history, open your heart and mind and use your imagination. An actor needs to have that innate ability, which I call the Acting Gene. Some people have it and others don't…that is why actors should understand that they have a gift. The same is true for comedy. Next to the Acting Gene is the Funny Gene. You must have an innate ability to be funny, no matter how developed it is. If you have it, I can teach you to be funny. I can help hone your skills and be a successful, working actor.

Q: How does comedic acting differ from all other forms of acting?

• **Comedy is all about the rhythm, the pace and the timing.** It requires you to be specific in your work. Sitcom acting takes precision. You can't drop words, or add words or pauses or ignore the punctuation because it throws off the rhythm and then the piece isn't funny. There are similarities in sitcom acting and dramatic acting in that the basic acting techniques still apply. You still have a "want, obstacles, intentions, stakes, etc." But in dramatic acting, there is more "leeway" in how an actor interprets the script. That's not the case with comedy. There is no mumbling, no long pauses (unless written in), no unnecessary static. Each word and piece of punctuation is there for a reason and it must be followed to get the most out of the jokes and to keep the comedic flow. Comedy is not easy and that's why many people say it's a lot easier to find a good dramatic actor than a comedic one.

Q: Why is it important for all actors to study comedy?

- **If you want to work on television, you have to study comedy.** Right now, there are three types of shows (not including reality television). At one end, there are the dramas like the *CSI* and *Law & Order* shows. At the other end, there are the sitcoms like *My Name is Earl* and *Two and a Half Men.* And then in the middle, there are the dramadies, like *Desperate Housewives, Grey's Anatomy* and *Boston Legal.* We are seeing a lot of TV shows being produced with more comedic plotlines, dialogue and characterizations. Even soap operas are adding humor. Therefore, it is easier for a well-trained actor with comedic training to get work.

Q: Who are the Eight Characters of Comedy?

- **They are eight specific character archetypes** that can be seen in any and all sitcoms (and dramadies) dating back to the dawn of television. They are not stereotypes by any means. Each character on every show has something unique that the actors and writers bring to him or her. But they also have something in common, certain personality traits that make them who they are and make them easier for us to identify. These are characters that actors and writers can use to "bring the funny" to a role or a show.

- **The Eight Characters of Comedy are: The Logical Smart One**—This is the most responsible and reasonable of the characters, most commonly the wives on sitcoms. Think Deborah Barone on *Everybody Loves Raymond.* **The Lovable Loser**—One of the most important of the characters, like the Logical Smart One, the Lovable Loser is vital for every show. He or she tries to do good, but often messes everything up. Think Lucy or Earl or Chandler. **The Neurotic**—The over-thinking, over-analytical ones: Think Monica, Frasier or Meredith Gray on

Gray's Anatomy. **The Dumb One**—Very simple, happy people who are very childlike in nature. One of the best is Joey or Kelly Bundy on *Married...With Children*. Another good example is Randy on *My Name is Earl*. **The Bitch/Bastard**—The mean, cynical ones we love to watch rip into the other characters. Think Carla from *Cheers* or Louie from *Taxi*. **The Womanizer/Manizer**—These are the sexy, flirtatious ones that only have sex on their mind. Edie on *Desperate Housewives* or Charlie on *Two and a Half Men*. **The Materialistic One**—Often the rich snobs who value only material goods and can't understand why others don't. Think Hilary on *The Fresh Prince of Bel-Air* or Gabi on *Desperate Housewives*. **In Their Own Universe**—The space cadets, those crazy, wild characters who seem to come out of left field, but are always funny. Kramer, Phoebe, Jack and Karen from *Will & Grace*.

Q: How can comedic actors use these characters?

- **I came up with these eight characters to help actors understand who they are and where they fit in.** Actors are able to organically gravitate toward a specific character, whether it be the Logical Smart One or the Neurotic, hone that character and then get work as that character. They will help you find you niche and they will give you some structure when you're called in to audition. I've seen it work many times over the years. In television, it's all about being real. You are not on stage; you are on a small screen, close up. Therefore, when you walk into a casting session, you want to make sure that they can see right away that you understand the character and that you're right for the part.

Q: What other pieces of advice can you offer comedic actors?

- **Learn how the jokes work.** Learn what a "Turnaround" is and how understanding "Triplets" can make you funnier. These are two comedic techniques that I designed to help actors "find the funny." Comedy is like any other craft. You must study it and get familiar with how the process works and then practice, practice, practice. Also, know you're basic acting techniques, study as much comedy as you can and watch as many sitcoms as you can. I recommend *Friends, I Love Lucy, Everybody Loves Raymond, Cheers, Will & Grace, Seinfeld* as well as many of the ones on TV today; you want to know what you might be called in for. You can learn a lot by watching these masters at work.

• **Mary Lou Belli is a director who specializes in sitcoms,** including *Eve, Girlfriends, The Hughleys, One on One, Major Dad,* and *Charles in Charge.* She is co-author of *The Sitcom Career Book: A Guide to the Louder, Faster, Funnier World of TV Comedy,* a must-have for people learning about the business of comedy.

Q: What do comedic actors need to be successful in terms of acting ability?

• **As the saying goes "Dying is easy, comedy is hard."** It's true. So to be a good comic actor you must first be a good actor. Some individuals who have come from stand-up backgrounds where they were funny first (D. L. Hughley, Paul Reiser) took acting seriously and rounded themselves as performers who were both funny and had acting craft.

Q: How is the business side different for comedic acting?

• **Actors on sitcoms that last many seasons** and get syndicated make a LOT of money. If one is lucky enough to be in this position, an actor can set himself up for life by working this opportunity both financially and as a solid base for work when that sitcom is over.

Q: Briefly describe the process from audition to actual filming.

• **The process from audition to filming** a multi-camera sitcom usually is pre-read, audition, getting cast. Then a normal work week would be: Monday, you table read and rehearse. Tuesday and Wednesday, you rehearse with revised script and do a run-thru. Thursday, you camera block and preshoot. Friday, you review camera blocking and perform in front of a live audience.

Q: When actors watch sitcoms, what should they be looking for to help them learn?

• **Actors should be able to analyze** what makes something funny, from knowing the basic elements of a joke (the set-up and punchline) to the common types of jokes that appear in sitcoms. (runs of 3, misleads, etc.).

Q: What sitcoms do you recommend?

• *I Love Lucy, Mary Tyler Moore, All in the Family, Cheers, Two and a Half Men, Frasier, Friends.*

Q: Any other advice for breaking into comedy acting?

• **Learn the technique then make it invisible...**Nothing kills a joke worse than seeing it coming. Practice makes perfect.

• **Carol Leifer started out as a stand-up comedian** and has appeared 25 times on *Late Night with David Letterman*. She was a writer/producer on *Seinfeld, The Larry Sanders Show* and a writer for *Saturday Night Live*. She also co-created and produced *The Ellen Show*. Carol continues to do stand-up and occasionally opens for Jerry Seinfeld on his concert tours.

Q: How do you turn a stand-up act into a sitcom character?

• **I feel the stand-ups** who have made the best transition to sitcom characters never stray very far from their "stand-up persona." What makes people laugh about the stand-up is a good indication of a direction to go in creating a sitcom version of the person. Embellishing their stories and setting them in a real-life situation is the job of a good creator. But the beauty of a stand-up is that they already have a story to tell! So the creator just needs to expand and mold their universe, and create believable and funny characters around them.

Q: How do you develop a stand-up act?

• **My best advice to someone who wants to do stand-up is to go out and do stand-up!** Whether it's in a class or a coffee shop or a comedy club, wherever someone will give you the most stage time. You only get better by doing it over and over and over again.

Q: How does a stand-up comic get noticed?

• **Obviously, the goal is to get on in the clubs** where agents and managers frequent. For example in L.A. where I live, trying to get good enough to go on at The Improv or The Laugh Factory. If you live in a different city, get on at the most popular club in your area. But ultimately, it seems to really make it you would need to move to L.A. or N.Y., unless your fan base is so big that it doesn't matter.

Q: What are some auditioning turn-ons and turn-offs?

• **When actors come in to audition,** an easygoing, relaxed personality is always comforting to see. I know actors get nervous, but the producers/casting people are put off by nervous behavior. That's not to say if you are nervous, some actors have good ways to hide it and the producers never know it! But tension in the room when the actor walks in is a big turnoff.

• **It's obvious when an actor is a pro.** They come in with a good, positive, confident energy. They give a brief and general "Hi!" to everybody and then they get on with it. It's great when an actor displays some natural charm, but it should be organic and not "pre-thought" to the situation. Believe me, there's nothing worse than an actor who comes in and asks everybody's name or wants to shake hands, etc. The actor doesn't realize how many other actors come in on a daily basis and usually the room is just tired. It's not a cocktail party, it's work.

Darlene Westgor is a standup comedian and in 2006 won the "Funniest Mom in America" title on *Nick at Night*. One of her prizes was to have a sitcom produced around her standup character. I was the dialogue coach on the production, helping Darlene deliver her first on-set acting role. I asked her for the following interview.

Q: How did you get started?

- **I started out in Improv classes** in Minneapolis and I just fell in love with the process immediately. For me it was perfect! Thinking on your feet; hanging with other funny and creative people. I made friendships that will last forever. I wrote and produced a couple of plays and then started putting up sketch comedy shows in any venue that would have us. I started Stand-up in 1995 and it has certainly been rewarding! For me, connecting with people in the audience and knowing that they understand and relate because we all have the same quirks and dreams and fears—is simply intoxicating.

Q: What is the first step to developing a standup act?

- **There seems to be an open mike stage** in virtually every city. I suggest going a few times as an observer. This is an excellent way to get a handle on how the open mike is run BEFORE you hit the stage for the first time! Make at least a couple of friends at the club. The biggest part of open mike nights is the networking and brainstorming that goes on before, during and after the show. This is a helpful way to write material and share ideas with other comics. For many comics as well as myself, those Monday nights became a lifestyle for many years. Talk about laughing with friends!! I would suggest taking an improv class before—or simultaneous to—stand-up. It gives you a handle on stage presence, which is very important.

Q: Do you really have to finish at three minutes when the light goes on if you are getting laughs?

- **Only if you want to work at the club again.** I can't begin to tell you how many times I've heard comics say, "I don't get it. I can't get booked at that club! I did the open stage and I killed! I went over a little bit but it's because I was KILLING! Why won't they return my calls?" Uhhh. Because you were disrespectful! My advice. Stick to your time. First of all, trust me, you weren't that funny and now you've let the club owner know that you can't adhere to simple rules. Even if you were killing, that set has been forgotten and your disrespect remembered.

Q: How many minutes did you use to compete in the *Funniest Mom Show*?

- I believe there were 13 or 14 of us and we each did 7 minutes. I was killing though, so I did 8 minutes. (Kidding, of course...) In the last round there were five of us doing four minutes each.

Q: You were the MC at a club for a while. Why and how was that helpful?

- It is helpful because you can work on material all the time. The MC sets the tone for the show and it's valuable to watch the booked comics having fun together.

Q: How does a comic find a manager and is that one of the first steps?

- It is a Catch-22. It's hard to get management until you have a lot of credits and of course it's nearly impossible to get credits without a manager. But if you're just starting out, you can get gigs with other comics without management. So don't worry about it right away.

Q: When should a comic quit their regular job and pursue the comedy circuit full time?

- When you've been headlining for the same kind of money that you would make as a corporate attorney! Unless of course, sleeping in your Echo sounds appealing. Most of my friends do comedy full time but they have been doing it for many, many years and they also do other things as well, like write and produce shows.

Q: When you shot the pilot, was it scary?

- Scary as hell; exhilarating and exhausting are a few words that would describe the experience. For me, not knowing what the experience was going to be like was probably a good thing. It allowed a certain vulnerability that was needed for the part.

- **Judy Carter, standup comic, author and master teacher** has appeared on over one hundred TV shows. She is the author of *Standup Comedy: The Book* (Dell Books) which has sold over 200,000 copies. Her latest book, *The Comedy Bible* (Simon & Schuster), the definitive guide to making a career out of making people laugh, was featured on *Oprah* and *Good Morning America*. Fifteen years ago she formed Comedy Workshop Productions, which runs comedy classes nationwide. Carter also produces the annual California Comedy Conference in Palm Springs, California, which is attended by top Hollywood VIPs including executives from HBO, Warner Bros, William Morris Agency and others.

Q: Tell me about the book.

- *The Comedy Bible* is the ultimate guide for anyone wanting to know how to turn their sense of humor into a comedy-making career, whether they want to do standup, write, or do a one-person show.

Q: Do you have specific things to say about actors doing stand-up?

- If you look at TV sitcoms, they are all using stand-up comics because they know audiences don't lie. There's a certain confidence that stand-ups have to bring to a producer. They can make an audience laugh right there and then. Or an agent can bring an actor to a producer and say, "Yes, this person knows how to make an audience laugh. I saw it myself."

- As a stand-up, it is much easier to showcase your talents because when you have an act, you don't have to wait to be cast in a play. You can go to a showcase yourself. It's obvious why casting directors prefer to go to a club. At a showcase at the Improv, they'll get to see 20 people in two hours, eat nachos and drink. It's true. They talk, schmooze, mingle and maybe have sex with someone they've met when they are done. That rarely happens in waiver theater.

- You can have a video of yourself doing stand-up and get work that way. I can't tell you how many students I have with development deals because they put up their showcase video at our sister casting site, standupdemo.com.

- Create an act. Decide what the sitcom would look like that you are in. For example, if you look at *Everyone Loves Raymond,* you can see that everything all the characters that Ray Romano talked about and acted out in his stand-up act became real actors in the sitcom that he became the center of. Who are the people that are in your arena of life? What is your life like? Who is your family? If you look at Mary Tyler Moore, her family was the people she worked with. Her problems were due to being a single woman. Roseanne's sitcom came right out of her life and the characters in it. It's a sitcom development dream.

- Back to *Roseanne*, it was her immediate family, trying to eke out a living and deal with men in this sexist world. If you put yourself in the center, who are the people that you have issues with? You start acting them out in your life and you start showcasing that. It's a great way to empower your career and hold the reins on your creative destiny. You're not waking up each day saying, "How can I get somebody to see me to give me a job?" You wake up each day creating material that will lead someplace.

Q: How do they learn to create material if it doesn't come naturally?

- **Get help.** Comedy is a craft that is learned. You have to have talent, but you also need assistance is shaping your talent. We have standup classes and also for people not in L.A. we offer a DVD series to assist funny people to turn their problems into a killer act. We talk specifically about how to arrange that material in stand-up material format. It's a very specific formula and structure that has to have a set-up to interest the audience and relieve itself in a laugh within 30 to 40 seconds because of the nature of television. You've got to keep people from channel surfing. Part two goes into those techniques.

- **Also included in the DVD is "How not to bomb."** Once you've put your act together and you're going to go out and perform it, you need specific techniques to let go of fear. Part four is how to go and market your act and start making money, which is a very separate issue.

- **CD ROM, Five Steps to Writing A Joke, comes with a little workbook.**

Q: What about the fear?

- **Actors that I speak to are dealing with fear.** "Oh, there's no one else on stage." What they find is the audience is their friend, and they become the other character in a scene. They learn that it's not about giving a monologue, but having dialogue with the audience. You just don't know how the audience is going to react. The same way in a play. You really don't know how the other actor is going to read a line, but you just have to be alive and respond.

Q: Do you have to be funny yourself?

- **Most people who make good stand-up** comics are people who aren't the center of attention but are the people who are watching and noticing the "weirdness" around them. They are the ones outside of their family, the ones who have a crazy family and who aren't very involved, but watch and comment later on what happened. It's the observers of life, but not necessarily the ones that are very funny, who are the stand-ups.

Resources

To download and print an updated version of this and all resource lists, go to actingiseverything.com.

Also look at the Improvisation Teachers Section.

Scott Sedita Acting Studios, 323/465-6152, scottseditaacting.com, email: scottsedita@aol.com, 526 N Larchmont Blvd., L.A., 90004. Scott teaches a one-day Comedy Intensive that includes his Eight Characters of Comedy, how to breakdown a comedy script, how to identify and deliver a joke and how to find your "Comedic

Note." This one-day intensive I believe is a must for all actors. Scott's sitcom class is great, I took it for six months and even though I've been coaching on sitcoms for 20 years I learned so much. Many other classes taught at the Studio. Todd Rohrbacher specializes in comedy improv.

Lesly Kahn Studio, 323/969-9900, leslykahn.com. Offers group classes and private coaching; prices vary-though on the high end. Specializes in comedic training, comedy intensives and general TV acting clinics. Highly regarded. Manager Steven Nash considers her notable.

Janice Kent's Sitcom Audition Technique Intensive, 818/906-2201. janicekent.com. $420 for 8 weeks. Beginners classes and Advanced. Hone your audition technique by: *Finding your signature; Facing your fears; Learning script analysis; Finding the HOT choices.* 2006 Students have appeared Desperate Housewives (series regular), The Office (series regular) Campus Ladies (series regular),Veronica Mars, Scrubs, Commander In Chief, Glory Road, etc. Also works privately; great for those important sitcom auditions.

Suanne Spoke, 818/487-1860, suannespoke.com. Hosts a Sitcom Audition Technique workshop for $100. Focuses on analyzing and breaking down sides. Often has reputable guest teachers help with the seminar, including casting directors, directors and other coaches. Suanne is a wonderful actress; look at her comedy reel on her site.

Caryn West, 323/876-0394, Caryn's Space for Actors, 7506 Lexington Ave., West Hollywood, 90046. A wonderful coach, Caryn teaches a 10-hour Comedy Skills Intensive, which emphasizes preparing for sitcom and single-camera comedy work. Cost is $200. Anything Caryn does is THE BEST!

Judy Carter, Comedy Workshop Productions, 310/915-0555, comedyworkshops.com. Judy guarantees a performance at a comedy club and a video of your act. *The Comedy Bible* includes a test to find out if you're funny. She offers free class auditing as well as regular e-mails about up-to-date casting info. Private consultation also available.

Sandy Holt, 310/271-8217. She is a *Second City* alumni, has a looping group and teaches improvisation, character work and on-camera sketch comedy. I asked Sandy for advice for struggling actors. She laughed, "Marry a rich person so they'll pay for your classes. Be willing to do whatever it takes. I don't care what age you are or what you've been through; follow your dream." Private coaching to work on material, timing and on-camera persona. $80 an hour.

Steve Kaplan's Comedy Intensive, 818/718-7570, kaplancomedy.com, email: SKComedy@aol. com. $325 for a 2-day intensive workshop and private coaching for $100 an hour. Workshop for professional actors, writers and directors designed to "move beyond intuition and guess-work" and give artists "the tools to understand why things are funny, how to adjust things that don't work, and how to make sure that your audition or performance succeeds." He created the HBO Workspace, founded New York's famed Manhattan Punchline, developed writers such as David Ives, Howard Korder, Peter Tolan, David Crane and Ted Tally, and directed and coached actors such as Mercedes Ruehl, Illeana Douglas, and Oliver Platt. He has taught comedy at Yale, NYU and UCLA and has been called the Stanislavski of Comedy.

Harvey Lembeck Comedy Workshop, 310/271-2831, harveylembeckcomedyworkshop.com. Prices vary for ongoing classes. Three levels but aimed for the trained working actor who wants to specialize in comedy. Teaches how to play comedy legitimately in a scene. Using improv as a method to teach comedy, work on stage 3 to 4 times a night. Robin Williams said, "I looked around the class and said I'm home, they can't hurt me now, forget therapy." Former students include John Ritter, Jenna Elfman, Bryan Cranston, Kim Cattrall.

Paul Ryan at Dennis Lavalle Studio, 818/783-7940, paulryanproductions.com, email: paul@paulryanproductions.com. All levels. Classes start at $225 a month. Master comedy acting classes, sitcom character development, comedy improvising, comedy timing, sitcom auditioning techniques, cold readings, comedy scene work. He gets many celebrities speaking at his classes. Also does a TV hosting class on the last Sunday of the month. Author of: *The Art of Comedy...Getting Serious About Being Funny.*

Comedy Dojo, Chris Barnes, 310/393-6686. comedydojo.com. $250 for 8 weeks. Chris has put together an acting technique you can take from the classroom to the stage, to the audition and onto the set. Actress Aimee Garcia recommended this class to me when we worked together on *All About The Andersons*. She found his comedy character definitions very helpful. Chris has an impressive resume, including a stint as a writer for *SNL*.

Cynthia Szigeti, 818/980-7890. Former head of the Groundlings' training program, and of Acme Comedy Theatre's improv workshops. Students have included Lisa Kudrow, Conan O'Brien, Alex Borstein and Julia Sweeney. She coaches actors and stand-ups privately. Prices vary.

Shari Shaw Actors Studio, 818/766-0346, sharishawstudios.com. On-going classes that applies Method acting to comedy. Prices vary; classes for all levels.

BOOKS

Order on my website or: Samuel French Bookstore, 323/876-0570 or 818/762-0535 or the website: samuelfrench.com.
The Eight Characters of Comedy: A Guide to Sitcom Acting and Writing by Scott Sedita.
The Sitcom Career Book: A Guide to the Louder, Faster, Funnier World of TV Comedy by Mary Lou Belli and Phil Ramuno.
Stand-Up Comedy: The Book by Judy Carter.
The Comedy Bible by Judy Carter.
How To Be a Stand-Up Comic by Larry Charles and Richard Belzer.
SeinLanguage by Jerry Seinfeld.
Successful Stand-Up Comedy: Advice from a Comedy Writer by Gene Perret.

VIDEO STORES

Video West, 818/760-0096. 11376 Ventura Blvd., Studio City, 91604.
Video West, 310/659-5762. 805 Larrabee Street, West Hollywood, 90069. **These video stores are the best!** Bargain days Tuesday, Wednesday and Thursday, $1.29 a tape. Have them give you a tour of the store; they've got classics, independents, foreign, art house, comedies, stand-up comics. Just about anything you need to research. Fantastic!

PRIVATE ACTING COACHES

• **Many actors routinely work with a private coach** when they are preparing for an audition. In fact, many agents and managers will not sign an actor unless they agree to coach for all important auditions. The time to get your coaching is before your first reading. If you are called back, the auditioners liked what you did. Sometimes, though, they might ask you to take the script and bring a character back with a whole different attitude. Your coach can help you discover a new way to approach the character.

• **A good time to seek an audition coach** is when you are getting lots of callbacks but not landing the jobs. The coach may be able to give you that extra edge of confidence to put you over the top.

• **When working on projects,** actors will often hire their coach to prepare them for the role before shooting starts. They will work on the entire script so when they are shooting out of sequence the actor will know and remember the work they had planned for each scene. Often on a film or a single-camera television show, you may shoot the first and last scene the same day. You may be shooting the nude love scenes your first day on the project, even the first day of meeting your partner. For several seasons of *Seinfeld,* Michael Richards worked with his coach, Joanne Linville, preparing for each episode.

• **You may need coaching** if you are a new actor and have been given a job as a result of your fame in another field, such as sports or modeling. When I was Joan Darling's assistant, she coached, among many others, Joe Namath, for his first film after his football career. Some of the personalities I've worked with are Catherine Oxenberg when she was on *Dynasty;* Debbie Maffett, Miss America, when she landed her first television job hosting *P.M. Magazine*; stand-ups Thea Vidale, on her sitcom *Thea* and Darlene Westgor on her Nick at Night sitcom.

• **A beginning actor** who is shy may want to have private sessions before joining a class.

• **Working with a good acting coach privately** will help actors develop their craft quickly. They will learn how to deliver a sustained performance, as every moment will be concentrated on them.

• **In our business, most of the acting** we do is one-on-one, whether it is for a casting director, or a camera. There may be a room full of producers, writers, the network executives and a director, but the actor will be playing to one person and the group will be watching you work alone. When you are on set, you are playing with the other character or characters in the scene and the camera is watching you.

• **One of your considerations** when thinking of studying privately might be the cost. The average price is $70 to $150 per hour and at least twice that much if you are being coached on the set or for a role you are being paid for. Most acting classes are around $50 a class where you might have ten minutes or so focused on just you. For $100, you can have an hour focused on you. We all have to decide how to spend the money we set aside for advancing our craft. I do believe it is good to be in a class; there is the group dynamic that you don't have when working privately, and you learn from the group. So perhaps you will set your budget up to meet twice a month or even once every two months with a private coach to test how you are doing under that type of pressure. You will reach a point where you will be going quite often to a coach, preparing for your auditions. Pilot season can mean actors having two coachings a day and many auditions a week. I hope that becomes your reality. Sounds like fun, doesn't it?

• **I video tape when coaching.** I believe actors learn faster if they are able to see their work, observe their own strong and weak points and see what they look like, just listening. They take the tape home and continue to learn from watching their work, what they have delivered well and my notes. Many times an actor will bring a scene they have prepared and it is dynamic—there is nothing for me to fix. I then marvel at what they did, ask how they did it and have them do it again. I say, "It's not broken, I'm not going to try to fix it so we can spend an hour; I'm just charging you for a half hour today." I keep the actor's tape running the whole time so they can take it home and listen to me telling them how wonderful they are and why. I don't mind the missed half-hour's income; I enjoy the actor's growth.

• **Most of the coaches** listed below are written about in greater detail in the *Acting Coaches* section.

Private Coaches

To download and print an updated version of this and all resource lists, go to actingiseverything.com.

Judy Kerr, 818/505-9373. JudyKerr.com. $100 an hour. All levels, acting techniques and audition work. I coach actors for auditions. I also coach actors who want to study acting privately. A beginner who wants an understanding of what it is to act before taking classes; or an experienced actor who wants an hour devoted to them to further develop their technique. I give the actor a script ahead of time; they work on it and bring it in having done the best preparation they know how. I coach on video so they keep a tape of their acting along with my critique and instructions of how to make it better and how to deliver stronger acting choices. The actors then review their tape at home and learn more. I also teach a private one time, one-and-a-half to two-hour career coaching/guidance meeting for $150 to $200. This is based on the resources and principles in this book but geared for you individually—what works for your particular needs.

Caryn West, 323/876-0394. $100 or $80 if currently enrolled in class. http://groups. yahoo.com/group/CarynWest-ActorsLA. She is great at preparing you for your auditions. Caryn has coached me many times for auditions.

Scott Sedita of the Scott Sedita Acting Studios and the coach on "Fight For Fame," 323/465-6152. scottseditaacting.com. $90 for an hour and $45 for a half hour. Author of *The Eight Characters of Comedy.*

Jeffrey Marcus, 323/965-9392. jeffreymarcus.com. $100 an hour. "My coaching is designed to assist you in finding truthful behavior in the dry dust of the words. Change fear to excitement in one session."

Cherie Franklin, 818/762-4658. $85-$200 an hour. Cherie is an inspirational teacher; I've worked with her often. She's also an on-set coach.

Stuart K. Robinson, 310/558-4961. $100 and up. Great with commercials, auditions, script writing and directing for demo reels and business strategy.

Janice Lynde, 323/650-0515. janicelynde.com. $75-$150 an hour. Teaches a wonderful, fast, simple audition technique, as well as coaching for a specific role you have been cast in.

Jamie Rose Studio, 323/799-1183. jrosestudio.com. $100-$125/hour. Her teaching methods draw from acting coach Roy London and her extensive professional experience.

Kimberly Crandall, 310/463/7136 kimberlycrandallactingcoach.com. $75 an hour, $45 a half-hour. "At the end of your session you will feel so confident about the upcoming audition you will start to 'love' the audition process itself."

Clair Sinnett, 310/606-0813. Actorsworking.com. $100 an hour for career consulting and audition preparation. Author of *Actors Working: The Actor's Guide to Marketing Success.*

Mala Powers, 818/980-5400. chekhovpowers@earthlink.net. $75 an hour. Mala is a Hollywood Walk of Fame honoree, author and director specializes in the Michael Chekhov Technique of Acting. Audition preparation and coaching for specific stage and film roles. Characterizations through the use of Imaginary Center, Imaginary Body, Psychological Gesture.

Joel Asher, 818/785-1551. Joel-Asher-Studio.com. $100-$125 an hour, but free when you are taking his scene study class.

Anthony Caldarella, 310/828-6898. Director/writer, acting coach, imdb.com. $100 an hour. "I focus on helping the actor break down the script and to ask the questions to inspire character discoveries."

Sandra Caruso, 310/476-5113. tft.ucla.edu, sandracaruso.com. Private coaching and audition preparation, $50 an hour. Professor of Acting at UCLA School of Theater, Film and Television.

Brian Drillinger, 310/828-9107. $90 an hour. He helps the actor strengthen their ability to prepare and execute a great audition by learning how to make physical and emotional choices. Also offers private voice lessons for $75 an hour.

Bernard Hiller, 818/781-8000, bernardhiller.com. $85 per hour. He prepares actors for auditions and is also available for on-set private coaching. He will help you find a way to bring your unique quality to any role.

Rae Allen, 310/396-6734. Tony Award-winning actress and director. $125 per session on camera.

Jill Jaress, coach and career consultant, 310/828-7814. jaress@adelphia.net. $120 an hour. Audition preparation as well as business techniques.

Sandy Holt, 310/271-8217. $80 an hour. Audition preparation. Geat with sitcom material.

Leigh Kilton-Smith, 323/650-4204. $150 an hour for consulting and coaching. Also an on-set coach.

Janice Kent, 818/906-2201. janicekent.com. $90-125 per hour. Recommended by many top-level agencies and managers, she specializes in sitcom, but coaches everything.

John Kirby, 323/939-5284. $75 an hour unless paid by a studio or agency. Works privately on auditions, bookings and on-set coach. Also does career consulting.

Warner Loughlin, 310/276-0555, warnerloughlin.com $160 an hour, unless paid by studio. On-set film and television coaching for actors and directors.

Allan Miller, 818/907-6262. $125 an hour.

Mike Muscat, 818/904-9494. $75 an hour at his office and $100 at your home, he coaches on camera and offers a money back guarantee. Helps stage actors adjust to film acting.

Wayne Dvorak, 323/462-5328. actingcoachdvorak.com. Private coaching is $60 session.

Cynthia Szigeti, 818/980-7890. Prices vary. Former head of the Groundlings' training program. Coaches actors and standups.

John Sarno, 818/761-3003, hollywoodacting.com. Teaches classes and privately; focus on method acting and auditioning. Prices vary. Recommended by agent Bonnie Howard.

Joanne Linville Studio, 310/248-4825. Teaches technique for all levels of actor; Offers scene study and private coaching; $100 an hour. Michael Richards credits Joanne for his work on *Seinfeld*.

Check the Acting Coaches, Audition Coaches, Comedy Coaches, Improvisation, Voice Teachers and Commercial Classes sections for class listings and other teachers that will sometimes offer private coaching sessions.

Improvisation

• **I believe every actor** should have some improvisational training. Many casting directors look for the ability to improvise on your resume. I have been hired for several acting jobs solely because I knew how to improvise. In television it is almost essential because you have very little rehearsal time; nor is there time for the director to tell you how to play a scene.

• **Improv is also good** for breaking down barriers you might have in revealing yourself, so it is helpful to study it at the beginning of your acting career—you get off to the right start.

• **Todd Rohrbacher** is often called in as an assistant casting director for improvisationial projects. In the audition he sets up a premise and then improvs with the actors. Todd is the Founder and Artistic Director of *Captain Creamsicle's Laughateers* and is an alumnus of *ACME Comedy Theatre's* Main Company. He teaches all levels of improvisation as well as on-camera comedy and audition technique at Scott Sedita's Acting Studios. He is a sitcom dialogue coach as well as an animation writer.

Q: How does studying improv help with auditions?

• **There will always be scripted comedies**, but one of the ways sitcoms are being rejuvenated is with improv. *Curb Your Enthusiasm* popularized the semi-improvised half hour comedy. A few more have come along since: *Significant Others, Sons and Daughters* and *Free Ride.* There is a freshness and reality to improvised comedy that audiences find appealing. These are great jobs to book because you really get to bring your voice and ideas to the role you're playing. But if you're not a trained improviser, you won't be in the running!

• **Shows that are entirely scripted may bring improv** into the audition process just so the director can get a stronger sense of your abilities and see how well you work on the fly. It's hard to avoid at least some improv as you audition for comedic roles. In short, executing comedy requires the ability to make fast, brave, distinct choices. It also requires precision timing, pace and rhythm. Improv training helps you to hone those skills.

- **Improvising helps you evolve into an "entertainer."** Actors are often perfectionists so they get in their heads, self-criticize during auditions, focus on rejection…the list goes on. Entertainers are more fluid, better prepared for the unknown and are more likely to have fun with the long term process of steadily building a career. Think of Jim Carey, Robin Williams, Ben Stiller, Lisa Kudrow and Will Ferrell. Yes, they are all good actors, but they have taken a step beyond that label to become the industry's highest paid entertainers. They know how to improvise. If you want to book work in comedy, you should too.

• **Jeff Doucette**, founding member of the ongoing *Improv at the Improv* and veteran of Chicago's *Second City*.

Q: How does improvisation help actors?

- **There is a common misconception** that improvisation is about being funny. When actors are working on their feet, they often make the more comic choice, but that is not by any means the only valid one. Wonderful improvisations often center on more dramatic situations and emotions. Improvisation is a technique of acting. Acting is playing. As actors, we play parts in plays, screenplays, or teleplays. Spontaneity is the natural by-product of play. Improvisation opens the door to spontaneity by focusing on playing and solving problems in the moment. Through the process of improvisation, actors learn their own acting technique naturally by learning how to push their own buttons. They learn scene structure and character development. They unlock their creativity and open their imagination.

- **Learning the lines and breaking down a scene** can only give an actor a game plan. Once the camera is rolling, once the lights come up on the stage, the actor must trust his choices and find the truth in the moment. He must play the part. Improvisation teaches an actor to trust his instincts. An actor trained in improvisation learns to love being out on a limb. He's not afraid because he knows that if the branch gives way, there will either be a net to catch him or he will discover that he can fly.

- **Improvisation also helps the actor in everyday life** and in almost any audition situation. By learning to play with people and trust his instincts, an actor can overcome fear and learn to project his personality in a positive and constructive way.

Q: How should an actor pick an improv teacher?

- **First of all, the actor has to decide what he wants.** There is comedic-performance oriented improv and there is improv aimed more at the acting process. Both are good, but many actors are intimidated by the comedic improv classes. They feel that they have to be clever, quick and funny, or are intimidated by the competitiveness of the class.

- **Obviously you should talk to the teacher.** But ask specific questions and listen carefully for the answers. The more you know what you want out of a class the more specific you can be with your questions. You're not going to "get" the whole course in an interview, but how you relate to the teacher will give you a feeling of how it might be in the class.

- **Take advantage of an audit.** You can get a feel for the teacher, the class and the other students. If auditing isn't permitted, try to talk to as many students as possible. Most will say they love it, but try to pin them down and find out why they love it. See if you can get them to be specific. This will give you a better idea of what it is they look for in a class. It may or may not be what you are looking for.

• **Sandy Holt improv/cold reading teacher,** acting coach, actress, comedy writer and co-owner of a voice casting company, began her career performing with *Second City.*

Q: Why is improvisation important for the actor?

- **Improvisation is the springboard to your imagination.** I get actors to unlock the part of their brain where the creativity is, to break through the cliches. Improv is like jazz—you pick up on the riff that's happening and go with the dance and bring your magic to it. I get actors to find their own magic. Sandra Bernhard told me when doing *King Of Comedy,* she used all the skills she learned in class. She got the part because she brought her own excitement to the work, her own stamp.

- **Improvisation is also valuable for writers and stand-ups.** If a writer is having trouble with a script, we improvise to see what isn't working. Is it the action? Too wordy? Are the characters authentic? I had writers from *Cheers* come to my class. They were having trouble pitching ideas. By getting them into improvising and playing different roles, they really increased their pitching skills. Stand-up comedians find out what's funny about them and what makes them special.

Q: How would you describe your ideal student?

- **Someone who wants to play,** is willing to take direction, wants to participate, loves to get up and is willing to work through resistance. Actors should use their improv class as a safe place to make mistakes, work through blocks, get their courage up, take risks, go through their discomfort, and move through fear, so they can tap into the most wonderful, craziest part of themselves. When I interview actors wishing to join my classes I ask what they need to work on. Some people say, "I'm going up for auditions but I don't nail the job." So we work on how to nail the job. I work with actors on camera because this is a film business. I work on appearance and image. When you walk into a room, what do they see?

Resources

To download and print an updated version of this and all resource lists, go to actingiseverything.com.

Todd Rohrbacher at Scott Sedita Acting Studios, 323/465-6152. scottseditaacting.com. 526 N. Larchmont Blvd., Los Angeles, 90004. Improv class designed for film and television. Cost is $35 per class. Todd works in improve basics, games and exercises but also shows actors how to tailor their improve skills to the film medium, especially in auditioning.

Acme Comedy Theatre, 323/525-0233. acmecomedy.com. One of the bigger improv companies in town. Classes start at $350. Acme will place you in one of its five classes, from basic improv to sketch writing and performance.

Gary Austin, 800/DOG-TOES, garyaustin.net. Gary is the original founder of The Groundlings. He is a famous coach and teaches around the country. His prices are very reasonable and you should take at least one session with him. Many stay for years.

Bang Improv Studio, 323/653-6886. bangstudio.com. 457 N. Fairfax Ave., Los Angeles 90036. Specializes in scene and character building. Beginning classes with improv exercises and games, start at $275 a month and decrease with each new level up to the Master Class.

Jason Bowers, jasonbowers.com. Email: jbo@jasonbowers.com. Classes are $140 a month and focus on short and long form improv and improving in a casting session.

Comedy Dojo, Chris Barnes, 310/393-6686. comedydojo.com. $250 for 8 weeks. Actress Aimee Garcia recommended this class to me when we worked together on *All About The Andersons*. She found his comedy character definitions very helpful. Chris has an impressive resume, including a stint as a writer for *SNL*.

Andy Goldberg, 310/283-4027. offthewallcomedy.net. 12—16 week classes. Author of *Improv Comedy* as well as member of the *Off the Wall* improv group since 1975. Ongoing class applying improv techniques to character development.

The Groundlings, 323/934-4747. groundlings.com. 7307 Melrose Ave., Hollywood, 90046. $450 for 12 sessions at the beginning levels. A performing group producing many working actors specializing in comedy. Go see a performance and get an idea of what is possible in improvisation. Students audition for the basic level, then are invited to the intermediate class. Auditions are not required for the pre-beginning-level class.

Sandy Holt, 310/271-8217. See the *Audition Technique Section*. Combines improv with audition technique.

Kip King, 818/784-0544. kipking.actorsite.com. $350 for 10 weeks, returning students $300 for 11 weeks. One of the original Groundlings. Helps you bring yourself to each character you play. Especially helpful with comedy. Uses improv with commercials and comedy.

Harvey Lembeck Comedy Workshop, 310/271-2831. harveylembeckcomedyworkshop.com. Three levels but aimed for the trained working actor who wants to specialize in comedy. Teaches how to play comedy legitimately in a scene. Using improv as a method to teach comedy, work on stage 3 to 4 times a night. Former students include John Ritter, Jenna Elfman, Bryan Cranston, Kim Cattrall.

Second City Training Center, 323/658-8190. Email: training.la@secondcity.com. secondcity.com. 8156 Melrose Avenue, Los Angeles, 90046. Lots of different classes at varying prices. See website for information.

VOICE AND
VOICE TEACHERS

To an actor a word is not just a sound, it is the evocation of images. Your job is to instill your inner visions in others...and convey it in words.
—Constantin Stanislavski

The voice is the audio reflection of your soul. Expanding the voice opens the artist and the soul. —Bob Corff

• **Acting is a vocal art**; our voices are used to interpret and depict scripts. Most actors need voice training in order to have complete control of their speaking voice. In many plays, actors need to use their voice for a considerable length of time. In film and TV, a big yelling scene may come after 12 or 16 hours of work; your voice should last through all of that. Another skill that must be in the actor's tool kit is the ability to speak with a general American accent; without it you will be very limited in the roles you will be considered for. You can add other accents and dialects for even more versatility. Of course, speaking other languages helps too.

• **Sal Romeo, a popular acting coach says:**

  • **As an actor, it is necessary to free one's natural voice** so the truth of feeling comes through. Much of what is done in film and television today is shot in close up and really all you've got is your voice to bring the nuance and emotional truth to the work. Vocal relaxation and use of language enhances and brings truth to one's performance. Many of us have been raised with tension in our voices; we put on a nice personality that hides our feelings in order to please. Often that voice is pitched from two or three notes to even an octave higher than our real, natural, true voice. When you learn to relax the tension in the voice, the emotional truth rings out in a richer, more resonating sound.

- **Tom Todoroff, film producer, acting, dialogue and dialect coach, says:**

  - **Basically, all you have to act with is your breath.** If you're not connected to your breath, it's possible to speak but you are saying words that don't come from where you feel things. I can understand you, but I'm not receiving your words where I feel things. The breath sends off vibrations that the other actor and the audience feels.

- **Gary Catona, voice builder, says:**

  - **The voice is a character,** as identifiable as your physical appearance. Your voice should be an expression of who you are, as an actor and as a person. When a person acts and a singer sings, they are indulging in an athletic activity. It is athletic because you are using muscles. In a sense, an actor is somebody who is a vocal athlete and you have to look at his or her voice in that light. Vocal exercises are important; exercise is necessary to improve your voice.

- **Bob and Claire Corff, well known voice teachers, say:**

  - **Enriching and improving your voice alters the way you feel** about yourself and the way people respond to you. Voice is the purest representation of you, revealing levels of confidence and attitude. The voice is one of the first and most powerful characteristics people respond to. A strong and self assured voice commands attention and respect.

  - **Developing an effective voice is as important** to a person and an artist as developing a toned and healthy body. Practicing the proper exercises from one to three weeks can make a striking improvement in any actor's voice. This can have as dramatic an effect on their performance and confidence as having plastic surgery.

- **Godeane Eagle, speech pathologist and voice teacher, says:**

  - **Actors are their own instruments,** and in order to play that instrument, it has to be in tune. Some of the problems are: not using the voice to the fullest, lack of confidence, vowel shapings or vowel projection, and the sound of the voice. If, at the end of a performance or rehearsal, the performer is feeling strain or pain in the throat area, he or she is doing something incorrectly. Voices can be stressed to the point where they simply stop.

- **Ben D'Aubery, dialect and accent coach, explains the difference between dialects and accents:**

  - **Dialect is regionalism**—as far as emphasis on the words and pronunciations as used in language. You have an accent when you use your own language regionalisms on someone else's language. For instance: a German learning to speak English would be speaking with an accent. But if a Californian goes to the South and speaks as a Californian, it would be considered a dialect. If English is your native language and you go to another country where English is spoken, you would be speaking a dialect, because your "English" would be a regional difference on that country's "English"—Irish, Scottish, Australian, etc.

• **Accent** means when you take on a foreign language, you're speaking with an accent—Spanish, Italian, Russian, etc.

• **When listing dialects and accents** on your resume, make sure you list them correctly.

• **Godeane Eagle,** believes ear training is the first step when working with accents.

  • **It's necessary to take the actor to the piano** and check how he or she recognizes pitches; it must be known if they can match a pitch, or even hear a pitch. Ear training makes people aware of fine-tuning differences in sound, such as between 'pen' and 'pin.'

• **You can train your ear for the proper language or dialect** you wish to use. A good source is Dove Books on tape. The books are read by well known actors and authors. If someone says they want you to play an Elizabeth Ashley or Tom Hanks type, you can get a tape of that actor reading a book or parts of a book and pick up some of what their essence is. Also check out any of the free dialect websites; some of the best are listed below.

• **Shopping for the right voice teacher** is important because working with your voice is extremely intimate and personal.

• **Godeane Eagle believes:**

  • **It's necessary** that the voice teacher be someone with whom you feel comfortable, someone who cares about you and is interested in your voice. The speaking voice is very sensitive, delicate, and will respond negatively to negative teaching. Actors can learn both privately and in small classes, though beginners frequently need one-on-one because they need total attention.

• **Tom Todoroff recommends:**

  • **Meet with three different coaches** and take a class with each—see who you connect with.

- **He also spoke of the discipline required for voice work:**

  - **Your voice is a series of muscles** like other muscles in your body and it responds to exercise. When you go to the gym or take a dance class, your body becomes more elastic, more coordinated; your voice is the same way. If you don't work on it, it doesn't take care of you. An actor needs to work 20 minutes each and every day on their voice. To be an actor and not work on your voice is akin to being a dancer and saying, "I don't go to dance class" or a pianist who says, "I don't believe in scales or practicing." So much of what I teach beginners in the first classes has to do with the benefits of discipline. Discipline allows you incredible freedom.

- **For information on work in voiceovers,** read the *Voiceover Section.*

Resources

To download and print an updated version of this and all resource lists, go to actingiseverything.com.

DIALECT WEBSITES

thedialectcoach.com. Joel Goldes. Excellent site.

iwasthere.org.uk/page_18.htm. Click into Links then into International Dialects of English Archive. You will find two different printed texts and then downloadable voices reading the text in many different dialects. MP3 files. You can study these and train your ear for the dialect.

Ku.edu/~idea/index.htm. The International Dialects of English Archive at the University of Kansas has over 500 free dialect samples from all over the world.

uncc.edu/english/clc/index1.html. Oral histories from different parts of the country.

dialectresource.com/. Brief samples of some dialects; tapes of many different dialects to purchase, available from their website or Samuel French bookstores.

m-w.com. The website for the Merriam-Webster Dictionary provides correct audible pronunciations of words.

polyglot.lss.wisc.edu/dare/dare.html. On this site, Dictionary of American Regional English, click on Audio Sample and you will hear several different people with accents reading a short passage.

http://web.uvic.ca/ling/resources/ipa/handbook.htm. Downloadable audio files of language illustrations. Many languages.

VOICE TEACHERS

Joel Goldes, 818/879-1896. thedialectcoach.com. Amazing coach. Ccoaching $85 an hour. Good news is you can work with him over the phone anywhere in the country. He will send you a CD of your phone conversation. If you have a regional accent, you can work with him on developing a standard American accent. Also specializes in standard dialects (New York, Southern, British, etc.) and more obscure dialects (Nigerian, Bantu, Finnish, Asian). He's worked with a ton of stars, including Jennifer Garner, Mike Myers, Josie Maran and Tom Arnold. Lots of free dialect tips on his website.

Bob Corff, 323/851-9042. corffvoice.com. $80 a half hour. If you mention this book he will give a special rate of $70 a half hour. For actors and singers, works on giving your voice color, strength and stamina. Working on breathing, diction, accents and accent reduction, sibilant "s" and other speech problems, proper placement, lowering your voice and widening your range. Small group classes and private sessions. Author of audio tape/CDs, *The Bob Corff Speakers Voice Method* and *The Bob Corff Singers Voice Method*. Also wrote *Achieving the Standard American* Accent with wife and associate Claire Corff. Some of his famous clients include Antonio Banderas, Glenn Close, Hank Azaria, Samuel L. Jackson, Faye Dunaway, Sally Field and Salma Hayek.

Claire Corff, 323/851-9042. corffvoice.com. $45 and up. She teaches the Bob Corff method. Speaking, singing and accent reduction. She's fun and easy to be with. Many of my students as well as my husband, and I have improved greatly while working with her.

Rowena Balos, 310/285-8489. rowenabalos.com. Sliding scale but around $75 an hour for private. Basic Introductory Voice Workshop is usually $240 to $265, and includes book and audio tapes. Works on accent reduction. Former head of voice department at NYU. Recommended by Caryn West.

Barbara Bragg, 323/876-6702. Class and private coaching prices vary. Trained in Linklater voice process and most of the classical dialects. Has worked with both film and stage actors. Caryn West recommends Barbara for vocal production and articulation.

Linda Brennan, 818/829-2338, vasta.org. $90 an hour. Helps with accent reduction as well as dialect and accent coaching, especially American and European languages. Has worked with a number of celebrities and on a number of movie sets, including American Pie, The Brady Bunch Movie and The Scorpion King

Sam Chwat, In New York, 212/242-8435. (Pronounced schwah.) nyspeech.com. People Magazine says: "Speech pathologist to the stars, accent-uates his celebrity clients." Adam Sandler in *The Waterboy;* Julia Roberts in *Mystic Pizza;* Leonardo DiCaprio in *The Basketball Diaries;* Robert De Niro in *Cape Fear.* He's recorded three audio books about accent elimination. Order through New York Speech Improvement Services, 1/800/SPEAKWELL.

Ben D'Aubery, 818/783-1951. $45 to $60 an hour. Private and group lessons, specializing in accent reduction and acquisition. I worked with him at the West Coast Ensemble Theatre to develop a North Carolina accent; he was excellent. He can deliver a crash course to get you ready for an audition in a short amount of time. Standard English, Cockney, Scottish, Irish, Aussie, French, German, Russian, Italian, Spanish, Yiddish, American Southern, New England, New York and Caribbean. On *Seinfeld,* he helped the Jamaican jogger (whom Elaine fouled up) create his accent.

Bill Dearth, 818/761-1051. speechmech.com. Specializes in learning and losing accents and developing speaking voices. "Your voice is as important as your picture!" Highly recommended by commercial teacher Carolyn Barry.

Brian Drillinger, 310/828-9107. larrymossstudio.com. Private coaching available. Recommended by acting coaches Larry Moss and Michelle Danner and actress Jode Edwards. Brian begins by working privately. You learn to connect with your full breath and work through a series of exercises that become a vocal warm-up you can use the rest of your career. Once you've learned the warm-up, you join the advanced class and work on acting material from a vocal perspective. In class you will work to create a clear channel of breath, emotion, and voice. Brian believes, "You must have an emotionally connected, fully expressive voice; it is the primary connector between you and the audience."

Godeane Eagle, 310/450-5735. $50 to $75 an hour. Godeane holds an M.A. combination in music, theatre and clinical speech. She teaches singers and actors who want to sing. She teaches stage voice, projection, and is very mindful regarding voice and throat protection. She works with students of all ages, including young children, and is trained in speech defect correction and accent reduction. She was my special teacher and helped me find my real voice. I am eternally grateful.

Libby Jordan, 310/428-2992. $75 an hour. American dialect coach, she works almost exclusively with Australian, English, and New Zealand actors who require a natural-sounding American accent. She also works with American actors who need to perfect a new dialect, whether British or American. Her technique focuses on how the breath, tongue, lips, placement of the jaw and intonation all determine how our dialects sound. Libby says this method quickly teaches you how to physically change your speech patterns effortlessly so you can slip into any American dialect easily.

Saul Kotzubei, 323/965-8333. voicecoachla.com. Private coaching and classes on a sliding scale, averages between $90-$160 per hour. Lead trainer in the revolutionary Fitzmaurice Voicework training which combines basic voicework techniques with yoga and other forms of body-based and meditative practices. Works with many stars.

Patrick Munoz, 323/512-3841. $75 an hour for private. $150 for studio work. Teaches privately and at the Scott Sedita Acting Studios, 323/465-6152. scottseditaacting.com. Three one-hour sessions, $210. Learn to breathe properly and lose any regionalism and accent reduction. He incorporates several techniques including Skinner and Linklater plus his own unique approach. Works with many actors who are trying to rid their speech of regionalisms, clear up their speech and learn new dialects. Also works as an on set dialect coach. Very highly recommended by Talent Manager, Steven Nash. Private clients include Penelope Cruz.

Tom Todoroff, 310/281-8688. tomtodoroff.com. See Acting Coach section.

VOICE AND DIALECT TAPES/CDS

The Bob Corff Voice Method, corffvoice.com. *The Bob Corff Speakers Voice Method, The Bob Corff Singers Voice Method, Achieving the Standard American Accent* and *Voice Method for Singers.* Also "Learn Accent Series" for English, Irish, Southern, French and more. Sold on the website or at Samuel French Booksellers, Take One! and Skylight Books. "With the confidence that comes from having a strong, powerful voice there are no limits to what you can achieve in your career." Casting director Reuben Cannon says, "Your success as an actor or singer will be greatly determined by your vocal skills. Study with a master—Bob Corff."

Sam Chwat's SPEAKUP! Programs, 1/800-SPEAKWELL, nyspeech.com. Three different tapes: *American Regional Accent Elimination; Spanish Regional Accent Elimination; Asian Middle Eastern, Indian-Pakistani Accent Elimination.* Call for more information.

Jerry Blunt audio tapes of accents and dialects available at theatrical bookstores. These tapes are very conversational and easy to learn from.

David Alan Stern, 800/753-1016. dialectaccentspecialists.com He teaches from a very academic point of view on these tapes. His books and audio tapes are available at theatrical bookstores or from the website. They will probably have a tape for any dialect or accent you need.

SINGING TEACHERS

Morgan Ames, well known composer, singer and producer, recommends Lis Lewis and Rosemary Butler to the professional and studio session singers she produces and arranges for. They work strictly with the singing voice.

Lis Lewis, 818/623-6668. thesingersworkshop.com

Rosemary Butler, 310/572-6338. rosemarybutler.com. Works also with teens. Call for rates.

Bob Corff, 323/851-9042. corffvoice.com. Offers private coaching in all styles, covering vocal technique, breathing, relaxation and removing the "break" through vocal exercises that strengthen the voice to build stamina and increase vocal range. Bob also teaches Singers Performance technique to help feel more comfortable on stage. Has worked with Glenn Close for *Sunset Blvd.* and Antonio Banderas for *Evita.*

Suzanne Kiechle, 818/769-5880. $125-$150 an hour. Very famous singing coach who has worked with Tony nominees. Christina Applegate said she couldn't sing at all before working with Suzanne. Suzanne says, "A majority of people don't know how to use their voices, the mechanics behind it. I show the how." She can teach you to sing, no matter what kind of music. She also helps you deal with nodes and other vocal problems without needing surgery. Highly respected.

Auditiontrax.com. Caryn West recommends this site for audition piano demos or to learn a song.

BOOKS AND MATERIALS

The Total Singer by Lisa Popeil, 818/906-7229. popeil.com.
The Secrets of Singing by Jeffrey Allen, 800/644-4707, ext. 22. vocalsuccess.com.
Tom Todoroff's recommended reading list: *Voice and the Actor* and *The Actor and the Text* by Cicely Berry; *Freeing the Natural Voice* by Kristen Linklater; and *Speak With Distinction* by Edith Skinner.
The Brand Library, 818/548-2051. 1601 W. Mountain Street, Glendale, 91201, at the top of Grandview Ave. Hours: T & Th 1-9, W 1-6, F & Sa 1-5. They have a vast supply of records, tapes, CDs, print music and art books available for loan-out.
Theatrical bookstores sell books and tapes to help you with standard American speech as well as dialects.
Travel Stores, for tapes of instruction on how to speak other languages. Usually the instructor has the accent of the language they are teaching.
Working Actors' Guide lists voice teachers for speech and singing.

• **Tongue Twisters** can sometimes be a very good warm-up for your voice on the way to auditions or before getting ready to act in class, on the stage or set. Memorize your favorite ones to be able to use them anytime. Godeane Eagle gave me these two favorites of mine: "Blueberry pie with peach ice cream" and "Strawberry shortcake with whipped cream." Really move your mouth, pucker and smile. Tom Todoroff's favorite is: "Eleven benevolent elephants." Try some of the following twisters. Use a tape recorder to make sure your pronunciation is correct. Also, check out actorsite.com for many more famous, and more obscure, Tongue Twisters.

TONGUE TWISTERS

- The lips, the teeth, the tip of the tongue.
- Which witch, what watt?
- A big black bug bit a big black bear.
- Loving Lucy likes light literature.
- Some shun sunshine, do you shun sunshine?
- Bad blood (ten times very quickly.)
- Flesh of freshly dried flying fish.
- I slit a sheet, a sheet I slit. Upon a slitted sheet I sit.
- Lemon liniment, lemon liniment, lemon liniment.
- Aluminum, linoleum
- Unique, New York

CREATE YOUR LIFE

BE YOUR OWN LIFE COACH

• **You can learn how to create your life,** as you want it to be. You are responsible for your thoughts, for your life. Are you willing to accept that responsibility?

• **This section is for those who are seeking ways** to improve their life. If you are one of those, here are some of my favorite tools. Just as we are all alone in front of the camera, we are all alone in life itself. As I see it, our goal is to become the best that we can be in living the life we design. If you agree, this section could be helpful.

• **What you need to know to master acting** is exactly what you need to know to master your life. Being a good actor is about making specific choices when interpreting a script. Similarly, having the life that you desire is about making choices that contribute to your life's plan. We are constantly making choices, whether we realize it or not. In fact we are the sum-total of our life choices. In order to make the best, most thoughtful choices we must have a plan, a design for our life.

• **Most of us want to be authentic,** follow our instincts, take risks and have a good time. Many times we have baggage that prevents us from doing that. As actors we have to know our characters completely in order to understand why they act the way they do. We certainly must know ourselves just as completely. What is authentic, what is unique about you? These are the discoveries to be made.

• **Go for your dream—what is stopping you?** Here are some ways to learn how to give yourself permission to take risks, to jump off the cliff, to be authentic. Who wants to jump off a cliff that someone else has chosen for you? I encourage you to have the passion to design your life as you see it. That can be a life of joy, grief, troubles, ease, romance, wealth, poverty, fame, sadness or any combination.

• **The tools below have helped me** as well as countless others in living the life they have designed. To live an authentic life one must accept the total responsibility for it. There is no passing the buck, placing blame or playing the victim. When you make a choice that wasn't for your greatest benefit you must examine that choice to see why you didn't honor your plan. Did you go for the quick fix, the easy out? Did you allow an outside pressure to get to you? This process of self-examination is what helps you grow into being fully authentic.

Tool #1 – Rewrite your life stories.

• **Many times we tell stories about ourselves** that do not serve us well. Such stories may prevent us from realizing our full potential. When you have unflattering stories about yourself, perhaps ones that were told at home, rewrite them. Often, we've actually made up the negative stories in our heads, and we can re-think them. I'll give you one of my stories and how I rewrote it. I believed that my father didn't love me and that he never approved of me. My father has been dead 30 years. Yet, I never resolved my problem with him. Finally, I rewrote the story. Now I say, "my father didn't love me the way I wanted him to and couldn't give me the approval I needed."

• **As I worked with that story** I saw that the man my father was would never have been able to love me like I wanted to be loved. All those years of wanting approval had been a waste of time. I had wanted blood from a turnip. I forgave him for being who he was and the next step was to find something to be grateful for; I'm told the two greatest healing actions are forgiveness and gratitude.

• **As I thought about it,** I came to have gratitude for my legs. I have my dad's long thin legs and have been complimented on them all my life. Fortunately, as one ages, the last to go are the legs. So as the face and body have succumbed to age, the legs are holding up pretty well. This may sound like a simple tale but it was years of hard work to arrive at a place of healing. What I thought of as my father's disapproval had held me back from taking risks. When I was able to forgive and find some gratitude, it gave me freedom to become more authentic, to jump off the cliffs I chose, not the ones I thought he wanted me to. It doesn't matter what is true; you are the one who decides what is true about your life's stories.

Tool #2 – The Four Agreements

• **These agreements will help you** learn how to take responsibility for everything you say and for all of your actions. Again, these seem simple but it is your devotion to them that will bring about profound change in your perception of life.

Four Agreements

The Four Agreements, A Practical Guide To Personal Freedom by Don Miguel Ruiz. I believe the knowledge gained from this book enhances an actor's life and career. Buy the book. Here is a sample.

1. Be Impeccable with Your Word

Speak with integrity. Say only what you mean. Avoid using words to speak against yourself or to gossip about others. For example: When you say you are going to show up for a rehearsal, you are there; you don't cancel at the last moment. You will be careful and thoughtful about what you say you will do.

2. Don't Take Anything Personally

Nothing others do is because of you. What others say and do is a projection of their own reality, their own dream. When you are immune to the opinions and actions of others, you won't be the victim of needless suffering. For example: When you are told you are too old, young, short, tall, pretty, fat, thin, whatever, you will still feel good about yourself! That is their opinion, their world.

3. Don't Make Assumptions

Find the courage to ask questions and to express what you really want. Communicate with others as clearly as you can to avoid misunderstandings, sadness and drama. With just this one agreement, you can completely transform your life. For example: You will never end up with the wrong sides/script in the audition room; you will always ask, "Have there been any changes?"

4. Always Do Your Best

Your best is going to change from moment to moment; it will be different when you are healthy as opposed to sick. Under any circumstance, simply do your best, and you will avoid self-judgment, self-abuse and regret. For example: When you have prepared for your audition you will never have to leave the room feeling badly; you will have done your best.

Tool #3 – Self-Esteem Builders.

I believe the following esteem builders are a great way to find out what is authentic about you. The reason that most actors hold themselves back from success is their lack of self-esteem. Others can help you with self-confidence. You do a good job; then, when others tell you so, it can encourage you; you find courage to step out a little more. On the other hand, self-esteem is something that you must build yourself. I'm grateful to my friend and therapist Jackie Jaye-Brandt for allowing me to use them.

Self-Esteem Builders ©
Jackie Jaye-Brandt, M.A., MFT
© copyrighted information Jackie Jaye Brandt, MFT

Jackie Jaye Brandt, M.A., MFT, 818-505-1664, jackiejayebrandt.com. Individual, couples and group therapy and lectures for the Motion Picture & Television Fund.

1. **Give up, forever, the notion of being a victim**...of your circumstances, your relationships, your career, etc. Being a **victim** is a state of mind that needs to be replaced with being a **creator.**

2. **Find a Way to Take Responsibility** for all your Actions and Consequences: Understand that until you accept this, you will find yourself constantly feeling victimized, out of control and burdened. Responsibility gives us *control* over our lives. It is understanding that we always have *choice*.

3. **Be Willing to Give up Being Right:** Needing to be right is a full-time job, and a needless waste of an enormous amount of energy.

4. **Start Investigating and Questioning Belief Systems:** Those who know it all have nothing they can learn. Give up sentences like "I've always been this way", "I can't do... (i.e., auditions)", or "I wish I was someone who....". This simply *locks in* your belief system. "*You become what you believe...You attract what you believe is possible, and you always get what you expect!*"

5. **Learn to have the Proper Conversations with Yourself:** These are usually manifestations of your belief systems. Speak positively and visualize positively, rather than being worried about failing or the "what-if's." Have conversations like "I love to audition", "I am at my best in business meetings", "I love exercise" (even if you don't believe it for a minute....you will learn to believe it with enough time).

   Be grateful - This is diverting your mind from thinking about what's missing in your life to seeing the reality of what you *do* have. It's not Pollyanna thinking, but rather directing your mind to a place where good feelings reside. **Remember, you're having a conversation anyway.** Why should it be easier to always move toward the negative? Feeling grateful takes **practice**, especially if you're more inclined to, or in the habit of, noticing what's **missing** in your life.

6. **Personal Integrity:** Everyone's sense of what is right and wrong is personal, but your *body* will tell you as well. Start tuning into what is right for you, so that your actions are congruent with who you are (your values).

7. **Stop Comparing Yourself to Others:** This is a huge problem for people, especially in Hollywood. Comparing sets you up to feel like you're not enough. If you **must** compare yourself, compare yourself to yourself (as you were last year, ten years ago, etc.)

8. **De-emphasize Material Possessions:** They don't love you, comfort you or bring you great joy. They are just *things*. Detach from the "I'll be happy when..." mentality.

9. **Press through Fear:** Each time you **have** your fear and do it anyway, you build self-esteem. Fear is simply a signal that you're truly alive and challenging yourself. Every time you press through the fear, you've exhibited courage. Courage builds self-esteem.

10. **Forgive Yourself and Others** for all the Things You're Still Holding Onto: Forgiveness does NOT mean: it was okay, it was right, the person shouldn't be punished, you are condoning their actions, you are reconciling the relationship. It simply means that you are choosing to let go of your feelings of resentment forever, in favor of moving forward.

11. **Become aware of, and take action** on, your in-completions. **Action** can include (1) Education/Classes/ Growth Groups; (2) Therapy (individual or group); (3) Promises (i.e., "I'll return to school when the kids start high school").

12. **Resolve to Accept Yourself Unconditionally**: If you have some cleaning up to do, get to it. Unresolved stuff stays with you forever. Then, after an inventory and the appropriate amends or completion work, no matter what you've done, **forgive yourself** and move on. You are the only you in the world. Accept that you are the best you, you can be, and, as such, a work-in-progress. You've done the best you could do, given what you've known. And when you know better, you'll *do* better. Accept your weaknesses, as well as your strengths.

13. **Get and Polish your Communication Skills**: Otherwise you will stuff your emotions, gather up and store anger, and question what is and isn't real. Communication skills allow you to turn criticism into requests and to express yourself without alienating others. This must also include *SETTING BOUNDARIES ...we teach people how to treat us!* Communication skills are the number one way to increase self-esteem on a daily basis!

14. **Challenge Yourself/Take Risks/Grow**: Part of creating self-esteem is feeling adept. When you try something new, challenge yourself to something difficult, keep going after you miss the mark a few times, you build your self-esteem enormously. Each of these experiences builds on itself, so that you can call it forth to reinforce yourself at any time.

15. **Find your Gift/Passion and Pursue it**: Everyone has a gift or gifts. It can be acting, music, art, candy-making, teaching children, etc. Find out what it is that gives you passion, and pursue it, as a vocation or an avocation.

16.   **Set Goals:** First get clear on your value system. From there should spring your goals. Goals give us direction, purpose and reason to celebrate ourselves. They also allow us to have our dreams come true. Give up the failure mentality. It doesn't really exist, except in our minds.

17.   **Celebrate your Accomplishments,** the Attainment of your Goals & your Successes: Learning to acknowledge yourself is vital. We've certainly learned how to beat ourselves up!... only acknowledgment actually moves us forward.

18.   **Reset your Goals:** Many people, once they've achieved a goal, sit back and decide to rest, relax, and say "okay, I did it". Unfortunately, you will soon feel hollow. Keep at least one goal in front of you at all times. The more goals the better... only work on a few at a time, however, to avoid overwhelm.

19.   **Create and Nurture Love and Support Systems:** If you have toxic family members or don't have solid, loyal friends, it is important to create them. Everyone needs people to talk to and trust (in addition to their spouse). As we get older it seems harder to create friends, and it's not...it just takes effort and trial and error. It is also important to have good advisors, since nobody is an expert at everything.

20.   **Take Care of Yourself:** This includes vigilant exercise (#1), proper nutrition, stress education and yearly physical exams. Make sure your body supports your mind.

21.   **Laugh at Yourself:** Since we have already given up being right, the next step is to accept ourselves and our humanness. It is utterly silly to take life so seriously when we have such a limited amount of time to enjoy ourselves. Laugh as much as possible every day, especially at yourself. The less seriously you take yourself, the less seriously you'll take everyone and everything else.

LIFE AND CAREER
COACHES

- **Career and Life Coaches** have come to be a very important part of an actor's team. I wrote the first edition of this book in 1981 for my students because I felt they needed career coaching in order to compete at the highest levels. In the last several years many classes, seminars and workshops have been established solely to help people promote their careers. One of the largest areas of private coaching is now in building careers. Career building in no way replaces talent development, nor would any career coach of merit make that claim. I think career coaching is valid and necessary in this competitive field. Individuals must decide how much energy they want to put into their art and how much into the business. Sometimes we can do both at different stages of our life. The truth of the matter is, it is always hard work. Perhaps a career coach can guide you in answering where best to focus your time.

- **From a *New York Times* article by Mireya Navarro:**

  - **Whenever Bryce Dallas Howard teased her dad**, the actor and director Ron Howard, about how much actors are paid, he'd say, "It's so that they can afford their therapist." But decades after her father made it in Hollywood, Ms. Howard, 25, is making her own way in acting, and she's therapist-free. She sees a life coach instead. Ms. Howard, while filming "Spider-Man 3," said her coach helps her navigate the demands of show business on her own terms, including making time for writing and protecting a degree of privacy during press interviews without losing her cool. "It's not about rehashing the past," said Ms. Howard, who said she's "really into self-improvement." She called Sherri Ziff Lester, her coach, after a manager friend passed on her name last year. "With Sherri," she said, "it's, 'Let's talk about this week.' She asks me a series of questions so that I see my priorities and decide what I need to do."

• **Wendy Haines is my life coach.** When I took her one-day Goals and Success Workshop, it was research for this Gold Edition. I felt it my duty to investigate for my readers. I thought, "I'm doing fine in my life; what other goals do I have?" Wendy showed me the possibilities that would open up if I would just reach for them. I learned so much in one day. Then I took one private session over the phone and now I talk to her every two weeks for a half hour. She has helped me write this 11th Edition with joy and ease unlike any of the other editions. She has coached me in starting my *Acting Is Everything Workshops* in other cities and even countries. I didn't need therapy; I needed help with the day-to-day actions in my life.

• **When Wendy and I talk, I tell her what has been going on,** which helps me remember. Life can speed by and one of my failings has been lack of celebration. Wendy is helping me have more celebrations in my life; then we plan strategies for the next two weeks. One of the most valuable lessons she has given me is permission to have time for myself and to indulge in pleasures I might withhold from myself. Each person's issues are individual, which is why a life/career coach usually works privately with their clients.

• **Wendy further explains what she does as a life coach:**

  • **The career path of being an actor is not an easy one.** Some actors may find themselves great at doing "all the right things"—great headshots, good representation, great acting coach, good at marketing themselves, etc, and still not see the results they are seeking in their career. Some actors believe they'll just get "discovered" and leave it up to everyone else to make them successful and find it's not happening. In either case, there are important sources of learning, insight and support an actor can access that will bring them beyond these places into the realm of big success. This is where life coaching and the Goals and Success Workshop I created come in.

  • **The path of being an actor can pose many challenges:** it can be easy to get caught in the drudgery of the day-to-day pavement pounding, day-job juggling and solitary world of acting. You often go out and do your best work and never get any feedback. It can be tough. Or the phone just won't ring and the feeling of being powerless in your own career takes over. There's a quote I love: "The good news and the bad news is that success and fulfillment is about YOU!"

- **In my workshops and also in my private coaching,** I work with people from what I call an "inner" perspective; to recognize that we can only be as successful (or fulfilled) as we believe we can. When we engage in our careers from this perspective, we can become empowered and accountable for creating our success. It is more about how we "show up" in our careers and our lives than anything going on around us. So, I guide people in exploring ways that they may be limiting themselves or getting in their own way. We are often not even aware of how we hold ourselves back. It is equally important to know exactly what our BIG DREAM for our life looks like, to be clear about where we are going. I guide people, through tools and practices, to begin to "live into the skin" of the self they see in their big dreams. My workshops and coaching are designed to empower actors to do all of these things. In my experience, this is the REAL work of being a successful actor.

- **I consider myself to be a life and career coach.** I believe it is all connected, especially for actors. Our "product" is US... our heart, our soul. It's a vulnerable product to "sell" at times. So, I see the acting career as being a very personal path. I also work from a holistic perspective. We can all make a task list and try to stick to it in order to achieve our goals. But when we are willing to observe ourselves in the process, we will gain insight and clarity about how we may be invisibly holding ourselves back. Where we hold ourselves back in one area in our lives, we are sure to find we do the same in all areas in our lives. I find it essential that we pay attention to our career and our life as a whole in order to bring it all together and step into a life that is successful and a life that is fulfilling—the life we want to live.

- **Laurie Johnson is a life coach, as well as a working actress.**

Q: How do you know if you need a life or career coach?

- **There are two ways I approach it.** One is if you feel a block somewhere. If you feel like your shoe is nailed to the floor in a particular arena and there is some obstacle in the way. The second way is you are not feeling blocked but you don't know what the next step is. Everything is going great and I want to kick it to the next level. You can't quite see what that next level is or how to do that. One is handling an obstacle and one is a design conversation. The kind of obstacles I've dealt with are: trouble in auditions, fear, can't seem to move into action.

- **For some people it can be, "Am I in the right career?** Is this really my passion? Am I doing this because I told my high school friends and parents I am going to do this, so now I have to?"

• **Linda Salazar, Life Coach** and founder of Awaken the Genie Within asked one of her clients to tell me how life coaching was helpful.

  • **I always felt that I was really bad at auditions.** I got nervous, which affected my concentration, therefore not allowing me to be focused in the moment. The result was just an average audition and I always left the room beating myself up, analyzing and criticizing my performance long after it was over.

  • **I got a call from my agent about hosting a TV show.** My first reaction was sheer terror, self-doubt, I couldn't do it. And then, excitement set in at the realization that this is my dream job. With Linda's techniques and tools to manage my energy and her constant support, for the first time in my career, I was able to prepare myself, channel my energy, and really focus beforehand so I was more than ready on the day. And after it was over, I walked away feeling wonderful. I didn't analyze or continually go over it. Which, in itself, is such a great feat for me. For the first time ever in an audition, *I* was in control. And you know what else? I got the job!!

  • **Linda assists me in fully realizing** that I have done quite well for myself in my career up to this point in time. This allows me to really acknowledge and appreciate all the positive aspects of my achievements throughout my life and career.

• **Laurie Sheppard is a master certified Life coach and Career Strategist.** She founded Creating At Will® in 1994.

Q: How do you work with the clients you coach?

  • **I assist my clients in looking at the whole pie** rather than one slice of their life, so their career and personal goals integrate smoothly. But all of my clients hire me initially for their career development or career transitions. My work is about positive change. I assist clients to clarify their *Next Big Thing* and develop a strategic action plan to get there. *The Next Big Thing* is what's most important for you now, a valued and worthy objective, which challenges and rewards you.

  • **While achieving your next big thing** you are able to maintain a connection to yourself, trust yourself, and have a certainty about your choices. We are bombarded with distractions as well as opportunities. We need a peaceful heart as well as a discerning eye and well-designed map to keep us on course. Making clear choices for changes, rather than being at the effect of changes, gives us the necessary edge to expedite, as well as enjoy, the journey. My clients are more confidently accepting, more effortlessly maintaining their focus and direction, and able to repeat steps for the next challenge.

• **Career/Marketing Coach Sam Christensen's** course is called **Image Process.**

Q: **Tell me about the unique course you teach.**

• **I have students that have just stepped off the bus** two weeks ago, and I have people who have been at this for 30 years who are trying to focus. I begin with a basic introduction of how marketing works for any product and then adapt it to acting. I then work on an image system, which allows people to figure out how they are perceived by other people outside of themselves. For example, with Greta Garbo, there was always mystery in her photographs: the clothes she wore, the publicity the studio did for her. The studios used to develop themes with an actor.

• **Suppose an agent represented Goldie Hawn.** Goldie Hawn thought she was a serious actress and she wanted to play Juliet. The agent took her because she's kind of a giddy blonde. Meanwhile, the photographer is attracted to her and he's trying to catch all the sexiness. Instead, if Goldie, the agent, photographer and haircutter are all in agreement around the theme that Goldie is wacky, upfront, bright, lively and a little suspicious, then everybody's talking the same language.

• **The actors come up with a set of words which are the primary themes** of what happens when they walk into a room—the stuff they bring to every part before they start making adjustments. It's the stuff that ought to be in a photograph of them.

• **For instance, in one of my classes,** there was an actress whose words are "urban, perplexed, genial, comic, direct, and impatient." Somebody else who is "tempered, amused, a tough-nut to crack, straight-shooting, embodied." Another person who is "hard-core, a mutt, motley, I land on my feet." Here's somebody who is "simmering, wild-eyed, mad-cap, conspiratorial, I know where the body's buried." These are not descriptions I give them. These are things that they choose through a rather involved process.

• **All of a sudden the actor has a language** and qualities to talk to the agent about so the agent can go out and use those same kinds of descriptions. When the actor comes in to meet the casting director, the actor is what the actor is comfortable in being, the actor is what the agent has introduced, he is what the pictures look like and everybody is in agreement. Improvements show up in all kinds of ways, not just in getting jobs.

Resources

To download and print an updated version of this and all resource lists, go to actingiseverything.com.

GROUP CLASSES FOR DEVELOPING YOUR LIFE AND CAREER

Wendy Haines, 310/395-3246. wendyhaines.com. IGNITE Your Career – The Goals and Success Workshop: Learn how to succeed from an inner perspective. This interactive one-day intensive will give you the training, tools, and hands-on experience to transform your career on the spot! You will walk out with a system to keep you on course to start living the life and career you desire! Do you want to—Be successful and fulfilled? Erase limitations that keep you stuck? Get empowered with tools to be your most effective self? Clarify your true purpose and set goals effectively? Wendy also offers: IGNITE II—The Master Class: This six-week course extends your knowledge from IGNITE I—allowing you to deepen your understanding and practice in an intimate, advanced environment.

Dee Wallace, 818/876-0386. deewallacestone.com. Dee has healing work based on balancing your energy so you are never in reaction, but always in creation. When you drop into the negative, you can't attract what you want. She offers a step-by-step approach, not just theory. Workshops are held once a month in Burbank for $100. Private sessions are $60/hour. Dee has awakened me to all the possibilities of claiming and creating my life. Since working with her I can get myself out of the lower vibrations when I choose and make the choices that bring much more pleasure and success into my life. Life was good before taking her workshops and now I have shifted into high gear.

Sam Christensen, 818/506-0783. samchristensen.com. 10440 Burbank Blvd., North Hollywood, 91601. Specializing in image definition and career marketing for actors and comics. Sam's studio offers the *Image Process* which includes an initial meeting, a four-day intensive and monthly results workshops all for $695. After you complete the process, private consultations are $125. "Today craft and talent are expected from the actor. Ultimately, it is their personal uniqueness that gets them hired and gains them an audience. An actor's ability to identify and market their unique qualities is 'make or break' in our business." Also offers acting and audition classes and a gallery featuring 40 of Hollywood's best photographers.

Scott Tiler's The Fall and Fly Class at Scott Sedita Acting Studios, 323/465-6152. scottseditaacting.com. 526 N. Larchmont Blvd., Los Angeles, 90004. The Fall and Fly is an empowerment class for actors. It consists of a series of exercises specially designed to help actors become energized, focused and free. It comes from the idea that if you take the risk and allow yourself to let go, you will Fly higher than you ever thought possible. It is also a vital support system for all of those looking to gain the strength, discipline and vision necessary to maintain an acting career in Los Angeles. Students are encouraged to develop action lists, set goals and develop mission statements. Exercises include: Meditation, Visualization, Writing, Drawing, Movement, Improvisation, Character Work and Yoga.

Artist's Way Workshop, 310/839-3424. creativelife.com. $350 Remove seemingly insurmountable barriers to artistic confidence and productivity. Offers a few different workshops all based on the book.

Breck Costin, BCC & Associates, 323/848-9665. bccfreedom.com. 8033 Sunset Blvd., #8000, Los Angeles, 90046. Private, $300 an hour. Monthly *Conversation*, first of the month on Mondays, $40. Also offers courses of varying lengths and costs on such topics as personal freedom, financial freedom, aging with grace and the art of communication. "Come to be coached, get your questions answered and gain clarity about your life."

Flash Forward Institute, 818/558-5917. flashforwardinstitute.com. Tools: How to get mentors, referrals, bookings and deals. They brag about how quickly their system works in helping you achieve your entertainment goals. Network with high-powered Flash Forward alumni from agencies, networks, studios, production and casting companies. They offer very inexpensive introductory courses as well as longer intensives on a number of topics; typically in the $425 range.

PRIVATE LIFE AND CAREER COACHES

Judy Kerr, 818/505-9373. judykerr.com. Private one-time class $150. I critique pictures and resumes, help you choose clips for your demo reel, steer you toward teachers, photographers and services specifically suited for you, as well as guide you on long and short term goals in Los Angeles. If you wish, I will also send you a script ahead of time so you can prepare it and test your audition skills. For people out-of-town, $50 half-hour phone consultation. See website.

Wendy Haines, 310.395.3246. wendyhaines.com. Coaching with Wendy Haines is a personalized way to step into and create the life you desire. Wendy's individualized approach is designed to meet you where you are and give you access to Wendy's vast base of tools and knowledge that becomes your springboard for moving ahead. Working with Wendy in this manner offers precision and personally-tuned support, insight, accountability and empowerment to keep you on track and on purpose—for you to truly create the results and life you desire. I love working with Wendy; life has really been enhanced with her on my team.

Linda Salazar, 310-375-4800. awakenthegeniewithin.com Linda, a film industry professional for 27 years, can truly help actors and understands their issues. "Awaken the Genie Within" proprietary life coaching method guides actors who require all their power and focus for more successful audition and performance experiences. Linda's Certified Life Coaching gives you tools and practical strategies to use right away. Master the management of your emotions so you can regain control over your career and the unpredictable life we lead in this industry. Learn to quiet your inner "Gremlin" and "awaken your Genie" to experience an ongoing sense of calm, ease and fun—which ultimately makes you more successful, too. Coaching services are available by telephone from the comfort of your home—either one-on-one or in groups.

Laurie Sheppard, Creating At Will® 310/645-2874. Creatingatwill.com. Master certified Life Coach/Career Strategist. Laurie coaches by phone to clients worldwide. She calls her clients to save them long-distance fees. Her programs and prices are on her website under *Current Programs*. Her free monthly career tips ezine is available by signing up on her website homepage.

Clair Sinnett, 310/606-0813. Actorsworking.com. $100 an hour for career consulting and audition preparation. Author of *Actors Working: The Actor's Guide to Marketing Success*. Clair has been a long time casting director, still works as an actor and coaches world-wide.

Eve Brandstein, Coach for Career and Life Matters, 310/499-4111, evebrandsteinproductions.com. First session is two hours for $250 and then its $125 an hour. Eve is a psychotherapist, hypnotherapist and life coach. Her experiences in the entertainment industry—she was a casting director and is presently a producer/director/writer—gives her special insight in helping her industry based clients. One aspect of the therapy is called Narrative Therapy; she helps you rewrite your life's stories. Her motto is "What you believe is how you will live."

Jill K. Allen, 818/207-6115. BigRedJill@aol.com. $150 for a one hour consultation, but the first meeting is free. If you prepay for a month at a time, you get a discount. Specializes in working with creative people in the entertainment industry, from actors to dancers to writer/producers, composers, etc. Helps you to reignite your passion, put an end to your procrastination, coax out clarity and help you to let your genius soar. Jill has experience working as an actor, in the agencies and studios, as well as a Masters Degree in Organizational Behavior. Consults over the phone or face-to-face.

Barbara Deutsch, The Barbara Deutsch Approach, 818/508-9078. bdapproach. com. She works with actors, writers, directors and producers. Private sessions, $150 an hour. Actors' workshops, *Breaking The Rules, Your Own Way,* $240 a month. She moves your career to a higher level. *In The Biz,* interactions and role playing, giving you sustainable tools to take you from good to great. Also in Vancouver, Toronto, N.Y., Las Vegas and London.

Harriet Greenspan, 818/266-6698. buddyskid@aol.com. $125 an hour. A casting director for the past 20 years, she includes acting coaching, career issues, relationships, money and health matters. "Strives to help students create rewarding lives." Harriet has an uplifting personality, is great to be with and knows all aspects of the business.

Terry Lichtman, 805/528-8282, actingcareercoach.com. Terry was a very successful agent in Los Angeles for close to 30 years and guided many successful careers. She offers advice on building a career.

Laurie Johnson, lauriejohnson.com. Four sessions, $300. They are one-hour taped sessions. You walk away with a tape for life. "Once you finish the four sessions, that can be it or you can maybe come back for one. If there is a new issue we do another set of four." Also the author of *Rich By Choice Poor By Habit*. Check out her website for more information on Laurie and her Passion Principles.

Janice Kent, 818/906-2201, janicekent.com. Coaching in person, 1 hour session $80 or phone 1/2 hr. $40. With over 30 years of experience as an actor, director, acting coach and life coach, Janice has incorporated her Life Coaching training into her approach to teaching audition technique. Her combination of Meisner and Spolin Improv techniques, along with insight and heart, encourage growth in skills and the ability to make choices that are risky and playful. This process helps the actor to identify and unblock the fears that stop the actor from making those choices and booking the job.

Melissa McFarlane, 818/729-7872. electrickites.com. $175 a month for group class and up to $1,500 a month for private. An International Certified Co-Active Life Coach, and on a mission to bring extraordinary change to ordinary lives. She has over 15 years experience as a coach, trainer and professional actress, working extensively in the area of professional development with a diverse spectrum of individuals including actors, producers, directors, writers, lawyers, salespersons, creative types and CEOs of small businesses. Melissa and her company hold workshops as well as private sessions in person and over the phone.

Kathleen Noone, 818/980-7234. kathleennoone.com. $85 per hour. Emotional coaching and entertainment business counseling. Over 40 years as an Emmy Award winning actress working as a primetime series regular, daytime series regular, episodic appearances, MOWs, films and theatre. "I have experienced the tremendous highs and lows and developed good techniques to help in relationships with agents, producers, writers and actors. We face the struggles of employment and unemployment as well as our own demons when dealing with a business that doesn't honor our talents."

Jill Jaress, coach and career consultant, 310/828-7814. jaress@adelphia.net. Jill specializes in teaching new actors how to break into the business and working actors how to increase the number and quality of their bookings.

IN BOSTON
Lori A. Frankian, Business Consultant for Actors, 617/437-0334. lorifrankian.com. In Boston, works one on one or via telephone. Lori says, "When actors work with me, they will: Gain the direction, respect, motivation they deserve as well as a solid understanding of how to pursue work/training with reputable professionals in Boston, New York and Los Angeles. Talent will develop and maintain their goals, receive personalized strategies and learn how to carry them out successfully. Learn the who's who, the how to's and what not to do's when it comes to networking, auditioning, marketing and training." She successfully prepares her clients for the move into the Los Angeles market.

Stage Presence, Body Awareness, Body Movement

• **The moment you step on stage** or in front of a camera, you must become larger than life. This ability comes from the control you have over your body. We are born with the capacity to use our bodies perfectly but somewhere along the way, many of us learn bad body habits. I don't think there is an acting institution or acting teacher who does not recommend some type of body movement class. We act through our bodies; acting is an athletic event.

• **In the beginning of my career**, an acting coach told me I would never be able to work as an actress because I was "sunk into myself," I had no presence. I had spent a great deal of my life trying not be seen—very detrimental for an actor. Your presence, your appearance, really does make the difference in getting jobs. It is the way you present your *package* when you walk in the door that will make a lasting impression.

• **He was the right kind of acting teacher** because he not only told me the problem but gave me the solution: The *Alexander Technique*. It took me about four lessons before I began to get an understanding of how to hold my body properly. Once you learn the technique, it is yours. I studied constantly for two years because I was in bad shape, but then it became mine.

• **Good stage presence becomes a habit**, just like bad posture. This technique has helped me in everything I do, whether it's yoga, ballet or lifting weights. It is a specific, unique body technique that will increase the amount of space you take up in a room and what you *radiate* in person, on the stage, or in front of a camera.

• **After about ten years I had to go back for more lessons;** I was "sinking" again. This time I went with the SIKE Technique that incorporates Alexander Technique and other traditions. It took me about a year to really discover good stage presence again. There are also many other health and pain relieving benefits with the SIKE Technique.

THE ALEXANDER TECHNIQUE

• **F. M. Alexander was an Australian actor.** When he lost his voice while performing, he went to specialists and was told there was no solution. He decided to look for the cure himself. He spent many months in front of a three-way mirror to try and detect the exact reason for the hoarseness in his voice. He discovered the hoarseness came as a result of vocal misuse and an overall pattern of body misuse. He could clearly see it in his mirror but he couldn't feel it. It became clear he could not correct his voice without changing his mental concepts and the way he used his whole body. He noticed the muscles at the back of his neck pulled his head down and caused a chain reaction of pressure down his spine. This created tension throughout his entire body.

• **Alexander then developed a technique** to help himself and over the years trained many actors and taught others to teach his technique. The changes he noticed in himself and his students included: a release of excess tension in the body, a lengthening of the spine, greater freedom and flexibility in movement, more efficient breathing, elimination of vocal problems and improved posture and appearance. His most famous directive and one his teachers give over and over again is: "Let my neck be free to let my head go forward and up, to let my back lengthen and widen." When you learn to move in this fashion you will acquire better posture, grace of movement, better balance and coordination in your body for all of your activities.

• **The *Alexander Technique* is taught** at many institutions, including The Juilliard School in New York, ACT in San Francisco, SMU in Dallas, UCLA and USC in Los Angeles. Juilliard graduate Kevin Kline says, "The many obvious benefits that the technique afforded us as actors included minimized tension, centeredness, vocal relaxation and responsiveness, mind/body connection and about an inch and a half of additional height." Andre Rotkiewicz, movement teacher at KD Studio Acting Conservatory in Dallas, says, "It makes you, the actor, aware of your mannerisms so you can control and change your actions. You will become more neutral and able to take on more characters. The connection with the mind and body will let you become more universal." Alexander said, "Every man, woman and child holds the possibility of physical perfection; it rests with each one of us to attain it by personal understanding and effort."

• **Lyn Charlsen, certified *Alexander* instructor says:**

> • **Performers need to be conscious of what they're doing** with their bodies, because that is their means of expression. It really becomes the tool for the expression of their art—whether that's somebody holding a violin, an actor on stage, or a singer. The way that we are using our body translates into the sound of the guitar, the sound of the voice, or the expression of the face.

> • The *Alexander Technique* can increase an actor's physical coordination and allow him to express himself fully. The elements of choice and consciousness enliven performance skills and make it possible for people to do what they intend. What's so wonderful for actors to know is that their instrument is so finely tuned that they can really be spontaneous.

THE SIKE TECHNIQUE

• **Dr. Mallory Fromm and Therese Fromm of the SIKE Institute** explain this unique body work, which is a healing art and a means of correcting poor body behavior, harmful to the quality of presence, movement and voice.

> • The *SIKE Technique* combines two healing and alignment techniques. The first one is *Physio-Synthesis*, created by an osteopathic physician to restore structural balance in order to improve the body's contour, grace in movement, circulation and breath control. The second technique comes from Japan and is based on the precise use of Ki (or Chi) Energy to send energy directly into the nervous system to command muscles and ligaments to move and shift bones and organs.

> • This technique relaxes the upper body, head and neck by strengthening the actor's body from the ground up. Inner core muscles extend the spine which lifts and supports the head up and off the top of the neck, producing a "floating" sensation. The body is grounded and light at the same time. Application of Ki Energy to the head and solar plexus produces mental clarity and heightened concentration. Thus a unity of mind and body is achieved. In this way stage presence is enhanced through the natural projection of character, substantiality, and intensity.

> • The *SIKE Technique* for actors is a series of weekly or bi-weekly treatment and instruction that, as the actor gains confidence, tapers off to seasonal treatments to maintain an integrated body structure. The ultimate goal is to make the actor independent of the practitioner.

MOMENTUM

- **Ebba-Marie Gendron, acting teacher** and practicing, registered dance/ movement therapist has developed *Momentum*. She works with actors and other artists who wish to strengthen their art and deepen their self-knowledge through movement. She explains *Momentum*:

  - **It is in connecting to the body through movement** that we connect to the deepest part of who we are—the place in us from which our creativity as artists springs. Movement allows for open, honest and spontaneous connection to both ourselves and others.

  - **Our feelings, past experiences and imagination** are directly held in the body. Opening the body to this material sets the stage for deeper internal awareness and subsequently, greater spontaneous flow of impulses through action. This ability directly translates to character development, scene study and performance.

- **There are a number of other methods as well,** including Pilates and yoga methods of all shapes and sizes. A couple of others are:

  - **The Feldenkrais Method** says that our thoughts, feelings, actions, sensations and emotions are all related to our self image. The method helps people improve knowledge of themselves and the quality of their actions. Coming from a very scientific approach, the focus is on awareness and the process of understanding one's body.

  - **Laban Movement Analysis** suggests that movement reflects human behavior and that no matter what we're doing, the body is never still. This method breaks down movement possibilities and what they mean, as well as encouraging movement efficiency based on the desired result.

Resources

To download and print an updated version of this and all resource lists, go to actingiseverything.com.

American Society for the Alexander Technique (AmSAT), 800/473-0620. amsat.ws. Check website to find a teacher in your area. Workshops and classes are also listed on the site. This is the only organization of authorized or certified teachers of the technique in the United States. Teachers can only be a member of this society if they have gone through a three-year, rigorous, approved training course.

Dr. Mallory Fromm and Therese Fromm of the SIKE Institute, 818/992-0713, sikehealth.com. $90 per treatment. Workshops are announced on the website. Mallory is the author of *The Book of Ki: The Healing Principles of Life Energy* and *Qi Energy for Health and Healing*. Therese is a graduate of England's Royal Academy of Dramatic Arts and has experience with Feldenkrais Technique, Alexander Technique and is a certified practitioner of *Physio-Synthesis*. My husband continues to do extensive work with Mallory, and I have my regular tune-ups with Therese.

Momentum, Ebba-Marie Gendron, 310/770-2825. Classes are held at the Sal Romeo Acting Conservatory. Open to all actors. This ongoing movement workshop focuses on the freedom of expression achieved through relaxation, kinesthetic (bodily) awareness and the use of voice. The classes are led by Ebba-Marie Gendron, MA, DTR. She pulls from her extensive and varied movement training to uniquely synthesize the work of Jerzy Grotowski together with dance/movement therapy, yoga, creative movement and voice to create a powerful creative exploration for the actor. Private sessions are available for $50 an hour.

Michael Frederick, 800/295-9296. alexandertechniqueworkshops.com. Internationally recognized, Michael has taught Alexander Technique in the U.S. and Europe since 1978. He is also an expert in Psycho-physical Re-education. His annual Serra Retreat Alexander Residential Workshop in Malibu is a week-long study in the technique and applying it to your individual goals. Cost of the retreat ranges from $970 to $1,295.

Lyn Charlsen, Alexander Technique, 818/786-3944, Van Nuys. $60 for a private class. She is a special teacher and was my first introduction to this type of body work. She has worked with many actors.

Debby Jay, Alexander Technique, 818/763-1193. alexanderexperience.com. Debby has been teaching the Alexander Technique for 16 years, including seven at the Howard Fine Acting Studio. She now teaches private lessons in Studio City/Valley Village. Specializes in helping actors become more grounded and expansive, two qualities that are essential in pursuing the art and business of acting. Lessons are $70 and a sliding scale is available.

Larry White, Alexander Technique, 310/394-3177. Specializes in scoliosis.

UCLA, USC, **Howard Fine Acting Studio** and many other colleges offer group classes.

South Florida: Roberto Mainetti, 305/438-9379. 1918 Southwest 17th Terrace, Miami, FL 33137. $50 hr.

Scripts for Workshop Scenes and Monologues

• **Choosing the work you want to do in your scene study class** takes effort but it is very rewarding; you get to act the roles that attract you, roles you may not otherwise have the opportunity to portray.

• **Take chances! Stretch! Can't hurt!** It also really helps to read scripts. Even if you read 15 scripts to find one scene, you will have learned more about which characters interest you.

• **DVDs and videotapes of movies are a great source for scenes.** Many times there are deleted scenes on DVDs that may have a scene your audience won't recognize. Books are useful. When you pick a scene from a novel you'll have a good background of the characters. Non-fiction books may inspire you with an idea to write a scene or short film of your own.

Resources

To download and print an updated version of this and all resource lists, go to actingiseverything.com.

SCRIPTS ON-LINE

whysanity.net. There are hundreds of monologues that have been transcribed from movies. My lovely student Carol Hernandez told me about this site and the ones below. This one solves the "where to find a short monologue" question.

Themonologueshop.com. They have hundreds of original and classical monologues with a monthly subscription service of $6.95.

Scriptcrawler.com. Script search engine for movies, TV, radio, anime and stage plays.

Artofprogramming.net/resources/movies.html. Movies and script resources.

Bookcity.net. Hollywood Book City (located on the world-famous Hollywood Walk of Fame) has been the place to go for books, movie scripts, television scripts and other collectables for more than 25 years!

Simplyscripts.com/links.html. Links to movie scripts, screenplays, transcripts and excerpts from classic movies to current flicks to future films. Great resource.

script-o-rama.com. Drews Script-O-Rama.

dailyscript.com. Daily Script features a new script every day, or search the huge database. Free.

screentalk.org. Screen Talk.

movie-page.com. Movie Page.

vl-theatre.com. The Virtual Library for Theatre and Drama.

screenwriting.about.com. Free Scripts.

zzippeddskripptzz.com. Many film scripts. A one-time $15 sign-up fee. You have to remember your password to get back in after signing up.

chezjim.com/writing/monologues.html. Free adult and teen original monologues. Actor Jim Chevallier has written many monologues he invites others to use. He also sells a book *The Monologue Bin.*

Academy of Motion Picture Arts & Sciences Library, 310/247-3035 for general information; 310/247-3020 for general reference. 333 S. La Cienega, at Olympic, West Hollywood. M,Tu,Th,F 10-5:30; closed Wednesday and weekends. You must present a valid ID such as a passport or driver's license. No personal belongings are permitted, but they provide storage lockers. For film scripts: read the scene into a tape recorder or hand-copy and take home to type—there is no photocopying unless the script has been published. Laptop computers are permitted, but no carrying cases. Great place to go.

American Film Institute, Louis B. Mayer Library, afionline.org. 323/856-7654. 2021 N. Western Ave., north of Franklin, Hollywood. M-F 9:30-5:15; W until 7:15; Sa 10-4:30. Library is closed during the summer and odd hours during Christmas and Spring breaks. No copying of unpublished scripts, but you can copy published ones. Books, periodicals, clipping files, festival files, motion picture collections, seminar transcripts, oral history transcripts, special collections.

Movie World, 818/846-0459. 212 N. San Fernando, Burbank, 91502. Every day 11-6. Books, posters, magazines, photos, autographs, memorabilia and scripts.

Script City, scriptcity.com, 818/764-4081.Outside of California 800/676-2522. Ask them for a catalogue; it's all mail order. They have thousands of movie and TV scripts, directories, guides, books, audio/video seminars, etc.

Samuel French Theatrical Bookstores, samuelfrench.com. 323/876-0570. 7623 Sunset Blvd., Hollywood. M-F 10-6; Sat. 10-5; Closed Sunday. Valley store: 818/762-0535, 11963 Ventura Blvd., just East of Laurel Canyon, Studio City. M-F 10-9; Sat. 10-6; Sun 12-5. For plays, get their free catalogue. They also sell many published film and television scripts.

Larry Edmund's Theatrical Book Shop, 323/463-3273. 6644 Hollywood Blvd., Hollywood, 90028. M-Sa 10-6.

Dramatists Play Service, 212/683-8960. 440 Park Ave. South, New York, NY 10016. Call, ask for a catalogue; they will mail it.

The Drama Book Shop, dramabookshop.com, 212/944-0595. 250 West 40th Street, New York, NY 10018. Many seminars and book signings held in their Arthur Seelen Theatre. A great store!

• SCENE AND MONOLOGUE BOOKS

• *Check my website for the newest books, actingiseverything.com. It's a good idea to buy two copies of a scene book; then you and a partner can read all the scenes together—good practice.*

99 Film Scenes For Actors, edited by Angela Nicholas. The interview with acting coach Mark Monroe on how to pick scenes for class is worth the price of the book. I love this book. Definitely buy two.

The Ultimate Scene and Monologue Sourcebook: An Actor's Guide to Over 1000 Monologues and Scenes from More Than 300 Contemporary Plays by Ed Hooks. This reference book should be on every actor's and acting teacher's bookshelf. No monologues, but tells you where to find them.

The Monologue Index: A guide to 1,778 Monologues from 1,074 Plays edited by Karen Morris.

The Perfect Monologue by Ginger Howard Friedman. Forward by Michael Shurtleff.

Contemporary Movie Monologues: A Source Book for Actors edited by Marisa Smith and Jocelyn Beard. Over 95 monologues from contemporary films.

Film Scenes for Actors edited by Josha Karton.

The Actor's Book of Movie Monologues edited by Marisa Smith & Amy Schewel.

Uptown Character Monologues for Actors: Powerful Original Audition Pieces by Glenn Alterman and many other monologue books. glennalterman.com.

• **Many screenplays are in book form**—sometimes several scripts by the same writer or director.

Monologues

• **Monologues can be a very important acting tool.** I've seen many actors land an agent, manager or a role in a short film because they delivered a "killer" monologue. This information is strictly for the film and television industry. For theater monologues talk to your coaches about what type of monologue to use.

• **Choose your monologues carefully.** Select one that is perfectly suited to you; how you could be cast in a film or television show today. The length should not be over 90 seconds no matter how good it is; one minute is fine. The piece should give the information in the first sentence or two of who you are and the situation you are in. I think it is best not to give an introduction.

• **Another option is to write your own.** This can be a great exercise in creating a character for yourself and showcasing your strengths as an actor. However, if you're going to write your own, it must be good. Write and re-write like you would a scene; make sure the character is interesting and compelling. If you are asked what the monologue is from, never say you wrote it. You can say it is from a short film you did or a workshop scene a coach gave you.

• **Any piece you choose** and adapt, whether from a monologue book or one you've created, must be acted truthfully—as in all acting. Your delivery must look like a conversation and you should even be prepared for the other person to speak. Sometimes you will deliver your piece directly to a person (always my favorite choice), a chair or into the lens of a camera. Regardless, you must act as if you are talking to a real person.

• **After rehearsing your piece** and getting feedback from your friends, it is good to perform under pressure. Do it in front of your class, your coach certainly, your manager or the assistant, your make-up artist, photographer. I love the story Jerry Seinfeld tells of how many times he rehearsed the material he did for his first appearance on the Johnny Carson Show. That was his big break and the right monologue in front of the right person may be a big break for you.

• **Bob Fraser, author of the marvelous on-line book** *You Must Act!* youmustact.com, offers some hints on how to create your own piece.

  • **Here are some good places to look for material:** Court TV. Some of these trials have fascinating characters. Books. One great thing about novels is that the characters often talk at length and when they do, it's usually something dramatic. Old movies. Again, the writers of the older films were allowed to go on a bit. Use your recorder to capture these gems. Interviews. There are many newspaper and magazine stories where the subject is interviewed and tells a good story. Do your own interviews with people. Ask them how they met their spouse. What did they do in the war. Autobiographies are a good source. If you're looking for a funny monologue, look at books written by funny people. Drama and memory pieces are even more available in autobiographies. While you look, keep in mind the three main things every performance monologue must contain:

  • **Story. Character. Emotional impact.** In fact, the successful monologue will be just like a successful movie or play. It will contain a beginning, a middle and an end. A good way to accomplish the mind-set of a good monologist is to start thinking like a comedian. A well-structured joke contains all the elements of a full length entertainment.

  • **Story.** Don't make the mistake of thinking that the viewer has any information up front. They don't. So your choice has to contain the entire story. The opening line or two should set up the whole piece. Hook us. Give us the back story. Tell us who the character is. The next line or two should present the dilemma, the conflict. The end should always be a "snapper." The punchline of a monologue is extremely important. Find a good one. I'm not talking "joke" here. I'm talking about the "exit" line, "The button," The last thing you say and do.

• **Jim Chevalier of Monologue Bin**, jimcheval.com, has hundreds of monologues on his website that you may want to use or adapt.

• **Below are some monologues I've adapted** for the workshops I teach in cities around the country, and these are the instructions I give with them: "I provide these because I know they are short. You are welcome to change words, substitute words, make these your own without adding any time to them. With a monologue you always want it to represent your age range and type."

Woman - Sports nut – Serio-comedic

This guy looked liked a good catch. Handsome, money, good family but he is such a disappointment. You are complaining about him to your best girlfriend or sister.

I thought this guy was going to be the love of my life, but I've about had it. Sports! It is all he ever thinks about. He's possessed. I knew it from the first he was into games, but I never suspected anything like this.

On our first date he insisted I come back to his apartment and when we got there he showed me his collection of baseball cards.

He even has this Watchman TV he takes everywhere so he won't miss sporting events. The other night at La Boca (put in an upscale restaurant you know) he set the damned thing up right in the middle of the scampi and pasta (put in your favorite meal) and started watching the fight and making bets with the waiters. It was sick, trying to eat and watch some dude/guy with a nosebleed.

And his obsession is screwing up our relationship too. He has a problem sexually because he is so preoccupied with sporting events. Yeah, he may be bowling 250. . . but in the bedroom he is throwing gutter balls!

Woman - Actress to Producer - Dramatic

She has been called back three times for an awful low budget script, now he's telling her he may be able to give her the part if she goes out with him.

Look, Friend, let me give you a little quick history: I came out here a little over two years ago. I hitched out, as a matter of fact, with this tattooed pervert in a rusted-out RV who tried his damndest to get me into the back of the thing for over two-thousand miles. But I didn't cave in. And I haven't caved in since I've been here, in spite of hearing every proposition from some of the biggest of the big-time scumbags.

I came out here with the intention of making it in the business because I think I have some talent. If I don't, after a fair shot, it's back to Dayton and a job at GE.

I may not be working right now, may not be "up for a series," but I'm also not up for you! Not now, not ever. If I make it, whatever "making it" is—and I'm beginning to wonder altogether—I'll make it on my feet, not horizontal.

Man or Woman - FBI Agent to Lover/Crook - Dramatic

The agent has fallen in love with the gangster she was investigating.

Tosses a thick file in front of the gangster.

There's your explanation of why I'm leaving. Check it out. Everything anyone ever wanted to know about crime organizer Sonny/Sunny Bonito. I'm good, you have to give me that. Or at least I used to be. And I would've gotten away with it, too. I could've sent you up for the rest of your life.

I broke the first rule: never get involved with a suspect. I suppose you seduce every cop who tries to arrest you? What about D.A.'s and judges? Who says crime doesn't pay.

That file is all yours, don't worry, no one but you has seen it…there aren't any copies. You should get out and forget all about me. That's my plan, too. I'm being "reassigned." Some desk job as far from the action as they can put me.

Goodbye, Sonny/Sunny. I won't forget you. And for whatever it's worth, the bit about falling in love with you? That was no act, not part of the assignment, nothing I ever meant to happen… I'm not that good.

Man or Woman - Dramatic

Forgive you? You're asking me to forgive you? Our relationship was so beautiful, so perfect, I don't think you realize how powerful it was. You changed my life, you were that person for me. When you first started to get so busy, it dawned on me that I might not be that person for you.

I can't ever go back to loving you the way I did before you cheated on me. Look, my love wasn't strong enough the first time around and now you're asking me to forgive you? Whether or not I can is not going to be what keeps us apart. I could always forgive you, but I could never forget. So I don't want to see you again, I don't want to get any voice mail messages, and I don't want you calling and hanging up. I've moved on with my life, I can live without you.

Man - Surveillance Guy – Drama

Tough, charming, confident. There should be a twist at the end where we see he could be really scary.

You want to know what I do? Cameras, microphones, surveillance, like Orwell's "1984."

Do you know that Uncle Sam can look right into your life? Your private life? Open up the doors to closets you don't want open, any time he wants, any where he wants, But he doesn't do it himself, he brings in guys like me. My boss, this guy Keller, he runs the team. Think of him as the Michael Jordan of surveillance and undercover work. The final word on the subject, the Supreme Court.

But then there's Jake, he's my idol he's cool, really cool, like Steve McQueen was cool, you know, loner, lover, rebel, the man himself. But then there's Alex . . . (whew) smokin' hot. But don't play her cause if you do she'll rip your heart out like that Indian high priest did in Speilberg's Temple of Doom. Yeah, I've got the coolest job in the world.

You just better hope that our phone never rings and someone drops us your name.

Man - Psyche – Serio-comedic - Adapted from Jim Chevalier's Monologue Bin.

To his best friend or brother. Always has an excuse why he can't commit. This time he can't leave his dog, no matter how much he says he wants this relationship.

You know it's not my fault, right? This time I was ready to commit. 100%. My bachelor days were as good as done.

The plan was, while I was down here, Alice would be looking for a house. It had to be big enough for Psyche, my dog, who's very sweet, but she's touchy about change. It's just a bit much for her in certain respects.

So, Alice calls and tells me she's found the perfect place. Only, it won't be free for another six months. But that's okay, she says, because we can stay in the studio in the meantime. I ask, "What about Psyche?" She says, "I can find someone to take care of her for six months." Six months! I know Psyche's not going to like that.

I've pretty much told Alice, she hasn't left me a choice. This is an issue I'm not willing to compromise on. It may work out. But right now, it looks like it's back to me and Psyche.

How to Rehearse and Prepare for Scenes, Monologues, Audition Material and Acting Jobs

• **Your job as an actor is to make dialogue sound like the truth.** Sometimes that's easy and other times it's not, but it is always doable. You decide what is the truth of the script; you choose how to tell that truth. When you don't really figure out the script your performance won't look truthful—it will look general, non-specific, vanilla, like you are just saying the words with a fake attitude.

• **Eli Wallach, talking of creating the reality in acting**, said: "If I ask you to sing *Happy Days Are Here Again,* the same words but I change the circumstances. If I say to you, 'Sing it like you've just been given a raise or won the Academy Award,' you'll sing one way; if I say to you, 'Your wife of 30 years just died—now sing *Happy Days Are Here Again.'* You sing it without me prompting you as how to sing it…and that's one of the secrets of good acting."

• **Making the choices for your interpretation** of the script is your "acting work." How you choose your acting work will come from what you have learned in basic technique acting classes, from what has worked for you in the past and from your instinct. As always, making these choices is what allows you to give a very specific, unique performance, whether for a finished project or an audition. I am instructing you from what I have studied, used in my own acting and taught my students. I ask you to use acting tools that come from your own life experience, your own reality. Other acting techniques are just as valuable; use what works for you.

• **Never start to memorize lines until you have chosen your acting work.** If you memorize the words before choosing the work, it will tie you up so you won't be able to really investigate all that is waiting to be discovered. This is true whether you have twenty minutes to work on a script or three weeks.

• **Read the whole script** (if available), then read your scenes again out loud to hear the words; all the roles, not just your lines. Read the copy or sides over many times. Don't "act" at first; listen to what your instincts tell you about the script.

• **When you are auditioning for a television series** that you haven't seen or don't know the tone of, you can view an episode or several at Jan's Video Editing, 323/462-5511. Jan's has copies of all of the shows.

• **Look up any word you are not familiar with** at m-w.com, Merriam-Webster's Collegiate Dictionary. Enter your word, write down the meaning and then click on the little speaker icon and a voice will pronounce the word clearly for you. If it is a new word, you need to learn to pronounce it. Record it several times on a tape recorder. Listen to the word and repeat it out loud many times so it will sound like your everyday language. When your character is a doctor, lawyer, politician or in the military, they will have a specific vocabulary that rolls off their tongue.

• **Decide the given circumstances of the script.** This means what, when and where are the circumstances? Look for every clue possible. It is important what the other characters say about your character. *Given circumstances* are all the things the story (script) tells you about the events taking place and the characters taking part. Such as: What happened right before and after this scene? What was I doing? What was I saying? How old am I and the other characters? What is my relationship to the other people in the scene and to the people mentioned in it? How do I feel physically? Emotionally? What do I want? What is standing in the way of my getting what I want? What is the emotional event going on in the scene? What is the place like? Is it home? Is it a place that is uncomfortable and why? Are the ceilings high or low? Is it hot or cold? Ask and answer every possible question you can think of.

• **When all the given circumstances** aren't in the script or scene, use your imagination to create them. Your choices should be *hot* ones: passionate, filled with feeling. You either *love or hate* yourself, the situation and the other characters. Be specific: this character is afraid of the dark, has hot flashes, is sexually aggressive, shows affection by teasing, feels betrayed by his sister, hopes the sweat stains under his arms aren't showing, has to go to the bathroom but doesn't want to leave the room, etc. The more specific you are the more you will be able to pack into your interpretation of the script.

• **If the role you are auditioning for is a day player part** with just a few lines, then you may have to make up all of your given circumstances. For instance: This is an accountant who loves his job, a bank teller who has a hangover, a garbage collector who is an opera buff, a doctor who is very proud of his education, a socialite who has a drinking problem, a musician who is afraid of becoming deaf, a ballerina who is obsessed with her feet. For most day player roles you will be the only one who knows these things about the character.

• **Nina Foch, famous actress, director** and private acting coach says, "I never tell people what to do. But I ask them every possible question and I get them to ask themselves every possible question. When they leave me, it's unlikely they'll be asked any questions they're not prepared to answer. They're prepared." Be as thoroughly prepared as you can. It may help you to write the given circumstances on your script as you discover them.

• **You must figure out what the author means** in each and every line so you know how to personalize it, or relate it to your own life.

• To *personalize* the scene is to make the lines mean something to you personally so it looks like you are speaking the dialogue truthfully. Use the lines of the scene as a *code* for what you would say, did say or wished you had said in your own life. If the scene situation is like a situation that you have experienced in your life, it's fairly easy and there won't be much acting work involved. If it is different from your own life, then choose a similar or parallel situation.

• **When you are personalizing,** you will be talking to the other character in the scene "as if" they were your: sister, father, lover, enemy, someone you betrayed, who betrayed you, and so on. It doesn't matter if the scene says you are talking to your sister and you (because of the circumstances) decide to talk to a male principle you had in grade school. If need be you can personalize one part of the script as one person and then switch talking to another person more appropriate for another section.

• **Harvey Keitel, speaking of** *acting as if*:

  • **Improvisation was always a very good tool for me to use.** It helped to bring me closer to the role; to find the role in me. To learn about the life of a pimp *(Taxi Driver)*, I found myself a pimp and we improvised. I played the girl and he the pimp, and he showed me how a pimp would treat one of his girls and then we would reverse the roles. So first I had to research what a pimp is; then I can play it *as if* I'm a pimp. The notion of improvisation, the notion of *as if* is very simple: to do it as if I'm your brother, as if I'm your father, as if I'm your husband—sort of a jumping-off spot, the *as if*.

• **For auditions, the next step is rehearsing the lines,** thinking of the pieces of acting work you've chosen. Try several different approaches and personalizations; if the director gives you some direction during the audition, you will not be fixed on just one way of performing the role. Highlight your lines, saying them as you are highlighting. Underline your cues. Sometimes it is not a line, it is a phone ringing or a kiss or a doorbell. You want to memorize those cues so you have a reaction planned, even though they don't actually happen in the audition room.

• **The lines are not the most important thing;** they can get people off the street to simply read the lines letter-perfect. They are looking for an actor who can create a *relationship* with the person they are reading with. Most of the time in auditions, you are not reading with another actor but rather a casting assistant so you will usually have to create the whole relationship yourself. You can do this by being very specific about the choices you make. You may also read with an actor who is good or not so good. Play "in the moment," listening and reacting to your fellow actor but also keeping your work specific.

• **I believe you must memorize the script** for an audition and only look down at the script once or twice during the interview. (Always hold the script—even if it's memorized.) I know for some actors this skill isn't easy to acquire, but to compete, you must give a full performance of the material. Anything less and someone else gets the job.

• **Memorize in a flat monotone**; say the lines over and over but don't use your acting work. By using a flat monotone to memorize, the words will just be instruments to get across the script's meaning and you will never get stuck doing just a line-reading audition. Memorizing this way will allow you to be flexible at the read.

• **The next step will be to choose some sensory work.** This means using one or more of your five senses to make the circumstances or your personalizations more vivid for the audience. When you are auditioning you may not have time to get to this step. Sometimes you can plan it out and sometimes a great piece of sense memory, maybe the smell of your first lover, will come to mind as you step into the auditioning room. These types of inspirations are a gift from the universe; use them.

• **When you have rehearsal time, choose sensory work** to make the given circumstances and your personalizations very specific and unique to your own life. The way to choose sensory work is: if the character is insecure, macho or afraid, think of a *real* time in your own life when you felt insecure, macho or afraid. Then *make an effort* to wake up the memory of that time through one or more of your five senses: the *smell* of the room; the *touch* (what your fingers remember) of an object from that place or a piece of clothing you were wearing; the *sound* of music that was playing or a horn honking; the *taste* of food you had eaten; the *pain* in your heart or foot; the butterflies in your stomach; how the moon *looked*; that specific event in *your life* when you felt insecure, macho or afraid.

• **Rehearse the scene** a few times, trying some of the pieces of sensory work you've chosen; see how each piece can change the way the scene plays. Try several different pieces. Then when you're ready to perform the scene, monologue or audition material, you'll have an idea of what works best. You must still remain free enough to act *in the moment* when everything is working beautifully and you are living the scene; or free enough to choose a new piece of sensory work at the last moment because you had a wonderful flash (driving in your car) of what the scene is really about. Trust your instincts.

• **If this is a scene for an acting class,** a rehearsed scene for an agent's office or a showcase, the next step is to get with your partner to rehearse. Discuss and agree on the given circumstances for your two characters. Remember, the events that you are personalizing from your own life will be very different from your partner's and you should never discuss them; you can diffuse your personal choices by talking about them. Your choices are your tools, your treasures, your actor's secrets; they can't possibly help anyone else and the only way you can lose them is to discuss them.

• **Next, if you must, cut the scene.** A showcase scene should be four minutes or less and a class scene five or six minutes (acting minutes, not reading minutes) with a beginning, middle and end. Do not add lines or words unless you must to set up or end a scene.

• **Rehearse in a professional way;** be considerate of your partner. Never be late. Arrive with your homework done. Scene partners may find it very useful to improvise scenes that could have happened outside of the script. Such as: when they first met; last Christmas; two years later; when they were caught in a snowstorm, etc.

• **Sally Field says:**

  • **Rehearsal is a most exciting time for me,** delving into what you can create, and when the director calls 'Action,' you take flight, leave your body, and are no longer on this planet.

• **Never give or ask another actor for acting notes. It is most unprofessional, and will not be appreciated by anyone.** Community theater actors are famous for this. You may discuss the scene or script endlessly but you must make your own choices. Tell your partner, "I'm going to try something different this rehearsal." Never ask anyone for a line reading and decline when someone wants to give you one—these are choices *you* must make. That is what being an actor is all about. If you need some help thinking of choices to make, call your coach or an actor friend and ask for help. I still have to do that, even though I'm hired as a coach to help actors make their choices. Sometimes you need that outside perspective.

• **Find an activity to be doing during the scene or monologue.** *Never pretend* to do something. One time when I was directing a very important show, an actress during rehearsals always pretended to be embroidering. I had assumed that during performances she would really be doing it. On opening night she was still pretending and I sat in the audience, dying. There is so much pretending in acting; anything you can really do—do it. Pick an activity that is logical for the character. Fix food, cut up an apple or cheese, find an article you really want to read in the paper or magazine, repair your radio, polish your nails, clean your gun, wax the furniture, shave, put makeup on, etc. Again, try several different things; never settle on the first one. Always investigate.

• **Finally, memorize the lines.** The work above will give you a good idea of what the scene is about and what you are talking about; it will make the memorization much easier. *The lines are not the important part of the scene; the relationships are what is most important.* Yes, you learn the lines word-perfect; that is the only way to be professional. The lines are more like the costume; they are just tools to help get the story across, but not the whole story. The actors who bore us are the ones who are just saying or reading the lines.

• **When you have been** *hired* **for an acting job,** *always* show up on the set or sound stage with your lines memorized. That is your job as a professional actor. The exception is a stage play where you have the opportunity to rehearse and grow in the character before you learn lines. This luxury is what makes working in a play so much fun. You are allowed to discover your character.

• **Memorize word-perfect: it is a valuable habit.** (*See the Memorizing Section for more details.*)

MEMORIZING

• **Many actors who come to me for private coaching** show up without their lines memorized. They usually say, "I've heard it's best not to have the words memorized so it looks like you can do more with the script when the lines are memorized." Either the actors have been taught by a teacher who doesn't know what auditioning in Los Angeles is all about, or what they really heard was, "Always hold your script in your hand during the first audition." You hold it in your hand because, in case of nerves, the lines fly out of your head or you hit an unexpected emotional moment and lose the lines. The people auditioning you will feel more comfortable when your script is in your hand, they know you won't have to scramble to find your script and interrupt the audition flow. It is always acceptable to forget a line and to look at your script to pick it up. Stay in character and in the moment, look at your script, see what the line is and go back to playing the part.

• **Bonnie Gillespie is an author and casting director.** Her books include *Casting Qs: A Collection of Casting Director Interviews, Self-Management for Actors: Getting Down to (Show) Business* and *Acting Qs: Conversations with Working Actors.* She specializes in casting SAG indie feature films. Her weekly column, *The Actors Voice,* is available at Showfax.com. Bonnie has given me a few quotes of how certain casting directors feel about actors showing up for auditions without the script memorized. As always, look everyone up on imdb.com so you can see their casting backgrounds.

> "**Material is available way ahead of the audition.** I put the script in the lobby, I put the sides up on the fax services. There's no excuse. We know how many people want this job, so it's awful when someone who has booked an audition isn't prepared for the opportunity. Get all the sides for all the characters. If you're up for a lead role, you can bet you'll learn about your character from reading all the sides." **Michael Donovan, CSA, CCDA**

"**Be prepared, obviously. Have the lines as memorized as you can.** Some actors need the security blanket of holding onto those sides, and that's fine, but have a good handle on the material." **Julie Selzer,** CSA

"**I want to see you invested in your career.** I want a performance, I don't want to see you doing a cold read." **Bob Morones,** CSA

"**I personally want you off book.** This is so my director can work with you. Ninety percent of the time, we don't prescreen. I want you at performance level because when you read for me, the director is there." **Donald Paul Pemrick,** CSA

"**I can smell a cold reading in an instant,** generally at the end of the actor's first or second line. I'm more than happy to give you the time to work on it." **Lisa Miller Katz,** CSA

"**To come in, especially for a producer session,** and not be prepared? It's inexcusable. You wouldn't do that in any other profession. You wouldn't do that with a board meeting. This is the career you've chosen. Take it seriously." **Michael Greer,** CSA

"**Not that one has to memorize the scene,** but an actor has to take the time to decide on choices before coming in. An audition is not an attempt. You need to make a choice and go with that choice, right or wrong." **Pam Dixon**

"**I am amazed when people are off book.** It doesn't matter whether you hold the sides in your hand or not. I can tell the difference between reading and being prepared. And being prepared includes knowing what you're auditioning for. This is especially important when you come to producers. Don't come in and gush about the show, but at least see it before you come in. Or call friends and ask them about the show. You have to know its tone. This is part of your homework." **Patrick Rush,** CSA

"**You can tell who's winging it.** Get the sides as soon as you can, and really make a choice, even if it's wrong. Just let me see that you've made a choice. We can always redirect you." **Lori Cobe-Ross**

"**Don't come in here saying you just got the material.** Remember that producers don't ask the scattered actor back. Without exception, I find it's the well-prepared actor who gets the part." **Julie Ashton**

• **If it is hard for you to memorize—never, never mention it.** No one wants to hear it. Actors who memorize easily may not understand and think you are a fool. You'll hate them because it seems they'll have an advantage. Other actors who have trouble learning lines will resent you for bringing it up. They also won't trust you to learn yours because they know what the fear is like. So, for your own sake, keep it to yourself how hard or easy it is for you to memorize. It is the *ultimate* actor's secret. Discussing it does nothing but damage. Assume that other actors memorize and you can too; it just takes practice, time and effort. Being a good actor has nothing to do with how easy or difficult it is to learn lines.

• **Some actors go through torment memorizing.** So what! You go through this trial alone or with a loved one at home who will hold book for you. Memorizing is just a mundane part of your acting craft that must be conquered silently, without complaint.

• **William H. Macy** says, "It should look as if you're making up the words and you've never said them before and it's happening in real time right before your eyes, even though it's not. It's scripted."

• **An industry insider** said he wished actors would conduct themselves like Richard Gere who arrives on the set at the beginning of a project with "two suitcases and the script memorized."

• **Memorize lines in a flat monotone.** Do not memorize in an acting way or you'll be stuck with that rehearsed line reading. You won't be free to add sensory work and personalizations to change the meaning of the piece. The writer's words are a code for what you are feeling and experiencing from your own life. The actor gives the piece meaning by using specific, personal acting choices. When a director asks you for a different reading of a line, be able to change your acting choice immediately. Make several choices before settling on one so you'll be prepared. Keep trying different acting work with the same words to see what unique things, what new insight; you can bring to the script.

• **Highlight your lines in yellow** and draw a dark line underneath so they stand out. If you have a stage direction between two of your lines, draw a line on the left linking the two lines so you won't stop talking because of some instruction (she picks up the glass, etc.). Memorize the writer's lines word-perfect. This is professional. No one is holding book in acting class, but in an audition the people in the room have lived with the words for perhaps weeks, certainly days, they know when they hear something that is off. On the set, the script supervisor is watching each word. A word of caution; do not stop an audition because you have misspoken. If your acting is brilliant no one will care that you've inadvertently missed or changed a word.

• **Set aside blocks of 15 to 20 minutes** of solid, concentrated memorization time. Hold a piece of paper over everything but the first line. Say the line and then look to see if it's right. When it is, add the second line and do both together until they're memorized, then add the third line, etc. Memorize your cue line also; if you don't know the cues you won't know when it's your turn to speak. Another good way (to augment the above) is to tape-record the piece in a flat monotone voice. You can record all the parts; just change your voice for each one. You can act the other roles if you want but, again, yours is spoken in flat monotone. Now play the tape over and over—in your car or while you're doing the dishes. When you have the lines down, record a tape leaving a blank space for your lines and then say your lines with the tape; you'll learn the cues this way.

• **When I was the dialogue coach on** *Seinfeld,* Jerry used to love being tested. He felt the key was learning all the cues. So if I could give him a cue from any place in the script and he knew the line—he won. He would also take Ginkgo Biloba (said to be a memory-enhancing herb) in the afternoon on show day and then right before we started shooting the show.

• **Still another technique**—write or type out all the lines except yours. Just type the character's name where your lines go. Have a bunch copied and then write in your lines like filling in the blanks. Check to see your accuracy. Writing the lines in longhand helps get them in your memory.

• **Speed drills are good, on your own or with your scene partner.** This is Joan Darling's "bla bla" exercise. Say the lines as fast as you can, NO ACTING. If you can't think of the line, say "bla bla bla" till you do or it's the other actor's line, then jump back in with yours. The secret is: the words tumble out of your mouth with no meaning—then you are free for acting.

• **Get the words into your body.** Set up a rehearsal space similar to where you'll be acting. Move around the space as you are doing the lines.

• **To practice, memorize something every day** until you perfect the memorization craft. Soap opera actors have to memorize a new script every night.

• **Look for books on memorizing** and learn other people's techniques. All is fair in the pursuit of learning lines—more tools for your tool kit.

• **I also believe it helps** to put your script under your pillow when sleeping.

• **Not knowing your lines can stop you from being an actor—toughen up!**

Resources

To download and print an updated version of this and all resource lists, go to actingiseverything.com.

m-w.com is the Merriam-Webster OnLine Dictionary. Look up all words you don't know the meaning of. Click on the speaker icon and hear the word spoken correctly. If it is a difficult word in a script you can record it many times on your tape recorder and hear it over and over.

learningannex.com. They offer many courses of industry related topics including memorizing.

Vicki Mizel, "Brainspouts," 213/840-6754. vickimizel.com. Private $65 hr. Holds seminars on her memorization technique geared toward actors, $99; also has a four-week series of memorization classes for $375. $89 for the memory tapes. Vicki says, "Through stimulating and strengthening your mind, you will turn the main ideas into tangible pictures allowing you to memorize, retain and recall monologue and script copy easily. You will be able to get off book in minutes for auditions or once you've landed the part. Besides just learning to get off book, the memory system truly deepens all aspects of the work.

ACTING BOOKS

AND

TAPES

All of the following theatrical books may be purchased at bookstores, theatrical bookstores, amazon.com or from my website, actingiseverything.com.

Samuel French Theatrical Bookstores, 323/876-0570. samuelfrench.com. 7623 Sunset Blvd., Hollywood. M-F 10-6; Sat. 10-5; Closed Sunday. Valley store: 818/762-0535, 11963 Ventura Blvd., just East of Laurel Canyon, Studio City. M-F 10-9; Sat. 10-6; Sun 12-5. For plays, get their free catalogue. They also sell many published film and television scripts.

Larry Edmunds Theatrical Book Shop, 323/463-3273. 6644 Hollywood Blvd., Hollywood, 90028. M-Sa 10-6.

To save space, I have only written descriptions of my favorite acting books. To see descriptions of all the other recommended books and to download and print an updated version of this and all resource lists, go to actingiseverything.com.

• MY PERSONAL FAVORITES

The Eight Characters of Comedy: A Guide to Sitcom Acting and Writing by Scott Sedita. This book is a necessity, there is nothing else like it. Scott is now L.A.'s comedy guru.

How to Get Arrested: A Motivational Story for Actors by Michael Wallach. The author teaches actors the correct show biz path to follow in an entertaining and delightful tale.

Acting Qs: Conversations With Working Actors by Bonnie Gillespie and Blake Robbins. These are great interviews that help you understand the Casting Director's relationship with the actors.

The Sitcom Career Book: A Guide to the Louder, Faster, Funnier World of TV Comedy by Mary Lou Belli and Phil Ramuno. This book is so important if you have ever thought of working on sitcoms. I know this world and have worked on sitcoms as a coach for twenty years but every time I pick the book up I learn something new.

Acting With Impact by Kimberly Jentzen. Respected coach and director has documented her techniques. Very valuable.

The Intent to Live: Achieving Your True Potential as an Actor by Larry Moss, the famous New York and Los Angeles acting coach and Director. It is endorsed by Leonardo DiCaprio, Swoosie Kurtz, Tobey Maguire, Helen Hunt and my favorite Jason Alexander.

Ten Minutes to the Audition by Janice Lynde. Janice is a working two-time Emmy-nominated actress. She also is an Acting Coach and director. This is a small book that you can review right before the audition – check over the Actor's Checklist which is 20 pre-audition "Dos and Don'ts."

Winning Auditions – 101 Strategies for Actors by Mark Brandon. A shared collection of actors' trade secrets and tricks of the trade.

Actions: The Actors' Thesaurus by Marina Caldarone and Maggie Lloyd-Williams. Highly recommended by acting coach Caryn West, it helps actors choose the actions to play.

Actors Working: An Actor's Guide to Marketing Success by Clair Sinnett. Contains valuable exercises and worksheets to aid the actor in preparing a custom marketing plan. Includes a bonus CD.

Casting Qs: A Collection of Casting Director Interviews by Bonnie Gillespie. These are great interviews that help you understand the Casting Director's world.

Self-Management for Actors: Getting Down to (Show) Business, Revised 2nd Edition by Bonnie Gillespie. This will help you manage your own career before you have an agent or manager. Bonnie and her husband Keith are featured prominently in this book. Her self-management techniques work.

Acting Out: Your Personal Coach to a Money Making Career in Television Commercials by Stuart Stone. A top commercial casting director offers invaluable information in this book. One of the best on the market.

Let The Part Play You by Anita Jesse. She is a teacher, famous for her audition techniques. Her exercises will make you a better actor and give you an understanding of the acting process. Love her exercises on learning to focus and concentrate.

The Power of the Actor: The Chubbuck Technique by Ivana Chubbuck. The 12-step acting technique that will take you from script to a living, breathing dynamic character. Endorsed by Halle Berry, Garry Shandling, Elizabeth Shue, Eva Mendez, Jessica Biel and Eriq LaSalle.

Your Face Looks Familiar: How to Get Ahead as a Working Actor by Michael Bofshever. Michael has been a working actor, acting teacher and director for thirty years and knows what he is talking about!

Breaking Into Commercials, 2nd Edition The Complete Guide To Marketing Yourself, Auditioning To Win, and Getting the Job. by Terry Berland and Deborah Quelllette. Foreword by Jason Alexander. An excellent book by a casting director and teacher. To the point!

How To Audition For TV Commercials: From the Ad Agency Point of View by W.L. Jenkins. Lots of good tips.

Working Actors Guide. A great big book full of Los Angeles resources.

Thomas Guide.

• OTHER ACTING BOOKS AND TAPES

Acting For The Camera by Tony Barr.

Acting In Film by Michael Caine.

Acting Is Believing: A Basic Method by Forster Hirsch.

Acting: The First Six Lessons by Richard Boleslavski.

Acting Truths and Fictions: Straight Talk about the Many Myths, Myth-Conceptions and Mistakes that Affect Actors' Development and Professional Careers Today! by Lawrence Parke.

Action! Acting For Film & Camera by Robert Benedetti.

Act Right: A Manual for the On-Camera Actor by Erin Gray & Mara Purl.

The Actor's Menu: A Character Preparation Handbook by Bill Howey.

An Actor Prepares by Constantin Stanislavski.

An Agent Tells All by Tony Martinez.

Audition by Michael Shurtleff.

Call Back: The Complete Guide to Preparing and Performing the Audition that will Get You the Part! by Ginger Howard Friedman.

The Craft of Acting: Auditioning. A video tape by Allan Miller.

Hitting Your Mark: What Every Actor Really Needs to Know on a Hollywood Set by Steve Carlson.

How To Audition by Gordon Hunt.

How To Get the Part Without Falling Apart by Margie Haber.

If You Don't Dance They Beat You by Jose Quintero.

If You Want To Write by Brenda Ueland.

The Inner Game of Tennis by W. Timothy Gallwey.

Killer Monologues by J.P. Pierce.

Method or Madness? by Robert Lewis.

Michael Chekhov: On Theatre and the Art of Acting (audio) Edited with **A Guide to Discovery** by Mala Powers

My Life in Art by Constantin Stanislavski.

The Mystic in the Theater by Eva Le Gallienne.

No Acting Please by Eric Morris, author of **The Craft Of Acting** and **The Meg Approaches.**

On Acting by Sanford Meisner.

On the Technique of Acting by Michael Chekhov. Preface by Mala Powers. Includes a biography of Michael Chekhov by Mala Powers.

A Passion for Acting: Exploring the Creative Process by Allan Miller.

The Playing Is The Thing: Learning to Act Through Games and Exercises by Anita Jesse.

A Practical Handbook for the Actor by Melissa Bruder, Lee Michael Cohn, Madeleine Olnek, Nathaniel Pollack, Robert Previto, Scott Zigler. Introduction by David Mamet.

Screen Acting: How to Succeed in Motion Pictures and Television by Brian Adams.

Sense of Direction by Bill Ball.

Stanislavski's Legacy by Constantin Stanislavski.

Strasberg At The Actors Studio: Tape Recorded Sessions Edited by Robert Hethmon

Strasberg's Method, As Taught by Lorrie Hull: A Practical Guide for Actors, Teachers and Directors by S. Lorraine Hull.
The Technique Of Acting by Stella Adler.
To the Actor by Michael Chekhov, edited by Mala Powers.
Towards A Poor Theater by Jerzy Grotowski.
Your Film and Acting Career: How to Break Into the Movies and TV and Survive in Hollywood by M. K. Lewis and Rosemary R. Lewis.

• BOOKS LISTING TEACHERS

The Selective Hollywood Acting Coaches and Teachers Directory by Acting World Books. Detailed information. Do not purchase these types of seminar books produced by Keith Wolf. They have a picture of a wolf on the cover. The information is not current.
Working Actors Guide, published every year.
Back Stage West ads. Request their latest back issue featuring the workshops and teachers in Los Angeles. They also feature some Northern California teachers. There are issues with all the college training programs and summer training opportunities.

• GUIDE BOOKS, HOW-TO BOOKS AND TAPES

Acting as a Business by Brian O'Neil.
Acting Strategies for the Cyber Age by Ed Hooks.
The Actor's Encyclopedia of Casting Directors by Karen Kondazian.
The Actor's Guide to Getting The Job, an audio tape, By Carolyne Barry and Kevin E. West.
The Actors Guide to the Internet by Rob Kozlowski
Actor's Interview Log: *Where Am I Going? Where Have I Been?*
The Actor's Picture/Resume Book by Jill Charles with photographer Tom Bloom.
An Actor Succeeds by Terrance Hines and Suzanne Vaughan.
The Agencies: What the Actor Needs To Know by Acting World Books.
Agents "Tell It Like It Is!" a video tape by Joel Asher.
The Audition Book by Ed Hooks.
The Backstage Guide To Casting Directors by Hettie Lynne Hurtes.
Back To One: How To Make Good Money As A Hollywood Extra by Cullen Chambers.
The Book: An Actors Guide to Chicago.
Book on Acting: Improvisation Technique for the Professional Actor in Film, Theater & Television, by Stephen Book.
The Camera Smart Actor by Richard Brestoff.
Casting Directors "Tell It Like It Is." video tape by Joel Asher.
Curbside L.A.: An Offbeat Guide to the City of Angels from the pages of the L.A. Times by Cecilia Rasmussen
Directors on Acting, video tape by acting coach, director Joel Asher.
Discover Yourself in Hollywood by Lilyan Chauvin.

Dreams Into Action: Getting What You Want by Milton Katselas.

From Agent to Actor by Edgar Small.

Getting The Part, video tape by acting coach Joel Asher.

The Glam Scam: Successfully Avoiding the Casting Couch and Other Talent and Modeling Scams by Erik Joseph.

Hollywood Agents & Managers Directory by Hollywood Creative Directory.

Hollywood, Here I Come!: An Insider's Guide to a Successful Acting and Modeling Career in Los Angeles by Cynthia Hunter.

Hollywood Scams and Survival Tactics by Lilyan Chauvin.

How To Be A Working Actor: The Insider's Guide to Finding Jobs in Theater, Film and Television by New York casting director Mary Lynn Henry.

How To Get Publicity by William Parkhurst.

How To Sell Yourself As An Actor by K Callan.

How To Work a Room by Susan RoAne.

The Job Book: 100 Acting Jobs For Actors edited by Glenn Alterman.

L.A. from A to Z: The Actor's Guide to Surviving and Succeeding in Los Angeles by Thomas Mills.

The Los Angeles Agent Book: Get the Agent You Need for the Career You Want by K Callen.

Making It in New York City by Glenn Alterman.

Meditations for Actors: for the actor within us all by Carra Robertson.

The Practical Dreamer's Handbook: Finding the Time, Money and Energy to Live the Life You Want to Live by Paul & Sarah Edwards.

Ross Reports: TV Commercial Casting guide, Comedy Casting Guide and Personal Managers Directory are among the great ones.

Seminar Books by Acting World Books. I love these and recommend all of them: **The Selective Hollywood Acting Coaches and Teachers Directory, The Agencies, Publicizing Yourself, Personal Managers**, etc.

Survival Jobs: 118 Ways To Make Money While Pursuing Your Dreams by Deborah Jacobson.

True and False: Heresy and the Common Sense for the Actor by David Mamet.

Voice and the Actor by Cicely Berry.

Walking in This World: The Practical Art of Creativity by Julia Cameron.

The Working Actor's Guide edited by Karin Mani.

Working in Hollywood by Alexandra Brouwer & Thomas Lee Wright.

The Writer's Journey: Mythic Structure for Writers by Christopher Vogler.

Your Handwriting Can Change Your Life by Vimala Rodgers.

Fake Cigarettes, Smoking, Fake Tears, Sweating and Funny Teeth

CIGARETTES

• **Some people say** that you have to be or have been a smoker to be believable smoking in a role. I don't know this to be true. When I think of Daniel Day-Lewis in *My Left Foot* portraying the feisty Irish artist Christy Brown born with cerebral palsy, I believe a great actor can do anything. Smoking while you are acting without using nicotine is definitely possible and believable. I was a smoker and it took many tries and years to rid myself of the longing. If you don't smoke, I encourage you not to start. If you do smoke, quit.

• **Health issues aside,** the nicotine craving can hurt you as an actor. You will be on a set where no one in the cast smokes and you can't get out to have a cigarette; the distraction can hurt your performance. On an audition your preoccupation with when you will be able to have your next smoke will take needed energy away from your focus. You may have to leave acting class to have a smoke just at the moment when the teacher has something to say that will help to transform your acting.

• **If you must smoke** in a play or film, use herbal cigarettes; they are non-addictive. Even if you are a smoker, it is wise to use the herbals for take after take. They burn faster and look real. The only drawback when working in the theatre is they may smell like marijuana. Many health food stores and smoke shops sell the herbals. When working on a set, let the prop people know well ahead of time that you will need herbal cigarettes. As a safety measure, have some of your own.

• **On a set**, matching the length of the cigarette for each take is an issue. The prop people will take care of the proper length for the master and close-ups, which can start at different spots in the scene. Ask props to use the gizmo that lights the cigarette, so they can get it going at the right length and hand you the lit herbal cigarette. You must keep track of the drags you take, your attitude, the placement of your hands, when you use the ashtray.

• **William B. David** was a reformed smoker and had to smoke during his seven seasons on *The X-Files* as the "Smoking Man." He used the above methods in order to remain a non-smoker. He says, "For any given scene one might smoke 30 to 40 cigarettes."

• **Magic-trick cigarettes** are an alternative for the theatre. They are expensive and bought in magic shops. You blow in them and they emit a powder that resembles smoke. They really are believable and the audience doesn't suffer from the second-hand smoke.

TEARS

• **You learn in acting class** how to reach the emotions where tears are likely to come from. When they don't come and the director wants them or the audition script calls for them, you will have to create the tears however you can.

• **Some actors tell me they learn to** look out of their eyes in a certain way that the tears just flow. Actress Janice Allen, when looking at a person, adjusts her eyes as if to see a picture in a mass of dots to bring tears. If you are not familiar with that type of picture, do some research and find one and practice.

• **On a sitcom**, you can get away with giant sobs and putting your hand over your eyes and make it look like you are wiping away the tears. There is a famous *Seinfeld* show where Jerry's girlfriend never stops crying. The actress was worried about not really crying. I asked what she did in the audition she said, "I just faked it." I said, "Well, continue doing it; you got the job." She was hilarious.

• **Ammonia Inhalants** by North Health Care, at most drugstores, can help. They are for reviving people when they have fainted. One sniff makes your eyes water.

• **Also try liquid Binaca** loaded up on your finger or knuckle. Rub your eye with it to start tears.

• **A fresh cut onion** in a plastic bag in your pocket can help. Get the juice all over your hand and rub it in your eye.

• **No matter how you get yourself to tears,** you have to make sure that the true emotion is there to support it. Crying simply for the sake of crying will come across as poor, forced acting. Some of the most powerful scenes are those in which the actors appear to be trying not to cry. If the scene does call for actual tears, then yes, you need to produce them. But no matter how you get yourself to cry, what will help you sell it are real, true emotions you put into your acting work.

UNDERARM SWEATING

• **Prescription Drysal** applied once a month will change your life. Underarm sweating is very uncomfortable so an actor must find a way to prevent it. Shots of Botox have been known to help with sweating by paralyzing the glands.

• **Many actors have had great results** with a product from drugstores called Certain Dry. They apply it two to three times a week at night. Some men have said they use Secret or other women's deodorant to keep them dryer. With any product you do have to be aware of the risks with certain deodorants and antiperspirants that have been reported by health experts. A natural deodorant is always best, but you will change your life if you are not sweating during your important meetings and when you are acting.

• **Continue to look for a solution** that works for you until you have this pesky problem conquered.

FUNNY TEETH

• **Dr. Bukks for personalized funny, fake teeth.** Many styles, including hillbilly, homeless, missing teeth and buck. Most are $35. drbukk. com, 800-925-BUKK. Call for a brochure. Chris Cooper did it best in the movie *Adaptation*.

Section Two

Pictures and Resumes

How To Take Great Pictures

• **Your 8x10 pictures put you into the acting business;** they are your most important career marketing tools. An 8x10 picture or a small online image is usually your first introduction to the people who will be calling you in for interviews and auditions, and casting you in their productions. You must have pictures, they must look like you, and you must like them so you never have to apologize when handing them out.

• **Color pictures are recommended when submitting for castings** in Los Angeles. Black and white pictures are used for specialized submissions.

• **Agents, casting directors, producers and directors** will arrange to meet you because of something they see in your eyes, attitude, look or style. An actor always brings an 8x10 picture to every interview; or at least has them available in the car. Actors at a higher casting level no longer bring a picture. Agents and managers send headshots to the casting office electronically.

• **Consider your photo shoot** an important acting assignment. You will be investing a great deal of money, time and energy. Preparation is the key. To research various looks, characters and attitudes you can play, use the pictures from the websites, tear pictures out of magazine ads, watch shows, commercials and rent movies. Gather the appropriate clothes for these aspects of yourself from your wardrobe, thrift stores and new purchases. Don't borrow clothes; what you use for your photos will soon be your audition wardrobe. Have the clothing items altered, cleaned, ironed and ready.

• **Here are recommendations from renowned photographer Ray Bengston** for different looks to consider when shooting headshots.

Men
- **Scruffy/Tough Guy:** Unshaven, garage mechanic, criminal, grunge, undercover cop
- **Business Man:** Suit, power look, glasses
- **Dad:** Smiley, warm, casual shirt and khakis
- **Sexy Leading Man:** Best outfit
- **Goofy/Nerdy Guy:** Grad school geek, Laptop/software whiz, witty techie

Women
- **Down and out/victim:** No makeup or hair styling whatsoever
- **Casual Mom:** Smiley, warm
- **Working Class:** Blue collar look, earthy
- **Secretary:** Quirky, cute look, funny assistant
- **Business Woman:** Power suit, hard-edged, ice queen
- **Sex in the City:** Attitude, sure of herself
- **Lawyer/Doctor:** Nurturing professional

• **Your first step is shopping for a photographer.** Study the photographer websites in the following listings and on my website: JudyKerr.com. They use their best pictures in the latest Los Angeles styles on the sites. Look at the pictures of people who look like you. If you have blue eyes, check out the blue-eyed actors to see how the eyes look. How do they handle your gender, ethnicity and age bracket? If you are 18, don't look at the 30-year-olds. If you are 40, don't look at the 20-year-olds. If you are a woman, don't look at the men's shots. Print out shots that you would like to achieve for yourself. Narrow your photographer choices down to three and interview them.

• **The photographer's personality and environment are very important.** You must feel comfortable in order to take the risks of letting the camera see inside you. Certain personalities click with our own and others make us uncomfortable. Your instincts will tell you what feels right. Don't ignore your gut feeling and go with someone because all your friends got great shots or the photographer is famous.

• **The price for a photo shoot** can be from $150 to $900 plus makeup for women and also men who need it, though some photographers do their own. My students and I have obtained good pictures from photographers in all price ranges. If the picture helps you get interviews, it has done its job. Pictures are one of your biggest expenses and greatest payoffs. This is the place to use a good percentage of your available promotion dollars.

- **Respected photographer Tom Lascher advises:**

    - **The three issues to consider when choosing a photographer are:** first, look at the pictures and imagine whether you would fit in this photographer's style. The second factor is whether you and the photographer want to go in the same direction. If you're thinking femme fatale and he's thinking ingénue or you're thinking villain and he's thinking leading man, you may spend the whole session tugging in different directions. Third and most important is whether or not you can have enough of a relationship with the photographer to be able to use the photographer not just as a technician but as a scene partner.

    - **The goal of the headshot** is to suspend the disbelief of the casting director, so that he or she sees beyond the photograph and feels the presence of the person/actor it represents.

- **Prominent photographer David LaPorte says,**

    - **A good picture is about truth.** This is expressed as an open and accessible energy. When you are open and available there is an effortless expression of information. This is a business of seeking the truth at every given situation. It is essential that this energy is also revealed in your headshot. Without it, the picture is lifeless and doesn't carry that special quality of who you are as an actor.

- **The most important feature in the photograph are your eyes.** We must be able to see inside you, see your thoughts. Models' eyes, for the most part, fade into the picture. Actors' eyes must draw the viewer in, move them in some way and make them curious about you. The viewer needs to think they can read your thoughts.

- **Have your hair styled, colored, permed and treated** at least a week before the shoot. The exception is men doing long and short hair looks in the same photo session; they will shave and get their hair cut in the middle of the session. If you are planning to do your own makeup, have a makeup designer show you how to do it and purchase the right products. *See the Make Up Artists Section.* Do this a couple of weeks ahead of your shoot and practice, practice, practice.

- **To look as good as you can on the day of your shoot,** get a week's worth of daily vigorous exercise and plenty of sleep, especially the night before. Wear sun block, you don't want a tan on your face. Be alcohol and drug free for a week before the shoot. Train for the session as a highly competitive athlete would.

- **The most important thing about your picture** is that you are looking straight into the lens, eyes open. Pretend or personalize the camera as someone you are eager to talk to, for a specific reason. Let your guard down, no defenses; be at your most vulnerable. Let the camera see inside you. Project the attitudes you, your agent and acting coach think are appropriate for he characters you will be cast to play. The focus should be *very sharp*.

- **Casting director/acting coach Clair Sinnett says:**

  - **Don't just do smiling and non-smiling looks.** What you need in a picture is attitude, feeling, thought behind the eyes. Actors should have two monologues prepared when they go to a photographer. One, a dramatic piece that really touches them, makes them angry, hurt or even makes them cry. And second, a comedic monologue that makes them laugh. When actors don't have monologues, as a short cut they can think of the worst day they've ever had, for theatrical pictures; the best day, for commercial pictures.

  - **Do your own hair and makeup** the way you do them on a day-to-day basis. Look like your picture when you walk in the office.

- **Caryn West, respected Los Angeles and New York actress and acting coach, advises:**

  - **Make up a 4x6 index card** with some expressions of attitude or one sentence thoughts to say to the camera; use these when you are feeling self conscious or feel you've dried up.

  Sentences such as:

  - I love your eyes too.

  - I have a wicked sense of humor.

  - I "butt breathe" and love this. *(See the Audition Technique Section for Caryn's explanation of "butt breathing")*

  - Life is short and precious and I take myself all too seriously in these situations, so I'm giggling now.

  - Do you come here often?

  - My wife/husband loves me, so there.

- **In general, Caryn advises:**

  - Get a teeth whitening/cleaning. Bring a small boom box and your favorite CD. Get a full body massage, finishing one or two hours before the shoot. It really relaxes your face and eases overall tension.

• **The first picture you need** is a commercial and/or theatrical color headshot that looks just like you will look when you walk in the office.

• **If you have a great body,** male or female, and like to show it off, you will need a body shot. Consider tennis, bike riding, dance, workout clothes or one of your own personal skills that require body-fitting clothes. If you do stunts, you need pictures of you doing martial arts, jumping from a building, firing a gun, whatever your specialty. If you want to be considered for sexy roles where nudity or partial nudity is required, take pictures in a tiny bathing suit or an outfit that plays up your body. Do not mail these shots! Give them out personally when it is appropriate to the role. You will also have them posted on your website and with your membership casting site. These ¾ shots don't show up as well as headshots when submitting via e-mail or the Web.

• **Kevyn Major Howard, well-known photographer.**

• **Q: What is your approach to shooting headshots,** and how do you instruct actors to prepare for a shoot with you?

  • **The headshot is the critical tool,** which transports the actor's charisma and talent to the decision makers within the film industry. If you mirror what great artists do in film, you make it easy for them to hire you.

  • **My approach is an accurate and exact replicate** of what cinematographers and directors have been shooting for the past 75 years. It is the art form of putting people on film. The focus is on the eyes because the eyes communicate emotion and emotion is what sells films. I know how a great headshot can impact an actor's career. Thirty years ago I was so disenchanted with my headshots that I dared take my own, and the rest is history. I have had the pleasure of working with some of the greatest icons in film. Stanley Kubrick hired me as one of his lead actors in *Full Metal Jacket* based upon my headshot and my talent as a photographer and actor. I have also worked with legends Frank Sinatra, Clint Eastwood, Charles Bronson, Ron Howard, James Caan, Willem Dafoe, to name but a few. Dreams do come true—with talent, imagination, knowledge and vision.

- **On how to prepare**, there are the obvious answers to your question such as get plenty of rest, don't drink the night before, clothes should be pressed etc., but let's get down to the real deal.

- **There is nothing to prepare.** Simply show up. You can't be anything but what you are, being what you are is your gift. An actor's job and craft is simply to live truthfully in the moment under imaginary circumstances, this is the actor's art. If you can see the camera, then the camera can see "you." If you try to predict the outcome, you'll end up looking like an actor who is acting for the purpose of doing an actor's headshot. The great actors of film have touched us not by pretending to act, but by truthfully revealing their raw vulnerability and artfully embarking on mankind's emotion. So just be you.

- **All pictures need attitude.** Look in the camera lens, let the camera see inside of you, and then imagine you are talking to someone you know who would make you say things like:

"I want you."	"You make me angry because..."
"Come here."	"I'm so embarrassed."
"Get out of here!"	"I'm ready."
"I hate you."	"I love you."
"You devastated me."	"You feel so good."
"I'll pay you back."	"You're so sexy."
"I'm bad."	"You're so cute."
"Please forgive me."	"Come on, let's play."
"You are so bad."	"Let's party!"
"I'll never forgive you."	"Where's the party?"

- **Another picture might be upbeat**, with a smile that makes you look happy, perky, in love with life, with lots of energy in your eyes. When looking in the lens, say things like,

"Hey!"	"This is the best!"
"Oh!"	"Yummy!"
"What a great day!"	"What a bargain!"
"What a surprise!"	"I got the job!" etc.

- **Do whatever it takes to get your energy up.** Talk to the camera as if it is your puppy, pet bird, best friend or mom; find what works for you and then do the acting.

• **Makeup artist Rita Montanez** designed the following clothing list for photographers she works with.

CLOTHING LIST

Bring a lot of clothing so we can figure out what works best for you!
• Solid colors work best (no prints, patterns or stripes), texture works well.
• Long sleeves are best for headshots, never wear short sleeves if you are uncomfortable with your arms.
• Mock turtlenecks, nothing bulky.
• White, black and gray t-shirts work well under denim shirts, sport jackets, etc.
• For women, jewelry is simple, studs and small earrings. No watches or rings.
Commercial
• Think The Gap, Banana Republic, J. Crew, etc. Casual and comfortable, layered looks.
Theatrical
• Dark colors are inherently more dramatic.
• For women: bodysuits, simple shirts with clean lines. Cleavage is not always appropriate. If a suit has been suggested, again, simple clean lines. Large shoulder pads are out.
• For men: blazers with collared shirts or t-shirts. Suits for an upscale look. Ties are good for a detective, a cop and a business look.

• **Photographer Ray Bengston suggests:** Clothing should fit the character. Solids and mid tones are best. Bold stripes, patterns, whites and blacks are not great. Then again, it depends on the market or character. If you're doing a goth or punk look you would probably wear a lot of black. If you're a doctor you might wear a lab coat. It's best not to have too many props or a wardrobe that looks cartoonish. It's all about being real.

• **The above descriptions** of pictures are for the Los Angeles market. If you are in another city, research the trends in your area. If you are moving to Los Angeles, plan on having your professional pictures taken here. If your pictures are from New York, Austin, Chicago, Minneapolis or Miami, chances are they will work. Headshots from other cities, most likely won't work here.

• **For commercial interviews in some parts of the country**—not Los Angeles, your agent may want a composite. These can be three or four shots on one side or a commercial headshot on one side and several commercial-type situation shots on the back. When my martial artist daughter, Cynthia Kerr, lived in Dallas, she used a one-sided composite made up of two pictures—one wearing a tank top and karate pants, doing a perfect side kick, the other a glamour head shot. Composites have your name, your agent's name and oftentimes your measurements.

• **When it is time for your first pictures** and your funds are limited, contact art and makeup schools and colleges to investigate how to become a model for the photography students in exchange for photos. We list a couple of places in the following resources list.

• **Or ask a talented friend with a good digital camera** to shoot a trial roll in an outdoor setting with good lighting. Look at the photos on your computer, crop and enhance them, then burn a disk with the ones you like and have them developed at a drug store or one-hour photo place into 4x6s to see the real quality. All this can be done cheaply and may result in an okay head shot to get you started.

• **The following photographers** are all talented and well-respected, but I have never found one that everyone has been satisfied with. Make sure the photographer you choose guarantees their work. This means if you and your agent did not get the shots you need, they will re-shoot for the price of supplies and makeup artist only.

• **Try not to be discouraged** if it takes more than one photo session to get an 8x10 you love. Use these picture-taking events as a time to learn something about acting in front of the camera. Your personal preparation and ease with the photographer will make all the difference in the success of the shoot. It can be very tough not to have your pictures come out as you dreamed they would. I have been through agony myself, with my daughter Cynthia and many of my students. When I was shooting photos for this book, one of the photographer's pictures were awful. Obviously, he's not in the book, but I had seen many of his pictures that I loved. Try to diagnose what didn't work. This isn't to look for blame, but to educate yourself. Blame will not solve anything and can lead to self-pity, which can kill your spirit. Pick yourself up, save more money and go for it again.

• **Hugh Grant** says, "I'm terrible at having my picture taken. I'm always furious and unpleasant."

• *Headshot Secrets Revealed!* is a terrific online book by Bob Fraser. It gives excellent instructions on how to do everything regarding headshots. Headshotsecrets.com, money back guarantee.

• **The next step is choosing the right shots to reproduce.** If your photographer has given you the disk, select your favorites, burn a CD and have 4x6 prints made. Do not ask anyone but an agent or manager to look at a full CD of all your pictures. Have the prints made up at a drugstore or one-hour photo place. If you have been given an online proof sheet you will probably be able to print out your own prints. Now you are ready to get opinions from experts in the business to help you choose your shots for reproduction: your acting coach, photographer, an agent or casting director. Keep track of each person's picks and then make your choices. I suggest you choose last so you can see how others perceive you.

•**Photographer Ray Bengston adds,** "When you don't have an agent or manager to tell you what looks, what pictures to reproduce or put online, learn how to sell yourself. Watch television and see where you fit in, know what markets you're right for. The more specific you are, the more successful your shots will be. With submissions being online, agents like to submit the proper picture for the part. I think the biggest mistake actors make is doing looks just for the sake of doing looks or doing a look because one of their friends did it."

• **Now you are ready to reproduce your master picture.** Burn a disc from your computer or choose online, whichever way you have your proofs. Take it to the reproducer, chose border style which includes no border, font and size for your name, make it a small size name. Many flaws can be corrected by retouching. *See Photo Retouching Section.* When you are happy with the shot, the reproducer will run off as many copies as you need. I think photo prints are best because you probably won't need more than 100 each of a couple of looks. If you are an actor who uses several hundred photos a year then by all means, have lithos done. For the price break you have to run off more than 250 of each master.

• **If there are pictures you hate**, you have my permission to destroy them no matter how much they cost. You don't want a picture you hate to be anywhere in this world; you never know when it will turn up to embarrass you.

PHOTOGRAPHERS

To download and print an updated version of this and all resource lists, go to actingiseverything.com.

Actingiseverything.com/links/photographers
nowcasting.com. Photographers' gallery.
actorsite.com.

Here are photographers who have pictures featured in the book:

Bob Bayles, 818/997-8518. bobbaylesphotos.com. $150 for 80 JPEG images burned to a disc, which you'll receive at the end of the session. He likes to shoot with available light. 3-4 wardrobe changes. Use your own makeup artists. His studio has a very comfortable atmosphere. Bob really tries to work with you to get the shots you want, and help you be at ease throughout the session. He has shot many of my students and they have all gotten the shots they need. *See photos of Suzanne Wallace Whayne and photos of Keith Johnson in the Photo section.*

Ray Bengston, 661/253-4908. eyekool.com. $300 for three looks and $400 for six looks. Price includes a full resolution CD of the entire session. Only moves on to the next look once he feels he has the shot. Coming from a casting and acting background, Ray approaches the different looks as categories, finding shots that will help showcase the client in their particular market. He believes each shot should say something different. Ray has been shooting for years, works with commercial casting directors and agents. See what he has written about the different shots you want to try and capture. *See photos of Caryn West in the Photo section.*

Mark Bennington, 323/655-1929. benningtonphotography.com. $400 and shoots color film but can convert to black and white. Will do 8-11 different looks. Former actor who understands what an actor's headshot needs to say. He says, "What I do is capture images of a real person in character. To me, the 'real' mom or businessman or mechanic or cop or whatever doesn't mean an actor standing in a studio or a perfectly lit alley way holding a corny prop. It means being real with yourself and knowing what you sell." *See photos of Caryn West in the Photo section.*

Shawn Flint Blair, 323/856-6105. photographybyshawn.com. $350 for headshots (also offers professional makeup for $150). Shawn shoots digital and client will get a disc with photos two days after shooting. Comfortable, easy, relaxed session with 2-3 clothing changes. Shawn also shoots business headshots and a number of other styles. She says, "I love seeing a client relax, have fun and enjoy the process of a photo shoot. Capturing their personality is my goal." *See photos of Brittani Taylor in the Photo section.*

David Carlson, 323/660-0028. davidcarlsonphoto.com. Basic package is $350 and includes 3-4 looks, CD of shots, online proofs and about 700-800 images. David also shoots children ($300 for those under the age of 12). He specializes in natural light, but does offer studio lighting. He also offers group discounts. David is terrific to shoot with, very laid back but makes sure he gets all the shots needed. He shoots in a neighborhood that provides great backdrops. I love the look that he got in my photos. *See photos of Judy Kerr and young actors Melodie Gorow and Aaron Gorow in the Photo section.*

Mary Ann Halpin Photography, 323/874-8500. maryannhalpin.com. $495 plus tax for digital, three different looks in a three to four hour session. Reviews images throughout the shoot on large screen to check wardrobe, hair, makeup and emotional intention of the actor. Encourages actors to come camera ready, but does offer hair and makeup artists. A $200 nonrefundable deposit required. She says, "If an actor says, 'This is the most fun I've ever had having my pictures taken,' then I feel I've done my job!" The music and snacks are great. She is the author of the books *Pregnant Goddesshood: A Celebration of Life* and *Fearless Women: Midlife Portraits*. *See photos of Suzanne Wallace Whayne in the Photo section.*

Michael Hiller, 323/960-5111. michaelhiller.com. Prices range from $375 for three looks to $450 for four. Shoots digital (film by request). Makeup is available for $125. He uses mostly natural light, but exceptional studio lighting is also available. Having been an actor for more than 20 years he really knows what it takes to get your shots to work. I love his shots and I use one on my business cards. I always get great feedback from it. Michael says, "I fully guarantee two things: my work and that you will have a fun and productive session." *See photos of Judy Kerr and photos of Denise George in the Photo section.*

Rich Hogan, 323/467-2628. richhoganphotography.com. Digital rates start at $395 for three looks and 180 shots. He says his clients can choose "digital or film, black & white or color, headshots or body shots, commercial or theatrical, creative and edgy or clean and captivating." The new photographic techniques Rich uses are getting incredible reviews from the people in the business. It took him two years to perfect this technique, but the results are amazing. He's shot Tina Turner, Magic Johnson, Big Boy of Power 106, Jay Thomas, Playboy and Penthouse models of the year. *See photos of Brittani Taylor and photos of Kevin Anthony in the Photo section.*

Kevyn Major Howard, 323/664-9564. KevynMajorHoward.com. He is touted as the "King of the Hollywood Headshot" on the Discovery Channel show *The Human Face*, hosted by John Cleese and Elizabeth Hurley. Kevyn shoots digitally and often offers promotions. A successful actor, Kevyn is one of Hollywood's most sought-after photographers. He believes the eyes are the windows to our souls and brings that belief to each and every shot. When you shoot with Kevyn it begins early morning, he likes the light, and with several other actors. The makeup and hair stylists, Nicole and Ladi, start right in, it is like being on a set. Kevyn's style is totally unique and I loved shooting in the atmosphere he creates. He created my golden image for this golden book. *See photos of Judy Kerr in the Photo section and the author shot on the back of the book.*

Mark Husmann, 213/680-9999. greatheadshots.com. $750. Shoots digitally, viewing the shots as you shoot. Mark says, "My clients leave with 150 to 200 great shots." Every shot is in color and black and white for versatility. View your shots online, making your own test prints of your favorites; you can e-mail them to your agent, manager and acting coach for their input. All multiples are made from the original digital file. Makeup and hair artist is $200. He shoots inside a studio, using the natural light. Mark shoots two people a day and he meets people prior to shooting so they will feel comfortable on the day of the shoot. "I tell people to try and keep the pictures as simple as possible; the photographs should be about them, not the clothing, the makeup, or the background." *See photos of Denise George in the Photo section.*

Stefanie Keenan, 310/309-7828. stefaniekeenan.com. Price is $300 for unlimited digital photos. Does hair and makeup herself. Stefanie prefers a simple, natural look. A former model, she knows what's needed in a photo. As part of the shoot, Stefanie will change locations up to four times and allows for as many clothing changes as needed. She prefers shooting outside, but will shoot inside as well. *See photos of Brittani Taylor in the Photo section.*

Suze Lanier, 323/460-4060. suzelanier.com. Prices start at $225. Shoots both digital and film. Includes one 8x10 copy, complete with retouching, ready for reproduction (will provide same day for a small fee). Suze also has one of the coolest studios in L.A., complete with a ranch and million great spots for shots. She has been an actress since she was a child and understands the ins and outs and ups and downs of the business. Plus she is fun to hang out with. She was voted "one of L.A.'s top headshot photographers by *Backstage West* and has worked with an endless number of celebrities including: Ashlee Simpson, Taylor Ball, Soleil Moon Fry. She says she "shoots for fun!" *See photos of Keith Johnson in the Photo section.*

Diana Lannes Photography, 213/427-8096, Studio: 323/465-3232. dianalannes.com. $250 to $350 depending on the package. Diana works out of the Hollywood Raleigh Studios office that she shares with her husband, photographer Randall Michelson. She shoots with natural or studio light and they do all their own printing and retouching with gorgeous, flawless results. Clients are able to view their photos during the shoot and they can take home the whole photo shoot plus finals on a CD for $25. Professional Makeup available, $125. *See photos of Denise George in the Photo section.*

David LaPorte, 310/452-4053. davidlaporte.com. Two rolls for $275, $95 for makeup. Includes proofs and negative. Also shoots digital and includes CD. You order your own 4x6s and 8x10s. Unconditional guarantee means you and your agents have to love the photos or he will re-shoot. He helps people to just be themselves; that's why agents and managers love his work. "Bringing out the personality helps market the actor." Very likeable, open and truthful. Shoots just two to three people a day. Several of my students have used David and I loved their photos. They said he was great to work with. *See photos of Suzanne Wallace Whayne and young actors Melodie Gorow and Aaron Gorow in the Photo section.*

Kevin McIntyre, 818/293-9200. kevinmcphotograph.com. Kevin shoots color and black and white digital. Prices range from $235 for two looks to $365 for six looks. CD provided at the time of the shoot. Retouching available for an additional charge. Kevin also shoots fashion, weddings and music bands. "His ability to adapt to any pace and personality is complimented by his easygoing manner; the product intensely and simplistically captures the honest essence of a client." He is a natural light devotee and is recommended by many top agents. Kevin is very relaxed and shoots in a lovely atmosphere. So many of my students have gotten great shots from him. *See photos of Judy Kerr and young actors Jackson Tovar and Austin Tovar in the Photo section.*

Jeffrey Nicholson, 323/850-7468. theshotphotography.com. Prices range from $495 for four shots to $695 for six shots. Hair and makeup are available for an extra fee. Jeffrey shoots all ages. He has shot over 5,000 actors and models all over the country. Emphasizes an actor's eyes. Shoots in L.A. and New York. He says on his website, "A great headshot that creates stronger representation and auditions for you is priceless. I am all about making your shots extra special and separating you from the pack." Brittani loved shooting with him and she recommended he be listed in the book. I'm so glad she did. *See photos of Brittani Taylor in the Photo section.*

Robert Raphael, 310/486-7881 or 310/855-0048. headshotsbyrobert.com. Four looks with makeup for $375. Robert has been a makeup artist for 20 years, working with many of the top photographers, giving him an insight into what a great headshot is all about. Shooting in his salon, The West End, he uses natural light, studio beauty light or theatrical set light. "The color headshots are an added dimension for commercial head shots. Works very well for actors with honey brown or red hair, hazel eyes or to bring out what you really look like. Many managers, agents and casting people are asking my clients to print in both B&W and color." *See photos of Suzanne Wallace Whayne and photos of Kevin Anthony in the Photo section.*

Wayne Rutledge, 818/731-2903 or 206/550-1820. rutledgephoto.com. $350 Shoots digitally then copied on a CD disk, 3 looks, 4x6 proofs. Wayne works in Orange County, Los Angeles and Seattle. "I shoot till I'm happy and the client is happy as well." Kevin also an experienced model tells me, "Wayne was able to coax emotions and vulnerability out of me that no one has ever captured before." Wayne shoots in Orange County and Kevin enjoyed the event of getting out of town for a photo shoot. Very highly recommended by agent Carlyne Grager. *See photos of Kevin Anthony in the Photo section.*

Paul Smith, 323/463-8864. paulsmithphotography.com. Packages start at $450. Shoots all digital using natural or studio light. Makeup optional for $150. Clients can view their photos during the session; online proofs available 24 hours later. Being married to an actor, Paul understands the necessity of a relaxed working environment. By creating such a space, he allows for a fun and spontaneous shot, giving actors the freedom to focus on their internal thoughts and stories. *See photos of Kevin Anthony in the Photo section.*

Jonathan Vandiveer, 323/630-0344. jvimages.com. Prices start at $250. Jonathan will shoot up to four looks and price includes online proofs and session download. He says, "I work with the actor in a very collaborative way, going through the images as we work, helping with wardrobe, talking about marketing goals and strategy, and helping to direct and coach to create and capture real moments. The goal is to capture images that convey who the actor is as an individual in a way that clearly sets them beautifully apart and ultimately gets them calls." *See photos of Denise George in the Photo section.*

Where to model for photographers:

Amy Ward, Award Studios, 310/859-2779. aawd.net. 1541 Westwood Blvd., L.A. 90024. Internationally photographer is often looking for models for her makeup class. Books weeks in advance. Each session lasts about three hours and includes makeup work done by 2 to 3 artists (Amy stresses she only needs models with "excellent" skin). The major benefit is that makeup is free and all models get 8x10 prints for $25!

Westmore Academy of Cosmetic Arts, 818/562-6808, 877/978-6673. westmoreacademy.com. 916 W. Burbank Blvd., Ste. R, Burbank, 91506. Every couple of months, students at the Academy are looking for makeup models. The upside is that you get a free makeup session and photos that could potentially be used as a headshot. The downside, according to those who have participated, is that the students may tend to use too much makeup, especially for men, as they are experimenting and learning. They take just a few photos and there is often a long wait. This is worthwhile if you have time to kill (bring a good book). You will be learning more about the business.

Other recommended photographers:

Armen Asadorian Photography, 818/789-9825. armenasadorian.com. Prices range from $180 to $550. Wide variety of photo packages and very artistic feel to the work.

Mark Atteberry, Idyllic Photography, 818/386-1266. idyllicphotography.com. $395 to $525 for up to four looks. CD included. Mark only shoots one client a day.

Lesley Bohm, 213/625-8401. bohmphotography.com. Digital packages start at $450. Makeup and hairstylist, $150. She's shot many of the current stars on soaps.

Frank Bruynbroek, 818/755-7933. fbsiteonline.com. $450 digital session with as many changes as needed. Money back guarantee. Proof sheets on line. "I approach the headshot session as if it were a publicity shoot."

Brad Buckman, 323/466-2700. bradbuckman.com. Prices range from $495 to $595 for up to four looks. Uses a variety framings, lightings and backgrounds.

Dakota Photography, 877/721-2667. dakotaheadshots.com. $425 for digital shots and up to six clothing changes. Unlimited shots. Shoots in Palmdale.

Kenneth Dolin, 310/429-2876. kennethdolin.com. Price ranges from $350 to $399. Proofs online. Kenneth says a headshot, "must capture some special part of the actor, some inner life, the thing that makes that actor absolutely unique." He offers a 10% discount to clients who got his name from Judy Kerr!

Gayle Garnett, 310/712-3911. photographybygayle.com. Digital and film, black and white or color. Time is spent discussing how you will market yourself.

Greg Crowder, 310/471-3232. gregcrowderphotography.com. Shoots film and digital. $350. Location shots. Also shoots in San Diego 619/892-4965.

Terri Hanauer, 310/459-1859. terrihanauer.com. $225 per roll for color, includes proofsheet, negatives as well as a CD of images. A wonderful photographer. Terri keeps up to the minute on what the industry needs are in Los Angeles as well as in Canada. If you will be working in both markets, definitely see her.

Melinda Kelley, 818/728-1461. melindakelley.com. $325 to $375 for up to five looks (includes CD). Melinda is listed as one of the top headshot photographers by Backstage West.

Tom Lascher, 818/762-7634. lascherphoto.com. $300 (plus $100 for makeup) for 100-200 shots. Acting coaches Sal Romeo and Michael Nehring give Tom the highest of recommendations.

Mara, 818/781-8933. $350 for up to five looks. Makeup included in price. Shoots digital with minimal retouching. She's been a photographer for 30 years. Mara was a New York model; she is beautiful and makes you feel beautiful.

Chris Millar, 323/469-4432. dramashots.com. $200 for up to four looks. Digital with proofs provided the following day. Good at preparing actors for the shoot, telling them what to plan for and what they need in a headshot.

Donald Norris, 818/693-9114. norrisphoto.com. $399 for three looks, about 120 shots. Digital and proofs online. He knows what looks are hot.

Michael Papo, 818/760-8160, 818/764-0907. michaelpapo.com. Prices range from $235 to $600 and include makeup and negatives or digital disc. Michael has over 25 years experience and is also a career advisor. One of the best always satisfies.

Marina Rice Bader, 310/859-4687. marinarice.com. Digital $325, multiple looks. Approaches each session as a fun publicity shoot.

David Sobel, 310/308-5957. davidsobel.com. Shoots digital. Prices for clients from Judy Kerr range from $185 for 3-4 looks to $285 for 6-7 looks. Uses natural light and shows clients the shots during the shoot. As an actor, David knows the importance of capturing an actor's personality, attitude and essence. Recommended by agent Bonnie Howard.

Pamela Springsteen Photography, 323/930-9003. pamelaspringsteen.com. $500 for three rolls, no prints included. Makeup artist available. She shoots many celebrities and CD covers, works in a studio and starts with Polaroids. Pam keeps a very low profile on her headshots but they are always fabulous. She's a special favorite of mine.

Jillian Griffiths of J Thomasin Photography, 323/691-8689. Price ranges from $175 to $275 for up to five looks. Jillian says, No fake smiles allowed."

Guy Viau, 310/202-1257. guyviauheadshots.com. Prices range from $215 to $575 and include proofs, negatives and one 8x10 print.

Other Photographers With Good Reputations

John Corbett	323/654-9427	johncorbettphotography.com
Michael D'Ambrosia	310/444-7391	michaeldambrosia.com
Kelsey Edwards	323/936-6106	kelseyedwardsphoto.com
Erin Fiedler	818/415-1533	erinfiedler.com
Handeland Tesoro	818/623-7200	handelandtesoro.com
Michael Helms	818/353-5855	michaelhelms.com
Robert Kazandjian	323/957-9575	kazphoto.com
Kim Kimbro	323/769-5588	kimkimbrophotography.com
Michael Lamont	818/506-0285	michaellamont.com
Maggie Smith	310/454-1545	maggiesmithphotography.com
Peter Solari	323/934-9930	solariphoto.com

In South Florida: Bob Lasky, 305/891-0550. boblasky.com. He is wonderful; ready for the Los Angeles market. I taught workshops in South Florida and all the actors who shot with him had excellent pictures. For anyone acting in this area, check out his website. Everything you want to know about South Florida is there. When L.A. bound, don't put his name on repros.

In Austin: Fabrizio, 512/483-8000. fabriziophotography.com. Good reputation. When I did a workshop in Austin I saw many of the great photos he did for actors. His shots are Los Angeles ready! Don't print his name on reproductions.

Other Cities: *See the Cities Outside of Los Angeles section.*

• **The following pictures are presented here** to demonstrate different types of 8x10s used for theatrical, commercial and child actor interviews and auditions. I think it is informative to show you pictures of the same actor taken by different photographers. Each photographer chose the photos to be used, the makeup artist and whether retouching should be done. Retouching for all headshots done by photographer unless otherwise noted. Notice how each shot tells a different story. Imagine how many stories your pictures will tell.

My special thanks to the photographers,
makeup artists and retouchers for their
time, energy, creativity and
the donation of their services.

Actor	Photographer	Hair	Makeup
Judy Kerr	**Kevyn Major Howard**	**Ladi Labidi**	**Nicole Bolin**

Photographer
David Carlson

Hair and Makeup
Rita Montanez

Photographer
**Michael
Hiller**

Hair and Makeup
**Laura
Connelly**

Photographer
**Kevin
McIntyre**

Hair and Makeup
**Rita
Montanez**

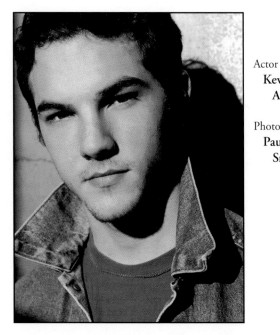

Actor
Kevin
  Anthony

Photographer
Paul
  Smith

Photographer
Robert
  Raphael

Photographer
**Rich
Hogan**

Photographer
**Wayne
Rutledge**

Actor
**Brittani
Taylor**

Photographer
**Jeffrey
Nicholson**

Hair and Makeup
**Elke
Von Freudenberg**

Photographer
**Stefanie
Keenan**

Hair and Makeup
**Stefanie
Keenan**

Photographer
**Shawn Flint
Blair**

Hair and Makeup
**Shawn Flint
Blair**

Photographer
**Rich
Hogan**

Hair and Makeup
**Dawn
Mattocks**

Actor
Denise
   George

Photographer
Jonathan
   Vandiveer

Denise did her own makeup

Photographer
Michael
   Hiller

Hair and Makeup
Laura
   Connelly

Photographer
**Diana
Lannes**

Hair and Makeup
**Meredith
Cross**

Retouching
**Randall
Michelson**

Photographer
**Mark
Husmann**

Hair and Makeup
**Colette
Taber**

Actor
**Keith
Johnson**

Photographer
**Bob
Bayles**

Photographer
**Bob
Bayles**

Photographer
Suze
Lanier

Photographer
Suze
Lanier

Actor
**Suzanne Wallace
Whayne**

Photographer
**Mary Ann
Halpin**

Hair and Makeup
**Mitzi
Druss**

Photographer
**Robert
Raphael**

Hair
**Fernando
De Jesus**

Makeup
**Robert
Raphael**

Photographer
Bob Bayles

Suzanne did her
own makeup

Photographer
**David
LaPorte**

Hair and Makeup
**Laura
Connelly**

Actor
**Caryn
West**

Photographer
**Ray
Bengston**

Hair and Makeup
**Anacia
Kagan**

Photographer
**Ray
Bengston**

Hair and Makeup
**Anacia
Kagan**

Photographer
**Mark
        Bennington**

Hair and Makeup
Victorio

Retouching
**L.A.
      Retouchers**

Photographer
**Mark
        Bennington**

Hair and Makeup
Victorio

Retouching
**L.A.
      Retouchers**

The previous 14 pages have featured what could be called *theatrical shots* and the next pages could have been called *commercial shots.*

These labels are disappearing. Currently, agents are making less distinction between the shots. Actors have the freedom to submit the pictures they choose.

Beginning on the next page are shots that can be seen as having a little more energy, a little more character, a little more fun.

Following the adults are the child actor shots. As in true show biz form, the children featured are in the book through their connections. They are my grandchildren.

Actor: **Judy Kerr**
Photographer: **Kevyn Major Howard**
Hair: **Bolin Labidi**
Makeup: **Nicole Ladi**

Photographer: **Michael Hiller**
Hair and Makeup **Laura Connelly**

Photographer: **David Carlson**
Hair and Makeup: **Rita Montanez**

Photographer: **Kevin McIntyre**
Hair and Makeup: **Rita Montanez**

Actor: **Kevin Anthony**   Photographer: **Rich Hogan**
Photographer: **Paul Smith**

Photographer: **Wayne Rutledge**   Photographer: **Robert Raphael**

Actor: **Brittani Taylor**
Photographer: **Jeffrey Nicholson**
Hair and Makeup: **Elke Von Freudenberg**

Photographer: **Shawn Flint Blair**
Hair and Makeup: **Shawn Flint Blair**

Photographer: **Stefanie Keenan**
Hair and Makeup: **Stefanie Keenan**

Photographer: **Rich Hogan**
Hair and Makeup: **Dawn Mattocks**

Actor: **Denise George**
Photographer: **Jonathan Vandiveer**
Denise did her own makeup

Photographer: **Diana Lannes**
Hair and Makeup: **Meredith Cross**
Retouching: **Randall Michelson**

Photographer: **Michael Hiller**
Hair and Makeup: **Laura Connelly**

Photographer: **Mark Husmann**
Hair and Makeup: **Colette Taber**

Actor: **Keith Johnson**
Photographer: **Bob Bayles**

Photographer: **Suze Lanier**

Photographer: **Bob Bayles**

Photographer: **Suze Lanier**

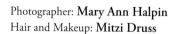

Actor: **Suzanne Wallace Whayne**
Photographer: **Bob Bayles**
Suzanne did her own makeup

Photographer: **David LaPorte**
Hair and Makeup: **Laura Connelly**

Photographer: **Robert Raphael**
Hair: **Fernando De Jesus**
Makeup: **Robert Raphael**

Photographer: **Mary Ann Halpin**
Hair and Makeup: **Mitzi Druss**

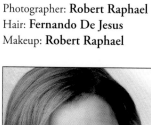

Actor: **Caryn West**
Photographer: **Ray Bengston**
Hair and Makeup: **Anacia Kagan**

Photographer: **Mark Bennington**
Hair and Makeup: **Victorio**
Retouching: **L.A. Retouchers**

Photographer: **Ray Bengston**
Hair and Makeup: **Anacia Kagan**

Photographer: **Mark Bennington**
Hair and Makeup: **Victorio**
Retouching: **L.A. Retouchers**

Actor: **Aaron Gorow**
Photographer: **David Carlson**

Photographer: **David Carlson**

Photographer: **David LaPorte**

Photographer: **David LaPorte**

Actor: **Melodie Gorow**
Photographer: **David Carlson**

Photographer: **David Carlson**

Photographer: **David LaPorte**

Photographer: **David LaPorte**

Actor: **Jackson Tovar**
Photographer: **Kevin McIntyre**

Actor: **Austin Tovar**
Photographer: **Kevin McIntyre**

Makeup and
Makeup Artists

• **While women always need a full makeup** for their photos, men seldom need full makeup, just a little help.

• **Men will need** translucent powder to remove shine and maybe an eyebrow pencil to fill in their brows. It is most important that a man doesn't look like he is wearing makeup in his photos. Other imperfections can be removed in retouching.

• **Makeup artist Lorraine Altamura tells men:**

   • **For photo shoots,** 95% of Caucasian men can use Revlon's Love Pat in the Suntan tone found at any drugstore for about $10. It is a moisturizing powder and can be put on dry or wet. If you put it on wet, just dust off the excess when it dries. Don't put it on your lips. Joe Blasco's Natural Blue Neutralizer I, found at professional beauty supply stores, is a mild beard cover and great for eliminating dark circles under the eyes.

• **Robert Raphael,** makeup artist and photographer, talks about eyebrows.

   • **The many looks** your brows can have would surprise you. Where your arch is placed can make close set eyes appear further apart and can help a heavy lid to appear lifted without cosmetic surgery. Your brows and lashes may need to be colored. Pale blondes look better with a deeper ash brow and redheads need a touch of brown. Men can really benefit from natural eyebrow grooming. Defined brows and lashes will give your eyes a stronger expression when you are acting.

• **Lorraine Altamura,** makeup artist, talks about lips and hints on how to work with your makeup artist.

- **I use a product called Young Lips** to smooth on the lips first. This will keep your lip color from bleeding. Next apply lip pencil and then lipstick.

- **Come with your eyebrows tweezed or waxed.** Don't tweeze the top of the eyebrows; the natural shape duplicates the top line of the upper eyes. When you strip that line away, it takes away your personality. Do your eyebrow, mustache waxing and facials at least a week before the shoot. Your face goes into shock for three or four days after these procedures. Get your hair styled at least two weeks before the shoot to be sure the style works. If you want your hair to grow another inch, then wait; you want these photos to last for a long time.

- **Rita Montanez, makeup artist, designer and teacher, tells actresses:**

  - **Makeup is incredibly important when it comes to photography;** the right makeup shows that you are professional. If you don't have a makeup artist for your photo session, make sure that you know how to do your own properly. In black & white photos you have to create a lot of contrast because normal makeup will not show up. You use more, concentrating on shading, using grays, browns and blacks. Color photography is different because it's more natural; something you can wear everyday.

  - **Always take your own makeup kit on a shoot** so you're prepared if the makeup artist doesn't show up for some reason. In interviews, your makeup can be the same as for color photography. For commercials, you need to look natural. On soap opera interviews, you want a glamour look. If there's a little bit of chubbiness or excess chin area, learn how to contour in order to complement your face.

- **Anne Archer** *(Fatal Attraction, Clear and Present Danger)* thinks actresses should learn to do their own makeup. She likes to do hers at home so she can leave for the studio a little later. She has two complete sets of makeup; one is set up at home and the other is organized in a portable bag she always carries with her.

- **Most makeup artists in beauty salons or department stores** will give free makeup lessons if you buy from them. Hold a mirror so you can watch what they do; ideally, they will draw a step-by-step chart for you. If you aren't buying products, a lesson is usually less than $100. Makeup by a professional artist for a photo shoot can range in price, but averages between $50 and $150.

• **Rita created the following chart** for my readers and students. Rita has listed commercial products but she has developed her own line of great products that are reasonable and can be purchased in person, by phone or on her website.

MAKEUP CHART FOR
COLOR PHOTOGRAPHS
by Rita Montanez 818/509-5733. makeupbyrita.com.

• Use makeup sponges for best results.

• Foundation should be applied lightly and evenly over entire face. Blend well (no masks).

• I like putting concealer on after the foundation, so the dark circles and other things that the foundation did not cover, can be concealed.

• Powder sets your makeup and keeps shine down. A large brush is my favorite way of applying powder. Powder comes in loose form and in a compressed form (compact). They both work well.

• Eyebrows. Keep them groomed. You can have a professional clean them up for you. Or if you like doing them yourself, make sure that they're done prior to your photo shoot. Fill any gaps in your eyebrows (sometimes there's a little less hair in certain areas) with color from eye shadow using an angle brush ... very light-handedly.

• Eye shadow. Using an eye shadow brush, apply a soft color over entire lid — preferably a neutral shade, and a darker color against the lash line. Blend the darker shade into the corner of the eye and a little into the crease of the eye.

• Eye liner. I like using two different methods. For a more natural look, line the top of the eye with a soft pencil and go over it with a matching eye shadow (brown, grey or black) applied with an angle brush. The second is a gel eye liner, forming a finer line, not softened.

• Curl eyelashes if they're straight, then apply a light coat of mascara.

• Blush and contouring. Use a blush brush to apply powder blush to the apple of the cheek to keep a natural look. Contour to get more defined cheekbones, brushing the contour color under the cheekbone. You can use a bronzer or a taupe shade for contouring.

• Lips. Putting lip liner softly on the whole lip always helps lipstick stay on longer. Apply a creamy lipstick over the liner. A gloss also works.

• Many of the products above are sold by MakeUp by Rita. Lessons are also available.

- **Rita further advises during your photo shoot.**

  - **Check all of your makeup during the shoot.** Use either powder/foundation on a puff or loose translucent powder on a puff for touchups. A great deal of attention and focus on your makeup will make a world of difference in your pictures. Hint: a little Preparation H hemorrhoidal creme will take down puffy eyes.

- **Lorraine shares further tips:**

  - RCMA (Research Council of Makeup Artists) is the best creme foundation for photos; mostly pigment and less grease for more coverage and less shine. MAC cosmetics have very good colors. If you can't go to a beauty supply store and get RCMA, then MAC is a good choice. The foundation doesn't have to go down the neck but put a little blush or contour powder in the middle of your neck, and to contour the décolletage line.

  - **We use three tones or shades** on the eyes and several tones on the face: foundation, highlight, contour and blush. Also use three tones on your lips. For instance: a deep rose, almost burgundy on the outer edge, a lighter rose to blend it all in together and a beige on the inside bottom lip to highlight and pucker the lips; it makes them more interesting. When you're touching up, use a creamy lipstick pencil that's just a shade or two darker than your lip color; filling in your lips with pencil color is the trendy thing to do. You can use just a tiny bit of foundation on the hot spot of the bottom lip.

  - **Put your lipsticks in little round pots** that screw together or in little plastic flip top pill boxes with several compartments. Buy the pots at the professional beauty supply and the pill boxes at the drug store. Scoop out the lipstick from the tubes with a plastic spatula or knife and put them in the containers, microwave them for a few seconds and the lipstick will quickly melt to the bottom of the containers. Use a brush to combine your own lipsticks for interesting looks.

  - **Cleanliness is very important,** especially for people who have sensitive skin. I sharpen all my pencils as I put them back. I use disposable mascara wands that go into the tube once and are discarded. Bring your own mascara; if someone has conjunctivitis and the wand goes back in the tube, the mascara is contaminated. Use clean sponges with the creme foundations. I use a spatula or side of the brush to take it out of the pot and put it on my pallet (hand) so the sponge doesn't go back into the pot. The Board of Health says the Hepatitis B Virus can stay alive on a piece of paper for eleven days. AIDS virus stays alive on cuticle snippers through general washing; it has to be killed in a 10 part water, 1 part Clorox solution.

• **Robert Raphael is a talented makeup artist.** I had my first makeup lesson from him over 20 years ago. I still use the special brushes I bought from him. He talks more about makeup.

- **Makeup can make your best features pop.** When applying your own makeup, bring your best features forward first. Your so-called flaws will diminish without much effort.

- **For Women:** Schedule your eyebrows to be shaped a week before your photo shoot. If there are any areas of facial hair that appear to cause shadows, waxing can eliminate the hair for up to six weeks. You can also have the photo retouched.

- **Mascara:** From dark brown to black. Painting only the upper lashes is a more youthful look in photos, as well as omitting the liner from the bottom lid. When it comes to television and film this rule does not apply.

- **Eye Brows:** Fill your brows in with a powder shadow a shade lighter than your brow color. Match only your brow shade if there are no brow hairs, such as at the end of your brows. If the brows appear too dark when finished, simply apply ivory shadow or translucent powder over them.

- **Keep all shadows,** blush and lip color matte. Avoid all frost colors.

• **Rand Rusher, R.N., C.N.O.R.** leafandrusher.com Botox, Collagen, Cymetra, Perlane and Restylane injection specialist at Leaf & Rusher Medical Clinic in Beverly Hills, talks about the best way to take care of your skin.

- **Commit yourself to the basics:**
- **Water**
- **Cleanse**
- **Sunscreen**
- **Moisturize**
- **Anti-oxidents**—using vitamin rich moisturizers are the best anti-aging effects. Anti-oxidents help eliminate free radicals caused by environment, smoking, pollution. Topical vitamins work faster, within hours, to replenish the body, while oral vitamins can take weeks to show significant effects. This is why Dr. Leaf and I have developed a skin care line, called Leaf & Rusher, to provide necessary anti-oxidents for daily skin regiments. For more information, please visit leafandrusher.com.

MAKEUP KIT
by Rita Montanez

Foundation in your shade.
Concealer for dark circles.
Pencil concealer for other things to hide.
Finishing powder and puff.
Blush for healthy glow or
Bronzing powder for a natural tan look.
Eyeliner, soft taupe or gray pencil.
Mascara.
Carmex or lip balm on lips before liner.
Neutral lip pencil as lip liner.
Lipstick close to liner color.
Powder brush to blend all of the face powders.
A sponge and Q-tips for clean up.

Resources

To download and print an updated version of this and all resource lists, go to actingiseverything.com.

EYEBROW SPECIALISTS

Robert Raphael, 310/486-7881 or 310/855-0048. robertraphael.com. The West End Salon, 520 N. La Cienega Blvd., West Hollywood, 90048. Brows are $20 and up. Makeup for photo shoot is $100 and up.

Diane Barletta of Salon Oasis, 818/876-0633. 22941-C Ventura Blvd., Woodland Hills, 91364. Actress Jode Leigh Edwards says, "When I went to Diane, my eyebrows had been destroyed; they were lopsided and I'd been burnt by the wax. Diane is very gentle, and the shape is always perfect for my face. I would drive to Timbuktu for her. I won't let anyone else touch my eyebrows!" Rates available upon request. Diane does all types of body waxing, facials and massage.

Jacqueline Shepard, 323/939-8969. Located at Chroma Makeup Studio, 9605 S. Santa Monica Blvd., Beverly Hills, 90210. $32 for eyebrow tweeze rather than wax; Lash tinting, $25-$30; brow tinting, $12; lip wax, $12; individual false eyelash application, $25. Chris Kerr and Cathy Kerr say she's the BEST!

Elke Von Freudenberg, 323/525-1429, makeup.gq.nu. Brittani Taylor recommends Elke for eyebrows. "She is super affordable, does an amazing job on my eyebrows. She has me spoiled; it's one-stop shopping for grooming!"

MAKEUP ARTISTS

Photographers will usually have professional makeup artists they recommend.
• *The following professional makeup artists will go on your photo shoots to work with you.*

Rita Montanez, 818/509-5733. makeupbyrita.com. Hair and makeup: $125 for a general shoot. I've worked with her many times. Besides being available for your photo shoot, she gives private lessons in how to do your own makeup. Private lesson are $150 and last about 1-2 hours. You learn color, B&W photography, natural and glamour looks. $150 for special occasion. You get a 20% discount on her professional line of cosmetics when you take a lesson. She will personalize a makeup kit to suit you. Rita works with many photographers. *See Judy Kerr's shots taken by David Carlson and Kevin McIntyre in the Photo section.*

Laura Connelly, 310/473-3355. Makeup and hair. $100 and up, depending on time and locations, for a general photo shoot. She likes to stay the whole shoot to keep an eye on the hair and makeup for the photographer. She specializes in natural, pretty makeup that really enhances one's own unique beauty. Makeup for a special occasion and private lessons, $100 and up. I loved the way Laura styled my hair for Michael's shots so I hired her to teach me how to do it. She showed me, then had me do it myself with my own equipment. *See Judy Kerr's and Denise George's shots taken by Michael Hiller and Suzanne Wallace Whayne's shots taken by David LaPorte in the Photo section.*

Nicole Bolin, 818/429-1466. nicolebolin.com. $100 and up. Nicole's specialties include beauty, character and special effects makeup, as well as hair-styling. She does a lot of work for film in television (including work on *Pirates of the Caribbean*), but also does print work, weddings and special events. *See Judy Kerr's shots taken by Kevyn Major Howard in the Photo section.*

Shawn Flint Blair, 323/856-6105. makeupbyshawn.com. $150 and she stays the whole shoot, approximately two hours. A true artist, she works in all media (video, film, photography, commercials). Shawn says, "I work with each client, giving them the look they want with makeup and hair. The only thing I do not offer is blow drying hair straight; I use a straight iron for that." She works with photographers doing promotional shots, headshots, catalogues, music, etc. Available for private lessons, $150 about an hour and a half. There is a FREE step-by-step makeup lesson on her website plus many other features including before and after shots. Also private sessions for any occasion including weddings, special events, award shows, etc. She is a professional photo retoucher as well. *See Brittani Taylor's shots taken by Shawn in the Photo section.*

Meredith Cross, 818/406-2735. Works with photographer Diana Lannes. Trained in doing makeup for headshots, still shoots, commercials, television promos, music videos and films in Los Angeles and Colorado. Encourages a relaxed environment and enhancing an actor's natural beauty. She says, "Makeup is fun and exciting. It is part art and part magic. It lets you ask the question, who would I like to be today?" *See Denise George's shots taken by Diana in the Photo section.*

Mitzi Druss, 323/376-3666. mitzidruss.com. Prices vary depending upon the job. Mitzi has over 15 years experience doing makeup for film, television, print and theatre. Her specialties include personal styling, period work and light special effects. She is also a certified skin care specialist and a stand up comic. *See Suzanne Wallace Whayne's shots taken by Mary Ann Halpin in the Photo section.*

Dawn Mattocks, 323/251-3305. makeupwithmattocks.com, festquest.com/dawn_m. Makeup and hair $85 (up to $150 for two looks). Graduate of Otis Parson School of Design with over 15 years experience as a makeup artist. Has worked on several projects and special events, including TV shows, music videos and commercials. *See Brittani Taylor's shots taken by Rich Hogan in the Photo section.*

Anacia Kagan, 818/749-6644. $125-$200 per session. Anacia has worked with photographers as a hair and makeup artist for over 13 years. She has developed techniques to help compensate for any type of lighting. She says it's important to "create light with your face." Her specialty is helping clients create a character without going over the top. *See Caryn West's shots taken by Ray Bengston in the Photo section.*

Stefanie Keenan, 310/309-7828. stefaniekeenan.com. Photographer who includes makeup in her session fee of $300. Stefanie prefers a simple, natural look with her photos and holds the same philosophy to hair and makeup. *See Brittani Taylor's shots taken by Stefanie in the Photo section.*

Robert Raphael, 310/486-7881 or 310/855-0048. robertraphael.com. The West End Salon, 520 N. La Cienega Blvd., West Hollywood, 90048. $100 and up for a photo shoot. He does great eyebrows $20 and up. He carries a great line of makeup, still gives makeup lessons and the salon has all the services. Plus he's a very wonderful photographer. *See Suzanne Wallace Whayne's shots taken by Robert in the Photo section.*

Victorio, 213/949-2534. Works at Sephora on Hollywood and Highland. 323/462-6898. Hair and makeup is $150-$450. Several years of experience in the business, working with celebrities and beginning actors alike. He says, "I hate the word 'client.' When I work with someone, I tell them I can be their brother or their sister. I work with them and make them comfortable." *See Caryn West's shots taken by Mark Bennington in the Photo section.*

Elke Von Freudenberg, 323/525-1429. makeup.gq.nu. Makeup for headshots is $95 in studio and $150 on location. Eyelash application is $10. Elke has worked in the industry for over 15 years and has done makeup for several celebrities and special events, including the Emmy's and the MTV Movie Awards. *See Brittani Taylor's shots taken by Jeffrey Nicholson in the Photo section.*

Alicia Ali. Contact her through Rich Hogan at 323/467-2628. Hair, makeup and photo styling. She works mainly with Rich but is available for outside shoots. She also gives private lessons.

Helena Cepeda, 310/991-0422. $100 for makeup and hair. Helena has an extensive background as a makeup artist and stylist. She works often with celebrities; she was the resident makeup artist for *The Vagina Monologues* and does freelance work on Lifetime's "Biographies" and ABC news. She is experienced in working with hair on camera—will go on sets. She has a great eye and can create both a subtle, natural look or go to the other extreme. She also does weddings and special events.

Sara Chameides, 818/400-7229. $100 and up for makeup and hair. Very experienced in styling (fashion background). Sara has been a makeup artist for over 10 years in all capacities, print in B&W and color, film, video, stage, and personal appearances. Happy to consult/shop for an actor getting their makeup kit together. $75 for makeup design and lessons.

Alisa Chompupong, 323/528-8755. Makeup is $150 for up to four hours with light hairstyling available upon request. Has experience in film, videos, editorial and commercial print, television, fashion shows and celebrity work. Trained at the prestigious Parson's School of Design in New York. She also creates looks and character designs for Barbie and Polly Pocket dolls.

Dara Dupuy, 310/403-9233. laphotosession.com. $150 for hair and makeup. Also does headshots for $250 per session (hair and makeup included). She says, "I feel it is important to stay for the whole shoot, sustaining perfection. Making subtle changes such as flipping the hair gives you different variations to choose from. I believe it is in your best interest to shoot multiple 'looks' ranging from natural to glamorous during your photo session."

Yolanda Frye Skin Care, 310/275-3981. 632 1/2 N. Doheny Dr., Los Angeles, 90069. Black and white photography and special event makeup, $75 at the shop, $150 at the photographer's location. See her special facials and notes about her full service skin and nail services, in the Age Defying section.

Eryn Krueger, 818/414-1314. $150 for a four-hour shoot. $200 for hair and makeup. $100 for an hour makeup and hair session at the photographer's. She'll leave you instructions on how to change for a more glamorous look. Eryn certainly knows the glamorous look; Emmy nomination for helping to create the "looks" on General Hospital. She also works in video, commercials, film, stage and print.

Anne Marso, 310/281-1904. $150 and up for hair and makeup. In the business for 15 years, she does B&W and color print; also videos, commercials, features, fashion and weddings.

Naja, 310/770-9525. $100 and up, makeup and light hair, from natural beauty makeup to more creative looks. She stays for the whole shoot for touch-ups and bump-ups. She does head shots, commercials, videos and printwork. She believes that it's important to work in a relaxed, friendly and comfortable environment.

Kari Nicole, 310/592-6914. makeuponlocation.com $125-$250 for makeup and hair at the photo session. Extensive professional training in all aspects of makeup: fashion, beauty, fantasy, character and special effects. Makeup for film, television, theatre, fashion and weddings. Call or e-mail for scheduling.

Colette Taber, 818/749-8997. illuminatedbride.com. Works with photographer Mark Husmann. Prices start at $150. Has over 18 years of experience doing makeup for headshots, celebrities and advertising work. A true professional with an emphasis on natural beauty. *See Denise George's shots taken by Mark Husmann in the Photo section.*

Sandy Williams, 818/752-2582. Pager: 818/327-9036. Makeup and hair for photography sessions, $90-$150. "I believe actors should have a real say in how they want to look, especially their hair, because they have to duplicate it. We go from looking very natural to upscale glamour." Special occasion, award show makeup, $300. She also does film, rock videos, commercials, television.

• *The following makeup artists sell makeup and give lessons at their place of business.*

Cynthia Roman Beauty, 310/276-5558. leafskincare.com. Leaf & Rusher Medical Clinic, 436 N. Bedford Dr., #104, Beverly Hills, 90210. Makeup application and lessons; post-op makeup applications and lessons; facial waxing and brow shaping. Endorsed by many celebrities and affiliated with the top Plastic Surgery Office in Beverly Hills. Cynthia has developed her own line of products. "Though inner beauty is timeless, our outer beauty is timed."

Kim Nguyen at Barney's, at the Vincent Longo counter. 310/276-4400. 9570 Wilshire Blvd. My friend Samantha Harper loves the Vincent Longo line and Kim's expert makeup techniques. She is wonderful for finding subtle yet striking combinations of eye, cheek and lip color as well as foundation for your skin type and coloring . She gives lessons and does private work for shoots and special events. $100 to $200.

Cinema Secrets, 818/846-0579. cinemasecrets.com. 4400 Riverside Drive, Burbank, 91505, in Toluca Lake. M-F 8-6, Sa 10-5. $75 to $150 per lesson for a one or two hour session.

Naimie's Film & Television Beauty Supply, 818/655-9933. naimies.com. 12640 Riverside Dr., Valley Village, CA 91607. M-W 9:30-6, Th-Fr 9:30-7, Sat 9:30-6. $55 for makeup application. This is where most of the studio makeup and hairstylists get their supplies. The regular retail store is on the top level. 10% discount with your SAG card.

The Color Company, 818/760-7798, 800/315-0108. jillkirshcolor.com. Jill Kirsh manufactures her own color coordinated line, has worked with several big name celebrities and appeared on QVC and many television shows. For $250, she will go to your home and got through your closet, helping you find the best outfits as well as fabrics to enhance your color photos. Further, she provides you with a individually designed makeup kit you can take with you to the shoots (includes blush, eye shadows, lip gloss, mascara, lipsticks and lip and eye pencils). Kit costs $75. *See the Wardrobe Section for more about her color charts.*

Westmore Academy of Cosmetic Arts, 818/562-6808, 877/978-6673. westmoreacademy.com. 916 W. Burbank Blvd., Ste. R, Burbank, 91506. Every couple months, students at the Academy are looking for makeup models. The upside is that you get a free makeup session and photos that could potentially be used as a headshot. The downside, according to those who have participated, is that the students may tend to use too much makeup especially for men, as they are experimenting and learning. They take just a few photos and there is often a long wait. This is worthwhile if you have time to kill, bring a good book. You will be learning more about the business.

Amy Ward, Award Studios, 310/859-2779. aawd.net. 1541 Westwood Blvd., L.A. 90024. Internationally renown photographer is often looking for models for her makeup class. Books weeks in advance. Each session lasts about three hours and includes makeup work done by 2 to 3 artists (Amy stresses she only needs models with "excellent" skin). The major benefit is that makeup is free and all models get 8x10 prints for only $25!

PROFESSIONAL BEAUTY SUPPLY STORES

For regular or stage makeup and hair supplies, beauty supply stores are your best bet. All of these stores will give a 10% discount to actors with a SAG card. They also provide mail order service.
Cinema Secrets, 818/846-0579. cinemasecrets.com. 4400 Riverside Drive, Burbank, 91505, in Toluca Lake. M-F 8-6, Sa 10-5. Owner Maurice Stein has been in the business over 30 years. Makeup artists and hair stylists work there part time, so you have professionals helping you.
Naimie's Film & Television Beauty Supply, 818/655-9933. naimies.com. 12640 Riverside Dr., Valley Village, CA 91607. M-W 9:30-6, Th-Fr 9:30-7, Sat 9:30-6. $55 for makeup application. This is where most of the studio makeup and hairstylists get their supplies. The regular retail store is on the top level. 10% discount with your SAG card.
Frends Beauty Supply, 818/769-3834, 213/877-4828. frendsbeautysupply.com. 5270 Laurel Canyon Blvd., North Hollywood, 91607. M-Sa 8-6, closed on Su. Makeup and hair supplies, all brands.

SPECIAL MAIL ORDER

Alcone Makeup Supply, 800/466-7446. 212/633-0551. alconeco.com. 235 West 19 Street, Manhattan, NY 10011. Request catalogue online. They are the largest store and outlet on the East Coast. There is no sales tax for out-of-state sales, which balances the shipping cost.

BEAUTY SUPPLY STORES WITH THEATRICAL MAKEUP

Larchmont Beauty Center, 323/461-0162. larchmontbeauty.com. 208 N. Larchmont Blvd., Los Angeles 90004. The very best; I love this store. 10% SAG discount on most products. My favorite.
Bay City Beauty Supply, 310/393-3709. 320 Santa Monica Blvd., Santa Monica, 90401. M-Th 10-7; F&Sa 9-8; Su 10-7. Good prices. Big inventory.
Diamond Beauty Supply, 818/761-1778. 11988 Ventura Blvd., Studio City, 91604. M-Sa 9:30-5:30; Su 11-4:30. Wonderful store, carries all the good products and they are very knowledgeable and helpful. Full service beauty shop in the back including an African-American specialist, hair extensions, facials, waxing and makeup.
La Peer Beauty (formerly M.P. Beauty), 323/934-7500. 6244 Wilshire Blvd., L.A., 90048. Corner of Wilshire and Crescent Heights in a strip mall. M-F 10-7, Sa 10-6. A small store but packed with products. Second location at 8950 W. Olympic Blvd., Ste. 113, Beverly Hills 90211. M-Sa. 9-8, Su. 11-6.
MAC Make Up Store, 310/271-9137, 800/588-0070. maccosmetics.com. 133 NoRobertson, Los Angeles, 90048, across from the Newsroom Cafe. M-Sa 10:30-7, Su 12-5. They give a 30% discount to actors for a year—sign up in store; bring a photo copy of your Union card. Also sold in the Beverly Center at the MAC store and at Hollywood & Highland. Without discount, sold at Nordstrom's and Macy's department stores. The creme foundation is wonderful, especially for your photos; covers everything. The powder colors and lipsticks are excellent; I see many makeup artists on the set using all their products.
Number One Beauty Supply, 310/656-2455. 1426 Montana Ave., #3, Santa Monica 90403. M-Sa 9-7; Su 10-6. They have all of the Hard Candy shades. Jennifer Aniston, Courtney Cox, Holly Hunter, Michelle Pfeiffer, Robert Wagner, Mary Steenburgen and Anne Archer visit this store, just to name a few. Body jewelry, a self-painting kit for tattoos, is big with the celebs.
Studioworks Inc., 818/848-1838. mystudioworks.com. 814 N. Hollywood Way, Burbank, 91505. Marilyn Phillips has about 30 years experience working as a hairstylist in the film industry. Her new store services many top sitcoms and feature films. Carries just about any and all hair and makeup products that an actor could want or need. And if they don't have it, they'll order it for you.

PHOTO RETOUCHING

• **The photos you use for your headshot** should closely resemble you. As you mature, your wrinkles will get you roles but as a young person, lines and shadows on your photos that look like wrinkles will hurt your chances of being called in for your age appropriate roles. Your retoucher can advise you according to your specific needs. The cost can range from $20 to $60 for an uncomplicated job. As always, get an estimate of the cost before proceeding.

• **Digital retouching** is very popular with photographers who are shooting with digital cameras. My only caution is to be careful not to take away too much personality. With computers it is very easy to make a picture look perfect which is not always in your best interest. When the photographer is doing the retouching rather than a lab, it is personal because they shot your pictures and know your personality and what you look like in person.

• **Photographer Mary Ann Halpin** believes that most pictures are enhanced by having the whites of the eyes lightened and the eyelashes defined. She further suggests that if you have a great shot but the eyes are slightly out of focus, they can be sharpened by a retoucher and thus save the picture.

• **Nichan, master artist, retoucher.**

Q: Why get pictures retouched?

  • **We clean the shadow inside a line or wrinkle.** We remove any blemishes or undesirable marks.

  • **If the mouth is in-between** opening and closing we restore it to normal.

- **When a picture is out of focus**, we sharpen the eyes by adding more lashes and by adding white to the eye, and on the edge of the pupil.

- **If the hair looks thin** because the light hits it very strongly, we can add more detail. We can remove hair that is out of proportion or in the wrong place.

- **When the background is too distracting** or there's something missing, we can change it—even remove the whole background and put in a new one.

Q: How do you shop for a retoucher?

- **The best way is to see the retoucher's work and get the prices.** Your picture is something you are going to use for a couple of years. Five or 10 dollars over a two-year span is not going to affect you that much.

Resources

To download and print an updated version of this and all resource lists, go to actingiseverything.com.

Shawn Flint Blair, 323/856-6105. artist2design.com. Starts at $35. b&w and color photos; manual and digital retouching. Shawn is the only makeup artist we know of who also does retouching. She has been doing retouching for over 15 years and also does graphic and Web design. Her makeup website is makeupbyshawn.com. *See her photos of Brittani Taylor in the Photo section.*

L.A. Retouchers, 323/663-3394. laretouchers.com. Orders are done primarily online. Packages range from the Lil Nip-N-Tuck, which includes teeth whitening, line softening and blemish and stray hair removal for about $28 to what they call the Joan Rivers, which costs up to $55. Their motto is "You. Only better." *See Mark Bennington's photos of Caryn West in the Photo section.*

Randall Michelson, 323/465-3232. $45 to $75 for the average headshot, including a final print. He does digital retouching designed to maximize the impact of your headshot. Complexion, shadows, flyaway hairs, contrast, background, eyes, clothing problems, fat and thinning hair can all be corrected in a natural way. Randall's retouching work is included with the photography of Diana Lannes. *See photos of Denise George in the Photo section.*

Mary Morano, 323/466-4079. 424 N. Larchmont, L.A., 90004. Minimum $35 for headshots. Call to set up appointment. b&w and color retouching on headshots.

Multi Image, Gail Rudy, 323/466-1266. 1607 El Centro Ave., Suite. 14, Los Angeles, 90028. Color, b&w retouching on headshots and any photos used for reproduction. Digital and conventional; free consultation. Two day turnaround. Old photos restored. In business since 1977.

Cameron Murley, 818/760-6756. 12260 Magnolia Blvd. Suite #3, Valley Village, 91607. Flexible hours and turnaround time. Free estimate. Full service retoucher; art background. Mainly does digital retouching. Charges around $60 an hour depending upon complexity of project. Full satisfaction guaranteed. Can reconstruct bodies and faces. Restores and rebuilds old photographs. Treats each picture as an art project.

Nichan Photographic Services, 818/508-8566. 12555 Hatteras St., North Hollywood, 91607. B&W and color retouching on headshots. Does not do digital, as they say, "only the old-fashioned way." Cost is about $50-$60 per picture. Some services available while you wait. Complete retouching services; techniques include etching, bleaching, dyeing and airbrushing. He is indeed an artist and has been retouching for many years, the favorite of many photographers.

RJG Photo Retouching, Rodney Gottlieb, 310/202-0150. Los Angeles. B&W and color retouching on headshots, $75 an hour. $60 for the average 8x10. Airbrushing. Digital retouching. For changing the background, taking fat off the face, removing flyaway hairs, the range is slightly higher. He will quote the price before he does the work. 24 years experience.

Barbara Clayton Turner Studio, 323/464-4015. 1570 1/2 Gower, north of Sunset, in Hollywood. Photographer Frank Bruynbroek recommends her work.

Eliott Photography and Retouching, Elliot de Picciotto, 323/876-8821. elliotphotography.com. 1151 N. La Brea Ave., West Hollywood, 90038. Is also a photographer and does headshots. Price is $30 per headshot for his clients; $25-$55 for other customers, depending upon the amount of work. Recommended by actress/coach Caryn West.

Photo Labs and
Picture Reproduction

• **Photo labs take your pictures** from digital files and film rolls to make proof sheets and 4x6 proof prints, some even put your proofs online. They produce your border or borderless matte 8x10 masters for retouching and reproduction, plus many other services. Printed proof sheets aren't used much any more. All of these labs do multiple prints and some do lithographs. The labs listed here take mail orders.

• **The original 8x10 master picture** must be of excellent quality. When you mass-produce the picture, quality is always lost; you cannot avoid it. Go to a duplication lab that specializes in photo reproduction. Most pictures will need to be retouched at least a little before being reproduced. *See Photo Retouching Section.*

• **Take very good protective care of your masters, digital files and negatives.** If masters get bent you will have to pay for another one. I keep each of mine with a piece of cardboard in an 8x10 labeled envelope, in a labeled folder in my file drawer. I am able to find my master and negative at a moment's notice.

• **In general, your 8x10 headshots** should be printed on photographic paper because we usually run off 100 copies at the most. Color lithos, like those printed by Reproductions, usually require 250 minimum for a price break. You would need that many only for a mass mailing or drop-offs. *(See Actorsite)* Most of the theatrical casting submissions are done online and all of the commercial submissions are done online. Pictures are used when you go on auditions and when submitting to agents and managers. Many working actors no longer need to bring pictures to auditions. See Will Estes' resume in the Resume Section; he doesn't even have a copy of the picture his agents use for submissions. We all long to reach that level; as of this writing I still bring a picture and resume to all auditions.

• **The photographic paper choices** are glossy, matte or pearl, with or without borders. Your duplication lab will show you what is available. Sometimes fancy borders cost more, especially the "sloppy" or "full frame" borders. Use what your agent wants or what you think will sell you and sell the picture best. Be creative; stand out.

• **If you are looking for an agent**, you may need two different photos, perhaps run 50 of each. Use photo copies, not lithos. A new agent may want new pictures or new shots mastered and reproduced. You may decide on marketing strategies when submitting to theatrical agents that are different than just a headshot. Do not do mass mailings to agents. When you have a decent resume and are SAGE (Screen Actors Guild eligible) send your materials to theatrical agents. For the commercial agent, you don't need experience, but commercial classes on your resume helps. *See the Agent Section.*

• **Your professional pictures must have your name on the front.** The photo reproduction service will do this for you. Don't put your agent's name on your pictures because if you change agents the pictures become obsolete. Your agent's and manager's information is always on your resume, which will be securely attached to the back of your picture. When a picture you are sending out is for a very important project, write your phone number on the back of your picture in case it gets separated from your resume.

• **Do not put the photographer's or reproduction lab's name on your photos.** If the photographer takes your picture for free then you can advertise them on your reproductions. Really look for this in the proofing. One of my actors had a problem at Isgos. They had not put the photographer's name on the proof but when she picked up 400 copies of four different pictures the photographer's name was on all the reproductions. She was very disappointed and Isgos said they couldn't do anything; "The photographer insists his name is on the reproductions." So inspect everything and ask questions.

• **The labs listed here**, in order of preference, are reliable but there may be other good ones. Compare each lab's work. Quality can always change, that is why you proof. Look at the papers and finishes and collect samples. Write the name of the lab and prices on the back of the sample picture and keep this in your picture reproduction file. This knowledge will be valuable because you will have pictures run for different uses. Have the reproduction lab do test shots. Test shots are several samples of what the finished reproduced picture will look like. Proof the shots and pick the exact skin tone and look you want. Your educated instinct will tell you which of the test shots is best. Doing test shots usually doubles the delivery time.

Photographic & Reproduction Terms

• **Border:** 1/4" or more of white around the picture.
• **Sloppy Border or Full Frame:** Shows sprockets of the film around the picture.
• **Bleed:** Picture covers all the paper.
• **Black Line:** Added to border around the picture.
• **Overlay:** White name on dark area or black name on white area of picture.
• **Litho Line:** Your name, or other information.
• **Line Negative:** Name in border of picture.
• **Copy Negative:** Negative made from master print.

Resources

To download and print an updated version of this and all resource lists, go to actingiseverything.com.

See websites for services, current pricing and turn around time.

Argentum Photo Lab, 323/461-2775. argentum.com 6550 Sunset Blvd., Hollywood, 90028. The do every type of photo lab work plus photo reproductions. They have a wide selection of layouts, fonts and papers. I use them all the time and always run into someone I know at 3PM when there is a line waiting to proof and pick up. The service here is excellent, they really care, they hire great people. They will put your disk up online for $10. This is a very handy service, you can mark the photos and just send a select few to those you wish to help you choose. You can print out copies on your computer for comparison.

Reproductions, 323/845-9595 or 888/797-7795. reproductions.com. 3499 Cahuenga Blvd. West, Los Angeles, 90068. Also in New York. Their prices include all setup fees. They never add on charges for layouts or adding a black line. Great photo reproductions and the best color lithos. They keep your scans for two years; call with your reorder, it will be ready in two days. New orders take four working days. I'm sure that is without proofing. I think it is always worth an extra day to proof. They were the first in town to do these digital scans. The service is great and they are quick to make things right without an argument.

Nardulli, 323/882-8331. nardulli.com. 1710 La Brea, Hollywood, 90046. M-F 8AM-10PM, Sat. 9-4. All work is custom including bleeds, sloppy borders and border with lines. Wonderful lab, wonderful work. All work is custom and the prices reflect that. Ten percent discount for repeat customers. The tests are free and ready in three days, then two days to complete the run. Top of the line reproductions.

Isgo Lepejian Custom Photo Lab (Isgos), 818/848-9001. isgophoto.com. 2220 W. Magnolia Blvd., Burbank, 91506. M-F, 9-6. Orders may be taken at their smaller location, 323/323/876-8085. 1145 N. La Brea Ave. Hollywood, 90038, half block north of Santa Monica. M-F, 9-6, Sat. 11-4. Processing and 8 ½ x 11 proof sheet, 4x6 proof prints in by 1 p.m. back by 4:30PM.

Paragon Photo & Digital Imaging, 323/933-5865. 323/937-1922. paragonphoto.com 326 S. La Brea Ave., L.A. 90036.

Photo Business Cards: 4over4.com for the absolute best photo business cards. They are color on both sides a heavy paper and shiny coating. $89 for 1,000. *See page 215 for more biz and post card printers.*

Resumes

• **First and foremost**, your resume is selling you and it should represent you in a professional way. The purpose of your resume is to give the reader a brief description of you and your professional experience. You must have one to go along with your picture when you are seeking interviews and auditions.

Resume Form

• **At the top**, centered: put your name in bold letters
• **On the left side** of center, in a column, put in smaller print than anything else:
> Height:
> Weight:
> Hair: (color)—not necessary with color photos
> Eyes: (color)—not necessary with color photos

• **In the center** of the page under your name, include any union affiliations: SAG, AFTRA, AEA. These union titles do not have to be big. Your work on the resume will make it obvious that you belong to the unions.
• **On the right side**: how to contact you: your agent's name and telephone number. If your agent doesn't mind, you can include your contact number. and email. If no agent, your cell number. You must have a Los Angeles number: 310, 818, 323 or 213. Don't question this; just do it if you are going to live here. This is actually the most important item on your resume. In smaller print, list your email address under the phone number. Do not use a shared phone number and you must have voice mail on your cell phone. Do not put your home address or age range on your resume.

• **Now comes the fun part**—your experience and training. Always list the project with your highest billings first, then the others in lesser order. Do not use all capitals. Small caps can work. You want to make your resume very easy to read. Make sure the font you choose is easy to read. Don't skip any spaces to accommodate a title or billing just use one line for each production you are listing.

• **List films first.** First column: film title; center column: your billing – lead, supporting or cameo; (cameo would be a one or two line part), third column: the director. When listing a student film, use the director's name, not the school. You can use a little italic word above the directors saying Directors instead of dir. Before each one. If you must list extra work then clearly state it.

• **Television.** Left column: title of show; center column: billing; star, guest star, co-star; (co-star is the lowest television billing) right column: director and/or network.

• **Stage or Theater.** Left column: name of play; center column: lead, supporting or ensemble if it is a play we know, after the billing put a slash and the character name: Lead/Stanley; right column: the name of the theater—unless the director is famous, then list both.

• **Training.** First, list the teacher you are studying with currently; then any other acting teachers. You can list any specialty class, such as voice or commercials, and the teacher's name. Last line, list your college first, then your degree.

• **Special skills,** including any foreign language (level of proficiency— fluent or conversational), accents, dialects, firearms, martial arts and any sports or training that might make you special—computers, medical lab, sharp-shooting, pilot's license, CPR, etc.

• **White Space.** It is important to have white space at the bottom when you don't have a lot of experience. You want to look like you are building your resume. Certainly when you have oodles of credits there won't be room for white space but in the beginning don't try to look like you have done it all, it just looks like filler.

• **If you have not acted professionally,** in place of Film/Television/Stage, put Acting Workshop Scenes and list scenes and characters you have performed in acting class. Now your task is to develop credits to put on your resume; student films, plays and projects you produce yourself are a way for your resume to grow rapidly. Do not think of seeking an agent until your resume indicates that you are able to land work yourself.

• **It can take two years** (after obtaining your union cards and agent) for your resume to reach a fairly comfortable professional place. It does grow! Enjoy the process.

• **Sylvester Stallone's pre-Rocky resume credits:** *A Party at Kitty and Stud's,* 1970; *Bananas* (unbilled bit), 1971; *The Lords of Flatbush,* 1974; *The Prisoner of Second Avenue* (bit), 1975; *Capone,* 1975; *Death Race 2000,* 1975; *Farewell My Lovely,* 1975; *Cannonball,* 1976; *No Place To Hide,* 1976; *Rocky* (writer and actor), 1976. No wonder he had nothing in the fridge. The legend goes that he turned down $250,000 for his Rocky script and got very little for it in order to act in the movie. The reason he wrote the script was to get a break as an actor in the biz, and he didn't sell out.

• **Harrison Ford's early resume:** *Dead Heat on a Merry-Go-Round*, 1966; *Long Ride Home*, 1967; *Luv*, 1967; *Zabriskie Point*, 1970; *Getting Straight*, 1970; *American Graffiti*, 1973 (memorable but too small to lead to anything other than more character work); *The Conversation*, 1974 (just a few moments but very daring); *Heroes*, 1977; *Star Wars*, 1977—this is the role that led to his many leading man roles.

• **Michael Keaton:** *Night Shift*, 1982; *Mr. Mom*, 1983; *Gung-Ho*, 1986; *Batman*, 1989; and then the big time.

• **Some copy services will typeset** and laser-print your resume. There are services that advertise in *Back Stage West*. If you are computer savvy, typeset and print your own resume. Your resume must be trimmed to 8x10 to fit on the back of your 8x10 picture. Pink's photocopying does great, fast, reasonable work. *See resources.*

• **Have just a few resumes photocopied** each time, unless you're sending out a large mailing; you'll be adding things often. Copy services charge more to use color paper; if you are using color paper it is cheaper if you provide your own. Make sure the color you choose is easy to read and will fax clearly. Ask them to charge you the rate for white copies. Everything is placed on your resume in order to be easily read and understood.

• **Always have your resumes cut to 8x10** so they will fit on the back of your 8x10 picture. Attach the resume to your picture, back to back, facing out. Use double-stick tape, spray glue or staples. **Staple from the picture side and hide the staples in the borders so they won't draw the viewer's eye away from your face.** Place two staples on top and two on the bottom about two inches from the left side so when a three-hole punch is used, the picture and resume will go into the punch easily. *Never submit a resume that is not cut-down to the exact size of the picture.*

• **Another option is to print your resume directly on your headshot** using a laser printer. It may take a little time, but can look more professional and less bulky. This can be tough to do and at a $1 a picture you may not be willing to try it, but some are expert at doing it.

• **When submitting your package** for a particular role, put a Post-It note on your picture with the name of the role you want to audition for. A cover letter is not necessary, unless there is particular reason why you are right for the role. Also put the name of the role on the outside of the envelope. More and more actors are using clear envelopes so casting directors can instantly see their headshot and the roles they're interested in. Actorsite has designed my favorite envelopes for mailers, they are all clear with no edges to catch. I expect these types of submissions to be fewer and fewer. Most casting directors want online submissions. You'll still be submitting to agents and managers.

• **At all times keep pictures,** resumes, and a roll of double-stick tape or stapler in a zippered briefcase in your car! You may get a job because your pictures and resumes are with you.

• **Alex Stone, a 25 year veteran of film and TV,** talks about picture and resume submission packages.

Q: What are some tips to help actors gain interviews?

• **The casting person** will get a huge stack of submissions, so you have about a second for your photo to grab their eye. The choice of a good photographer is crucial: the money you spend there is never wasted. After that, good reproductions. The resume is important. It should be truthful, factual, neat, clean, and the same size as the picture.

• **Some resumes are almost unreadable** because of exotic computer typefaces or faded Xerox copies. One actor listed a special skill as "requitball." Typos or misspellings are not acceptable. You must have a professional looking resume. Duplicate your resumes on light colored paper. Avoid bright orange, red or green; a casting person may need another copy of your resume and these colors won't fax or photocopy well.

• **A lot of people use the "special skills" as icebreakers.** It's an excellent technique because the more odd skills you have, the more chance you get to talk to the casting person.

• Fine art	• Bartending
• Sign language	• CPR
• Canoeing	• Dog showing
• Baton twirling	• Sculpture
• Nursing	• Trampoline
• Wire welding	• Chainsaw and wood splitting
• Skydiving	• Accents and weird noises

- California State Champion Cheerleader
- Beijing opera dance techniques (If I had this person in the office, I'd say, "Tell me about Beijing.")
- For Dracula, they were casting people who could speak a Middle-Eastern language, not just put on the accent. An actress got a role because she knew enough words to string together and they liked the sound.

RESOURCES

To download and print an updated version of this and all resource lists, go to actingiseverything.com.

See Working Actor's Guide *and* Back Stage West *for many other resume design businesses.*

Actorsite, 818/782-2800. actorsite.com. 5656 Cahuenga, North Hollywood, 91601. Acting group that provides a number of services, including dropping off headshots and resumes in their custom clear envelopes. The envelopes are $50 for 100 and I love them. You can call or drop in and see if they have them in stock.

Pink Copy Center, 818/762-8100. printyourscript.com. 12080 Ventura Place #2 (Laurel Canyon & Ventura Blvd.) Studio City, 91604. $15 to set up a simple resume; go in with it written out. $25 to scan and make a photo resume with up to four pictures. If you have your resume on your computer, bring in the disk and it will just be $25 for the photo setup. Shawn has owned this copy service for years and is always looking for ways to help actors with their marketing skills. Copying, printing, color copying, digital output, digital B&W copying. Discount for actors. Also prints scripts.

Smart Girls, 818/907-6511. smartgirlsprod.com. 15030 Ventura Blvd., #914, Sherman Oaks, 91403. Acting resumes created in a half hour, $75. Changes to existing resumes for $25. They also do professional cover letters. They save work for easy updating. Many office services for actors and screenwriters.

Keith Johnson

Hair: Brown
Eyes: Blue/Grey

323-397-7576
actingkeith@cricketfeet.com

Height: 5' 10"
Weight: 180

Film & TV

The Bank Robbery	Photo Lab Customer (Featured)	Dir.: Gary McAuley/SunWest
Pobre Ana (non-broadcast)	Roberto (Supporting)	Blaine Ray Productions

Theatre

Señor Menudo (Staged Reading)	Various Characters	Director: Robert Thompson
The Big Quirk (Staged Reading)	Various Characters	Director: Zac Baldwin
Arsenic and Old Lace	Teddy	Thebes Players (MI)
Dracula	Arthur Holmwood	MATC (WI)

Commercials

No current conflicts.

Training

Michael Donovan:	Private Coaching; On-Camera, Commercial Technique, Character Development, Cold Reading
Doug Warhit:	Private Coaching; Scene Study
MATC (WI):	Wm. Patrick Barlow & Roger Herian; Stage Combat, Character Development, Dialogue, Scene Study, Improvisation

Special Skills

Japanese Swordfighting (Kendo/Kenjutsu), Martial Arts, Archery (Longbow/Hunting), Soccer, Skydiving, Hiking, Really Bad Golf, Swimming, SCUBA, Ping Pong, Horseback Riding (Western), Conversational Japanese, Some Spanish Dialogue, Former US Marine (Infantryman, Squad Leader, Weapons Expert, Water Training, Survival, Distance Shooting… extreme distances… like a mile… really)

Keith Johnson's first resume when he had been in Los Angeles nearly a year. Read his story in the *Living An Actor's Dream in Los Angeles* section.

KEITH JOHNSON

Film (selected)

Stock Tape	Lead	Director: Anton Musant
SockDoc	Lead	Director: Greg Lee
A New Tomorrow	Supporting	Director: Carey Corr
Room: 214	Supporting	Director: Marc Higa
A Dull House	Supporting	Director: Ali Kiani
A Song for David	Supporting	Director: Ed Kay
A Head of the Game	Supporting	Director: Tom Breedlove
Pregnant Pause	Supporting	Director: Stephen Whitehead

Television (selected)

CSI: Miami	Co-Star	Bruckheimer TV/CBS
Scene of the Crime (season 2)	Star	Authentic Ent./Learning Ch.
Scene of the Crime (season 3)	Co-Star	Authentic Ent./Learning Ch.
Surgery Gone Wrong (season 1)	Co-Star	Film Garden Ent./Discovery Ch.
Surgery Gone Wrong (season 2)	Co-Star	Film Garden Ent./Discovery Ch.
Murder Trial: The Nightstalker	Co-Star	Granada Media/Learning Ch.
Pobre Ana	Co-Star	Blaine Ray Productions

Theatre

Sockmuffin the Elf	Santa Claus	Dir: Brian Tyree/Hudson Thtr.
Searching for Splash Barbie *	Sam	Dir: Austin "Rocky" Kalish
The Trojan Women	Soldier	Dir: Brad Mays/Ark Theatre
It's Gonna Rain Chillun	Lucifer's Guard	Dir: Jerry Jones

Training

Adam Marcus:	Scene Study (ongoing)
Damona Resnick:	Audition Technique, Cold Reading
Doug Warhit:	Scene Study, Character Development, Audition Technique
Tim Wade:	Scene Study, Character Development
Richard Tatum:	Voice Over, Vocal Characterization, Commercial Voice Over Technique
Michael Donovan:	On-Camera, Commercial Technique, Character Development, Cold Reading

Participant in weekly staged readings with Naked Angels, Film Makers' Alliance.

Special Skills

Japanese Swordfighting (Kendo/Kenjutsu), Martial Arts, Archery (Longbow/Hunting), Can Crack Knuckles Take After
Take, Soccer, Skydiving, Hiking, Swimming, SCUBA, Ping Pong, Horseback Riding (Western), Conversational Japanese,
Some Spanish Dialogue, Former US Marine (Infantryman, Squad Leader, Weapons Expert, Water Training, Survival,
Distance Shooting... extreme distances... like a mile... really)
* as part of the Bitter Truth Theatre's Festival of One Acts

abby casey talent
310.454.8533
501 almar avenue
pacific palisades ca 9 0 2 7 2

Print Agent: Kathleen Schultz Associates
818.760.3100

4705 Laurel Canyon Blvd., Suite 306 Studio City, CA 91607 • Phone (818) 487-1800 • Fax (818) 487-1849 • E-mail OTALENT@aol.com

Keith's resume four years later. This represents a driving ambition, fueling his desire to find work as an actor.

ELI SCHWARTZ

Height: 5'3"   323/555-5555
Weight: 108   eli@elischwartz.com

Films   *Directors*
Forever   Lead   Jeremy Bein
Snapshots   Supporting   Sol Roth

Theater
The Miracle Worker   Helen Keller   Fl., Katy Award
Water On The Moon   Lead   F.A.T.E. Theatre
Lovers and Other Strangers   Lead   Florida
Bye Bye Birdie   Lead   Florida
The Sound of Music   Lead   Florida
You're A Good Man, Charlie Brown Lead   Florida
The Prime of Miss Jean Brodie   Lead   Florida
Old Jed Prouty of Bucksport Maine Lead   Florida
Letters To Kelso   Lead   Florida
Brighton Beach Memoirs   Lead   Florida
110° In The Shade   Lead   Florida
Oliver!   Lead   Florida

Industrial Films
Child Abuse Prevention
CPR Training
Car / Bike Accidents

Training
Judy Kerr's Acting Workshop, Class Assistant

Special Skills
Various Southern Dialects, New York accent, British accent
Competitive Gymnastics: Bars, Floor, Tumbling, Unicycle Riding,
Snow and Water Skiing, Firearms, Singing, Piano, Bartending and Waitressing

Eli Schwartz's resume shows a young adult, new to Los Angeles and just starting to audition for film work. Meanwhile, she stresses her theater background and her leading roles in major shows out of town.

360 N. CRESCENT DRIVE, NORTH BLDG, BEVERLY HILLS, CA 90210 TEL: 310-288-8000 FAX: 310-288-2000
500 FIFTH AVENUE, 37TH FLOOR, NEW YORK, NEW YORK 10110 TEL: 212-703-7540 FAX: 212-764-8941

WILL ESTES

FILM

U-571	Dir. Jonathan Mostow	Universal
HARD SHELL	Dir. Jean de Segonzac	Independent
NEW PORT SOUTH	Dir. Kyle Cooper	Independent
TERROR TRACT	Dir. Clint Hutchinson	Independent
BLUE RIDGE TRAIL	Dir. James Rowe	Independent
THE ROAD HOME	Dir. Dean Hamilton	Independent

TELEVISION

LAW & ORDER: SVU	Guest Star	NBC
REUNION	Series Regular	FOX
AMERICAN DREAMS	Series Regular	NBC
DIVE FROM CLAUSEN'S PIER		Lifetime MOW
SEE YOU IN MY DREAMS		CBS MOW
THE FAMILIAR STRANGER		Lifetime MOW

TRAINING
Kevin McDermott, Center Stage LA
Tim Colceri, Improvisation
Judy Kerr, Private Coaching
Diane Hill Hardin's Young Actors Studio
Improvisational Theatre, Music Center ON TOUR Program

WWW.PARADIGMLA.COM
WWW.PARADIGMNY.COM

Will Estes started working in commercials at age nine and successfully made the transition from child to adult actor. His resume looks low key. He has one of the most powerful agents in town. The more status you have, the less you emphasize your accomplishments. Will has been a series regular on eight shows. *See his interview in the Child Actors Section.*

PRINTING AND PHOTOCOPYING

• **A valuable relationship** can be built with your reproduction people. They will be very helpful in the promotion of your career.

• **In the printing department**, you can have postcards printed with your picture and a space for a message. Have five hundred or a thousand printed blank and then when you want to print a message, you can just run off five or a hundred, whatever you need, or handwrite short "thank you for the interview" notes. Let people on your mailing list know what you are doing or wish them a "merry new TV season" or any other idea you come up with. Print your picture and resume on 5x7 cards or on cards the size of business envelopes. Leave an area for the address or label. It is better to send mail that doesn't have to be opened or send items in odd size envelopes.

• **Have picture business cards made up.** So important to have these with you when meeting people; later they can see your face and remember who you are.

• **When you do a play or showcase**, send out flyers or cards to let casting directors know you are acting somewhere. Even if they never attend, your name and picture cross their desk. It is good to send something to all the casting directors once or twice a year. The best times, I believe, are mid-July, the beginning of the television shooting season, and the last of January, the start of pilot season.

• **A very clever actress** printed 8½ x 11 white mailing envelopes with an inch and a half by three inch imprint of her eyes in the lower right hand corner with "look into my eyes..." underneath.

• **Picture mailing envelopes are available with a clear plastic** side so your picture can be seen before the envelope is opened. Bob The Printer and Pink Copy Center carry these, as well as many other places. My favorite is by far, Actorsite, actorsite.com.

• **You can design your own note cards** with a picture on the front and then open it up to write inside. Christopher Paul Ford sent my favorite. It was a great picture of him printed vertically, his name and phone number in black in the bottom border. In the left corner, in white, it says, *The journey of ten thousand miles begins with a single phone call.—Confucius Bell.* Clever, fun and inventive.

Resources

To download and print an updated version of this and all resource lists, go to actingiseverything.com.

4over4.com, 1,000 biz cards $89, 2-sided color and coated. 250 cards free. My favorite. Other types of cards printed as well.

New Image Print, 323/965-9382, newimageprints.com. 727 N. LaBrea Ave., Los Angeles, 90038. 1,000 color 4/4 business cards, $75; 1,000 color 4/4 post cards, $169. This is a great price for cards to your industry mailing list.

Vistaprint.com. Good online printing.

Actorsite, 818/782-2800. actorsite.com. 5656 Cahuenga, North Hollywood, 91601. Acting group that provides a number of services. The only place these fabulous custom, clear envelopes can be purchased is from Actorsite directly. Drop by and take a look at them, you will love them. $50 for 100.

Pink Copy Center, 818/762-8100. printyourscript.com. 12080 Ventura Place #2 (Laurel Canyon & Ventura Blvd.) Studio City, 91604. M-F 8:30-6. Sa. 9:30-3. Copying, print- ing, color copying, digital (Fiery) output, digital b/w copying. They give a discount to actors. They will copy a message on your picture postcards at a cheaper cost than having them printed. Very helpful. They also do resumes and photo resumes.

Alpha Printing & Graphics, 310/273-9460. alphaprinting.biz. 9030 West Sunset Blvd., West Hollywood, 90069. They scanned my resume, put my agent's logo on it, printed 200 copies and trimmed them. A good bargain, and it only took ten minutes. Validated parking.

Bob The Printer, 818/766-9379. 4850 Vineland Ave., North Hollywood, 91601. M-F 8:30-5:30, closed weekends. Complete business printing, script copies, color copies, full and self serve copying, faxing, mail boxes. Very helpful, big busy place.

Charlie Chan, 323/650-7699. charliechan.com. 8267 Santa Monica Blvd., West Hollywood, 90046. Also, 323/850-5407. 7402 Sunset Blvd., L.A. 90046. Also, 213/380-6121. 3974 Wilshire Blvd., L.A. 90010. M-F 8:30-6, Sa 10-4. Self or full-service copying, offset printing, computers and laser printers for customer's use. Friendly, helpful, fast service. Talk to general manager, Alex, for your special printing needs and designs. Postcards, business cards, flyers, velox and halftones, etc.

Copymat, 323/461-1222. copymathollywood.com. 6464 Sunset Blvd., Ste. 100, Hollywood, 90028. At Wilcox. M-F 8-10 Sa & Su 10-7. Color, oversize and laser copies; high-speed duplicating; professional binding; self-service typing and worldwide fax service.

Henry's, 323/464-7228. 6110 Sunset Blvd., Hollywood, at Gower Gulch. M-F 8:30-7, Sa 9-5. Self or full-service copying, offset printing. Friendly, helpful, fast service.

Kinko's, 800/254-6567. fedexkinkos.com. Many locations. Open 24 hours, 7 days a week. I find, in general, their photocopying work is not up to my standards but with their 24 hr. service, in an emergency, they have saved me. Where I find they do have excellent services is in their computer departments. The employees are knowledgeable and helpful and the computers work well.

Nuprint & Graphics, 818/509-0003. 3962 Laurel Canyon Blvd., Studiio City.

SECTION THREE

WORKING AS AN ACTOR

GENERATING ACTING WORK

• **Section Three is about creating acting opportunities** for yourself. You have been training, you've figured out your type, how you see yourself being cast. You have your 8x10 color or black and white photos that look like you and you have your resume. Now you need more experience. Maybe at this point on your resume, you only have plays you did in college, high school or community theaters in your hometown. Perhaps the only experience on your resume are a few workshop scenes. This section is all about helping you build up that resume.

• **Through your training**, you know that you can understand a script and you've learned how to breathe life into the dialogue using your unique personality. You have delivered good performances in your workshops. Your teachers and the other actors look at you with awe and say, "You moved me; you are good." There is a voice inside that says, "Maybe I can get a director to cast me in a project and I can deliver a performance on stage or in film."

• **Many actors want to look for an agent at this point.** Agents are in business to make 10 percent from the fees you generate. When you are earning money from acting, then it is time to put your team together. But now is the time to gain experience and get your career tools in place for this long career ahead of you. *See the Career Team Section.*

• **Billy Bob Thornton arrived in Los Angeles struggling and broke.** He took a job as a waiter. First night on the job, as he worked a Beverly Hills banquet, director Billy Wilder, a many time Oscar-winner, walked up to him and said, "So you wanna be an actor? Look, I hate to disillusion you. You don't have the looks for a leading man. Learn to write. Then write your own movie—and write yourself a good part in it." Years later, after Billy Bob had learned to write, he wrote *Sling Blade* and was nominated for best actor and won the Oscar for best writer. He had been kicking around for years but with *Sling Blade,* he became an "overnight success."

• **Amanda Peet,** talking to a group, said, "No matter how many acting classes you take, how many times you stand alone in front of your mirror at home rehearsing, no matter how many Katharine Hepburn movies you watch, the only way to learn your craft is by acting—on stage or in front of the camera. And I'm of the school that work sparks more work, which all actors hunger for."

• **Mars Callahan,** at 31, co-wrote, directed and starred in the feature film *Poolhall Junkies.* It took him ten years to get it made and then another two years to get its theatrical release. Mars says, "I guess I just never gave up. If anything, that's it: Never, ever give up." He and a poolhall friend wrote the script when he was 19. They did get options over the years because the script was good but it just didn't go. Mars kept working on his acting, landing small roles and started studying directing. He directed a film short, which even got him a small directing job. Finally, when the opportunity came he was ready to direct and old enough to play the lead. Originally, he wrote it to play the younger brother.

• **Mars went on to advise actors** in an interview in *Back Stage West,* "You've got to be out there doing something all the time. An actor acts. How many monologues do you have memorized? Can you do something from Tennessee Williams? Can you do something from Shakespeare? How many accents can you do? Can you sing and dance? Work at it. Write a one-man show. Do a play. Work begets work."

• **Pamela Munro, an actress** who has worked in many independent films and tons of stage productions, talks about how online casting has helped her career:

> • **Whether represented or not, I have always gotten most of my work for myself.** Over the years I have tried every avenue I could think of to do this, but the one that has been the most successful has surely been using the Internet. It's been a godsend for me, especially as I have been re-inventing myself lately as an actress and making the difficult transition from ex-ingénue to character woman. I don't think the younger actors have any sense of what a closed shop casting was 20 years ago. It's much more open now.

> • **I have managed to cover 80%-90% of the submissions myself,** electronically. This saves money on pictures, postage and time— even gasoline. Electronic networking also is much more efficient than old fashioned face time, although it has to be backed up by personal contact.

> • **I have landed juicy supporting parts** in indie features and other TV and commercial work. This makes me more desirable for an agent or manager, as I have proven myself to be capable, dedicated, energetic—and *castable.* That means money for both of us. The electronic window on casting has given us an extremely valuable tool to orient ourselves in our careers, whether by self-submissions or by keeping track of what's out there.

• **Nia Valdalos** is the actress and screenwriter of *My Big Fat Greek Wedding*. I met Nia on a show I was coaching; she played a ditsy receptionist. She is so talented; in this little role I saw her create something new for every rehearsal. She had just arrived in town because her script had been optioned. She told me her story and that she was waiting on the go-ahead for shooting the film. I am including part of her interview from *O Magazine* as an inspiration for us all.

> • **What I know for sure is** that in your lifetime you will hear the word "no" much more than you will hear the word "yes." People say no when they don't want to think in a different way, and when they don't know what else to say.

- **In my career,** I have been asked to leave theatre school, not gotten past the first round of auditions for an acting job, and then been told I was unattractive and therefore would never make it as an actress. As if looks have anything to do with good acting. They told me that it would be impossible to cast me in a part since there were no roles written for someone who looked like me. So I set out to create that role.

- **I got on stage, and I started telling stories** about the one thing I knew best: my family. When the play sold out, I was approached by companies to turn it into a movie. I asked to play the lead and write the screenplay. They said no.

- **Then Rita Wilson and Tom Hanks** came to my show and what did they say? They said yes. Yes, they were going to make it into a movie. Yes, I would be the writer of the screenplay. And yes, I could play the lead.

- **What have I learned?** That secure people say yes much faster than people who operate out of fear. That some people believe thinking in a different way is an interesting choice. That if you keep saying yes to yourself, one day someone might just say it to you.

- **I am telling you these stories** because I don't want you to play a victim of the industry. I want you to have the kind of courage these actors have. You will find many actors who whine and say, "I can't get an agent. I don't have any auditions. Someone else has all the luck. I never get any opportunities." I want you to talk about the script or idea you are writing; about the scripts you've downloaded; about the weekly script reading group you've organized; about the volunteer work you are doing; how excited you are over the scene you are rehearsing for class. Yes, create your own acting opportunities when you are between roles.

Casting Sites, Membership and Informational Sites

• **Online casting services** put actors' pictures, credits and sometimes short video or voiceover reels on their websites. Some sites charge for posting pictures; others don't. Some are free when you are in the Union or if you have representation. Some are strictly for the casting and agent communities to use and others will accept email submissions from actors. Some have casting notices that you can submit yourself for. I think if you can afford it, they are all good investments. If you get one job, it will pay for five, six or more years of postings.

• **I believe in marketing.** As in any business, it pays to advertise. When you do not have representation and are looking for acting roles on your own, it is important to have access to where the jobs are.

• **There are many online membership groups.** I've investigated these below and believe they can help your career. Many have informative actors' forums. However, always take anything you read in chat rooms with a grain of salt; you don't know who is doing the writing. Remember we all have opinions; when you hear one that rings true with you, it probably is. If you hear something that you wish were true, it most likely isn't. Acting websites are popular as a place for actors to ask industry people career questions, talk to other actors, post their headshot, resume and bio and most important, submit for castings.

• **Purchase your own name** as your domain name: JudyKerr.com, for instance. Always try to get the dot.com, it is the easiest way for people to find you. If you are going to be famous, buy all combinations of your name: .com, .net, and .tv, at godaddy.com. You will want to have your own website—if not this moment, certainly sooner than you think. *Go to Personal Websites for more information.*

• **When making online submissions for castings** or to agents or managers for representation consideration, label the downloadable file with your name. People who open attachments are taking a chance of downloading a virus. If you need to send an attachment, the reader is more likely to download it if it has your name on it. Also, when it is downloaded onto their desktop, your name will be visible and when they are considering you, the file will be easy to find again. Most such downloads are labeled a generic "Pic.doc" or "headshot.doc." Make sure yours will be welcome and identifiable. Many people in the industry won't open outside attachments at all, so a good policy can be to paste your resume and a small headshot or a link that leads to your website in the email cover letter.

• **All of the organizations in this chapter** are reliable businesses. Do your own investigation before giving money to any sites. It is helpful to be registered with as many as possible. If you must choose one or two, then select by doing your research and following your instincts.

Resources

To download and print an updated version of this and all resource lists, go to actingiseverything.com.

ONLINE CASTING SITES:

These are the main sites; they have great reputations in the industry. They are a "must join" for any professional actor wanting steady work. I also encourage beginners to join these sites, but be aware that when submitting for castings here, you are competing with professional working actors.

Breakdownservices.com, Actorsaccess.com, Showfax.com, 310/276-9166, 310, 385-6920. All three sites are part of the same company, working together. Agents and casting directors use Breakdown Services for their online submissions service; this is where most daily castings are listed. Actors Access is where actors can submit themselves electronically for commercials, TV shows and movies—both union and nonunion. Actors can also set up detailed profiles and link up to a feature that will notify them when a submission fitting their description is posted. Showfax is where actors can get sides for most projects. I suggest joining Showfax.com for $70 a year; then you can submit for free through Actors Access.

Nowcasting.com, 818/841-7165. 60 E. Magnolia Blvd., Burbank, 91502. They post union actor pictures and resumes on the site for free. Nonunion, unrepresented actors are charged $2.50 a month. Members receive casting notices almost on a daily basis and can submit to the projects and roles they are right for online. $10, $15, or $20 a month membership packages. Free unlimited sides and actors can check out five minute clips of the shows to help get a feel for the audition. They don't charge for casting directors to post their projects so many independent, nonunion and student casting directors will favor this site for posting casting notices. They offer labels for casting directors and agents. Great site. The resume clips are the most outstanding in town. Download "Online Demo Reels" from actingiseverything.com for in-depth information.

Lacasting.com, 323-462-8000. 6671 Sunset Blvd., Hollywood, 90028. Beau Bonneau developed this online casting service which is now the most widely used for commercials among agents and casting directors. Agents sign their actors up for free for the basic account but if you plan to submit yourself, sign up for the member plus account for $5 per month. If an actor wants to change or add a picture it is $25. Set up fee for unrepresented actors is $50, free hosting for six months, then a $10 monthly fee. They also have theatrical castings. You have to register with your birth date; this troubles me. If you wish, give a birth date that reflects how you are cast.

imdb.com and imdbpro.com. In Hollywood, the Internet Movie Database is used for a lot more than simply finding out trivia about your favorite actors. imdb.com is free to all, though there is a charge to post your picture on the site. If you've done any kind of project, it's important to post your picture and credits, you can continually update your listing. When signing up the first time do not put your birth year on it. The imdbpro $12.95 a month, has listings of over 65,000 industry people, current updates of projects in production, box office information, industry news and message boards for people in the industry. All of the casting directors and most industry pros subscribe and use it all the time.

Playersdirectory.com, 310-247-3058. 1313 N. Vine St., Los Angeles, 90038. Before the age of electronic profiles and submissions, the Academy Players Directory used to be the place to get seen. Many agents and casting directors do still look at the yearly set of books, which feature actor photos and credits for union-affiliated actors only. The Directory, which is part of the Academy, includes a searchable database and electronic submissions, in conjunction with Nowcasting.com. Yearly cost is $75.

MEMBERSHIP SITES

For beginners and seasoned pros alike. I am a big fan of these sites. I do my showcasing at Actorsite.

Actorsite. Run by Jack Turnbolt. actorsite.com, 818/762-2800. 5856 Cahuenga, North Hollywood, 91601. This is a great membership site. $40 a month or $299 a year. Lots of helpful information and actor chat rooms. Free to members: monthly headshot sessions, agent workshops, several acting classes a week, invited industry speaker guests who donate their time, and getting great advice from Jack who is always around. Wonderful supportive group of actors. Also information and resources for kids looking to break into the business. Great reputation, good investment. Free daily newsletter to all filled with uplifting information and encouragement. Extra fees: headshot dropoffs to casting directors, Casting Director Showcases, always focused on education. They also have the best clear envelopes for mailing your submissions. Jack designed and had them produced, you can't buy them anywhere else.

Actors' Network. actors-network.com. 818/509-1010. Studio City, 91604. $50 a month. Free Monthly Orientations where you'll learn all about the Network and how business is done in Los Angeles, a great way to spend two hours. The Actors' Network has a combination of tangible resources, leadership, expertise and reputation. They endeavor to alleviate confusion about the business and provide a unique perspective through curriculum style activities, topical discussions, and goal setting groups. The Network schedules industry guests from casting, agency, management and producers offices who volunteer to speak and educate actors. This 15-year company creates an actor community that is professional and supportive. They focus on what an actor CAN do rather than on what actors cannot. Members report their successes continually. Whether new to Hollywood or wanting to get to the next level, actors find the business mindset and resources to succeed. On the website, members post and update an online profile viewed by the industry and retrieve daily updated contact information on all casting, agent and manager offices. Owned and operated by Kevin E. West and Paulo Andres.

RECOMMENDED SITES

Great sites for beginners to help learn more about the industry, get your face out there and hopefully get some auditions.

Backstage.com. *Back Stage West,* $12.95 a month. Lists tons of casting notices each week, especially in theater. I believe you should be subscribing online if you are actively seeking auditions because you will get their advanced casting notices a couple days before subscribers of the actual publication. One of the member features is your free page on their website. Plus, the site has tons of past and present articles online to answer any question an actor might have.

Richard Azurdia's site, richardazurdia.com Casting notices and industry info. Lots of ethnic castings plus much more. Great group. Richard is a working actor. Networking, wonderful Web links, lots of opportunities. Sign up for his newsletter: razurdianetwo rk@yahoogroups.com.

Actorsbone.com. Paul Molinaro runs this interesting site. $20 a year to post up to three pictures and resume, updated every month. Also has an actor forum section. Paul has been running the site since 1999 and has met many industry people. Many actors have been cast through the site. What I like best is the Shorts Festival—they accept shorts on video or film. Bonnie Gillespie recommended this site to me. She finds it very valuable.

Actorplace.com. One of the few FREE online sites. Actors can post headshots and a profile, submit for castings via e-mail and set up their own personal Web page on the site. Recommended by acting coach Caryn West.

OTHER SITES:

These are other sites that actors have used and recommended. Still, I want to remind you again to do your homework when contemplating signing up for these sites. Talk to other actors or industry people and figure out if these sites are helpful to you and worth the money.

Actorspages.org. Free site for both union and nonunion actors. Post headshot and resume. Searchable database allows casting directors to search by name, representation, project, etc.

Thecastlist.com. Membership site. They post pictures, have casting notices and other audition information.

Castpages.com (formerly castnet.com), 888/582-4201, ext. 3603. Membership site, free for SAG members. Nonunion membership is around $500 plus with a monthly dues plan. Includes free sides, talent search, agent submissions, resume updating, casting notices with email submissions. This is now an international site and there have been many changes. **I do not recommend for L.A. nonunion actors.**

Craigslist.com. Listings for everything from jobs to apartments to dates for just about every major city in the country. The L.A. Craigslist does post some projects, from student films to studio casting. But be warned, anybody can post here and some of the projects could be bogus.

Creativeactors.com. Creative Actors Alliance, 310/840-2240. Membership fee is $60 a year. Besides other benefits, they will post two pictures, a resume and a reel on their Affiliates Page.

Exploretalent.com, 323/785-2020. 8033 Sunset Blvd., Hollywood 90046. Membership fees vary based on the services. They have relationships with many casting directors in town so electronic submissions are getting looked at. Also allows for actors to post resume and headshots, which they will touch up if you desire.

Gigdirectory.net. Bills itself as "Like a Craigslist but designed for the arts and entertainment industries." Lists jobs and acting gigs as well as helpful articles and message boards.

Hollywoodoperatingsystem.com, 310/289-9400. 400 S. Beverly Dr., Beverly Hills, 90212. Membership is $29.99 a month for six month commitment and $19.99 a month for a year. Includes unlimited submissions, 10 photos and a Hollywood Operating System magazine subscription.

IndieClub.com. Actors, directors and crew alike can get information on current projects (mainly independents), post profiles and chat with each other.

Mandy.com. Similar to Craigslist but specifically for entertainment industry. Posts all kinds of job openings as well as extensive casting.

Myspace.com. Very popular social site, but many actors are using MySpace to post their own acting Web pages and to link up with other industry people. A valuable site for networking and free. Very hip and "in."

Nosotros.com. A nonprofit organization formed to promote Latin actors. The membership is $50 a year. Members may post their headshots and resumes for $30 to $50 a year. You can have your posting connected to your own website and email for free if you wish. If you are Spanish-speaking I would think this is a must.

Therightcast.com. Very user-friendly. Set up resume and headshots for just a buck a month and check out sides for mostly smaller projects. Also posts other acting links and info on shows and showcases.

Starsearchcasting.com, 800/927-1639. 4360 E. Main St., Ventura, 93003. A newer site, offering services for free. Post a profile with headshots and resume to be seen by agents, casting directors, production companies and photographers looking for models.

Talentinla.com, 818/507-0775. Free. Post a profile with headshots and video.

Talentpimp.com. 8033 W. Sunset Blvd., #3000, Hollywood, 90046. Talent P.I.M.P. is "your Pipeline Into Motion Pictures." $35 for a year. Combining elements of MySpace/Friendster with typical acting websites, this site provides a great place for actors to hook up not just with other actors, but also with some industry people. You can post a profile and also check out a number of free listings, including audition info and jobs.

THE BUSINESS OF
COMMERCIALS

• **A commercial career is a tough, competitive,** ever-changing specialty career. Commercial acting classes are essential. You will also benefit from taking improvisation classes, as well as studying basic acting craft.

• **Working in commercials** can change your life. One good national commercial can be worth roughly $35,000 a year or more. If you were to book three or four nationals in the next year, just imagine how much your financial world might change. The security of having money in the bank can give you the confidence to continue pursuing the acting career of your dreams. Some actor's careers consist solely of commercials or voiceovers; it is what they love to do.

• **Hugh Leon, successful commercial agent with Coast to Coast Talent Group says:**

  • **If you are not in class, you're not serious about making a living** working in commercials. I don't care how many commercials you book, you still need to study, to get in there and practice. You are always going to learn something new by looking over new copy, getting in front of the camera and staying current. When you take classes from various casting directors and top commercial acting coaches, you learn what is going to get you a callback when you audition. Improv is also a huge part of commercial acting. I strongly encourage actors to get involved in an improv class or troupe.

• **Stuart Stone, one of the busiest commercial casting directors,** a great commercial workshop teacher, and author of *Acting Out—Your Personal Coach to a Money Making Career in Television Commercials* says:

  • **When there is no dialogue in the commercial,** it is great to find actors with good improvisation skills. The actors who have "what it takes" can always be counted on and we continually book them. They have developed themselves, are prepared and have taken the appropriate classes and workshops. Understanding the audition process and *how* to audition is what can often make the difference in booking the job.

• **If you want a commercial career, be an expert in commercials.** Watch commercials at different times of the day and night. Where are you going to make your money? Figure out what your type is. Are you the spokesperson, young mom or dad, fast-food counter guy or girl, granny or gramps, blue collar worker, executive, athlete, model type, the comedian? Maybe you fit several types. Knowing your types and the spots you will most likely be cast in will help you sell yourself when you start interviewing with agents.

• **Keep a notebook; study the actors who look like you** and are in the same age category. What is the product, the style of campaign, the type of people, what was their behavior, why did they book the job? Write down the copy (dialogue in commercials) and practice doing the commercial yourself. What type of clothes are they wearing? Clothing terms are usually:

  • **Casual,** meaning what you might wear to clean your house or mow your lawn, dockers and T-shirt. No jeans or denim shirts.
  • **Nice casual,** which is what you would wear out to dinner and a movie with friends—dockers with a nice shirt or sweater.
  • **Upscale casual.** This look is casual and classy.
  • **Upscale.** Dressy and classy.
  • **Business/Spokesperson.** Suit and tie for men, tailored dress or suit for women.
  • **Hip/trendy look** means the latest fashion trend.

• **Your notebook will help you when you get an audition** for Coke, Xerox, IBM, Folgers, Citibank, etc. You will have a sense of what the campaign is and what the client might be looking for when they are auditioning you.

• **Stuart K. Robinson, respected and sought-after commercial coach,** who teaches the skills, techniques and philosophy of how to book the job, says:

  • **The reason most actors are not successful** is that they don't know what the client (the person/people who represent the product which is being advertised) wants. The client will tell you what they want you to do, but they do not tell you what they need. In order to be competitive in the commercial business, the actor must be an expert at three things:

  • **First,** you must be able to diagnose what the client needs without being told.

- **Second**, you must be able to create the behavior to answer that need.

- **Third**, you must be able to execute that need before the camera.

- **Once you have an idea of the type of characters** you can play and you have taken enough commercial classes to be consistently good, it is time to shop for an agent. You now need a promotional package. This consists of a great headshot, a resume and a powerful cover letter.

- **Terry Berland, casting director** and author of *Breaking Into Commercials* says:

  - **The package is the most important part.** This is what we first see of you. It must be put together well and give a real and true depiction of you as a professional. Sometimes all we have to go on is the picture and the resume so make sure that package is the best it can be.

- **Your commercial headshot is the most important tool** in your promotional package; it is your ticket in the door. Your picture will be one in a thousand that passes the desk of a casting director or agent in any given week; you must grab their attention in a millisecond.

Q: What is a good commercial headshot?

- **Commercial agent Hugh Leon says:**

  - **I like personality shots.** I should be able to say 10 things about who that person is, whether this person is a smart-ass, intelligent, crazy, warm and loving or shy—something about that person. A commercial actor can have multiple pictures—a business shot, a casual shot, an athletic shot if you are athletic and a zany/crazy shot if you are a character, etc. But make sure they're not "schticky" or cheesy. And no props.

- **Stuart Stone likes pictures that have great energy. He adds:**

  - **Your picture should look like you do** at any given moment of the day. I want to know what I am getting when I call you in. I like natural shots. We're not looking for your wedding picture. We want you to look like how you look 80 percent of the time. Don't waste your time or money getting all made up or touching up your headshots. In fact, that can hurt you because if you come in and don't look like your picture, you might get turned away at the door. Your pictures should be more real, how you look most of the time.

Casting director Michael Donovan has cast over 1,000 commercials,

- **The picture needs to look like you, as you do** *normally*—not under that specific lighting with that special makeup, etc., and not at your most glamorous. I should be able to look up at you as you walk in and not be surprised! Just be yourself when you're getting your pictures taken.

- **In terms of what's most important, your eyes need to connect.** When casting directors are going through hundreds of photos, your picture gets a matter of seconds under their noses. When you look in someone's face, you look at their eyes—same thing applies to headshots.

- **Stuart K. Robinson says:**

  - **Anytime I look at a headshot and I know what the person is thinking,** that is a great photo. A photograph is not meant to capture a look on your face. A photograph has to capture your quality, a specific feeling.

  - **To take a great shot you have to have a thought.** "I am so happy to be here." "It is good to see you!" "It's my birthday!" You have to have a feeling about what is going on, so the photographer can capture that feeling. That thought will be real joy, true pride, warm love, real power, great satisfaction or whatever it is you are trying to capture.

  - **Thoughts create great photos; posing creates portraits.** Let the picture show your acting ability. Bad pictures do not come from bad photographers. Bad pictures come from bad acting.

  - **To get a great shot you have to prepare for your photo shoot.** Interview photographers. Do not just pick one because someone tells you to go to them. Meet them, make sure you feel comfortable in their company. Look at their work, see what they think is a good shot. Do the eyes talk to you? Are the pictures saying anything? You want a photographer who gives you the motivation, freedom and comfort so you can have specific thoughts, one who knows when to snap the photo.

  - **Before the shoot, decide what categories you want to capture,** what thoughts to have in your head in order to do that. Bring to the shoot your favorite music and photographs from your life that can help you trigger the moods you want to feel. Do not rush your session—take all the time you need. Remember, this picture is going to open up the doors to your career.

- **Commercial agent Blair Taylor says:**

  - **The biggest problem with most headshots** is that they're supposed to reflect an actor's personality and unfortunately, they rarely succeed in doing so. If I see a picture and I "get" them, I'll call that person in. That's what the headshot is supposed to do; tell me about yourself.

  - **Sometimes it's the actor's fault.** I'll often see a beautiful or interesting actor with a "dead" picture, meaning there's no personality in it. It's well-lit and the actor looks great, but there's nothing there. You can tell that the actor was more worried about what was going on around them than what was going on inside them.

  - **Sometimes it's the photographer's fault.** I have an issue with photographers who get too wrapped up in a trademark style. It's sad, but sometimes we can recognize the photographer before we recognize the actor and that's not helpful to the actor. That's why it's important for an actor to choose a photographer that's going to help them pull out their unique personality.

- **Good examples of commercial pictures are in the photo section.** *Also, see the individual photographers listings in Section Two.*

- **Casting director Stuart Stone talks about resumes:**

  - **Put everything you can on your resume** and be proficient in everything you list under special skills. That means be above average and not that you're good at it because your uncle was a professional at the skill. I look under training to see if you have taken commercial workshops, improv or any other training. Do you have theatre credits? List plays you have done, no matter how long ago or how small the venue. We like to see on your resume that you are studying and working.

- **The third tool in your package is a powerful cover letter.** *See Cover Letters in the Career Tools section for instructions and examples.*

- **Now your package is together.** How do you get a commercial agent, or at least an appointment to meet with one?

- **There are three ways to get an appointment with an agent.**

1) The standard way. Mail your headshot, resume and cover letter to agencies. Or in some cases you can email them (if they say they will accept email submissions) or send them an email directing them to your acting website. These methods are not very effective unless your materials are so dynamic that they just have to see you as soon as possible.

- **Beverly Long, casting director and teacher says:**

  - **There are books with the names of agents** and a little blurb about
    each agent in the city. There are probably 200 commercial agents
    in Los Angeles. You can't send your picture out to every agent, but
    with some help you can narrow it down. That is what I try to do in
    my classes—narrow it down and give you maybe 10 to 12 choices of
    agents who will be likely to represent you.

2) The scenic route way. Doing theater or showcases and hoping
someone sees your work, that you impress them and they suggest
a meeting.

3) Referrals, the most effective way. When an agent is told by someone
they respect that they should see you, they will. How do you get referrals? You ask! If you know someone who has an agent or who knows an
agent, ask him to introduce you. Make it known that you are looking
for an agent.

- **When you get an interview with an agent, you want to go in there**
and really sell yourself. What usually happens is, we try to be on our best
behavior and answer the agent's questions without letting our personality out. The agent then wonders what is so special about this person?
Go into that office knowing exactly where you are going to make your
money, act and look your type, dress your type. Be extremely clear about
the roles you are going to book and the categories you are going to work
in. Talk about commercials you love. Talk about what their part is in
the business; you are an expert too.

- **Tell stories about yourself.** Look around the office and learn about
them. Try to find a common denominator and establish a relationship.
Most agents will take you on because they like you and like being around
you. It is not always about your acting ability.

- **Neil Kreppel, long time, respected commercial agent from
Commercial Talent Agency.**

**Q: How do you build a relationship with an agent? Should you ask
them to lunch?**

  - **Make an appointment,** come in and just talk so we can get to know
    each other. As for lunch, at this time in the agency, we are really too
    busy to go out to lunch. If someone wants to bring in something for
    us to have lunch together that would be all right.

Q: What is the actor's responsibility?

- **They should always have pictures here** with their resume stapled on the back. They should immediately confirm with us the information we have given them about an audition. They should always arrive early for their appointment time and of course, they should book some jobs.

Q: How can the actor help the agent?

- **We expect clients to be very professional.** We want them to have trust in us. It is all right if you fax occasionally or call about a casting that you have heard about and wonder if you have been sent out. Sometimes you have been submitted and sometimes you may not be what the casting director has asked for. We don't like people to be annoying, calling every day about submitting them for projects because they have seen the breakdowns.

- **Commercial agent Hugh Leon** talks about what he expects from the actors he represents.

  - **I expect the actor to give me the right pictures**; I need the marketing tools to get you out there. I don't want to hear, "I don't have the money to get better pictures." Once I have called you with an audition, don't ask me to rearrange the audition time to meet your schedule. Don't miss an audition—this is not a hobby, this is a career; it should be the number one priority. If it is not, get out! Do the best you can, be professional and go into your audition prepared. Don't call me 20 times a day. Keep good records, write down the audition information, who you saw, where you went, what you wore, so if I call you a week later with a callback you are ready to go. Have a Thomas Guide in your car— I'm not a map. Keep your cell phone on you at all times; you should be reachable 24-7. Confirm auditions. Be grateful that I got you an audition. Remember, I work for free until you book a job.

- **Once you have signed with an agent**, it is a good idea to start marketing yourself to casting directors. They are the ones who will call you in to audition.

- **When Cynthia Kerr's agent took her on**, she had postcards printed. Her picture on the left; under the picture her name and under that SAG. The message was on the right with her agent's logo under it. "I'm ready to work! Just signed with Gold/Liedtke Associates for commercial representation. Looking forward to auditioning for you soon!"

- **Stuart Stone, CCDA, casting director, talks about marketing:**

  - **Postcards with your picture on it are a great marketing tool.** I don't have to open an envelope, your picture is right there. Write a note, let me know you just signed with such and such agency, or you will be on a TV show (with date, time and channel) so I can watch, or that you are in a play. You can send postcards or fliers every few weeks. I will become familiar with your face, so when your agent submits your picture to me, I can recall who you are. I am aware of who you are and if you are right for the part, I'll call you in. You can also knock on my door and say, "Hey, I just wanted to introduce myself." I don't mind an actor doing that, because most actors do not take the initiative. The mistake is trying to get into a conversation when I am busy; it is bothersome.

- **Casting director Michael Donovan, CSA, CCDA,** when asked about receiving unsolicited pictures and resumes, responded:

  - **No problem with my office.** But I really resent it when an actor does not include a cover note of some sort. It could be very brief, and hand-written. It should *not* be a "form" letter, in which you have written in the casting director's name, or a letter that says "Dear Casting Director." An actor wants to be treated as an individual—so treat the casting person the same way. The same applies to letters sent to agents' offices.

  - **We also accept submissions from actors without agents** or even nonunion actors; that is how we meet new people. At one point, I'm sure Dustin Hoffman was nonunion.

COMMERCIAL AUDITIONS

- **Danny Goldman, CCDA, casting director, director and teacher, describes his job:**

  - **The function of the casting director** is to show the director, the agency and the client a variety of people—the types they ask for and some alternatives. We have seen as many as 200 people for one part. The final decision is made by the client, the agency and the director when the director is a star director. The casting director has no say whatsoever. If the dialogue is really bad, those actors that can come in and solve the problems of the dialogue are the ones who get the job.

- **When your agent calls you with an audition,** they are going to give you some valuable information. They will tell you the date and time of your call, the casting person/company and their location, as well as the product, the wardrobe you should wear and the type of character they are looking for (i.e. young mom, clerk, spokesperson etc.). You must write all this information down and use it to help prepare yourself for your audition.

• **Plan your wardrobe** based on the information your agent gave you and from your own research on the product and type of character they are looking for. Dress for the part. Don't forget your headshot and resume.

• **Use your Thomas Guide** or download a map from your computer with directions to the location. Plan to arrive at least 15 minutes before your call time to go over any copy you will need to rehearse.

• **When you arrive at the audition, check the storyboard** (a series of hand drawn pictures showing each scene of the commercial) and see if there is any copy you need to prepare for the audition. Diagnose the script quickly with the techniques you have learned from your commercial training. Don't worry about memorizing the copy.

• **Once you feel prepared to audition, sign in** on the Exhibit E SAG/AFTRA Commercial Audition Report, (sign-in sheet). Print your name, Social Security number (SAG membership number can be used instead of Social Security number for security purposes), agent, time of actual call, time you arrived, your initials, whether it is your first call or a callback. The sex, age and ethnicity questions are optional; the unions use these to track casting trends. Always be sure you sign out when you leave. If the audition runs longer than an hour, you may be entitled to compensation from the production company.

• **Next, fill out the size card if one is available.** This is used for callbacks to help size up groups or pairs and also for the wardrobe people when you book the commercial, so be accurate. You do not have to put your address or Social Security number on the card. After you complete the size card, the casting director will probably take a Polaroid of you. These usually look pretty bad—don't get upset over it. The casting people say they only use them as a reference to help match you up with your video audition.

• **When the paperwork is done, continue to work** on the audition copy. Rehearse out loud, get comfortable with the words and your actions. Make the material about you. Own it! Keep a positive attitude; do not let other actors in the room distract you. Compete for the job.

• **Carolyne Barry, commercial actress, teacher and casting director says:**

> • **Good commercial acting is good acting, only speeded up**; it is the pauses that are tightened up. When auditioning, you must spend time with the copy as you would a cold reading. You must motivate the copy, know who you are talking to and determine your objective.

• **Casting director Stuart Stone suggests:**

> • **Always know what has happened in this character's life** the moment before you start talking and what is going to happen after the last moment of the scene. Make the piece real to you, then it will be real to us. Give the most feeling you can to the copy and still be honest. This is the ideal in commercial acting.

• **Stuart talks about improvements actors can make.**

> • **It makes things tough when actors arrive at castings** where there is dialogue and they do not take the time to work on their lines. They get caught up in conversations and gossip in the waiting area and forget why they are there. When they come into the studio to audition, they become frustrated or discouraged because they gave a bad audition.

• **Terry Berland, casting director says:**

> • **Confidence is so important in getting the job.** Some actors come in with confidence and you can see right away they know what they're doing. They're grounded, they know how to connect immediately, they don't come in with any baggage, they're efficient and they're prepared. The confidence carries over into the reading. They know how to hit their mark, add dimension to the space and texture to the performance.

• **Casting director Michael Donovan says:**

> • **Be specific in your choices for the commercial copy.** So many actors I see walk into the audition concerned with what the producer or casting director wants. I want the actor to show us what they want to bring to the copy. The most important thing I teach in my classes is to make specific choices and be confident in them.

• **I asked Michael how he felt about actors** hearing about a casting session and arriving and signing in like they belong there.

> • **If an actor happens to come to an audition** with a friend and sees that there is a session going on that he would be right for, I don't mind the actor asking if they can be seen for the spot. There is a big problem though if the actor just signs in, "crashing the session."

• **Stuart Stone also responds to actors dropping by the office.**

  • **I often do not mind actors who stop by to drop off a postcard and say hello.** They must realize though, we are usually very busy and do not have time to get into a conversation. When an actor has heard about a part we are currently casting and they want to audition, I request they go through their agent for many reasons. If they do not have representation it is important that they ask before they sign in. To just sign in without asking is *crashing* the audition, it is not professional and very much frowned upon. If the actor is right for the part, I am glad to let them audition, but check first.

• **You are auditioning when you enter the audition room.** Be in character. Your behavior, body language, tone of voice and emotions should reflect the situation in the commercial scenario.

• **There will be a mark on the floor where you should stand.** Most likely it will be a piece of tape in the shape of a "T." Stand on your mark with the "T" between your feet and look into the camera. If a cue card (the copy written in large print placed near the camera) is provided, look it over. Some words may be different from your script. Get familiar with the sentence structure so you know where to look when you need to read the next line.

• **Not all auditions have copy.** Many times you are asked to improvise a scene or tell a funny joke, or the casting director will ask you a question like, "Name three people living or dead that you'd like to have dinner with and why?" Do not panic, just say the first thing that pops in your mind. If the question does stump you, keep a constant connection with the camera. This will allow your personality to show and remember, you can always make something up. The people looking at the tape are looking at your personality and how you will fit it with their product. They often watch these tapes with the sound turned off.

• **The casting director or the camera operator will give you directions.** As you listen to them, look into the camera and picture someone you know in the lens and let the camera see inside you.

• **You will be asked to slate your name.** Slating is your introduction and your opportunity to let the clients know, within the first three seconds, you are what they are looking for. After you slate your name, the casting director or camera operator will often ask for profiles. This means they want to see your face from different angles. The director or camera operator will then say "action" and you start the scene. Go for it!

• **The casting director is not always in the room** during the first call audition, but don't think they're not watching. Most casting facilities have video feed from the audition room to the casting director's office down the hall. Listen to all directions given to you and work them into your audition. You must be flexible; they are also looking to see if you are able to take direction.

• **After the audition say to yourself,** "I took a shot today at a $35,000 job today," and then forget about it. You may hear from your agent in a couple of days that you have a callback. Congratulations. A callback means you are a finalist for the job and you get to audition again, this time for the clients, the director, producer and advertising agency. When you go to the callback, dress and look the same way you did for your first audition unless your agent tells you differently. Figure out why they called you back, so you can give them more of the same behavior. The director will most likely be directing your audition. One of the things they will be looking for is how flexible you are, how well you take direction and how easy you will be to work with.

• **After your callback, your agent may call you to say** you are on "avail/first refusal" or they have put you on "hold." "Avail/first refusal" means the casting director wants to know if you are available to work on a certain date. It is not legally binding; the actor can accept other work. When the actor is put on "hold" they are asked to schedule a specific day to work. The actor and employer have made the commitment; it is legally binding and payment must be made whether or not the actor works on that day.

• **You booked the job! Your agent or someone from the production company** will call you with the days you will need to be available for the commercial shoot and the time and date of your wardrobe fitting. You will be paid hourly with a one-hour minimum for the fitting. At your fitting appointment you will be given the date and time of the shoot and location for the commercial.

• **When you arrive on the set, find the second AD** (assistant director), who will have your SAG contract and let you know where you need to be. I suggest asking them for today's call sheet. It will have the names of everybody who is working that day. I also find it helpful when writing my thank you notes because the addresses of the advertising agency and production company are usually on the call sheet. You should file this away. You may need to refer to it years later when you are working with some of the same people again. Make sure you read your contract carefully. If you are unsure about anything, call your agent before signing. Have the production company fax a copy to your agent.

• **Always be professional, polite, prepared and eager to work.** Stay relaxed and comfortable. If you are not working on a shot, stay close by and let the AD know where you are at all times. When they call for you, be ready to work. Have fun; this is what you have been working so hard for.

• **When and how much do we get paid?**

• **An on-camera principle actor gets paid a session fee** for each day of work or for each commercial produced, whichever is greater. Currently the SAG union session fee is $535 for an eight-hour workday, excluding mealtime. The ninth and tenth hour are paid at time and a half. The eleventh hour and beyond is known as golden time and is paid at double-time. The session fee must be paid within 12 working days.

• **The session fee allows the advertising agency** the right to use the commercial for 13 weeks. The actor cannot work for a competitive product during the same period of time.

• **Holding fees or fixed payment fees** are paid every 13 weeks to maintain the rights to the commercial and the actor's exclusivity to the product. The amount is equal to the session fee. If you do not get a holding fee after 13 weeks it means you have been released and then you can book another commercial with a competing product.

• **When the commercial is aired, you are due residual payments.** There are several different types of residual payments and they are paid on different scale levels depending on how the commercial is used. Some of the different categories are: network use, cable use, national, regional, local, wild spot, dealer use.

• **It is not uncommon in commercials to receive a "buyout" payment.** This means you will be paid a single fee for the shooting and airing of the commercial. No residuals. These are usually commercials that are sold to foreign markets.

• **Your pay checks usually get mailed to your agent** and they will take out their 10 percent of the union session fees, holding fees and residuals. The agent then mails you a check. When you have a good national commercial running, it is fun to go to the mailbox.

• *For more information on payment for commercials, check out sag.org.*

COMMERCIAL CLASSES

Stuart K. Robinson, of Robinson Creative, 310/558-4961. $350 for five weeks. Teaches commercial audition technique for five weeks and film and television audition ongoing. Class size is limited to 16 students. Stuart is the kind of teacher who inspires his actors to greatness. As a commercial teacher, he is a genius, His theatrical classes are very special too. Many of my students have taken his class and loved it. He gets to the heart of figuring out why the producers/directors need this character in the script and what is the character's function. He teaches a motivating, positive acting philosophy, very focused on actors landing the jobs. Actress Brittani Taylor says, "He is one of the most inspiring teachers! When I have any question about my career, I always ask him because he has been in this industry long enough to know the answer, or know someone who knows. He keeps me prepared for the competitive and tricky world of commercials." His classes always have waiting lists—good luck.

Stuart Stone, CCDA, casting director, 323/866-1811, commercialacting.info. $300-$350 for four weeks. His *Acting Out* commercial workshop teaches you how to audition so you get the callback; and then on the callback, how to book the job! Copy reading techniques, cue card skill, overcoming obstacles and working with props. He also teaches students how to market themselves. He provides valuable insights and actors seem to book more jobs after taking his class. Stuart is fun and my students have loved his classes. He likes to call in the people he has taught; he doesn't forget you. Because of his busy casting schedule, classes are just a few times a year. There is usually a waiting list. His book, *Acting Out: Your Personal Coach To A Money Making Career in TV Commercials,* is geared to actors everywhere, whether working in your home town area or preparing to move to Los Angeles. His website is full of helpful information for actors.

Terry Berland, CCDA, casting director, 310/571-4141. TerryBerlandcasting.com. Author of *Breaking Into Commercials: Complete Guide to Marketing Yourself.* Six-week on-camera, $350. She teaches how to apply your unique personality and develop a confident approach. Learn on camera how to create dimension in this one-minute commercial medium. She also talks about the process of choosing the right actor for the job. Class includes meeting an agent. Also does a voice over workshop.

Carolyne Barry's Commercial Audition Technique, Improv and Acting workshops, 323/654-2212. carolynebarry.com. Intro, Intermediate and Professional levels offer individualized and comprehensive instruction. Program includes Improv for Commercial Auditions, a Commercial Casting Director's Workshop and Cold Reading. Six to twelve weeks starting at $335. Carolyne and her staff focus on developing the individual talent of each student, building a solid "craft" and promoting confidence. They have successfully trained thousands of working actors. Recommended by agents, casting directors, managers and working actors. *Carolyne and Kevin E. West of the Actor's Network have produced an audio tape: The Actor's Guide to Getting The Job,* great to listen to on the way to your auditions.

Michael Donovan, CSA, CCDA, casting director, 323/655-9020, 8170 Beverly Blvd. Suite 105, Los Angeles, 90048. $275, with a $25 discount for referrals. Michael Donovan has cast over 1,000 commercials as well as film, television and theatre and runs this well-respected workshop. Three-week class.

Megan Foley, CCDA, casting director, 818/216-9350, meganfoleycasting.com. $150. Teaches a commercial intensive, a one day, eight-hour class on camera, that covers all aspects of the commercial audition as well as the business of managing a commercial career. As a bonus, students get to sit in on a casting session with Megan.

Bernard Hiller, 818/781-8000, bernardhiller.com. He has done over 200 commercials and teaches actors how to become successful in the commercial field. $225 for four on-camera sessions. Private commercial training is also available. All levels welcome.

Kip King, 818/784-0544. kipking.actorsite.com. $350 for 10 weeks, returning students $300 for 11 weeks. One of the original Groundlings. Helps you bring yourself to each character you play. Especially helpful with comedy. Uses improv with commercials and comedy. Guest casting directors, agents, celebrities and voiceover pros. Private coaching, $75 per hour. Chris Katan from *Saturday Night Live* is his son.

Lien/Cowan, CCDA, Michael Lien and Dan Cowan, casting directors, 323/937-0411. The office casts hundreds of commercials a year. $150 for a one-day, six-hour class on either Saturday or Sunday, includes snacks and a pizza lunch. Class is taught by associates Jan Bina and John Smet. 15 actors per class. Two teachers, two studios, lots of on-camera time. They critique pictures and have the actors read actual copy from commercials they've cast. They show the call back tapes of people who got the commercials. *$ In Commercials TV and Movies* is a book they offer online at the website.

Beverly Long, CCDA, casting director, 818/754-6222, beverlylong-casting.com. Teaches commercial, television and film casting for children and adults. Eight weeks for $300. I took my first commercial class with Beverly many years ago. She is very knowledgeable, fun and a great teacher. Many of my students have taken her classes with great results.

Sandra Merrill, 323/662-7720, sandramerrill.com. Five-week commercial class that focuses on acting specifically for commercials, including dialogue, improv, camera and cue-card techniques and in-depth examination into finding your character. Small classes. Also offers consulting and private coaching at $35 for a half hour. She has worked in the industry as a casting director, agent and manager for over 20 years and has cast some of the most popular commercials. I audited her class, very good.

Fawnda McMahan, Commercial Break, 818/906-9611, commercialbreak@sbcglobal. net. One-day workshop that covers the business side of commercials, including a screening of top commercials produced to study for trends, information on casting directors and other key contacts, strategies for marketing yourself and answers to your questions. $95. Small class size.

John Sudol, 818/505-1223, johnsudolstudio.com. Teaches acting basics, scene study, audition technique for improving your reading skills and a commercial seminar all about the business. In his commercial seminar, he focuses on how to get an agent and succeed in front of the camera. John is a well-known and respected acting coach and independent director. Highly recommended by many top industry professionals.

Blanca Valdez, CCDA, 323/876-5700. Casting director for most of the Spanish speaking commercials. This is a huge market. She teaches a class that can be hard to get into but keep calling. Tell them I sent you. It is worth the wait. If you speak Spanish, you will want to know Blanca Valdez.

BOOKS & TAPES

Order from Samuel French Bookstore, 323/876-0570. SamuelFrench.com.

Acting Out: Your Personal Coach to a Money Making Career in TV Commercials by Stuart Stone.

The Actor's Guide to Getting The Job, an audio tape, by Carolyne Barry and Kevin E. West. $24.95. carolynebarry.com.

The Agencies: What the Actor Needs To Know by Acting World Books.

The Actor's Picture/Resume Book by Jill Charles & Tom Bloom.

An Actor's Workbook: Get The Agent You Need And The Career You Want by K. Callan.

.Acting In Television Commercials by Squire Fridell.

Acting In the Million Dollar Minute by Tom Logan.

Breaking Into Commercials: Complete Guide to Marketing Yourself by Terry Berland.

Commercials, Just My Speed!! by Vernee Watson-Johnson.

How To Audition for TV Commercials: From the Ad Agency Point of View by W.L. Jenkinss

Word of Mouth, a Guide to Commercial Voice-Overs by Susan Blu & Molly Ann Mullin.

Ross Reports Television and Film: Agents, *TV Commercial Casting Guide* by Backstage.

West Coast Performer's Complete Personal Managers Directory by Acting World Books.

FILM AND TELEVISION AUDITIONS, INTERVIEWS AND CALLBACKS

• **If auditions scare you,** join Actors Access at breakdownservices.com, nowcasting.com and lacasting.com. Check for audition possibilities daily. Buy *Back Stage West* each Wednesday afternoon or Thursday morning. To be really on top of it, subscribe on-line at backstagewest. com and check daily for new projects. Send your pictures and resumes either hard copy or online, to all the projects you are right for, and go on every audition/reading you can. You will be more comfortable doing auditions only after doing a lot of them. Give the interview and reading all of your attention and focus at the time. Then let go of the audition. The director or producer will either hire you or not. You will get jobs to build your resume.

• **Paul Newman** says, "If you want to survive, you have to show your ass. You can't walk in and play it safe."

• **Luke Perry** (*Beverly Hills 90210*) had 216 auditions before landing his first job.

• **To some actors,** *interview* and *audition* are two of the most terrifying acting words. To others, they are very exciting words because they are the actions that lead to landing acting roles. Perhaps with more understanding, you will realize how the other people involved (agents, casting directors, directors, producers) do their jobs and what exactly *your* job is as an actor. The fact is, auditions cause stress; it's how we handle the stress that makes the difference in landing the jobs.

• **Get your script or sides ahead of time.** SAG guarantees that you can get them at least the day before your interview. Often, though, in the case of episodic television, the script is still being written. In this situation, make arrangements with the assistant at the casting office to pick up your script as soon as it's available. This may be only an hour or two before the interview. For a fee, you can download your sides on Showfax.com. I suggest you subscribe online to Showfax.com and Nowcasting.com, and get your sides 24 hours a day. Sometimes your agent has the script and will fax the sides to you. *For instructions on how to prepare your script for auditions see Section One: How To Rehearse And Prepare.*

• **When you are auditioning for a television series** that you haven't seen or don't know the tone of, you can view an episode or several at Jan's Video Editing, 213/462-5511. Many classic shows can also be viewed on the Internet, either on the official show sites, the studio websites or places like apple.com where you can download show clips to your iPod.

• **Whenever you walk into an office** for an interview, whoever you are meeting is hoping 100 percent you are wonderful and will:

• **Make them a lot of money,** as in the case of an agent or manager.

• **Make an impression on the producer or director** that a casting director is having you meet. Casting directors' reputations depend on introducing new discoveries (you) to their employers.

• **Fit the director or producer's concept of the role.** They are all rooting for you!

• **This is absolutely true.** I worked many hours in casting sessions when I was an assistant to director Joan Darling. Directors hire excellent casting directors so they will screen out the bad actors and thus save them a lot of time. The casting directors' reputations depend on the caliber of actors they bring in. However bad, untrained and scared, actors do end up coming in for readings. They are usually friends of the producer or director, the director's assistant, someone the network thinks is up and coming, a waiter at Canter's because he has been so nice and has a good look, etc. When you get an opportunity to read, be prepared and take full advantage of it.

• **The one person in the room** who may not be rooting for you could be you. You don't think you're good enough. You don't deserve to get a break. Someone in the waiting room is perfect for the role. You got here by mistake. You are faking it when you act. You are too fat, thin, old, young, short, tall, blonde, dark, ethnic or not ethnic enough. These are all personal issues that need to be faced and worked on. Self-doubt has killed many promising careers. You are in charge of your thoughts. If your thoughts aren't encouraging or supportive, learn how to change them.

• **So, if you've met the casting director** and they've called you in to read for the director, you are a good actor or have a great look. That is not in question. If your agent has obtained the reading without you meeting the casting director first, you are a good actor represented by an agent with a good reputation. If you've obtained the interview in one of the other ways, say "thank you very much" and enter the office knowing that you have acting work to do. Let the fear be there—let it be part of the character.

• **Commit to the acting choices** you made when you read the script. Be open and vulnerable, and you will do a good acting job. Listen without any defenses to directions you may be given and deliver them to the best of your ability. This is your job as an actor. You may not get the role (most of the time you won't) but this is not proof of whether or not you did a good job. There may have been another actor who was better suited to the role.

• **Mira Sorvino said the first time she auditioned** for the hooker role in Woody Allen's *Mighty Aphrodite,* she didn't get the part. Woody thought she wasn't sensual enough. Then, while she was in London, she found out he was there and still auditioning. She went to King's Road, bought trashy clothes and mules with plastic flowers, fluffed out her hair, dredged up a cartoon voice, went to see Woody and wowed him. She eventually won the supporting actress Oscar for the role.

• **Ned Bellamy**, character actor, played the role of Eddie, Elaine's psychotic employee, on *Seinfeld.* He made the character choice to use a raspy, creepy voice. I asked Jerry if Ned had used that voice at the audition. He said, "Yes, and I was quite surprised when he showed up at rehearsal and that wasn't his real voice." I asked Ned about it. Moments before the audition, he decided on the voice and asked casting director

Marc Hirschfeld if he should use it. Marc said, "Why not?" Ned had a couple of questions to ask about the role and used the same voice to ask them because he didn't want to break the illusion of the character. Besides being a wonderful actor and looking the part, his choice of using that voice may have been what gave him the edge over the other actors auditioning.

• **Katie Holmes** (*Dawson's Creek*) is from Cleveland. She had done some school plays and then, in her junior year, she and her mother went to a talent convention. She did a monologue, they liked her, sent her to Los Angeles. She auditioned for the film *Ice Storm* and got it. After shooting it and returning home, she auditioned for pilots by recording her reading on video tape and sending it to her agent. Her mother read the other characters off camera. She said she kidded James Van Der Beek, saying he was good but her mom really knew how to play Dawson.

• **Gail O'Grady** (*American Dreams*) auditioned for the part of the secretary on *NYPD Blue*, wearing a '60s hairdo, false eyelashes, a tight angora sweater, bright stirrup pants and adding a heavy New York accent; she was inspired by characters in the film *Working Girl*. She said, "I know this woman, she's very physical. And I knew nobody else would show up like that." They auditioned over 100 actors for the part. The three-episode role turned into a regular role with Gail receiving an Emmy nomination.

• **David Schwimmer** (*Friends*) wanted the part in the film *The Pallbearer* from the moment he read the script. He was obsessed. A dozen actors were up for the role. One morning the film's director, Matt Reeves, found a tiny coffin on his desk. The message inside: "I'd kill to be in this movie!" It was signed David Schwimmer. Persistence paid off.

• **Debi Mazar** (*GoodFellas, Jungle Fever*), in an interview, spoke of her audition with Spike Lee for *Malcolm X*. She wore a blond wig, 1940s makeup, platform shoes, and landed the part of Shorty's girlfriend. She said, "I thought Spike would like to see the character the minute I walked in the door. It was a great audition."

• **Poppy Montgomery** auditioning to play Marilyn Monroe for *Blonde*, a CBS miniseries, decided to take a gamble. "I didn't do the breathless Marilyn voice, I came in with a ponytail, a white T-shirt and jeans." She was playing the younger Norma Jean Baker, the pinup girl. Out of the 100 actresses auditioning, the producers chose her.

• **Casting Director Tom McSweeney** says, "We love actors; they're our livelihood. We love to find new people. There's nothing more fun than giving an actor a break. I don't want to see actors suffer; I want to see them work; I want to see them happy."

• **Tuesday Knight** was working as a receptionist at Orion Television. "Somebody from the show *Fame* saw me. They were looking for a combination Deborah Harry/Madonna–so they had this big cattle call. I saw it on TV, about 3,000 girls. Then the next day they saw me in the office and they hired me. It was like a dream. I was a regular for a while."

• **Director Ron Shelton's original plan** for Woody Harrelson's date in *White Men Can't Jump* was to be a snooty Ivy League girl. Rosie Perez showed up for an interview and blurted out to him, with feeling, "I can't audition today! I'm having a bad hair day!" That grabbed his attention; she got the role.

• **Regina Taylor** auditioned for *I'll Fly Away*. She felt she was very different from the part until she started thinking of her grandmother and her family. "When I finally sat down to audition to a room full of suits in Los Angeles, I told them I wasn't ready to do the scene, that I felt like talking. They said, 'Sure, talk.' I told them about where I came from, about the faces of the people who raised me. When I was done talking, no one said anything. Someone thanked me. I got up and left." A month later she was in Atlanta filming the part of Lily Harper.

• **Anna Maria Horsford** *(Amen)* says when she went to audition for the part of Sherman Hemsley's ditsy daughter, she wore a pink bathrobe, a pair of little-girl teddy bear slippers and carried a supermarket tabloid under her arm. Her reasoning was: if the character doesn't work, then what does she do? She watches soap operas and reads the gossip sheets.

• **Mariska Hargitay** auditioned for the TV series *Tequila & Bonetti*. Executive Producer Donald Bellisario, said, "I vividly remember the day she auditioned and gave a sly twist to a tragic monologue about a dead husband. The other actresses played it straight, but Mariska played it with laughter. She told this horrible story as if it were a joke, and as she continued, tears started to streak past her smile. She got the part."

• **Edward Norton** brought the stutter into the audition for *Primal Fear*. It was not in the script, it was his invention.

• **Kissing and sexual scenes are hard to carry out** when you are in the auditioning room. Bonnie Gillespie, author of *Casting Qs: A Collection of Casting Director Interviews*, told me of an interview situation that casting director **Jane Jenkins, CSA** often shares.

> • **I have vivid memories** of Vincent D'Onfrio's audition for *Mystic Pizza*. The sides called for the character to roll around on the floor with Lily Taylor's character in a heavy make out scene, followed by an abrupt confrontation by her father. Most actors felt the need to grope me, grab me, or roll around on the floor by themselves. Vincent got down on one knee and did the whole scene as if it were his close up. When you have one of those physically demanding, complicated scenes that is impossible to do in an office, do your close-up.

• **Susan Rutan** *(LA Law),* referring to every character she auditioned for said: "You can get away with anything you are comfortable with. If you think you're pushing it, then you are. Never hit a casting director. Never touch them. Commit, commit, commit. I know that whenever I fully commit to a choice, I either get the job or get a chance to do it another way." When talking about her *LA Law* audition, she said:

> • **There was a clue in the script:** "She would chew off her right arm for Arnie." I took that and committed to that part of the personality. I didn't know anything else about her. There were four little scenes. One was where she came in, in the morning, and there was this big smell in the office. I brought an empty spray can with me and I sprayed it around the room and used it. I'm not sure props are always right, but they were right for this moment. As I was leaving, Greg Hoblit said, "You made us laugh." They didn't know she was funny. I made a choice; I risked—but you have to do it. Otherwise when you go in to read and just do what the stage directions say, you're doing what everyone else is doing.

• **It takes guts to go with your instincts** like that; but in these cases, the actors ended up launching their careers with long-running television series. It certainly was worth it. I'm sure there were times these actors didn't get jobs using outrageous choices, but the few successes are worth the many failures.

• **Casting Director Cathy Henderson, CSA**, says:

> • **I think the actor who usually gets the part** will be someone who walks in and does it as if they were walking on the set, somebody said "Action" and they did it. Making it their own and making it real.

> • **A great deal of the reason** why one person will continually get a job and someone else won't is very often not how talented someone is, but more that they grasp what the director and producer are doing that day, which is trying to hire several people for specific roles, and not that they're waiting for someone to come in and blow them away. I mean, it's great if that happens, if the part calls for it. But lots of times your part doesn't call for you to come in and blow somebody away. They want somebody natural, somebody who has good chemistry with the rest of the cast and somebody who makes it real.

• **Casting director Clair Sinnett** says actors should ask, "Would you like to see what I've prepared or is there something specific you would like to see?"

• **If you know any directors or casting directors**, you might ask if you can volunteer to be a reader for them. As a reader, you will read all the other roles with feeling to the auditioning actor. You will be a partner to play off of. The time you spend in a casting office will be a real eye-opener to the casting business. It is also valuable to volunteer as an intern in a casting office.

• **Joe Reich, casting director**, when asked how an actor should hold a script during an audition replied, "I only care that the actor does hold the script. It is axiomatic that when you memorize the script you will always forget a line, usually at the most crucial point (and usually at an important audition). So even if you do memorize, please carry the script and spare yourself that agonizing moment."

• **Absolutely do not look at the script when you are talking or listening.** I cannot say this strongly enough. The time to look down is when the other person reading with you has finished their line and you don't know what your next one is. Start your reaction to what has been said to you and then look down and "grab" the words. Look at the other person and take the time to play the lines. Don't just say them. Use all your acting work and choices. Remember, the lines are not important; the acting is. I believe it is best to memorize the script.

• **Kathleen Freeman**, the late character actress and teacher, taught me a very valuable exercise for quickly learning to pick up your lines from a page. Read out loud from a newspaper. Hold your thumb near the copy. Look down, pick up words. Look up in a mirror or into the room and try to make real conversation with those stiff words. Newspapers work better than magazines, because they are written in a dryer form. If you do this 10 minutes every day for three months, you will become very good at picking up words off the script.

• **Wallis Nicita, producer** and former vice president of Warner Bros. Casting, says, "In casting, it is a new person every 10 minutes, eight hours a day, five days a week. You get one take to hit your emotional level and then, good-bye, thank you very much."

• **Improvisational Projects: Todd Rohrbacher** is often called in as an assistant casting director for improvisational projects. In the audition he sets up a premise and then improvs with the actors. Todd is the Founder and Artistic Director of *Captain Creamsicle's Laughateers* and is an alumnus *ACME Comedy Theatre's Main Company.* He teaches all levels of improvisation as well as on-camera comedy and audition technique at Scott Sedita's Acting Studios. He is a sitcom dialogue coach as well as an animation writer. Here he talks about auditions for improvised shows.

> • **The most common mistake actors** make during improvised auditions is to overplay the joke and neglect the honesty of the circumstances and relationships in the scenario. It is the actor's job to create a history and relationship with other characters the same as if it were a scripted role. Even if the role is comedic, you still have to show a range of emotions and have a character arc. You should start in one place emotionally and end in another. Whether the circumstances call for it or not, find a reason to switch it up emotionally during your audition. You won't book a series regular role by playing one note. From the beginning you have to include the warmth, affection, friendship, love or sexuality—whatever feelings you would have for the character you're playing against—as well as the humor.

> • **Also, improv auditions get stale quickly** if you beat around the bush or "slow burn" into the premise. If you are given an idea to work with, get to it quickly. Think in terms of starting in the

middle of the scene as opposed to the beginning. The premise you are given is likely to have some conflict. Identify that conflict and address it immediately. Remember that many people (Casting Director, Director, Producer, Creator, etc.) have to watch your audition played back on tape. They don't want to wait around for you to get to the point. They don't want to see you "warm up" on tape. Do that before you come into the room. Have energy and a few ideas on how to attack your scenario right away. Doing simply this much will put you at the head of the pack. Believe it or not, the priority for these types of auditions is NOT to be funny. It's important to show your comedic abilities, but you have to be honest and believable first. The best advice I can give is to break down your character the same you would for a dramatic role and play it and the circumstances as honestly as you can.

• **There is nothing to be afraid of except your own ego.** You are a business person, a career person, a professional dealing with other professionals. Take up your full space, ask questions if you don't know something. It is okay not to know.

• **Take care of the people interviewing you.** Interviews are also difficult for some of these people; they are shy too. The reason they ask a question is to find out about your personality and who you are, not necessarily what your credits are.

• **Come to love the question** "What have you been doing?" If you can love that question and come up with an entertaining, positive, happy answer you've got the interview 90% down.

• **Casting director James F. Tarzia speaks of general interviews.**

  • **During a general, I'll read the actor's resume** and ask them to tell me about themselves. I don't want them to tell me what's on the resume, I can read what's there. I want to know if there is a well-rounded human being here, or are you one-minded and focused on just being an actor? If you're not a well-rounded human being, then there are no dimensions to you. I want people to be three-dimensional.

• CALLBACKS

• **When you go back for another reading,** wear the same clothes, hair style and make the same acting choices, unless you have been asked to read for another part. The time to use an acting coach is before the first audition, not for the callback. They have called you back because they liked how you looked and what you did. The exception would be if they told your agent they didn't like your acting and wanted you to play the role in another way. At this point, a coach could be of great help to open your mind to another point of view in choosing your work.

• **Casting director James F. Tarzia says,**

> • Of course, we all know about actors on callbacks—they never seem to do it the same way they did it when they first auditioned. There must be this thing about it: "I got a callback, I think I'll rework this totally different from what I did the last time." But I liked what you did, don't change it, please don't change it, because I'm going in before you and saying to my director, "This is the most brilliant reading I've seen, I mean he was just absolutely great," and the actor will come in and do something *totally* different, and I'm like, "What are you doing?" My director is looking at me going "Uh huh, okay." It's a surprise and we don't want to be too surprised. So leave it, don't change it.

• **There are acting jobs** and you will get yours. This is your career path and you must take each one of the steps. There is a natural progression. Yes, some people seem to get luckier breaks. *Yay!* They will get there faster and help us. Everyone likes to have their friends working with them. It makes for a happier family on the set.

• **After the audition, have an appointment in your book** to go to: facial, dance class, rehearsal, movie, lunch, etc., so the interview becomes just another event in your day. Write down the people you've met, put them on your networking address list, send thank you notes if appropriate. Remember the things that you did right and for the most part, don't talk about your auditions.

• **Try to keep your interview scenes** (sides) from your film and TV auditions and the copy from your commercial auditions. File them in your notebook. When you work on a project, keep the scripts; years down the line, you will love having them. Maybe your career will someday be valuable enough for a library donation. We never know until it's over.

Resources

Mobile Mailbox, 323/848/9721, mymobilmailbox.com. 1483 N. Havenhurst, Los Angeles, 90046. This is an inexpensive messenger service; Biff Yeager is the actor/owner of the company. Actors can submit themselves for projects they hear or read about that are currently casting. To quote the brochure, "We are a unique messenger service developed several years ago as a once-a-day, fast pickup and delivery service. We pre-sell our own special delivery stamps as low as $1.25 each. Anything that fits in a 10 x 13 inch envelope may be sent by affixing the required amount of stamps and depositing the envelope into one of our conveniently located drop boxes around the Los Angeles, Hollywood, Century City, Beverly Hills, North Hollywood and Burbank areas!" You must register with MMB and buy your stamps before you can put your submissions in their drop boxes.

GetMoreAuditions.com. 310/921-6000. They are a marketing service that submits actors' headshots to producers, major casting notices and directors for a weekly fee plus postage. You receive a detailed report listing your submissions. Founded in 1997, over 90% of their clients book auditions or jobs. Clients have auditioned for or booked: Alias, ER, CSI:NY, CSI:Miami, West Wing, Without A Trace, The Shield, Cold Case, The Practice, House of Sand and Fog, Planet of the Apes, One Night at McCool's, General Hospital, Days Of Our Lives, and Passions. As well as IBM, Hertz, Doritos and Chevrolet commercials and numerous Independent films. GMA service is Member of the Better Business Bureau. Mention you found GMA through this book and you will get an additional week free!

• *See Casting and Membership website section for other auditioning resources.*

CONQUERING FEAR

- **John Wayne said:**

  - **Courage** is being scared to death and saddling up anyway.

- **If you haven't** already thought of your own ways to get through some or all of your interview, audition and performing fears, here are some tried and true ones. Use them all and add your own until you can walk through your fears. These are *not* the most important moments in your life; they are just simply moments.

- **Jeremy Irons**, Oscar winner for *Reversal of Fortune,* says about acting:

  - **A lot of it is like hang gliding**—you just hold on and hope it works. When I talk to acting students, I always read them this poem: "Come to the edge, it's too high, come to the edge, you might fall, come to the edge—so they came. And they flew." I want to keep coming to a high edge. That's why I've made the choices I have. Sometimes I will fall, and sometimes, please God, I will fly. But I wouldn't want to get so scared that I come to a low edge I can just step off easily.

- **Meryl Streep said:**

  - **Characters that are in precarious life and death circumstances** are dangerous characters to visit with your body and soul. It's dangerous to go there. We spend our whole lives as real human beings trying to get beyond the fears and the terrors that are there, everywhere, for us. To be an actor is to want to visit those dark places, the scary parts.

- **Time.** When you know the time and location of your interview, start planning backwards. You want to arrive and park your car one half-hour before your scheduled appointment time. That means checking the address in your Thomas Guide and figuring your exact route and leaving for your destination in plenty of time to find it. As a rule, on your way to the audition, the traffic will be the worst it has ever been in history. Always give yourself a break and allow the most time it could take—not the least.

• **Bill Macy,** (mature character actor) was doing a presentation of a scene from *Maude* at the Television Academy to honor Norman Lear. Three days before the event we were talking and he casually mentioned he had just come back from a trial run to make sure he knew exactly where the Academy was, where he would park and how long it would take him to get there. Now this is from an ex-New York cab driver who starred in his own TV series for seven years and has worked decades in films, television and on stage. Still, this veteran is clocking how long it will take him to get to his destination for this important event. He says, "It makes me feel secure to know where I'm going." He gets secure so he can walk on the edge of the cliff in his acting. He loves taking risks, that's why he's so funny!

• **Keep a coin purse** in your glove compartment so you'll always have quarters and dimes for parking. I also keep a few coins in my appointment book.

• **Keep a magnetic lock box** hidden on the outside of your car with your car key and house key in it—never be locked out of your car or home before an audition or set call. If you haven't already done this, please put this book down and do it right now. You can get the lock box at most drug stores, key shops, Target, Pep Boys, etc. and keys can also be made at most of those stores.

• **In getting ready to leave the house,** whatever preparation it takes to turn you on to yourself, do it. This may involve some of your *actor's secrets* or simply deciding what to wear, ironing it, primping, playing positive tapes or music, reading something inspirational.

• **If you have an early appointment** and you aren't any good in the morning till you've been up for three hours and have had four cups of coffee, it means you are up $3^1/2$ hours before the appointment. Luckily, when you work in film and TV and your call is for 6 or 7AM, you can just take a shower, wash your hair and go to work. The hair and makeup people take care of the rest and give you a chance to wake up.

• **Okay, you're prepared**, parked in your car a half-hour ahead of time. Now relax. Just sit with any fears, tears, giggles, anger or whatever comes up; you may start to cry or laugh. Experience all of it because beyond those feelings and tensions are the knowledge of who you are and the energy to use all of yourself. Allow plenty of time for this, then take down all of your defenses, be willing to let whatever happens to you happen. Go into the office, sign or report in with the assistant, and check to make sure there aren't changes of dialogue in the sides you are reading today or pick up your copy or sides if you don't already have them.

• **If for some insane reason you weren't able to get your script ahead of time,** find the restroom so you can say all your lines out loud. Figure out what the scene or copy is about (the situation), who the characters are and to whom they are talking. Find similar experiences and characters in your own life and act as if you were talking to them under these given circumstances. Memorize as much of the material as you can—at least the first couple of lines.

• **Then go back to the office**, relax, observe everything going on but don't expend your energy talking with the other actors until you have read and are on your way out.

• **Practice these "punctuality" muscles** by being at class on time to get ready to act—whatever that takes for you: coffee, socializing, talking to your teacher, etc. Also practice this with any appointments. This will help you figure out what it takes for you to be at your most comfortable, relaxed, unique best.

• **On your drive to the interview** or before, start thinking of your stories. Have an answer to "What have you been doing lately?" It is very important to have a wonderful story to tell about each entry on your resume, as the interviewer might use it as a guide for conversation.

• **Stories.** These are *positive* stories about your life, your career, the weather; it doesn't matter. If anyone mentions the smog, you haven't noticed because of some other positive thing you *have* noticed. If it's raining—isn't it grand how fresh it smells.

• **Make the stories short**, interesting and geared to show off who you are. You just got back from a great vacation, skiing, surfing, Las Vegas. You're taking a class in anthropology and are going on a dig next week.

You can use things that happened a few months back as if they were last week; a story is more exciting if it sounds like it just happened. Funny incidents entertain. The most trivial information can be made humorous. Show biz gossip stories are good: shows you've worked on, stars you've worked with. Just make sure the story revolves around *you* and not who or what you are talking about.

• **Love of yourself.** Give yourself the *permission* to be wonderful. Your uniqueness is the gift, yes gift, you are giving the audience, whomever they may be. Keep putting yourself on the line; don't be afraid to be outrageous, or to be willing to just say the lines. Most of the time you are going up for parts that are exactly like you.

• **I've asked my students to make a copy of the following speech** on a bright colored piece of paper and put it in their wallet. Every time they take out some money, they see the bright color and think of not being afraid.

Adapted from Marianne Williamson's writing about fear.

Our deepest fear is not that we are inadequate.

Our deepest fear is that we are powerful beyond measure.

It is our light, not our darkness, that most frightens us.

We ask ourselves: Who am I to be brilliant, gorgeous, talented and fabulous?

Actually, who are you not to be?

Your playing small doesn't serve the world.

There's nothing enlightening about shrinking so that other people won't feel insecure around you.

We were born to make manifest the glory that is within us.

It's not just in some of us; it's in everyone.

And as we let our own light shine, we unconsciously give other people permission to do the same.

As we are liberated from our own fear, our presence automatically liberates others.

DEALING WITH REJECTION

• **Through my spiritual work and inner growth,** I have found positive ways to accept not getting an acting job I've wanted. I don't forget the jobs and I still wish "they" had wanted me, but I have come to accept the fact that they didn't.

• **I hate dealing with rejection** but I can tolerate it, even though it hurts. Sometimes I do stew about it, rationalize that somehow it's for my own good, get angry and/or feel sorry for myself. I've learned, if I'm really in self-pity, to give myself a time limit, whether it's 15 minutes or two days. It usually doesn't last the full time but sometimes it does and then time is up and I let go of it. I really do believe I have a choice in my thoughts.

• **There have been times in my life** when I have allowed the depression to take over for longer periods, but not anymore. Time seems too precious to me now; I've got so many things in my life that fulfill me. I still don't have enough acting or coaching jobs. When I do get one, I really celebrate the whole event.

• **Sometimes you can have a job and lose it.** In my spiritual work, we are taught that events happen for a reason. When we lose one thing, something better will come along. When you have been fired or the pilot you were counting on going to series didn't go, it is hard to see what might be better. This is a time in your life where you really have to do the hard work of keeping yourself in the game.

• **Hilary Swank talks about the day Aaron Spelling fired her** off *Beverly Hills, 90210.* "I was on the eighth season and around the 16th episode, Aaron said, 'Hilary, it's not working.' I went home and cried all day, weeping, 'If I'm not good enough to be on *90210*, then I shouldn't be an actress at all!'" Three weeks later, she landed her Oscar-winning role in the independent film *Boys Don't Cry.* Hilary says, "You must trust fate. If I hadn't been fired, I wouldn't have been open to take the role."

• **Bill Macy, a well known mature character actor** was cast as one of the regulars on an ABC show called *Regular Joe* with Daniel Stern. They shot the pilot and word was everyone was hot for the show. At the last minute in May, it didn't make the fall schedule. Then in August it was back on for a mid-season replacement. All fall the news was, "It was a go." Then they started dropping characters and changing the storyline. Then just three weeks before the show was to go into production they told Bill they were replacing him with Judd Hirsch and paying off his contract.

• **Bill has been around a long time** so he was sad but went to play golf and get on with his life. The next week he auditioned for a movie he hadn't been available for until then. Callbacks and dealmaking ensued. Finally the deal was signed on the day he had been scheduled to start shooting the series. The movie was *Surviving Christmas* with Ben Affleck, James Gandolfini, Christina Applegate and Catherine O'Hara. This ended up being a great turn of events. Bill believes, "When one door closes, another will open."

• **When we follow the second agreement in** *The Four Agreements* book by Don Miguel Ruiz and don't take anything personally, we reach a higher level, we learn to trust, we work even harder. Rejection is tough and we get tougher.

• **Dr. Sherie Zander** instructs actors on ways to deal with rejection.

   • **Everyone must face rejection**, but for the actor rejection is a constant companion. It cannot be avoided. No one is immune. It not only affects the beginner, but the seasoned actor as well. Success, fame and fortune don't keep the experience and pain of rejection away. Rejection must be faced and dealt with so that it will not destroy the motivation and self-esteem that are necessary in order to maintain an acting career.

   • **No one likes rejection.** It can be discouraging and hurtful. It may lead to insomnia, depression and despair. Because it is so prevalent and so destructive, it is critical that you, as an actor, discover how to detach from its harmful effect. But, how is that possible? You are told not to take rejection personally, but how do you differentiate who you are from what you do?

- **When I work with actors who are struggling** with this issue, I begin by taking a look at possible sources of rejection in childhood. Often the healing of early emotional wounds will provide the emotional stability that is required to move through rejection with less pain and stress. You may need to get to a good therapist.

- **I work with attitude and perspective.** Because every success will be preceded by many rejections, it may be helpful to view each rejection as a stepping stone rather than a setback. Remember that every rejection brings you one step closer to success.

- **There are many practical things** you can do to keep rejection from getting you down. Finding a safe way to release feelings of anger, sadness, hurt, fear and guilt is a good place to start. You may need to cry or yell, hit a punching bag or pour out the feelings on paper. This will serve to clear your mind and body and prepare you to carry on in spite of disappointment.

- **You may find a creative outlet** for all of that rejection energy—write a poem, write an article, draw, paint or sculpt. Physical exercise will help. Get the sleep you need and eat regular, healthy meals. Take this opportunity to do things that are fulfilling and refreshing.

- **Turn your focus away from thoughts of failure** and onto improvement. Take time to study and explore your craft. This is the time to continue the mechanics of finding new work—phone calls, mailings, photos, networking. Make a decision to learn what you can from this rejection by doing the following:
    - **Make an effort to find out** why you were turned down.
    - **Notice any positive things** that came out of this incident.
    - **Make two lists:**
        Things I can change.
        Things I can't change.
    - **Utilize the practice of meditation and prayer.**
    - **Decide to go for the next opportunity and try again.**

- **I would encourage you to prepare now for that day.** You can do so by making sure you are living a full life. Take time to develop deep and lasting friendships. Nurture and enjoy family relationships. Involve yourself with other actors in study or support groups. These are the persons who will help to lift your spirits when discouragement and despair threaten to bring you down.

- **You have many choices.** Refuse to allow rejection to ruin your day or your future.

LIE ABOUT YOUR AGE?

• **In film and television, you will play within a few years of the age** you are thought to be, unlike theater or projects in other parts of the country. Never give an age range of more than a few years. 15 to 19, 18 to 22, 21 to 25, 27 to 32. People in this industry will not buy broader age ranges unless you are a definite character actor. It is the look they want; your age doesn't matter. I have found that actors in cities outside of Los Angeles will give age ranges of 10 years. That just doesn't work here.

• **Honesty is always the best policy!** But that doesn't mean you have to tell your age. *However,* if you are 30, look 22 and are reading for a part that is 22, *if* you are asked how old you are, you might give the age the part calls for or say, "I play 22." You can only do this if you are very comfortable with it. It is hard for a casting director to bring you in to meet the director and producer for a 22-year-old role if they know you are 30. Remember, you will be laughed at if you look 30 and claim to play 20 to 30. You must judge your age according to how those in-the-know in the industry perceive you.

• **I don't recommend lying;** I recommend side-stepping the question because once you tell someone your age, they always think of you as that age.

• **It is usually best** to do what your agent wants you to do. They will be selling you at a certain age. When you are hired, someone in the production office will end up knowing your age because of the ruling that you must show your driver's license, passport, or birth certificate to prove your right to work. SAG has been trying to get this rule overturned.

• **Stuart K. Robinson, noted commercial acting teacher,** successful actor and director highly recommends that you never tell your age. He believes that if you are asked outright, "How old are you?" which is against the law, that you avoid answering. I love watching Stuart teach; he has the perfect body language and verbal language to avoid telling his age. For example, "I don't tell my age." or "It is a long tradition in my family, we never tell our age." or "You tell me, do you think I look the right age to play this part?" or "Don't you agree, I'm in the age range to play this part?" or "I believe I look the age to play this part. If you disagree, I'm out of here." Stuart is a master at pulling this off with style.

• **In legal terms, according to SAG,** a performer should never be asked their age or ethnicity. The only exception is if the producer needs to know whether or not the performer is a minor or if the actor speaks a certain language.

• **I am one to blurt out my age.** You really have to always play it as you see it. We can change our minds on how we see things. If you decide not to tell your age then you will have to keep it a secret from most everyone. Angelina Jolie has been pulling off younger for years. One of my students graduated from UCLA with her younger brother. My student was 25 and Angelina was still selling 22. Every article about her has a slightly different age. I'm not saying she isn't what she says she is, but she may not be.

• **There is no denying the fact:** the younger you play the more opportunities you will have to work. This will not change, so each of us has to make peace with this issue. There is no use in trying to change the business; you can only change yourself, your thinking, your age.

CASTING DIRECTORS

• **Casting directors are mentioned all through this book** because they are usually the people who bring you in to meet the producers and directors of film and television projects. *(For more about commercial casting directors, see the Business of Commercials section).*

• **Lori Cobe-Ross, is an independent feature film casting director.**

Q: What does a casting director do?

> • **I read the script** with the director or writer, work up the breakdowns of the characters and specifically what we want or what we need. I submit the descriptions to the Breakdown Service, they send this information over computer or fax to all of the agents. From that, the agents submit actors. That same day, particularly on a feature, I receive hundreds of pictures and resumes. I don't interview all of the actors, but I look at everything.

Q: Do you prefer seeing actors through agents?

> • **Unfortunately, 99 percent of the time, I have to say no to the actors.** If I see a hundred people, only one is going to get the role. So it's a lot easier to talk to the agents, without saying directly to the actor why they weren't right. Also, actors without agents would be at a disadvantage making their own deals because they're not really equipped to do that, whereas, agents are.

Q: Is making the deal the most important part of your job?

> • **For the producer it is;** for the director it's getting the right actor for the part. I work for the producer and the director. To me they are of equal importance, though I would think getting the right actor is more important.

Q: When actors are reading together for a role with kissing and such, should they do it for the audition?

- **People are afraid to ask questions about physical movement.** Some actors are afraid to look each other in the eyes. You really need to act physical. You should talk about it ahead of time. You could say to the actor, "Is it okay if we kiss?" or "What do you want to do?" Make sure you are both willing to do it. Then ask the auditioners what they would like to see.

- **Lori wrote a letter** to the editor of *Back Stage West*. I think it is important for all actors. It is reprinted here with her permission.

  - **Casting is a business.** We casting directors do our part and the actors need to do theirs.

    1. **Always bring a picture and resume** with you to every audition. Come on—keep some in your car.
    2. **Get a contact number with a Los Angeles area code.** Some casting directors might not want to make a long distance call. Why risk losing an audition?
    3. **Don't call a casting office** unless you are running late for an audition or it is some emergency. Our job is to find the best actor; we are not career counselors. After talking to agents and managers to schedule, negotiate, and book actors, auditions, preparing and approving sides, and dealing with our producers and director, there is little or no time left in the day.
    4. **Don't make excuses once you are in for an audition.** If you aren't prepared, *don't audition*. Ask for more time. I'd much rather give you time than see you stumble through the material. We don't know who has had the sides for an hour or a week; we assume you've spent time on the material.
    5. **Be kind to the casting assistants.** I don't need to say more.
    6. **It's fine to ask questions in an audition.** If you have unanswered questions about your character, you cannot do a good job.
    7. **One last hint** that I learned from my best friend, casting director Mark Paladini: If you go to an audition and you know the casting director, and it is just the two of you in the room, it is fine to chat, reminisce, schmooze...*but* if there are others in the room just do your audition and answer any questions you're asked. You don't want the producers, director or others to think that you were brought in as a favor. You want them to think you're there because you are one of the best choices for the role.

• **Bonnie Gillespie, a casting director and author** of the books, *Casting Qs: A Collection of Casting Director Interviews, Self-Management for Actors: Getting Down to (Show) Business,* and *Acting Qs: Conversations with Working Actors.* She is also a career consultant on the business of acting. I asked Bonnie for some specific quotes to demonstrate how much the casting directors are on the actor's side. She chose the following from many, many hours of interviews she has conducted.

• **Carol Lefko:** "Actors think that casting directors are not on their side. We are! We have a problem and they are our solution!"

• **Ellyn Long Marshall:** "Our eyes, minds and hearts want you to be what we need. It's not known what is needed. You bring it in and show it to us."

• **Delicia Turner:** "I tell my actor friends, 'Look, if you're good, you're making my job easier.'"

• **Mike Fenton, CSA:** "We don't bite. We don't invite an actor in hoping he'll fail. The sooner we find an actor who scores, the better for us."

• **Laura Gleason, CSA:** "I know how difficult the process is. I respect actors and really enjoy them as people and I want them to do so well."

• **Iris Grossman:** "We want you to be the one who's going to get the part because then the job is done. I want you to come in and get it."

• **Julie Hutchinson, CSA:** "Our fantasy is to make a major discovery and stop looking."

• **Amy Lippens, CSA:** "We want you to be good. We want you to be right for the part. It's about being creative and having fun."

• **Marnie Saitta:** "When an actor comes in and feels nervous, I want to say, 'Hey, you're doing me a favor, coming in here and making good choices. You're inspiring me.'"

• **April Webster, CSA:** "We try to make this a safe place, so that the actor feels that he or she has the right to try something out. I want you to do your best work because that makes my job go smoothly."

• **There is so much valuable information** that can help you with your career. When you go to showcases, take notes; the casting director will often say something of a personal nature. You can mention it in your thank you letter or when you have an interview two years later. You can, for instance, inquire whether their child won his Little League championship or not.

• **When you see a film or television** show that you especially like the casting of, write the casting director telling them what you liked in particular. Their addresses can always be obtained through Breakdown Services or other membership groups.

• **One of the biggest challenges for an actor is getting seen by a casting director.** There are many right and wrong ways to go about doing it, but the majority of casting directors say blind submissions aren't very effective. Rather, most meetings come from agent referrals, casting director workshops, the occasional open call and postcards that inform casting directors what you've been working on. Casting director Terry Berland says, "Actors creating their own projects make them stand out."

• **Carol Lefko casts independent features,** including *Dark Heart* and *The Drop.* Carol is very well-respected and has a great view of the industry. She tells a great story about being the first female ever in the CBS mail room and how she got her first casting assistant job by dressing in the same colors of the casting director's office.

Q: What's the best way for an actor to get seen by a casting director?

• **I still think the best way to get seen by a casting director is by doing good theatre.** And that's tough in L.A. I go see a lot of theatre and if I see somebody who sparks my interest, I will bring them in. It's a great way to check for new talent. There's a reason why many of the biggest television and film stars are also theatre actors.

Q: What exactly is that "spark" you're looking for?

• **I look for actors who have a strong grasp of the character they're playing.** I like the ones that bring their own interpretation, that make the character their own, that do something novel. I keep the playbills and make little marks next to the actor names. I realize that it's tough for actors to get into meet casting directors, so if I see somebody good or if somebody is recommended to me, I'll take the time to meet them.

Q: What do you look for from an actor when they meet you?

• **What really draws me to an actor is confidence, preparation and somebody who looks good.** Actors must have confidence, and it's not necessarily an acting thing. It's a confidence in who they are. I can't stress that enough. It also doesn't always come with just experience. It's deeper than that. It's about knowing who you are as an actor and as a person and being able to translate that in an interview. And if you're reading for me, you must be prepared. I'm one of those casting directors that expects you to have the material memorized because that really shows that you want the role. If you're ready, it also helps build up your confidence. And, I hate to say it, the actor needs to look good. We work in a superficial industry and looks leave an impression. If it's a guy, I want to see a good haircut. If it's a girl, have the right amount of makeup. Wear good clothes. Show me that you care and that you want to leave an impression. Remember, you typically have only one chance to wow a casting director so make the most of it.

• **Joey Paul, CSA, film, television and stage casting director:**

Q: How should the actor approach a general interview, when they are just meeting with the casting director and not auditioning?

- **For the most part, actors take the wrong psychological approach.** If they walk into a general interview and a casting director has to say to them, "So, tell me about yourself," they're not off to a good start. Part of the reason that a general interview might go very well is that a real dialogue of action and response occurs between two people, just like in a regular scene. If a general interview is one where the casting director is just asking questions and then passively sits there and listens to the actor talk about their life or their day, etc., it is not very conducive to making a long-lasting impression. Everybody likes to talk about themselves, particularly people in show business, who are oriented toward, and proud of their accomplishments. The goal of a general interview should be to find a common bond, something that both people can jointly discuss. The actor should be asking questions, too.

- **Questions like,** "I am familiar with some of your work; it's amazing what you do. Is casting everything you thought it would be and is it a creative and fun process for you?" or, "I was curious; how did you first get started as a casting director?" I think that if an actor seems interested in the casting director, they'll have a better chance of the casting director being interested in them. People always respond well when somebody says, "You know, I saw such and such film that you cast and I felt... How long have you been casting this project? Are you still looking for such and such? I notice the artwork in your office is of a southwestern taste" Coming from a business point of view, I don't think of that as flattery. That kind of discussion lends itself to being able to remember the actor better, but only if it comes from a real and genuine place.

- **For me, there's nothing worse** than when actors come in, sit in my office and don't say a word. Nothing, not even bad small talk like, "Boy, the traffic was busy getting here today. What was it like for you after the earthquake?" To me a general interview is kind of like a blind date; you have hopes that maybe this time it might work out. You hope there's a possibility that you could make a friend. Maybe this person will like you and remember you. If you were to go on a blind date and all the person did for 20 minutes was talk about himself, you'd walk away saying he couldn't care less about me. All the regular things also apply: be yourself, don't be somebody you're not, be real and honest, have a sharing dialogue. If they ask a question, you ask a question, or start off the conversation with a question.

Q: So you're really talking about personality development?

- Yes, because ultimately if an actor becomes a major, major star, one of the reasons may be because they have an incredible personality in addition to their talent. Robin Williams is a perfect example of that. I tell students of mine that they should see a general interview in their mind the same way they would if they were going to appear on David Letterman or Jay Leno. If they aspire to be a celebrity someday, then that aspiration has to be with them today. The reason that kind of success happens is because that's who they are now.

- Actors who are shy and would rather do the acting work than be in situations where their personalities must carry them, shouldn't do general interviews. Whoever represents them or is helping them to promote their careers should put the emphasis on trying to get them the audition. Let the actors do their magic in the reading and leave.

Q: When going in for an audition, should the actor immediately start to do the audition or try to get a general conversation going first?

- I have never been impressed by an actor, regardless of whether it's a call back or an initial meeting, who wants to try to create a general interview situation prior to their audition. Particularly if they assume that we're going to sit down and talk before they read. I firmly believe that less is more. There are ways actors can develop a certain kind of control over auditions, rather than coming in like victims. One of the ways they can do this is by truly looking at the audition as a journey.

- With the entrance into my office they have the opportunity to take me on a little fantasy journey that will be created by what they do. If actors are in control of this journey, they will have a better chance of my going along fully for the ride. When they come in and decide they want to talk, tell stories, do whatever before they read, they've put a heavier burden on themselves. They hope that I am following them, am attentive and they are holding my interest for that entire story, talk or whatever. After we're done with that, they've got to go back to a somewhat neutral place, so they can get into the character that they're reading.

• **Look at that audition as if it were a bunch of line-to-line dots** on a piece of paper. They have to take me along from dot to dot to dot to dot on this journey, which is comprised of their story and all the points of interest. Once they've finished the story there's another dot they've got to carry me to, back to that neutral place so they can be the artist. Then they've got to take me to the next dot when they begin to perform, and all the little dots that are within that performance. They hope for that entire journey, I'm with them. It's a much heavier burden doing all of that, because if they say anything that's the least bit of interest to me, it's going to be much more difficult to get me back on track and hold my attention. Whereas, if they simply come in and just begin to do their magic, the role, it's like the curtain comes up, they do the audition, the curtain comes down and they leave the stage or my office, as it were. They have a greater chance of maintaining my attention and now that they're gone and I was so enraptured with what they did, I have the potential of thinking, "Wow, I want more. That was great." The only way I can get more is by bringing them back.

• **Tony Shepherd was the Vice President of Talent for Aaron Spelling Productions for 14 years:**

Q: What do you see when an actor is entering the casting meeting?

• **If you're in the business of buying talent,** a casting director, producer or director, you can see the talent in the actor in 30 seconds or less; it's that indefinable something. You feel it; you know it. I look for a twinkle in the eye. You can't create that; it comes from within. I think the best actors are people who understand what they are about, understand what is going on in the world around them and how they relate to that world.

Q: How can an actor make the best impression?

• **Boring people make boring actors.** Work on yourself, process your life, examine how you relate to other people, how you communicate. Learn how to work with and motivate yourself and use that person from within. Acting is just a little bit bigger than real life. You are going to use who you are in everything you do. If you aren't focused, centered, honest, a risk-taking person, what kind of an actor can you ever expect to be? What you do in your daily life is directly reflected in what you do as an actor.

• **80 percent of jobs are lost,** not because the actor is right or wrong for the role or they can't act, but because something has gone wrong and they come in less than 100% focused. You don't know why, it's just that the person isn't right. In casting sessions, listen to what we say about actors: "He's cold, he has an edge, he has no warmth, he has no vulnerability, he has no strength." We're not talking about the person's acting ability, we're talking about the person, what they bring of themselves to the role they are playing or reading for. If an actor sits in a room with me and is interesting, exciting and there is a sparkle, a twinkle, an energy and a vitality about them, I can tell you right now they are going to work; it's only a matter of time.

- Finally, in your auditions and acting work, find tragedy in the comedy and humor in the drama.

• **Richard DeLancy casts, among other things, *Unsolved Mysteries*.**

Q: What will cause an actor to lose a job or not be called in again?

- **Being late. That's my number one pet peeve.** I believe that an actor's job is the interview. If you can't make the interview, then... A lady was late for her interview with producers. She was so perfect for the role but if she's going to be late for her interview with the producers, I cannot guarantee she is going to be at work on time. In New York, if you are late for your audition, you are no longer going to be considered for that role. That's the discipline I like.

• **Eventually, hopefully at some point, you'll be recognizable enough to "take a meeting."** This is when you get to the point where you're not a huge star, but people, especially casting directors, are aware of your work. This works a little different than those initial casting director meetings when you're an up-and-coming actor. But the advice is similar: Be prepared! Bonnie Gillespie wrote an amazing article on taking the meeting in her weekly column *The Actor's Voice* for Actor's Access in February, 2006 (you can look it up in the archives). In it, she mentions how it's up to the actor to be prepared and knowledgeable about everyone who might be in the room, have things to talk about other than themselves and to follow up after the meeting.

• **Clair Sinnett, independent casting director, says:**

- **Learn the business. See at least one feature film a week**, if that's the area that you want to go into. Watch television. What are some of your favorites? Who does the casting of those shows? That's the "business of the business." Know who the casting directors, directors and producers are in television as well as feature films. Once you know who they are, try to find out a little bit about them so you can send them a personal cover letter that accompanies your picture and resume every time you write them. Remember, your picture and resume is your liaison between their desk and you.

Resources

To download and print an updated version of this and all resource lists, go to actingiseverything.com.

Casting Society, castingsociety.com. Look up the members; many of their resumes are listed. They may be more up-to-date than the imdb.com listing. The site also provides an up-to-date listing of what shows casting directors are working on, invaluable information. A special actor's section provides lots of news and other resources.

Casting Directors Directory, by Breakdown Services. 310/276-9166, breakdownservices.com. 2140 Cotner Ave., Los Angeles, 90025. $45 a year for a subscription of two directories a year with updates snail-mailed every two weeks or e-mailed weekly. Casting directors move around very fast; this directory is the leader in providing the most current information because CDs use the Breakdown Service every time they're casting a new project. It also gives you a list of all the television shows and who casts them as well as CD resumes. **Casting director mailing labels** (300) for $17. You can send out notices of a film, television show or play that you would like them to see you in or just to hear that you are working. Again, your name crosses their desks. As always, check reputations. You can never have too much correct information.

Now Casting, 818/841-7165. nowcasting.com. 60 E. Magnolia Blvd., Burbank, 91502. This is a membership organization run by Union actors. As a member you can download information from their Casting Director Guide; Casting Director Labels, list of current projects and who is casting, casting director interviews, casting notices emailed to you as they receive them: you submit electronically. They also post your pictures, resume and demo reel and qualified members receive a discount at the casting director workshops. Updated agency information and labels. Membership ranges from $10-$20 a month.

Actorsite.com. Run by Jack Turnbolt. 818/762-2800. 5856 Cahuenga, North Hollywood, 91601. $40 a month or $299 a year for membership. Lots of helpful information and actor chat rooms. Free to members: monthly headshot sessions, agent workshops, several acting classes a week, and getting great advice from Jack who is always around. Extra fees: headshot dropoffs to casting directors, Casting Director Showcases, always focused on education. Great resource.

Casting Qs: A Collection of Casting Director Interviews, www.castingqs.com. by Bonnie Gillespie, the current casting columnist for *Back Stage West.*

Casting Directors Master Map by Actor's Toolbox. It is a fold out map showing the locations of all the casting directors and whether or not they accept drop-offs or mail-in submissions. Updated monthly.

The Actor's Encyclopedia of Casting Directors, by Karen Kondazian.
The Back Stage Guide To Casting Directors, by Hettie Lynn Hurtes.
Casting Directors' Secrets, by Ginger Howard.

CASTING DIRECTORS
TALK ABOUT
PILOT SEASON

COMPILED BY BONNIE GILLESPIE, AUTHOR, *CASTING Qs:*
A COLLECTION OF CASTING DIRECTOR INTERVIEWS

• *Pilot season is a very big deal in Los Angeles. Over 100 comedy and dramatic pilots may be shot during "pilot season" which runs typically from January into April. All the completed pilots will be viewed by May. That is when the networks decide on their fall schedules. The number of pilots chosen to go into production in July depends on how many returning shows each network has. Typically, 25 pilots will be picked up for the fall schedule. The network will order six to twelve shows to be produced. Many of the shows that premier in the fall will be cancelled before their third episode airs. There are usually several more pilots in limbo for mid-season replacements; they won't go into production until the fall.*

• *For casting directors, agents and many actors, pilot season is the busiest time of year. I asked Bonnie Gillespie to contribute the following chapter because she talks to and interviews the casting directors who are at the core of this frenzy of casting.*

• **Bonnie Gillespie, an author and casting director,** has taught seminars to working actors in Atlanta, New York, and Los Angeles. Her books include *Casting Qs: A Collection of Casting Director Interviews, Self-Management for Actors: Getting Down to (Show) Business*, and *Acting Qs: Conversations with Working Actors*. Bonnie specializes in casting SAG indie feature films and provides career consulting services to actors. She is co-founder and co-host of Hollywood Happy Hour and co-founder of the Flickering Image Short Film Festival. Her weekly column, *The Actors Voice,* is available at Showfax.com.

BONNIE'S CONTRIBUTION BELOW

CASTING Qs PILOT SEASON—TIPS FROM CASTING DIRECTORS

What I've learned, in talking to both casting directors and actors about pilot season, is that the stakes are high, the pressure is on, and the rewards can be unfathomably good. Of course, after six trips to producers, getting told, "We went another way," can be a crushing blow.

My advice on how to keep (relatively) sane during pilot season? Spend as much time as you can in preparation for your auditions; allow plenty of extra time to commute, park, and find your way to the audition location; and be graciously patient. Remember that pilot season affects everyone in this town, and no one should take any of that personally.

In an attempt to uncover the absolute must-haves for actors during pilot season, I contacted several casting directors with track records including TV series and pilot casting. What follows is their advice for the physical tools, the emotional strength, and the perspective on timing essential to weathering auditions through pilot season and beyond.

CONTRIBUTING CASTING DIRECTORS:

Check imdb.com for the casting directors latest credits.

Patrick Baca, CSA, who has cast several pilots and series, as well as many features.
Jeanie Bacharach, who has cast several pilots and series.
Matthew Barry, CSA, former actor who mainly casts features.
Deborah Barylski, CSA, who has cast many pilots, series, and feature films.
Jackie Briskey, CSA, who has cast soaps and series.
Lori Cobe-Ross, who has cast series and films.
Donna Ekholdt, CSA, former actor who has cast series and served as a casting executive.
Bonnie Gillespie, former actor who primarily casts independent films.
Peter Golden, CSA, pilots and series as well as overseeing a team of network TV casting directors.
Elisa Goodman, CSA, who has cast dozens of MOWs and features.
Cathy Henderson, CSA, who has cast features and pilots.
Marc Hirschfeld, CSA, pilots and series, and overseeing a team of network TV casting directors.
Lisa Miller Katz, CSA, who has cast many network sitcoms.
Mark Paladini, CSA, former actor who has cast several series.
Kevin Scott, CSA, who has cast several series.

Dan Shaner, who has cast several series and pilots.
Mark Teschner, CSA, former actor who casts soaps.
Michael Testa, who has cast several series and pilots.
Elizabeth Torres, CSA, who has cast several pilots and features.
Katy Wallin, CSA, who casts features and reality TV shows.
Paul Weber, CSA, who has cast several pilots and series.
April Webster, CSA, who has cast many series, feature films, and pilots.
Bonnie Zane, CSA, who has cast many pilots and series.

A STRONG HEADSHOT

"A good picture is your first priority. Good pictures are extraordinarily important. Don't let your lover or your mother pick the one they want on the mantle. Your head shot should say, "I'm a very good actor," to me when I look at your eyes. Let us figure out what to do with your hair. Just look like you can act." - **Cathy Henderson**

"There's a certain depth to you that comes across in your pictures. I look at the picture and resume thinking, 'Do I want to get to know this person better?'" - **Kevin Scott**

"The Casting Society of America conducted a survey of its members in 2004. The preference of headshot style is clear: Fully 99% of commercial casting directors insist on color headshots (it seems their clients require it), 95% of theatrical casting directors *do not have a preference either way* (so make your own choice, defer to your agent, etc.), and 100% of all casting directors surveyed said the most important thing is looking like your headshot (no surprise there)!" - **Bonnie Gillespie**

CONFIDENCE

"I'm looking for strong persona, charisma, distinct choices with the character, and star quality. I don't care if it's just one line. I want to see an air of confidence about you." - **Marc Hirschfeld**

"I'm looking for you to have] a comfort level with yourself. You need to feel comfortable in your own skin." - **Kevin Scott**

"I like to call it charm, but it's really a sense of humor about yourself or a sense of irony within the role that you need. Remember that it's not a personal issue when you don't get cast. It's not a statement of the quality of your work." - **Donna Ekholdt**

"It's often not about talent, but about who's *more right* for the role. Just let it go and trust that you have something unique and when it's your turn, it's your turn." - **Mark Teschner**

"Getting a callback is an indication of your talent. Be glad. You have to keep your own center and realize that getting a callback is an accomplishment. Every time I work on a pilot, I get thousands of envelopes. Piles and piles and piles! It blows my mind." - **Jeanie Bacharach**

"The hardest thing is to stay present. That's a hard process. There's whispering, there's note-taking. Keep your focus. Connect to your reader. Remember who you are, not who they want you to be. Have integrity and fill the room with your energy. Take the space. Know you're a contribution to the project. The right thing will happen. Know that casting directors are nervous at those meetings too. Be clear on your technique and focus on the task. It's not about getting the job." - **April Webster**

Actors have heard, time and again, that a good auditioning mindset is, "Behave as if you already have the role." Here's my take on that, from a callback situation on an indie feature film I was casting. We had already cast the male lead in the project. In selecting actors to play the other roles, we wanted to check chemistry between the actor hired for the lead and those who, potentially, would share the screen with him. So, we hired the lead actor for the day of final callbacks. That way, we could see him play with our top choices for the other roles and match/contrast them in all those important ways (looks, type, build, chemistry).

Here's what became obvious after just a few actors came through the room for their callbacks: There is no mistaking the auditioning actor who truly *has* the role, when you see him playing with the one who actually has already been hired.

See, our male lead had no "junk" in his head. He already had the role and was just coming to work that day, doing the part with sides in hand, playing with other actors and helping us evaluate their work. That is a beautiful thing.

So, when we saw actors who were hung up over a change they'd decided to make in their read between pre-reads and final callbacks or how much they were counting on a job like this or whatever other "junk" they brought into the room with them, we were all uncomfortable. We were watching them *try* to get the role. And we could see how high they'd made the stakes for that experience. That's *not* fun to watch.

However, it is exactly that factor that made the *right* actors stand out. When an actor walked in who had no "junk" in his head, who didn't *show us* how high he felt the stakes were for booking this gig, and who just *played* along with the lead, it was beautiful. At those moments, we were watching two pros at work. We were watching two working actors playing off one another, enjoying the process, and simply showing off their goods for an appreciative group.

The actors who came in knowing that—for the 15 minutes they were in the room with us—the role *was* theirs, were the ones who got hired for all the other roles. - **Bonnie Gillespie**

PREPAREDNESS

"You have to treat an audition like a job. Go in prepared. Be professional. Take that audition seriously. If you're given the opportunity to read the script, read the script." - **Katy Wallin**

"Don't feel, in a cold read situation, that complete wardrobe is necessary. It's a cold reading. We don't need sets, wardrobe, or props. Props are a real distraction and they show your lack of experience. Ask whatever questions you have *before* reading. Don't kick yourself after reading by wondering what the answers would've been if you had asked the questions." - **Jackie Briskey**

"Get the material ahead of time. Study it. Make a choice. Come in here and do it." - **Kevin Scott**

"Try to be as prepared as possible during pilot season. It is about the only time of year that a script should be readily available in the casting director's office, so there's no excuse for not having read and prepared the script as much as possible. Ask questions of your agent or of the assistant in the casting director's office. Know the tone of the show. Is it similar to something already on the air? There's no such thing as too much information. All of this will be helpful during an audition." - **Lisa Miller Katz**

"Remember that a sitcom really is just a 22-minute play. When you're preparing for an audition, have two or three ways of doing the role in your back pocket. The producers don't always know what they want, so they may just ask you to try something else. Have something else ready. But know that most of the time in television, they don't want you to deviate from the script." - **Deborah Barylski**

"I want to see someone who has an understanding of the text, who is good with the language, who has made strong choices—whether [those choices are] right or wrong. I want to see that you've thought it all out."
- **Jeanie Bacharach**

"Remember that, in casting a pilot, we are looking for someone that an audience will care about every week. Make your character special, someone we will want to care about and therefore want to see week after week." - **Lori Cobe-Ross**

LISTENING

"Do you listen? The most important thing about acting is what's going on in your eyes. Are you listening and reacting or just doing your lines? I know the difference." - **Jackie Briskey**

"If I'm reading with you and I pause, mid-line, and you jump in, thinking it's your cue, I know you aren't listening. If the phone rings, you should pick it up after you've *heard* the phone ring or looked to it as if the ring drew your attention there. Those details are important to the reality you should create for us. Be a good observer of people. Borrow from what you observe. It's the little things that could add to a character exactly what it needs." - **Peter Golden**

PILOT SEASON TIMING

"We get busy. I will add a casting director to our office for pilot season. The stakes are very high. Actors become overwhelmed and their priorities are skewed out of line. Be fully prepared. Your agent can help by not scheduling 12 appointments in one day. Don't be so attached to the outcome that you are depleted and your energy is gone, and you're not present for your auditions. That just adds tension." - **April Webster**

"Within four to six weeks of getting the script, we're shooting the pilot, so sometimes our casting directors hold auditions with just an outline and one scene. The actor will go from reading for the associate to the casting director, to the producer, do a callback, maybe read for the director, get to the studio level, and then final choices go to the network, all just in a few weeks." - **Peter Golden**

"Many people have multiple appointments on busy days during pilot season. If you feel the need, ask for more time. Usually that will be an option. If you're an actor who seems like you don't care about giving a cold reading, you'll be quickly dismissed during pilot season; a time when reading 100 actors a day is the norm." - **Lisa Miller Katz**

"Limit how many auditions you attend in a day. Preparation for an audition is so important, because things can move very quickly. A preread in the morning can lead to a producer's session, a studio session, and a network session within 24 hours. I don't agree with the mindset that you can *wing it* for the preread and if you get a callback, then you'll start preparing. If you connect with the material and confirm your audition, you should show your commitment from the very beginning of the process by preparing for the audition. So many times I've heard actors say, 'I didn't read the script because I had four other auditions today.' That's like going on a first date and saying, 'I would've showered but I had a couple of dates earlier.'" - **Mark Paladini**

"Listen, we enjoy doing pilots, it's just the process is so nerve-wracking. It's insane!" - **Michael Testa**

"They've talked about it for years, spreading it out a bit. Why it can't be six months instead of just three months is beyond me." - **Dan Shaner**

"Actors need to realize that although you may be the single best thing since sliced bread, the director loves you, the casting director wants to marry you, and the producer is about to call his real estate broker for that $11 million house in the hills [that sometimes] the *creative executive* doesn't 'get you' and the casting director has to start all over again. The lousiest actor in your acting class—the one with acne, bad hair, horrid breath, who won't even make his own funeral on time—will get the job because the same *creative executive* thinks that he's 'it.' So, you go home and cry and want to move back to the city from which you came and become an assistant manager at your local Home Depot. But you can't. Because as an actor, you have to keep trying. You have to understand that even if you didn't get the job, the casting director will remember you and push you and insist that smart people hire you because you have talent." - **Matthew Barry**

"Pilot season is like Las Vegas. It's the one time of year when, all of a sudden, there are more slot machines available for you [as an actor] to play on. Anyone can hit it big. Even the little old lady sitting next to you can land a pilot. If you don't hit the jackpot this time, you know there is always next year. Hopefully, you'll be a more experienced player by then." - **Patrick Baca**

"With pilots, it's always challenging to find new leading actors in the age range of 30 to 40. Right now, we're searching for an attractive leading lady in her thirties. The challenge is matching the right actor to the right role, because a lot of these actors don't have a lot of success until the right role comes along. In casting a lead character, I'm most likely not going to be surprised anymore. We have to find someone who has been around, who is established, but who hasn't yet been matched to her perfect role." - **Bonnie Zane**

"Pilot season is hard. Actors have too many auditions in a day and the test process just sucks. You've got to cut people some slack, during pilot season. Sitting in the room, we'll all say, 'This sucks,' but we're not making changes to the process. It's just the way it is. There's a lot for the actors to deal with, but there are actors who still book and do it, so the test process really separates the men from the boys, so to speak."
- **Elizabeth Torres**

"What I love to do is work with the studio and network in the pilot process. The work is creative and we come to a consensus. It is really a collaborative process, but casting is sometimes like fighting with your family. You will go through the process and then all be gratified when you've raised a good kid." - **Paul Weber**

"If casting sees a million people and the pilot is still not cast, it may work in your favor to go in at the end of their casting process, because at least they've narrowed their choices down and they have probably defined what they really want. The good news is, some things don't happen for a reason—and better, more exciting things come to you unexpectedly: you weren't right for that part, they write you a new part, the writer-producer remembers you on the next project he is doing, someone is having dinner with someone who is having trouble with casting and someone remembers and recommends you, whatever. So always do your best with integrity, commitment, your word. Never take anything personally—and don't forget to bring a cookie to the casting director if you have an appointment at 4 PM, chances are, they will need sugar and a good latte to make it through the night!" - **Elisa Goodman**

Don't Try Pilot Season Too Soon

Finally, I'd like to share an excerpt from Self-Management for Actors about making premature moves with regard to pilot season. **Bonnie Gillespie**

So very many actors from out-of-market believe that Los Angeles is "calling" them for pilot season before that is true. *Most* actors who move to L.A. for Pilot Season end up leaving after four months, angry that they spent all sorts of money for temporary housing and a long-term rental car only to sit by the phone, never getting out for more than a handful of auditions.

What I've always recommended is that actors move to Los Angeles *for good* when they are ready to pursue a film-and-television life fulltime. Now, before I go into all of the qualifiers for that statement, let me say that I *do* support the idea that some actors are perfect for pilot season *visits* if they are busy, working actors coming in from New York (or even from Toronto) with bicoastal representation. There absolutely *are* actors who can—and do—come to town and take pilot season by storm, head back to their hometowns, and live as even bigger fish for having had the experiences here. Those aren't the folks I'm talking about.

I'm talking about the actors who believe they can pick up from wherever they live with no agent or manager, no SAG card, very few credits, no demo reel, and a clearly-out-of-market headshot and come to L.A. for pilot season expecting something to happen. *Can* something happen? Of course. And, as I've said before, legends are built upon the fact that lightning does, occasionally, strike. But until you have enough credits in your local market, coming to Los Angeles to pursue a film and television performance career is simply a dream killer. And this business is hard enough as it is for that anvil to fall on your head too!

It's much better for you not to attempt a pilot season short-term move but instead build credits (and your bank account) to a point where a permanent move to pursue a lifetime career as an L.A.-based actor is feasible. Then, it's not about pilot season (which is crazymaking for even the locals, in terms of volume of auditions and hectic scheduling constraints). It's about the long haul. And you want to be an actor who "made it," right? Not an actor who "made it to L.A. for four months and came home bitter about it."

Because so much of casting is relationship-based, it is always advised that you have a team for you here before making the move. Many people find their first year here *very* lonely, if they've headed here with money and a plan... but no connections. So, start building relationships by making regular visits for networking events, showcases, and projects you can grab from where you already are. Get to as high a level in your current market as possible and then let the folks on your local team help you with the transition (via introductions and appointment-setting) when that time comes.

Also, when you do make the move, if you have never experienced a pilot season here, time your move at the *end* of pilot season—when everything slows *waaaaaay* down (say, after mid-April) so that you can get your bearings and be *ready* for the *next* pilot season, come mid-January. Actors who move here in November or December thinking they'll be ready for that immediate pilot season end up being frustrated, confused, and burned out from having put forth much futile effort, for the most part. Also, be sure to plan to give L.A. (or New York, for that matter) at least 18 months, never "just a year." That's a setup for failure, as it takes 13 months to get the lay of the land and to really know what you're do-ing—no matter where you live!

Consider your lifetime goals carefully before making big moves. Pro athletes train for many years as non-pros before they suit up profession-ally. Make sure you're ready for the big leagues before you get yourself here as nothing but a benchwarmer.

Casting Director & Agent Cold Reading Workshops

• **Cold Reading workshops give actors an opportunity** and a place to show themselves to people in the industry. Some in Hollywood feel it is unfair to ask actors to pay to meet casting directors, I believe we are paying to meet an industry person and to learn more about them. The workshops are cheaper than most acting classes and you do get to act and give your headshot to someone who could possibly call you in for an interview. For many actors, it is the only way to get seen by a casting director. Certainly for the costar television roles, this is the way be seen. Most of the casting directors will call in actors who don't have an agent. Because there is no negotiation, they typically pay union scale plus 10%. In some of the workshops I've even heard casting directors say they will call in nonunion people; it always surprises me.

• **Here is a general description** of how the workshop companies below operate. You need to audition and get accepted into the workshops. The workshops are about three hours long; there can be up to 18 actors a night. You sign up for a specific casting director or agent's office because of the type of projects they cast or the type of clients they represent. When you arrive, you sign in and are given the sides, an acting partner and about fifteen minutes to prepare. The casting director, associate, assistant or agent will come in and usually tell you something about the projects they cast or the type of clients they represent and how their particular office runs. You take notes to be used when you contact them over the years.

• **Then the readings start.** You are in the room watching the actors perform their scenes and you hear the industry person give notes and adjustments. Sometimes the actors will do the scene again. Acting coach Caryn West gives out a list of "dos and don'ts" to the actors who take her Audition Workshop. I keep the list in my workshop notebook and review it when preparing my script. Caryn is a big fan of showcasing and has been called in and cast by casting directors she has met. A couple of her hints are: Bring a picture that is most appropriate for the shows they cast, and sit in the back and very quietly work on the script, letting in new ideas.

• **Yes, they cost money,** but so does everything else you do to promote yourself. Consider showcase costs as marketing expenditures. If you don't have very many credits and don't know many casting people or agents, promotion is the name of the game. I landed my first agent at a "prepared scenes" showcase. I was called in and cast for a situation comedy by a casting director I had met at a cold reading workshop a year-and-a-half before.

• **Kathyrn Joosten,** imdb.com, moved to Los Angeles and credits all of her work to her workshops at Reel Pros. Look at her resume and see the work she has landed. She says the minute she is out of work she goes back to doing the casting director workshops.

• **Good things do happen from casting director workshops and showcases,** but you can't count on anything except getting to act for a few minutes. That, in essence, is what you are paying for. It is very hard to get a casting director or agent to come see a play. It costs to send out your flyers, make follow up calls and offer free seats that you often end up covering. I believe it is best to make peace with the cost of doing business; this is marketing.

• **When showcasing, I strongly suggest** you read your script and rehearse at least once through on your own. Decide the given circumstances, what the script tells you about the scene, and what your character needs and wants. Then rehearse with your partner. Set up whether one of you is entering, whether you are standing or sitting, give the scene a little blocking. When at a good showcase you will be working with experienced actors. Most of the actors will nearly memorize their lines; they will look at the script very few times while performing the scene for the casting director. You must practice reading scripts every day and learn to look down and grab the lines. Also work on memorizing every day so it becomes second nature. It is like riding a bike—it seems impossible at first and easy after you know how to do it. Train like an Olympic athlete. Go for the gold!

• **The term "cold reading" is not an accurate description** of what you are doing. You are giving a warm reading. A cold reading means performing the scene as you are reading it for the first time. Under a true audition situation, you have your script the day before an audition and are expected to give a finished, polished, opening night performance in the office of the person or people you are auditioning for. In the workshop atmosphere, the casting director knows you have had only a few minutes to make your acting choices.

• **I believe** you should feel pretty confident about your cold reading skills before being seen at a showcase. Learn about auditioning from your acting teachers, have a few auditions, land a few roles, become SAG eligible, and then show yourself to casting directors at workshops. When you have acting experience, the casting director will have more to work with and will remember you as a good actor.

• **Sharon Lawrence** said when she first came to town she did casting director workshops. She chose the casting directors very carefully, picking shows she felt she would be right for. Sharon met casting director Junie Lowry-Johnson's assistant; they called her and she booked a guest star spot on the series *Civil Wars*. When a part came up for a district attorney on *NYPD*, Junie remembered her and brought her in for the interview. She was cast and then became a regular for several seasons.

• **Rebecca McFarland** was one of George's girlfriends on *Seinfeld*. It was her fourth Los Angeles job. She had moved here the year before with a college degree, many theater credits and SAG eligibility. A friend asked Rebecca to audition with him for an agent he wanted—the agent took her and not him. When I met her on *Seinfeld* she told me she was getting her work by showcasing every week and being called in by the casting directors. You will see by checking her credits how much she has worked in these years since that beginning year. She has developed a working actor's career.

• **Casting director's jobs depend on bringing in actors that read well.**

• **I know many experienced actors**, including myself, who have landed auditions and roles from showcasing. Again, go, watch and decide for yourself if you feel showcasing is a worthy place for some of your marketing dollars.

• **One of my students sends a picture, resume and short note** to the casting director before he does a showcase, typically saying, "I'm looking forward to meeting you at such and such showcase."

• **A theatrical agent talks about the value of cold reading workshops with casting directors.**

> • **When your agent sends your picture and resume to a casting director,** that casting director may have received 700-2,000 submissions for the same role. First, they bring in who their bosses told them to. The second group of actors are friends who could do the job. The third group are professionals who work all the time who they know can do that job. And the last person is the unknown picture in the pile that they have no knowledge of. My feeling is, you can jump from kindergarten to first grade if you can do the cold reading workshops with the casting director. I think they're extremely valuable for the good actor. Out of 16-20 people they see in a workshop, they're looking for the gem. If you're very good, they're going to remember you. You've now put yourself past the picture and resume that's been put across their desk by an agent. You're now a human being and they know a little bit about you.

• **Actors who don't understand** how a casting office works think that showcasing for an assistant or associate isn't as authentic as auditioning for the casting director. Most casting offices have a casting director, an assistant and an associate; they may have several associates depending on how busy the office is. The casting director is out looking for more jobs and negotiating with the agents. They train the people in their office to work in their style so they can trust them to go through the hundreds of submissions for each role and pull out the people to audition. The showcase producers at a legitimate top-level group like those below will screen the people they bring in. They depend on their reputations to stay in business. You go to the showcases that attract the top-level people. There are plenty of showcasing outfits that do not have high standards. Don't go to them. Pick and choose the people you want to audition for; you never have to blindly pay for a showcase of someone you are not interested in meeting. As in most career choices, you are in charge.

• **Beware of scams when looking into showcases.** There are some unethical people who call actors that have submitted their pictures to casting directors. The actors are told, "You need to showcase with me in order to work." Do not accept phone calls from people you have not submitted to, who say they don't know how they got your picture or who gave it to them. *See the Scams Section.*

Resources

To download and print an updated version of this and all resource lists, go to actingiseverything.com.

The following groups have good reputations. Investigate carefully; reputations can change.

SAG & AFTRA **members** are eligible for the union showcases. sagfoundation.org, aftra.org.

Actorsite, JP Turnbolt 818/762-2800. actorsite.com. 5856 Cahuenga Blvd., North Hollywood, 91601. You must audition for the showcase. Showcasing is just a small part of the services they offer for actors. Agent Carlyne Grager highly recommends this showcase for the actors she represents. This is the place I showcase because I like working with the other actors, everyone is friendly and encouraging. I believe Jack attracts the best guests. I always get auditions when I am actively showcasing. *In compliance with the LAAWC guidelines.*

Reel PROs, 818/788-4133. reelpros.com. 13437 Ventura Blvd., Ste. 220 Sherman Oaks. "The Workshop for Professional Talent." Run by actors, for actors. They take great pride in the showcase and have a very careful audition process. Actors are placed in one of two groups; RP2 for actors who play ages 18-26 and Players for actors who play 27 and up. Through cold read and acting work, actors acquire credits. If they're good, they're asked to join the Main Arena, if not, their membership is terminated. Workshop prices start at $34 with series packages available. $50 annual membership fee. *In compliance with the LAAWC guidelines.*

Act Now!, 818/285-8522. actnownetwork.com. 14140 Ventura Blvd, Ste 203, Sherman Oaks, 91423. Their audition process consists of three cold readings by appointment only. Costs vary but average around $50. Directors, agents and casting directors. Staff provides ongoing guidance and support to help each actor set and meet their professional goals. *In compliance with the LAAWC guidelines.*

Casting Network, 818/788-4792. castingnetwork.net. 12500 Riverside Dr., #202, Studio City, 91607. Free orientations & cold reading auditions. $30 plus per session, discount when you buy a series. Many sessions a week. Directors, agents and casting directors. Call for their brochure. Strong acting background and/or union affiliation required. *In compliance with the LAAWC guidelines.*

In the Act Productions, 310/839-8311. itaproductions.com. 10820 Washington Blvd., Culver City, 90232. Audition required. There is a $45 processing new member fee for those accepted and a $30 annual membership fee. This also gives you your own web page on Casting911.com for one year. Prices vary depending upon the workshop. *In compliance with the LAAWC guidelines.*

One On One Productions, 661/263-2887. oneononeproductions.com. 451 N. La Cienega, L.A., 90048. Office hours: M-F 11-5. Average $28 and up, special for series. Audition required, they are held each Wednesday between 1-3:30, no appointment necessary. Guests include casting directors, agents, directors and producers. *In compliance with the LAAWC guidelines.*

Talent To Go: talenttogo.com. This is a prepared scene showcase different from what I have been talking about above. Several managers I know like their clients to present scenes through this company. So look at their website and see if it might be something for you.

• *For Audition Material and Cold Reading Teachers, see Section One.*

Nudity,
The Casting Couch
and Sexual Orientation

NUDITY REQUIRED

• **Julia Roberts, John Travolta, Sandra Bullock, Cameron Diaz**, Freddie Prinze Jr., Sarah Jessica Parker, Sarah Michelle Gellar, Andy Garcia, Scarlett Johanson, Kirsten Dunst, Winona Ryder, Alicia Silverstone all put no-nudity clauses in their contracts. Many actresses use black electrician tape on their breasts so the camera operators won't shoot what they're not supposed to. Geena Davis advises, "If there are parts of you that you don't want the crew to see make sure the tape is very visible."

• **If you play a leading actress** you will most likely need to make the decision of whether or not you will do nudity in your career and under what circumstances. Diane Lane in *Unfaithful* and Kathy Bates in *About Schmidt* were nominated for 2002 Oscars. Christina Ricci in *Prozac Nation*, said it was "really difficult." Jenny McCarthy has built a career using her *Playboy* centerfold as a launching pad, although now she says she won't do nudity. Darryl Hannah and Jamie Lee Curtis both made the transition from nudity-required "B" movies to big budget mainstream films. In Debra Winger's first movie, she had her top off *(Slumber Party '57)*. Sylvester Stallone was nude in *The Italian Stallion*, a low-budget soft-porn movie. Many actors have appeared nude, yet they haven't hurt their careers—in fact they may have propelled them: Richard Gere in *American Gigolo*, Minnie Driver in *The Governess*, Camryn Manheim in *The Road To Wellsville*, Tim Curry in *The Rocky Horror Picture Show*, Isabella Rossellini in *Blue Velvet*, Natassia Kinski in *Cat People*, Glenn Close in *The Big Chill*, Kim Basinger in *9 1/2 Weeks*, Sharon Stone in *Basic Instinct*, Emma Thompson in *The Tall Guy*, Heather Graham in *Boogie Nights* and others. Holly Hunter won the 1993 Oscar for *The Piano* where she had a beautiful nude love scene and Harvey Keitel exposed his penis. There are some roles where a body double was used. Jane Fonda in *Coming Home* and Julia Roberts in *Pretty Woman* used body doubles.

• **There are the low-budget,** teen-exploitation, horror or comedy movies. Often, an actress' career can get locked in this genre and—because they have done one or two—that's how they will be cast. The producer will say, "You did it for that movie, so you have to do it for mine." Elizabeth Berkley got typecast after she did *Showgirls.*

• **If you never want authentic nude pictures of your body on the internet,** then never allow yourself to be photographed nude. Alyssa Milano, Pamela Anderson and Dr. Laura Schlessinger went through law suits because old boyfriends had sold shots of them nude. Leonardo DiCaprio sued *Playgirl* because they used frames of his nude butt from his movie *Total Eclipse.* Charlize Theron's pictures ended up in *Playboy* because she had signed a release for pictures taken for her portfolio before she was famous.

• **Once you consent to work nude,** it is very difficult to take the decision back. Matthew McConaughey posed with his girlfriend in the nude in exchange for a few roles of headshots for acting pictures. When Matthew became a big hit, the photographer threatened to sell the photos. Beginning bids were half a million dollars. Remember the Vanessa Williams scandal—losing the Miss America crown because of the *Penthouse* magazine pictures? She survived and has gone on to become a major singer-actress. When Suzanne Somers was at the height of her sitcom success with *Three's Company,* *Playboy* ran pictures that she had modeled for when she needed money to raise her son. What is there to consider in making the decision? If it's a strong moral dilemma, don't compromise yourself. If it is not a moral issue, discuss it with your agent or manager in relation to your career. If you choose to do it, the things you have to consider are:

> • Are you able to be nude in front of the cast and crew of a movie set?
> • Will the scenes be shot in a tasteful way?
> • Is the nudity important to the story line or there just for the sake of nudity?
> • Videotapes and DVDs of your movies will live forever.
> • The time it will take to keep your body looking great.
> • Be honest with yourself; come to a decision you can live with.

• **I was director Joan Darling's assistant** when she directed William Katt and Susan Dey in their first nude love scenes in the feature film, *First Love*. Joan, a wonderfully sensitive director, discussed the design and choreography of each move. After the first day of shooting, the actors seemed to get used to it. They were both beautiful and in full body make up. After a week, cast and crew were all very bored and eager to get them out of bed and on to the rest of the shooting.

• **David Niven** said to one of the actresses he was doing a love scene with, "I'm sorry if I get aroused and I'm sorry if I don't." Now that is a true gentleman for you.

• **Olivia d'Abo** discussed her role with Armin Muller Stahl in *The Last Good Time*.

> • **After the film was edited,** the director asked me to reshoot the scene of me walking out of the bathroom and this time actually dropping the towel so the audience could see what Armin was reacting to. I decided that it was important to the film. When nudity is totally organic and motivated by the scene and the actor is comfortable within their own skin and vulnerable in that moment, it works.

• **I asked Olivia about having love scenes with such an older man.** She said, "He's got baby's eyes, it made me want to mother him, to take care of him." She also talked of her deep respect for him as an actor. These feelings also parallel the plot of the film.

• **Liv Tyler removed her top in** *Stealing Beauty*, but declined to do so in *Onegin*.

• **Leonardo DiCaprio;** *Total Eclipse* and *The Beach*. "Nudity is really tough but you have to do it if it's part of the film."

• **Mira Sorvino was nude in** *At First Sight*. When asked about it on *Entertainment Tonight* she said, "Have a sense of humor about it. Trust the people you are working with and have a generally good atmosphere on the set."

• **Daryl Hannah hid behind hair extensions in** *Splash*. She said, "If there was a role I really wanted to play and that was the only way I could get it, hell, I'd do it. Though I would really rather not."

• **Nicole Kidman and Iain Glen were both naked on stage** in New York doing the play Blue Room. Iain did nude cartwheels. *People* magazine asked Iain, "How did the decision to appear naked come about?"

> • **We shook hands and said, "I'll do it if you do it."** And that's when we went for it, really. It's a very strange feeling being naked. It does make you feel vulnerable. But the thing that grounds us is trying to be inside the scene so that it's not about a thousand people watching you but one person—the character—watching you.

• **Bridget Fonda's first film was a NYU film,** *Aria.* There were 10 different directors directing 10 minute segments based on opera arias. There was no dialogue, just nudity and death. She "went for it all, first time out."

• **Gwyneth Paltrow says she used a body double** in a brief strip scene in *Great Expectations* because, "I would have had to not wear a bra, and I just didn't want to do that in front of the crew."

• **Angela Bassett says she was asked to undress** for *How Stella Got Her Groove Back.* She decided to keep her private parts private. That way, the audience "can put their own ideas of love and sensuality into it."

• **Halle Berry,** was lying facedown naked in *Introducing Dorothy Dandridge.* When asked if it was a body double or her body she said, "I'm not really comfortable with nudity in films. I doubt I'll do it again, but because that is how Dorothy was found dead, to stay true to history, I had to do it." She of course did do it again for *Swordfish* and her Oscar-winning performance in *Monster's Ball.*

• **Sally Field** said in an *Actors' Studio* interview: "What is the big deal about taking your clothes off? It's about the acting work."

• **Holly Hunter** in an *Actors' Studio* interview, when asked what it was like to do the sex scenes in *The Piano.*

> • **Very easy. The sex scenes became integral to the story.** It was necessary to the movie to see the unveiling of those characters. No big deal—by then the crew were all family.

• **Julianne Moore was asked** in the *Los Angeles Times* how her family dealt with the many times she has done nudity, especially in *Boogie Nights.*

> • **My mother has always said,** "I'd much rather see you naked than dead." It's funny, but it's true. What's really disturbing, when you look at a movie, is seeing a dead body. But how scary is it to see your daughter walk across a room with no clothes on? Not very. But if you see her shot up a million times or have her head cut off, that's scary.

• **You just hope you're in a situation that's safe.** I did a nude scene in *Body of Evidence* that was just awful. I was too young to know better. It was the first time I'd been asked to get naked and it turned out to be completely extraneous and gratuitous. Ugh. It was a terrible film and a terrible performance by me. It was about nothing, and I didn't need to be doing it.

• **Ashley Judd** said that she won her applause prior to filming a lengthy nude scene. She arrived on the set in a robe and blithely announced, "Hi, I'm Ashley and I'm going to be nude for the next 12 hours. I'm not embarrassed and I hope you won't be either." The actress then dropped her robe and said, "This is my body." The ovation swelled.

• **Faye Dunaway,** in an *Actors' Studio* interview.

  • **What is really difficult is to reveal your soul,** your pain, your vulnerability. That's what has to happen, no matter whether you have clothes on or not. Nudity comes with the territory of movies. The actual clothes on or off is less important than the emotional nudity. In bed usually exposes moments of extreme vulnerability and openness—that's what is difficult.

• **Jennifer Jason Leigh says:**

  • **I don't have a problem with nudity** if I think it moves the story forward and says something about the character. But no matter how truthfully and honestly it's portrayed, it still seems to bother people.

• **Kate Winslet, when asked how comfortable she was** with her first nude scene in *Jude*, said:

  • **Not at all! No way! Oh, it was awful.** I was so nervous, I starved myself for a month beforehand. I went through all the paranoias: "My bum's massive. My breasts are saggy. I've got a spotty back. Chicken arms. I can't do it." I just had to keep remembering that the scene was a real turning point in the story and to get on with it. At the end of the day, you forget that you're completely naked.

• **Stephanie Stephenson,** after landing a choice role in the touring production of the Broadway musical *Les Misérables,* quit the next day when she learned she would also have to play a prostitute in an ensemble scene.

• **I have a friend who is very cute.** His first day on the set in his first starring role in a *Showtime* movie, he was required to be completely nude, making love with Laura Flynn Boyle. They didn't know each other and, right off the bat, they were both totally nude and in bed. He said it was uncomfortable but got on with the task and was proud of his work. Incidently, he is gay; but this was an acting job, not a date.

• **Selma Blair** has done scenes with nudity in films like *The Sweetest Thing, Storytelling* and *Cruel Intentions*. In an interview with *Back Stage West*, she suggests;

> • **Don't be nervous about your body.** If you're comfortable in it, then everyone around you will be comfortable. It's really just another costume you're putting on for the day.

• **Nudity can be a perfectly wonderful part of artistic expression** or it can be in poor taste and a career risk. It is such a personal decision—I suggest you search and follow your heart. Trust your educated instincts. *See manager Tami Lynn's remarks in the chapter on Personal Managers.*

• **The Screen Actors Guild nudity clause** states that an actor should always be informed of nudity in a project before the first audition. Also, total nudity is not required at auditions. Performers are required to give their consent on still photography, sex acts and the use of body doubles. Also, performers should expect a "closed set," meaning the only people in the room are those that are needed to film the scene. Many actors will expand on this clause, requiring a "nudity rider," which gives the artist the right to approve the final cut of their love scenes.

• **Bonnie Gillespie, a casting director** and author of *Casting Qs: A Collection of Casting Director Interviews, Self-Management for Actors,* and *Acting Qs: Conversations with Working Actors.* In one of her weekly columns, *The Actors Voice*, at Showfax.com, she talked about how to protect yourself when doing nonunion projects.

> • **So, you agree to star** in a (nonunion) film based on your interest in the script as it existed as of a particular date. Great. You sign a contract in which you state you'll perform the services of an actor in the designated role in the project of a particular title based on that script and your meetings with the principals involved (producers, director, writer, other actors, etc.). In the contract, there is no mention of nudity and in the script you're holding, there is no nudity for your character (implied or explicit). But you show up to set one day and are asked to do the scene nude.

> • **Okay, this is where the script comes into play.** If nudity is not spelled out in your contract and there is no nudity in the script upon which you made your decision to participate, there shouldn't be any nudity asked of you on set. This is why it's important to hang onto the version of the script that existed as of your contract date, since revisions could

suddenly cause you to be topless (all the more reason to be sure your contract spells out that you're agreeing to do a role based on a script that existed as of a certain date). That way, if you are told that you have violated your contract, you are being bullied! If nothing in your contract or the script says otherwise, you can assume that you signed on to do a fully-clothed role.

• **So, even though you don't have SAG backing you,** you should still always have someone look over your contract, whether it be an entertainment attorney, small business legal aid or an agent/manager friend. Obviously, each person has a different level of expertise with this sort of thing (and accountability for the advice given), but until you have the backing of SAG, you should still check in with others if you are ever unsure of a contract's language.

CASTING COUCH

• **The so-called casting couch still exists.** There are people who will promise actors roles in film and television in exchange for their bodies and there are actors who will go for it. There are also actors who will make the offer first. Sometimes it works—the actor gets a job, but most often the actor gets no job, loss of self-respect and loss of reputation (a fragile commodity when you're trying to build a career.) I've seen actors waste enormous amounts of time trying to take this way to a career that resulted in one or two minor jobs and loads of broken promises.

• **Be honest with yourself**—have a fling if you choose because you think it might be fun and worth the risks, but don't fool yourself. With very few exceptions, the "casting couch" has not been a winning journey.

• **There are SAG regulations governing franchised agents** or sub-agents which make it a violation as a condition of representation "to request of an actor a nude or semi-nude interview, or to request that an actor engage in sexual activity." Any breach of this regulation should be reported immediately to SAG.

• **Agent Bonnie Howard of Howard Talent West** received a package addressed to "Mr. Howard." In it was a pair of sexy, new panties, a piece of candy, a condom and a letter requesting an interview.

• **Talent agent Wallace Kaye** was tried, found guilty and sentenced to five years and four months in jail for sexual attacks on eleven aspiring actresses and models ranging in age from 20 to 35. He would engage them in various improvisational scenes that were sexual in nature. The "auditions" were scheduled in the early morning or late evening behind locked doors. At a certain point in the scenes, he would force himself on them, putting his tongue in their mouths, fondle and kiss their breasts, grab their buttocks—all while they were physically restrained.

• **The law says that sexual harassment exists** when attention is unwanted or unwelcome. The moment your relationship with someone changes for you, and you say so, you are a victim of sexual harassment if that attention continues.

• **Sidney Poitier** advised Denzel Washington at the beginning of his career: "Be very careful of how you start in Hollywood. The first two, three or four movies will determine how the town looks at you. The choices you make then will affect the rest of your career."

• **Eve Brandstein**, producer, casting director and author of *The Actor: A Practical Guide To A Professional Career,* was a guest on my cable show. One of my students at the time, Cynthia Geary *(Northern Exposure)*, asked:

Q: Does the casting couch exist?

- • **There is something like that going on all the time.** The casting couch exists in life, not just in a casting director or producer's office. This particular profession you're involved in is a very seductive profession. I believe what an actor brings to the audition or to the interview or movie is a certain amount of sexual energy, the creativity, charisma, beauty, the specialness of the person. You have to use that to make your work great, and that is sexy and at the same time you're trying not to be seductive. So you're doing two things—you're sending the message "Pay attention. Hey, how do I look? Do you notice me?" So there is something confusing; some people get mixed messages. Then there's the good old fashioned situation where you're attractive to somebody or you find them attractive. By the way, the casting couch goes both ways; it can be a two-way experience. Nobody is an unwilling victim.

- • **Bottom line is it's a personal decision.** I recommend you walk out of the room if somebody's putting the make on you as an actor. I don't think it's worth the risk. A lot of times it turns out to be a very bad thing for the actor. The person in power is certainly less at risk. If you feel you're being harassed or asked to do something that is obviously inappropriate for that interview or that audition that deals with your sexuality, I say get out of the room as politely and nicely as you can. Do not be offensive; leave. You are dealing with someone who has problems you do not understand and it could possibly even turn against you. Leave but follow it up. Make sure your agent knows. Report it to someone.

• **A young actor I know arrived in town from Texas** with a list from his teacher of a few people to look up. I was one of them. We met and he enrolled in class. Three days later, I got a call from him. He was ready to leave town. He had met with a casting director who was on his list and the man was very nice and helpful. He asked the actor to pick him up at his home to go out to dinner to talk further about his career. The actor was very pleased to be having dinner with this well-respected person in the industry within his first week of hitting town.

• **During dinner, the casting director** spoke of specific actors he knew who were not gay but had sex with male casting directors in order to land their roles. My friend was shocked at the conversation and revelation and said he could never do anything like that. When they arrived back at the casting director's home, he invited the actor in to pick up some scenes to practice with. When they got inside, the actor stayed for a time talking, still reveling in being in this man's company. Eventually the man put on a porno tape and tried to seduce him. The actor fled, didn't sleep that night and called me early in the morning. I pointed out that perhaps he had been too nice during the dinner conversation when his instincts sensed it was going in a sexual direction. I also pointed out the casting director was wrong to take advantage of his profession in trying to seduce him. To give the casting director a break (a very big break), perhaps he felt the actor was hanging around waiting to be hit on.

• **It's been ten years since this incident** and the young actor has gone on to a very nice career in all areas of our business and may be on his way to stardom. I'm sure he smiles now at his naiveté.

• **Make the decision as to how far you will go sexually** to land a part before you are in a situation where you must decide in the moment. Most actors have never faced a casting couch situation; I hope you never do. I hope it's always your talent, look and personality they want.

SEXUAL ORIENTATION

• **I believe in freedom of choice in matters of personal sexuality.** "To thine ownself be true." However, if an actor is perceived as gay due to certain types of mannerisms, this can be limiting to the actor's castability in certain types of roles.

• **On my cable show, an actor asked Eve Brandstein:**

Q: How do you advise actors who are gay in how honest they should be with their agents and casting directors?

> • **It depends;** I certainly don't think it's something you have to bring up since it's a personal issue in a very professional circumstance. If an actor has heard that they are perceived as gay, it may create a closing-in of how they'll be cast. If you don't want your casting possibilities perhaps narrowed, it's perfectly okay to make a decision and adjust to how you are perceived.

• **I would like to add to Eve's comments** that an actor must always be working on their image and must understand it is important to learn how you are being perceived. It's hard to look at ourselves honestly, but it's necessary.

• **An actor once came to me for private coaching** because he had accidentally overheard the people in his theater group laughing and talking about him, saying he would be foolish to think he would be considered for a certain role because he was so obviously gay. The actor didn't understand what this meant. When he told me the story, he was choking back his tears. He had left the company and had been off sulking for a few weeks but then decided to face the truth of how he was being perceived.

• **When I met him, he did display mannerisms** that were probably inappropriate for the wide range of roles he was physically "right" for. The fact that he actually was not gay had nothing to do with his image problem. When we got on camera, he talked and walked and did some of his stand-up comedy act. Then I played back the tape so he could observe himself. He quickly developed an understanding of his own body language and appearance and was able to adjust his physical expression to create a more effective image. I saw him a few years later. He was fine and had gone on to a wonderful working career. While gay actors certainly play powerful, masculine roles, no actor can get such specific roles without the appropriate image.

• **Another actor was sent to me by a commercial casting director** who said "The actor is wonderful but with his mannerisms, he will never land a commercial." This actor happened to be gay, but the concern to me was not sexual orientation, but rather the actor's physical believability playing certain types of characters. After studying and analyzing the way he came across, he made some adjustments which improved his castability in a wider range of roles for his physical type. Within a year, he had landed eight commercials and continues to have a very lucrative commercial career.

• **What about playing a homosexual?** You and your agent must decide what's best for your career. You must decide if you can be comfortable showing affection in or out of bed with a person of the same sex if the script calls for it. Also, you must consider the idea of being typecast. Tom Hanks won the Oscar for *Philadelphia*, playing a gay man dying of aids. Hal Holbrook played a homosexual father in *That Certain Summer;* Matthew Broderick in *Torch Song Trilogy,* Aidan Quinn in the television movie, *An Early Frost.* William Hurt won the Academy Award for *Kiss Of The Spider Woman.* Will Smith *(Fresh Prince)* played a gay man in *Six Degrees of Separation,* but refused to do the sex kiss as it was written in the script, so they used a camera angle that looked like they kissed. These roles certainly didn't hurt the actors, but all of them had previously played roles as straight men.

• **More roles are opening up for men and women gay characters.** Ellen "came out" on her show. *Will & Grace* was a hit. There are also edgier, meatier gay roles on shows like *Queer as Folk* and *The L Word.* Prime time sitcoms and dramas are also seeing an influx of metrosexual roles.

• **Agent Bonnie Howard went to a play, *Bar Girls*,** in which all the characters were lesbians—very sexually explicit. One of the women was seeking representation and asked to meet her. Bonnie assumed she was gay. She said, "No, I'm an actress." Bonnie signed her on the spot because she had been so convincing.

• **You do not have to divulge your sexual orientation;** it is nobody's business. You are an actor, and if you wish to play gay and straight characters, it is your choice.

WORKING ON THE SET

Download the On-The-Set Glossary of Terms from my website, actingiseverything.com.

• **Katharine Graham said it best,** "To love what you do and feel that it matters...how can anything be more fun."

• **First and most important, you have the job**. It is yours. You might as well act on that instead of thinking, "Oh no! Someone is going to take this away from me." Yes, it can happen—sometimes actors are replaced after casting, because someone (producer, director, etc.) changed their concept of the character.

• **One day on** *Seinfeld,* all the actors and crew were on the New York street rehearsing a scene. A guest actor was back on the stage complaining, wondering how long he was going to be there, generally pestering the 2nd A.D. Jerry happened to hear over the walkie-talkies that there was a problem. He called the line producer, asked her to fire the actor and call casting to bring in someone else. The next season, this actor was the star of his own show and all the gossip was how horrible he was to work with. His show lasted just one season.

• **So yes, your worst fears are possible**—you can lose the job. But the odds are in your favor that you will do the job. Let go of the idea that somehow you won't live up to the role and that you can't deliver what is necessary. You can do it like no one else in the world can. Use your energy to focus on *how* to do the job, not in fear of not being able to do it. Make that role come to life through you.

• **Fear starts with a "what if" thought**. "What if I mess up?" "What if I'm not good?" Stop these thoughts and instead, create thoughts of how wonderful you are going to be. "I'm going to be satisfied with my performance." "I'm wonderful at what I do." Fear is a misuse of your imagination.

• **Jerry Seinfeld told a good/bad story on the set one day.** The first sitcom he was hired on, as a regular, was *Benson*. When he came to the set for the table reading of the fourth show he would be shooting, the assistant director called him over and said they had forgotten to call him and tell him he was fired. He had to leave the stage. He said, "That is when I knew I had to have my own show, so that could never happen to me again."

• **When doing a situation comedy,** there will be a table reading. If you have a significant role, you will be at the reading. Prepare for it like you did for your audition. If you can't get the script the night before, see what time you can pick it up from the office. Go sit in your car or the commissary and mark your script and rehearse your role. The writers need to hear you deliver the lines so they can see what works. Dress close to what you wore for the audition and look like you looked when they gave you the job. You are the guest; you want everyone to see why you were cast.

• **In order to study the finest of sitcom acting,** record or TiVo *Seinfeld* reruns or buy the DVDs. Each of the characters has a different form of comedy. Study how they deliver the lines; notice how it is not about the line, but the delivery. Of course, *Seinfeld* also had brilliant writers. More about comedy in the *Comedy* chapter.

• **Bobbie Eakes of *The Bold and the Beautiful* was a student of mine** when she first moved here. She had been Miss Georgia. Being cast on the daytime drama was one of her first acting jobs. She was on the show for 10 years; she talks about when she first started.

> • **The main thing for me when I was starting out and still very green** was, you fake it. You try to let them think you are completely confident even if you are nervous because they just want to know that you are going to be able to take the ball and run with it and do your job. Just try to be confident or exude confidence, even if you are not.

• **For your first time working on a set,** here are a few hard and fast rules that cannot be broken:

• **If you accept a job, you must show up on time** and you must stay there until you are told you can leave or at wrap time. Always report to the Assistant Director when you arrive and when you leave the set for any reason. Sign out with the A.D. at the end of the day.

• **Being on time can be a chore.** Make a trial run before the first day, if possible. Check out where the parking will be. If you are going on location there should be a map attached to the call sheet. If you are not on the set, have them fax it to you or to your copy service where you receive faxes. You will probably have a ten or fifteen minute walk to the set from your car—wear comfortable shoes to get there. You may be delayed checking through security at the studio gate. Allow yourself the longest time it could take to get to the set, not the shortest.

• **Never look directly in the camera**; never talk or move when they have called "rolling" unless you are in the scene. Talk very quietly on the set, even when the camera is not rolling.

• **Never walk through a door** when a red light is on; it means the camera is rolling/shooting.

• **If you have an injury**, do not leave the set without reporting it to an assistant director. This happened to me. My finger was broken. I didn't realize it because I had been acting and the adrenaline was going. Luckily, the makeup person insisted I report it. Surgery was required to correct the break, which would have been very expensive if I hadn't reported it on the job.

• **When you are shooting you must focus** all your concentration on your acting work. You will be getting direction on where to hit your mark. You have to keep track of an activity you are doing to make sure you do the same thing on every take so the editor can cut in and out of takes. This may be your toughest assignment, there is usually so much activity going on around you.

• **Buy the book,** *The Camera Smart Actor* by Richard Brestoff. Read it the night before every new job. Take it with you. If you get scared and feel like you don't know what you are doing, you can read it in your dressing room.

• **Michael Richards, Kramer on** *Seinfeld*, in an interview with the *Los Angeles Times* said:

  • **It is hard work. Deep down I always enjoy the process,** but I find you have to work very hard to get to the moments where you surprise yourself—spontaneous moments where something comes through that wasn't in the script, the table reading or any discussions. That's always exciting. It feels holy.

- **Mira Sorvino said in an interview:**

  - **I was absolutely neurotic doing *Mighty Aphrodite*.** Every night brought a new nervous breakdown. I'd cry and talk to God, I was so nervous. Then the next day, I'd show up and do my scenes.

- **Director/writer/coach Anthony Caldarella,** imdb.com, talks about how an actor prepares on set before shooting the scene.

  - **Relaxation on camera is crucial.** You've done homework on the script, now stay relaxed and flexible, so that you can truly work off your scene partners and collaborate with the director. Remember, you were chosen for the role, for who you are and what you did in the audition. If you have made new discoveries about your role, tell the director or just show him what you want to do.

- **In an interview in the *Hollywood Reporter*,** the three following actors talked of what it takes to deliver on the set.

  - **Robbie Benson:** At a moment's notice, you can be transformed into another world. Ten seconds before the director says "Action!" you are yourself, yet with that one word, you put your entire soul into what you're playing. It becomes an obsession, especially when it works and you know that it's working. You realize that your performance contributed to the film in that one moment. Even if they cut it, you think about that one moment that works. That moment carries you through all the bad moments. It's like baseball and that one perfect crack of the bat. You're going to keep swinging to hear that crack once more.

  - **Rutger Hauer:** Actors make films for the same reason people go to see them—it's a chance to share the dream, the drama, the comedy, the horror, the fantasy of life. The audience wants to buy it and we want to give it. The key element is "Don't act." The moment the camera comes on, the moment it starts to roll, the actor's third eye goes into focus and he or she begins to live the part.

  - **Susan Blakely:** Besides knowing your craft, there should be the ability to be spontaneous, to be intuitive, to feel how much you are projecting in front of the camera compared to what you project in real life. The spontaneity is so important, especially in television because you don't do much rehearsing, if any. You need to be open and loose so you can change things and react at the right moment. The best actors are able to be creative on their feet.

• **When you are the star of a project you will set the tone** for the whole on-set family. I admire the actors who show up on time and ready to go; it is rude to be late, to keep sixty people waiting for you.

• **In television there will be times** when, as a guest, you won't be able to rehearse with the star because they don't want to work that hard anymore. Give it your all, when rehearsing with the stand-ins. Don't let a situation like this hurt your shot on that show.

• **Gossip—the crew is full of it,** and when you are a guest you will be the target of some of it. There is so much empty time to pass and people who have been together for a long time have talked about everything there is to talk about so they are looking for anything new. Try to be a welcome addition to every set you go on.

• **Members of the crew often don't understand the way actors work.** They can't understand why you don't hit your mark and say your lines perfectly every time so they can go home. Don't look to them to judge your acting. The director and other actors can be trusted much more, although you may not get feedback.

• **Director Robert Altman** was asked how actors act? He responded:

  • **They bring their personality to it.** Anybody can do this; it's just if they will. They can act if they get past that barrier of self-consciousness. All the experience you need is in your head. If they have the opportunity to do it and they have the confidence, they can break that shell and let the truth of themselves show. It's all in everybody's mind, it's in everybody's computer. We all sit there and say, "I'd do this or I'd do that"...that's all it is.

• **Steven Spielberg asked Dee Wallace** why actors get so weird on the set. She gave him this explanation:

  • **Actors are like race horses;** they are trained to get in the starting gate and go. When in hair, makeup, and wardrobe, they are getting ready and when the gate doesn't open for five hours, they get worn out.

• **William H. Macy,** when asked if there was such a thing as over-preparing, told *Back Stage West*:

  • **Perhaps not over-preparing, but useless preparation.** I've been guilty of it, and I think many actors are. You're going to play the Pope, and so you start trying to figure out: What does it mean to be the

Pope? What does the Pope read? What was the Pope's childhood like? What does the Pope do when he prays? And I think the mature actor ultimately realizes, "There's no way I can know any of that, and even if I did know it, there's no way I can act on it. I *am* the Pope—end of story." So that ends my preparation. Sure, you've got to figure out how Catholics do the service and all of that stuff. But that ain't about acting; that's about physicalizations and anybody can do that. Who is the Pope? You are the Pope. Quit auditioning. You've got that role.

• **The set is the most grown-up place to be.** At first appearances it seems that there are a lot of people to take care of you; Wardrobe, Makeup, Hair, Script Supervisor, Dialogue Coach and the Director. Make friends with these people; they are your allies. But these people will not necessarily always know what you need. You must take care of yourself.

• **The costume designer and wardrobe assistants** can really help you. Your wardrobe is so much a part of your character you have to be comfortable in your clothes. Do not settle for just anything; keep pushing nicely till your clothes are right for you. If the director is dead set on a certain outfit you can't stand, get the designer to help you become comfortable in it. Within limits, you can help design your makeup; it will depend on the look of the film, but you do have a say.

• **Costume designer Tom Baxter suggests:**

  • **If you are a visitor on the set**, guest starring or supporting, treat everybody the way you would like to be treated. If a wardrobe person asks you if you have clothes to bring in, tell them honestly what you have and if you think it will work or not. A lot of times they will think, "They said they had that so I don't have to cover that." Then you get there the next day and you find out they did have a white shirt but it was short sleeved and looked like a rag. It wasn't a white shirt you could use as a dress shirt. For the smaller parts you are always going to be asked to bring in your wardrobe, unless the show needs something specific or it's a period piece. When you get in and out of the clothes, hang them up. The wardrobe people aren't there to be maids; they are there to do a job. It's really quite a complicated one.

  • **Be someone everyone likes.** If you have a bad attitude, it doesn't work. The most successful people I've seen in television are the people who have that spark about their personality.

• **On one of the films I worked on,** I had to ask for a different makeup person. He was so negative; every morning I spent my energy warding off the negativity. One day, he got drunk in the afternoon and started making sexual remarks. I had a week's work left and knew I couldn't go through that turmoil anymore or my acting would suffer. I went to the head of the makeup department and he put me with someone else. The makeup person is the one you will spend your first hour with each morning—he or she is important. On a situation comedy, I like to be one of the first to be made-up.

• **Handle hair the same way.** You know what your hair will and will not do. My hair is curly so I know if they are straightening it out with hot rollers they can't keep them in too long or it will go even curlier. I have a friend who goes to the set in her own hot rollers because her hair is really straight and it takes longer to curl.

• **The script supervisor** has your lines and can help you match lines for other takes if you happened to change a word or two. Assume you are giving directors what they want unless they say otherwise. If it isn't *your* scene, you may not get much attention; learn to give it to yourself. Don't rely on the outside world to tell you that you're wonderful; assume you are. After you assume you are wonderful, then see what else you can find. It may be another acting choice or something special to do with one of the props. Make every tiny little thing count. Keep adding things you would do in your real life; some will work, some won't—take the chances. All kinds of surprises can happen in the editing room. Because of the master or a change in the concept of the scene, they may need to use your close-up because you were the most interesting and had the most life about you during the scene.

• **Your dressing room is your home** away from home. Bring with you things that make you feel comfortable. There is usually an abundance of time so you need things to fill the time. Depending on your type of dressing room, you can expand what you may need to feel safe and content. It's the place to prepare your acting work first and foremost. It is also the place to rest and conserve your energy, meet with other actors, work on your scenes, go over lines, have someone in to share lunch, make your phone calls. I try to keep most of my outside life away from me unless I'm having a real easy shooting day.

• **Jennifer Grey**, *It's Like, You Know...*, during the first week we were back from summer break she went to Pier One and bought some great tables and a rug. She covered the ordinary couch with a lovely blanket and pillows. She brought in some pictures and favorite lamps. She made the rather drab place adorable and homey. She also snuck her little dog LuLu into her dressing room everyday for company.

• **I bring any little snacks** I need that I won't be able to get on location or at the studio. I bring incense because I like to make the room smell like me. I bring my own makeup (just in case) and, of course, a hairbrush. I always bring a book to read that I love at the moment—something to look forward to get back to reading. I bring a good tablet to write on. Sometimes I use it as a kind of journal; other times to just simply write over and over "I can do this role," "Everything is working perfectly," or any other affirmation I may need at the time. Usually there is a bed or couch to lie down on; if not, bring an air mattress the next day so you can stretch out. I always bring an inspirational book or two. Sometimes, if I'm feeling insecure, just by opening a positive book a passage may catch my eye and make all the difference. Be careful of eating meat or sugar; it gives your body too much work to do and can take away from your acting energy.

• **When on location**, there is the additional burden of finding something to do because you don't go home at night. You go to a hotel room that you have had to make into a safe, homey place. A camera can really get you involved with everyone else. I like a Polaroid because you can give pictures to the people right away. If you do this, you must ask the still photographer and cameraman for permission to shoot. Also ask if there are any rules you should know about—when or where not to shoot.

• **Sally Field** said that the first time she worked with Burt Reynolds she filled books writing "I am worthy for Burt to like me" and other such affirmations. Obviously it worked; they had an affair that lasted several years and films.

• **You are the star in your own life** and you are the star in the role you are playing. When it comes right down to it, you are the one who the audience sees on the big screen, little screen, or stage. Your instincts are there to guide you. Keep your mind open, take in all the information anyone has to offer and then make your own decisions as to what is best for you.

• **No one can act your role for you.** Your job is to be prepared and to make yourself comfortable or uncomfortable, whichever appeals to you.

• **If you do get scared trying to figure out a script** or getting a handle on the character, pick up a phone—call your coach or another actor and talk about it. Joan Darling tells a wonderful story about a role she was in a panic over. She couldn't see what the part was about. She went to see her old friend and teacher, Walter Beakel and raved on for the whole evening about not knowing what to do. He finally said "It's easy—she is a Jewish mother." Joan saw immediately what he meant. She went out and bought a big mommy purse and filled it with things Jewish mommies have in their purses and she was home free.

• **I worked with Sharon Farrell** on a pilot where she was playing a ditsy social reporter who was very interested in how she looked. The part was flimsy, so the day before shooting she went to a drugstore and spent $100 on makeup. When she came to the set, she had all these new things to play with that ended up making the part very funny.

• **So don't panic: there are solutions to every acting problem.** Just ask the universe for the answer and you *will* come up with the solution. And after all, this is the fun part of acting, solving the problems.

• **Now you have the job:** wardrobe, makeup, hair, director and best of all, the other actors. The best thing that can happen is you can play totally *in the moment*. This is where acting is at its easiest; it feels like flying. No matter how you may have prepared, leave yourself open for the wonderful surprises that happen when the camera starts to roll or the curtain goes up. Playing in the moment is what creates the real magical moments in any performance.

• **I talk so much about acting work** because when you are in trouble your work is your insurance. Just like life insurance, hopefully you won't need it. All your work is there if you need it, but it is okay to have everything going beautifully.

• **When I was coaching Dennis Erdman** (now a very accomplished director) in *Friendly Fire*, he called me from location. He said, "I don't know what happened; everything is gone. I was wonderful and then today I couldn't do anything." As we talked, it came out that he had been shooting for seven days and it was easy and fun. All the emotions were there, and he hadn't done anything but relax and hit his marks. Of course he wanted it to be that way, as we all do, but sometimes something happens for whatever reason (doesn't matter) and we *run dry*. All he needed was to start using the acting work. Well, he went back on the set the next day, used his work and came up with the same great acting he had been delivering. After that he had days when he would *fly* and days when he needed to call on his craft every moment he was shooting. Both ways work for the audience.

• **The more acting jobs you do**, the easier and simpler they get. If you are not feeling scared, that is okay. Yes, you may miss the feeling but you will get over it.

• **On every project** there is an abundance of ego trips, power plays and politics. Ideally, the actors won't be involved in them. The director usually tries to keep these undercurrents away from the actors so you can do your job better. Of course, the gossip is always interesting and I am not saying not to listen to the stories going around. Sometimes they can be the most entertaining part of the job. Don't get emotionally involved. If something is going on between some of the actors or even between you and another actor, it is most difficult to keep your personal emotions under control. But do it. Let's say, for example, you must insist on something you need to be able to perform and you can't get it—let it go. You will gain somewhere else. I'm not saying not to fight for what you want; but if you lose the fight, lose it and forget it. That way it can't really harm you. Feel good about the times you win and even let go of those too and move on to the next event.

• **Hopefully, your set will be a happy one** and a *family*. All sets end up being families but not necessarily the type of family we want. Whatever you can do to turn the people around you into the family you want, do it. Sometimes you may have to shield yourself from this family and other times you will die and cry when the project is over and you have to leave this family.

• **Relaxation. Keep relaxing and feeling all your feelings.** Don't cover up fear, anger, tears, frustration, joy, ecstasy. Relax and experience all of yourself. Then go out and use all of it. If you are feeling joy and the scene is about sadness, then let the joy be there over how sad you can be. If you are feeling angry and the scene is about ecstasy, be in ecstasy over being able to feel such anger. Most of the time after your relaxation and full experience of your feelings, you will come through to the perfect emotions for the scene. Do not censor or cover up your feelings from *yourself*. Sometimes it is very appropriate to not let others see your feelings. You can have all your defenses up off-camera but never on-camera.

• **One of the things I liked best about Jerry Seinfeld,** he was able to really feel and experience his feelings when they were happening. I saw him get angry a very few times and I saw him get his feelings hurt a couple of times. He dealt with it in the moment and didn't seem to carry any resentment. On the last day of shooting the show, I asked him how he felt. He said when he started driving to the studio that morning he had cried the whole way in. He then let it go and had a great day and evening.

• **We usually get what we intend to get.** Intend to have a good time doing your job.

• **When it's a wrap for the day,** find some way to entertain yourself and be good to yourself. We all have our own unique ways; use yours. Again, there are no rules to follow except your own.

• **Drugs and alcohol** will shortchange you and the people you're working with. *STAY IN REALITY.* Actor Kelsey Grammer, in the middle of a scheduled shooting season, went into rehab at the Betty Ford Center. There were probably 20 employees the production continued to pay until he could work again. While that was good for Kelsey, there were seventy or eighty crew members with mortgages to pay who were without jobs because all of the other shows had their crews for the season.

• **Safety, safety, safety.** Actor Kenneth Steadman was 27 years old; he had moved to Los Angeles to pursue acting five years before his death. His career seemed to have great promise, he had been on *NYPD Blue* and *Baywatch* and a guest star on the premiere episode of *Maloney*. He died while guest starring on *Sliders* when a dune buggy he was riding in overturned. The dune buggy had seat belts, but he wasn't using his. Take care of yourself on the set; wear the seat belts, let the stuntmen do their jobs.

• **Firearms Safety:** After actor Brandon Lee's death, SAG put out some guidelines for using prop guns on the set.

  • **Use simulated or dummy weapons whenever possible.** Treat all guns as if they are loaded and deadly. Unless you are actually filming or rehearsing, all firearms must be secured by the prop master. Never engage in any horseplay with firearms or other weapons. Do not let others handle your gun for any reason. Never point a firearm at anyone, including yourself. Always cheat the shot by aiming to the right or left of the target character. If asked to point and shoot directly at a living target, consult with the property master or armorer for the prescribed safety procedures. If you are the intended target of a gunshot, make sure that the person firing at you has followed all these safety procedures. If you are required to wear exploding blood squibs, make sure there is a bulletproof vest or other solid protection between you and the blast packed. Check the firearm every time you take possession of it. Blanks are extremely dangerous. Even though they do not fire bullets out of the gun barrel, they still have a powerful blast that can maim or kill. If you are on a set where shots are to be fired and there is no armorer or qualified prop master, go to the nearest phone and call the Guild. A union representative will make sure proper procedures are followed.

• **Reviews can be killers.** If you decide to read them, do you believe the goods ones and discount the bad ones? Glenn Close says she can't read them because even if they are good for her but mean to another cast member, it hurts her. I know many actors, myself included, that have gone to bed for days over bad reviews.

• **To read the TV ratings:** The first figure is the number the show comes in (currently, out of 131 shows); the next figure is percentage/share. For instance: *Seinfeld* one week was #2 with 22.0/34. *The Single Guy* was #7 with 16.3/26. A single ratings point equals 970,000 households, or 1% of the nation's 110 million TV homes (as of 2005) in the Nielsen Media Research universe. Share is the percentage of sets turned on at a given time that are tuned in to a particular show.

• **I want to encourage you to think of acting as a life-long career.** Brenda Blethyn did six films in the year following being nominated for an Oscar for *Secrets & Lies*. She did *Secrets & Lies* when she was 50 years old; it was the third movie of her career. Some actors do work in their older years; don't buy into "Your career is over at 40."

Dialogue and On-Set Coaches

• **Whenever someone asks me what I do** and I say I am a dialogue coach, they ask, "What does that mean?" Or they think it is a dialect coach, who corrects speech or teaches accents or dialects, which it is not. Each dialogue coach may give you a different job description. On some shows, I have been the acting coach where I prepare the actors for the director, rehearsing and helping them to make their acting choices.

• **On most shows,** I am there to run lines and rehearse with the actors, to help them memorize their lines and incorporate any line changes or new scenes that suddenly arise. Typically on sitcoms, there are changes each day and even while shooting, there may be changes between takes. Sometimes I just read the cue lines flat; other times I read the full lines of the other characters, close to the way the characters will be saying their lines so the actor I'm reading with can work out their moves, timing and reactions.

• **Sometimes we will have non-actors as guests on a show.** I usually work very intensely with them not only to help them to learn their lines but to help them sound real. When former Los Angeles Mayor Richard Riordan appeared on *It's Like, You Know...*, he had all of his scenes with A. J. Langer, who played Lauren. As I was running the lines with them, the Mayor said about himself, "Oh that didn't sound real." A.J. gave him such a great tip. She said, "Try to make each line just a little different, have a different attitude on each one." That was such an easy way to think about the lines. He understood what she meant and really gave a good performance and got laughs.

• **Each actor has their own personality** and their own way of working. The coach must try to be very sensitive to their needs because there is much more that goes into the acting process than the words. Some actors like me to be close by all the time (Jerry Seinfeld, Olivia d'Abo and Jennifer Grey); others prefer to work mostly on their own and ask me to run lines with them occasionally. Still others may like to just sit down and go over a difficult scene or some may just want to go over the line changes.

310

• **Jason Alexander, who played George on *Seinfeld*,** has a photographic memory; it seemed like he could look at the lines once and have them down. Before he shot a scene, I would hang around, available to run lines with him, although I knew it wasn't necessary. I'd run the lines with the guest actors as many times as they wanted, then I'd ask Jason to run them once with the guests. It would be tedious and unnecessary to run them more than once with him. I don't know how Jason made the despicable George likeable, but he did. Jason received a lot of fan mail from women because they thought he was adorable, which Jason is in real life.

• **Julia Louis-Dreyfus was a blast to work with.** Maybe because I have three daughters around her age; maybe it was her curly hair (I also have curly hair). It certainly was her sense of humor and talent. I loved it best when we had a new script or were blocking and shooting and taking one scene at a time out of sequence. She would come into the makeup room and say, "I don't know the lines, I haven't looked at this." So for the next hour while she was getting her hair done, she would get the entire script down and have an idea of how she wanted to play each scene. She learns very fast and starts out running her lines flat and then, about the third time through, she follows her instincts and begins to flesh out her role. When she went on the set, she turned it up another 100 degrees and nailed it.

• **It seems to me Julia can make any line work.** I remember in one script Elaine had the line, "Tim Whatley." Jerry says he's talked to Tim Whatley and she responds, "Tim Whatley!" with so much emotion and body movement, the audience immediately got it that she is nuts about him, he is adorable and she would do anything to get him, loose woman that she is.

• **Michael Richards (Kramer) is so very talented and funny.** He was my first buddy when I started on the show—he had the flu that week and really needed my help. I think he may have worried more than anyone about his lines, but he always got them. He had so much to figure out besides the lines—the timing of his physical humor is so precise. It looked easy, natural and truthful, but he planned it meticulously. When he had a complicated scene to work out, we would go over it many times. Yes, there are surprises, like when he jumped out of a window while chasing Newman and just about ended his sex life. I think the most important thing for him is to be truthful; he was always working to achieve that.

• **In one scene, Kramer was supposed to be taking pictures** of George to impress the girl at the one-hour photo place. We were shooting the scene without an audience so Michael hadn't had any rehearsal. He had many props in the scene, supposedly lights to set, a fan to move and turn on, pictures to take from different angles and George to convince to relax and loosen up. Very precise movements, lines to be said and marks to be hit all at the same time, so the four cameramen shooting the show can each get their shots. Since there had not been a rehearsal, I had to run lines with Michael, anticipating the pace that Jason might use. It was so entertaining to watch Michael work out the crazy stuff he does and fun to be a part of his acting process.

• **Jerry Seinfeld was very particular** about getting each line exactly as it was written. Because he had the final decision of each word in each line, he liked to have the lines rewritten just the way they would be spoken. Each week I would pick out my favorite line in the show; most often it was one of his lines and wasn't really a joke line, it was a payoff or an attitude he had. Before each show, we would run through his scenes and then before each scene was shot, all the actors ran through as much of the scene as time allowed, as they were getting touched up with hair and makeup on the set. I tried to keep track of any problem lines and point them out to them before shooting.

• **Jerry is a "money player;"** he was great in rehearsal but when the cameras rolled, a whole new energy and dimension came out. When he was acting, he was also producing the show, deciding on how the scene was to be played. I don't know how he did it; he had control of it all, and yet he seemed to have a very good time working. One of my favorite things about Jerry is that he didn't mind looking like a fool. He could write the show so he always looked good but it was funnier when his character looked shallow. On show days, he liked to have a precise schedule which included light meals. His assistant, Carol Brown, made sure he had everything he needed to be comfortable. He meditated before each show. Jerry seems to have endless energy—I never saw him look tired on the set except the second to last show when he got sick and lost his voice. It was the first time in nine years we had to postpone the shooting for one day.

• **On *The Single Guy*, we had a good time**; the pace wasn't as fast and there weren't as many scenes as *Seinfeld*. Jonathan Silverman started working as a teenager and has never stopped. He is great on the set and is concerned about all of the cast and crew. When we did the pilot, he had *Single Guy* hats made for all of us, which is unusual for an actor to do on a pilot, but it made us all, cast and crew, a family.

• **Ernest Borgnine was so much fun**; he loves to laugh and has a thousand stories to tell. He used the script cover he's had since *Marty*, the movie for which he won his Academy Award. He brought in his Oscar to the set one day so we could see it. The set chair that he uses was made in Mexico for him when he was working on *The Wild Bunch*. At his age, he had plenty of energy, loved to work and was able to keep up with everyone on the set. He was always prepared with his script; we just ran lines a few times.

• **Shawn Michael Howard's first series regular role** was on the *The Single Guy*. He liked to run all of his lines in the script from the beginning to the end. He would get his lines down perfectly and then when we were shooting he would throw in some lines that he thought might work for his character. The producers encouraged him to do this because they were still developing the character.

• **Ming-Na just fascinated me.** *Joy Luck Club* was one of my favorite movies and the serenity and mystery of the character she played was so beautiful. But on *The Single Guy*, she was snappy, hip and New York sarcastic. It is interesting to watch her listen. There is always so much going on in her mind; she listens actively.

• **Joey Slotnick (Sam on *The Single Guy*) had a great amount of energy**, sort of an engine running inside. He always had some activity, something that was going on in the scene. He had a small role in the movie *Twister*, but every time he came on the screen, he was full of where he had been and where he was going. The same was true for *Blast From The Past*—he was so funny as that intense religious hippie, and that engine was running inside.

• **Olivia d'Abo *(The Single Guy)* was great to work with**; she loved to rehearse so I got to spend a lot of time with her. She was always working out her activities and because she was new in the second season, she was trying to discover more things about who her character was. In one scene we were shooting late at night, she had to fly in the door, find out Johnny wasn't going to stop a friend's marriage, hit several marks as she was all over the room, tell a long story filled with emotion and then flop into the chair. The scene was playing too long so the producer decided to cut part of the dialogue. They cut a chunk out from the top and then a piece out of the middle of the monologue which changed the blocking. It is hard to remember cuts like that but Olivia tackled it like, "Oh, boy here we go; this is a challenge and fun." Each take was hilarious, it was always like it was the first time she was doing the scene; whether it was a different turn of her head or inflection in her voice, she kept discovering new things each take. Actors must develop discipline, concentration and focus.

• **I work with all of the guest stars on the shows,** which I hope all of you reading this book will be at sometime. Almost all the guest stars are good, have great respect for the shows and are happy to be there. It is important to remember that as a guest star, you are there just for that show, so always check out the set, the cast and crew, figure out where it is designed for you to fit in. There is always a chance that if they like working with you, you could be called back to do your character for another show.

• **If you get scared, just keep breathing** and there will probably be someone who senses it and will help you, though you don't want to seem needy. Occasionally actors have had panic attacks. They put so much pressure on themselves, they sort of short circuit. I don't think anyone else on the set has been aware of it and that is how I like to it to be. I will hang out with them, keep coming back to them, run their lines, laugh at their jokes, assure them that they can get through it. They always do.

• **It is important that you do your rehearsals at home** because you never know what your shooting day is going to be. On *Seinfeld,* an actor was doing one scene on a no-audience, block-and-shoot show. He was playing a repair guy making a telephone call to Kramer; working a half day, doing one scene and leaving. This was a show shooting on location all over the studio lot. I ran lines with the actor and we rehearsed where he would be shooting until he felt comfortable with the hard hat and the phone on the pole. He was a big fan of the show and was fighting his disappointment at not being able to work with the cast. The scene played great, just what the director wanted. There were two takes and then the crew moved on, so anti-climatic for the guest. It helped this actor immensely that he came in prepared, he had done his acting work, figured out who, what, when and where. If he had been planning on discovering his character during rehearsal, he would have been caught short.

• **The actor who played the cable guy** on that same show was wonderful. He had several long monologues outside Kramer's door, during the last one there was quite a dramatic emotional change; he convinced Kramer to open the door and they hugged. He almost cried, yet he was funny. The preparation, talent and guts to do that take after take was remarkable. I must have rehearsed those monologues fifty times with him so he could try a lot of different acting work he was thinking of. The crew applauded at the end of his last take—it is unusual to move the crew.

• **When you are a guest on a show, come in absolutely prepared.** We had one actress who could hardly tear herself away from other stuff she was doing (reading a magazine, eating, talking) to rehearse. She would have a wad of gum in her mouth, casually go off her lines like they didn't matter, and just think she was so cute. Of course, this drove me nuts. I would try to work with her but she always wanted to get back to me later. Finally, right before the show, she was ready to work with me. Well, my policy is to take care of the guests first so I can be fully available for the members of the cast who have so many scenes and a story line to think about. This girl had given a hard time to many of us on set who were trying to do our jobs. When you come to play on a team, jump in and be a team player.

• **One actor had fully prepared his work,** but in rehearsal he was completely flat. I knew he would be replaced if he didn't deliver the character. I took him aside to run lines and encouraged him to do all the stuff he had worked on. He said he was afraid of being too big. I said, "Go for it, they will tell you if you're too big." Well he did, and was so funny, they brought him back to do another show.

• **I love working as a dialogue coach,** I work closely with the script supervisor who, among other things, is in charge of making sure any missed or muffled lines are re-shot so they don't lose a line or word the writer or producer wanted. Not everything can be fixed in the editing room. If a show doesn't have a dialogue coach, the script supervisor will run lines with the cast, in addition to their other work. I'm happy to say the script supervisors I've worked with are always glad I'm there to help the actors.

COMMERCIAL
PRINT MODELING

• **Print work is an additional source for actors to gain experience** and make extra money. Commercial print is a still picture of a commercial. It is the type of advertising you see in newspapers, magazines, on billboards and buses. Print models get paid by the hour. In the Los Angeles, market, models are paid between $150 and $200 an hour. There are no residuals but, depending on the format and product identification, it is not unusual to be paid a bonus on top of the hourly rate.

• **Aaron Marcus is an actor, commercial model and author** of *How to Become a Successful Commercial Model.* He says:

  • **A lot of very successful commercial models are actors.** Photographers love hiring actors because they can take direction and provide a variety of believable emotions and layers of expressions.

Q: What is the difference between commercial modeling and fashion modeling?

  • **Everyone knows about the fashion model**—tall, thin, very unusual and exotic looking. To even be considered as a fashion model, you must have very specific physical requirements. For commercial print work they hire everybody; there are no height, weight or age requirements. Fashion models normally promote high-end designer clothes; commercial models advertise everything else.

Q: How can someone get started in the commercial print business?

  • **The most basic way would be with an 8x10 headshot.** Call the agents in your city and find out if they handle commercial print. Ask if they have open calls, or if you should submit by mail. Once you get an agent you will need to get a zed card, also known as a composite sheet. This is a collection of photographs that shows a variety of ways you can

316

look and the different categories you can play. The agent can help you decide on the categories that would be marketable for you. The zed card is your calling card. It is what the agent submits to a photographer or an art director in order to get you work. It is not uncommon to get hired from your card, without having to audition.

Q: How do you audition for print work?

• **The audition for commercial print modeling is called a "go-see,"** because you go and you are seen. When your agent calls you with the audition information, make sure you find out what they are looking for, and dress the part. When you walk in the room you want them to say, "Yeah, that is the person for this job." Before signing in, look over the layout of the ad (copy of ad). It shows what the clients are looking for. Study it. What does this person look like? What are their facial and body expressions? Is there any copy, any words to the ad? Know the kind of expressions you want to show. When you feel prepared and ready, sign in. In most situations you will have a Polaroid or digital shot taken and they will staple it to your composite sheet.

• **When you book the job, it is important that you understand the ad** and how it needs to be delivered. I view commercial print work as any other acting job. I say words or sounds that will allow me to feel the emotion that I need to present. It will make the shots look very powerful. When you are in touch with your expressions and emotions, there is believability in your eyes and your body will move naturally. Some photographers might say, "I really don't want to see any kind of talking." Then you need to do an internal monologue. The key is to have some life going on in your brain.

Q: When do you get paid?

• **The client pays the advertising agency,** the advertising agency pays the photographer, the photographer pays the agent. Once the check clears, the agent takes out their 20% commission and then the model gets paid. In most cases it takes 90 days to get paid.

• **At the shoot there are two forms you need to fill out.** One is a voucher and the other is a model release form. The voucher is the contract that you sign at the end of every job. You get a copy, your agent gets a copy and the person paying you gets a copy. The other form is the model release form. Basically it says the photographer can use your image any way he wants to. You must get familiar with these forms, learn to fill them out correctly and make the necessary changes. If the changes are not made, you could lose a tremendous amount of money.

• In his modeling guidebook *The Good, The Bad & The Beautiful,* James Pentaudi says commercial work is for all ethnic types. "The key factors in a commercial look are versatility, believability and likeability. Models have a ready and able smile, good skin, good teeth, softer bone structure, a more two-dimensional All-American or Everyman's face."

• While researching the print modeling business, I talked to several actors who supplement their acting income as "fit models." Fit modeling is basically a garment industry job. Every company that manufactures clothing uses fit models to make their patterns. The fit model goes to the factories and works with the designers. They drape their designs on them and decide what trim to use or what buttons would be best. Then the model goes to the fit room and tells the pattern maker what is uncomfortable, what is too tight or too loose.

• The hours are flexible; the manufacturers will work with your schedule if you are the size they need. The required size is "average" but one company's average might be a size eight for women, another's a size two. You do have to be well proportioned. The pay is $75 to $85 an hour minus the agency commission which is 15 to 20%. Models can work for several manufacturers; many fit models work non-stop.

• Natasha at Peak Models and Talent, says her company handles many actors that add to their acting income by fit modeling, print modeling or working conventions as hosts and hostesses. You can send a picture and resume along with snapshots, your measurements and the type of work you are interested in, to Peak Models and Talent, 25852 Mc Bean Parkway, #190, Valencia, 91355. The website is peakmodels.com.

Resources

How to Become a Successful Commercial Model by Aaron Marcus. howtomodel.com. 410/764-8270.
The Good, The Bad & The Beautiful by James Pentaudi. A guide to breaking into different parts of the modeling industry. To get a copy, call 800/375-4994.
The Modeling Handbook by Eve Matheson
Ross Reports Television & Film: Commercial Casting Guide by Back Stage West.
The Agencies: What the Actor Needs To Know by Acting World Books. Use this guide to look for an agent. Their listing will specify if they do print or not.
The Working Actor's Guide, L.A., Aaron Blake Publishing.

VOICEOVERS FOR COMMERCIALS AND ANIMATION ACTING

• **Voiceovers and animation acting** take a special acting energy, coming from a different perspective. You should be a well-trained actor before studying voiceovers; it is a *very* lucrative field to get into.

• **You must have an agent for this work**; there are several of them in town. This is another very tough field to break into—you need a very special voice and talent. Some voiceover actors have said that a voiceover gig can bring anywhere from 10 to 500 voice artists in for an audition. Plus, more and more celebrities are doing voiceover and animation work. However, industry experts said they are always looking for new voices from people who have an understanding of how the business works. And with the number of cartoons on TV, there are an increasing number of opportunities for kids of all ages as well.

• **Also, look for experience and opportunities everywhere**—from friends' projects to company websites. An actor told me of a friend who gained experience recording telephone messages for businesses for experience and now makes quite a bit of cash in the industry.

• **I recommend taking classes with casting directors.** Look in *Back Stage West* for ads. If you get in the circle of people who are doing voiceovers, you will learn a lot about it.

• **Self-promotion online also seems to be key**; set up your own website with audio clips. Go to voicebank.net and listen to the many demo voice tapes that are online and you will get a feel for the type of talent this work demands.

Voiceover Classes

To download and print an updated version of this and all resource lists, go to actingiseverything.com.

Susan Blu, 818/783-9130, blupka.com. Great classes, she knows the business. Studio: 818/501-1BLU for voiceover demos. Susan is the author of *Word Of Mouth, A Guide To Commercial Voice-Overs.*

Terry Berland Casting and Voice Box Studios, 310/571-4141, terryberlandcasting. com. "The place to go to move your voiceover career forward. The most progressive up-to-date creative workshops, seminars, marketing and networking strategies in the industry." Terry is co-author of Breaking into Commercials 2nd Edition. THE book on commercials.

Dolores Diehl, The Voiceover Connection, Inc. 213/384-9251. voconnection.com. Teaches workshops in all phases of voiceovers, commercial, narration and animation, from basic to advanced levels. All basic classes taught by Dolores. Agents, casting directors and performers teach the intermediate to advanced to pro levels. Demo seminars, workouts and simulations.

Michael Bell's Voice Animation Workshop, 818/784-5107. "In my class, you will learn to paint the picture with your voice, test the limits of your pipes and your imagination and rediscover the fun of eating the scenery! Above all discover who's hidden inside, let them out and make them pay!" A voiceover actor with tons of credits, he teaches just a couple of workshops a year.

Hollywood Actor's Studio, Eric Stone, 323/460-2580, actingconnection.com. Focuses on the technical aspects of voiceover work. $150 for first session and $90 each after that.

Braintracks, 310/472-4480, braintracksaudio.com. Provides in-depth training on basic voiceover work to animation to creating characters to understanding the business. Will also help you make demos. A little pricey, $130 for an hour session.

Joni Gerber, 323/654-1159. Private classes for all levels. One of the top working voiceover people.

Sandy Holt, 310/271-8217. Teaches voiceover/looping workshops and produces voiceover demos. Also teaches cold reading.

Voice Acting, voiceacting.com. Offers lots of different kinds of classes covering all aspects of the industry.

OTHER IMPORTANT SITES

Voicebank.net. Voiceover demos plus much more

VoiceStarz.com. Classes on line, plus a lot of information.

Voice123.com. Job listings and a place to create a voiceover profile.

VOICE COACH

Robert Easton, "The Henry Higgins of Hollywood," 818/985-2222. He is also known as the dialect doctor. He has coached many, many famous actors over many years.

BOOKS

The Agencies: What the Actor Needs To Know by Acting World Books. This is the authentic, well-researched agent guide. There are other publications that look like this one—don't be fooled. You will find agents who specialize in voiceovers.

Word Of Mouth, A Guide To Commercial Voice-Overs by Susan Blu.

Voice and the Actor by Cicely Berry. This is not necessarily about voiceovers, but about using your correct voice.

Voice-Overs: Putting Your Mouth Where the Money Is by Chris Douthitt.

LOOPING

• **Looping is another acting tool** to add to your tool box. Many actors have never heard about this lucrative work. Looping is done on a post-production sound stage; the actors replace or add voices to film and television productions after they have been edited. Loopers need strong improvisational skills because the main function is to supply the voices of the extras that are seen in the background. There are a few looping groups, but they are very hard to break into. In general, TV shows may use just five actors and films may use six to 12 actors for all the voices.

• **The more lucrative looping gigs** are those where an actor rephrases lines for films making the transition to television. For every cuss word or other word that doesn't pass the censors, a looper needs to ovedub it with something else like "I don't give a shoot!" These voice actors need to sound like the characters they're dubbing over. A typical contract for this kind of work is around $800 for about four hours of work.

• **There are several different modes** of looping such as "Wall to Wall," "Doughnut," "Pass By's" and others. You will be taught these in a workshop or you may get the chance to observe a looping group in action.

• **The most important tool is your looping notebook.** This is where you write down sentences you might use in conversations at an airport, hospital, bowling alley, boxing match, nightclub, singles joint, computer room, office, dance studio, etc. You look for potential dialogue everywhere. Any lingo or jargon of different occupations is very valuable. Extensive research is usually required for each job you do, depending on the situation of the film. This all adds information to your notebook. Long time, experienced loopers arrive on the sound stage with several huge notebooks.

• **Toby Stone of Sounds Great looping group:** "When I worked on *Backdraft*, I needed to find out all about Chicago, including street maps. Then I called the burn unit ward at Sherman Oaks Burn Hospital to find out what the vitals are on a burn victim. What kind of drugs they would give, what kind of salve they would use." This information went into her looping notebook to be used for that job, and saved for any other project involving burn victims. This authentic type of conversation is what makes looping believable.

• **When you take a workshop,** the teacher will hand out sheets to begin your looping notebooks, including Police Codes and Traffic Violations, Police Dispatch, Police Precinct, Phones, General Conversation, Forensics/Crime Scene, Airport Pages and Airport Terminal Conversation.

• **In looping, the conversation can't be all that interesting** because the audience doesn't want to be aware of what the background voices are saying. There's a fine line between not being boring and having new things to say, something with a little spin to it. It's like walking and chewing gum at the same time. There are different kinds of restaurant conversations; it may be a Denny's kind of lunch place or it may be a very fancy upscale dinner kind of place. Depending on what you are seeing on the screen, you may change your voice or the type of attitude you have. If there are only six loopers on the sound stage, you have to be able to sound as if you are everyone in every situation.

• **Even if you are not planning** to seek actual looping work, I think all actors will find taking a workshop helpful because you could be called in to revoice or loop your own lines on film and television projects due to sound or other technical problems. With the experience you gain in a looping workshop, you can go on any sound stage knowing looping etiquette, what will be expected of you and what terms are used. Self-confidence is a real key to looping.

• **Sandy Holt** owns a looping group, *Loop Ease,* and runs looping workshops. "Sometimes we have to revoice a main character. We may do a teenage or baby's voice, also different dialects. All the actors in the company are incredible at improvisation. We're quick and creative on the spot; you have to be able to improvise while you're looking at the scene on the sound stage screen."

• **Loopers earn Screen Actors Guild minimum and residuals.**

Resources

To download and print an updated version of this and all resource lists, go to actingiseverything.com.

LOOPING WORKSHOPS

Loop Ease, Sandy Holt. 310/271-8217 Voice casting director. She holds weekend looping seminars on a professional sound stage.

Loop Troop, 818/239-1616, looptroop.com, 859 Hollywood Way, #411, Burbank 91505. Has database of looping talent and also offers day-long seminars on looping. $275.

Contact SAG **for current list of Looping Groups.**

STUNT AND ACTION ACTING

• **Just like the acting profession, it is very hard to break into stunt work.** Stunt coordinators are the directors of the stunts on the set and usually make the hiring decisions. Unlike the acting profession, there are no agents for stunt talent: you can market yourself directly to stunt coordinators. Yu have an advantage if you are a world class gymnast, martial artist, motorcyclist, etc. Stunt people work under the SAG union and have the same benefits as actors. There are many stunt organizations and they all have strict membership requirements. You must be sponsored by a member to be considered.

• **There are groups of stunt people** who work out together. Find out how to meet them and get invited to their workouts. It's a real networking feat to get to know and hang out with the stunt community.

• **If you're not interested in stunt work,** stage combat training will come in handy when doing theatre or working in action films. Martial arts classes are a great way to shape and tone your body, as well as your mind.

• **James Lew can claim to have been beaten up by everybody in Hollywood!** His list includes Jackie Chan, Jet Li, Mel Gibson, Tom Cruise, Steven Seagal, Jean Claude Van Damme, Madonna, Charlie Sheen and many more. He is a member of the Stuntmen's Association. His martial arts training began at age 14, first in Korean style Karate. He studied a combat style developed by a Green Beret combat instructor, a Chinese style called "White Eyebrow" after the appearance of the original Grand Master and Kung Fu "Five Animals" style, the five animals being Tiger, Leopard, Snake, Dragon, and Crane. His favorite parts of the martial arts training are the traditional weapons: sword, spear, staff, whip chain many other Chinese weapons. Weapons are an extension of your body and a fantastic way to develop your balance, speed, agility, flexibility and power.

• **James is very well respected in Hollywood** as a top stunt coordinator, fight choreographer, second unit director and actor. James has now added to his resume as a writer, director and producer, his independent movie, *18 Fingers of Death*. He put together all his years of experience and connections to get his movie made and signed a distribution deal with Universal Studios. James formed his own action company, "Hong Kong Wire Action Team," handpicking the top action talents in the business to bring the best creative action to the entertainment industry.

Q: Tell me about your job as a stunt coordinator/fight choreographer.

- **I first read the script to digest the story.** Then I read it again to break down the action and write down my ideas. Always keeping in mind the tone of the movie, the story and the appropriate style of action to serve the telling of the story. My job responsibility is to bring the director's vision to the screen. The director may want to elicit a certain emotional response from a particular action scene or fight scene. If it's a real brutal intense fight scene, emphasize the pain element through the raw emotion of revenge. If it's comedy, find a situation to throw the "banana peel" on the ground. When you choreograph an action scene that people fall or something breaks, you give it a different flavor. As a stunt coordinator my job is to bring the most exciting action for the budget but all done with safety as the priority.

- **Technology has provided exciting new avenues** for action entertainment. I was hired to create the fight choreography on the video game, *Matrix, The Path of Neo*. There were over 700 different choreographed sequences needed for the game. It was done completely with the fight talent performing and being recorded through "motion capture." The talent wears special body suits with markers placed on strategic spots all over the body. The computer captures every movement precisely and the animators can bring to life any action characters for the video game. This same technology is used in many of the action scenes in the movies.

- **When I was working on *Undercover Blues*** with Dennis Quaid and Kathleen Turner, we had two weeks in pre-production for them to train. Rather than trying to give them a general training program, I felt the most efficient approach was to only work on the exact moves they were going to perform in the fight scenes. This meant that the fight choreography had to be designed before we started training.

- **It was a blast training Brad Pitt for his movie, *Troy*.** He plays Achilles, the greatest warrior in Greek history. The producers wanted to add "style" to his fighting techniques. I combined the traditional fighting style of that era with some Kung Fu techniques and came up with some pretty cool moves. The challenge was to bring a distinct style to his fighting without making Mr. Pitt look like he stepped off the set of *Crouching Tiger*. The goal was to guide him to the level of proficiency that he would not think about his movements but rather just feel his natural reactions as Achilles would fight.

Q: What training do you recommend for actors who want to do their own action work?

• **The most basic skills a stuntman** must train in are fighting skills. This also holds true for an actor wanting to perform his own action. Fight scenes are the foundation to build upon to becoming an action actor. A martial arts program would be a very wise investment because it teaches you how control your body, how to fall down without hurting yourself. The styles vary with different schools, different instructors. It's best to audit a class and get a feel for it. Ballet is great for developing fluidity and beauty in movement. For stunts, gymnastics is very beneficial because you need to experience rolling and tumbling. On the original movie, *Buffy, The Vampire Slayer*, I trained Kristy Swanson for her martial arts fights. She had dance training and was comfortable with graceful movement, so I had a foundation to build upon. I would incorporate some dance principles to her training to make it her own fighting style.

Q: Is it hard to break into stunt work?

• **It's like getting a credit card without having credit.** People always want to know what you've done. Get some experience, get something on your resume. If you have a special ability, if you're a champion at something it will definitely help open doors.

• **My first job** was on the original *Kung-Fu* series. They were looking for martial artists and I had that special ability they needed. Then other projects came along, and I had a credit. Your last job is your audition for your next job. If the stunt coordinator liked your work he will not only hired you again but will recommend you to another stunt coordinator looking for someone with your abilities.

• **Make a demo tape of yourself in action.** With the economical costs today of digital video cameras and editing software available you can put together an exciting reel of yourself performing the action of your expertise. There is no excuse for not have a demo reel. As in an acting reel, it should be under five minutes long. The production value is not as important as great content. It is your talent that matters. Get your action reel done, no excuses. So, if you have an opportunity to meet a stunt coordinator and he asks for your demo reel you can give it to him.

Q: What is the audition like?

• **The martial arts or stunt audition** is the same as an acting audition. They're always looking for that spark, something special. So you want to come in with a lot of intense energy, to come across like you can really hurt the person that you're going to fight in the film. They'll ask you to do a demonstration. You need to get across in your body language and your eyes through sense memory or personalization that your opponent is someone that you really want to hurt, take care of, defend against. Have a 30 second to one minute choreographed and very well rehearsed sequence ready. It will be played to a casting director/producer/director so play the moves to the best advantage towards that one direction. You can think of this audition like delivering a monologue.

Q: What advice do you have for martial artists or others wanting to break into action acting?

- **You must train in an acting class.** It is crazy for anyone to think that just because they are a successful martial artist or an athlete that they can be successful in movies. There are always exceptions that someone without training makes it in the movies and just as there is always someone that wins the lottery. I don't think anyone in their right mind would think that just because they are a great actor they could enter into an *Ultimate Fighting Championship*. Even if you are hired to perform a fight scene without any dialogue acting classes will still be beneficial to bringing real emotions while performing the fight scene.

- **There's a big difference between movie martial arts and real martial arts.** In real fighting you don't want to telegraph to your opponent, "I'm going to right front kick or throw a right upper cut punch at you." In film, you need to show the audience, "This is the kick that I'm going to use." Present it then go through with it. To make it a little more theatrical, you have to overemphasize certain moves. This is necessary because we are cheating the "hits" and using camera angles to create the illusion of making contact in the fight scene. You can almost think of performing a fight scene with the same emphasis on form, power and speed as you would in performing your form or kata.

- **To be successful, the key word is persistence. Never give up.** A martial artist learns through proper training how the power of discipline leads to achieving your goals. If you want to master a jump spinning heel kick, learn the proper technique and then do it over and over. There is a big heavy door to get through and into the movie business. Keep kicking, kicking and kicking until you kick it down. That's what I did for a long time and continue to do today.

Q. What about women in the stunt business?

- **Never has there been a better opportunity** for a stuntwomen or an action actress than today. The popularity of "chicks kicking butt" in the entertainment world is at an all time high and it is here to stay. The doors have been kicked down by blockbuster movies such as *Crouching Tiger, Hidden Dragon, Charlie's Angels* and television shows like *Alias* and *Buffy The Vampire Slayer.*

- **My advice to any women interested** in the action world would be exactly the same for the men. Total commitment to training to the level of a world class athlete is your best foundation. What distinguishes the successful stuntwomen is their ability to be just as good as a successful stuntman.

Q. What are your thoughts on achieving success in this business?

- **The first and most important point** to always remember in the stunt business is that it is a "business." Any business plan should include short term and long term goals. Your marketing approach can make or break your company. Survive with passion and persistence in your belief of yourself. But the one most vital thing you must do is. . .have fun!

• **Simon Rhee is a 7th Degree Black Belt** in Tae Kwon Do and a 4th Degree Black Belt in Hap Ki Do. He has been involved in the movie industry as a Martial Artist, Stunt Coordinator, Fight Choreographer, and actor, as well as instructor to many celebrities. Master Rhee owns one of the top Tae Kwon Do centers and has trained thousands of men, women and children since 1980.

Q: Tell me about working with Madonna.

- **I was hired** by Mr. Eddie Braun to work on the *007: Die Another Day* Madonna music video. There were two of us and the script required that we push Madonna into the water and throw her against a wall. We had to manhandle her and he wanted someone who could act and look menacing without hurting Madonna. To look more menacing one of us had to get a military haircut, and I had to be bald. I was paid $1,250 extra for shaving my head.

Q: Was Madonna afraid at all?

- **I don't think she is afraid of anything.** We rehearsed for two days, and after she saw how we were handling her, she felt very comfortable that we weren't going to hurt her in any way. One time we tied her to an electric chair, and she was halfway tied down and the director told her to struggle more. While she was struggling, she kicked me in the head with her boot. We didn't rehearse that, but sometimes stuntmen have to take that.

Q: As a stuntman, do you ever get hurt?

- **Yes, I do.** A few years back, I was doing a TV series called *Dark Skies* and I had to ride this machine called an air ram—you step on it and it catapults you into the air and then an explosion follows you. One time I was about to step on it and the explosion went off a little early and the debris went into my eyes. Another time, on *Lethal Weapon 4*, I had to fall onto the freeway from a moving car and I banged my shoulder—but you survive and you move on.

- **It's better to be an action actor**, because the production will always provide you with a stunt double so you won't get hurt. When you do your own stunts there is definitely a chance of getting hurt.

Q: What is the best training for an action or stunt actor to have before they arrive in Los Angeles?

- **If you want to be an action actor**, you will have to know how to act. Make sure you have a good acting coach. It's very important to take acting classes. In a movie I did called *Best of the Best* there is a scene at the end where I am handing a medal to my brother and I'm crying. We had to shoot that ten times and every time we shot it I had to cry. That's not that easy.

- **Pick some kind of martial arts training.** You are selling your image in Hollywood so you've got to look that image. It will take a minimum of six months to get good at martial arts. You also need weight training for definition. It's like taking acting lessons; you don't learn everything in one day.

Q: What was the first movie that you were in?

- **I worked on *Octagon* with Chuck Norris.** I was a martial artist extra and I got to do some karate stuff. I saw myself up on the screen for maybe one second. *See the website for all of Simon Rhee's films.*

Q: How do stunt actors get work?

- **I have been doing this for more than ten years**, so a lot of stunt coordinators know me. They will call me directly and ask me for my availability.

- **The way to find jobs** once you are in Los Angeles is through EIDC, www.EIDC.com, which is a permit office. They post where productions are shooting. You can go to the office or to the website and download addresses. I go to the website, find out what films are shooting and who the stunt coordinator is and then give them my picture and resume.

- **Shoot a demo reel** that demonstrates your martial arts, fencing, highfalls to an airbag, mototcycle tricks, whatever your stunt skills are and submit the reel to stunt coordinators.

Resources

James Lew, jameslew.com. Complete filmography, bio, photos etc. With links to many of the top action actors' website.

Simon Rhee, 818/224-3400, simonrhee.net. 22880 Ventura Blvd., Woodland Hills, 91364. Considered one of the best Karate studios, many celebrities have studied with Master Rhee. He is also a prominent action/stunt actor, *Best of the Best I & II,* and other films.

Film Fighting LA, 310/558-1143, filmfightingla.com. Bob Goodwin offers workshops for about $60 a piece. He has worked with a number of stars, including Christian Bale for *Batman Begins.*

Hong Kong Wire Action Team, hongkongwireactionteam.com. Providing creative action for the entertainment industry.

The Stuntmen's Association, stuntmen.com

Stunts Unlimited, stuntsunlimited.com.

International Stunt Association, isa-stunts.com.

Stuntwomen's Association, stuntwomen.com.

United Stuntwomen's Association, usastunts.com.

Women Stunt Professionals, V10stunts.com

Los Angeles Fight Academy, 4lafa.org. Also has listings of other links.

Academy of Theatrical Combat, theatricalcombat.com.
Beverly Hills Karate Academy, 310/275-2661. 9085 Santa Monica Blvd., West Los Angeles 90069. Emil Farkas teaches motion picture stunt fighting and all forms of martial arts stunts. He is a stunt coordinator and frequently casts stunt people from his classes.

Tim Weske's Swordplay Fencing Studio. 818/566-1777. swordplayla.com. timweske. com. 64 E. Magnolia Blvd. Burbank, 91502.

Extra Work

• **All actors should work** at least several days of extra work at the beginning of their careers. New actors have no idea what it is like to be on an actual film or television set. No person or book can explain what it is like to be working on location or on a sound stage. As an extra, you are part of the action and become familiar with studios and locations, not to mention the learning experience you get from watching professionals at work. An actor told me about working background on *Catch Me if You Can*, sitting in an airplane seat behind Tom Hanks and Leonardo DiCaprio as they discussed their intentions with director Steven Spielberg. How valuable is that?! If you are working part-time jobs to support your career, why not include extra jobs?

• **Keep a very low profile on the set,** that way no one will remember you as an extra. There is still a bit of a stigma attached to being an extra in Los Angeles; in New York it is not unusual to be an extra one day and a guest star the next. I want to caution you, I've seen actors get hooked on extra work and they end up a year later without having moved their acting careers ahead, they are exhausted, overworked and underpaid. You can get all the education you need with a maximum of 30 days.

• **There is a strict on-the-set protocol.** Never go on the set until you have read *Back To One: The Movie Extras' Guidebook (see Resources.)* As an extra, you are the lowest in the pecking order so your needs will barely be considered. Bring water, snacks, sunscreen, chair and reading material with you. Have anything you might need packed in your car—clothes to layer, sun glasses, reading material, playing cards, loose change and small bills; anything you might need to be comfortable.

• **Your best friend on the set is the second assistant director (2nd A.D.).** Report in as soon as you arrive and always let the A.D. know when you are stepping away from the set. When you are called, answer immediately in a loud voice that you are on your way and start walking with haste to where you are needed. The A.D. will most likely tell you where to move and what to do during the filming. I have overheard a second AD tell the third A.D. that she never wanted to see a certain extra on the set again because he wasn't cooperative. Everywhere you work, you are building a reputation; make sure you can be proud of it.

• **There is a possibility of getting your SAG card** through extra work. When you get three SAG vouchers, you are eligible to join SAG. A voucher is your pay record and is a three-page multicolored form. Each project has a limited number of these vouchers to hand out each day and every nonunion actor doing extra work wants one. The best advice is to do your job professionally with a great attitude. SAG has been threatening to end this voucher system.

• **Or, if they decide they need someone to say something** like, "Hey, pull that truck over here," there is no time to go out and hire an actor, so they point to one of the extras. That means you get paid SAG minimum for a line and are eligible to join SAG. Plus, you'll get residuals on that work for many years. If you are asked to do a line, do not leave the set without the day-player voucher which contains the daily rate, currently about $725.

• **Samuel L. Jackson** was a stand-in for Bill Cosby for three years on the original *Bill Cosby Show*. He said he learned so much about the camera working on the show.

• **Rob Morrow** (*Northern Exposure*) had been on *Saturday Night Live* in 1980 as an extra, playing juror #11 in a skit with Jane Curtain, Bill Murray and Garrett Morris. Twelve years later, he guest-hosted the show.

• **Judith Light** (*Who's The Boss*) began her career with a five-year role on *One Life To Live*. She landed that role after being an understudy on the soap. She took the understudy role—which is not even on-camera—because she was broke. Lucky for her.

• **Bruce Willis** in 1990 was on a TV show honoring Frank Sinatra's 75th birthday. In 1980, he was a photo-double and stand-in (extra) on Frank's movie, *First Deadly Sin*. Bruce said, "Frank had been such an inspiration on the set, talking to the actors and extras, telling stories of working on *From Here To Eternity."* Bruce went from a film extra to a multimillion dollar superstar in those 10 years.

• **Other actors who worked as extras** at the beginning of their careers are Ben Affleck, Matt Damon, Sharon Stone (Woody Allen's *Stardust Memories*), Bruce Willis, *(The Verdict)*, Brad Pitt (*Cutting Class*), Anjelica Huston, Dustin Hoffman, Kevin Costner, John Wayne, Bette Midler, Gary Cooper, Marlene Dietrich, Clark Gable, Robert Mitchum, Jean Harlow and Sophia Loren.

• **Casting director Marvin Paige**, who cast *General Hospital* for years, said in an interview:

  • **I don't refer to our people in that category as "extras."** I refer to them as atmosphere people. The point is, I want every cast member to be an actor. I don't just want a body standing there because, among other things, if they aren't actors, there's always a chance they'll trip over the scenery. People who have the training and background respond much better to direction so I prefer to have people who really are pursuing acting careers even in small roles. For example, we have an actor who plays a bartender; sometimes he has dialogue and sometimes not. But he's been working with us three or four years and that's an actor's number one goal—getting work.

• **Cullen Chambers, actor, background artist, author,** has helped tens of thousands of people work as extras over the years. His best selling book, *Back To One: The Movie Extras' Guidebook*, is a manual with step-by-step instructions.

Q: Why would an actor want to work as an extra?

  • **It's the first step toward an acting career.** It's like starting in the mail room and working your way up. You gain knowledge, experience and technical insight into the film making process. I've had to do more acting in the background on certain films than in principal roles; as a fireman, fighting fires, rescuing people in earthquakes, warping across the galaxy on the bridge of Starship Enterprise. You become aware of where the camera is and how to make a cross very precisely take after take so you won't block an actor who's delivering lines.

Q: How does a person get started?

  • **By registering with one or more of the extra casting agencies.** I've listed over 100 agencies in my book and rated them. You'll also find agencies advertised in trade publications. Some agencies charge a fee. Scams abound in this business—don't register with any agency that charges more than $20 or insists on expensive photos. You can have your extra pictures taken for $25 by the best in the business.

Q: What tools does an extra need?

- Here are a few: 3x5 color photos, telephone, an answering machine or service and/or a pager, dependable transportation, *Thomas Guide* Mapbook, and wardrobe which can be picked up at yard sales or thrift shops. Put together a business and formal look and some period outfits from the '50s, '60s, '70s, etc. It's all tax-deductible.

Q: What are some of the rules for an extra when on the set?

- **Number one rule is listen.** The director or assistant director's job is to tell you exactly what to do. Be on time. Bring three changes of wardrobe, pen and paper, book, small change, snack, and a folding chair. Sign in and out with the assistant directors or their assistants. Don't talk to or bother the principal actors—those with lines.

Q: How much does a nonunion extra make and how often can they work?

- **If they hustle, five to seven days a week.** The lowest pay is $6.75 an hour, $54 a day plus overtime and bumps which are for special bits. $101.24 for 12 hours. On many shoots you do work overtime.

Q: How can you work on your favorite TV show?

- **The end credits list the Unit Production Manager**, Stage Manager or Assistant Director, and where the show is taped or filmed. Call the studio. Ask for the show's production office and ask for the production manager or A.D. Say you're interested in working as a background actor and ask what extra casting agency they use. Then contact that agency and follow up as instructed in my book. *Cullen also lists the casting companies of every show in his monthly magazine. See below.*

- **Wardrobe designer and costumer Tom Baxter gives a few hints to extras:**

- **If you are working as an extra the best thing to do is to be polite** to the wardrobe person. A lot of times they can get you silent bits; sometimes they can even get you a line if you fit into a costume they have. I can't tell you how many times an extra who fit the mailman or cop uniform has gotten lines because I said that's who fits the costume. If you are wearing wardrobe from the studio's department, take care of it; watch where you put it down and never leave it lying around. We lost a jacket on a show that was loaned to an extra and he won't be back on the show again. The jacket cost more than he made. Make sure all of the clothes you bring to wear are clean and ironed perfectly.

• **I spoke with Judi Keppler of Judi's Casting.**

Q: What do you think it takes to be an extra?

• **People have no conception of the discipline and hard work it takes.**
A lot of people aren't used to getting up early. When we were doing a
two-day commercial shoot, our call time at the Johnny Rocket Cafe
was 5:30 in the morning. It takes money. You need money to survive
when you're not working. There's no guarantee you're going to work
next week.

Q: Do you have any special advice for extras?

• **If an extra is really intent on getting ahead**, they should not only
register with the different agencies, but they should learn how to
network a little bit so they are not just a photo on a piece of paper.
They have to get an identity and a reputation with the agency and
that takes time. And yet, it's a fine line because they can't be a pest.
I've had actors who would call me up in the morning and say, "Do
you need any cigarettes? Do you want a cappuccino?" They were very
smart. You can't bring people flowers and booze, it's too tacky. But
little things like, "I've got a half a day free. Can I come by and do
some filing or something?" Those people you remember, obviously,
and try to take care of them. It's a matter of perseverance, which
means you don't give up.

• **Stand-in**. The stand-in takes the place of the principal actor, freeing
them from tedious hours of lighting and camera blocking. They also
are there to protect and take care of the actors they replace—by showing them any blocking changes. The stand-ins tend to get more respect
on the sets they work on because they are there week in and week out.
They are part of the crew.

• **Extra casting agencies** are listed in *Back Stage West*; I've listed a few
here to get you started. All agencies require two forms of identification:
social security card, driver's license, passport or birth certificate and either
a 3x5 or 4x6 color picture of you against a white background.

• **Calling Services.** Most of the people I know who are doing extra work
say they have to use calling services to get their jobs. The service calls the
agencies for you and books your work for the next day. They call your
machine or beep you to tell you where to report. There is usually a fee
for starting the service and then a monthly fee of around $60.

• **SAG is still investigating** the call-in services and the accessibility of SAG vouchers. As in all areas of the business, changes can happen very fast. Investigate everything thoroughly. One of my students got her three SAG vouchers in a couple of weeks while she was interning at Bill Dance's Extra Casting Service. The interns in the office are first to hear about a film or television show that is giving out SAG vouchers. You have to work all the angles to get what you need.

Thanks to Cullen Chambers for many of the resources below.

Resources

To download and print an updated version of this and all resource lists, go to actingiseverything.com.

Cullen Chambers, 818/558-1196. backtoone.net. *Back To One: The Movie Extras Guidebook*, *$24.95* or *Movie Extra Work For Rocket Scientists*, a pocket-sized version of *Movie Extras Guidebook*, $18.95. The books can be purchased at theatrical bookstores and many newsstands in Los Angeles, or you can call and mail order. Free trial subscription to the monthly *Hollywood Industry Insider Magazine* when you order a copy of either book. To receive a free Extra Pay Rate Schedule ($5 value) send a self-addressed, stamped envelope to Back To One, Attention: Pay Scale, P.O. Box 753, Hollywood, CA 90078. It fits in your wallet so at the end of day you can figure out how much you made. It also lists some extra casting agencies and other information.

Rich Hogan's Photos for Extras, 323/467-2628. At Hollywood and Vine. The best. Prices start at $25 for 3x5s. He registers extras for Sunset Casting and Idell James Commercial Extras. Also a great headshot photographer; see the photo sections.

Filmla.com. This is a website that delivers a show sheet that tells where productions are filming that day on location in Los Angeles. You have to register to receive the information. This would be helpful if want to go to sets to see if they can use you as an extra that day.

Screen Actors Guild Extra scales: $126 in 2006. Stand-ins make $141. Commercial extras and stand-ins make $292.

AFTRA Extra daily rates are: General extra network sitcom, $92; 30-minute serial, $108. 60-minute serial, $140.

AFTRA Extras Casting File. This is a file of pictures and resumes of paid-up members who are available to do extra and stand-in work on AFTRA programs. Producers and casting representatives call and request names and home telephone numbers from the file. To submit: send your picture and resume to Extra File, c/o AFTRA, or drop them off at the membership counter. Sometimes you may be hired without being in AFTRA. You can work 30 days without being a member and after that they will deduct the union payments from your paycheck. Two of my daughters worked on *Facts of Life* as extras, joining this way. Some situation comedies hire AFTRA members as extras or "Under 5s" (under five lines). Pick up an AFTRA show sheet (printed monthly) then contact the production companies and find out who casts the extras. Call the person, ask if you can send a picture and/or come in for a meeting. Some Soap Opera Casting Directors attend cold reading showcases, so you can meet them that way. You can also send in a picture, etc. They will be listed on the show sheet.

EXTRA CASTING AGENTS

People registering for extra work must bring two original IDs: driver's license, passport, voter registration card, birth certificate or social security card. If in a union, bring union card. Also, bring exact cash or money order.

Central Casting, 818/562-2755. ep-services.com for information on how to register. 220 S. Flower St., Burbank, 91502. Fee: $25 union and nonunion. Cash only, exact change. For union members, bring your current union card. 818/562-2700 for address and directions only. This is the main extras agency in town; they cast extras for over 90 percent of TV shows.

Lacasting.com, 323/462-8000. 6671 Sunset Blvd., Hollywood, 90028. Popular casting site now offers Extras Connection free to members to, as they put it, "help you pay the bills between your principal bookings." Simply go to the office, sign up for extra work and they will take two digital photos of you.

Actorsaccess.com, 310/276-9166, 310/385-6920. Now offers Extras Access, which allows you to look up extras casting calls, build a profile and submit for projects. Free membership lets you load two pictures and pay $2 per submission. The regular membership costs $50 a year, allows you four pictures to post and all submissions are free.

Back to One Casting, 818/558-1196. casting@backtoone.net. Union and nonunion, commercials and print work. $25 photo imaging fee.

Uncut Extra Agency, 310/444-2929. uncutcasting.com. $50 signup fee.

Christopher Gray Casting, 323/658-1530. christophergraycasting.com. 8271 Melrose Ave. Ste 100, L.A., 90046.

Bill Dance Casting, 818/754-6634 or 818/725-4209. 4605 Lankershim Blvd. #401, North Hollywood, 91602. billdancecasting.com. Fee: $25. Everyone says good things about this casting company. They also use interns if you want to learn all about extra work.

Idell James Casting, 310/230-9344. 15332 Antioch Street, PMB #117, Pacific Pallisades, 90272. Pictures: send 8x10 with resume. Union members for commercials. Likes beautiful young people. Very selective.

Producers Casting, 310/469-0229. Fee: $35, must be SAG member. Casts for commercials. Very selective.

Jeff Olan Casting, 818/377-4475. 14044 Ventura Blvd., Ste. 209, Sherman Oaks, 91423. Fee: $25 computer imaging. They will call you in; they prefer not to work with a call-in service. Jeff has been doing this for years and works hard for his people.

Sunset Casting Registration, 323/467-9326. Nonunion commercials. EZM Studios, 1680 Vine St., Rm #1110, Hollywood, 90028. Registration Fee: $35.

Burbank Casting, 818/504-6213. burbankcasting.com. Looking specifically for models between 18 and 28. $40 registration fee.

Kids! Background Talent, 661/964-0131. 207 S. Flower, 2nd Floor, Burbank, 91502. $30 registration and they take a 20% commission when the children work. Parents and children can get a good feel of what the business really is by working at least a few days as an extra. If you want your children to work extra jobs you will pay 15% to 20% as commission to the extra company. Adults wouldn't stand for this but I guess they figure the kids don't need to earn a living and they get the parent along to take care of the child for free.

SAN DIEGO

Background San Diego, 858/974-8970. There are several shows that shoot there. There is an information line giving full information and how to register. Free.

CALLING SERVICES

Extra Management, 818/972-9474. Tell them Cullen Chambers from *Back To One* sent you for $75 off the startup fee. Otherwise, union fee is $160 and nonunion is $85.

Studio Phone, 310/202-9872. 10624 Regent St., Los Angeles, 90034. P.O.B. 661669, Los Angeles, 90066. The oldest calling service. Union only. Registration Tu,W,Th by appointment. They do take some nonunion extras and will try to help you get your three vouchers.

FREE REGISTRATION EXTRA CASTING COMPANIES

To register at the following agencies, send a 3x5 color snapshot along with your general information.

Creative Extras Casting, 310/203-7860. 2461 Santa Monica Blvd., #501, Santa Monica, 90404.

Xtraz Casting, 818/781-0066. P.O. Box 4145, Valley Village, 91617.

Short Film Projects

including

Student and Graduate Films

• **Chris Cooper** is a character actor who works all the time. Some of his roles include his Oscar-winning performance in *Adaptation*, the cruel father in *American Beauty* and the sheriff in *Lone Star*. He grew up in Kansas City and started working backstage in regional theatres there. He moved to New York, studied, worked on and off-Broadway and eventually an NYU student film led to his big break. Director/writer John Sayles cast him in his student film, then used him in other small roles and later wrote the lead in *Lone Star* for him.

• **Acting in student films** and projects can be your gateway to an acting career. It is not always easy to get a copy of the finished work—it usually takes a great deal of persistence on your part. One way to increase your chances is to have a professional contract for the producer/director to sign, laying out any financial compensation that was discussed and guaranteeing you a copy of your work. Make sure you have this signed on the first day of rehearsal when everybody is still excited about the project. Check for free downloadable contracts at holdonlog.com, and for a fee at findlegalforms.com and filmtvcontracts.com.

• **Student films are not always shot** under the best of circumstances; the directors are learning too. And very rarely do you get paid for your work. But if you are lucky and end up on a director's reel, you could be seen by every producer and agent in town, and possibly be seen at many film festivals. There is a possibility of being spotted and cast in a major production because of your acting work in a promising graduate director's reel.

• **If you are a beginner, you will gain valuable experience** in front of a camera—experience you cannot get in acting class or anywhere else. If you are a seasoned actor, you may get the chance to play a leading role, portraying the type of character that you may not be cast as in a commercial film. Circulating that film or being seen at the screening may have casting people thinking of you for a wider variety of roles.

• USC, UCLA, AFI (American Film Institute), The Los Angeles Film School, Cal Arts and Loyola Marymount are the finest film schools in the world and their students need actors for their projects. They advertise in *Back Stage West* most heavily at the beginning of each semester or quarter. Crew work is also available. It is valuable to meet these future filmmakers when they are starting out. I wonder who acted in George Lucas' first films at USC.

• **When working on a student production,** expect long delays and mistakes. You will learn how to size up a situation and to pick and choose the projects that you think will benefit you. Often student directors want actors to rehearse scenes from well known films to take into their directing classes. I feel it is of value to do this; their professors are working directors who may be in the process of casting a film you would be perfect for. You must open yourself to opportunities as often as possible.

• *Back Stage West* **writes an occasional column** about the hot talents in independent and student films. One of the things they reported on was the annual Student Academy Awards held by The Academy of Motion Picture Arts and Sciences. They honor student filmmakers from all across the country in four categories of filmmaking: alternative, animation, documentary and dramatic film. Past winners have come from Dartmouth, Rhode Island, NYU, Harvard, Stanford, Yale and Los Angeles. Also, the Academy of Television Arts & Sciences Foundation's annual College Television Awards included winners from AFI, Brigham Young, NYU, Missouri, Florida, Columbia and Northwestern. Bottom line, you can act in or produce student films anywhere you live.

• **Ang Lee, director of** *Sense and Sensibility, The Ice Storm* **and** *Brokeback Mountain,* did his graduate film at NYU, winning the school's annual competition. The film caught the eye of a William Morris agent, who signed him.

• **Actor Al Sapienza was advised not to work** for first-time directors for no pay. He didn't listen and acted in director Danny Cannon's first film, *Strangers*. Four years later, Cannon gave Al a co-starring role in his film *Judge Dredd*.

• **Harvey Keitel** was studying at the Actor's Studio in New York in 1965. He answered an ad placed by film student Martin Scorsese, who was looking for actors to appear in *Who's That Knocking at My Door?*, a film he planned to make. Of course, they've gone on to make five feature films together. That student film was the turning point in Harvey's career.

• **At the 1991 Academy Awards**, Adam Davidson won an Oscar for his 1990 short film, *Lunch Date*. In his acceptance speech he said he was so surprised; he just did a 10-minute film for his film class and all "this" happened. He thanked the actors for contributing their talents.

• **Allen and Albert Hughes did a five-minute**, $250 short film that served as Albert's film school project at Los Angeles City College (LACC.) He used that as his demo reel. The 21-year-old twin brothers made their feature film debut co-writing and co-directing the $3 million New Line's *Menace II Society*. Suddenly every studio in town wanted to hire them as writers and directors.

• **Make it a priority** to gain experience by landing work in short films. Landing these roles is just as competitive as any other part of the business. This is where networking can come in handy. Get on some of the crews, come to know the filmmakers.

Resources

To download and print an updated version of this and all resource lists, go to actingiseverything.com.

filmfestivals.com. Gives schedules of all the film festivals.
48hourfilm.com. Make a film in two days of competition.
Downloadable Contracts: holdonlog.com, findlegalforms.com and filmtvcontracts.com.

Back Stage West and backstage.com list many student films that are currently casting; answer the ads. But also, you might submit your picture and resume to each school, each semester on the chance that you would be perfect for a project a student may be casting. On the website you can get their Film Festival Guide.

Signatory Workshops, 323/549-6064. sag, 5757 Wilshire Blvd., 1ˢᵗ Floor, Los Angeles, 90036. Held the second Thursday of every month from 6-8pm. They will walk you through the signatory process of sag's Low Budget Agreements from start to finish.

Anita Jesse's Studio, anitajessestudio.com. Produces two short film festivals a year. You do not have to be a member of the studio to participate in the productions. The acting in the films is very good.

TriggerStreet.com, Kevin Spacey has created a web site devoted to encouraging new filmmakers. Top industry people participating include Mike Myers, Sean Penn, Annette Bening and Bono. Elaborate online workshop and showcase for those who don't have a showbiz track record. View short films and scripts.

Flickering Image Festival, actorsbone.com/shorts. Event for filmmakers of shorts.

Film Independent, 310/432-1200. ifp.org. Nonprofit organization dedicated to helping and promoting independent filmmakers.

FILM SCHOOLS

American Film Institute, 323/856-7600. afi.com. 2021 N. Western Ave., Los Angeles 90027. Lots of good stuff comes from here, a great place to circulate headshots.

Art Center College of Design Film Department, 626/396-2274. artcenter.edu. 1700 Lida St., Pasadena, 91103.

California Institute of the Arts School of Film & Video, 661/253-7825. calarts.com. 24700 McBean Pkwy., Valencia, 91355. P&Rs are posted on the casting bulletin boards.

California State University Northridge (csun) Cinema and Television Arts Department, 818/677-3192. csun.edu. 18111 Nordoff St., Northridge, 91330. Also has schools in Los Angeles, San Bernardino and Long Beach.

Columbia College Hollywood, 818/345-8414. columbiacollege.edu. 18618 Oxnard St., Tarzana 91356, Attn: Library. Actors receive a copy of their work.

Los Angeles City College (lacc) Department of Cinema and Television, 323/953-4000 x2620. lacitycollege.edu. 855 N. Vermont Ave., Los Angeles, 90029.

The Los Angeles Film School. 323/860-0789. lafilm.com. 6363 Sunset Blvd., Los Angeles, 90028, Attn: Headshot Files. This is the newest film school, opened in the fall of 1999.

Loyola Marymount University School of Film and Television, 310/338-3033, lmu.edu. 1 LMU Drive, Los Angeles 90045

University of California Los Angeles (ucla) Department of Film, Television and Digital Media, 310/825-5761. tft.ucla.edu. 102 East Melnitz Hall, Box 951622, Los Angeles, 90095, Attn: Gary Bailard.

University of Southern California (usc) School of Cinema-Television, 213/740-2211, Attn: Production Program. usc.edu. University Park, LUC-404, Los Angeles, 90089.

DEMO REELS

• **Actors seeking agents, managers** and auditions in Los Angeles need a demo reel. For actors with credits, this is not a problem—you simply get tape or DVD copies of films and television shows you have worked on and have a dynamite editor put together a three to four minute entertaining reel featuring your best acting work. Also, condense the reel down to one minute for just a sample of your work. Short individual pieces of 30 or 40 seconds serve well as online acting resume clips. On your website you can use several different lengths of clips so industry people can click on and see more of your acting if they choose.

• **A good demo reel will consist of** several scenes from network shows or feature films showcasing your acting strengths. These scenes must all feature your closeups; the story of the clip does not matter. The acting is the most important element on your reel, though professional production value is necessary as well. Your name and where to contact you, (agent, phone number or website) should appear at the beginning and end of the reel.

• **If you have not worked in film and television** or you can't get the footage from the projects you have worked on, you must get creative. Most agents, managers and casting directors say unless you have a network quality demo reel, don't bother. Yet, they still want to see your acting on camera. I believe rules are made to be broken.

• **Bonnie Howard, theatrical agent,** says, "On demo reels I want to see a name, headshot, no montage—just some really good acting of no more than three to four minutes long."

343

• **Steven Nash, talent manager and producer, says,** "Keep your reel short. Get to the point of each clip. This is not your greatest hits DVD, it is a marketing tool designed for best impact to its target audience. These are busy casting professionals scanning quickly for potentials."

• **Kimberly Jentzen, acting coach and director, says,** "Show a short excerpt from a scene, deliver the best part, that great line delivery and we'll assume you carried the scene. Include (if you have one) a strong snippet of you with any well-established actors. Unless it is a well-established actor in the scene, do your best not to have shots of anyone else on the reel but you. If you have the footage, make two reels, one for comedy and one for drama. A bunch of consecutive great moments of you make a great promo."

• **Starmaker Jay Bernstein says,** "Get an acting partner, shoot two minutes of a wonderfully acted original drama piece and two minutes of a good original comedy piece. Bottom line, fabulous acting with good material will showcase you well." Jay advises new actors to be well-trained before letting anyone in the industry see you. He says, "They will remember you."

• **There are a number of companies** that can help you create high-quality footage for a demo reel. Among them are Stuart K. Robinson, PerfectReel Productions, My You Me Productions and coach/director Joel Asher. See the Resource List for more.

• **A student of mine had an interview at a commercial agency.** They were interested but would have to see something on tape. He went to his commercial teacher, Stuart K. Robinson, who also happens to be a terrific writer/director/producer, and asked for help. Stuart knew that one of this actor's strong suits was comedy—a nerd. He suggested shooting a one-page scene similar to *Swimming With The Sharks*. The tape is less than 90 seconds, but it starts with the actor in a suit and tie looking like a big shot with his feet on the desk, talking on the phone …until the actual boss comes is which sends him scurrying around like the nerd he was portraying. The scene was original, funny, directed and edited well and the actor landed the agent.

• **If you produce a project yourself,** you need talented, creative people with you. Research carefully. You might get several actors and hire an excellent camera crew and split the expense. This is not cheap, but when a producer or director asks you for tape, you will have something of quality to show them. Of course, you have to look very good (lighting and makeup) and above all, the acting has to be of superior quality. See if you can get your acting coach involved in the project. Remember to keep each of your edited scenes one minute to 90 seconds long for your reel.

• **Producer Bob Fraser says,** "If your footage looks amateurish, pros will dismiss it and all who participated, especially you since you asked them to look at it."

• **When picking your footage, get help.** Cutting scenes yourself can be difficult so get the help of your acting coaches and a very creative editor.

• **Study other demo reels.** Planet Video does excellent work. You can make an appointment, go by their office, put on a pair of headphones and look at many of the demo reels they have edited. This will give you an idea of how you want your reel to look.

• **Look at demo reels** on the websites below. All the businesses below have video for you to view at their facilities. I cannot emphasize enough that no matter how much money you invest, if the acting is not excellent you are wasting your time.

WEBSITE AND RESUME REELS AND CLIPS

• **Actors post headshots, resumes and demo reels** so interested industry people can simply click on a link and get a sample of the actor's work. Shorter clips are easier, technology wise, to view.

• **Short reels** provide just enough to show your look on camera, how you've been cast before and if you delivered the moment needed in the scene. For more information on demo reels, download the 10-page article at actingiseverything.com.

• **Many of the major casting sites provide online demo reel services.** Breakdown Services has affiliated with a company called Reel Access to provide both short and full-length demo reels, costing $230 or more. Now Casting sets up full or short demo reels in an easy to view format for about $60. Now Casting also allows you to tie in resume clips cheaply.

• **You will need to have** a shortened version as well as a standard reel so you are ready to provide whatever a casting director, agent or producer needs. The resources below can provide both standard and one-minute reels.

HOW TO GET FOOTAGE FOR WORK YOU HAVE DONE

• **When you do a project where a copy** of your work is promised, have a professional contract for the producer/director to sign, guaranteeing you a copy. Make sure you have this signed on the first day of rehearsal when everybody is very excited about the project. Check for downloadable contracts at holdonlog.com, findlegalforms.com or filmtvcontracts.com.

• **It is often a difficult task** to get copies of your work, though the copy is usually the reason you are working for free. Ask the director or producer what kind of tape or format you will receive your copy on. Also ask if it will be possible to get unedited takes of your closeups. Provide new, high-quality tapes, Beta-SP, ¾", Mini DV or a high grade ½" VHS tape. Also have blank ready-to-record-on CD and DVD disks. Label these and give the producer or editor the type of format they request. Perhaps they will give you copies as you are shooting or while they are editing. For your demo reel purposes there is no need to wait until the filmmakers are finished editing and with post production.

• **Buy tapes and DVDs** at Best Buy or Edgewise Media; it is important that they are new. When you get a tape copy, take the best possible care of it. Play this original master tape just once for the transfer because each time a tape is run it loses quality. You will probably have to go to a tape editing facility to have it copied. It is worth the expense.

• **If you're in a film that is available on video or DVD**, rent it, cue it up and have an editing company copy your scenes, bypassing the anti-copy code. When you are copying shows from television to use for your reel, use a new high grade tape and record on SP, standard play, speed. This will give you the best quality from your home machine for editing. For the highest quality, pay to have a company record it on DVD, ¾" or Beta tape for you; that is called an air check. Jan's Video is the best. *See Resources.*

• **Take your footage** to an editing company with a sharp editor and put your piece together using fades and all their goodies to enhance the production value.

• **Packaging counts for a lot**; you want to look very professional. Label your DVDs, jewel cases, tape boxes *and* your tapes in bold letters with your name, phone number and picture. Create a good looking presentation for your box. Slip it inside the plastic cover and you are set.

• **An editor can freeze a single frame** on your tape and download it for you, so you will have a production still to use for promoting your movie coming out or telling people when your television show is airing. This is especially valuable when you are in a scene with a star. These are also good photos to show in interviews, when you are talking about working with a well-known actor.

• **Demo reel editors charge by the hour**, so make sure you do everything you can to have your footage organized and a plan for what order the scenes or shots should be in.

• **Bonnie Howard, Theatrical and Commercial Agent.**

  • **Until you have a demo reel of your work** that you are proud of, that can help you to get roles and shows a range of your talent, you are better off without one. Tapes are generally requested (a) if you are not available for a reading, (b) to see the range of your talent, (c) to show your work to a director who may be out of town, already shooting on location.

Resources

To download and print an updated version of this and all resource lists, go to actingiseverything.com.

Screen Actors Guild, 323/549-6064. If you are making a short film, attend a Signatory Workshop, held on the second Thursday of every month from 6 to 8 PM at SAG, 5757 Wilshire Blvd., 1ˢᵗ Floor. Here you will learn how to produce your film under the SAG deferred payment plan. It's always best to use professional actors.

Watchreels.com. This is a site with many types of demo reels; included are the directors, directors of photography and editors. Good research site.

Planet Video, 323/651-3600, planet-video.com, 838 North Fairfax Ave., L.A., 90046. D.C. Douglas and David Conner are Avid editors extraordinaire, top in their field. $75 an hour for editing. $25 for your Beta Master. Archiving your demo is free. Go watch their demo reels after you have gotten all the wonderful, informative data off their website. The website takes you through the step by step process of how to get the best demo reel. When I interviewed David, he said he could deliver almost any actor's reel within a four hour session, $300. If you want to design your reel yourself, you know exactly what you want and are ready to go with your tapes cued to the best performance, you can get it done in two hours or less.

Production HQ, 323/867-6769, productionhq.com. 1104 S. Hayorth Ave., Los Angeles 90035. Jay Lee does great editing for demo reels. I've been impressed with the reels I've seen. My students tell me Jay is very easy to work with, inventive and reasonable.

Jan's Video Editing, 323/462-5511, jansvideo@aol.com. 6381 Hollywood Blvd., Ste. 430, Hollywood, 90028. M-F 9-6. Make an appointment, Doreen will give her recommendations and assign you an editor. She believes actors need 1-½ to 2 hours for first time reels. You only pay for the actual editing time you use. All the editors are very well trained and have years of experience. Jan's Video will aircheck your shows for you from the air on ¾" or Beta tape, $20 for an hour show, $15 for ½ hour. Best of all, they may have a copy of a show you did years ago, which would be impossible to obtain from any other source. Jan's has the most extensive library of tapes anywhere—most network series and all movies of the week taped from satellite. They can take stills from your videos. They can transfer formats from any country to our formats and they can put your reel on any format you may need. Jan's has been producing demo reels longer than any other editing house. *Entertainment Tonight, Inside Edition, Extra* and *Access Hollywood* are always calling to grab something from their archives.

Stuart K. Robinson, 310/558-4961. $80 an hour for ongoing students; $100 an hour for others. He meets with the actor or actors to see what the short film needs to say about the type of characters the actor can best market themselves as. He then writes a script and they meet to rehearse. Stuart believes that the preparation should not be mixed with the shooting. He shoots with his small crew, then edits and scores the short film when it enhances the scene. He teaches a motivating, positive acting philosophy and is very focused on actors landing the jobs.

PerfectReel Productions, Michael McClure, 818/341-8474, PerfectReel.com, 3749 Cahuenga Blvd. West, Studio City, 91604. Basics: Shooting, $59 per hour; Editing, $49 per hour. Options: Custom written scene, $50; Actor provided per scene, $55; Crew Provided per scene $50; Location, $45; Acting Coaching, $45. Their website is full of information on shooting demo reels. In answer to, "Can I put this on my resume?" He says, "Of course, we are a legitimate production company known for our larger projects as well. Treat it like a short film. If we get any inquiry calls, we'll back you up."

Kati Lamkin, editlady.com, works with Actorsite, 5656 Cahuenga Blvd., North Hollywood, 91601. $180 for a 4 to 10 minute reel on a mini DV and master copy DVD. Additional charges for capturing more footage and custom designs for packaging. Daughter of actress Kathy Lamkin who says, "She's got the creative eye, freelances in casting and knows what catches a casting director's eye."

My You Me Productions, 310/820-1772, myyoume.com, 2050 S. Bundy Drive, #104, L.A., 90025. They do air checks. They shoot demo reels on locations or at their studio; audition tapes; blue screen; demo reels to computer CD ROMS; check them out. They create websites including pictures resumes and demo reels. Founded by actor Richard and Miyumi Heene, this company is dedicated to helping actors achieve their marketing goals.

Joel Asher Studio & Michael Communications, 818/785-1551. Joel-Asher-Studio.com. Actors At Work Demo Reels. Writing, directing, producing, editing, graphics and titles, packgaging, duplication—the complete demo reel. His informative, instructive video tapes he has produced are: *Getting the Part, All About Cold Readings, Casting Directors "Tell It Like It Is," Agents "Tell It Like It Is"* and *Directors on Acting!*

Potty Mouth Productions, 323/468-8361, pottymouthproductions.com, 1845 Canyon Dr., #1, Hollywood, 90028. Home of the $100 cash special for demo reels, including 8 DVD copies with case, face labels and DV master. Professional Digital Video Production. Shoot and edit your scene for $150-$200. David McClellan is an independent producer/director. "I shoot and edit projects for independent companies on a daily basis. I try to be fair in my prices and give repeat clients and referrals discounts." Good website, very informative.

Halpin-Croyle Studios, 323/874-8500, maryannhalpin.com. By appointment. Mary Ann Halpin, well-known for her individualized headshots and her accomplished videographer husband, Joe Croyle have developed a technique of shooting additional footage to enhance the footage you have.

Firepit Productions, 818/558-6622. Richard Corbin produces professional digital video audition tapes, specializing in Demo Reels for actors seeking hosting auditions. Shooting, $60 per hour, custom written scenes, editing services, and coaching available for an additional cost.

Dino Ladki, Casting Director, 310/289-4962, thecastlist.com. $90 an hour or $45 for half-hour, after the half-hour he bills in ten minute increments. Dino will rehearse and coach you on your audition and you leave with a VHS copy of your best take. He also shoots material to be used in your demo reel or to be posted on The Cast List site. Also, just a good place to go to see how your auditions are coming across in the actual audition room. It is one thing to do an audition in your acting class but going to Dino and putting audition material or even a monologue on tape will give you valuable feedback.

Duplication Station, 818/848-0994, duplicationstationinc.com, 2208 W. Magnolia Blvd., Burbank, 91506. Good for tape and DVD duplication as well as some post work, if needed for footage. Very friendly. Recommended by Karen Clark.

Dub-it, 323/993-9570 or 888/993-8248, dub-it.com. 1110 North Tamarind Ave., Hollywood, 90038. Video and CD-ROM duplication and conversion. VHS custom packaging, only orders over 2500. Minimum of tape copies is 50. When you are doing large quantities, this is the place to go.

EZTV, 310/829-3389, eztvmedia.com, 1629 18th St., Ste. 6, Santa Monica, 90404. M-SA 10AM to 7PM. Both studio and location production. They shoot demo reels at their facility. Prepare actor's reels and all dubbing, copying and editing in all formats. No air checks.

Larry Eisenberg, 323/254-5312, larryeisenberg.com. See the site and view several demo reels. Editing $40 an hour. "Every reel is a unique and entertaining production." Larry graduated with a Masters in Film Directing from Cal Arts. He says he financed his education by cutting demo tapes for actors.

Post Wanted, 818/246-9700, uniquefilms.com, 440 Western Ave., Ste. 206, Glendale, 91502. They produce actor demo reels. The price is comparable with the other listings. $1500 a day for two to three pages, plus editing. They use a three or four member crew; everything is professional.

Pro-Star Media, 818/509-9316, prostarmediagroup.com, 11366 Ventura Blvd., Studio City, 91604. M-F 10-6, Sa 12-5. Editing and copying, 10-minute tapes, air checks $45 an hour for ¾", $20 an hour for ½". Avid-computer digital editing system.

Ross Hunt Productions, 818/763-6045, rosshunthbtv.com. 12440 Moorpark, Studio City, 91604. Demo reels, inexpensive quantity duplication. Editing for $95 an hour. They also have a green screen where you can film.

Speed Video Duplication SVD, 310/828-2239, 2400 Wilshire Blvd., Santa Monica, 90403. Video copies from DV, VHS, S-VHS, ¾" Betacam SP, Betamax, 8mm. Hi-8 and VHS editing for demo tapes. Air checks.

Edgewise Media (formerly Studio Film and Tape), 800/959-5156. edgewisemedia.com, 1215 N. Highland Ave., Hollywood, 90038. Hours: 8AM-Midnight, Sunday 9-4PM, Tapes for any use available. Call ahead and they will have your order ready.

The Tape Company, 800/851-3113, thetapecompany.com. Takes orders on the site and over the phone.

Point 360, 323/957-5500, point360.com, 1220 N. Highland Ave., Los Angeles, 90038. 24 hours a day, 7 days a week. Any copying from any type of format. These are the top of the line machines, including film to tape. The best quality. No editing or air checks.

World of Video, 310/659-5959, 866/900-DUBS, wova.com, 8717 Wilshire Blvd., Beverly Hills, 90211. M-F 8AM-9PM, Sa 11AM-4PM. Demo reels. Editing and duplication for all formats, digital effects, film-to-tape and freeze frames. Avid editing, $119 per hour. Linear editing, $89 per hour. Air checks.

Phillip Kelly, 323/493-8644, davinstarr@adelphia.net. $225 for a full demo reel; $75 per one-minute speed reel. Includes all work and copy on a fully integrated menu-based DVD. An actor himself, Phillip knows the importance of a solid reel so he takes the time. Actor/ writer Jim Martyka says he is a great value. He will email you samples of his work.

Scott Cushing, 310/600-9220, onebedroomproductions.com. $60 an hour to work on your demo reel, no matter the length; prides himself on finishing high quality work quickly. His specialty is filtering through footage to find the best performances as well as cleaning up poor quality footage. Numerous clients have booked from his tapes. Also edits short films and pilots. Recommended by acting coach Scott Sedita.

Open Door Productions, 310/207-8955, opendoorproductions.net. $100 for two hours, editing with Avid technology and including three copies. Offers all other editing services. Check out the website.

Quick Nickel, 818/752-4391, quicknickel.com. $135 for an edited reel up to four minutes long, a condensed one-minute version and two DVDs with high-quality custom packaging that includes your headshot. Tons of samples of their work online for you to view.

Best Footage, 323/782-8386, bestfootage.com. $275 for up to four hours of editing and two copies of your reel. Also will host your reel online for a small fee so it will be available for anyone to view with a click of a button. Recommended by acting coach Jeffrey Marcus. If you mention his name, you get a 15 percent discount.

Carey It Off Enterprises, 818/782-4700, 818/687-0728, carey-it-off.com, 7220 Woodman Ave., #201, Van Nuys, 91405. M-F 9-6. Editing is $80 an hour, charged in 15 minute increments; airchecks for all network and cable productions dating back to 1997 range from $25-$60; duplication is $5 a copy. Also offers DVD authoring, web-ready video for acting sites and other production services.

Dubscape Incorporated, 310/202-2974, dubscape.com, 3614 Overland Ave., Los Angeles, 90034. Offers broadcast video and audio services as well as duplication for just about any kind of medium. Lots of services; check their website for prices on each. Recommended by actress Brittani Taylor.

SpeedReels, 323/931-1712, speedreels.com, 5225 Wilshire Blvd., Ste. 410, Los Angeles, 90036. They edit and condense your demo reel into a one-minute reel, which they set up on your own client website. Cost is $199 minimum; high-quality, but pricey.

Your Personal Website
Purchasing Your Name
Designing The Site &
Website Hosts

• **Having your own website** is a great marketing tool. You can send your link to anyone in an email, they can click on it to find your acting pictures, a resume and perhaps resume clips and a demo reel, and a direct email to you. You will want your website to look very professional, be easy to read and to navigate through. You will use your website address on all of your marketing materials.

• **Purchase your own name** as your domain name: JudyKerr.com, for instance. Try to get the "dot.com;" it is the best. Go to godaddy.com and see if your name is available. If you find your name is already taken, try searching again with a different domain extension (.org, .net, .biz, .tv, .info, .name, etc.), or by adding a dash in the name. For example, judykerr.com is taken. So with that name you might search for judykerr. net, judykerr.org, judykerr.info, etc. If this search also fails, you can try adding a dash to the name: judy-kerr.com, etc. Think about purchasing your name with several of the extensions if you plan on being famous. I wonder if bradpitt.tv is taken?

• **Designing, setting up and finding a host for your website** is necessary and it is an investment of time and money. The cost will depend on what you'd like to include on your site. Website developers offer different types of packages. Some just do the design while others will host the site as well. Research many actors' sites; keep a list of sites you visit and features you find appealing. When you find a site you like, the designer usually has a way to be contacted from the site. That is how I found Harry, my fabulous web designer—what a great day that was.

• **A designer from Actor Web Design** generously tells me: If you're game, you can purchase software like Dreamweaver, from Macromedia/Adobe. Those of you with a digital thumb will find the tutorial simple and informative, and you will have complete control over your site. When you use a web designer, a basic website should cost no more than $500. The more bells and whistles, the higher the cost.

• **Harry gave me these next two paragraphs** to help my readers find a good host when the newly designed website is ready to be launched.

• **To look for a host for your site** start with WebHostingTalk. com. This is one of the most reputable web hosting forums on the Internet. Click on the Web Hosting Forum link and read the reviews. When you find a hosting company that seems to offer something of value, check their site to see if they have telephone support. If not, send them an email to see how quickly they respond to your request for information. Good support is imperative. Anyone with a computer can start a hosting company. You want to be cautious **to** whom you give your credit card information. Check out their domain at the Registrar Godaddy.com. Type in the domain name of the host in question, you'll be taken to a page that states the domain name "is already taken, (click here for info)." Click on the link to find out who owns the domain. You'll arrive at a security page that states "Dear Customer, Please key in the access code you see displayed to the right in order to obtain the information you requested from our WHOIS database." You'll see an image consisting of numbers. Type the numbers in, and the information about the domain owner will be displayed. With this information, you can further determine if the host is legitimate by looking at the address and phone number. Call them if they offer a toll-free number. Beware of scammers—they're everywhere.

• **I highly recommend,** when looking for a hosting provider: Make sure they offer cPanel, (Control Panel). With cPanel, the actor can add and remove email addresses, create his or her own blogs, forums and guestbook, and lots of other neat stuff, including configuring backups of the site in case of emergency. To find cPanel hosts, type: "cPanel hosting providers" in Google, then search for the right prices. When you find one, send an email off to the company FIRST to see what kind of response time you get with an answer. If you don't hear back within an hour or two, don't waste the time or money.

Resources

To download and print an updated version of this and all resource lists, go to actingiseverything.com.

Harry's list of hosts he knows to be reputable, with longevity, and reasonable:
HTTPme, httpme.com (expensive but lots of space for video clips)
DownTownHost, downtownhost.com
LunarPages, lunarpages.com (multiple domains for one low price, toll free number)
Idologic, idologic.com
HostingMatters, hostingmatters.com
Clook, clook.us
HostGator, hostgator.com
A good article for searching for an honest host: whreviews.com/searchstrategy.htm
Skynethosting.net, hosts sites.
Godaddy.com to purchase the name for your site.
WebHostingTalk.com for reviews of web hosters.
Actor Web Design recommends for web hosting: actors.thewebhost.info for $6/mo.

Actor Web Design: actorwebdesign.com. Specializing in actor websites, creating branding, logo, reel editing, reel publishing to DVD, VHS and the Internet. Web design, promo material design, web hosting, computer consulting and more.

My You Me Productions, 310/820-1772, Myyoume.com, 2050 S. Bundy Drive, #104, West Los Angeles. Richard and Mayumi Heene create websites including pictures, resumes and demo reels. Dedicated to helping actors achieve their marketing goals. Just $80 to create a site and a one-minute video reel and $7.50 a month to host the site. You can use your own site name or use their site with a slash and then your name. I always believe it best to have your own name established. For just straight web designing without using their hosting, they charge $80 an hour without watching the clock too closely.

Wbsites4actors.com. Jonathan Levit designs websites for actors that include a homepage with one photo, a headshot page with two more photos, a resume page and a contact page all for $500. Design for additional pages including video are $75 each or $125 for a larger video clip. For designing sites not hosted by their company, he quotes a price according to the amount of work needed.

ActorsGetAWebsiteHere.com, 866/248-3313. Tom Hillman will design your site in a couple different of packages. The one-page with gallery is $99 to set up and $12.95 monthly while the six-page with mult-media content and a blog is $495 to set up and $19.95 monthly. Demo reels that allow viewers to skip to particular scenes. Rave reviews.

inSITEful.org, 310/359-2536. Web page designer that specializes in designing for creative people, including actors. Prices range from $300 and up depending upon what you need on your page. Includes hosting costs.

Jade Tiger Productions, 310/485-7285, jadetiger.com. 9903 Santa Monica Blvd., #942, Beverly Hills, 90212. Will help you design and maintain your site. Lots of samples available on their site for you to check out. Recommended by actress Tiana Hynes.

Also check out the Acting Websites section for a number of sites that allow you to post headshots, resumes and even demo reels and clips on their sites.

Producing Your Own Projects

• **If you find it hard to break into the business**, or if it's been a while since you have acted, you have the power to generate projects for yourself, whether it's an independent film or a theatre project. The people interviewed below are creating work in Los Angeles. If you are not in Los Angeles yet, start at home. If you are in Los Angeles, start now. If you aren't familiar with how stage or performance art is produced, apprentice yourself to directors and producers. They are always looking for unpaid hard workers in exchange for the education they will give you. *Back Stage West* lists ads for technical and back stage people all the time. The same is true for film and video projects. There are a number of independent projects that need crew help; working on these projects can give you some valuable experience and help you make your own films.

• **The advances in both commercial digital video cameras and the Internet** are helping everybody who ever dreamed of making a film. For a couple thousand dollars, aspiring filmmakers can get a decent enough camera for making a short digital video movie. Granted, these won't give you the quality of a 35MM film, but there are features on these cameras that can give you a low-end but professional-looking piece. Also, more and more filmmakers are posting their projects online, either on their own sites or popular sites like MySpace.com and YouTube.com, and gaining a following. These videos will look fine on computer monitors and television screens; the difference in quality will show up on the big screen, however. If you have some filmmaking experience and friends willing to work with you, why not make your own film? It's another way to keep working on your craft and be seen.

• **SAGIndie is a union outreach program from the union for independent filmmakers.** The group does film festivals, trade shows, panel discussions and even one-on-one meetings to help independent writers, directors and actors do their own projects. Most important, they provide guidelines for different SAG independent film projects. Author and casting director Bonnie Gillespie provided this helpful information on the different types of SAG Indie projects and what you, as an actor or producer, can expect when working on these projects. All information, including payments, as of May 2006.

SAG Short Film Agreement: Films 35 minutes in length or less with a budget under $50,000 that shoot entirely in the US can use the new SAG Short Film Agreement. This agreement allows all salaries to be deferred (this is the well-known copy, credit, meals deal) and also permits the producer to distribute the film at film festivals. Only if the film is bought for distribution beyond the film festival circuit, actors will receive deferred payments of $100/day.

SAG Ultra Low Budget Agreement: Producers with budgets below $200,000 for films shooting entirely in the US can use the new SAG Ultra Low Budget Agreement, which allows for six-day workweeks, reduced overtime, and SAG actors hired at a rate of $100 per day. These films qualify for distribution without producers having to pay "step-up" fees to actors, however there are residuals due to SAG members based on the film's distribution deals. Basically, if a SAG actor does a film under the ULB Agreement for $100/day and that film is later shown on TV or cable or sold in DVD or VHS format, that actor will receive a percentage of the distributor's gross receipts based on the number of days he or she worked on the film.

One of the biggest benefits to the filmmaker, in using the SAG Ultra Low Budget Agreement, is that actors don't have to sign off to allow any distribution deal to move forward. Because they were paid up front, they haven't loaned out their performances. This actually helps filmmakers who may lose a distribution deal on a film starring an actor who "made it big" since the filming of the project. One of the biggest benefits to actors working under the ULB Agreement is that they now are paid up front to do the work. Since distribution deals are often not reached, most actors doing films for no pay, hoping for back-end money, never see a dime. With this agreement $100/day is paid to each actor before the film is even finished, regardless of its future beyond that. A further benefit to the actor is that work done in ULB films goes toward Pension & Health Benefits.

SAG Modified Low Budget Agreement: This agreement is for films with budgets under $625,000 shooting in the US with initial theatrical release. There are also wonderful Diversity in Casting and Background Actor Incentives for the MLB contract which allow for higher total budgets (up to $937,500) if the Incentive terms are met (more info at the SAGIndie website). Daily rate is $268, weekly is $933. Residuals kick in for distribution beyond the initial theatrical market (again, for TV cable, and DVD/VHS release). This is the smallest-budget level at which a non-union actor must be Taft-Hartleyed to join SAG.

SAG Low Budget Agreement: For films with total budgets under $2,500,000 shot in the US with initial theatrical release, the SAG Low Budget Agreement provides a daily rate of $504 and a weekly rate of $1752. Same backend residual deal as above. Background actors receive $122 per day. Non-SAG actors may be cast in Low Budget films only with a Taft-Hartley Report from production. Again, there is a Diversity in Casting Incentive, which allows for an increase in the budget to a total of $3,750,000.

• **For theatre projects, once you have found material** that suits your personal style, honed, rehearsed and performed it, you may want to professionally tape or film parts of the production. A few minutes can be used for your audition tape, or perhaps you can find directors who need a 10, 15 or even 30-minute piece for their demo reels. Material is the hardest thing to develop. Once you have that, you may find all kinds of help from people who need to demonstrate their skills also.

• **Stacey Smithey, actress and producer**, has produced several plays. I asked her to write about what it takes to produce a play. She is always generating a place for herself to act.

  • **I learned how to produce theater by trial and error**. I found plays by going to Samuel French Bookstore and looking through their catalog of plays. The catalog breaks down plays by number of characters. It also lists the genre, a summary, past press quotes, any restrictions and royalty range (usually between $40 and $60 per performance and there is a security bond/deposit of $500 which you get back at the end). You can buy the catalog for $3. I then bought plays I thought were interesting and read them. I applied for the rights through Samuel French. You can send a letter to them stating the play, author, venue and number of seats, dates of performances, ticket price and type of performance (amateur, Equity, etc.). It can take anywhere from one week to five months to get a response, so start early.

  • **The most important choice is your material**, but the second most important choice is the theater. Call every theater in town and ask their prices, availability for performance and rehearsal. This is important because many theaters are not available at night for rehearsal as they are rented out for classes—and tech week starting at midnight every night makes it rough! It is better to pick a well-known theater, but they do tend to be much more expensive. You can also barter with the theater owner to bring down the price or throw in some extra rehearsal time. I have always paid less than the price they have asked. You can also ask to pay for the first two weeks up front and then pay the rest after you have opened and made some money. Some theaters want all the rent up front, but some will work with you and your needs. You can also find better prices if you are willing to do weeknight productions as opposed to weekend productions. It is usually half price if not 75% less. As a producer, you will want to make sure you have insurance. Theaters usually require this. It is about $425 for eight performances over a one month period.

- **You will need to cast and crew up your production.** A great way to raise funds is to split the cost among the actors. You need to agree upon this up front and you can't advertise this in *Back Stage West*. You can ask actors in your classes, friends, etc. You will need to find a director, lighting designer and operator, sound operator, set designer, graphic designer for postcards and flyers, press point person, box office/concessions attendant. Ask around—you will find these people. They will show up. It is wonderful when they do! Props and wardrobe are usually handled by the actors. You need a reservation phone number, reservation lists by date, cash box and cash change.

- **You will also need sound cues and music**, usually within your show. (Music within the play should be cleared through the music publisher. You can also ask unknown bands to use their music for free). It is also nice to have pre-show music, curtain call music, post-show music, and lobby music.

Other needs:

- **Rehearsal schedule**, usually four to eight weeks.

- **Other rehearsal venues** such as apartments, houses, etc..

- **Opening night reception** is nice.

- **Concession menu**, cookies, coffee, water, soda—you have to have a liquor license to "sell" alcohol, but many people serve it "for free" but accept donations.

- **Always bring extra toilet paper**, trash bags, paper towels—you never know!

- **Press Kit for reviewers and industry people.** This includes a press release, bios of cast and crew, actor's photos and press photos. They may want to feature your production and use still photos you provide.

- **Fax the press release** and invitations to press outlets for consideration for free listings and reviews at least one month in advance. Press outlets include *LA Times, LA Weekly, Back Stage West, Variety, Hollywood Reporter, New Times, Venice Magazine, Tolucan Times*—make follow up calls to make sure they received faxes and will be attending.

- **You may consider advertising,** but it is expensive. Only do this if you have a lot of money.

- **Lobby Board** with actor's headshots.

- **Awards.** Find out if you are eligible for the Ovation Awards, *LA Weekly* Awards, Drama Critic's Circle.

- **Program.** Include credits and bios of cast and crew.

- **Promotion.** Postcards, flyers, posters, map to venue and list of local restaurants you recommend. Opening night invites to casting directors and agents.

- **Web Tix offers your tickets at half-price** and On The House will give your tickets for free to their members and you get a free audience. This is good on press nights.

- **It is a joy to produce plays.** It is such a high when everything and everyone come together. Live theater is like nothing else! And as Judy Kerr suggested, "You will look back on this time as sweet!" The first play I produced was with Judy as director. How lucky we were to have such a wonderful, generous woman to direct, guide and lead us. It was a cherished time in my life.

- **Anne Etue is an actor, director, producer and publicist** for several theaters and projects. Anne directs and helps produce performers Amy Hill's and Nobuko Miyanoto's one-woman shows.

Q: How did you get interested in one-person shows?

- **Amy had some material** that she thought would make a good one-person show, and asked me to direct it. Her first show, *Tokyo Bound,* had a theme of her at age 18 going to Japan to find her mother's roots. We put the ideas on 3x5 cards and she would go away and start writing. I was initially a sounding board for her on whether or not I thought the material worked and I did some editing for her. She also had a dramaturge involved in the process.

Q: What's a dramaturge?

- **A dramaturge is a person** who looks at the script and helps to shape it. It's common in most theater companies to help research the material or go through the material and give feedback on whether it should be produced. One mistake a lot of people make is not to have a director or someone outside the piece to formulate it. Amy was approached by the Japanese-American Cultural Center and that was the first booking.

Q: Was that for money?

• **It wasn't much, but we always had some kind of compensation.** We decided that we had a good half-hour of material. Then we workshopped it at West Coast Ensemble. We had maybe 10 people in to give us some feedback in preparation for a run at the East West Players. Amy applied for a $9,000 grant from the Cultural Affairs Department; that's how the first run was partially funded.

• **When you get a grant, they don't just hand you a check** but at least it validates the goal; it's the green light to keep on working on it. We had a run and it was a huge success. Former *L.A. Times* critic Sylvie Drake came and saw it, loved it and gave us the front page. All of the reviews were outstanding. At the 99-seat level, it probably was one of the most successful one-person shows. In the program I was listed as Hika Keltamaki, stage manager; Elizabeth Bennett, promotions; Anne Etue, director. It was basically me and Amy. We had a lighting designer, a set designer, a music designer. Amy felt very strongly about paying everybody involved.

• **Another fertile ground for these one-person shows is festivals** in Canada. We did the Montreal Fringe Festival. We had tons of frequent flyer miles to take care of that expense. They put us up at someone's house who was connected to the festival, then we kept all the box office receipts every night. We did extraordinarily. Tickets were $7, seating 100+ people and every single night for two weeks we sold out. Each night they gave us $700 in Canadian money. Amy and I split it right down the middle and had a great vacation. Do the festival circuit if you can!

• **We could've gone all summer.** There were people that went from Vancouver all the way across Canada. We have been to Vassar College, Boston College, Arizona State University, Michigan State University, and a whole slew of schools.

Q: How do these colleges know about you?

• **Every year, there's a Western Arts Administrators Conference** called WAA. At the conference there are people who book for public venues, but the biggest number are people who book for the art centers. For example, UCLA has Royce Hall and the Wadsworth Theater, so the guy that runs that would be at the WAA Conference. We showcase a bit of the show at the conference; you get 15 minutes.

• **The college circuit has been a big thing for us.** We were at the Public Theater in New York. George Wolfe came to see *Tokyo Bound* when we did it at East West Players, and liked it. A number of theaters have solo performers' festivals. Louisville has a *Solo Performers Festival*; San Francisco has *O Solo Mio*. You don't make enormous sums of money, but they do pay. They'll be willing to subsidize your airfare and find you a place to stay.

Q: Any other advice for getting seen?

- There are now a lot of "spoken word" venues in L.A. like Sit 'n Spin (sitnspin.org) which goes up every Thursday at the Comedy Central Stage at the Hudson Theater. People read original material and often it is a good platce to try out solo material. There are other spoken word venues in L.A. that you can submit to as well as online sites that accept personal essay, like Fresh Yarn (freshyarn.com). These spoken word venues and online sites give you good exposure and a forum as you are developing your solo material.

Resources

To download and print an updated version of this and all resource lists, go to actingiseverything.com.

Anne Etue, 323/669-0553. She is available for directing, producing and publicity work.

SAGIndie.com. Part of the Screen Actors Guild dedicated to helping independent filmmakers. Lots of information and help on the site.

The Larry Moss Studio, 310/399-3666. larrymossstudio.com. 2437 Main Street, Santa Monica, 90405. All the teachers here encourage "story exercise," creating a 15-minute monologue of a story based on your life that is difficult to tell, with you voicing each of the characters. Many one-person shows have been developed out of this exercise.

Manhattan Monologue Slam. Mmslam.com. Originally conceived in New York, the slam also now takes place in L.A. Essentially, actors present their own monologues (either 30 seconds or three minutes depending upon how they qualify) to be judged in a competition. Winners get face time with industry bigwigs, including agencies.

Back Stage West, backstage.com. Produces an annual edition with theater and spaces suitable for rent. You can call them and get their most recent back edition with the theater listings. Also provides information on independent films, castings and film schools. A good publication for anyone interested in making their own project.

Time Six Theatre League Alliance and Web TIX, 213/614-0556. theatrela.org. Most Los Angeles theaters belong to this group and they also take individual members. There is a monthly newsletter and you can keep up on everything that is going on in the theater in Los Angeles.

PUBLIC ACCESS CABLE TELEVISION

• **Anyone living in Los Angeles County** can produce their own half-hour public access television show. Some studios charge $35 plus the cost of a 3/4" video tape, while other studios are free. If you provide a 1/2" tape, they will record the show on both formats at the same time for no charge. The best bargain in town!

• **It is possible to serve as a non-paid intern.** Most of the technical people are interns, thus the programs are not network quality. They offer small workshops where you'll get actual hands-on experience with cameras, lighting, technical directing (TD) and even directing. You can apply by calling the cable company. I interned for about nine months when I first started producing my public access show so I would be familiar with all aspects of production. Many of the full-time employees at the cable companies started out as interns.

• **The cable companies offer classes for producers** in how to operate remote 3/4" camera equipment and how to use the editing bays. There is currently no charge for editing or using remote equipment. Cable company rules change frequently but any amount they may charge will be reasonable.

• **I've been producing** *Judy Kerr's Acting Is Everything* since 1985. My students do audition material and monologues; it helps them gain three-camera experience and exposure to industry people. I have streaming video on my website where these informational shows can be viewed.

• **I also do talk shows,** interviewing prominent people in the acting business who have information for the acting community at large. My students present questions to the guests. Sometimes we have guest teachers designing exercises for the actors.

• **You can produce any type of show you wish.** Why not give yourself, your friends and associates an opportunity to do some acting or talk show work? For very little money, you can learn about the television industry from the inside out. All of the studios have day, evening and Saturday hours available in which to tape your shows.

• **When you're ready to produce a show**, you can rehearse in front of your home camera. In fact you can tape your whole show at home and use the cable facilities to transfer from your camera's format to 3/4" tape and edit the pieces into a 28-minute show. After your tape airs with the cable company that recorded it, you can take the tape to each of the other studios and they will air the tape for no charge. You can even get a several-week regular time slot at many of the studios.

• **All possibilities are open to you and your imagination.** I've coached many public access producers, working with them on-camera, guiding them and offering tips so they can avoid mistakes in their first few shows.

• **Here are a few studios to get you started.** Call and they will mail the guidelines, the producer meetings schedule, and provide information on the classes and intern programs. See you on TV.

Resources

To download and print an updated version of this and all resource lists, go to actingiseverything.com.

Private Hosting Coaching: Judy Kerr, 818/505-9373. $100 per hour.

At this printing, none of these studios are charging for producing shows.

Adelphia Cable, 310/315-4444. adelphia.com.. 2939 Nebraska, Santa Monica, 90404.

Adelphia Cable, 323/255-9881. adelphia.com. 3037 Roswell, Eagle Rock, 90065.

Adelphia Cable, 818/781-1900. adelphia.com 15055 Oxnard St., Van Nuys, 91411. Free; you furnish the tape.

Comcast Cable, 323/993-8000. Comcast.com. 900 N. Cahuenga, Hollywood, 90038.

Time Warner Communications, 818/998-2266. timewarnercable.com 9260 Topanga Canyon Blvd., Chatsworth, 91311.

THEATER AND THEATER GROUPS

• **Working in the theater is a way to keep acting**, networking and giving yourself the opportunity to be seen by someone who has the ability to hire you for film and television work. *Back Stage West* and the online casting sites list auditions for plays. Go to all the theater auditions you can; it gives you a place to practice your auditioning skills.

• **After Robert Redford** had turned down the role of Benjamin in *The Graduate.* Director Mike Nichols remembered seeing Dustin Hoffman in an off-Broadway play, playing a hunchbacked German transvestite, and flew him to Hollywood for a screen test. Dustin was cast to play his Oscar-nominated role. He was 30 and it was his first major movie role at a salary of $750 a week. He earned $20,000 in all and applied for unemployment benefits afterward.

• **Harry Belafonte told an understudy success story.** "In 1945, I worked as an assistant janitor; Sidney Poitier was a dishwasher. In our first play at the *American Negro Theater* in Harlem I had the lead and Sidney was my understudy. One day the young man covering my job called and said he couldn't work that night. I went off to haul garbage and Sidney went on to play my part. That performance turned out to be on the night a director from Broadway came to scout our company, saw Sidney in my part, and signed him on the spot for a role in *Lysistrata*, launching his brilliant career."

• **Kelsey Grammer** (*Frasier*) was doing an off-off-Broadway show of *Lonely Hearts*. Opening night was the first blizzard of the season, there were three people in the audience. One of those people was the casting director who cast him in *Cheers!*

• **Beverly Long, actress turned commercial casting director**, was in *Rebel Without a Cause*. "Every actor in the entire city went on the auditions for *Rebel*. I had done a few TV shows and Corey Allen (now a director) and I were doing a play. The director saw us and cast us both. This is why I tell actors to do plays—you never know who is in the audience."

• **Chazz Palminteri** is a real inspiration to me. *A Bronx Tale,* directed by Robert DeNiro, written by and starring Chazz was released in 1993. Five years before that, Chazz was a nightclub bouncer, TV bit player, living in a crummy North Hollywood apartment. "I was angry, I wasn't going anywhere. I went to a drugstore, bought some pads of legal paper and started writing." He took his first five-minute bit and performed it at his theater company's workshop. Although it was well received, he kept writing and taking it back to class. Eventually he had a 90-minute one-man show he performed to critical raves at both the West Coast Ensemble Theater in L.A. and Playhouse 91 in N.Y. He was hot. Everyone wanted to buy his story. He held fast. He had $200 in the bank but he wouldn't sell unless he could write the screenplay and star in it. Robert De Niro had seen the play in L.A. and called him. They met and made the deal.

• **There are many theater groups.** Choose one where you feel comfortable; a good way to find friends who are working together towards common goals. You'll usually need a short scene or monologue to audition. Certain companies may want a classical and a contemporary monologue. Go to the theater you are considering joining and see a production to find out if you like the acting and the production values.

• **When you have landed a play for the first time**, throw yourself into rehearsals, learn your lines fast so you have more time to play with the words. Show up prepared to rehearse. Take care of yourself. Have food and water and the comforts you need so you are free to have the fun rehearsals can be. Your rehearsal time is often much more fun than the actual running of the play.

• **Stage managers are second-in-command** and often in charge after the opening night. Show them every respect you can. Always let them know when you arrive. If there is a sign up sheet, as there will be at all Equity productions, sign it. When the play begins its run, the stage manager will give you half-hour, 15-minute and 5-minute calls. Always acknowledge that you heard them with a "thank you" or some verbal word so they know that you heard it. This is proper etiquette. Stage managers can be your best friends if you get into trouble during the play. Be kind to them.

• **The last week before the play opens,** rehearsals are hard because you are into tech rehearsals with the lights, costumes, sound, curtains. The last dress rehearsal before opening will be awful. The second night is usually a let down from all the energy that went into opening night. But no matter what, keep your energy up and give it your all because once again, you never know who's in the audience.

• **On your first dress rehearsal night, set up your makeup space.** You want to make it a safe place to return to between scenes. Take a box of tissues and a couple of lunch size paper sacks. You can tape one of the sacks to your dressing table in case there isn't a handy trash container. Take paper cups, straws and a bottle of water. Share your water and cups. Lay your makeup products out on a hand towel. I like to use a small glass for my makeup pencils, a regular pencil and a pen. Take a writing pad, post-it notes and scotch tape.

• **When you get your opening night notes,** tape them up on your mirror. Also tape something that is special to you, a picture of someone who loves you, or a saying that gives you inspiration. Get little opening night gifts for everyone. It might be a rose, candy bar, bag of jelly beans, T-shirt with the play's name on it, helium balloon, balloon on a stick with something printed on it, a little miniature prop (kids' toys) that pertains to the person's role. Write a little personal note to the actors, director and tech people. This will make your opening night even more special.

• **Your curtain call is the last time the audience sees you.** Go out with great joy, no matter how you think your performance went. Often, you won't get many rehearsals on the curtain call. If you have any influence, insist on a well thought out and rehearsed one. You owe it to the audience so they can honor you. Bask in the applause; let yourself hear it, stay in the moment. It is what we act for, to hear the approval. Do not judge yourself; do that in your car on the way home. You can always improve and you will the next night, next week or the next play.

• **When you have a small part,** there is bound to be a let down after you open. In rehearsals the play seemed all about you, now you see it's really the people in the leading roles who carry the play. Keep making sure you find something new you want in your scenes. Bask in the glory when you are on stage, and next time maybe your part will be bigger.

• **If you have a large role,** don't let up. Keep putting all the energy into your acting choices. If the reviews are good, yay! If they aren't, console yourself and make the reviewers eat their words. Many actors choose not to read reviews till after the run of the play or never because they feel if you believe the good ones, then you have to believe the bad ones.

• **Each time you have a performance** the audience is different and it is such an adventure. What holds you up is your acting technique. No matter how you are feeling or how you think things are going, you will take the audience on a journey if you keep concentrated and focused on your work and your acting choices.

• **Never whistle in the theater.** Never say *MacBeth* in the theater. Develop little good luck charms for every run.

Resources

To download and print an updated version of this and all resource lists, go to actingiseverything.com.

The Regional & Off-Broadway Theatre Guide, aclbooks.net. The Guide lists over 270 theatres around the country that have seasons from September to June with information on how to submit, when holding auditions and dates and shows. There is also a Summer Guide available. Total package of five issues is $82.50. Other packages available on the website.

On The House, 310/399-3868. $195 a year for 2 tickets; many shows every week.

Time Six Theatre League Alliance, 213/614-0556. theatrela.org. Kevin Remington Executive Assistant 213/614-0556 Ext. 10. This service provides up-to-the-minute information on what's playing where. You may also purchase half-price day-of-show tickets by phone. Tu-Sa 12-4. Mark Taper, Pantages, Kodak Theater, The Geffen, Pasadena Playhouse and other under-100-seat Equity houses.

Back Stage West, backstagewest.com. prints an annual issue featuring all the theaters and theater companies in town. You can call them and get that back issue.

• LOS ANGELES PROFESSIONAL THEATERS

Geffen Playhouse, 310/208-6500. geffenplayhouse.com. 10886 Le Conte Ave, LA, CA 90024.

Mark Taper Forum, 213/972-7353. TaperAhmanson.org. 135 North Grand Ave, LA, CA 90012. Casting Director: Amy Lieberman.

Pasadena Playhouse, 626/792-8672. pasadenaplayhouse.org. 39 S. El Molino Ave., Pasadena, CA 91101

Laguna Playhouse, 949/497-2787. lagunaplayhouse.com. 606 Laguna Cyn. Rd., Laguna Beach, CA 92651. Wally Ziegler, Casting Director.

• THEATER COMPANIES

Actors Co-Op, 323/462-8460. actorsco-op.org. 1760 N. Gower Street, Hollywood, 90028. Send a picture and resume. Auditions for membership are held once a year in the spring. They require two contrasting monologues no longer than 2 minutes in length, from published plays only. On the call back you can do the same monologue or a different one, a cold reading with one of their company members and an interview for a seven person committee. This is one of the top companies in town. No initiation fee, dues are $20 a month. Paul Stuart Graham, Managing Director.

The Actor's Gang at the Ivy Substation, 310/838-GANG (4264). Theactorsgang.com. 9070 Venice Blvd, Culver City, 90232. Artistic Director, Tim Robbins. Award winning theater. On the Board: Robert Altman, Annette Bening, Robin Williams, Susan Sarandon. Presents fine award-winning productions.

Actors' Forum Theatre, 818/506-0600. actorsforumtheatre.org. 10655 Magnolia Blvd., North Hollywood, 91601. Applicants can audition every last Saturday of the month from 12:30-1PM, or come to a workshop that meets on Tuesdays from 7:30-10PM. Dues $25 a month. No set season. Theatre looks for a variety of new plays. Workshop presentation on Thursday nights.

A Noise Within, 323/953-7787. anoisewithin.org. 234 South Brand Blvd. Glendale, 91204. This theater presents classic American plays as well as Shakespeare. They have a 26 member resident company. New members are accepted by invitation only and not until you have worked a year with the company. They will, however, audition for roles that cannot be filled within the company. They teach all levels of actors in their Shakespeare classes and have a summer program of the classics for teenagers.

Ark Theatre Company, 323/969-1707. arktheatre.org. 1647 S. La Cienega Blvd., L.A. 90035. Will take chances in their shows, well-praised around town. Occasionally looks for new members; check website to see if and how to submit.

Colony Theatre, 818/558-7000. colonytheatre.org. 555 N. 3rd St., Burbank, 91502. If you are interested in auditioning for the Colony Theatre, look for audition notices at backstagewest. com and on the Equity hotline. Company membership will be by invitation only. Dues are $15 per month. Must work two mailings within four months of production, attend company clean-up weekend, usher six times and work a full running crew within first year of membership. Shows are selected with company members in mind. Industry comps are given to cast members. No workshops; they produce plays. Very prestigious company.

Company of Angels, 323/883-1717. companyofangels.org. 2106 Hyperion Ave., L.A. 90027. Auditions are held twice a year at various dates. Send a picture and resume to: Audition Committee, Company of Angels P.O. Box 3480 Hollywood, CA. 90078 Initiation fee is $35 and dues are $35 a month. This is one of the oldest companies in town. They have many productions going on for the members to appear in. They don't have workshops but do have play readings; always looking for material.

The Company Rep at the American Renegade Theater, 818/506-7550. Thecompanyrep. org. 11136 Magnolia Blvd., North Hollywood, 91601. Hope Alexander is the artistic director of this multicultural resident company creating both modern and classical works and developing new plays and playwrights. They hold auditions twice a year. Send photo and resume to The Company Rep, P.O. Box 807, North Hollywood, CA 91603. Audition consists of two monologues, one modern, one classical. Membership dues: $40 a month (plus $25 initiation fee for new members, due upon acceptance into the company). Classes and workshops offered as announced. Requirements: Company Members are required to attend bi-monthly company meetings, participate in work calls and fulfill tech and committee work commitments. The Company produces a five-show season; they have an active Playwright's Lab and also encourage their members to develop projects of their own.

Lonny Chapman Group Repertory Theatre, 818/769-7529. lcgrt.com. 10900 Burbank Blvd., North Hollywood, 91601. Group has a long history in L.A., look for plays that are "eclectic and offbeat." Many of their productions come from the group's New Playwright workshops. To join, mail headshot and resume to Audrey Sperling.

Open Fist Theatre/Los Angeles Playhouse, 323/882-6912. openfist.org. 6209 Santa Monica Boulevard, Los Angeles Ca 90038. They hold auditions two or three times a year. Send photo and resume c/o Scott. They will call you with details for the auditions.

Theatre 40, 310/364-3606. theatre40.org. 241 Moreno Drive, Beverly Hills, 90210. Located on the campus of Beverly Hills High School. "For more than 26 years, Theatre 40 has been one of this town's most stable and consistent actor-run professional theater ensembles," *Daily Variety.* Mail picture and resume c/o Robert Cohen, P.O. Box 5401, Beverly Hills, 90210. In order to become a member, an actor must present an audition for the Artistic Committee. Active members pay dues of $20.00 per month, and support the company by ushering at productions, fulfilling a job on a committee and helping with the Adult Educational Theatre Appreciation Classes.

Theatre West, 323/851-4839. theatrewest.org. 3333 Cahuenga Blvd. West, Los Angeles, 90068. You may submit your pictures and resumes to be considered for membership. A couple of months before the auditions, generally in the winter, the membership committee reviews the submissions received and on the basis of your experience you may be invited to audition for membership. Only the membership actors are in the productions. Initiation Fee is $60, dues are $40 a month. Free professional workshops are offered to their members: Monday night actor's workshop, Tuesday morning Shakespeare, Tuesday evening writer's workshop, Wednesday night musical workshop, Saturday morning associates workshop.

West Coast Ensemble, 323/876-9337. wcensemble.org. 3151 Cahuenga Blvd. West. Ste.107, Los Angeles, CA 90068. Les Hanson is the artistic director. Auditions twice a year. Send a picture and resume, attention: New Members. They will notify you when the auditions will be held. You do a four minute scene for Les and then have an interview with the membership committee. Lots of workshops and productions to get involved in. Initiation fee is $100, monthly dues are $45. Plus you must donate five hours work time each month. You can reduce your dues to $35 by doing 10 hours a month. You must perform one production job a year. They offer a great intern program for beginners; if you are interested in that, mention it in your letter.

Write Act Repertory Company, 323/469-3113. writeactrep.org. 6125 Carlos Ave., Hollywood 90028. John Lant is artistic director and has worked all over the Los Angeles theatre scene. Write Act focuses mainly on original pieces, lesser known works by established writers and adaptations. The company also does a number of workshops and readings. Board members include Ian McKellan, Debbie Reynolds, Kelsey Grammer and many more. Membership cost is $40 per month. Members also help work on the shows and fundraisers. Will take new members occasionally. Check website for submission details.

LIVING AN ACTOR'S
DREAM IN LOS ANGELES

• **Many aspiring actors take my advice** but most don't; it isn't easy to work as hard as the people in this section have. Will they be stars? I don't know but it warms my heart to see that they are choosing to live the life of their dreams. If they don't become stars, I trust they will find joy living their lives as artists. The tools you use to master the craft of acting are the same ones you use to master your life—isn't that handy?

BRITTANI'S STORY

Brittani Taylor moved here two years ago. I asked her to keep an account of her adventures in Los Angeles. She came from Sedona, Arizona at 19 with two years of college, some training and theater experience. She had headshots and her parents pledge to help her get started in Los Angeles. When I met Brittani at our initial career coaching session, I immediately recognized her ambition and drive; she also has a great personality, sense of humor and style. She wanted advice on how to go about launching an acting career. The information and coaching I gave her is the same I have given to everyone who comes to me for career coaching. Bottom line; it takes hard work, self-discipline, determination, perseverance and the ability to not get discouraged when faced with rejections. Brittani has a dream and she wants to fulfill it. See Brittani's pictures in the Actor Headshot section.

• **I have wanted to be an actress since I knew what an actress was** and my love for the craft and performing never really went away. After doing every play I could in Sedona, Arizona, I won an art scholarship to Arizona State University. Since Phoenix has a commercial/theatrical market, it got me thinking again about pursuing my career.

• **I started taking a local acting class**, and my teacher suggested that I go to Los Angeles for a summer and see if I could make anything happen. After discussing this with my parents, they said maybe instead of going for a summer, I should just move here and go for it. They knew that I wouldn't be happy doing anything else.

- **Once the seed was planted, I just ran with it.** I read multiple books, including Judy's, to prepare for the move and lived with my wonderful second cousins in Sunset Beach for my first two months. It worked out great because it gave me a chance to figure out what part of Los Angeles I wanted to live in. I have the most amazing, supporting family. My parents help me out financially when I need the support. In their words, they are putting me through "acting college" which is way cheaper than me going to college out of state anyway.

- **I found my first studio apartment in Burbank** and moved in by myself. I tried to make sure that I was in class at least two to four times a week, because film and television acting is way different than my theatre training. Good photos are the key to everything, I soon learned, so I had a couple of shoots with different photographers to capture the different characters I would be likely to play. I registered myself on Now Casting, LA Casting and Actors Access because you can submit yourself for auditions, which led to several student and independent films.

- **I got my SAG card,** interned at a talent agency, which signed me theatrically and commercially. Through Judy, I found out about showcasing at Actorsite and Reel Pros, professionally run operations with high quality actors and guests. I regularly showcase for casting directors and their associates.

- **It is really important to market yourself,** so I have tried to make a point of "postcarding" new info to commercial and theatrical casting directors every two to three months. I discovered Samuel French, the most amazing bookstore with incredible books to help answer any acting question you could ever have. I have found that taking care of my body helps in my acting, not only physically but mentally, so Griffith Park and Gold's Gym are my favorite places to work out.

- **My first year was amazing!** I networked a ton, learned a lot about myself, bonded with fellow actors and industry people, and fell in love with Los Angeles.

3 MONTH DIARY (October-December 2005):

OCTOBER
October 1: Wrote a rough draft cover letter for new commercial representation.
October 3: Walked Griffith Park, Interned at ZPP Talent Agency and prepared script for Caryn West's Audition Technique class.
October 4: Approved headshots at Argentum Photo Lab before printing and also picked up new business cards. Audition technique class.
October 5: Picked out fancy envelopes for commercial agent mailing, started drawing in pastels again.
October 7: Faxed commercial cover letter to Stuart K. Robinson to edit. Lunch with another actress.

October 8: Address envelopes to send out to potential commercial agents, an all day task!

October 9: Showcase Reel Pros 2, guest was Kari Kurto of Dava Waite Casting, did really well, good comments.

October 10: Thank you postcard to Dava, typed her info into my showcase database. Prepared script for Caryn West class. Met with a photographer for potential test modeling.

October 11: Goal's Lunch with fellow actress (where we meet and set goals for the following weeks). Audition class with Caryn West. Open audition for UCLA, did a monologue.

October 12: Picked up new commercial headshots at Argentum, they did an awesome job! Prep for high fashion photo shoot with the Art Center of Pasadena.

October 13: All day photo shoot at Art Center.

October 14: Stuart K. Robinson Commercial Semi-Private Class, got edited cover letter back from him, helped approve everything before my commercial agent mailing. Worked on script for a USC grad film audition.

October 15: Fixed commercial resume with Stuart's changes. Audition Red Ace Cola Project, went really well, did everything I planned. Stapled headshots with new resumes for commercial agent mailing.

October 16: Mailed commercial agent packets.

October 22: Prepped clothes for another High Fashion Shoot, Art Center of Pasadena.

October 24: Did acting drop off. Photo Shoot Art Center. Prepared script for class.

October 25: Gathered clothes for shoot for the book. Audition Technique class.

October 26: Shoot with Shawn Flint Blair for the book.

October 27: Mailed comedy headshot to Kari Kurto for her files/pilot season. Interned ZPP.

October 28: Commercial Semi-Private class with Stuart K. Robinson.

October 29: Showcase Reel Pros 2 with Sibby Kirchgenssner of UDK and Libby Goldstein of Junie-Lowry Johnson. Went to the movies with another actress.

October 30: Prepare script for audition. Prepared two more scripts for Caryn West. Thank you postcard to Libby and Sibby. Updated showcase database. Meet with photographer Stephanie for the book.

October 31: Meet with Rich Hogan to discuss looks for the book. Audition for *Thelma and Louise*, USC, went so well they had me audition for another student film while I was there. Stapled new headshots. Prepared script for Caryn West.

NOVEMBER

November 1: Audition Technique Class.

November 2: Received two calls for meeting with top commercial agents. Prepared script for an audition.

November 3: Meeting Rod Baron of Baron Entertainment. Lesson with Caryn West for audition for independent pilot *Large* that I self-submitted on, nailed it.

November 4: Couriered postcard to Amy Reece, who I have showcased for in the past. Found out I was accepted by Baron Entertainment, I have a new top commercial agent!

November 5: Open Call for *So You Want To Be a Soap Star*. Finished gathering clothes for shoot with Stephanie.

November 7: Photo shoot with Stephanie for the book.

November 8: Callback for lead in the pilot *Large*, again went amazing. Audition Technique Class.

November 9: Meeting with new commercial agent, signed paperwork. Call from casting director on *Large* that I am going to next step, testing.

November 10: Uploaded new commercial pictures and changed the representation at

LA Casting and Breakdown Services. Commercial Semi-Private Class. Showcase Reel Pros 2.
November 11: Baron Entertainment is going to represent me for Print also, so
dropped off 4x6's for zed card. Gathered clothes for shoot with Rich Hogan. Design
resume for Baron Entertainment and staple hardcopy headshot they requested.
November 13: Lunch/movie with another actress.
November 14: Shoot with Rich Hogan for the book.
November 15: Got back 4x6's from Baron for Zed, dropped off hardcopy
headshots.
November 16: Looked at contact sheets from one of the test shoots at Art
Center, picked my favorites. Played tennis with a photographer.
November 17: Work on script for an audition. Set up Zed Card for printing at Isgo
Photo Lab. Industrial Pictures industry mixer with a family friend who is a director.
November 18: Goals lunch with fellow actress. Audition for *The Coke Accord*
went really well.
November 21-29: Sedona for a well-earned vacation and Thanksgiving.
November 30: Approved Zed design before printing at Isgo Lab.

DECEMBER
December 1: Did a drop off. Commercial Semi-Private Class.
December 3: Showcased Reel Pros 2 for Eileen Kennedy of La Padura and Hart,
good feedback.
December 4: Showcased Reel Pros 2 for Alison Mize. Movie and dinner with a
fellow actress.
December 5: Found out that pilot *Large* is being delayed because of script
issues. Postcarded Alison and Eileen. Updated showcase database.
December 6: Picked up Zeds, ISGO photo lab did a great job! First commercial
audition with new agents for NBC promo. Private lesson with Judy Kerr.
December 7: Acting Goals Lunch.
December 8: Purchased Commercial Casting mailing labels from Breakdown
Services. Commercial Semi-Private Class.
December 9: Dropped off Zed and Christmas gifts to Baron. Movie and dinner
with another actress.
December 10: Filled out postcards to announce new representation, using the
casting labels from Breakdown Services.
December 12: Mailed commercial postcards. Open call for Nous Model
Management. Picked up re-order on headshot from Argentum Photo lab.
December 13: Open call for Q Model Management and Next. E-mailed pictures to
L.A. Models.
December 14: Open call for Wilhemina Models.
December 15: Prepared script for lesson with Judy. Interned at ZPP, dropped off
theatrical agent Christmas gift. Commercial Semi-Private Class. Open call at
Click Models. Showcase Reel Pros 2 with Debbie George.
December 16: Lesson with Judy. Open call for independent film, told to call when I
get back into town to set up an audition.
December 17: Lunch, movie with another actress.
December 18: Showcase Reel Pros 2 with Allen Hooper. Updated showcase
database. Packed to go home for Christmas and New Years.
December 19-Jan 7th: Vacation.

KEVIN'S STORY

Kevin Anthony's manager Jake Azhar sent Kevin to me when he was ready to introduce him to agents and asked me to coach him on two monologues. I was very impressed with his talent, personality and look; he landed the agent. Acting/Career/Life Coach Kathy Young wrote Kevin's story of how he worked on becoming an actor before he moved to Los Angeles and then what happened when he got here. See Kevin's pictures in the Picture Section.

- **Kevin Anthony Deegan,** an enthusiastic freshman, walked into my Drama I class at Westminster Christian High School in Miami and announced, "I wanna be an actor!" His warm personality and charm caught my attention, earning him a supporting role in our play, *Nobody Heard Me Cry*. His sophomore year, he was cast as Jem Finch, a lead role in *To Kill A Mockingbird*. His charisma and contagious smile won him the part but he was clearly lacking discipline, motivation and a sense of direction. I encouraged him to focus on the "fundamentals" of acting: reading the script, memorizing his lines and making clear character choices.

- **In Kevin's junior year,** he played supporting roles in *The Odd Couple* and *The Crucible*. I helped him prepare to attend UCLA's "Performance for the Camera" Summer Workshop. That week in California changed his life. Kevin was more determined to take practical steps toward fulfilling his dream.

- **Senior year,** he was in my Honors Drama Class and the fall was dedicated to rehearsing the lead in *All My Sons*. Many hours were also spent writing, directing, acting and editing our school's first student film, *A Take on Me*. With five months to graduation, we met to discuss practical steps. I explained the importance of establishing a spiritual foundation. His next step was to apply to acting schools; we sent applications to CalArts, American Musical and Dramatic Academy, and the American Academy of Dramatic Arts. We prepared monologues for school auditions in New York and Los Angeles. He received acceptance letters from AMDA and AADA. After visiting both schools, he determined that the American Academy of Dramatic Arts in L.A. was the best choice. Kevin concluded the school year as the lead in *The Lion, The Witch and the Wardrobe*.

- **In July,** we decided on the best place for Kevin to live. He found an apartment in West Hollywood, giving him easy access to AADA as well as auditions. Continuing to build on his spiritual foundation, he visited Bel Air Presbyterian Church. One day while waiting in the parking lot at his apartment, he met Jake Azhar of the Hollywood Management Company. After becoming friends, Kevin eventually signed with Jake for management representation. Jake introduced Kevin to contacts in the industry including photographer Paul Smith who took his first L.A. headshots. With professional headshots and a manager helping shape his career, he was on his way to reaching his goals.

• **Kevin had full-time acting classes,** studying acting technique, movement, comedy, voice and speech. In addition, he enrolled in a weekly Bible Study Fellowship class, which fostered discipline and good study habits. At the end of the school year we discussed his priorities. Soon after, he decided to enroll in Santá Monica College to pursue a full-time degree. The decision to leave AADA would allow him to begin going on auditions and making headway in the industry. In September, Jake introduced Kevin to Judy Kerr and he began private coaching sessions to further fine-tune his skills. Kevin also took Stuart K. Robinson's Commercial Class.

• **In November,** having added considerable training to his resume, Jake felt that Kevin was ready to begin auditioning for agencies. He prepared two monologues and auditioned for the Morgan Agency and Amsel, Eisenstadt and Frazier (AEF). Having received offers from both, he decided to go with AEF. The unique charisma I saw in Kevin as a ninth grader, combined with his Los Angeles studies, had paved the way for him to live his dream. AEF has kept Kevin busy auditioning. He continues to depend on career guidance from his manager, Jake Azhar of the Hollywood Management Company and I continue to guide him as his life coach. His "I wanna be an actor" dream has become reality. Having built a firm spiritual foundation, Kevin's dream has expanded into a greater vision. He writes, "My call is to advance the industry by creating quality work with redeeming value to restore hope to audiences and ultimately, the world."

KEITH'S STORY

Keith Johnson told his story in the Tenth Edition and updates it in the following pages. An actor in his thirties, he tells of the events that led to changing his life completely in order to follow his dreams. Keith has not been a student of mine but I met him through his now wife Bonnie Gillespie. I was so intrigued with Keith's pursuit of his dream that I asked him to write his story in hopes of inspiring others who think their lives have fallen apart. You can pursue your dreams no matter your age or what obstacles seem in your way. See Keith's pictures in the Actor Headshots section.

- **In February of 2001**, I was living in Grand Rapids, Michigan and my life was shattered. In late January, my wife informed me that our seven-year marriage was over. Two weeks later, the bank I was working for was bought out by another bank and I was going to be let go.

- **I went from knowing** what the next 20 years of my life was going to be, to sitting alone in an empty, 3 bedroom/2 bath house with no idea what the future held. I took stock of the things that I hadn't been doing for lack of time.

- **In March,** I signed up for an adult soccer league, started spending serious time writing "my great novel" again, and started looking to audition in local theatre. I had done one play in my life, five years earlier, *Dracula*. I really liked acting, but it was not my dream, or so I thought.

- **In April,** I met a bunch of people on an Internet discussion group about an online humor magazine. One of those people, a writer for the magazine, was Bonnie Gillespie. I became drawn to Bonnie's wit, charm, sass and intellect. I learned she worked in the Entertainment Industry, and she learned I thought acting was fun.

- **In May,** with Bonnie encouraging my pursuit of acting, I was suddenly open to the idea of dreaming differently. There was good chemistry between us, we had a lot in common and started talking on the phone. We decided to meet in person in the middle of July. My plan to take a year off to figure out who I was went out the window; I was in love. Fortunately for me, Bonnie was too.

- **She kept encouraging me** to explore the acting life and to come out to L.A. when my job in Michigan ended. She told me to come out to Hollywood, and she would make me famous. I fell for it. The thought was very appealing to me, and I was starting to dream about a career in show business. Bonnie helped me prepare to audition for the part of Teddy in *Arsenic And Old Lace* at my local community theatre, and I got it.

• **As summer went on with rehearsals**, it became clear that acting meant more to me than I thought it did. I made plans to move to L.A. when my job and my play were finished. As if it were a sign from heaven, my job ended on the Friday before the play was to close on Sunday.

• **I showed up closing night** in a fully packed Ryder moving van. We put on the show, struck the set; I said my good-byes, and drove forty-one hours to Hollywood. That was the end of October, ten months from the date that my life had flipped upside down.

• **I came to this town 35 years old with no training**, two non-professional plays under my belt and a dream. This is not the usual recipe for success when moving to Los Angeles.

• **In December**, Bonnie wrangled me a job as a production assistant (P.A.) on a SAG, Modified Low-Budget feature film. I had never been on a film set, seen professional actors or a film crew. Bonnie's advice was to stay quiet, listen to what everyone was saying, and do whatever I was asked. We felt confident that I'd make a good P.A. because I spent four years in the Marines; I could reasonably follow orders.

• **I was a great P.A.** I learned what I needed to know to be comfortable behind and in front of the camera. I learned who's who and what's what. I learned about film crew etiquette and terminology. I got the chance to experience a lot of environmental setbacks, personnel setbacks, personality conflicts, and everything you might think of on a decently professional set.

• **Also in December, I took my first acting class.** I did four weeks with a coach who taught me the basics of scene study and character analysis. He made sure I understood what he meant and why it was important.

• **January of 2002** saw me working for the Sundance Film Festival in Park City, Utah. Bonnie not only works as a newspaper journalist, but she also worked for the Sundance Institute as their Archive Director for the Sundance Collection, so she arranged for us to volunteer for the festival.

• **In February, I got my first headshots.** Again, Bonnie's experience in the industry meant that I had little research to do in order to find good value for my money. She had been shopping for photographers and lithographers for years, and she handed me to her best-value people.

• **In March and April,** money was running low, so I took a full time job doing computer consulting. One of the reasons that I have no stress involved with my acting career is that I came to the industry with a ton of marketable skills, so I will never have to worry about making a living. The way I look at it is this: unless stardom strikes I'll always make more money at my day job than I do acting. That's just a fact of my life.

• **In May,** Bonnie and I started heavily pushing my acting career. She submitted me on everything for which I might be right. We sent an honest cover letter with every submission. It said I didn't have a lot on my resume, but I had already lived a life and brought that life to my acting. It also listed my training and I was pursuing more training.

• **The combination** of my headshot, resume and skillful submissions by Bonnie led to getting lots of auditions, and it continues to this day. In the last five months I have been auditioning five to eight times a week, and have booked over twenty different projects. Over a dozen of those were paying gigs!

• **January 10, 2003,** I had my TV debut, one of my non-union crime reenactment shows aired on The Learning Channel. I sent 100 postcards to casting directors and at least two tuned in. A casting director called the next day and wanted to know when I got my SAG card. I told her that I hadn't yet. She booked me for three days of voucher-earning extra work. While on the set, another casting director called and wanted to know if I was available to work on her Oxygen Network TV show for the following week. Yes!

• **Nine months after getting my first headshots,** with a SAG card and decent 2002 income from acting. I am the luckiest man in the world.

Keith added to his story in March 2006.

• **Joining SAG was a real change for me.** I was, at that point, working nonunion where I'd get offers to play roles. I'd get a call that would go something like this, "Hi Keith, my name is so-and-so and I was just talking with such-and-such, who you worked with nine months ago on this-and-that. Well, I need an actor, and he said you'd be perfect.

Would you look at my stuff..." It was a great place to be. I had established a series of relationships that got me consistent work. But being nonunion, it was mostly low/no pay, used for making and solidifying relationships that would hopefully pay off in the future.

- **I went from getting offered parts in small films** to scrambling to make new relationships in the ranks of the union production world with people who didn't really need or desire to take a chance on me. I went from auditioning five to eight times a week to auditioning, maybe, five times a month. Still, the projects I auditioned for were better paying and had more potential for an immediate impact on my career (I was now starting to work for people who were already at the place I wanted the nonunion guys to get to eventually). For the first eighteen months, it was difficult to see my joining SAG as a good thing. I was on the lowest rung of the ladder... but it was a better, higher ladder.

- **That year and a half was spent learning the lay of the land**, getting up to speed and starting to make new, union relationships. Things started to change for me in early 2005 when a relationship I'd made in 2004 started to bear fruit. I signed with a manager (my first representation in my four-year career) that I'd met at an industry event a few months before. Almost immediately, she was able to get me into casting offices for series TV that I hadn't been able to crack... ever. It seems that once someone in this town is willing to take a chance on you, others will too. I got auditions and callbacks and producer sessions. Also, through my new manager, I got into an incredible acting class.

- **I've been in that mode for the last year.** I am auditioning more and more regularly now as my relationships and reputation get more solid. Changing gears was hard, but since being a professional actor was and is my goal, it was a change I had to make. It's all starting to pay off; I just shot my first network TV co-starring role, on *CSI: Miami*. It aired on May 1st...my fourth anniversary as a working actor.

- **I still wake up happy every morning**, the luckiest man in the world.

JIM'S STORY

Jim Martyka is an actor and a freelance journalist who moved here from Minnesota in 2003. He has booked a number of commercials and independent films as well as a guest star spot on The Discovery Channel show "Reasonable Doubt." He also writes for people in the entertainment field.

- **You need to start now!** No matter where you are, what market you're in pursuing your acting dreams, you need to start working toward your successful career in Los Angeles right now. That was the message I got when I first read Judy's book, which really gave me the courage to move out here in the first place. In my three years in L.A., I've learned quite a bit about how to survive and thrive in this city and I can now look back and appreciate the efforts of what I did in Minnesota and how it has helped me work toward multiple careers out here.

- **Keep auditioning.** When I decided I wanted to be an actor, I was 22 and had no experience whatsoever. So one day, I went and got the newspaper and looked for classes and auditions. Later that week, I was in a one-day commercial class and three auditions for community theatre shows. Luckily, I booked a good part in one and got hooked. I kept auditioning and pretty soon that led to independent films and even commercials. I auditioned for everything, including open calls. A year before I moved out here, I begrudgingly forced myself to get to an open "cattle call" for a Pontiac commercial. Sure enough, there were hundreds of people there. But I booked it and a couple weeks later, I had a few thousand dollars and more important, I was SAG eligible!

- **When I got to L.A.,** that motto of "keep auditioning" paid off because I already had a pretty decent resume, SAG eligibility and the discipline to take advantage of every opportunity I could. Whether it's theatre, film, commercials, whatever … "keep auditioning."

- **That said, know who you are and work on that.** I know I am talented enough to do drama and even a little classic work. But I am a Matthew Perry-type and my niche is comedy. When I first got out here, I thought, like most others who move out here, that I could do everything. But I quickly realized that there was simply too much competition. So I decided to focus on my strength, comedic acting. I studied with a couple of coaches, including Scott Sedita and really discovered how I could make a mark. The overall goal for me is to build a successful career in my niche and then branch out.

- **Talk to everybody.** This was always pretty easy for me as I have been a journalist for several years, but it's amazing how much of a difference this can make. This is something I practiced in Minnesota, which was a smaller market, and it paid off because pretty soon many of the major players in town (coaches, casting directors, agents, directors) knew me. That not only helped me get auditions, it also helped me prepare for Los Angeles as many of them put me in touch with colleagues they had on the West Coast. Now, out here, I go to as many entertainment industry functions as I can and no matter where I'm going, I carry headshots, business cards, a little notebook and two pens with me. And if there's somebody that looks like someone I should know, I make sure to say "hello."

- **Do it yourself.** In Minnesota, I formed a group called the Twin Cities Actor's Forum with three other acting friends. It started with the four of us getting together once a week to practice scenes and talk shop. Two years later, we had over 500 members, our own theatre troupe, relations with all the major agents and casting directors in town, celebrity speakers and a great reputation in the Midwest and even with some people out here. The Forum showed me what I was capable of by working hard and how it could pay off.

- **The same has been true in L.A.** Nobody is going to give you anything here; in fact, people are more likely to take things away. I've learned that I need to work hard and pursue everything I can with all my heart. For me, that means everything from securing a career as a freelance journalist so I have the time and flexibility to pursue acting, to working on keeping together a support group of former Forum members that are out here pursuing the same dreams. Most important, that means going to auditions and even submitting for things yourself, if necessary. That was how I got an audition and booked a great role on *Reasonable Doubt*.

- **Enjoy it all.** I am a very introspective person and I constantly think about the decisions I've made about pursuing this career. If you're reading this book, you're like me, there is no other option—"Acting is everything," to quote a fantastic acting coach and author. I knew it was always going to be hard, from that first community theatre audition, to moving out to Los Angeles, to trying to build a career. But it can often also be very rewarding, as are most triumphs over adversity. Celebrate every accomplishment, work hard, get yourself ready and move. There are too many opportunities to miss. And that's the greatest thing about living in L.A. If you work hard and you're prepared, every day could be the day that changes the rest of your life!

CARLA'S STORY

Carla Renata is an actress I met when I was the dialogue coach on All About The Andersons. *She had a small role and really made the most of it. I was intrigued with her acting and when I heard how she got the role without an agent I asked her to write a bit of her story here. Her website is carlarenata.com.*

- I moved to Los Angeles from New York where I had been very successful commercially and on Broadway during what turned out to be the worst pilot season on record in 1999. At any rate, I was fortunate enough to obtain a commercial agent through my agency in New York and one of the agents made some phone calls on my behalf that hooked me up with a theatrical agent.

- I struggled for a little while until I booked with the Los Angeles company of *The Lion King* (where I eventually went on to obtain an NAACP Theatre Award Nomination) and had a steady gig for nearly three years. A couple of months before the show closed, I was dropped by my theatrical agency, my manager moved to New York to sell ice cream and I found myself back where I started.

- Remembering that I had a very savvy background in public relations, I took my career into my own hands, booking three sitcoms in one month from mailings to casting offices. I found a new manager, a new agent and in 2004, I was chosen to participate in the CBS Diversity Showcase which changed my life and career. The day after the showcase, I booked a Guest Star on *CSI* and booked several other Guest Star spots.

- Unlike most actors, I have the ability to sing and dance, so when I can't get a job acting, I go do musicals or plays. I did my first play at the Geffen Playhouse in Spring 2005. I am now extremely proud to declare that I am a working, not-a-Size-2, African-American actress in Los Angeles and I intend to keep it that way.

KATHY'S STORY

Kathy Lamkin is an inspiration. I met her at Actorsite where she is an important contributor. When she isn't on location, she books the speakers who donate their time and information. Kathy became a working actor in Texas and then made the leap to Los Angeles. Leaving her very supportive husband behind to continue his NASA career and to run their business in Houston, she and her grown daughter moved here. She has to maintain two residences. I asked her to include her story because some of you reading this book may want to launch a Los Angeles career later in life. Kathy has a very sweet personality; everyone loves her, yet she is tough and courageous. kathylamkin.com.

- **I love making a living in middle age doing what I love.** It truly is never too late to live your dream.

- **Living in the rural South** and receiving only two TV channels, it was a miracle I ever saw an awards show. I dared to dream the impossible. By the time high school rolled around, I became a thespian and majored in drama at college. A life-long love affair with acting then went into full force.

- **After doing community theatre,** I discovered that I could get paid to act and performed with a touring troupe. One of the directors also directed industrials. He asked me to sit for a couple of hours at a typewriter looking like an expert typist and I got paid $100. I decided getting paid for being on camera was a good thing. I edited my resume to one page, went to an agency and the next day they sent me on my first audition…a little thing called *Lonesome Dove.* I got a callback and ended up at network for the role. The agency took me on.

- **My first speaking line** was in a German mini-series called *Miller and Mueller* and that got my SAG eligibility. I did not join the union right away because Texas is a right-to-work state. I did more industrials, extra work and commercials. I auditioned for projects in Austin, Dallas and Houston. It took a balancing act to keep everything going, but I had help from a supportive family and friends.

- **I noticed that Texans who went to L.A.** usually returned within a few months, defeated, with their savings gone. This made me cautious. I started taking workshops with L.A. casting directors and getting feedback. I noticed what they liked and didn't like and realized the Texas talent pool was as strong as in Los Angeles. The two biggest drawbacks for Texas talent were a lack of confidence and over-inflated egos. Many actors weren't taking control of their career or their acting.

- **I attended workshops out of town**, or even out of state, in addition to those instructors I brought into my acting school. In searching for the best instructors, I discovered L.A. casting director Terry Berland's class. I loved the way she taught and motivated students, who were soon booking commercials in Texas. Terry is based in Los Angeles and is the reason I'm here. She introduced me to everyone she knew, and I went on as many general interviews as people would let me in the door.

- **My first three months in L.A. were rocky,** I didn't have a year's income saved; I hadn't researched places to stay. But I did have the support and encouragement of my husband, Steve that things would work out. If not, then at least I would know I had tried my best. My grown daughter, Kati and I flew to L.A. for an audition. We found an apartment to share. Several days later my husband drove one of our cars out to L.A. so we could have transportation and some furniture for our apartment. While I returned to Texas for previous commitments on *Screen Door Jesus* and *Texas Chainsaw Massacre*, Kati got a job and I had my goals set for succeeding in L.A.

- **Although not a household name yet**, the work has steadily increased and my exposure is increasing. I have had to adjust to a different standard of living, but the outcome is worth it! I was nominated for a 2006 SAG Actor award and found out I could be nominated for an Oscar for *Kiss Kiss, Bang Bang*. I believe in the impossible that an Emmy nomination will come through for my role as Momma Boone on the *Nip/Tuck* Season Three opening show.

- **Family support is crucial to making it in L.A.** or anywhere—doesn't have to be "real family," adopt one that gives you support. Kati and I discovered a formula for success and we believe this formula applies to more than just acting.

- **The ABC's of Acting: Attitude + Believability + Creativity = Dollars, Energy and Fun!**

PAMELA'S STORY

Pamela Newlands talks about moving to Los Angeles from Scotland.

- **When I moved to Los Angeles,** I was seriously culture-shocked. For an industry that is spaced out over a relatively small geographic radius, it took forever to get anywhere. Once I'd gotten over the horrors of L.A. traffic, I was faced with a completely new rulebook here. My black-and-white headshots had to be replaced with color ones. In auditions, my accent had to magically become American, which was not so much magic as a lot of hard work. I quickly learned that actors who succeed are the ones who understand and apply themselves to the business of acting.

- **It was a lot to take in;** I began to feel pangs of frustration. It felt like mild indigestion, like a 10-pound bag of sand was lodged somewhere in my solar plexus. The final clue was when an actor came up to me in class and said my "energy field" was "like, trapped, man," and I needed to "like, shift it." Fellow actors often offered me their brand of spiritual self-help advice, but this time, I listened. It seemed a strange spiritual laxative, but I began to contemplate "actor's energy" and how other people read us.

- **During this time, I enrolled in a Meisner class.** The best acting, he believed, was made up of spontaneous responses to the actor's immediate surroundings. I learned to react more and "act" less. It gave me a sense of stillness. I realized that the most interesting choices do come from honest human emotion. I began to understand the power actors have to affect people. Our job is to fill in the white spaces between the words. The text is already there, but we bring it to life.

- **My frustration segued into self-trust.** Hollywood became much more navigable when I allowed my instincts to guide me. I stopped questioning myself and accepted that our differences are what make us unique. We turn our self-consciousness into self-awareness. Go with your gut, make a strong choice, commit and trust. I now ask myself, "What am I bringing into the room, and what am I bringing to the material?" We all feel overwhelmed at times, but I'm reaping the benefits of introspection. My energy is no longer "like, trapped, man." It's unclogged and boundless.

- **You must do something each day toward fulfilling your dreams—** there is plenty to do in this career you are creating for yourself.

Section Four
Professional Tools

Free Email Newsletters

• **This Professional Tools Section introduces you to the tools** you will need to create a business for your professional career. You are studying, you have your marketing tools (pictures and resumes), you've gained experience and you are now running your life as a professional actor.

• **Your career takes many roads.** No one road is the correct one; each actor's path is their own. I hope you are discovering many new paths in this book and, as you take a certain path, others will open up to you.

• **Talk to any professional person** at the beginning of their career and you will hear of the many hours it took to establish themselves. As a competitive actor it will certainly take all the hours in the day to hone your craft, create your business and make a living. I am astounded at people's gall who think they can be lazy and have a career as an actor.

• **You have chosen the actor's way of life** over any other. Be the best that you can be.

• *Following are free email newsletters where you can learn and keep up with the show business industry.*

• FREE NEWSLETTERS:

Judy Kerr's News Group: judykerr.com. L.A. Actor related news. Sign up at website. Free downloads, Online Demo Reels, Self-Esteem Builders, On-The-Set Terms. Also web links and recommended books.

Actorsite.com. Subscribe to the Actorsite Report at the top of the page. Uplifting news about working on your career. There are many free areas and forums to check out. Very helpful newsletter; you get a sense of the Los Angeles Market.

Cynthia Turner's Cynposis, cynopsis.com, Cynthia@cynopsis.com. This is a must—sign up via e-mail. The latest showbiz news everyday, from new shows to ratings to casting calls to job opportunities. Love getting this each day. Website features streaming video, pod casting and archives. Cynopsis goes out to 85,000 members in 25 countries every day. This is like having a free *Variety* and *Hollywood Reporter* at your fingertips.

Razurdia Network, razurdianetwork@yahoogroups.com. Casting notices and industry info. Lots of ethnic castings plus much more. Great group, Richard is a working actor. Networking, wonderful Web links.

Now Casting, nowcasting.com. Acting, casting and marketing. Great email magazine.

Bob Fraser's Free Newsletter, showbizhowto.com. Sign up for the Hollywood How To Newsletter, Packed with information, inspiration and motivation; all about success in the acting biz.

Bonnie Gillespie's The Actor's Voice, showfax.com. Bonnie's advice column is but one tool on this great site; lots of free information.

Jeffrey R. Gund, JeffreyRGund.com. jeffgmusic@mindspring.com. Request to be on his email list; say I sent you. Networking, day job and acting opportunities.

Casting Networks, lacasting.com. Newsletters and articles from experts advice columns to local events.
Daily Candy, dailycandy.com. Great to keep up on cool things going on around you, places, clothing, play, movie or book.
Hollywood Happy Hour. groups.yahoo.com/group/Hollywood-Happy-Hour. Yahoo puts you through the paces. News, schmooze, reviews, interviews and networking opportunities.

Academy Foundation, calendars@oscars.org. Newsletter for the Academy; great list of upcoming events and information on what's happening in the Academy. Great site during Oscar Season.

L.A.Events, events@goldstarevents.com. ½ price ticket source, request newsletter.

LAstagetix@lastagealliance.com. Newsletter of ½ price tickets for stage shows.

FilmRadar.com. Great e-mail newsletter and website that provides information on any and all film screenings happening around town. Also lots of fun movie info.

Planet Shark Productions, planetsharkproductions.com. They have over 200 show biz links. Free email newsletter.

Actor Insider, Commercialacting.info/blog. Casting director Stuart Stone's blog full of great information, stories and advice.

Holdon Log, holdonlog.com. Monthly newsletter with Actor Track Tips-n-Hints and special offers. Download contract to get copy of your filmwork.

Actortips.com, Weekly articles, tips, job and audition announcements and more. Great listings, like Top Undergraduate Acting Programs, etc.

Actorslife.com, Audition tips and advice, mailing labels, audition links, news and more.

About.com, Tons and tons of articles on every topic you can think of, including acting. Many of the columnists have newsletters.

SAG Actor Bulletin Board, sagactor.com. Lots of open discussion groups and the occasional articles on SAG related issues.

Behind the Celluloid Curtain, celluloidcurtain.com. Open discussion and information on the business side of the industry.

• OTHER NEWSLETTERS OF INTEREST:

Levine Breaking News E-lert, levinepr.com. Request newsletter at: Levinepr2@Earthlink.net. Great website links. A little too political for me.

BargainsLA.com. Susanne O'Conner writes weekly of the bargains in Los Angeles and Orange County. They are always real bargains of high quality merchandise.

Life coach Laurie Sheppard, Creatingatwill.com/newsletter/. Useful career information for career development at whatever stage you're at on your job path.

Electric Kites, electrickites.com. Newsletter and workshop listings for life coaching group whose goal is to "Electrify your Life!"

WMW Group, wmwgroup.com. corenetworth.info, Free newsletter and blog. Carol Woodliff, a hypnotherapist with background in acting and business. Practical tools to better lives.

Making A Living

- **An actor must have financial backing.** If you don't have a trust fund, supporting parents, spouse or angel, then you'll have to provide it yourself. Your "day job" will give you the cash flow to support you and your career. Like any other person in business, career expenses will always be a part of your life. You need enough to live on and to reinvest in your career.

- **Peter Elliott of Now Casting** wrote an article I very much agree with entitled *The Actor Cycle.* Peter allowed me to extract some of it to emphasize how important it is to learn a skill or find a type of job that will pay for the kind of life style it takes for you to live in Los Angeles, pursuing your dream. You can read the full article on the website.

  - **In order to survive in Los Angeles,** you have to have money. And even if you work as an actor at SAG scale on 10 different projects in a year, with two days on each project (which is a pretty good year for most actors in L.A. in the first 3-5 years) you would only make a little over $11,000. That's just not a living.

  - **We all need to make a living.** There can be a balance between a full-time job and an acting career. *Every* actor needs to have another marketable skill. And there is *no* shame in working a full-time job. Success is not measured in the short term, but by the duration.

  - **If you are a planner,** you arrive in L.A. with no debt, $10,000 bucks in your savings account, a car, high hopes and plenty of dreams about your career. You pay the $300-800 to get your car registration transferred to California and find a place [most likely a single] to rent for $750 a month, paying a deposit and first and last month's rent. You feel on top of the world and you still have $6,000-$7,000 in the bank.

  - **You spend the first three months** trying to figure out what the heck is going on. You need headshots, classes, subscriptions and union dues ($1,300 if you become eligible to join SAG). You start using credit cards as your bank account dwindles. You get some nibbles and say "It's going to break any time now!" But it stays just a bit out of reach.

• **Your credit cards are getting higher**, but you know you can make it happen. You take a part time job so you can be available for acting jobs and auditions. It pays $7-12 an hour. On your ninth month, you find your bank account dry and the credit card debt piling up. So you keep the low paying job, increasing to 40 hours and only charge what you really need.

• **Soon you find yourself** $20,000 plus in debt with a job that pays you a few hundred dollars a week. You start doing the math and figure out that you can't pay this off unless you make a major change in your life. For many, this is the time they move back home, file bankruptcy and are beaten by the city. But it doesn't need to be this way.

• **Don't wait until it's too late and don't sugar coat it.** The next break may be around the corner, but that won't pay the big bucks. It takes time to be an overnight success and you have to be able to give it the time you need. Be realistic and stick to your dream. It can happen, if you can last long enough.

• **Most actors end up earning money** in many different aspects of show business, adding hyphens to their names: directors, producers, writers, teachers, dialogue and acting coaches.

• **Some jobs actors have had:** Jenna Elfman, clothing manufacturer. She put rhinestones on jeans and vests. Julianna Margulies, when people died, would go in and pack up their belongings. Thomas Gibson worked in a bank vault, bagging coins. Tom Hanks, hotel bellboy (carried bags for Cher). Quentin Tarantino, video rental store. Ray Romano, washed trucks. Lucy Lawless, gold mining company, sawed rocks in half. Grace Jones, director's assistant. Ellen Barkin, waitress in Greenwich Village. Dom DeLuise, baby photographer. Elayne Boosler, waitress. Robert Duvall, post office. Meg Ryan, grocery checker. Harry Belafonte, assistant janitor. Sidney Poitier, dishwasher. Mary Steenburgen waitressed in New York for five years. Tuesday Knight, receptionist. Margaret Cho, Raggedy Ann Doll at F.A.O. Schwarz in S.F. Cameron Diaz, clerk at TCBY, the yogurt shop. Danny DeVito, hair dresser Mr. Dan. Michael Caine, donut maker. Bob Saget, deli clerk (he financed his student films in college from his earnings). Warren Beatty, brick layer's helper. Bill Cosby, shoe salesman. Sean Connery polished coffins.

• **Stella Adler, one of the greatest acting teachers, said,** "Waiting tables is excellent for the developing actor. To be a good waiter you need to communicate effectively with your customers, be responsive to their moods and needs and keep your memorization tools sharp." At the same time they are handling dishes, glasses and such. "A physical activity while responding to the others in your scene—exactly what the actor does."

• **Taye Diggs, Jennifer Esposito, Selma Blair,** Gillian Anderson, Sandra Bullock, Steve Buscemi, Jessica Lange, were waiters. Geena Davis and Julianna Margulies worked at the River Cafe; Geena says the owner used to say, "Relax! I can tell you're going to be a star."

• **Patricia Heaton, Amanda Peet, Ashley Judd and Gwyneth Paltrow** were hostesses. Bruce Willis and James Gandolfini were bartenders.

• **Brad Garrett** worked at T.G.I. Friday's restaurant in Woodland Hills for two years while working his way up with his standup act and acting.

• **Jeremy Gursey, at 19, when working at a coffeehouse** in Studio City, noticed the lines for ice-blended mochas. He decided to create his own version and take it to film and television sets. He saved $100 from three paychecks to buy a commercial blender and an ice chest. He said, "I figured if all else fails, at least I'll be able to whip up some damn good margaritas. At the time, I was charging $2 by the cup and I remember returning home with a fat stack of ones." One night, when watching *Seinfeld,* he scanned the credits for the line producer, called and worked his way in. He had somehow memorized all of our favorite blends. He would bring mine to the set because, most of the time, I couldn't get away. Everyone loved him. Last time I saw him, at age 24, he figured his company, Mocha Kiss, had prepared more than 75,000 coffee drinks on about 100 films and TV shows. His assets now include thousands of dollars worth of large-scale commercial cappuccino machines, a van and his own office. He and four employees shuttle between 12 and 20 productions a week. What would he really like to do? "Direct." He has several film ideas percolating.

• **Rachel Griffiths** says, "Oh, I was just a terrible waitress. So I became an artist's model instead because then all I had to do was take my clothes off, lie down on a nice rug and fall asleep. I was good at that."

• **While job researching,** a good exercise is to write down everything you love to do and see if you can possibly put them together in a job you would like. When you are on the job, you want to shine, to be the best at what you are doing. This will increase your chances to make more money, but most of all, you will be a champion at everything you do. This will raise your self-confidence and self-esteem; you will be contributing to a better work place. Striving to be the best that you can be is a valuable acting tool. You can train for it every day.

• **Keep your priorities straight**. If you are an actor, you need to be acting somewhere at all times. Pick a job that won't drain you physically or emotionally. It should give you some flexibility for auditions and the ability to take off for a few days if you land that one, two or three-day job. Generally, stage actors look for day jobs, and film and television actors look for night and weekend jobs.

• **It is in your best interest** to choose a job that is connected to show business or one that is in an area of town where people in the business will likely show up. There is the slim possibility that you will be discovered on your job—it does happen. At least you will make friends who are connected and interested in the biz.

• **Gretchen Mol**, in 1996, was working as a coat check girl at a restaurant named Michael's in New York—a lot of agents dine there. She says, "One day an agent asked for my picture and resume." She was cast in Woody Allen's comedy, *Celebrity*, and hasn't stopped working.

• **Ethan Erickson**, desk clerk at West Hollywood's Le Montrose. He was spotted by a casting director and starred for two years on daytime's *Guiding Light*.

• **Learn the skill of saving money** when you are working your "day job." An actor's paychecks can be few and far between. If you save your acting money and live fairly frugally, you can actually support yourself working relatively few days a year. *See Union section for pay scales.* Inexperienced actors will make a major purchase when they receive their checks for six week's work on a film, then have to scrounge next month's rent. We never know when our next acting job will be. Knowing how to manage money is one of the keys to an actor's success.

• **Here are some ideas for jobs** that have worked very well for people I know. Some of these jobs take research to find out where to apply for them.

- **Starbucks**, all of their employees are hand picked for their personalities behind the counter. A manager told me last month he had 150 applications and only seven suited their criteria. All employees have benefits and profit sharing packages that become 100% funded after you work there five years. Flexible working hours and if you love coffee – why not?
- **Fit Model.** *See the Commercial Print section.*
- **Substitute teacher** can make a good living; the hours are great for our business.
- **The airlines** offer flexible hours, great benefits, trips to New York for auditions.
- **Work in restaurants or upscale grocery stores** (Whole Foods, Pavilions, Gelsons, Trader Joes, Ralphs) in Beverly Hills, Brentwood, Encino, Malibu, Santa Monica, Pacific Palisades, Studio City, West Hollywood or West Los Angeles.
- **An actress I know** works 20 hours a week, for 1-800-DENTIST, making $15 per hour. She can switch hours for her interviews.
- **Mystery Shopping.** One of my students does this earning about $200 a month.
- **"Acting as if you are a patient"** for doctor's tests.
- **A dog walking and grooming company** is a good way to be your own boss.
- **Traffic School teachers** work on weekends and make $100 a day, a good way to work on selling yourself to people, practice speaking and comedy.
- **Work as a messenger or delivering food** to offices and studios; landscaping or taking care of office plants; a mail clerk in a big theatrical agency; a secretary at a public relations firm; a limousine driver or a runner in an entertainment attorney's office.
- **UPS** is a great place for actors to work because they have hours from 3:30 to 8:30 a.m. and pay starts at $8.50 an hour, quickly raised to $9 an hour with full benefits.
- **Night auditor** at a hotel, basically someone to watch the desk and check people coming in late.
- **Product demonstrator,** companies sometimes look for actors to pitch their products at events or popular streets.
- **Stage shows** at our local amusement parks, auditions are advertised in the trade papers.
- **Temporary agencies** furnish the studios with office workers.
- **People who know computers** can get jobs at night inputting information. The hourly rate is usually around $15 to $20.
- **Construction.**
- **A teller** at a Beverly Hills bank.
- **Assistant to someone in the biz**
- **Extra work.** *(See Extra Section)*

• **Dan Cortes** (*Suddenly Susan, The Single Guy, Melrose Place*) began his show biz career as a production assistant at MTV. He was going to be let go in a month due to cutbacks. He wrote a treatment, mailed a copy of it to himself and left it sealed, for the postmark date. Then he pitched the concept for a sports show with himself as the host. They said they weren't interested but in two weeks time they had developed the same show he pitched. The last day of his employment they were auditioning 15 guys for the host. One guy didn't show up on time, so they asked Dan to hop up on stage to hold the spot for the guy. Dan auditioned along with everyone else until the guy showed up. Two days later, the producer called and offered Dan the job. I asked him, why didn't you say I was the one who conceived it? He said, "I was grateful to get the job and knew they wouldn't give me a piece of it. If they had gone with another host and been a hit, eventually I could have gone to court with the treatment I had presented." Landing the job of the host was his opening into becoming known as a personality.

• **Andi Matheny**, one of the members of my theatre company, works in the Universal Studio Wild West Stunt Show. They have two casts of five, and five or six alternates for each role. They trained her and she rehearsed for a month. The auditions are advertised in the trade papers. As third and fourth alternate last year, she made $22,000. In a job like this you can always be available to take auditions because an alternate will fill in for you.

• **Steve Martin**, worked at Disneyland selling guides, then at Knotts Berry Farm at the Bird Cage Theater, learning balloon tricks and the banjo. Jack Wagner worked a stint as a Universal Studios Hollywood tour guide. And Wayne Brady worked a number of jobs at theme parks all over the country. Many actors say theme parks are at least a job that keeps them entertaining and feeling like they're working in the business.

• **A good looking married couple I know dress up** in Superman and Wonder Woman costumes and make a nice sum in front of Grauman's Chinese Theater charging tourists to have their pictures taken with them. Be warned, the characters on Hollywood Boulevard can get pretty competitive with each other. Other popular spots for street performers include the Venice Beach Boardwalk and the Third Street Promenade. Permit requirements vary in each city, check out city websites for most current info (in L.A., it's ci.la.ca.us). For costume rental shops, check out the *Style, Image and Wardrobe Section*.

• **Mel Harris** made $85,000 in 1985 on the $100,000 Pyramid. She used the money to pay bills and finance her career. Five years later, in her third year on *thirtysomething*, she was on the $100,000 Pyramid as a guest celebrity. So if you like game shows, give it a try. At the very worst, you can walk away with some cool prizes and a great experience. Jim Martyka, actor/writer, won an all-expenses paid trip to a four-star resort off Isla Navidad in Mexico, a nice break from the hustle and bustle of L.A.

• **Assistants and production assistants** are some of the best jobs an actor can have in the industry. However, these are often some of the most grueling jobs, with long hours spent doing "gopher" work with little or no credit. Nevertheless, it's a great way to meet people, to be on set and to learn first hand how the business works. Many agencies, casting directors and studios are also looking for interns. While many of these don't pay, if you're looking for a foot in the door and you have some extra time, these can be a great opportunity.

• **Craig Zisk**, a producer and director imdb.com, began his show business career as a production assistant (P.A.) on *Family Ties* during the summer of his junior year in college. After graduating, he held many different jobs. In 1995, he became the supervising producer on *The Single Guy*. After directing several shows in the first season, he became full-time director in the second season. He and Brad Hall, the creator of *The Single Guy* and *Watching Ellie* met working on *Family Ties*. This is how networking friendships are made in this business. Always do a good job, no matter what that job is; you will be remembered.

• **Script coverage** is another great job for actors who have a knack for writing. Studios and independent producers and directors are constantly looking for people to edit their scripts, write up a synopsis and offer feedback. As with all cool jobs they can be difficult to find and very competitive.

• **Catering, bartending, waiting, valet parking** and limousine driving jobs allow you the opportunity of seeing how successful people party. The hours are flexible and the pay is good. Like most jobs, you have to prove yourself in order to get the best parties and hours; a good place to work on your personality skills. Work for the companies that cater celebrity show biz parties. Read the gossip columns in the *Daily Variety* and *Hollywood Reporter* trade papers; they often mention who caters the parties and parks the cars.

• **Many actors do audience recruiting** for movie screenings and marketing research for studios. *(See Resources list)*

• **Professional TV-studio audience member.** You get paid for sitting in sit-com audiences. *See Temps on Time in Resources.*

• **Mystery shopper** can be a fun part-time job. You go undercover to stores you are assigned to and grade the employees and the condition of the store. Salary can be up to $100 a visit. You stay in the store 20 to 30 minutes and e-mail a two-page report within 24 hours.

• **Another great gig is working with local film festivals.** Many times, event organizers are looking for all the help they can get. The pay is usually low and sometimes, the work is volunteer, but once again, it's a great place to not only meet people in the industry, but also see some great films. The Los Angeles Film Festival hires interns and volunteers, lafilmfest.com. Also check out the American Film Institute, afi.com.

• **Jill Hennessy** (*Crossing Jordan*) was a New York subway and street performer, playing the guitar and singing. She made a living and felt like she was performing and it kept her available for class, auditions and work when she could land a part.

• **Bonnie Gillespie**, casting director and author of the book *Casting Qs: Self Management for Actors*, castingqs.com. She is also a career consultant on the business of acting and is a big fan of author Deborah Jacobson's book, *Survival Jobs*. Here are a couple of paragraphs from a letter she wrote to Deborah.

  • **The funniest realization**, upon reading your book, was that I had, at some point in my life, held no fewer than 30 of the odd jobs you detail. I never understood why people shook their heads at me in dismay, asking, "How can you do so many different things?" and, "When are you going to get a real job?" all while coveting the freedom and flexibility my job(s) of choice provided. Even though I'd already begun living a freelance lifestyle, while in my 20s, it wasn't until I read your book that I realized that there needn't be a stigma attached to that choice. What a wonderful discovery!

  • **Since clocking out on the last day** of my long-term temp assignment in 1999, I have held (usually six simultaneously) the following survival jobs: pet-sitter, interview transcriptionist, makeup artist, actress, singer, voiceover artist, hand model, hair model, Improv comedy traffic school instructor, Payroll/office manager, webpage designer, graphic designer, columnist, focus group participant, product tester, academic tutor, SAT course instructor, nanny, casting assistant, theatre director, film print archivist, restaurant reviewer, book reviewer, acting advice columnist, biz of the biz speaker.

• **Temp work is a popular choice for many actors.** Temp jobs provide not just some occasional income, but also flexibility, which aspiring actors need. A couple of pieces of advice when doing temp work; sign up with a number of different agencies so you consistently have work, try to figure out as best you can when you can work so you don't flake on the job and make sure that job itself is flexible.

• **Law schools and medical schools** are other places to look for temporary work and you might even get to do a little acting. Often times these schools are looking to hire people to play mock jurors, clients, patients, etc. to help train their students in mock trials or medical situations. Check out the medical and legal programs at UCLA and USC. The Keck School of Medicine at USC is at 323/442-3483 or usc.edu/schools/medicine and the David Geffen School of Medicine at UCLA is at medsch.ucla.edu (no phone calls). The UCLA School of Law Volunteer Witness Program can be reached at 310/206-1193.

• **Actress Stacey Smithey** says, "My advice to a new actor in town is to do extra work! It will allow them an opportunity to be on the set and make some money and contacts. And if they need more money, get a few temp jobs, catering, etc. but nothing that ties them down to a desk or responsibility. I wish I had done it that way, rather then the desk job way. I think I would be farther along by now."

Resources

To download and print an updated version of this and all resource lists, go to actingiseverything.com.

CATERERS
Along Came Mary, 323/931-9082. alongcamemary.com.
Black Tie Event Services, 310/337-9900, Ext. 4. blacktieevent.com.
Dine With 9 Catering, 818/769-1883. dinewith9.com.
Gourmet Celebrations, 310/266-0625. gourmetcelebrations.com
Scotty's Bartending & Waitress Service, 818/247-9968.
Wolfgang Puck Catering, 323/491-1250. wolfgangpuckcatering.com. Multiple locations around L.A.

EDUCATIONAL THEATRE

Kaiser Permanente's CareActors. Part time. Needs extensive theatre background. Training for physicians and health care professionals to improve communication skills and patient/physician skills. Kaiser also casts actors to portray health care professionals and patients in theatrical presentations and improv patient simulations. Photo and resume to CareActors, Kaiser Permanente Educational Theatre Programs, 815 W. Colorado Blvd., #103, L.A. 90041. 323/259-4391.

Kaiser Permanente's Community Services. Touring Theatre Company with 25 full-time actors includes benefits. Tour schools, need young-looking actors. Send P&R to Edgar Garcia Educational Theatre, 825 W. Colorado Blvd., #222, L.A., 90041.

L.A. Troupe, Theatre-In-Education. Classical adaptations aimed at middle schools. P&R to L.A. Troupe, 9991 Maude Ave., Shadow Hills, 91040. 818/951-6882. mysterytodinefor.com.

National Conference for Community and Justice. Presents plays to high schools. P&R to Peter Howard, NCCJ, 444 West Ocean Blvd, Suite 940, Long Beach, CA 90802 Equity contract. nccj.org.

Shakespeare and Friends. Small Equity company tours middle schools and high schools. P&R to Dee Nieto, 11824 Dorothy St., L.A., 9049. 323/820-2292.

Stop Gap, 17-19 actors play to youth, adult and senior groups. stopgap.org

Storytellers and Troubadours, people with a ready-to-go finished project. P&R to Ken Frawley, President, 2900 Bristol Street, Suite D-105, Costa Mesa, CA 92626 714/979-7061 From LA County Only 1-800-381-8481.

ENTERTAINMENT INDUSTRY JOBS

Audience Recruiters, 1800-A-JOB-NOW, EXT. 1416, movieviewjobs.com. Also research assistants. You have to answer questions on an automated line, and if you pass they call you in for a physical interview, where you take a test and, if you pass, you are interviewed. I've known many people who work here; its tough but you can make a living with your own hours.

Entertainmentcareers.net. Links to the studios and to other jobs. Membership costs about $4.95 for the first month and members get job notices a full day before the general public.

Entertainmentjobs.com. A little more expensive, membership is $39 for three months. But members get a directory of jobs from over 3,800 entertainment-related companies, as well as helpful articles and info on seminars.

Robert A. Brilliant, Inc./CBS Screenings, 818/386-6605 Ext. 18, seasonal.

Showbizjobs.com. Does have some free job listings, but membership, which costs $35 for six months, allows browsers to post resumes and search for jobs by category or company.

The studios: Check the websites for CBS, NBC, ABC, Fox, Warner Brothers, Universal, Paramount, Disney, etc. for job opportunities, both full and part time.

GENERAL

entertainmentcareers.net. All kinds of career advice.

Hiring On The Internet: JOBTRACK: monstertrak.monster.com. Computer proficiency. hotjobs.com.

Hollywood Creative Directory: free job board: hcdonline.com.

Mystery Shopping. **Feedback Plus, Inc.**, gofeedback.com. For other companies: mysteryshop.org, they have links to companies that use mystery shoppers.
Transcription Company, 818/848-6500. transcripts.net. They transcribe video footage into scripts, 24 hours a day. For those with good computer skills.
USC School Of Medicine, Dept. of Medical Education, 1975 Zonal Ave. KAM 200, Los Angeles, 90033. Actors portray actual patients to help train medical students. Strong improv skills a must. All ages, all types. Send picture and resume to Attn: Denise.

TEMP AGENCIES

Apple One, 213/892-0234, appleone.com. 888 S. Figueroa St., # 170, L.A. 90017; 818/247-2991, 325 W. Broadway St., Glendale, 91204. Many temp workers can be eligible for low-cost insurance!
Executive Temps, 818/563-2939. 2321 W. Olive Ave., Suite F, Burbank, 91506. "We Give Temps a Good Name."
Friedman Personnel Agency, 310/550-1002. friedmanpersonnel.com. 9000 Sunset Blvd., #1000, Los Angeles, 90069. Jobs in the industry, fees paid by employer.
Temps On Time, 818/845-3030. 418 E. Olive, Burbank, 91501. Full range of employment needs. They also work with major studios supplying people for audiences. You get paid for seeing the show!
The Job Factory, 310/446-3071. thejobfactory.com. 1744 Westwood Blvd., Los Angeles, 90024. Unusual jobs and flexible hours. They've been helping actors for 25 years.
Other temp agencies with multiple locations around L.A.: Adecco, adeccousa.com; **Career Strategies Inc.**, csi4jobs.com; **Kelly Services**, kellyservices.com; **Venturi Staffing Partners**, venturi-staffing.com

PARKING SERVICES

Chuck's, 818/788-4300. chucksparking.com. (The best).
Valet Girls, 310/457-6657. valetgirlparking.com.

THEME PARKS

Disneyland, Audition Hotline: 714/781-0111. disneyauditions.com.
Knott's Berry Farm, 714/995-0088. knottsberryfarm.com.
Legoland California, Audition Hotline: 760/918-5454. legoland.com.
Sea World Of California, 619/226-3842. becjobs.com.
Universal Studios Job Line, 818/866-4021.
Six Flags Magic Mountain, Audition Hotline: 661/255-4800. sixflagsjobs.com.

BOOKS

Back Stage West, Hollywood Reporter and *Variety* and other trades have weekly listings.
The Working Actors Guide (**WAG**), workingactors.com, has many listings of where to find jobs for actors in Los Angeles. Order books through Samuel French Bookstore, 323/876-0570. samuelfrench.com.
Development Girl by Hadley Davis.
How to Be a Star at Work by Robert E. Kelley.
Survival Jobs by Deborah Jacobson.

CHANGING YOUR NAME

- **There are two reasons to change your name:** One, you don't like it and feel it doesn't suit you; and two, your name is already taken in SAG (Rule 15). I stayed with Kerr, one of my married names, because it fit, I liked it and my children are named Kerr. A numerologist once told me I would have more luck if I added an "E" as a middle initial or spelled my name Judie. I tried to do it, but couldn't; it didn't feel like me. I like my name so I will have to make more of my own luck. Listen to all opinions and then make your own decisions based on what feels right to you. Part of developing self-awareness is following your own instincts; they are there to guide you.

- **Jay Bernstein, personal manager, writer and producer:**

  - **A limousine driver/actor once asked me,** "Should I change my name? It's Alexander Propapalis." I told him to change his name, no one should have to get through your name to get to your talent. They're not going to say we have to get . . . They'll just cut you.

- **Salma Hayek says years ago Hollywood producers shunned her** because of her nationality. "When I first started, they said, 'Just don't say you're Mexican. With your name and your looks you can pass for Lebanese. Work on your accent so that it sounds more Middle Eastern.'" She refused. "I was born and raised in Mexico; I'm Mexican."

- **Michael Keaton's** real name is Michael Douglas.

- **Goldie Hawn** was told, "You sound like a stripper." Goldie said "So?"

- **Actress Samantha Harper** had to change her name from Harriet Harper. Her fiance, at the time, suggested Samantha. The minute she tried it she says, "My heart sang and I knew it was for me."

• **Bill Macy** *(Surviving Christmas, Analyze This, Maude)* had to change his name from William Garber. Later, William H. Macy had to add an initial in order to keep his name intact.

• **Meg Ryan** was Meg Hyra; Tori Amos was Myra Amos.

• **If you must change your name** because of the SAG rule, then choose a name that means something to you or your family. I would consult a numerologist with a list of possible names you could live with. Look for numerologists at psychic fairs and the Bodhi Tree Bookstore's bulletin board. *(See Bookstores.)* As with anything else, be cautious. Consultants will each have their own opinion based on their personal studies. When you are eligible to join SAG, call and ask about names before you join.

• **Search for your name on imdb.com** before registering with SAG. You can also visit Academy Players and look in the books to see if your name is taken. You may use any name for performance purposes if you have the first claim on it. Vanessa L. Williams was forced to use her middle initial because Vanessa Williams (of *Melrose Place*) joined SAG first. However, Sean Hayes was able to drop his middle initial, although he is still listed as Sean P. Hayes in the SAG international database.

• **I asked actress Maddisen K. Krown,** who went through a name change, to tell of her experience.

  • **When I wanted to change my name**, I took the following steps: Purchased the book, *How to Change Your Name in California,* by attorney Lisa Sedano; visited my local Superior Court branch to pick up the Petition for Name Change forms; contacted the Society of Kabalarians at kabalarians.com for assistance.

  • **California adults have the legal right** to change our names by "Usage," which is done without filing court papers. However, I decided to take the legal route because it can be difficult to get federal and state agencies to accept the new name without the official authorization.

  • **Once I had decided on my new name,** I filed the forms with the Superior Court; paid a Court Filing fee of $214.50, plus $95 for the Order to Show Cause for Name Change to be published in a local newspaper. On my court date I received my name change decree. I registered the new name with the actor's unions.

  • **The Society of Kabalarians** assisted me in choosing my new name. Their name change recommendations are based upon the principle that "through knowledge of the relationship of a name to a date of birth, one's inner potential and the mental characteristics, personality traits, and conditions in one's life can be determined. The right change of name can change your life."

• **Joel M. Barkow** from SAG wrote in the SAG newsletter about name changes on Social Security cards.

> • **Applicants who have legitimate business needs** for using assumed names (such as performers using stage names) are allowed to request additional cards. Apart from filling out an SS-5 form, available at all Social Security offices, you merely need to submit documents at the time of application that show use of the old name and current use of your stage name. A driver's license or similar id would suffice for the former, while the latter can be evinced from a signed contract or pay stub using the assumed name.

> • **Since the employer submits only your Social Security number**—and not your name—you can wait to apply for the second card until you receive the initial pay check stub before filling out the necessary application. However, the transfer must be taken care of prior to tax time, when the IRS begins checking names against Social Security numbers. The second card is for ID purposes only—it is not a legal document and does not have the same effect as a legal name change.

• **In 1998, SAG approved changes** to its previously strictly-enforced Rule 15. They will continue to "urge membership applicants not to join SAG with a professional name that duplicates or can cause confusion with that of an existing member." I believe it is vastly better to use a name that doesn't closely resemble another actor's name.

Resources

To download and print an updated version of this and all resource lists, go to actingiseverything.com.

Legal Name Change, Los Angeles County, 213/974-5299. Call this line for recorded complete information of how to change your name legally. Currently the cost is $320, plus a publication fee which varies by publication.

The Society of Kabalarians, (a registered non-profit society) kabalarians.com. Discover what's in your name.

imdb.com.

sag.org.

my.ca.gov to download name change forms.

HOME BUSINESS OFFICE

• **As a self-employed, self-motivated actor,** you are now in business and this requires an office, a private phone line (not to be shared with anyone), an answering machine, voice mail or message service, a cell phone with a message service and an e-mail account. One lost message could mean the loss of a career break, as well as the loss of a day's income, which could pay for two years of phone service.

• **It's wonderful to have a separate room** for your office, but few of us have that luxury. So set aside an area devoted to taking care of business.

• **Your first order of business** is to get your pictures and resumes out to prospective buyers of your talent. Just as an employee shows up for work each day, you must make a commitment to look for acting work each day. It doesn't matter what that acting work is: big, small, paid, free; you are looking for experience in your new business. Free jobs are just as valuable as paying jobs in your career.

• **You need a desk or table, a computer** and file folder dividers, trays or file drawers. Designate a folder or tray for each different head shot, a place for letterhead stationary, business envelopes, 8x10 or 8½x11 envelopes, postage scale, stamps, appointment book, acting notebook, networking card file, and bookshelf. You need a computer; until you can afford your own, some libraries and copy service stores have computers and printers available for your use.

• **Keeping track of incoming and outgoing phone messages** is an important part of every business. I find a valuable book for this is Avery's #50-111 In/Out Call Log, 100 pages. When I pick up my messages I write them in the book. My personal technique for checking calls off when I return them allows me to use both pages for incoming calls.

• **When my book is full,** (about two years) I file it away. There have been times I've had to refer to old books for the phone number of someone I needed to reconnect with. This is a small community and we do come in contact with the people we've worked with again.

• **Use a file box or file drawers to set up your files.** *Some suggestions for file folder titles are:*

- • **Advertising/promotion.** Copies of any publicity about you.
- • **Articles of interest.** Keep pieces on people you know, or would like to know; information on projects you'd like to work on; story ideas, etc.
- • **Audition copy.** The sides and copy from your readings.
- • **Bank statements.**
- • **Cash receipts.** Keep for income taxes. Write any pertinent information on the back. Don't forget video rentals.
- • **Commercial pictures.** Print work from magazines you could have done. Ideas of how to dress for commercials.
- • **Correspondence.** Keep a copy of any letter you send out or receive.
- • **Income statements of earnings.**
- • **Manuals for equipment.**
- • **Master head shots and negatives.** Labeled in a folder, you never have to worry about where to find your negatives or digital disks.
- • **Phone lists.** Keep every phone list you're given from acting classes and productions you've worked on. Great for making a networking phone call.
- • **Pictures.** I keep a few of each shot within reach.
- • **Pictures of acting roles** I want to play or a characterization I think will help me. I take these along on my photo shoots to show the photographer.
- • **Publicity, general.** I save copies of trade ads that I may want to emulate.
- • **Receipts** from check and credit card purchases.
- • **Resumes.**
- • **Reviews.** Keep a copy of all reviews from every project you're in.

To download and print an updated version of this and all resource lists, go to actingiseverything.com.

Resources

BOOKS

Working From Home, 5th Edition by Paul & Sarah Edwards. workingfromhome.com. $19.95. 664 pages and is listed in the New York Review of Books Catalog of the best books in print. "On the subject of home-based business, this gets as close as possible to everything you need to know, from office layout to maintaining personal relationships. A must for anyone considering working out of the home."

The #1 Home Business Book by George & Sandra Delany. Out of print, but check online for used copies.

Small-Time Operator by Bernard Kamoroff, CPA.

AUDITION LOG BOOKS OR SYSTEMS

It is very important to keep track of all your auditions, who you met, where you went, what you auditioned for. At the beginning of your career it is easy but as you get very busy it is hard to keep track without a computer program or a log book.

Actor's Interview Log. A book to keep track of where you have been. $10

The Actor's Office, 818/692-0706. theactorsoffice.com. E-mail: support@the actorsoffice.com. Mac or Windows $50. Track auditions and submissions, print postcards, cover letters, mailing labels, agent and casting director addresses.

protalentPERFORMER 1.71, 973/809-3215. protalentperformer.com. E-mail: customersupport@protalentperformer.com. Mac or Windows $119.95. 21-day free trial. Tracks submissions, auditions, contacts, etc. Also advertises to singers, comedians, dancers, models.

Holdon Log. ActorTrack 2.0. holdonlog.com. Mac or Windows $99.95. Not only tracks auditions, callbacks and contacts, but also features a program that analyzes your information, providing you with statistics and, even cooler, trends in your audition and booking patterns! They often hold free seminars. Email and ask where you can attend the next one. They are very informative and instructional.

WEB SITES

Working From Home, workingfromhome.com. Paul & Sarah Edwards.

Work-at-Home Success, workathomesuccess.com. This site posts listings of companies that hire home-based workers, plus discussions of important issues, including effective ways to communicate with your boss on the telephone.

USED OFFICE FURNITURE

Steel Casey Traditional To Funk, 818/763-5667. steelcasey.com. 10624 Ventura Blvd., Studio City, 91604. M-Sa 11-5; Su. 12-4. This is the absolute best place for used file cabinets with and without style. Desks, great desk and computer chairs. My husband and I have custom designed desks but everything else we have purchased at Steel Casey's. I especially love the used horizontal files. They take up less space, hold more and are better suited to hold copy machines etc. than the vertical file drawers. Stock changes all the time and Casey can get you just about anything you need.

Advanced Liquidators, 818/763-3470. advancedliquidators.com. E-mail: sales @advancedliquidators.com. 10631 Magnolia Blvd., North Hollywood, 91601. M-F 9-5:30; Sa, 10-4.

CAREER TOOLS

APPOINTMENT BOOK / PDA / TIME MANAGEMENT

• **Always have your "book" with you.** Write every appointment down: classes, rehearsals, interviews, workouts, meditation, dates for movies, plays, etc. All your phone numbers and addresses, a place to jot down notes, career goals and future plans should be included. When you schedule your days, be sure to allow for driving time. Sunday night is a good time to plan for the week. Purchase a system that has a full page for each day and lists the time of day down the left side of the page; a place for a "To Do List" and a place to write down directions to locations. I use the *Day Runner* in a 5x7 *Filofax* book. The daily log is valuable for verifying your tax deductions. You can store the year's log in the same file as the year's copy of your tax returns. I use a computer program for names, phone numbers and addresses. I update this every few months, print the pages and replace them in my book.

• **Personal Digital Assistant (PDA)**—Electronic Palm Pilot Systems, also Handspring products. I use a Handspring Treo with the Palm Pilot System software. I store all the phone numbers in my life and lists of anything I might need with me. I carry the **PDA** in my purse so I always have the information with me. I do not keep my calendar events and appointments on it. I find I need to look at those elements laid out on paper for the day, week and month.

• **I asked actress Tricia Gilfone to write about using the PDA.**

> • A Personal Digital Assistant, or PDA, is a good tool. The advantage is all the information on your PDA is stored and backed up on your computer. When you enter new information or make a change on your Mac or PC, it automatically appears on your handheld when you synchronize, and vise versa. In the event of a computer crash or disappearance of your PDA, you always have your valuable networking information backed up. If you want to purchase a PDA but you're not sure if it's right for you, I recommend starting off with the Handspring Visor or the Palm Zire. Currently, these are the most basic and inexpensive on the market.

- **There are numerous companies** with a plethora of models to choose from, the most popular being the Palm Pilot (Palm.com) and Handspring (Handspring.com.) Research at pdabuyersguide.com. Click on the links page for other related websites. You can download hundreds of applications that allow you to view web pages, create detailed shopping lists, expense records, even de-stress with some cool games, Handango.com and tucows.com. Find everything from Dictionary/Thesauruses to Diet and Exercise assistants to GPS and Map software. Get the Rand McNally Streetfinder guide, Randmcnally. com, to find your way.

- **Another fabulous application** is Avangto.com. This software allows you to keep current with the latest industry buzz by downloading magazine subscriptions such as *Variety, Rolling Stone, TVguide*, as well as the latest local and world news from CNN, USA today, and *The New York Times*. Keep up on Oscar picks with Yahoo or Hollywood. com to get your local movie theaters and show times.

- **Acting coach/actress Caryn West** keeps track of every casting director showcase she does on her Palm Pilot list under "casting directors." While there she puts in their name, address, where she met them, the scene she did and anything special she wants to remember. She can transfer to her computer and print out a complete list or just the previous month's list. When her agent or manager is submitting her for a role she will email them the history she has with the casting director. She finds the PDA very valuable in keeping organized.

- **The important thing about having a system to keep appointments** is the time management aspect. Time management can make the difference in having a successful career. You can educate yourself; there are time management courses. I have worked privately with expert Dr. Jo Christner and have taken a course from Dr. Jackie Jaye-Brandt. It is fun to manage your time and it can relieve that feeling of being overwhelmed. It will help every segment of your career and life.

Resources

Most stationery stores have inexpensive systems and books. The following systems are more expensive and prestigious.

Franklin System, at Franklin/Covey Store: 800/819-1812. franklincovey.com. They hold time management seminars.
Time Design System, 800/637-9942. timedesign.com. 11835 W. Olympic #450, West Los Angeles.
Jackie Jaye Brandt, M.A., MFT, Corporate Communications and Psychotherapy, 818/ 505-1664. Jackiejayebrandt.com. 3575 Cahuenga Blvd. West, #213, Los Angeles, 90068. Stress management, communications training, time management, group workshops, couples, groups and individual counseling.

TELEPHONE / VOICEMAIL / CELL PHONE / FAX

• **You must have a private phone** with a 310, 323, 213 or 818 preface and message device, not to be shared with a roommate. If you share a phone number and message device, you will lose important messages. Don't do it. If you do not use a phone number that looks like you live in Los Angeles you will not be considered as serious about your acting career and will lose opportunities. You must also have a cell phone with a local preface. Have a car charger in case the battery runs down. At this writing, Verizon is said to have the best reception; it is what I use.

• **Keep the outgoing message short and to the point.** People wanting to interview or hire you hate to wait through cute, long messages. It is important that your name or phone number, not both, be on your outgoing message so your callers know they have not dialed in error.

• **When you can't be reached on your cell phone,** check in for messages every 60 or 90 minutes during casting hours 10-6. You never know who may have a last-minute interview for you.

• **Show business is a phone business;** when you call someone and get their answering device, say your name and phone number slowly and clearly first, as if someone is writing it down, then the rest of your message and then your phone number again. Voice mail systems often cut off but if you have given your name and number first, they know who has called. *Always leave your phone number,* even if you think they know it. Your calls will be returned faster! Why not make it the easiest thing in the world to return your call? With cell phones and voicemail there are often voice dropouts; act as though your message is important and make sure you communicate clearly. In the last few years, I have received many phones calls I haven't been able to return because one number could not be understood. Give someone a second phone call if you have not received a return call in two days.

• **It is great to have your own plain paper fax machine.** If you don't, you must have a place where you can receive faxes 24 hours a day. You never know when you will need your sides faxed to you for tomorrow's audition. I prefer my fax machine on its own phone line. Some email addresses allow you to receive a fax like an email.

COMPUTER / EMAIL / INTERNET

• **You must be computer savvy** if you want to be competitive in your marketing strategies. Before you have your own computer you can use one at a library. Get a free email address at yahoo. com, msn.com and many others. Don't make the address too complicated; it should be one that people can remember. My Yahoo name is JudyKerrActing. Use your full name; if it is not accepted, add a word or number to the end. Include your email address on your business cards and resumes. When purchasing a computer, I recommend Apple/MAC because of the ease of video editing and the great graphic applications. A PC will be cheaper and will do other functions just as well.

• **There is no charm in saying, "I'm not into computers."** You will miss out on casting, networking and friendship opportunities by not taking this educational step. You can do it. You learned to ride a bike and drive a car which opened up new worlds; so will a computer.

• **With all the work being done online these days, it's important to stay organized.** There is online casting, membership groups, actor profiles and a lot of it is done online. As you work, all of this information needs to be updated so it's important for you to stay on top of it. For help, check out mytalentsecretary.com. The Talent Secretary is a system specifically designed for actors to help them update and manage their many website profiles and online activity, all for about $132 a year.

• **Information for setting up your own website may be found in the** *Your Personal Website* section.

CABLE TV / TIVO / VCR

• **All right, you are an actor.** You must know who is acting and where. You are a student of acting. You must have cable or satellite, you must have HBO, PBS, Showtime, Sundance and Bravo channels at the very least. Of course, often you are not home to watch what you need to see, so you must have a TiVo/DVR and a VCR machine. This way you can view when it's convenient. The truly easy part of TiVo is setting the programs you want to watch. One touch and you can set a whole season of *Grey's Anatomy*. Each week the show will be there ready for you to watch. Go to tivo.com to get all of the information.

• **You will use your** VCR when you want to keep a copy of a commercial or an actor's performance. That is also done with a click of a TiVo button, when the VCR is set up with the TiVo. You will also need the VCR to view rental tapes or to watch your tape from acting class and my private on-camera sessions. These career tools make good gifts for loving families to give aspiring actors.

AUDIO RECORDER / VIDEO CAMERA

• **An audio tape recorder** can be used for learning lines, taping your teachers' feedback, or recording you and your acting partner rehearsing a scene. I like the kind that has a pause button and a small speaker so I have the option of wearing headphones or not when listening to it.

• **A digital voice recorder,** such as the Olympus W-10, is extremely tiny, and also takes digital pictures; very handy. There are iPod attachments for recording. A digital MDV video camera would also be a helpful tool. However, always take notes—recorders can break so you can't rely on them completely.

Tom Kelly, 818/730-1076 or 818/707-2424. Better prices than discount stores and he delivers, sets up and does repairs. He specializes in custom-designed systems. When he sells you equipment, he also trains you how to use it. Good bargains on computers, audio, video, used equipment and trade-ins.

BUSINESS AND PROMOTIONAL PICTURE CARDS

• **Keep photo business cards** in your jacket pocket, purse, wallet, glove compartment. They are an important networking tool. Whenever you meet someone, hand them yours and ask for theirs. There is nothing more awkward than looking for a pen and scrap of paper when someone asks for your phone number. Great free cards at 4over4.com. Also check out gotprint.com.

• **File the business cards you receive.** Make a note of the meeting place, what the person looked like, your conversation. I keep mine in $8^1/_2$ x11 clear-plastic sheets designed to hold business cards. The sheets are kept in a one-inch three-hole binder on my bookshelf, close to the phone and ready for instant reference. Your stationery store has different types of systems for filing business cards.

MAILING LIST / COMPUTER PROGRAM / CARD FILE

• **Start now and keep a 3x5 index card file of everyone** you come in contact with who is in the business. Include on the card where and how you met and something about them that will help you remember them 10 years from now. Also, if you read something about them or send them something about you, note it on the card with the date. Better yet is a computer address system that allows you to keep notes with the addresses. I have one on Filemaker Pro for my Mac. There is also a program for the Palm Pilot where you can make address labels and lists.

• **This is the beginning of your mailing list;** these are the people who will possibly help you get acting work. When you are doing showcases, you will get much more value from your money if you keep up with the casting directors you have acted for. When writing to them you can say: You saw me do a scene (give the name of it) at so and so showcase on (give the date).

• **I've heard it said:** it is best to mail your announcement, flyer, postcard, etc. on Tuesday or Wednesday because everyone else mails theirs on the weekend and the casting directors receive them on Monday or Tuesday. Yours will arrive on Thursday or Friday. Or better yet, mail them on your lucky day. I personally send a little spiritual wish with each one. Hey, we need whatever edge we can get.

THOMAS GUIDE / LOCK BOX / EXTRA KEY / AUTO CLUB

• **The Thomas Guide is your absolute bible** for directions. This book is very clear and easy to use. If you don't know how to read a map, have someone teach you. Buy the L.A./Orange County Edition of the Guide at any bookstore or newsstand. You can't trust other people's directions. You may also get directions at maps.yahoo.com and mapquest.com., although computer map programs are not entirely reliable. Also check L.A. traffic status online at traffic.com or sigalert.com.

• **You must have a lock box on your car** with a house and car key in it. Even though all of my students have this book and hopefully read it, some will invariably lock themselves out of their house or car. After you have keys made, test them.

• **I keep a regular car key in my wallet behind my driver's license,** and a house key in the glove compartment, as well as a secretly hidden house key.

• **The Auto Club Road Service Policy** is another protection you need for yourself. About $55 a year. Membership: 800/222-8794. Also check out geico.com road service.

PASSPORT

• **You may land a job** because you are the only actor who can leave the country immediately. Have an updated passport and be ready to go. New passports are about $97 at the time of this printing, renewals $67.

Resources

travel.state.gov. The Department of State's Internet site, includes state-by-state listings of all post office passport acceptance facilities. Also blank passport forms.
You can apply at some post offices or the L.A. Passport Agency at the federal courthouse. Ask at your local post office for the nearest location.
Federal Courthouse, 11000 Wilshire Bl., 13th fl, W. Los Angeles, 90024. M-F, 8-3.

Professional Work Habits

• **The chief cause of failure** is giving up what you really want for what you want at the moment.

PUNCTUALITY

• **Over and over in this book,** people being interviewed talk about the importance of being on time. This habit can make or break a career.

• **Garth Brooks** tells the story about when he had been in Nashville for a couple of years, he and his wife worked in a shoe store to make ends meet. He was scheduled to perform at 11:30PM at a songwriters' showcase. It was not a prime spot, as the record company reps usually left by 11PM. Suddenly at 9:30PM, the owner ran backstage and said, "You're up, Garth. Ralph Murphy, the second act, hasn't shown up yet." Garth jumped up on stage, sang his heart out, and Capitol Records signed him before the evening was over. Ralph is still looking for a deal.

• **Check in with someone** immediately when you show up for work or an audition to let them know you are there.

• **Practice being on time every day, for every event.**

ATTITUDE

• **In this business, if you get the job,** that means you are skilled and crafted in what you do. If you have to shoot a movie for the next 10 weeks, or do seven years on a television series, who do you want to work with? Most people will want to work with kind, helpful, considerate, nice, gentle, warm, fair, fun, funny, professional actors.

• **There are all kinds of attitudes to adopt.** My grandsons, Austin and Jackson, are often told to change their attitudes when they are acting inappropriately. Their faces and tones of voice change. Very early in their lives, they knew all about attitude and how to fix theirs. So do you.

HARD WORK

• **Oprah's week-day schedule** was described by *People Magazine*. Her success is a result of hard work. How hard are you willing to work for your success?

- • 5 AM: Four-mile run.
- • 7 AM: Breakfast, makeup, hair and prep for shows.
- • 9 - 2 PM: Tape two shows.
- • 2 PM: Lunch.
- • 3 PM: Business and staff meetings. Phone calls.
- • 5:30 PM: Four-mile run, Stairmaster, sit-ups.
- • 7-9 PM: Tying up loose ends of future shows. Dinner.
- • 10 PM: Prep next day's show.
- • 12 AM: To bed

PREPARATION

• **Always have a pen or pencil** with you. Without a "note taking mechanism," you are minimizing your potential, rather than maximizing it. We think we'll remember a person's name or a phone call we need to make, but we won't. Keep notes throughout the day. Each night, process those notes: sort, file, transfer. Develop your own system of keeping track of valuable information.

• **Your success requires extraordinary, extreme actions.** The universe is giving us "whispers" all the time, many times a day. There are opportunities all around you; don't let them pass you by. Have your antenna up, your nose in the air, your ear to the ground, your sights on success.

• **Swoosie Kurtz**, film, television and Broadway veteran stage actress, in a *Women In Film* interview:

  • **In television and film there's no rehearsal.** In a one-hour television drama you do a different scene everyday and once you do the scene,

you never do it again in your whole life. As far as preparation, if I
have the time, I sort of do the same thing for film and TV as I do
for the theatre, which is read the material over and over again, get as
familiar with it as I can. I don't mean in terms of learning lines but
just the overall picture of the piece. What is the theme? What is this
writer trying to say? And what is my part? What does my character
do? And does she change? And, if so, what changes her?

• **Joan Darling, Emmy award-winning director,** talks about preparing
for auditions.

> • **Have pride**—don't do anything less than the absolute best you can do.
> Work on the "given circumstances," pick two strong pieces of acting
> work, decide what function your character has in this painting. Am
> I the comic relief? Am I the villain? Do I drive the plot? If you know
> those very bold strokes and you know how to act, you can come in
> and give a pretty damn good performance very fast.

> • **I was in a television movie** with Dustin Hoffman called *Trap Of
> Solid Gold.* He had a tiny part as an accountant. There was so much
> texture to the portrayal; he so filled himself as an actor that when he
> first appeared, picked up his head and just looked at his fellow actor,
> you knew everything about his character. It was from the amount of
> work that he did. If you want to be doing leads, why not do all the
> work you do as if it were a lead?

CONCENTRATION

• **Being able to focus and concentrate** are two of your most important
functions as an actor. Anita Jesse gives exercises to develop these tools
in her book, *Let The Part Play You,* available at book stores.

• **Linda Buzzell, author** of *How to Make it in Hollywood; All the Right
Moves,* gave some phone hints in the *Women In Film* newsletter.

> • **Lack of focus** can create a reluctance to get on the phone because
> you're not really sure what you're offering or what you're asking for, or
> whether you want it if you get it! It might help to put your Hollywood
> pitch (pitch for your talents, services, script, whatever) up over the
> phone where you can sneak a peek if you freeze up.

> • **Start out by calling a few friends** just to break the ice and get the day
> rolling. By the time you punch in the number of that studio executive
> or agent, you're nicely warmed up and ready to schmooze. Make your

calls standing up and use your body to gesture as if the person were in the room with you. And smile! Research has shown that callers can actually hear the change in your tone of voice and will be more responsive. Making job search calls is a numbers game, not a reflection on your personal worth as a human being. It's important to remember that it may take 100 calls to land one serious job interview.

• **Phone etiquette is very important.** Return those calls promptly, before the end of the day. When you call and leave a message *always leave your number slowly, as if they were writing it down.* They will return your call quicker.

DISCIPLINE

• **When actors aren't acting,** they must be cleaning up their lives, their habits, their house, their bills, always preparing to go to work. Because when you are working as an actor, even in a class scene, you don't have time to do much of anything else. You can let everything else go and let your role consume you. All your discipline will go into your work. You will have trained yourself to have discipline by all the things that you intend to do each day and that you actually do each day. We ask 90% effort in acting—maybe it takes that much in life too—if you want to make a living as an actor. Effort has to do with commitment, intention and discipline.

• **Intention is keeping your agreements.** I intend to be curious, not judgmental; I intend to do my laundry; I intend to send out my pictures; I intend to change my life into positive stories; I intend to eat well; I intend to be on time, etc.

• **Not keeping your intentions** gives you anxiety which leads to guilt, which leads to failure. Don't waste energy on *trying* to keep intentions—just keep them. There is time for everything. Being in business for yourself, as actors are, takes a great deal of *self*-motivation; it won't be coming from anywhere else.

• **Discipline becomes easier** as certain sets of behavior become habits in your life. It has been proven: it takes about 21 days to unlearn a bad habit or to form a new positive habit. In those 21 days, it takes conscious effort and vigilance; but then the new habit is yours.

Actors' Secrets

- "Where there is mystery, there is power." - Charles De Gaulle.

- "Talent is never using two words when one will do." - Thomas Jefferson.

- "Whatever it is that makes a person charming, it needs to remain a mystery." - Rex Harrison.

- "Mystery creates wonder and wonder is the basis of man's desire to understand." - Neil Armstrong.

- Secrets are very valuable acting tools. They give you energy, power and mystery; they draw dramatic, wonderful attention to you. I have heard it said: "Very good actors never talk about their art; very bad ones never stop."

- Actors, as a rule, are great talkers; they spend time and energy talking about what they are *going* to do, giving away all their secrets. In fact they talk so much to so many people, they don't do what they were talking about because they've expended the energy through the talking.

- Learn to focus your conversation on what you are actually doing, not on what you are going to do. If you decide you're going to send out 20 pictures and resumes to agents, don't tell a soul until they are in the mail. When you have an audition, don't tell anyone but your acting coach. If you're planning to get a night job so you'll have your days free for auditions, get the job, then talk about it. So much energy will build up from your career plans that you'll be bursting to carry your plans out! When you take action, the payoff is that you can talk about what you are really doing. You become interesting to listen to, an inspiration.

• **Condense your stories**—get to the bottom line fast. You needn't go into boring details; assume the person you're talking with understands what you are saying. You can teach your mind to think in a concentrated form like a writer. The practice of conserving words can be developed without a loss of communication; in fact there should be an increase in communication. People (casting directors, agents, directors, loved ones) will want to hear more; they will ask you to explain if they don't understand. Don't give away more of yourself than is absolutely necessary. Mystery is an important asset.

• **When you have spoken a word, it reigns over you.** When it is unspoken, you reign over it. There's no point in speaking unless you can improve on silence.

• **In acting,** you may be thinking a paragraph or two in your mind but have only one line of dialogue to convey your thoughts. Dialogue is concentrated because a play, television show or film is limited in time. The writer knows the actor can portray much more than just the words and assumes that the audience will get the message.

• **By controlling the content of your conversation,** people will be more attracted to hiring and spending time with you. Be *responsible* for all of your words. Negativity is death to creativeness. Guard yourself! Talking about illness, everyone's flu, the car accident you just saw, the horrible interview, the awful casting person, smog, this town, traffic, lack of money—robs you of energy. When you hear this going on with yourself or the people around you, don't say anything about it or point it out; simply change the subject to something positive. It is difficult to drop old habits but change brings an *awareness* of self. Awareness is what actors are constantly searching for.

• **Finally, do not allow yourself** to make excuses or blame someone or something else for your reality. Take responsibility for the words you speak and the deeds you do. If this is a new concept for you, there are many self-help books available at libraries and bookstores on creating your own reality.

• **Albert Einstein** said, "The most beautiful thing we can experience is the mysterious. It is the source of all true art and all science. He to whom this emotion is a stranger, who can no longer pause to wonder and stand rapt in awe, is as good as dead; his eyes are closed."

Cover Letters
When and How to Write Them

• **Written communication is extremely important in this business.** When contacting people by letter or email you must sound professional, intelligent and personable. Have your personality show through; let them know you have a spark. A letter you write seeking representation or acting work is not the type of letter you would write to a corporate executive when seeking a position.

• **Katharine Hepburn** said, "Show me an actor with no personality and I'll show you an actor who isn't a *star.*"

• **An audience judges your acting** by the way you bring a script alive. When your writing meanders, contains grammatical errors and fails to get to the point immediately, the reader (agent, manager, casting director, producer, director) will judge your other skills and aptitude.

• **Technology has increased the volume** of communication, leaving little time for readers to do more than skim your writing. Getting to the point is essential.

• **Learn techniques to improve your writing.** Use short sentences. Lengthy sentences are ambiguous, tedious and needlessly time consuming. The first sentence should state what the paragraph is about. It is why I use this bullet and bold style. I know people will scan to find the points they are interested in so I try to make them easy to find.

• **Submissions to agents and managers** are almost useless without a cover letter unless your picture, or body of work, is so outstanding it speaks for itself.

• **Stuart K. Robinson, commercial teacher,** says in his commercial class that your submission package is very important. Here he talks of the agent cover letter.

- **A strong cover letter will tell me why I need to respond** to this right now. Cover three points in your letter.

- **First, what is great about you?** Do not wait for them to discover it. If it is that you just finished two major motion pictures, your career is about to unfold and you are looking to get into commercials, tell them that. It could be that you have just finished the greatest commercial class and you feel like, "Ahhh, I know my calling now." Tell them that. It could be as simple as, "Everywhere I go, people ask me if I am an actor." Anything that will make them go, "oooh."

- **Second, tell them why you do not have an agent.** Is it because you just moved here from another market? Or you have been in another business for a while and you are just getting started now as an actor. Or you have been with a smaller agency, or an agency that did not quite work for you and you want to move somewhere more proactive. Tell them why, if you are so great, no one has scooped you up before.

- **Third point, where you are going to make money.** Why are you going to book young mom spots or why you are going to book any spot that has soccer in it? Tell them the sure thing. Tell them why money is going to come in if they respond to this submission.

- **Cover these three points in three very short paragraphs.** Add some personality; that is a big plus, and you will have a strong cover letter. Some cover letters are very colorful and some are right to the point. Either way, you want to catch their attention and give them the good news right away.

- **My daughter, Cynthia Kerr, wrote the following cover letter:**

I have just finished the greatest commercial class in the world with Stuart K. Robinson. I am continuing to work with him in his semiprivate classes. Having revived and sharpened my commercial acting tools, I am ready to go out and be competitive.

I recently moved to Los Angeles after a successful commercial career in Dallas, Texas. I have booked many national commercials, including Mc Donald's, Chevrolet, Southwest Airlines and Applebee's Restaurants, to name a few.

I book young mom spots, teacher, part of a couple, housewife, lady next door and business woman. I am also a champion black belt martial artist, so any spots in that category are mine.

I am looking forward to meeting with you at your earliest convenience.

- **Actor Jordan Osher wrote this letter.**

  My name is Jordan Osher. On a trip to North Carolina, I booked a small part on *Dawson's Creek*. The episode's director proclaimed, "I love this guy! He looks just like Seinfeld!"

  My part was rewritten and expanded. I have recurred on several *Dawson's Creek* episodes, shot a motion picture in which I starred as a dorky, connoisseur of art and then made the decision to move to Los Angeles where I have been studying intensively in preparation for a career in film, TV and commercials. Both of my teachers, Stuart K. Robinson and Judy Kerr, admire and will vouch for my work.

  If you are looking for a character and leading actor who plays sidekicks (Anthony Michael Hall, Jason Biggs/*American Pie*), hip kids and various high school, college and beyond nebbishes, geniuses and heroes, I would like to schedule a meeting to continue my booking streak. Or at least call me in to see if you think I look like "little Jerry!"

- **Jim Martyka, actor/writer, wrote the following letter seeking representation.**

  I have worked with *(actor's name)* on several film projects and he has spoken very highly of you. He suggested I send you my picture and resume for possible representation.

  As you can see, I have some experience in film and commercials. Plus, I am SAG eligible and ready to join whenever needed. I have experience in dramatic roles but my main focus or niche is comedic character acting for film, television and of course, commercials. I am a Matthew Perry/Topher Grace type mixed with a unique Midwestern style. I have managed to book a good amount of auditions on my own through word of mouth, recommendations or various breakdown postings, but I need an agent to get me out auditioning more frequently.

  Included are a couple of headshots. I have other looks and a demo reel I can show you. I would love to meet at your earliest convenience. Please call or email at the numbers on my resume. Thanks for your time and consideration.

- **Steven Nash, talent manager** and president of the Talent Manager's Association, gives some hints for writing to a manager.

A cover letter must be very short, if you hope to have it read. Your objective usually is to get a meeting. Yes, do mention any important things about you that may attract interest. Your commitment to hard work and belief in yourself are not subjects to go into in this cover letter (as many do). These are things to talk about if and when you get a meeting.

Be sure to give your phone number and email address on your cover letter and on your resume. It can be effective to list two or three of your special points in your cover letter, so the reader can spot them easily. Do research on who you are writing to.

Dear Mr. Manager, *(of course you would have the correct name here)*

I am 17 years old and moving to Los Angeles in three months to pursue an acting career. I am looking for representation. A recent picture and resume is enclosed.

*Many roles in church, high school and community theater.

*Professional model in my local market.

*Speaker around my state for my church teen program.

*Currently studying with: *(Name well-known Los Angeles teacher if you live here)*.

I heard of you in *Acting Is Everything*. (This lets me know you already have some understanding of how the business works.) Please let me know if you would be interested in taking a meeting.

Thank you

- **If you do not have important points**, then once again be brief and hope your age, look, or professional presentation will be meaningful to the person you are writing.

- **I personally do not like gimmicks** like attaching toys to the submission. Let yourself stand out by having a simple professional looking presentation. Actors should not call to see if we have received their package. If we are interested we will call you. Please understand that we are hard at work serving our signed clients, and while we look at every submission that comes in, it may not be immediately.

• **When you are making online submissions** to castings or to agents or managers for representation consideration, label the downloadable file with your name. People who open attachments are taking a chance of downloading a virus. Many people have infected their whole system and they are understandably wary. Most people prefer you paste a cover letter, resume and photo in the actual email itself, thus alleviating the downloading process. Or, put a link in the email that they can click on to lead them to a website with your info and pictures. If you do need to send an attachment, put your name on it; the reader will be more likely to download it. Also, when it is downloaded onto their desktop your name will be visible and if they are considering you, the file will be easy to find again. Most such downloads are labeled a generic "Pic. doc" or "headshot.doc."

• **Letter writing is not a part of acting**, but it is a part of the business of acting. Always know why you are writing and what you are asking for. Good writing is about editing. If you haven't edited your letter several times, it's not ready. There must be perfect punctuation and spelling. Always have someone else proof your writing.

TRADE PUBLICATIONS

BACK STAGE WEST

• *Back Stage West* is a must-read for actors in Los Angeles. You may reach a level in your career where you don't need to read it, but you may still enjoy the interviews and ads. Even when I am not actively seeking acting work, I still feel like it is part of my job to keep up with all of our trade papers. I sure want my doctors, dentists and plastic surgeons to keep up with their trades.

• For your information: You may hear the name *Drama-Logue* when actors refer to our Los Angeles trade paper. *Drama-Logue* was the only paper of its kind in Los Angeles for 20 years. *Back Stage* is the paper in New York. They moved a branch to Los Angeles, thus *Back Stage West*. Five years later *Drama-Logue* and *Back Stage West* merged. The combined paper is published by the same company that publishes the *Hollywood Reporter* and the *Ross Reports*.

• There are listings for every type of acting work in *Back Stage West*. But they shine when it comes to auditioning for theater work. The membership online casting websites, including *Back Stage West,* have taken over much of the film castings.

• Send out your pictures and resumes as soon as you get *Back Stage West*. They post daily on their website. There are some newspaper stands that get the publication on Wednesday afternoon. There is a 24-hour stand in Hollywood on Cahuenga just south of Hollywood Blvd., and another one in Studio City on Laurel Canyon Blvd., at Ventura Blvd. For every job, hundreds of actors submit their pictures; as always, it pays to be early. It looks as if some day, all submissions will be done online.

• Put the name of the role you are submitting yourself for on the envelope and attached to your picture with a *Post-It* note. No need to include a cover letter, unless you have some pertinent information—the part is for a golfer and you are a champion, or you've worked with the director and you want to remind them of that. Just writing a cover letter to say you want the job is unnecessary.

• **The free jobs that give you the most value** for your time and effort are usually, but not always, Equity-Waiver plays and graduate school sync-sound films. If you need experience in auditioning, then audition for everything. One of my students, T. R. Richards, auditioned over 160 times in two years. He's been cast in over thirty student films. Needless to say, with his studying and auditioning experience, he is moving his career right along. My career started from the first ad I answered (*Drama-Logue* cost 25¢ then), a USC student film, playing a waitress. The lead in that movie, Rick Davis, led me to my best friend, Samantha Harper, who led me to my mentor, Joan Darling.

• **Michael Lerner,** Oscar-nominated for best supporting actor for *Barton Fink,* said he owed his success to the *Drama-Logue.* He was living in a one-room Hollywood apartment with a pull-down bed. The phone was down by the gas station. He didn't have a car, lived on unemployment. He read about a play audition and got a part in *Little Murders.* Director Paul Mazursky came to see the show, put him in his movie, *Alice in Wonderland.* Director Michael Ritchie saw that and cast him in *The Candidate* and his career was launched.

• **New actor Robert Restraino** read an ad for a lead actor with intense eyes for a non union independent film, *Motor Psycho.* He ran a photocopy of his picture and erased the color of his eyes to lighten them. He landed the audition and the job.

• **Kevin Costner** credits his start from landing jobs he auditioned for out of the *Drama-Logue.*

HOLLYWOOD REPORTER AND DAILY VARIETY

• **When you have started a serious career,** it is a must to read one of these every day. You decide which is best for you and subscribe. I couldn't do without either one because in the social columns, my favorite, the same gossip isn't repeated. It's nice if you can share the expense and paper with another actor. You can also read them at the Beverly Hills or Hollywood libraries.

• **This information can be valuable** when meeting a producer or director; you will be able to discuss their projects because you are familiar with them. I keep files of articles that interest me or that may come in handy at a later time. I also have a file on types of publicity I like so I can refer back to it when I'm designing my own ads or mailings.

• **Jay Bernstein, manager, writer, producer, publicist,** taught a course called *Stardom, the Management of, the Public Relations for, and the Survival and Maintenance In.*

Q: Why should actors read the trade papers?

• **It's important to be educated** in anything you do. You're meeting people at parties. You may never know that you're meeting a director or a producer or who that person is unless you subscribe to the *Hollywood Reporter* or *Daily Variety,* read the *Los Angeles Times Calendar* section, and *People* magazine to get a feeling of who everybody is. You can spend a whole evening talking to someone and not connect their name or face to show business because a lot of people don't talk about it. You might have made a different impression if you had known. There are too many people, too many names. Also, learn the history of this business.

Resources

To download and print an updated version of this and all resource lists, go to actingiseverything.com.

The Trade Papers can be purchased at almost any newsstand, 7-11 store or theatrical bookstore in the area.

Back Stage West, 800/562-2706. backstagewest.com. 5055 Wilshire Blvd., Los Angeles, CA 90036. Six months, $55.00; one year, $89; two years, $149.00. $1.85 per single copy at newsstands and 7-11's in the Los Angeles area. Some newsstands receive it on Wednesday afternoon around 2pm. It's owned by the *Hollywood Reporter. Back Stage* has been the bible in New York for many years.

Daily Variety, 323/857-6600 or 800/552-3632. variety.com. pubservice.com. 5700 Wilshire Blvd., Suite 120, L.A., 90036. $259.00 a year, three and six month prices available. Television productions listed every Thursday, film productions listed every Friday, cable listed every Monday.

Hollywood Reporter, 323/525-2000. hollywoodreporter.com. 5055 Wilshire Blvd., L.A., 90036. $229.00 a year for daily paper or $175.00. a year for Tuesday edition only. Film productions listed every Tuesday, television productions listed first and third Tuesday of every month. Their subscribers are affluent and trend setting: $180,000 average income; $659,000 average residence value; 26% are millionaires; 35% own real estate in addition to their primary residence. Sounds great doesn't it?

Los Angeles Times **Newspaper,** 800/LA TIMES. latimes.com. Every day, $11.96 a month; Sundays only, $8.20 a month. Another must. *Every morning,* read at least the *Calendar* section. It will provide you with openings for conversation and again, more knowledge about the business and people in it. Much of film and television content, as well as style, relates to current events in the world. Your competition is reading the newspaper.

BOOKSTORES, LIBRARIES
AND
DVD/VIDEO RENTAL STORES

• **We are changing every second of our lives.** All knowledge gained is growth, even when some of the knowledge is rejected as not being valid. Just the act of making the choices of what is good for us is molding our unique selves.

• **Reading is an important tool for an acting career.** In *Dreams into Action,* Milton Katselas tells how reading can enhance your career. He gives exercises on how to improve your reading. I highly recommend this book from this respected director and teacher.

• **Sandra Bullock** loves, *"The Greatest Salesman in the World* by Og Mandino. It was given to me by Matthew McConaughey on the set of *A Time To Kill.* It's really special."

• **John Singleton,** when living in South Central L.A., would catch the bus to Hollywood to go to the movies. "I'd hang out, spending hours in Larry Edmunds and Samuel French bookstores, read literature, wonder if I could ever be a part of the movie-making environment."

• **Downloadable books and books on tape:** For Los Angeles travel time, audio books will save your sanity. If you live in L.A. County, the biggest bargain is through the Los Angeles County Library System, 800/253-0591. They will send you catalogs with hundreds of unabridged fiction and nonfiction titles. Each title is a flat $10, which covers the rental and mailing both ways. Audible.com is the other best deal around. I pay $22 a month and download two books. Every once in a while they have a $10 sale and I usually buy 10 books at a time. I gobble books up, I'm reading the classics and biographies as well as bestsellers. I get them all on my iPod, another tool to help you deal with the Los Angeles traffic. Please mention I sent you, Judy Kerr email address: judykerr@mindspring.com, and I'll get points for new books.

THEATRICAL BOOKSTORES

These stores are very important to your career. Besides all the plays, they have many reference books, including Variety's *Who's Who In Show Business,* seminar books such as *How To Get An Agent, How To Publicize Yourself* and videotapes on *How To Make It In Show Business.* Give yourself a treat and spend a few hours there getting acquainted with all the information that is available. Have fun, they don't mind. You can order online or by mail from any of the following stores.

To download and print an updated version of this and all resource lists, go to actingiseverything.com.

Samuel French's Theatre & Film Bookshop, 323/876-0570. samuelfrench.com. 7623 Sunset Blvd., Hollywood, 90046. M-F 10-6, Sa 10-5. Valley location: 818/762-0535. 11963 Ventura Blvd., Studio City, 91604 (1 block east of Laurel Canyon.) M-F 10-9, Sa 10-6, Su 12-5. Closed some Sundays in the summer—call to verify hours.

Larry Edmund's Theatrical Book Shop, 323/463-3273. 6644 Hollywood Blvd., Hollywood, 90028. M-Sa 10-6. This is a real Hollywood bookstore—lots of history here.

Performing Arts Books 818/703-7311. Outside Los Angeles County, 800/900-3949. 21530 Sherman Way, Canoga Park, 91303. M-F 11-7; Sa 11-5.

The Drama Book Shop, dramabookshop.com, 212/944-0595. 250 West 40th Street, New York, NY 10018.

BOOKSTORES

Book Soup (Bookstore and Newsstand), 310/659-3110. booksoup.com. 8818 Sunset Blvd., West Hollywood, 90069, across from Tower Records. M-Sa 9-10 Su 9-7 Sunday Newsstand 9-5. The coolest—lots of celebs.

Bookstar, 818/505-9528. 12136 Ventura Blvd., Studio City. 9-10 every day.

Bodhi Tree, 310/659-1733. bodhitree.com. 8585 Melrose Ave., West Hollywood, 90069. A spiritual bookstore. New and used books. 10-7 (used books); 10-11 (new books) everyday.

Brentano's Book Store, 310/785-0204. borders.com. In the Century City Mall, next to the movie theaters. 10-9 M-Sa, Su 11-6

Cosmopolitan Book Shop, 323/938-7119. betterbks@aol.com. 7017 Melrose Ave., Hollywood, 90038. M-Sa 11-6. A wonderful used-book and magazine store. They will go to great lengths to find the publication you need.

Heritage Books, 310/659-3674. heritagebookshop.com. 8540 Melrose Ave., West Hollywood. M-F 9:30-5:30 Sa-Su Closed. A special place.

Psychic Eye Book Store, 818/906-8263. pebooks.com. 13435 Ventura Blvd., Sherman Oaks. M-Sa 10-10, Su 11-8. Also Burbank, Torrance. New Age, metaphysical, candles, incense and crystals.

DVD/VIDEO RENTAL STORES

These are stores that specialize in unusual videos, including classic movies and old television shows.

The Continental Shop, all things British, 310/453-8655. 1619 Wilshire Blvd., Santa Monica, M-Sa 10-6; Su 12-4.

Eddie Brandt's Saturday Matinee Video, 818/506-4242. ebsmvideo.com. 5006 Vineland Ave., North Hollywood, 91601. Tu-F 1-6, Sa 8:30-5, closed Su, 72,000 titles, from episodic TV *77 Sunset Strip* to Japanese sex epics *Notorious Concubine.*

Odyssey Video, 818/769-2000. 4810 Vineland Ave., North Hollywood, 91606. M-Su 9am-midnight. More than 40,000 movies to choose from. Tu & Th, 99 cents each. Hong Kong section which offers karate action flicks normally available only in Asia.

Rocket Video, 323/965-1100. 726 N. La Brea Ave., Los Angeles, 90038. 10-11 M-Su, will find films by request. Huge foreign section.

Tower Video, 310/657-3344. tower.com. 8844 W. Sunset Blvd., West Hollywood, 90069. Silents, B and C titles, cult, foreign and hard-to-find films.

Video Hut, 323/661-4680. 1864 N. Vermont Ave., Los Angeles, 90027. 10-11 Su-Th, 9-midnight F-Sa. Also Asian films and special requests.

Video Journeys, 323/663-5857. 2730 Griffith Park Blvd., Los Angeles, 90027. 10-10 everyday. Library of 14,000 movies, 1,000 foreign films, and television series collections, documentaries.

Video West, 818/760-0096. videowest.net. 11376 Ventura Blvd., Studio City, 91604. Also 310/659-5762. 805 Larrabee Street, West Hollywood, 90069. 10-12 every day. My favorite. These video stores are the best. Bargain days M-Th $1.50 a tape. Have them give you a tour of the store—they've got classics, independents, foreign, comedies, stand-up comics. Just about anything you need to research. Fantastic!

Vidiots, 310/392-8508. vidiotsvideo.com. 302 Pico Blvd., Santa Monica. Eclectic offerings at this alternative-video store. Large TV selection.

Web Sites and Order by Phone: B-Movie Theater, b-movie.com. Critics' Choice Video, 800/367-7765. Facets Video, 800/331-6197. Home Film Festival, 800/258-3456, homefilmfestival.com. Movies Unlimited, 800/466-8437, moviesunlimited.com.

LIBRARIES

Academy of Motion Picture Arts & Sciences, 310/247-3020. Oscars.org. 333 S. La Cienega Blvd., Beverly Hills, 90211. Closed Wednesday, open other weekdays, 10-5:30. Scripts. You can also look up actor's agents.

Beverly Hills Library, 310/288-2220. beverlyhills.org. 444 N. Rexford Drive, Beverly Hills, 90210. 10-9 M-Th, 10-6 F-Sa, 12-5 Su.

Brand Library, 818/548-2051. glendalepubliclibrary.org. 1601 West Mountain, Glendale 91201-1209, located in Brand Park, at the top of Grandview Ave. Tu 1-9, W 1-6, Th 1-9, F-Sa 1-5. A very valuable source for music and art books, records, tapes and over 4,000 CD's.

Burbank Central Library, 818/238-5600. Burbank.lib.ca.us. 110 N. Glenoaks Blvd., Burbank, 91502. M-Th 9:30-9, F 9:30-6, Sa 10-6, Su 1-5. Scripts for use in the library.

Career Transition for Dancers, Career Resource Library, 323/549-6660. careertransition.org. SAG Building, 5757 Wilshire Blvd., Los Angeles, on the 8th Floor. M-W 11-4; Th-F 10-6:30. Call for appointment to use the library or computer.

Glendale Public Library, 818/548-2040. glendalepubliclibrary.org. 222 E. Harvard Street, Glendale, 91205.

Los Angeles Central Library, 213/228-7000. lapl.org. 630 W. 5th St., between Flower St. and Grand Ave., downtown L.A. Largest public library on the west coast. Open every day; call for hours.

Hollywood Branch, Los Angeles City Library, 323/467-1821. lapl.org. 1623 Ivar Street, Hollywood, 90028. M-Th 10-8, F-Sa 10-6, Su 1-5. All aspects of the industry including scripts and books on acting.

Culver City Branch, Los Angeles County Library, 310/559-1676. colapublib.org. 4975 Overland Ave., Culver City, 90230. M-Th 10-8, F 10-6, Sa 10-5.

Los Angeles County Library System, Books on Tape Rental, 800-253-0591. colapublib.org.

North Hollywood Library, 818/766-7185. lapl.org. 5211 Tujunga Ave., North Hollywood, 91601. Large selection of plays; also books on acting.

Santa Monica Public Library, 310/458-8600. smpl.org. 1343 Sixth Street, Santa Monica, 90401.

Pasadena Public Library, 626/744-4052. ci.pasadena.ca.us/library/ 285 E. Walnut Ave., Pasadena, 91101.

Unions

• **Until you join a union,** there are no restrictions. There are many opportunities for work that are nonunion. They may not be under the best conditions, and the pay will usually be lower, but take a look at the ads for work in the online casting groups, *Back Stage West* and other sources. Are you really ready to give up all these opportunities of gaining audition experience, the possibility of getting good film on yourself, building a reputation and networking? Ask actors who have lived in a right-to-work State; their work almost dies if they join the Union.

• **Don't be persuaded by other actors'** impatience to join a union. You have your priorities; you are building a career. That means studying, auditioning, landing roles and developing a demo reel so you have a resume with legitimate credits and experience on it.

• **When you are starting out** and don't have a demo reel, in all likelihood you will not be able to land a theatrical agent even if you are in the Screen Actors Guild. It is easier to get a job on a nonunion project than on a SAG film. Do your nonunion work and your non-signatory student films now. Those young filmmakers are trying to get into their respective guilds too. A few years down the line the producers and directors who hire you for student and nonunion productions will be hiring you for union productions.

• **When you have enough experience** and are ready to join, you can become SAG eligible by landing a principal performer role in a SAG project or by obtaining three vouchers from doing extra work. You then become a "must join" and can put SAG(e) on your resume. At this point I would ask you to **not** join the union until you get that next SAG job. When you get that job, because you are a "must join," the union has to let you come in that day and pay the initial fee of $1,482 (as of 2006) and annual dues based on earnings. You can now put SAG on your resume.

• **I want to warn you** about some schemes actors have used to get into SAG using false credentials. The most popular is the sale of fake vouchers. These unlawful plans can get you barred from the union forever, besides costing you a lot of money.

• **If you have decided** you must live your life as a professional actor, there are benefits for joining the American Federation of Television and Radio Artists, AFTRA, as soon as you can afford it.

• **If you plan to do game shows**, get your AFTRA card first so you will be paid for appearing. The shows don't seem to mind at all if you are union and you'll receive union scale payment for your appearance. The real bonus is: after belonging to AFTRA for one year, that work on the game show will make you eligible for SAG.

• **There is a SAG employment status known as "financial core."** Many actors make the choice, for various reasons, after they have joined the union, to take the financial core option. If you live in a right-to-work state and are not a member of SAG, you may work both union and nonunion jobs. If you are a member of SAG you may not do nonunion work even in a right-to-work state. Taking a financial-core status means you pay 80% of your dues but you are not a member of the union, though you can work on SAG projects. It is a very drastic step and the union makes it difficult to rejoin if you change your mind. I am a loyal member of SAG, AFTRA and AEA and would never advise anyone to take financial core, but many actors feel they cannot work freely enough as a member. Investigate carefully what your advantages may be. Call the union to find out what your options are. An experienced agent I talked with says, "I have several professional actors who are core. They work a lot more and there is no down-side."

• **What does it meant to be Taft-Hartleyed into** SAG? Taft-Hartley is a labor law that basically says that you cannot force a person to join a union just because they did one job. If you go for a second union job, you are saying to everyone, "Hey, I'm interested in this as a profession." Now you have to join the union. Don't join the union until your second SAG job. You can do all the SAG deferred roles you can land; you do not need to be a SAG member to be eligible to work on them. If you are in SAG, you cannot do any nonunion work of any kind without penalties.

• **It is a catch-22.** You have to be in the union to get a job, and you have to have a job to join the union. SAG rules say that as long as they read 25 actors for a role, the production company will not be fined for giving a nonunion actor a job. If you are on a set and the director decides someone has to say a line and there is no time for casting, they can give you the line, a SAG contract and wages for the day. It is done through the

Taft-Hartley Law. You can get your SAG card as soon as the paperwork is in the computer at the union; or you can wait years to get it. Always save your paperwork though.

• **The Guild has only 90 days from the day you perform the lines** to file a claim on your behalf. If you are told by anyone that you have to wait for the film to be released because upgrades apply only if the lines remain in the film, *do not believe that person*! An upgrade is warranted if you are directed to speak while the camera is rolling whether or not your lines are included in the final edit. If in question, call SAG Production Services at 323/549-6811. **You must leave the set with a copy of the SAG contract.**

• **The contract can be found on the SAG website,** sag.org. The site also provides answers to general questions about joining SAG, benefits of being in the union and most important, pay scales. At the time of this printing, SAG contracts are scheduled for renegotiation within the year. Here are the major current pay scales for 2006. Check SAG website for most current info.

ROLE	PAY
Day performer	$716
Day performer – solo dancer	$716
Day performer – solo singer	$773
Weekly performer	$2,483
Weekly performer – solo dancer	$2,300
Weekly performer – solo singer	$2,483
Major role – ½ hour	$3,849 per week
Major role – 1 hour	$6,158 per week

• **Payment sometimes will depend** upon the number of lines you speak and how much camera time you have. Make sure you check with your agent to figure out your exact classification for a project and how much you should expect to get paid.

• **Commercial work has even more variables when it comes to pay.** As of 2006, the session fee for a commercial actor with a principle role in a commercial is $535 a day. However, that actor will get more money from residuals as the commercial or images from the commercial air on cable and network television, the Internet, billboards, radio, etc. SAG has the complicated pay scales on the website, but it's really up to your agent to help keep track of where the commercial's airing and how much pay to expect. Because of how confusing the commercial payouts can be, many actor's count on their session fees and the rest of the checks that come in are simply nice little surprises ... sometimes, thousands of dollars worth of surprises if the commercial airs for a while!

• **Many beginning actors in L.A. find themselves working in** SAG **Independent movies.** You need to be careful here because many independent films say they are "SAG Experimental" or something similar, which is nothing more than a tactic from independent directors to attract more professional actors. Still, there are a number of legitimate SAG Indie films and opportunities for SAG actors to work in these films without violating union contracts. In 2005, the contracts for these films changed. Here's what to expect. Remember, these are all SAG projects.

TYPE OF FILM	PAY (DAY RATE)
Student Film	Actor may defer pay
Short Film (less than $50,000)	Actor may defer pay
Ultra-Low Budget (less than $200,000)	$100
Modified Low Budget (less than $625,000)	$268
Low Budget (less than $2.5 million)	$504

• **The union websites** have all of the detailed up-to-date information available, so learn about the unions.

To download and print an updated version of this and all resource lists, go to actingiseverything.com.

Screen Actors Guild

Screen Actors Guild, SAG, 323/954-1600, 800/724-0767. sag.org. 5757 Wilshire Blvd., Los Angeles, 90036. (between Fairfax and La Brea) M-F 9-5.

American Federation of Television and Radio Artists

American Federation of Television and Radio Artists, AFTRA, 323/634-8100. aftra.org. 5757 Wilshire Blvd., Suite #900, Los Angeles, 90036. M-F 9-5:30.

Actors Equity Association

Actors Equity Association, AEA, **also called Equity,** 323/634-1750. actorsequity.org. 5757 Wilshire Blvd., Los Angeles, 90036.

AFTRA/SAG **Credit Union,** 323/461-3041. 6922 Hollywood Blvd., Hollywood, 90028. M-F 9-4. Have your residuals automatically deposited in your savings account. It is a great way to save. If needed you can always take money out. There are many advantages for an actor to be part of the Credit Union. They even make house equity loans.

Income Taxes
and Accountants

Since *Acting Is Everything*, many expenses you have are tax deductible. You don't necessarily have to be earning money acting in order to deduct expenses. A tax specialist will determine exactly what is right for you.

• **When you start filing your income taxes** as a full or part time actor, seek an Entertainment Accountant. They will be aware of all the current deductions. Your part is to save receipts and to mark everything you do in your appointment book. Should you ever be audited, you will need to justify every expense.

• **An entertainment tax accountant**, financial consultant and finance manager, answers some income tax questions.

Q: Why should an actor hire an accountant to do income taxes?

• **The laws are very complicated** and change every day of the year. There are specific areas of deductibility for actors that are unique and an accountant has to be knowledgeable about them and must stay current on the changes in the law. In my experience, most actors are not knowledgeable about this and basically give the government excessive money in taxes every year.

• **In general, an actor can deduct anything** that has relevance to his career; the normal deductions relating to such things as union dues, use of their car for business purposes, subscriptions, DVD rentals and books relative to their profession, going to theaters and movies where they can basically research current trends in acting, business travel, lessons on becoming an actor and numerous other specific items related to their unique career.

Q: Can you start deducting these expenses before you are earning money as an actor?

- **This is an area that is constantly changing** under the law. If the person is dedicated and exercising their efforts as an actor even though they are not earning money at this time, they can develop what is called business losses which they can utilize in one of the following ways: They can deduct those losses during the first two years of their profession and then accumulate any losses after that until they earn money. Generally this is not advisable because if they are not earning money the first two years the losses are not that beneficial.

- **I would recommend generally,** in the case of an actor whose career is accelerating, that they don't immediately utilize their beginning years' losses until they start to make better money because each deduction will create bigger tax savings. As they earn more money, they get into higher brackets. You list the losses on the year you spent the money but you put them into a reserve account that you can accumulate for future benefit. When you have future independent acting income, you can then extract those past losses and deduct them from your current income. It is necessary to list them in the year you spend the money, otherwise they are forever lost.

Q: How do you choose an accountant?

- **Clients usually pick an accountant on a friend's recommendation.** Then they decide to go with the accountant because they tell good jokes, have gone to the same college or for other wrong reasons. When actors are having a hard time deciding, I suggest they ask their potential accountant for three recommendations from current clients, three from former clients and the accountant's banker.

Q: How much does it cost to have your income tax done?

- **Accountants all have their own fees** based on the work involved. Minimum for a new client is $250. When actors start taking business deductions, their returns are no longer simple. Many new actors go to a general accounting firm like H&R Block and pay a smaller fee because generally their associates are not as qualified as an independent accountant.

- **It is a joyous day when your income tax return says occupation: actor.** It is a time to take a moment and reflect on where you have come from, to acknowledge that some of your dreams are coming true. My return says occupation: actress/acting coach/producer/author; it has expanded over the years.

- **Some tax deduction categories: Advertising and publicity,** pictures, photo reproduction, resumes, audio/video tapes, Academy Players Guide; commissions paid; **Professional fees,** tax preparation, attorney, bank charges; office supplies, business cards, postage; **Dues and initiation fees**, unions, theatre groups, website memberships, agent/manager fees; **Trade publications**, including Breakdown Services Casting Directors; **Research supplies**, plays, films, scripts, books; **Career enrichment**, workshops, classes, private coaching, video rentals, movies; **Wardrobe and makeup**, clothes, jewelry and anything else you use for acting; **Communications**, telephone, long distance calls, fax, e-mail, website; **Traveling**, auto, insurance, license, parking, gas, repairs, hotels, travel meals; **Business meals and business gifts**, $25 and less.

• At tax time, the trades run articles about actors' taxes and ads for accountants.

• *Working Actor's Guide* has listings for accountants, deductions and business managers.

Resources

To download and print an updated version of this and all resource lists, go to actingiseverything.com.

Feinstein & Berson: Scott Feinstein, 818/981-3115. feinsteinberson.com. E-mail: scott@feinsteinberson.com. 16255 Ventura Blvd., #625, Encino, 91436. CPA and Business Manager, has a strong client list consisting almost exclusively of SAG, AFTRA, IATSE and DGA members.

Pamela Price, 323/663-5727. 4527 Ambrose Ave., L.A. 90027. She used to be an actress and specializes in people who are in the entertainment business.

Scott Rubenstein, E.A., 323/658-5271. lataxservice.com. E-mail: scottrubenstein@pacbell. net 8350 Melrose Ave., Suite 201, L.A., 90069. Tax consultant. Scott has given seminars for SAG. He has many clients in the biz and photographer Alan Weissman recommends him.

Chuck Sloan & Associates, 818/769-2291. chucksloan.com. E-mail: staff@chucksloan.com. 11684 Ventura Blvd. #189, Studio City, 91604. Recommended by Tricia Gilfone. Chuck is an actor as well so he understands an actor's tax needs.

Actors' Tax Prep: David Rogers, 818/260-9884. actorstaxprep.com. E-mail: David@actorstaxprep.com. 4444 West Riverside Dr. #204, Burbank, 91505. Actor/writer Jim Martyka says he is one of the best, especially for those actors who are juggling multiple jobs.

SAG, Volunteer Income Tax Assistance Program (VITA). 323/549-6431. E-mail: ActorVITAla@ActorsToolbox.com. 5757 Wilshire Blvd., LA 90036. M-F 10-4. From February through April 15. Union members help fellow union members with their taxes. They hold classes in January for those who wish to be Tax Assistors. If you pass the test, you are qualified to help other members prepare their own taxes. Every paid up SAG or AFTRA member can apply for this free help. Those using the service will get guidance with their taxes in a classroom setting. VITA also provides online help and packets of information for members.

California State Board of Accountancy, 916/263-3680. dca.ca.gov. You can check to see if the business manager or accountant you are considering is licensed and in good standing.

Working Actor's Guide (WAG), available at theatrical bookstores, lists many well-known accountants.

Networking:
Organizations, Churches and Charities

• **Increase your friendship circles** and social involvements. If you are not naturally a socially involved person, then this will be another skill you will have to learn. Look for places within the show biz community where you can feel comfortable networking; clubs or restaurants you frequent, tennis courts like Plummer Park, gyms, acting class, dance classes, charity or volunteer work, baseball or bowling teams, seminars, workshops, etc. Where do you have your morning coffee? Seattle agent Carlyne Grager told me of one of her actors being discovered by a Warner Bros. producer because she had coffee at Priscilla's in Toluca Lake every morning.

• **The more people you know in the business,** the more likely you are to get a phone call from someone who wants you to work on a project. We all like to work with people we know and who are fun to be with. Also, by talking about the business, you pick up news and hints that will help you with your acting and career.

• **Publicist Joyce Schwarz** suggests attending or working at one charity event each month. Choose a charity that is close to your heart.

• **Camryn Manheim** says, "If you go to a play, don't go opening night; go during the preview week when everyone involved will be in the house." You may strike up a conversation with the producer, writer or director.

• **Jay Bernstein,** manager to the stars, taught a course called *Stardom, the Management of, the Public Relations for, and the Survival and Maintenance In.* He advises actors to read *Emily Post's Etiquette* book. There is much to be said about knowing how to be polite and correct in social situations. He says, "If you are a woman, join Women In Film, meet other women." In general, he advises men and women to learn to play tennis and golf. "You can show up at a golf course and make up a foursome." And think of all the celebrity golf and tennis tournaments you can play in when you are a celebrity.

Resources

To download and print an updated version of this and all resource lists, go to actingiseverything.com.

• ORGANIZATIONS

The Actors' Network, 818/509-1010. actors-network.com. E-mail: info@actors-network.com. 11684 Ventura Blvd., #757, Studio City, 91604. They are a professional, unique, business networking organization, created by actors. This is a membership organization I have a great deal of respect for. I believe dedicated actors can make a difference in their careers by working in this group. They have an office that you can drop by, check the bulletin board, look up something in the library full of all the current books and directories. Their members are pro-active and successful so you can create friendships with people who are on the same type of career path that you are on. Membership costs $50 per month, billed quarterly with a one-time initial processing cost of $50.

The Creative Actors Alliance, 310/840-2240. creativeactors.com. E-mail: talent@creativeactors.com. 8424-A Santa Monica Blvd., #192, West Hollywood, 90069. They hold a Monthly Showbiz Brunch. It is held at a restaurant. It's free; you pay for breakfast. On the website they tell you who the speakers will be at the next event. Actress Tiana Hynes tells me, "They are supportive, honest actors who realize the benefit of working together to uplift and challenge the entire group."

Film Industry Network, 818/985-5400. filmindustrynetwork.com. E-mail: info@filmindustrynetwork.com. 12400 Ventura Blvd., #166, Studio City, 91604. Open to individuals from all facets of the entertainment industry. "We create the opportunity for industry professionals to: make key contact, develop solid industry relationships and exchange vital resources." Meets the second Sunday of every month from 3 to 6 pm. $75 for yearly dues. Monthly meetings are $5-10 for members and $10-18 for non-members. Topics have been: *Show Runners; Packaging Yourself & Your Project;* and *Learn To Swim With The Sharks . . . But Not As Bait.*

Nosotros, 323/465-4167. nosotros.org. They hold networking brunches every three months. "An event for the entertainment industry professional as well as the Hollywood hopeful. It is 'a place where we aspire to inspire' and honor special guest speakers from every aspect of the entertainment business." You do not have to be a member to attend. Membership is $50 a year and meetings are the first Wednesday of each month. Online membership is available for $40 a year. If you are Spanish-speaking I would think you would want to be a part of this long established group.

Jeffrey R. Gund's Newsletter, JeffreyRGund.com. jeffgmusice@mindspring.com. Tell him Judy Kerr sent you and request to be put on the newsletter email list. Many networking opportunities.

Film Independent, 310/432-1200. filmindependent.org. 9911 West Pico Blvd., L.A., 90035. Annual membership $95. "This non-profit membership organization is one of the largest and most dynamic groups supporting quality independent filmmaking today." They offer seminars, top level contacts, member gatherings, luncheons.

Nebraska Coast Connection, 213/368-4622. nebraskacoast.com. Though created as a way to keep Nebraskans residing in L.A. in touch with each other, the group is open to all. They often have prominent industry guests, including Alexander Payne. Check to see if there are any organizations with former residents of your state or home town. If not, start one!

Showbiz Softball League, 909/867-2327. Balboa Sports Center, 5600 Balboa Blvd., Encino. Saturdays between April and October. Play, but also go to games! Usually features agents, casting directors and studio execs, and celebs are occasionally seen playing.

Entertainment Basketball Game: For men every Sunday at 5pm in Beverly Hills. For information, contact: Aurora411@earthlink.net.

Women In Film (for men too), 310/657-5144. wif.org. 8857 West Olympic Blvd., Ste. 201, Beverly Hills, 90211. Annual dues range from $35 to $1,075 depending upon the level of membership. You can volunteer to work in the office in order to meet people who later may sponsor you for membership. Great networking breakfasts and industry seminars and screenings.

Academy of Television Arts and Sciences, 818/754-2800. emmys.org. email: membership@emmys.org. 5220 Lankershim Blvd., North Hollywood, 91601. They will send you requirements to join; they are less stringent for non-voting members. Membership requirements are also posted on the website.

Audiences Unlimited Inc., 818-753-3470. tvtickets.com. email: tickets@audiencesunlimited.com. Free tickets to live TV comedy and drama show taping sessions (no game shows). Hours and availability vary, mostly at Valley locations. Details also available online.

• CHURCHES

Agape International Spiritual Center, 310/348-1250. E-mail: info@agapelive.com 5700 Buckingham Parkway, Culver City, 90230. agapelive.com. Services Sundays at 8AM, 10:30AM, and 6 pm Wednesday 6:45PM. New age, large following, many celebrities.

Bel-Air Presbyterian Church, 818/788-4200. belairpres.org. 16221 Mulholland Dr., L.A., 90049. Services Sundays at 9am, 11AM, and 6PM. Many programs for all ages of people, great singles groups, spectacular location and building.

Church On The Way, 818/779-8000. TCOTW.org. 14300 Sherman Way, and 14800 Sherman Way, Van Nuys. At Sherman Way and Van Nuys Blvd., Services Saturday at 6PM, Sundays at 8AM, 9AM, 11AM and 6PM. Interdemoninational fellowship in association with the International Church of the Foursquare Gospel.

First African Methodist Episcopal Church, (F.A.M.E.) 323/730-7750. famechurch. org. Email: famechurch@famechurch.org. 2270 S. Harvard Blvd., L.A., 90018. Services Sundays at 8AM, 10AM and 12PM.

First Baptist Church of Beverly Hills, 310/276-3978. firstbaptistbevhills.org. 9025 Cynthia St., West Hollywood, 90213. Services Sundays at 11AM and 6PM. Lots of actors and people in the business; very active membership.

Grace Community Church, 818/909-5500. gracechurch.org. 13248 Roscoe Blvd., Sun Valley, 91352. Between Coldwater and Woodman. Services Sundays at 8:30AM and 11:30AM. Fundamental Christian.

Hollywood Presbyterian Church, 323/463-7161. 1760 N. Gower, Hollywood. 90028. fpch.org. Services Sundays at 8:30AM, 9:30AM, 10:45AM and 11AM. Great choir. Lots of programs.

Hope Lutheran Church, 323/938-9135. hopelutheranchurch.net. 6720 Melrose Ave., Hollywood, 90038. Services on Sunday and Thursday. Also organizes a number of activities and trips for members. Carlyne Grager tells me the Sunday morning worship is a "concert" worship where music is the backdrop and added to enrich the expression of liturgy, sermon and lessons.

Hompa Hongwanji Buddist Temple, 213/680-9130. nishihongwanji-la.org. 815 East First St., L.A., 90012. Service Sundays at 10AM.

Kabbalah, 310/657-5404. Kabbalah.com. E-mail: losangeles@kabbalah.com. 1062 South Robertson Blvd., L.A., 90035. Every Tuesday and Thursday at 7PM, What is Kabbalah? This is where Madonna took lessons.

North Hollywood Church of Religious Science, 818/762-7566. nhcrs.org. 6161 Whitsett Ave., North Hollywood, 91606. Services Sundays at 8am, 9:45AM, and 11:30AM.

Self-Realization Fellowship Temple, 323/661-8006. yogananda-srf.org. 4860 Sunset Blvd., Hollywood, 90027. Services Sundays at 9:30AM and 11AM. 310/454-4114. 17190 Sunset Blvd., Pacific Palisades, 90272. Services Sundays at 9AM and 11AM.

Shambhala Meditation Center, 323/653-9342. la.shambhala.org. 8218 W. 3rd St., L.A. Teachings of Tibetan Buddhism, Wednesdays, Thursdays and Sundays.

Spiritworks Church, 818/876-0386. 260 N. Pass Ave., Burbank, 91505. Actress/coach Dee Wallace teaches a class here on clearing away blocks and allowing positive energy in your life.

St. Ambrose Catholic Church, 323/656-4433. st-ambrose.com. 1281 North Fairfax Ave., West Hollywood, 90046. Services Saturdays at 5:30PM and Sundays at 8AM, 10AM, and 12PM.

Synagogue for the Perfoming Arts, 310/472-3500. sftpa.com. E-mail: sftpa@verizon. net. 11727 Barrington Ct., L.A., 90049. Services first Friday of every month at the University of Judism, 15600 Mulholland Dr., Bel Air, 90077. Major industry attendance.

Zen Center of Los Angeles, 213/387-2351. zcla.org. 923 S. Normandie Ave., Los Angeles. Daily services and introduction to Zen practice offered on Sunday mornings at 8:15. Also a Zen Center of Orange County, 949/722-7818. zcoc.org.

• CHARITIES

networkforgood.org. Connects you to 33,000 volunteer activities. Thanks to dailycandy.com for this info.

Heal the Bay, 310/451-1500. healthebay.org. E-mail: membership@healthebay.org. 1444 9th St., Santa Monica, 90401. Memberships start at $35. Fighting for a swimmable, fishable, surfable Santa Monica Bay.

Meals On Wheels, mowaa.org. Several locations throughout L.A. Check website for location nearest to you. Provides meals to the elderly.

PAWS (Pets Are Wonderful Support), 323/464-7927. pawsla.org. E-mail: info@pawsla. org. 1546 Argyle Ave., Hollywood, 90028. Provides pet care for ill people with pets.

Project Angel Food, 323/845-1800. angelfood.org. 7574 Sunset Blvd., L.A., 90046. Provides meal delivery to incapacitated people with terminal illnesses.

Union Rescue Mission, 213/347-6300. URM.com. 545 S. San Pedro St. L.A., 90013. Provides food, shelter and clothing to the homeless. Need servers for Thanksgiving and Christmas.

Section Five
Career Team

Agents

• **Spike Lee said it best** on *Inside the Actor's Studio*, "Agents are not going to get you work if you are not established."

• **Your job is to establish yourself,** to make a mark, before you seek a theatrical agent. This book is written in sequence. First you study, you learn how to deliver a crafted, good performance, one you can deliver take after take. You have your pictures taken and develop a resume. You learn to audition by going to many auditions. You learn to work by working. You develop a demo reel, you prove that many directors have taken a chance on you, hired you and you have delivered. Maybe you've worked nonunion and made some money. Your next tool will be to become SAG eligible. You have developed your career tools; you are now ready to get your career team in place. An agent is usually your first team member.

• **There are the four distinctly different areas** of work requiring an agent. Theatrical, which includes work in film, TV and stage; commercials; voiceovers and print work. A few agencies handle all types of acting work; some handle just one area of the market. Many individual agents specialize in one field; some may handle actors across the board. An agency may have one or several agents working in each department.

• **Agents are protected by California law**; only they can solicit employment and negotiate actor's fees. Some are franchised by the unions—SAG, AFTRA and AEA. Keep checking sag.org and agentassociation.com for the most up-to-date information regarding signing agreements with agents. I must say as an actor, I belong to all three unions and, as misguided as I sometimes believe the union is, I still back them 100%.

• **If you are a commercial type**, it may be easier to get a commercial agent first. They sign many more people than a theatrical agent; some agencies have several hundred actors on their rosters. A good theatrical agent would handle 30 to 50 actors alone; if there are three agents then perhaps 150 clients for one agency. These are very general figures just to give you an idea how it works. One of SAG's guidelines for agents is to accept only union actors—yet, if you have a great commercial look they will stretch the rules. If you are 22 or younger, it is easier for an agent to accept you as a nonunion actor.

• **My advice is to read one of the several books** on agents which you can buy at a theatrical book store. Then design a short, unique cover letter. *See Cover Letters section.* Enclose your wonderful 8x10 photo that looks just like you, and your resume. Mail it to specific agents within the agencies that use the type of actor that you are.

• **When agents are interested,** they will call you to come in and meet them. Go in dressed looking like your picture. Something in that picture attracted them. What you have to offer the agent is your good training, background and the experience you have been able to get for yourself. They want hard workers because when you are first starting out, they are not able to devote much time to you; they concentrate on the actors who are making money for them. Agents make 10% of what you earn. They do 10% and you do 90% of the work of obtaining employment.

• *Back Stage West* has interviews on a monthly basis, talking to agents. Cut these out, save them, learn more about the way the business is run. Agent Billy Miller of Michael Slessinger & Associates told this story.

  • **When Jenna Elfman** (*Dharma and Greg*) **was looking for an agent,** her husband read an article in *Drama-Logue* about agent Michael Slessinger. He said, "Jenna, this sounds like the kind of agent you'd want to be with." She asked her commercial agent to set up a meeting. There wasn't a lot on her resume except a couple of student films and commercials. She had scenes from her student films on tape and they were great, so we decided to give it a try. And that's how we started representing her.

• **Anne Archer** (*Fatal Attraction, Patriot Games*) advises, when you have landed your agent:

  • **Learn how to keep friendly**, positive communication with your agent—always telling them the good news—something positive someone said, a great project you heard about, etc. Make them feel like you're a team. Be helpful; take responsibility for creating a warm relationship with your agent.

• **Paula Wagner**, at an awards dinner, remembered her meeting with Tom Cruise during her agent days at Creative Artists Agency 15 years ago.

  • **Tom wore a great sports coat** (borrowed) that covered a ripped T-shirt. . . he was living in and out of his car, and I was impressed with his intelligence, presence, self-assurance, decency, capacity for good, and, as I came to know him, his curiosity, courage and conviction.

• **Theatrical agent Harry Gold,** of Gold/Liedtke Associates Agency told Karen Kondazian in *Back Stage West,* what he thought an actor should know about this business.

  • **There's so much more that you can do to get yourself work** besides waiting for your agent to call. The more you know about the business, the more empowered you are. The more you know your place within the structure, the better you can play the game. There's so much material to read to stay current with what is going on. Read the newspaper every day to keep up with current events, the trade papers to know who the principal players are that are making the decisions today. I find so many actors have no idea who, for example, is running ABC. You can be sure Al Pacino knows the head of every studio. He works the business as well as anybody. It's about understanding the business, about trying to look at the trends so you can follow them and be a part of them in some way.

  • **The biggest stars in the world work the business.** It's a skill and it takes a certain kind of expertise. Seek to be in some kind of contact. You must be extremely resourceful in this business, even if you have an agent. The way you do it is by gaining a full understanding of the business and by networking well. If you can align yourself with good directors, good casting people that will help you get one extra little foot in the door, then you're playing the game a little bit.

• **Theatrical and commercial agent Bonnie Howard, owner of Howard Talent West:**

Q: How can an actor get an appointment to meet with you?

  • **A great 8x10 will attract attention.** By that I mean a color headshot, natural looking, very relaxed and not posing. I like to see more in a picture than *generic nice guy.* Something a little more specific, perhaps *grandfather,* or *driving instructor.* Something a casting director could look at and say, "Yeah, he would make a great IRS collector." Quirky is good, without going over the top, warm, confident. Leaning forward into the camera expresses confidence, enthusiasm, energy. If your picture is touched up, and you walk in with wrinkles that are not on the picture, it's disappointing and distracting. There's very little difference between commercial and theatrical shots. I'm using them all for everything and getting good results. I look at every single picture that comes into my office because I'm interested in finding new talent. Theatrical doesn't necessarily mean looking serious; remember, people smile in film and TV, too.

- **A well put together resume helps.** Don't put any extra work information on your resume. Instead of listing the type or name of the character you played, I would rather see the billing. If you were featured, co-starred, or even starred in something, brag about it and put that on there. Commercials should not be on a theatrical resume. The reason for that is you might sabotage yourself unknowingly. Someone might want to call you in for AT&T. If you have Sprint or Verizon on your resume, they may say, "That's a competitor company, let's not call him in." Only include modeling if you've modeled for a top designer, like Dior, in Paris or New York. I would leave broadcasting off, unless you're going for a voice-over agent. Student grad films are good. You should list the school that you did the film for. The resume should be the same size as the picture. I don't care whether the resume is stapled or glued to the picture; *I do care very much about grammatical and punctuation mistakes.* Have a professional proofreader read the resume before you mass produce it. Don't rely upon spell-check.

- I attend the UCLA and the USC student film screenings and I find talent there. Showcases are also good. I strongly suggest doing good plays in good theaters in a good role.

Q: On a day-to-day basis, what exactly does an agent do?

- **I subscribe to the Breakdown Service.** It's a breakdown of almost every project in production. There's a description of each character that they need to cast. I represent about 50 theatrical actors—from the age of five to the oldest actor, who is 85. I submit the appropriate pictures to the casting directors, electronically or by messenger, directly to producers or, if it's a pre-read, then I try to get auditions for the actors. The actor goes directly to producers and/or directors, or if it's a pre-read hopefully gets a callback. Once the actor goes to the audition, it's out of my hands.

- **I call casting directors to pitch my actors.** I receive calls requesting suggestions for roles not put out to all the agents. I meet with talent managers to discuss a client's career, meet with actors of interest who are looking for new representation, and meet with current clients to review our strategy and/or their headshots and promotional material and plans.

Q: What if the producer or director wants to hire the actor?

- Usually the casting director or business affairs department for a
  series calls me to make the deal. The price of the job is determined
  by the prior history of the actor's work. It starts out union scale
  plus 10 percent commission. A good agent will always try to raise
  their actor's fee. Lately, the industry has been very tight-fisted. I
  like commercials a lot because I get to see my actors working more
  frequently on TV, and I get a great deal of pride from that. I also
  like it when the checks roll in. On national commercials, the actor
  usually works one or two days, and sometimes the checks come in
  for more than a year. Residuals are a big part of the business.

Q: If I have an agent, how can I help them to help me?

- Don't bug them. Don't call them frequently to say, "Why haven't I
  heard from you?" My pet peeve is, "I was just calling in to see what's
  new." If there is anything pertaining to that actor, the first thing we do
  is call them. Most agents represent a large number of clients and it's
  very difficult if we get calls all the time. To help your agent, update your
  pictures; make sure your agent has a supply of pictures and resumes
  at all times. I don't mind if my clients come in and check their supply
  themselves; it's a big help to me. When you deliver your pictures and
  resumes, make sure your resume is attached to your picture. Update
  information, pictures and resumes on the electronic submission sites,
  promptly. They are being used more than 50% of the time.

Q: What about the actor's demo tape?

- Demo tapes should be as short as possible, and as high impact as
  possible. Just select the best work. Don't send it unless it is requested,
  because you probably won't get it back, unless you include an envelope
  with return postage. DVD is becoming the medium of choice.

- Wondering who the top agencies are? In 2002, the studios rated the
leading agencies according to their deal-making creativity and effectiveness. It was a tight race but CAA was slightly ahead, then Endeavor,
UTA, William Morris and ICM. These are still the major players today.
If you have one of these agencies representing you, you are at the top
of your game. But if you're just starting out or even in the middle of a
blossoming career, don't try to get representation with these firms who
have all the star talent and will pay little or no attention to you. Rather,
look for a reputable mid-sized firm with an agent that's going to send
you out and look out for your best interests.

• **I must caution you about certain scams.** *Never* sign with an agent who charges you any type of fee or insists you have pictures taken by a certain photographer or says you must study with certain teachers. This must be strictly a business arrangement and it is your responsibility to get out of the office if things don't seem on the up and up. An agent's fee is 10% of union work gross salary and residuals, period. They make their money when you work. When you terminate an agent, be sure to notify the unions. Some agents in this time of SAG uncertainty are having clients sign General Service Agreements, which are approved by the State Labor Commissioner. My understanding of that type of agreement is the agent can charge up to 20% commission.

Resources

To download and print an updated version of this and all resource lists, go to actingiseverything.com.

The Association of Talent Agents, agentassociation.com.

Screen Actors Guild, 323/954-1600, sag.org.

AFTRA, 212/532-0800, aftra.org. A national listing of AFTRA Franchised Talent Agents is available.

BOOKS

Reference books date quickly; purchase only the latest editions.

The following books may be purchased or ordered through Samuel French, 323/876-0570, samuelfrench.com.

The Agencies: What The Actor Needs To Know by Acting World Books. They list each agent within the agency. This is the best book when you are looking for a new agent.

An Actor's Workbook: Get The Agent You Need & The Career You Want by K. Callan. She is a working actress and has written several books for actors.

Personal Talent Managers

• **The professional talent manager is responsible** for all aspects of the client's career. This includes artistic development, promotion of their career, working towards short and long term goals, maximizing their income and protecting them.

• **The talent manager's role is to advise**, consult and guide your career all along the way. A good manager understands your needs and goals, and they use their skill to help you move toward your objectives. They sift offers, deciding which to pursue and which to turn down. They usually have the final say on the agent's negotiation with the casting director or producer.

• **A manager takes a percentage of the money you earn**—usually 15 percent. Typically, the agent takes an additional 10 percent. Some actors fear these costs, particularly when the paydays get very big. Instead of looking at how much you must "give away," think about this: When the paydays are big, that is when you can most comfortably afford to compensate your team. And consider how little of your income you must pay out to compensate your team. Plus they are working "on spec," meaning you only have to pay them when there is income. There are very few companies in America that get to pay their executives in such a manner!

• **Your manager works in every part of your life.** Managers have fewer clients than agents do and their clients sometimes speak with them daily.

• **A new actor would be very lucky** to get the services of an experienced manager. Agents focus primarily on the immediate audition. A good manager, by definition, looks at the longer term career development of the actor. An actor with opportunities needs as much expertise as they can get to make wise decisions and take advantage of those opportunities. How many actors broke through with that one big job and then were never heard of again?

• **When you hire a manager,** hire one who you honestly believe can help you achieve your personal career goals. This means you must not only set short and long-term goals, but also educate yourself on who the respected managers are and how you can appeal to them. Value yourself. Don't be lazy. If you are lazy there is not much hope for having a career no matter how much money you have to promote yourself. You need to work every day on the business side of your career as well as your acting craft. To do any less will minimize your chances of reaching the big career.

• **When your career and business** have been created in partnership with a manager, then you have been blessed with a business structure that works. I believe loyalty is a very important element in creating, developing and keeping your team. As your career expands you need that team more than ever.

• **Poppy Montgomery moved to Hollywood** from Sydney, Australia with no acting experience. She cold-called Julia Roberts' then-manager Bob McGowan to see if he'd help make her a star. She sent him pictures all the time. She says, "I think he thought I was kind of funny." Two months later, he signed her. Two years later, by the time she was 23, she was working steadily on ABC's *Relativity*, movies *The Other Sister, Life, This Space Between Us, Dead Man on Campus, Desert's Edge, Devil in a Blue Dress.* Her career continues to grow; she is now a series regular on *Without A Trace.*

• **Steven Nash, head of Arts and Letters Management,** came to management after years as an acting coach and a prominent producer/director in theatre and film. His clients have appeared in many major films, commercials and television series. He is President of the Talent Managers Association, produces feature films under the banner Arts and Letters Entertainment and has offices in Beijing, China.

Q: What is the difference between a manager and agent?

- **In the major markets, like Los Angeles,** the job of the manager is quite different from the agent. While everyone wants success for the actor, the agent's main focus is to pursue the audition for the actor. The professional talent manager is concerned with all aspects of the actor's growth, development and prosperity. The manager is like the C.E.O. of the company owned by the actor. It may be said that a manager does many of the services that used to be done by the studios for their contract players in the "golden age of Hollywood." Today, most talent agencies will usually only look at more established talent. So it is typically the manager, if the talent can attract one, who is ready to work towards the long-term growth, who will invest their time, expertise and contacts in building a talent that is young in their development. Then when a talent is ready, the manager works with the actor to find the right agent to bring onto the team. Once the career is established, then the manager is essential to the care of the actor's career.

Q: Why does an actor need a manager?

- **As I said in** *Acting World's Personal Manager Directory,* to break through to the big career in today's increasingly competitive market, an actor must have expert guidance at all steps of the journey. There are many people who call themselves managers, but I feel the professional talent manager is a breed apart. Managers who have true expertise and take a hands-on approach to developing and protecting careers is what to look for. If a "developmental" actor can enlist a quality manager early in their career, it would put them at a great advantage. Certainly for an established actor or star, the service and the responsibilities of the talent manager is far reaching.

Q: Tell us about the Talent Managers Association.

- **It was formed in 1954** as the Conference of Personal Managers. We changed the name in 2000 to the Talent Managers Association (TMA) to reflect the 21st century evolution of Talent Management. Members pledge to pursue the highest standards of professionalism and ethics in all we do. A member may not sell any goods or services to a client for profit. We are paid by commission only when our clients work. We also produce networking and informational events for industry professionals, with special events for the actor.

Q: What sort of actors do you look for?

- **Talented, of course, but I need to feel that I can help the actor** to achieve an important career. I am attracted to well-trained actors who are marketable and appealing. I also consider an actor's ability to pursue a career aggressively in terms of time and resources. A really great look is always of interest. On top of all that I have to feel they would be a responsible person to invest my time, expertise and resources in.

Q: Would you consider taking on a client who is fairly new to the biz?

- **While the last actor I signed had extensive film and television credits,** if I see the potential of a "new" person, I could be interested. The time and effort that I put into each of my clients is quite substantial, so I have to be ready to commit. I certainly have had some great successes with my developmental clients. Two of them, for example, have recently done major roles in big studio features.

Q: Where do you find clients?

- **Referrals certainly from industry professionals.** Our office also receives many headshots sent by actors and will call those that we are interested in at that moment—please do not call us. I go to theatre and showcases and occasionally teach industry workshops as well as university seminars. Everywhere I go holds the possibility of meeting an actor with strong potential. One of my clients I met at a party, then spotted in an independent film. His screen presence grabbed me.

Q: Do you only manage actors?

- **I sign people "across the board,"** meaning in all entertainment areas. Recently one of my actors booked a job directing a television pilot. Another actor wrote a screenplay which we sold.

Q: So you also manage writers?

- **Most of my clients** do work in related creative areas sooner or later. But please remind your readers that our office does not accept unsolicited scripts.

Q: How involved do you get in the actor's life?

- **I have been known to help find an apartment** and to help shop for a designer gown for an awards show. The actor and I are on a team together. I give support and guidance in almost any area, though I spend most of my time on their career and development. It takes all our best efforts to reach for the big career and then to hold onto it and grow it.

Q: Do you think your background as a director and acting coach helps your effectiveness as a manager?

- **Definitely.** I think my understanding of the acting process and the interpretation of material makes me more valuable to clients. I have been thanked by producers, directors and casting directors for appreciating their artistic needs or requirements.

Q: As a manager, what do you think it takes for an actor to get the job?

- **Getting the job in Hollywood** is initially about things other than acting.

- **There are so many trained actors today,** the competition is tougher than ever. Many good and deserving actors can rarely get an audition to "show their stuff." The challenge today is to be at your peak readiness on every level in case that key opportunity pops up. Then you must continually promote yourself. Until you are well-established, regular promotion is essential.

- **I believe casting directors at an audition,** working efficiently in their high pressure jobs, have sometimes decided whether you are in the running before you even speak. This is particularly true in one of the many film and television auditions where your audition scene is three lines, and there is no event in the scene to sink your teeth into. In addition to having an appropriate look, I believe you need to have a carefully focused edge, an essence about you that is clear and instantly captures the casting director's attention. One can and should develop this edge intentionally. Figure out your unique traits, and choose the ones to put forward. I call this *Image Definition*.

Q: Any advice for the young actor?

- **The cold reading, camera technique** and result oriented classes are very important, but it is also significant to study basic acting. Learn how to interpret material. When you pick up a script, have a technique for making artistic choices into actable elements. On a business level, be organized and aggressive. Don't just wait for the phone to ring. There is always something you can do to progress. A good manager will certainly guide you and be a source of ideas and inspiration.

Q: Any final advice for my readers?

- **I love actors and I love the creative process** of developing careers. I sign clients with the expectation of success and long-term relationships. An actor who comes to me needs to be on the same page and understand our roles together. This is not a business for those who must have instant gratification. Be ready to develop your artistry, skills and career over the long term.

- **If a quality manager** doesn't respond the first time you contact them, maybe keep them on your promotions list. There may come a moment when you are just what they are looking for. Also, there are sometimes actors that are not right for my management company that I do put into our film casting files.

- **The higher your career goes,** the more you will benefit from the expertise of a quality manager. Build your reputation with that manager.

- **Tami Lynn, personal manager/producer,** is past president of the Conference of Personal Managers (COPM) and became a lifetime honorary member in recognition of 30 years of personal management. She started the West Coast National Conference of Personal Managers.

Q: When is the right time to look for a personal manager?

- **When actors know that they need help,** they should seek representation whether they're just starting out or they are established.

- **A personal manager is one who guides** and gives direction to one's career.

Q: How does one look for a manager?

- **The best thing to do is to contact one of the organizations.** The TMA is based on the West Coast. Contact them and explain that you're looking for a manager. We usually have actors mail their pictures and resumes and I will present them to the organization. If there is some interest, then the manager will contact the client. If you want to investigate someone, ask the appropriate manager organization to have them checked out.

- **Every manager should, like an actor, have a biography.** You can see who their current clients are and other clients they have represented, how long they've been in management, what their record is. I give my clients my full biography.

Q: Could you name some of the people that you've managed?

- **Christina Applegate,** 11 seasons on *Married with Children, Jesse,* and many films. We've been together since she was seven years old. Valerie Bertinelli, Adam Rich, Mary Beth McDonough from *The Waltons* and Katy Kurtzman.

Q: In Christina's career, before she got *Married with Children*, was she in that sexy mode?

- **Yes, she made many guest appearances on episodics.** She's a beautiful girl. At the age of 14, her career zoomed, which is usually a difficult age to hit. She had beautiful long hair which she cut all off like a punk hairdo. All the girls had long hair, and she would walk into interviews with this short, very unusual haircut. She got cast in *Heart of the City*, which really showed her acting ability. It was a wonderful hour-long series. She stood out. When the producers of *Married with Children* wanted to recast the role of Kelly Bundy, they came to us.

Q: Should an actor sign a management contract?

- **Once both people have done their homework** and the manager wants the actor and the actor wants the manager, most definitely there should be a three year contract. It takes a year just to put the whole thing together.

Q: What happens when a manager signs an actor?

- **The first thing is to evaluate their acting ability** and to make sure they are working with a good drama coach, and they have pictures that work. Most likely, they will need new pictures. Then get their resume together. A lot of times an actor doesn't realize that there are things that should be included. They think that school plays and things like that are not important. Anything they've done is important.

- **A manager will probably be in touch with a client daily** if they're working. If the actor isn't working, the two would be in touch to talk about something specific coming up or they would be sure the client is doing what is needed for themselves. If there is a problem on the set, the actor calls the manager, not the agent, because of the personal involvement that you have.

- **We can open up an interview for them.** Then the ball is totally in the actor's court.

Q: For a general interview, what kind of clothes are appropriate?

- **The simplest clothes are the best.** Casual clothes from jeans to simple skirts for girls, and for guys, just jeans and T-shirts. It should be a totally relaxed, simple situation unless there's a specific role that they're going for. Then they would most likely dress for that role. They shouldn't be investing in expensive clothing.

Q: What happens when the question of nudity comes up?

- **In advising the actor on what roles to take,** unless it's something like nudity, there's no role that should be turned down when you're starting out. Absolutely no role. I've heard actors say, "I'm looking for a particular role, or a particular path," or "I don't want to do this or that kind of role." That's insane. I think they should take the roles that are there whether it be feature films, television or cable, because you never know what you're going to get from that.

- **When you're talking about nudity, that's totally different.** There's nudity and then there's nudity. Pornography is an absolute no. It's the lowest type of work. All that does is to put you in the context of being a nude actor. It degrades you. I have actresses right now who will do nudity. That's fine as long as it's done in good taste and there's a reason for it. I will go in and say, for instance, both actresses are fine with their breasts but they do not want to show their butts. I will make sure in the contract, that whatever part of their body they do not want to show won't be shown. I'm there whenever they do a nude scene.

• **Al Onorato, personal manager** with Unified Management, was a casting director for 15 years and one of the founding members of the Casting Society of America (CSA).

Q: When, in your opinion, is it time for an actor to get a personal manager?

- **There are a couple of schools of thought.** One is that you start right from the very beginning, to discover people who have x quality or x amount of talent and direct them toward the right productions, films, projects, teachers, etc. I've always thought, in this business you have to trust some people. I have to put trust in the people that I want to handle, and they trust that with my guidance they will avoid some of the pitfalls. Everything costs money. So when you're going to spend the money, you want to put it in the right area so you're not just spinning your wheels.

- **In today's market place** there are so many projects being done that you want to have as many opportunities as possible so having a team—agents and manager—working for you is almost mandatory.

- **On the other hand,** someone may have a career that's already started but has gotten blocked or typecast into one area of television or stage, and they can't make the move into the next area they want to be in. A manager may guide the career into a different direction.

- **When I meet actors**, sometimes they may not have had a lot of training but they have certain instincts that work for them and they are able to transcend all the training that other people have had for years. But they must then train and study.

- **There is a great demand for actors and actresses in TV who have comedy backgrounds.** If someone has the right look, their chances are greater at getting a shot than someone who has done only drama. More than ever, actors who have been on successful television series are making the leap into leads in movies.

Q: Where do you find clients?

- **Everywhere. I go to workshops, showcases, watch television** and see both big budget and small independent films. I travel across the country doing workshops and looking for talent. Along the way you find some people you think have a certain amount of ability and desire; those are the ones you encourage to pursue a career.

Q: When should actors move to L.A.?

- **If someone really wants a career** they have to go where the market is. That is Los Angeles for film and New York for theater. That old adage about "I'm not going to go there unless I have a contract" or "I'm not going to go there unless I have a job," well, that's really pie-in-the-sky thinking. Before someone gets a job there are numerous steps one must go through first: tapes, auditions, callbacks, interviews. In some instances, I try working with them long-distance by requesting that they put themselves on tape for projects. The eventual reality is they are going to have to be in Los Angeles or New York.

- **At the International Model & Talent Association,** we found a girl from Ohio who we felt had great potential. We started working with her this way, on tape. Eventually she and her mom spent some time in Los Angeles so she could be seen in person. She did land a role in an Ang Lee film.

- **In moving to NY or LA, people should be prepared financially and emotionally** because you are probably not going to support yourself as an actor right away. You must make necessary arrangements until that occurs. Patience and perseverance are extremely important. The belief that it is going to happen within a short amount of time may not happen, so be prepared to have lots of time on your hands that you fill preparing for those opportunities to audition.

Q: What do you do on a daily basis? What is your job description?

- We try to keep apprised of all the projects that are going on, whether it be television, theater or movies and the various roles in the particular projects.

- **Most all our work is on the phone.** It's checking and dealing with agents, casting people at the studios and casting directors on various projects. We also handle producers, directors and writers. In doing so, we're looking for opportunities for them as well as the actors. Our goal is to get our clients seen so we approach each project through casting, producers, directors or whoever necessary.

Q: Do you have any advice for actors?

- Acting in this business is very much like athletics. You have to do it. You've got to study. The best athletes and Olympic stars are people who have been nurtured and have had coaches along the way to help guide them and keep them away from bad habits and the wrong training. The people we revere in our business, Meryl Streep, Al Pacino, Anthony Hopkins and that caliber of actor, have trained and continue to grow as artists.

- **Don't believe people who say, "I'll make you a star."** It's not an easy process and if you want to be a star, hopefully you want to be an artist as well, not just somebody whose name is on a billboard but somebody who can point proudly to the work that they do. I think it's important to uphold dignity and principles. There are no guarantees.

- **What is so often the hardest thing** for parents or loved ones of actors to understand is that it doesn't happen overnight. Every time they say, "What have you done?" or "What are we going to see you on?" though it's done with love, it also puts the actor in a precarious situation, because they feel like they've got to prove something. People don't understand how long it takes.

- **Terrance Hines, personal manager, Hines and Hunt Entertainment,** acting coach and author of the best selling book *An Actor Succeeds, Career Management for the Actor.*

Q: What do you look for in prospective clients?

- I look for honesty, a sense of humor and a passion that fills the room. I like the actor to have good reasons why they want management. They should do their homework by checking out my company. They should have a support system in place and enough money to invest in pictures that look like them and enroll in excellent acting classes.

- **They should be open and honest** about who they are, with an understanding of how others see them. They should have a grasp on the business aspect of the entertainment world. Are they prepared to trust and listen to those guiding their career and are they able and willing to block out the voices that do not have their best interest at heart? Are they prepared for rejection? Do they understand that there are valleys as well as mountains in long careers? Above all, do they have a sense of humor to get them through the worst of times?

Q: How do you work for your clients?

- **Our company interfaces with a network** of producers, directors, writers, casting directors and executives. When you have clients on a series or in films, the casting directors or producers call to have lunch and discuss the show. This gives the manager the opportunity to discuss their client list.

- **I find that going with clients to an interview**, especially a producer callback or the network, has proven very fruitful. Discussing the choices of material, adjustments in the direction of the career, changing physical appearance and working on the acting tools take up much of the management day.

- **Management offers a landscape** where the actor can have a sounding board at his beck and call. Every artist needs to be encouraged to beat their head against the wall one more time.

- **Jake Azhar, President of Hollywood Management Company** on the Board of Directors of the TMA, Talent Managers Association.

Q: Tell me about your client base, where you find them and how you develop them.

- **I choose actors who have an honest commitment** to excellence and the drive to make life happen. Our combined power is the magic ingredient for success. I go to showcases, plays, screenings and acting schools around the world. I'm always on the lookout for the best and brightest. I found one of my best actors at a coffee shop on Sunset Boulevard.

- **My clients are anxious to work and work on themselves.** I know what my actors need when they start with me and am able to direct them to the right coaches. For newer actors, preparing them to meet casting directors is vital in this process. The manager/actor relationship is based on strong trust, and trust must be proved, guided and agreed to by both parties. A breach in trust must be studied and repaired right away.

• Casting director Joey Paul, CSA.

Q: What is your feeling about working with personal managers?

• **As a casting director**, I would love to spend more time finding new talent, but there are time constraints with the job that make that very difficult. Good talent that comes from the East Coast or Midwest regional theaters, who have their Equity and SAG cards but not a lot of TV credits, may have incredible difficulty just getting an agent. Smaller agents have difficulty getting their clients in to read for auditions. A personal manager who has both knowledge of the industry and certain relationships with agents, can get their clients representation. They can really make a difference in somebody's career when they're starting out.

• **Actors can benefit** from the manager's experience and relationships and save themselves a lot of time. The manager might steer them to a good teacher, a good photographer and help them to redefine their look into something that's marketable. Many actors come here thinking it's just about the acting or they hear it's all a look. They don't understand what a look is, what their look is. Many actors hear, "Well, you don't need a personal manager 'til you've got a career to manage." But there are personal managers who have developed careers right from the start. I think some of them are very worthwhile.

• **Anyone can be a personal manager.** It may be wise to choose one who belongs to the Talent Managers Association (TMA). Before hiring a manager, check around to be sure he or she has a good reputation. An inexperienced manager who has not built any successful careers will be counting on you to put them on the map. **Walk away from anyone who wants to charge a fee other than a percentage of what you earn.**

• **I want to alert you to some practices** that I believe are not helpful to your career. Breakdown Services Ltd. over the years has sued and won judgments against many pseudo/fake management companies who go into business solely to charge actors $50 to $100 a month for access to the casting breakdowns.

• **Actors defend paying these illegal fees** by saying it helps them to know what roles are being cast. I believe there are legitimate ways to spend money that will indeed really help your career. The Actor's Network costs $50 a month and the return is of great value. Casting showcases are a valid way to open yourself to casting opportunities; they average $25 to

$40 each. Alicia Silverstone moved to Los Angeles when she was 14 to live with her acting coach Judi O'Neil. Soon afterward she was spotted at an actors' showcase by manager Carolyn Kessler. Within a year she was cast in *The Crush.*

• **The best thing you can do for your career is to act** wherever you can make an opportunity for yourself. Submitting unsolicited pictures and resumes to casting directors is valid but one of the least likely ways to be discovered. Doing showcases, short films, student productions and hosting or appearing on public access shows are legitimate ways of being seen.

Resources

To download and print an updated version of this and all resource lists, go to actingiseverything.com.

Arts and Letters Entertainment, Steven Nash, ArtsandLettersEntertainment.com. 7715 Sunset Blvd., #100, Los Angeles, 90046. They will consider mail submissions, from age 15 to 24 only. They will contact you if interested. No visits or phone calls, please.

Tami Lynn Productions and Management, 818/888-8264. Fax: 818/888-8267.

Hollywood Management Company, Jake Azhar. 310/999-4747. They will consider email or mail submissions, from age 15 to 24 only. They will then contact you if interested. No visits, please.

Al Onorato of Unified Management, 818/954-9944.

Hines & Hunt Entertainment, Terrance Hines and Justine Hunt, 818/557-7516. Manages all types of actors but encourages character types to call.

Stein Entertainment Group, T.J. Stein, 323/822-1400, SteinEntertainment.com. 1351 N. Crescent Heights Blvd., #312, West Hollywood, 90046. Children, teens and young adults.

Talent Managers Association, 310/205-8495, talentmanagers.org. Their purpose is to promote and encourage the highest standards of professionalism and ethics in the practice of Talent Management.

The West Coast Performer's Complete Personal Managers Directory of Managers for All Performing and Creative Talents, an Acting World Books publication. At theatrical bookstores and actingworldbooks.org. This is much more than a directory; it has the information you need to shop for and land a personal manager.

Ross Reports, Working Actors Guide and *Hollywood Creative Directory* are other publications that list personal managers and are sold at theatrical bookstores.

PUBLIC RELATIONS
AND PUBLICISTS

• **No one knows who you are or what you are doing** without publicity. All the networks and most of the production companies hire publicists, formerly known as press agents. These publicists get the press to write about the TV shows, movies and the actors in the projects. Even so, many individual stars hire their own representative to handle their publicity.

• **Alicia Silverstone, Jenny McCarthy and Matthew McConaughey** are actors who became household names even before we saw the projects they were promoting. This is because a publicity machine had put their faces and names in front of the public with such repetition that we wanted to know who they were. The same was true of Sandra Bullock and Brad Pitt.

• **A publicist's basic responsibilities** include preparing written biographies of their clients to send to the press, keeping contacts in the media aware of any favorable newsworthy developments in their client's lives, taking the requests from newspapers, magazines and TV talk shows that want to interview their clients, and pitching story ideas about clients to these same requesters. The publicist can also decide how the public should see their client and proceed accordingly to create that image.

• **Rosie O'Donnell** mentioned in a live interview at the Oscar ceremonies that she was out of town and her publicist picked her gown and jewels. She flew in from location that morning and had the final fitting. Publicists can design the way their artists are presented to the public.

• **Marisa Tomei's** successful nomination for the Academy Award for *My Cousin Vinnie* was directly due to her publicity team. They took out trade ads and got tapes to all of the Academy voters. When she was nominated they doubled their efforts and she won the *Best Supporting Actress*.

• **Many actors choose a publicist** for their capability to keep them out of the news. Jason Alexander of *Seinfeld* told me when we were working on the show that he had been with his publicist for years because, "she doesn't like publicity." She didn't ask him to do openings and the type of things he didn't want to do.

• **When selecting a publicist,** as in other business choices, choose by reputation, personality and a mutual agreement on the way you want to be represented.

• **Liria Mersini is a public relations consultant and life coach currently working in Washington D.C.** When in Los Angeles, she coached individuals and led workshops on *Celebrity 101, The Power of Image and Creating Perfect Bios.*

Q: How do you help actors create PR?

• **My goal is to de-mystify the PR process and help my clients** create powerful packages. I work with actors before they are ready for representation, as well as established actors who are ready to make a change in their image. In both cases, I help actors understand the PR process and package themselves so that they can gain more control of the image they and their team put forward.

• **Understanding PR and the way it works can really help an actor** navigate the system and set reasonable expectations for their own PR campaign. Taking a workshop or interning at a PR firm is great exposure. It can take the mystery out of building celebrity and help a new actor think in terms of marketing.

Q: How does an actor start?

• **An important first step is to create a bio that reflects their essence,** especially before they've done a great deal of work. This is one tool that can clarify their whole package and set the tone for meetings with agents, casting directors, managers as well as publicists. The point here is to have your package of materials (you, your pictures, bio, resume, and tape) deliver a strong, consistent message. It is never too early to begin this process.

• **I work with actors on becoming experts on marketing themselves.** In this business there is so much pressure on actors to conform to someone else's idea of who they are when it is really their uniqueness that generates interest and builds celebrity.

Q: Where do you see actors getting stuck?

- **The biggest mistake I see, both in new actors and in celebrities,** is that they tend to abdicate their power to experts. Remember, a good publicist is an expert at the process of building celebrity. They have training, experience and, most importantly, contacts. However, you are the world's foremost expert on you. When an actor knows who they are and what they want from the publicist, they radically increase their chances for success.

- **Often, an actor will hire a public relations firm** because of the "A list" artists that firm represents. Sometimes this strategy pays off, but there are no guarantees. It is also common for actors to present themselves as blank slates and ask for guidance on how to be marketed. Either way, the whole power structure is off. The actor is only one of many clients on a talent roster and that can be disempowering, especially when there are bigger names on that roster.

- **The bottom line is, if you are an expert on you,** then you can really benefit from a good publicist's ideas and contacts. It can be a very exciting process. At $2,000 to $5,000 per month, it is definitely a costly one. Doing your homework can prepare you to get the most from this important relationship.

• **Publicist Kelly Bush** of ID Public Relations works in entertainment publicity, representing actors, directors, composers and writers.

Q: Does an actor hire you on a regular monthly basis?

- **The publicist,** like the agent or manager, is part of the team. When an actor has a strong team supporting them, they are able to focus on doing great work while their team does its job. It is important the publicist, agent and manager are in constant communication.

- **I have an ongoing relationship** with my clients just like the agent or manager. People sometimes think a publicist can be hired only once in a while. When there is an opportunity to make something happen for someone, what happens if they are not "on" at the time? It is important to consider publicity for the entire career—not just for a particular project. For example, magazines work sometimes up to 4-6 months in advance.

Q: When you get a new client and you are the first publicist, what is the procedure?

- **If the client has worked** for 10 years and never had a publicist, they've probably done a mish-mosh of interviews based on what they were promoting at the time. I approach the entire career. I start with smaller things and work towards magazine covers. I look at all the photographs that have been taken and biographical information or feature stories that have been written. I write a new bio that is very straightforward. If necessary, I put together a photo shoot so we have something we're happy to send out.

- **It's about presentation** and packaging. If a client has never done any press, it's exciting because you can do it right from the beginning.

Q: Is there a great deal of expense for new clients?

- **The client doesn't pay** for the magazine or newspaper photo shoots; the publications do. If we're promoting a film or television show, usually the studio will pick up expenses associated with the publicity. The client only pays publicity fees and expenses.

Q: How are those fees determined?

- **It's a flat monthly fee.** Publicists charge anywhere from $2,000-5,000 a month. There are perfectly reputable publicists that charge less but in my opinion, you get what you pay for.

Q: How do actors shop for publicists?

- **Their agent or manager will know publicists** the client would get along well with and whose work they trust. I would take no more than three meetings, otherwise it gets very confusing. Ask the publicist about their approach to things, or what they feel are important types of publicity, and you will get a pretty good sense of whether or not you agree with their ideas. If you trust your publicist, they can do their job and help take your career to a high level—which makes the agent's and manager's job easier. If a producer sees an actor in *Vanity Fair*, they may say, "If *Vanity Fair* thinks they're hot, then I want them in my next movie."

Q: When is it time to hire a publicist?

- **When the actor has something to promote.** A television show, a film, a theatrical production—with enough time in advance to do the proper job. Look at Rita Wilson from *Sleepless in Seattle*. She got a good amount of press with just a five-minute crying scene in the film. There have been a lot of small parts that stood out and received attention for the performer. A publicist can get your work in front of an editor, to convince them that your story is worth covering. The time to think about hiring a publicist is when you've done work you're really proud of.

- **My job is to educate** the magazine editors and television producers on who my clients are and why they should be on their shows or in their magazines.

Q: Does the publicist go to these interviews?

- **You accompany your client** on everything. For print interviews, I introduce the writer to my client and then I leave them. I'm there for every photo taken and every television appearance.

Q: Have you ever had a client who is really shy and publicity was difficult for them?

- **I don't put them in situations** where it's going to make them uncomfortable. I have clients that I would never put on *Letterman* or *The Tonight Show*. It's just not appropriate for them. There are a lot of other things you can do, though, that are more conducive for your client. If they're more comfortable with a one on one situation, everything they do is in print. They just don't do TV.

Q: How do you find clients?

- **The best way to get a client is to do a good job** for the ones you have and word gets out. Also, I go after clients. For example, at the film festivals you see movies before their theatrical releases. I hear about someone who is outstanding in a role, and I'll call their agent and say that I'm interested in meeting with this person.

Q: Do you have any advice for actors who don't have that movie or television project yet?

- **Do great work** and if you receive great reviews that gives you something to go on. I've met with people who wanted a publicist and once we had a meeting, I was able to tell them that it's not time for it yet. A person may have a supporting role in a successful television series and the media may have no interest in talking to them. The publicist really doesn't know what we can do for that person until we get out there and start working and see what kind of response we get.

Q: What advice can you give for actors who already have publicists? How can the actor help?

- **Doing press is almost like an audition.** You put on your acting hat and you're an actor. You put on your publicity hat and you're doing publicity. It's very different. You really have to know what you're doing. You really have to make an impression. The client can make a publicist's job easier by being good at it. It helps to see other people on TV shows like *Letterman*, read magazine and newspaper articles, see other actors doing press and the kind of impression you get after you read the article. You may say, "Do I like this person?" or, "This person sounded really arrogant" or, "This person I admire." You see someone doing a talk show and you say, "That was really boring."

• **You can learn from that.** You see a great actress like Geena Davis who brings on her inventions. That makes for good TV. These TV producers want to get great ratings. They want people to stay up late and watch.

Resources

To download and print an updated version of this and all resource lists, go to actingiseverything.com.

Working Actor's Guide, workingactors.com. Lists Public Relation Firms.

Guerrilla P.R. and *Guerrilla P.R. Wired* by Michael Levine are good books about doing your own publicity. guerrillapr.net

ID Public Relations: Kelly Bush, id-pr.com. 8409 Santa Monica Blvd., West Hollywood, 90069.

Studio Fan Mail/Tamkin Color, 310/275-6122. studiofanmail.com. Email: service@studiofanmail.com. 1122 S. Robertson Blvd., #15, L.A., 90035. When it is time in your career to have someone answer your fan mail, Jack Tamkin runs a wonderful business. They send out all color photos with authentic-looking autographs and personal messages. Their costs are lower than most black and white photos. When requested they will send a prospective client an interesting, thorough set of samples of their work.

Dick Delson & Associates, 818/763-2362. publicity4u.com. 4605 Lankershim Blvd., Suite 214, North Hollywood, 91602. Has worked with a number of celebrities and also worked on a number of Oscar-winning films over the years.

ENTERTAINMENT ATTORNEYS

• **It is an exciting time** in an actor's career when the future holds so much promise that an attorney is needed. Be certain that the finances and terms of your deals are properly in place so that you can calmly enjoy your hard-earned successes.

• **As actors' careers grow**, they must seek the best support people for their team. It is important to understand what an entertainment attorney can do for you before you need one.

• **Your attorney can advise you** of your rights in a given situation and negotiate a contract—money, billing and terms are complicated areas but it's vital they are handled to your best advantage. The ins and outs of an entertainment contract are so complicated and abstract that you need a specialist. It can be dangerous to your best interests to rely on a family attorney—or even your agent—who is not an experienced specialist. Attorneys usually charge by the hour and a good one will estimate costs for you. When seeking an attorney, ask your friends in the entertainment industry for their recommendations. We all hear the attorney-bashing jokes, but your personal legal matters are no joke and you need a caring, honest, loyal attorney. Interview several and then go with your well-tuned instincts as to who will work the best for you.

• **Chandler Warren, entertainment attorney,** began his career in New York representing the producers of *As the World Turns* and *Another World,* also dozens of stage productions on and off Broadway and over 50 independent feature films. Today he represents writers, directors, actors, producers and designers in all phases of film, television, stage and recording. He works extensively in low budget features in New York and Los Angeles, including the complicated area of film distribution.

Q: Under what circumstances does an actor need an attorney?

- **For example**, when an actor is required to sign a test option for a television series, it may bind him/her for the next three to seven years of his/her professional life. The agent can negotiate the basic terms of the deal, but it is important to have the fine points of the contract negotiated by an entertainment attorney.

- **When an actor is engaged for a series of commercials**, the agent will handle the basic negotiation but an attorney should review and negotiate the fine points. Otherwise, the actor could find his/her picture on the product's labels, billboards and cardboard cutouts in super markets and wonder what happened. Every phase of the use of the actor's name, likeness, voice, etc. has to be carefully spelled out.

- **When the actor is cast in a good role** in a motion picture, the producer may want additional options, etc. This should be reviewed on the actor's behalf. There are any number of things in most "standard" actor contracts that need to be negotiated.

- **When the actor is cast in a legitimate stage production**, often the producer will want options to take the actor along with the play as it moves. And there are billing considerations, housing, per diems, etc. to be negotiated. Or the situation may be reversed, where the actor wants the option to continue and this has to be negotiated so the actor is protected.

- **When the actor is also a singer** there are other pitfalls, as the music business is complicated and dog-eat-dog. Those contracts can tie up an actor and/or the actor's writing talents for many years. This is an area that must never be entered into without an entertainment attorney at the actor's side.

- **When an actor signs with a manager**, a lawyer is essential. A management contract can be in effect for a long period of time and usually encompasses money from all sources of the entertainment business. An actor has to be sure the contract allows him/her to leave if the manager is not fulfilling the job. Remember, an actor must never rely on an oral promise.

Q: How do you feel about agents?

• **I am a strong believer** in both agents and managers. Most attorneys are not acting agents; they don't get the Breakdown Service, they aren't in contact daily with casting directors, etc. But if an actor doesn't have an agent yet and has been cast in a series, a soap, a major part in a motion picture, or gets a recording contract, the actor only needs the services of an attorney. From that job, the actor may then secure a top agent or manager.

Q: In what other situations might an actor need an attorney?

• **No one should direct a play** without a written contract, especially if the play is a new one by a new playwright. What is the director's future option to direct? What is the director's billing? Should the director agree to a royalty pool? And so on.

• **An actor who writes a play**, or has a unique idea, will need a copyright. No one reading this book should ever lose sight of the fact that a copyright is probably the most valuable commodity a person can have; yes, even better than residuals because it lasts longer. Also, the writer needs to negotiate royalties, travel and per diems, billing, subsidiary rights, option terms, etc.

• **Actors often produce** their own 99-seat waiver shows in order to showcase their acting talents. All of the many legal headaches which every producer must face will have to be dealt with. No producer should remotely consider going into the producing business without an entertainment attorney who is familiar with legitimate stage contracts, SEC filing requirements, limited partnerships, etc.

Resources

To download and print an updated version of this and all resource lists, go to acting-iseverything.com.

Chandler Warren of Warren, Alpert & Beigelman, LLP, 323/876-6400. 7715 Sunset Blvd. #208, Los Angeles 90046. Extremely knowledgeable, fair, and easy to talk to. His walls are lined with pictures of famous actors and posters of shows he's worked on.

Los Angeles County Bar Association, 213/627-2727. lacba.org.

California State Bar Association, 213/765-1000. calbar.org. Ask for information on several attorneys who are listed as specialists in Entertainment Law.

Business Managers

• **As actors develop their earning capacity** and start saving money, the next person on their *career team* will be a business (financial) manager. Some actors or spouses of actors may have an educated background in business and time to research, but most of us need to seek a professional to manage our expenses and investments. Business affairs become very complicated when the actor is working on remote locations.

• **When you have landed that role on a series or a big movie** that is taking you on location for months, it might be time to look for a business manager. Gayle Futernick, in her *Drama-Logue* column, gave some great examples of when you would need some help.

  • **After 25 hours a day on a set spent learning your lines** and your marks, you aren't going to feel much like writing rent checks or doing budgets on Quicken. You need a new car, because you just can't drive to The Lot in your old, beat-up Chevy. Should you buy or lease a new car? Should you open a retirement fund? Maybe you should keep your bucks in a liquid, short-term investment just in case. Then again, the producer did smile and mention something about a starring role in the spin-off.

  • **Maybe it is time to buy a house.** Who is going to help you get a mortgage? Who is going to refer you to a reliable investment advisor? Who is going to reconcile your check book? Who is going to be on hold with the bank for 20 minutes while they figure out why your service charge quadrupled last month? Who is going to remember to deposit your residual checks in the investment fund and the weekly paychecks in the household account?

  • **Who has time to keep up with your paperwork? Not you!** You're busy getting to sets on time and interviewing with the press. They need you in wardrobe at 7AM for a fitting and you're supposed to lunch with your agent at Le Dome. Life is a bit hectic and right now you're spending your time shmoozing with the right people at the right parties.

- **Tax planning is not exactly your strong point** and you're not really sure how to build a spreadsheet that will remind you when to pay your bills. And mom lives too far away to help . . .

• **I love Gayle's writing and I think she makes her point very well.** As actors, we all hope and yearn for the predicament she outlines. Here are a few more of her thoughts on using the right business manager.

- **There are no generic answers.** These decisions depend on you and your lifestyle. If you tend to lose control with money, think about your future. Remember how hard it was to get this gig. Remember how many people are trying to become working actors. Unless you are an established mega-celebrity, be conservative with your finances and use your business manager as your money conscience.

- **While you need to be able to depend on your business manager,** it is not advisable to totally turn over the reins and never check his work. It is your money and your financial health that are important. Request and review periodic (monthly or quarterly) reports. You are paying them to provide services for you and to educate you about your financial matters. Trust is a mutual understanding.

- **There are no licensing procedures for business managers.** You may want to find one who is a CPA (Certified Public Accountant). The advantage is tremendous: CPAs have passed the CPA Exam and have work experience in the accounting field. They are licensed and regulated by the state, and must abide by professional ethics and complete 80 hours of continuing education every two years.

- **Business managers can charge hourly, a fixed rate or a flat percentage** of your gross salary earned as their fee. Typically, business managers charge five percent of gross income that is earned from your professional services as their fee. Thus their fee would not be based on amounts earned on investments.

- **If your annual income exceeds $100,000**, it is probably time to consider using the services of a business manager.

• **At the beginning of Oprah's success,** she had Bill Cosby on her show. When discussing finances, Cosby said, "In order to know where your money is going, always sign every check and investigate and approve each investment yourself." Oprah credits his advice for much of her prosperity. I'm sure Oprah has a business manager to keep everything in order, but she runs the ship.

• **Shaquille O'Neal**: "When you're dealing with money, you have to take half of what you make and put it away. Then take half of what you have left and put that away. So you've put three quarters of it away and you play with the one quarter that is left. If you invest wisely, safely and don't take too many risks, you'll be alright."

• **Some actors are not interested in handling their money.** If that's you, be selective in choosing your professional advisor. There are no regulations for financial managers so they have free rein. You sign your money over and trust they will do the right thing. Your hard-earned money could be gone; we have all heard the horror stories of business managers running off with all of their clients' money. On the other hand, most actors with money have been guided by financial consultants and managers.

Personal Manager T.J. Stein had an article in his newsletter by business manager, CPA Scott Feinstein about whether or not to incorporate. I am quoting some of the article to give you an overall view. Keep in mind this is general information and tax laws change every year.

  • **It comes down to one main issue, cost vs. benefit.** The costs of incorporation include initial one-time, out-of-pocket expenses plus on-going annual expenses such as legal and accounting fees and additional payroll and corporate taxes. On the other hand benefits of incorporation include the ability to establish a pension plan, the right to deduct medical expenses and the transfer of other expenses from your personal tax return to corporate tax return where there are no limitations and the financial advantages of fiscal year-end planning.

  • **The benefits fall into three basic categories:** pension plans, medical and business expense deductions and fiscal year-end planning.

  • **As an employee of a production company/studio** and the recipient of W-2 income, the only retirement account you can voluntarily set up is an IRA. Unfortunately, if you are a member of a union, and although you have the right to contribute to an IRA, the contributions would <u>not</u> qualify as a tax deduction. With a loan-out corporation, you can set up a corporate pension plan and take a deduction from your gross income of up to $30,000 per year. This would obviously save significant tax dollars.

  • **Your employee business deductions are included on Schedule A** of your personal tax return and, as such, are subject to several limitations. In fact, if your deductions are large enough you could be subject to what is referred to as an "alternative minimum tax." In simple terms, you could lose a significant portion of the tax deduction. With a corporation, there are no such limitations. The IRS generally respects the deductions of a corporation. In other words, the standards for proof can be greater on a personal tax return than on a corporate tax return.

• **As for medical and other personal expenses,** a corporation can adopt a medical reimbursement plan which allows the corporation to pay directly and deduct all medical expenses (less amounts paid by insurance) including expenses for mental health, eye care, chiropractic, etc.

• **Finally, a corporation can establish a "fiscal" year-end** as opposed to the required December 31 calendar year-end for individuals. This enables you to manipulate income by pushing back or accelerating income between calendar years, depending on your particular financial status each year.

• **Since there are no regulatory bodies** or other ways to check on financial/business managers, you must do some extensive research before making any financial decisions. Ask your accountant, attorney, agent, manager, successful actor friend or any other trusted friends in the business for their recommendations.

Resources:

To download and print an updated version of this and all resource lists, go to actingiseverything.com.

Feinstein & Berson: Scott Feinstein, 818/981-3115. feinsteinberson.com. 16255 Ventura Blvd., #625, Encino, 91436. CPA and Business Manager, has a strong client list consisting almost exclusively of SAG, AFTRA, IATSE and DGA members.

California State Board of Accountancy, 916/263-3680. dca.ca.gov/cba. You can check to see if the business manager or accountant you are considering is licensed and in good standing.

Working Actor's Guide (WAG), workingactors.com. Available at theatrical bookstores, lists many well known business managers.

SECTION SIX
CREATING YOUR STYLE AND IMAGE

STYLE, IMAGE AND WARDROBE
FOR ACTORS AND ACTRESSES

• **Much of who we are as actors** is defined by how we look, what we wear, how we present ourselves. Some of us are born or raised with a sense of style and taste; others develop it. You must look successful. If you are not naturally talented in this area, you will have to learn how to dress yourself to present the image that you choose to project. You can cultivate taste and create your own *look*. Read books. Watch the style shows on television. Consult a friend whose taste you like. Try different styles; decide how you want to uniquely present yourself. Always practice looking your best, whether your style is beach dude or conservative homemaker.

• **When I've taken style classes,** I studied pictures of styles that were flattering to me and learned what types of clothing suited me best. I have hired stylists to go shopping with me to teach me the clothing style and color foundations I needed to build my wardrobe. It has been a great help to me professionally to be able to present the exact picture of myself that was right for the occasion.

• **If your funds are limited,** go to resale stores, discount designer stores, department store sales and factory outlets. I have listed a few. There are also countless books available with stores and their locations. When buying clothes, the fabric and fit are most important. A student of mine said she never shopped because she didn't have money to buy clothes. She

473

had no idea what her size was, what current styles were up to date. You must educate yourself. Do lots of shopping and trying on, no buying. When you can afford to buy, you will know what and where to buy.

• **Consider the thought and money** that go into film wardrobes and you realize the importance of what you wear. Costume designers receive Academy Awards. When you are working on a production, see what tips you can pick up from the wardrobe design people. When I was shooting my first film—*First Love,* directed by Joan Darling—on location in Oregon, Donfeld (nominated for an Academy Award for *Prizzi's Honor)* took me shopping to show me what styles would be good for me. I still use the information I learned that day; basic rules don't change.

• **Angela Lansbury, film, stage and television star, said,** "I made peace with myself early and decided I was going to be a rare bird." She understood her style and image and capitalized on it. She started acting at age 16 and made all the transitions, carrying her image with her.

• **Costume Designer Linda Serijan-Fasmer created the wardrobe designs for the first season of** *Felicity.*

   • **Felicity was a bit of a wallflower the first season.** She wasn't supposed to be too sexy or adorable looking. But Keri Russell looked gorgeous in almost everything we tried on her. Body-conscious clothes showed off her size 0 figure, so it became apparent that not only her legs, but also her waist would have to be off-limits. She's an extra small so we bought mediums. Everything was oversized. Flattering colors lit up her face, which meant that colors had to be restrained—navy, rust, olive, and burgundy. Felicity's closet revolved around pants (Levi's 501s were her favorite, followed by Army surplus or Abercrombie & Fitch khakis and other straight-legged pants), cotton shirts and dozens and dozens of sweaters—textured, nubby cardigans, turtlenecks and crew necks in patterns and earth-colored solids.

   • **We bought every DKNY turtleneck made.** Man-style shirts from stores such as the Gap, Banana Republic and Nordstrom were usually not tucked in. Every single one was recut to look somewhere between fitted and baggy, but never with darts. Darts are too sexy. Her shoes were strictly utilitarian, either Converse navy sneakers or Birkenstock boots or sandals.

   • **Keri was also a stickler for character consistency.** She didn't want to wear anything with stretch or sheen or big, groovy collars. She didn't wear anything in her hair or paint her nails. When I bought her a stainless steel Swiss Army watch, she didn't think it was right. "It's like, too much."

- **Resident Advisor Noel Crane** (Scott Foley) wore Big Star, Lucky and Diesel jeans because they are most flattering to the rear end.

- *See Pictures and Resumes Section for clothes to wear on your shoot.*

- **Maude Feil, costumer, wardrobe stylist,** specializes in working with actors and actresses just starting to set their own style or in changing their style.

  - **I can put a man or woman together for about $1,000.** That includes my fee of $75 an hour. I know all the places downtown; I know where to get the look for less money. I work on commercials all the time and I'm used to staying within a budget. I can always work within your budget. There are just certain wardrobe pieces you have to have. I work with all shapes, sizes and ages. If a client needs special hair and/or makeup styling, I bring in someone from one of the network shows I work on, to consult with them. That would be an extra cost of around $150.

  - **I don't work with color charts myself;** I find it too confining. But many times a client will give me their book of colors and I work within those colors for them.

  - **One of my clients called me because he wasn't happy** with the roles he had been auditioning for, strictly senators. He wanted a broader range. He had an abundance of white hair and a very tailored conservative East-coast look. I went through his closet, picked out some things he could use, got rid of some of the Brooks Bros. shirts. We added some soft t-shirts and softer clothes, and I advised a buzz cut for his hair. He was very pleased, got new pictures and started auditioning for and landing a wider variety of roles.

  - **When I start working with someone, I get an idea of the look** they want to achieve, I pull magazine pictures, put them in a book. I'll look at their closet to see what they have. There is shopping, fittings, alterations, returns. I work with the client like I do when I am working for a director of a show.

- **Tom Baxter, Emmy-nominated wardrobe stylist, costume designer,** *Aldo Award* for "Most Influential Costumer in Fashion on Prime Time Television."

Q: What about audition clothes for the actor?

- **Let the dialogue in the script guide you.** For auditions, the actor should get the breakdown of the character from their agent and dress close to the person they are playing. For example:

- **Preppie, upwardly mobile, young male professional:** Go for the stereotype navy blue blazer, gray slacks, maybe a sweater vest with a tie and shirt, perhaps a crest on the blazer. A more casual look could be khaki pants, an oxford button-down shirt and a V-neck sweater. Visually, you need short to medium hair. If it says preppy and you have long hair, you might as well stay home, or wear a ponytail and tuck it in the back of your shirt.

- **A tough, over-the-hill broad:** if it's a comedy and the actress is busty, take advantage of that; a V-neck sweater and a pair of slacks with a big wide belt. She would be the girl sitting on a bar stool, 55 trying to look 35, with a cigarette hanging out of her mouth and a pink scarf tied around her neck. We did this exact look for an actress in *Pennies From Heaven*.

- **Upscale, trendy patron at an art museum:** For a woman 30-50, a suit would be nice; '40s gabardine styles obtained at resale or vintage stores. Guys in this setting can do it with a suit or khaki pants and a cotton blazer.

- **Men 21-50 with these few items can do anything.** A black blazer (sport coat), a navy blazer, one suit, a pair of khaki, grey, navy, black and white dress slacks. A business look with the suit, a nautical look with the blazer and white slacks (just stick a crest on the blazer on the pocket.) Put the black blazer with the black slacks and you have a black suit. The khakis with the black blazer and you have nice sporty look. Gray pants with the blue blazer you've got a nice business or preppy look.

- **Women's looks vary with their age.** 18-30 is one look, 30-50 is another look, and after 55 another look. Women need a rayon suit with a skirt. For the money, rayon looks and hangs the best and seems to be the easiest to alter. Make sure the skirt is a color that matches the jacket. Substitute a pair of slacks to make it more casual. A short or long black stretch evening dress for a young girl going up for sex-pot or modeling parts. Jeans, sweater or chambray shirt and sneakers. A sweatshirt for a housewife that lives next door. Secretary in a law firm, don't go in without a suit; you can always take the jacket off and put it on the back of the chair. It is a nice piece of business and something a secretary would do, unless you sit at the front desk—then it would stay on the whole time. Secretary in the car rental or super market manager's office: A skirt or a nice pair of slacks and blouse and cardigan or sweater vest. A tough secretary would wear jeans and sweater.

• **Gabrielle Zuccaro of Bleu Clothing** has advice for men's formal wear. My daughter Christina's husband Thomas Cobb is a graphic artist. One year he was nominated for an Emmy and of course needed to wear a tuxedo to the ceremony. Gabrielle told Christina not to rent one because, "they are awful." She said, "Buy one at a department store, have it altered to fit, then buy a beautiful black or dark gray shirt and a black tie. The black on black on black is a great look." It would serve an actor well to have good looking formal wear in his closet, you never know where you might be invited at a moment's notice and you can show up in "black tie" attire.

• **Illeana Douglas** (*Next Best Thing, Message in a Bottle, Grace of My Heart*) says she buys her t-shirts and sweaters in the children's department; "They fit much better."

• **The colors you wear** will determine how people perceive you, whether you look vibrant, washed out, cool or hot. This is valuable information when you are dressing to read for a specific role.

• **Have an expert or professional do your colors.** Your color consultant will hold different shades of all colors next to your face to see what looks best on you. Some color systems put people into four categories: fall, winter, spring or summer. Then there are variations within each season. (I'm a "gentle summer;" my husband is a "vibrant winter.") The expert will make an individualized color chart that you carry with you when shopping. If you stick to your color chart, you will be able to wear everything in your wardrobe mixed and matched; all your clothes will go together. This information will enable you to be a wise shopper and help minimize your expenses. Having your colors done is a one-time expense unless you change your hair color.

• **Know what your colors are.** It will make the difference between a photo that works and one that doesn't. You can help your professional makeup artist: When you sit in the makeup chair, describe what colors look best on you.

• **Jennifer Butler** has a unique way of achieving color and style harmony for her clients. She has created a system of personalized design and color analysis that draws upon her 4,000 swatch color system. She occasionally gives a free seminar on colors and style.

Q: Why are colors important?

- **How many times have you looked in your closet** and said, "I have nothing to wear!" even though you have a closet full of clothes. When you walk into a meeting, is your unspoken communication saying, "I'm approachable" or "Leave me alone!"? Do people think you are overpowering when your biggest challenge is overcoming shyness?

- **What may be a power color for one person** could signal romance in another. You can see what a dilemma this could cause. And if you send out the wrong messages, you may well be puzzled by other people's responses to you.

- **Have you ever noticed how one day** everyone you see tells you how great you look while on another day, you don't even get noticed? If you choose to wear clothes that are reflective of your personality and physical characteristics, you will experience more and more of those, "Gee, you look great" days. In fact, not only will those who see you notice how well you look but you, too, will see and feel the difference.

- **Color Consultant Jill Kirsh says:**

  - **People think having their colors done can be very limiting,** that they can only wear a few colors, but what you see when you have your colors done is that everyone can wear every color. It is just finding the shade of the color that works best for you.

  - **You need to find the right colors and shades, especially for headshots.** Actors don't realize how important the wardrobe is for a headshot. Certain colors mean different things. What you're wearing says a lot about who you are and sometimes that headshot is all a casting director or agent sees of you.

- **You can create different characters with the use of color.** When you have your colors done, you find out what colors make you look vibrant and alive, say for commercial auditions, but you also can create different effects for characters by using the wrong shade for you. What would you wear for a character that is out of step with the real world? For a trailer park resident? For a druggie? For a socialite? Homeless? Rich?

- **Tina Lynne, wardrobe stylist,** takes into account the color of your hair, eyes and skin though she doesn't adhere to a strict color palette. She believes everyone can wear certain shades of all colors.

Q: How do you dress a guy, 22-30, good looking, who has only worn jeans and t-shirts all of his life? What would it cost him to be "styled," including your fee and the clothes?

- **He will need a dressy look, a GQ look.** There is a great store called the Men's Warehouse. He can get a nice knock-off Italian suit that will make him look like a million bucks. Another basic sport coat, two pairs of pants, four shirts, four ties and one or two pairs of shoes, a nice belt, and he will look absolutely fabulous. The cost for the clothes might be $500. The cost for my services would be from $50 to $150 an hour, depending on where we have to go. For men, I also find the Beverly Center is a great place because they have hip looking, very Hollywood looking clothes. You don't have to get the name brands; you just have to know what looks good on you.

Q: How about an actress, thin, size 0-4, and 22 to 30, who doesn't know her image. How would you get her together for auditions?

- **When a woman walks into an audition,** she should be dressed for the part and comfortable with the type of person she's trying to portray. I coach them on how to wear the clothes and to project the image they want to sell. Depending on the build, the coloring and whether they have a hard or a soft look will determine whether we create a floral or a very simple kind of look.

- **Looking finished, put together, color coordinated** is probably one of the biggest keys in landing a role. Look at soap operas. When they decided to spend a great deal of money on the clothing, accessories, hair and sets, daytime TV changed forever and the ratings became huge.

- **If the client is on a budget,** I take them through Neiman Marcus and Saks Fifth Avenue so they can see what is available and what they like. That takes half an hour. Then I take them to a store that is reasonably priced and we match the look. You start with two skirts, two jackets, four tops, two pairs of shoes, one pants suit and two bags. You have one black dress. You can do this at a place like Ross or Loehmann's for $500, versus one Armani jacket for $1,000.

- **Loehmann's is a great place to start** because they have the more expensive clothing at a quarter of the price and you can get some fabulous basic clothes there. Jones of New York and Tahari (brands available at Macy's and Bloomingdale's) make some classy stuff that looks like Armani but is a quarter of the price. Marshall's and Ross are also good. You have to take the time to go through everything.

• **Dino Calabrese, clothing designer** and wardrobe, hair and makeup stylist, gives the following hints for actors with limited funds for clothes.

• **Thrift store shopping is great.**

• **Both men and women** should own: a pair of black slacks; a nice denim jacket, oversize so you can layer it; a pair of jeans; and a nice basic blazer, whether it's oversized or not, in rayon, not wool. Something in black is good and primary colors are good too. Combine colors, layer tank tops and t-shirts. Keep the same types of textures in your wardrobe; mix and match silks with lighter-weight rayons or cottons.

• **A basic skirt** should be gabardine or a lightweight fabric to wear with silk. Wear a t-shirt with the skirt and thick obi belt and you have a nice casual look.

• **Everyone should have a white shirt.** Plain form-fitting t-shirts can be worn under the shirt. Women need an A-line black dress. A pair of colored hose makes one outfit, belt it for another look, wear it as a tunic over a pair of bell-bottoms or pajama pants. A string of pearls works with a dress, sweater or t-shirt. Plain black boots with a medium heel to wear with skirts and pants are a necessity. Same with men—basic black boot; wear with tuxedo or jeans. Always keep shoes cleaned and shined and clothes pressed.

• **Take t-shirts**, skirts and jackets all in the same fabrics but different colors to mix and match. Use blue, green and yellow and tie it together with a multicolored belt and you look great but if the texture's off, it doesn't work.

Resources

To download and print an updated version of this and all resource lists, go to actingiseverything.com.

IMAGE MAKERS
Wardrobe consultants and Image Makers are listed in The Working Actor's Guide (WAG) and trade ads.

Bleu Clothing, owned by Gabrielle Zuccaro, 323/939-2228, bleuclothing.com, 454 S. La Brea, Los Angeles. Open 11-8 M-Sa., 11-6 Su. Bleu is one of the Editor's Picks in the book, *Where To Wear L.A. Shopping Guide.* My daughters are wild about her clothes and her eye for design. Cathy Kerr was at the Oscars one year, all over the red carpet and on all the pre-show cameras. Gabrielle had styled her, including what makeup to wear and what to do with her hair. She looked great, easily competing with the women who had spent many thousands of dollars. Gabrielle will help you find your own personal style. Twice a year she holds not-to-be-missed sales. Get on her mailing list and check out the website for new design arrivals.

Jill Kirsh's, The Color Company, 818/760-7798. jillkirshcolor.com. $300 for individual color consultation. Group rates available. Featured in *L.A. Magazine, The Best of L.A. List* as the best color consultant. Jill is known as "Hollywood's Guru of Hue." She drapes you with all the colors and picks out the shades of each color that are best for you, making a swatch book for you to carry. She helps actors choose the right colors for headshots and audition clothes; she will go to your place and look through your closet. She has developed her own makeup line and included in the fee, does your makeup showing you the shades that are right for you.

Jennifer Butler, Color and Wardrobe Expert, 323/931-2626, jenniferbutlercolor.com. 25 years experience in the art of color and design. She offers extensive services and is an expert on your whole image. She has introductory free seminars each month. She does wardrobe consultations, color palette design, shopping excursions and wardrobe classes. Check out her website which outlines her many excellent services. Very highly recommended. Why not check out her free seminar, you will gain new knowledge.

Deborah Gordon, Flying Colors, 818/784-2939. Wonderful color palettes. She creates quite a spectacular color notebook for your use. Call her studio for full information on her services.

Maude Feil, 310/545-0882. She helps you update your look by putting together the best outfits, be it for headshots, auditions, etc. She will rearrange your closets so you won't have to wonder what goes with what; go shopping with you; in fact, she will shop and bring you the things to try on and return what doesn't fit or you don't like. It is more expensive that way, but working actors often don't have the time to shop. She charges $150 for initial consultation and then $75 an hour. She says she can work with people's budgets.

Tina Lynne, Style Consultant, 323/939-9117. A specialist in the complete makeover, she can put you together from the inside out. She loves new actors and people new to town and is willing to work within a fairly small budget. Says she shops all the time and knows what is out there in the stores.

Web Newsletter Best Bargains Suzanne Conner, bargainsla.com. Only the highest quality of bargains. Subscribe to the free email bargain newsletter at the website.

SERVICES

• CLOTHING DESIGN

Shawnelle Eveningwear, 310/230-2032. She specializes in costume design for feature films and evening gowns for award shows. Gowns average $800 and up. She also does consultations for auditions and specializes in character development through wardrobe. By appointment only.

• ALTERATIONS AND CLEANERS

5 Star Cleaners & Laundry, 818/506-8960. 4356 Laurel Canyon Blvd., Studio City, 91604. M-F 6:30-7; Sa 8-4. Great service and great prices! Alterations.

Suke at Beachwood Cleaners & Laundry, 323/467-0021. 2699 N. Beachwood Dr., Hollywood Hills, 90068. Great cleaning, fast alterations and inexpensive.

International Custom Tailors, 818/509-9032. 12075 Ventura Pl., Studio City, 91604. Good prices. Kenny and Karin can alter just about anything beautifully. They are great people.

Studio 1 Hour Cleaners, 818/505-0828. 11302 Ventura Blvd. at Eureka, across from Bally's, Studio City, 91604. $1.50 per item. Surprisingly good work. Very good alterations.

• EYEGLASSES

Oliver Peoples, 310/657-2553. oliverpeoples.com. 8642 W Sunset Blvd., L.A., 90069. The absolute best in eyeglasses. You really can tell the difference. They are very expensive but guaranteed and they will fix them up if they get twisted or broken. I love mine and will always have a pair. Their non-glare coating is really the best.

Westside Opticians, 323/653-0243. 363 S. Fairfax Ave., L.A., 90046. M,Tu,Th 10-6; F 9-5; Sa 9-1; closed W&Su. The best styles for good prices. Jeff can fix anything.

Happy Eyes, 818/246-2202. happyeyesoptical.com. 114 E. Wilson Ave., Glendale, 91206. Recommended in Suzanne Best Bargains, Tony the owner is very helpful. Great bargains and great styles.

• SHOE REPAIR

Sunset Shoe Repair, Manuel Keshishian, 323/654-7743. 8036 Santa Monica Blvd., L.A., 90046. (Crescent Heights & Santa Monica) "We rebuild your shoes like new." There has never been a shoe or purse problem this man couldn't fix for me.

Garbo Shoe Repair, 310/394-6306. 1450 4th St. at Broadway, Santa Monica, 90401. Very reasonably priced. "If your shoes are uncomfortable, he won't let you out of here until he's got the pad just right."

• LUGGAGE SALES AND REPAIRS

Beverly Hills Luggage, 310/273-5885, beverlyhillsluggage.com. 404 N. Beverly Dr., Beverly Hills, 90210. Expensive but great.

H. Savinar Luggage, 323/938-2501. savinarluggageonline.com. 4625 W. Washington Blvd. between Crenshaw and LaBrea, L.A., 90016. Valley store: 818/703-1313. 6931 Topanga Canyon Blvd., Canoga Park, 91303. 30%-50% off Tumi, Hartmann, Boyt, etc. Also replacement hardware.

Langer's Luggage Shop & Handbag Hospital, 323/512-4710. langersdiscountluggage. com. 7447 W Sunset Blvd. L.A., 90046. The best; they can fix anything. If you ever have luggage damage at the airport, report it, then take it straight to Langers; they take care of everything.

Luggage 4 Less, 818/760-1360. luggage4less.com. 5144 Lankershim Blvd. near Magnolia, North Hollywood, 91601. Do not buy luggage until you check this place out.

• WIGS

JJ Wigs of Hollywood, (men and women) 323/466-0617. 6324 Hollywood Blvd., L.A., 90028. Rent a wig for photo shoots for $25 or $29 and they will style it and put it on you. They have wigs to buy for as little as $35. You can get a good one for $60-$70. The real hair and hand-tied ones go for up to $250.

Naimie's Beauty Center. 818/655-9933. naimies.com. 12640 Riverside Dr. North Hollywood, 91607. Discounts for actors.

Wilshire Wigs, 800/927-0874. wilshirewigs.com. 5241 Craner Avenue, North Hollywood, 91601. M-F 9-5:30; Sa 9-4. One block east of Vineland, off Magnolia.

TRENDY/UPSCALE/RESALE/VINTAGE/THRIFT SHOPS

The Ultimate Consignment & Thrift Store Guide, consignmentguide.com. Many links to other shopping information all over the country.

Aardvark's Odd Ark, (men & women) 323/655-6769. 7579 Melrose Ave., 90046. M-Th 12-8; F-Sa 11-9; Su 12-7. Other location: 310/392-2996. 85 Market St., Venice, 90291. Every day 11-7. Vintage and regular clothes.

Armani Wells, (men) 818/985-5899. armaniwells.com. 12404 Ventura Blvd., Studio City, 91604. M-Sa 11-6; Su 12-6. The best for men. This is the place for you to go. She knows how to style you.

American Rag, (men & women) 323/935-3154. 150 S. La Brea Ave., L.A., 90036. M-Sa 10-9; Su 12-7.

Baba, (women) 310/360-9494. 517 N. La Cienega Blvd., West Hollywood, 90048. Custom couture, exquisite fabrics, and warm salon. Custom prices start at $350.

Cherie, (women) 818/508-1628. 12526 Ventura Blvd., Studio City, 91604. T-Sa 10-5. Very upscale designer clothes on consignment.

Claudia's Boutique, (men, women & children) 818/980-3473. 11930 Ventura Blvd., Studio City, 91604. M-Sa 10:30-7; Su 12-5. Really packed in tight, but she seems to know where everything is.

Collectible Glitz-Miss La De Da's, 818/347-9343. 21435 Sherman Way, Canoga Park, 91303. One block west of Canoga Ave. M-Tu 10-5; Th-Sa 10-6; Su 12-5. The greatest and best priced vintage jewelry in L.A., many believe. Huge selection available with jewelry arranged by color and type. Specializes in vintage jewelry, costume jewelry and sterling silver. A little new modern jewelry is also available.

Council Thrift Shops, (men and women), ncjwla.org. 310/477-9613, 11571 Santa Monica Blvd., L.A., 90025. 323/938-8122, 1049 S. Fairfax Ave., L.A., 90019. 818/997-8980, 14526 Victory Blvd., Van Nuys, 91411. 323/652-2080, 455 N Fairfax Ave, L.A., 90036. 310/572-9158, 12120 Venice Blvd, L.A., 90066. 310/360-6505, 8520 W Pico Blvd., L.A., 90035. 310/452-2421, 850 Pico Blvd., Santa Monica, 90405. 818/710-7206, 21716 Sherman Way, Canoga Park, 91303. This is one of my favorites, really good brands at low cost. Excellent men's sport coats and suits. They will pick up your donations. They provide clothes for homeless women and children.

Fashion Institute of Los Angeles (FIDM) Scholarship Store, (men and women) 213/624-1200. fidm.com. 919 S. Grand Ave., L.A., 90015. M-F 9-6; Sa 10-4. The institute operates a year-round fund-raiser to support their scholarship programs. Local manufacturers and retailers donate new merchandise, some quality, some irregulars and the public is invited for some excellent bargains.

Great Labels, 310/451-2277. greatlabels.com. 1126 Wilshire Blvd., Santa Monica, 90401. M-F 10-7; Sa 10-6; Su 12-5. 11th and 12th parking in rear of building.

Iguana Vintage Clothing, (Men and women) 818/907-6716. iguanaclothing.com. 14422 Ventura Blvd., Sherman Oaks, 91403. 323/462-1010, 6320 Hollywood Blvd., Hollywood, 90028. Styles of the '40s, '50s and '60s. M-F 11-7, Sa 11-8, Su 11-6 for both stores. This is a huge store, very organized. Great shopping.

It's A Wrap! (men & women) 818/567-7366. tvclothes.com. 3315 W. Magnolia Blvd. Burbank, 91505. M-F 11-8; Sa-Su 11-6. Large busy store; they have a lot of clothes from the film and television industry. Definitely a place to take people visiting from your hometown.

Jet Rag, 323/939-0528. 825 N. La Brea Ave., L.A., 90038. M-Sa. 11:30-8. They have everything from every era. For current and vintage styles. Winona Ryder, Juliette Lewis and Drew Barrymore have been known to stop in.

Junk for Joy, (men & women) 818/569-4903. junkforjoy.com. 3314 W. Magnolia Blvd., Burbank, 91505. Tu-Sa 12-5. New and used vintage fashions, footwear & accessories. Kimonos, junk jewelry, gloves, bow ties, spats, hats and eyeglasses. Silly and ugly clothing of good and bad taste.

P.J. London, (women) 310/826-4649. pjlondon.com. 11661 San Vicente Blvd., Brentwood, 90049. M-Sa 10:30-6; Su 12-5. Highest fashion, lowest prices for clothes.

The Paper Bag Princess, 310/385-9036. thepaperbagprincess.com. 8818 Olympic Blvd., Beverly Hills, 90211. Very upscale; shoppers are said to be: Elle MacPherson, Shalom Harlow, Demi Moore, Elisabeth Shue, Parker Posey, Courtney Love, Madonna, Sofia Coppola, Jennifer Nicholson. Puccis, Pradas, Guccis, prices range from $25 to $6,000.

Pasadena City College Flea Market, 626/585-7906. pasadena.edu/fleamarket/. 1570 E. Colorado Blvd. at S. Hill Ave., Pasadena, 91106. 8-3 on first Sunday of the month. Like garage sales, it's free and showcases a somewhat haphazard mix of merchandise, offered by established circuit dealers and casual sellers who strew goods on the ground. The market is in four sections, three along the S. Hill Ave. side of the campus and the fourth off Bonnie Ave.

Polka Dots & Moonbeams Vintage Wear, 323/651-1746. polkadotsandmoonbeams. com. 8367 W. 3rd St., L.A., 90048 . Great vintage and funky new clothes for women. Great selection of vintage hats, bags, jewelry too. Lots of celebs.

Ragtime Cowboy, 818/769-6552. 5213 Lankershim Blvd., North Hollywood, 91601. Vintage clothing & costumes. This is one of the first vintage clothing stores in NoHo.

Ragtime on Green, 626/796-9924. 1136 E. Green St., Pasadena. Tu-Sa 10-6, Su 11-4. Jammed with inventory with low prices. Brand names, also.

Reel Clothes, (men and women) 818/951-7692. reelclothes.com. Used to have a store location but now does business exclusively over the Internet. Clothes that are returned from film and television sets. I have good luck with men's clothes here.

Repeat Performance, (men & women), 323/938-0609. 318 N. La Brea Ave., L.A., 90038. By appt. only. Fine vintage clothing and accessories in perfect condition. Specializing in '40s & '50s attire. No Rentals.

Rose Bowl Flea Market, 323/560-7469. Rose Bowl Dr., Pasadena. More than 1,500 vendors. Second Sunday of every month.

The AdDress Boutique (women), 310/394-1406. theaddressboutique.com. 1116 Wilshire Blvd., Santa Monica, 90401. M-Sa 10-6; Su 12-5. Clothes from very wealthy women who can't be seen in the same outfit twice, plus new clothes.

DISCOUNT SHOPS

Citadel Factory Outlet Stores, 323/888-1724. citadeloutlets.com. Right off the I-5, Los Angeles. From I-5 southbound, exit at Washington Blvd. From I-5 northbound, exit at Atlantic Blvd. North. M-Su 10-8. 44 stores. Ann Taylor, Geoffrey Beene, Bass, Eddie Bauer, United Colors of Benetton and many others.

DNA, 310/399-0341. dnaclothing.com. 411 Rose Ave., Venice, 90291. 323/882-8464, 7519 Sunset Blvd., L.A., 90046. For jeans and t-shirts, everything from Calvin Klein to Point Zero, for less. Huge discounts on Joseph jeans, Big Star jeans, Weaver's soft cotton loose-fitting t-shirts, etc.

Dressed Up!, 818/708-7238. dressed-up.com. 6000 Reseda Blvd., Tarzana. M-Sa. 10-6; Sun. 11-4:30. "L.A.'s only evening wear superstore." Designer dresses, cocktail suits, formal gowns and evening separates.

Loehmann's, 310/659 0674. loehmanns.com. 333 S. La Cienega, 90048. Just south of 3rd St. and across from the Beverly Center. M-Sa 10-9; Su 11-7. This is where Tina Lynne brings her image clients that are on a budget.

Marshall's, 888/Marshalls. marshallsonline.com. Call for store locations and complete information.

Marrika Nakk, 323/882-8278. marrikanakk.com. Very romantic, beautiful clothes. Call and get on her phone list and they will call to tell you of their sometime sales at her house in West Hollywood. Fabulous bargains!

Nordstrom Rack, (men, women & children) 818/884-6771. nordstrom.com. 21490 Victory Blvd., Woodland Hills, 91367. M-F 10-9; Sa 10-8; Su 11-7. Plus other locations. You can find real treasures here.

Rick Pallack, (men only) 818/789-7000. At time of printing, Sherman Oaks store had closed and they were looking for larger digs. Phone message provides updated information. They dress all the stars and design movie wardrobes. Twice a year they have a huge sale. Take advantage of looking like you are a successful actor.

Sichel Promotional Sportswear, 818/255-0862. sichel.net. 10847 Sherman Way, Burbank, 91352. They make many of the T-shirts, caps and jackets for film and TV crews. About two weeks before Christmas they put a couple of racks on the sidewalk filled with the left overs. They are a steal, relatives back home love to get these treasures. M-F 9-5.

COSTUMES AND PERIOD CLOTHES
RENTAL AND SALES

CRC Costume Rentals Corporation. Rental only. 818/753-3700. costumerentalscorp. com. 11149 Vanowen St., North Hollywood, 91605. Huge! Uniforms/research library, check them out.

Glendale Costumes, 818/244-1161. thecostumeshoppe.net. 746 W. Doran St., Glendale, 91203. Tu-Sa 10-6. Good prices.

Hollywood Toys & Costumes, 323/465-4444. hollywoodtoys.com. 6600 Hollywood Blvd., Hollywood, 90028. 4 blks. E. of Highland. M-Sa 9:30-7; Su 10:30-7. They have a huge selection.

Magic World Costuming, 818/700-8100. 10122 Topanga Canyon Blvd., Chatsworth, 91311. M-Sa 9-6.

Western Costume Co., Rental only, 818/760-0900. westerncostume.com. 11041 Vanowen St, North Hollywood, 91605. M-F 8:30-6. Probably the most famous and most expensive. They have everything you could possibly need.

Hair Stylists,
Manicurists and Waxing

For makeup stylists, eyebrows and makeup resources see Section Two, Makeup Artists.

• **As an actor, how you look** has a great deal to do with getting your career moving. You need a hair stylist who can be trusted to deliver your hair the way you want it each and every time. Sometimes you are hired for a role two or three months ahead of time and the director expects you to show up looking the same as when they hired you. You want a hair stylist who will please you if you are maintaining a look, as well as contribute their own ideas on how to develop the unique "you" to the fullest. Cultivate your relationship with this most valuable person on your team of personal professionals.

• **Fernando De Jesus of the West End Salon talks about hair:**

  • **It is important to have the right look** when showing up for a casting call. Style, shape and color should be current with today's fashion world. The product you could sell or the series you could star in partly relies on your look. Updating your image can make the difference in a director casting you for the role that may have gone to someone else.

  • **A step beyond the new haircut is the color.** Not only can it highlight your features but it can actually change your image to comic, that zany redhead! You can be as subtle as going from mousey brown to golden brunette. Take a good look at who is making it and ask yourself. "Does their look play a big part in their success?" "Yes!"

Stan Vogel (aka Red), one of my favorite hair stylists, comments:

  • **If there's anything constant,** it's the change on a man's head of hair. Whether he likes it or not it thins out, he loses it, the hairline changes, grey starts coming in. Men aren't that knowledgeable about what hair can do, so they need a lot more instruction. They might appear to be easier to deal with, but it's hard for them to accept change. Women are more adaptable. Culturally, it's cooler for women to color their hair, and we're getting there as far as men go; there is progress.

- **Attitude is everything. You can wear your hair the way you want,** as long as you have the right attitude about yourself. Barbra Streisand does all kinds of things with her hair and none of it is really right, but it's right because she's got the right attitude. If you're not satisfied within, it doesn't matter what you do on the exterior. All's fair in love and hair!

Resources

To download and print an updated version of this and all resource lists, go to actingiseverything.com.

The following professional hair stylists work with men and women.

STYLISTS AND SALONS

Stan Vogel (aka Red) at Louis Michael Salon, 310/275-1322. 413 N. Canon Dr., Beverly Hills, 90210. A good guy, never runs late, never cuts too much, very talented in all areas of hair work, a color expert. I love the highlighting he does for me and when I was a redhead, he kept it the perfect red. He blows hair really straight. Because I have curly hair, this is important to me; not everyone can do it. He's fun and easy to be with. *See his comments above.*

Ladi Labidi at Nick Chavez Salon, 310/247-1838, email: theladi@gmail.com, 9032 Burton Way, Beverly Hills 90211. Very highly regarded stylist who has worked with a number of celebrities. His work has also appeared on a number of shows from *Oprah* to *Home Shopping Network.* He has worked for the past 15 years as the key hair stylist with renowned local headshot photographer Kevyn Major Howard. Ladi's hair styling fee for headshots is $95 and he will remain on set for any touch-ups that need to be done during the shoot, $25 extra for any extreme changes. Truly one of the best in the business. *See Judy Kerr's shots taken by Kevyn Major Howard in the Photo section and on the back cover.*

Fernando De Jesus, The West End Salon, 310/855-0048. 520 N. La Cienega Blvd., West Hollywood, 90048. Fernando is from London; he specializes in corrective hair coloring. Beautiful custom stylized work. One of my students took in a magazine cover picture of Elizabeth Hurley to match the color and style; she got beautiful results. *See Suzanne Wallace Whayne's shots taken by Robert Raphael in the Photo section.*

Object Beauty Shop, 323/852-0978. 8237 W. Third St., L.A., 90048, at Sweetzer. Cuts start at $45. My daughters, long-haired Cathy Kerr and thin-haired Cynthia Kerr, love Hiroshi (his cuts start at $45 for men and $55 for women); he never cuts too short and you don't have to wait a long time for an appointment. Cynthia loves his special highlights. They rave about the massage shampoos. Hiroshi is a surfer so if you love the ocean you'll love this shop.

Anne Dutton at Shadow Hills Hair Salon, 818/415-4158. 9749 Wheatland Avenue, Shadow Hills, 91040. (A funky little shop way off the beaten track) $35 for a cut and style. Acting coach Anita Jesse says, "Anne listens more effectively than anyone I have ever had cut my hair; if she can deal with my hair she's a genius." Anita's hair looks great. This seems out of the way but it's not far—it's horse country and there is a great country coffee shop across the street. Makes you feel like you're in Texas.

Art Luna, 310/450-7168, 2116 Main St., Santa Monica 90405. Cuts and color, $150 and up. Clientele includes Claire Dane, Kelly Lynch and Candice Bergen.

Barber Shop Club, 323/939-4319. 6907 Melrose Ave., West Hollywood. Hot-towel shaves, shoe shines and games of chess. Listen to jazz while getting a haircut. Shaquille O'Neil, David Arquette and Vince Vaughn all are clients. *Featured on dailycandy.com.*

Brenda Ferreira at Studio B, owner/stylist, 310/395-8025. 1512 11th Street, Suite 206, Santa Monica, 90405. All services. She can be very trendy, if you want that. She will teach you how to style and manage the hairstyle she gives you. Her background is as an image consultant for men and women. She is good to talk to about how you look and how you would like to look. Great with men. $30 consultation fee.

Byron Studio, 310/276-4470. 407 North Robertson Blvd., Beverly Hills. Small, three-chair, Zen-like studio offering haircuts, styling, color and makeup. Byron Williams has styled Rene Russo, Sharon Stone, Salma Hayek, Kirsten Dunst and Robin Wright Penn. *Featured on dailycandy.com.*

Colin Booker, 310/657-9172. Works privately through referrals. He works on many film and television productions. Specializes in makeovers and redesigning your whole "look." Very highly recommended by actress/coach, Caryn West.

Julia Clay, 323/633-7328. Private and makes house calls. Highly recommended by stylist/facialist Tina Lynne. She is known for her transition free highlights and her unharsh custom coloring. She is an artist in all of her hair work. Reasonable prices, complimentary consultation.

Justin Anderson of the Neal George Salon. 310/275-2808, 9320 Civic Center Dr., Beverly Hills, 90210. My daughter, Chris Kerr, loves how he works with her curly hair and keeps the blonde highlights real. Many celebrities have been seen there, including Jennifer Aniston and Britney Spears.

Elements Spa and Salon, 323/933-0212, 110 S. Fairfax Ave. (Farmer's Market Place), Los Angeles, 90036. Richard Dalton was the official hairdresser to Diana, Princess of Wales for ten years. Providing glamour and the highest levels of service in a discreet, sleek environment. *Featured on dailycandy.com.*

Linda Kammins' Aromatherapy Salon, 310/659-6257, lindakammins.com, 848 N. La Cienega Blvd., Suite 204, Los Angeles, 90069. Th-Sa 11-6. Hair cut, hair balancing is $75, aromatherapy fresh hair oil treatment is $55. Services: Hair balancing, free-hand hair painting, natural enzyme coloring, botanical coloring, two-process coloring, fresh aromatherapy hair and scalp oil treatments, hair loss treatment, herbal facials and all-natural Linda Kammins Aromatherapy Products.

Luke O'Conner/ Owner of the Lukaro Salon, 310/275-2536. Lukaro.com. 323 N. Beverly Drive, Beverly Hills, 90210. Brittani Taylor's favorite hairstylist, he does Debra Messing as well as Brooke Shields, and a slew of other celebrities. Brittani says, "He is such a nice guy, full of energy, and he works magic on my curly hair."

Mauro, 310/273-0600, maurohair.com, 421 N. Rodeo Drive, Rodeo Collection, Beverly Hills, 90210. Consultation on a new look, 30 minutes, $65. Prices can be found on the website. Reasonable. My friend, Samantha Harper, has been loving his work for years. He does many celebrities as well as new actors just creating their individual "look." He has developed a great product line, as well.

Mijo Hair Studio, 323/822-2970. 8450 Santa Monica Blvd., West Hollywood, 90069. Tu-Sa 10-6. $25 for men's haircuts and $45 for women's haircut and blow-dry. They specialize in actors and models. Joe can blow curly hair dry to poker straight if you want it. Besides all of her great styling services, Mindy is an expert in color. For many years, she was the assistant to the top Beverly Hills guy. The prices are reasonable and these are nice people. Of course they do everything else, but love their specialties.

Pingatore Vern Salon, 323/932-8376. 7961 W. Third Street, Los Angeles. Enter from Edinburgh Ave. and go up the outdoor staircase. Gene Forget for men and women's great haircuts and expert color work in a low-key environment. Reasonable prices. Steven Nash says, "Gene is a skilled artist and cares a lot. He is sensitive to your special showbiz needs."

Quy Phu Nguyen of Empire Salon, 949/261-5856. 2967 Michelson, Suite K, Irvine, 92612. Monday thru Friday. Robin Gee says, "Quy gives great contemporary, fashionable haircuts that are easy to manage and to do yourself. He has a good sense of trends and being current. He listens to what you want, but always has great ideas of his own for you to consider."

Carlton's Hair Salon, 818/986-8750, carltonhair.com, 14006 Riverside Dr., #249, Sherman Oaks, in Fashion Square Mall. Hair cuts start at $50. Highly recommended by makeup artist Rita Montanez.

U Salon, 310/204-4995. 1772 S. Robertson Blvd., Los Angeles. Has both junior and senior stylists and prices vary depending upon which you work with. Cut and blow dry is $31-$53 depending on hair length. To blow long hair straight is $18-$37. Highlights are $65-$120. This is a wonderful place to save money and get the latest fashion updates. Owned by Umberto's of Beverly Hills. I understand that the creme of the crop hair stylists work here developing their skills so they can move up to Umbertos. My friends Elizabeth Beim and Linda Small love it. I've heard nothing but raves about this place and they are open on Sundays and Mondays—seven days a week.

Sheri Veges, 310/822-1367, hairlocs.com. For hair extensions. I've seen them and they are fabulous. They last until you cut them out.

RECOMMENDED STYLISTS FOR HEADSHOTS

Rita Montanez, 818/509-5733. makeupbyrita.com. Hair and makeup: $125 for a general shoot. I've worked with her many times. Besides being available for your photo shoot, she gives private lessons in how to do your own makeup. Private lesson is $150 and last about 1-2 hours. Rita works with many photographers. *See Judy Kerr's shots taken by David Carlson and Kevin McIntyre in the Photo section.*

Laura Connelly, 310/473-3355. Makeup and hair. $100 and up, depending on time and locations, for a general photo shoot. She likes to stay the whole shoot to keep an eye on the hair and makeup for the photographer. She specializes in natural, pretty makeup that really enhances one's own unique beauty. I loved the way Laura styled my hair for Michael's shots so I hired her to teach me how to do it. She showed me, then had me do it myself with my own equipment. *See Judy Kerr's and Denise George's shots taken by Michael Hiller and Suzanne Wallace Whayne's shots taken by David LaPorte in the Photo section.*

Elke Von Freudenberg, 323/525-1429. makeup.gq.nu. Hair and makeup for headshots is $95 in studio and $150 on location. Eyelash application is $10. Elke has worked in the industry for over 15 years and has done makeup for several celebrities and special events, including the Emmy's and the MTV Movie Awards. *See Brittani Taylor's shots taken by Jeffrey Nicholson in the Photo section.*

Anacia Kagan, 818/749-6644. $125-$200 per session. Anacia has worked with photographers as a hair and makeup artist for over 13 years. She has developed techniques to help compensate for any type of lighting. She says it's important to, "create light with your face." Her specialty is helping clients create a character without going over the top. *See Caryn West's shots taken by Ray Bengston in the Photo section.*

Stefanie Keenan, 310/309-7828. stefaniekeenan.com. Photographer who includes hair and makeup in her session fee of $300. Stefanie prefers a simple, natural look with her photos and holds the same philosophy to hair and makeup. *See Brittani Taylor's shots taken by Stefanie in the Photo section.*

Shawn Flint Blair, 323/856-6105. makeupbyshawn.com. $150 and she stays the whole shoot, approximately two hours. A true artist, she works in all media (video, film, photography, commercials). Shawn says, "I work with each client, giving them the look they want with makeup and hair. The only thing I do not offer is blow drying hair straight; I use a straight iron for that." She works with photographers doing promotional shots, head shots, catalogues, music, etc. Available for private lessons, $150 about an hour and a half. There is a FREE step-by-step makeup lesson on her website plus many other features including before and after shots. Also private sessions for any occasion including weddings, special events, award shows, etc. She is a professional photo retoucher as well. Samples are on her website. artist2design.com. *See Brittani Taylor's shots taken by Shawn in the Photo section.*

Mitzi Druss, 323/376-3666. mitzidruss.com. Prices vary depending upon the job. Mitzi has over 15 years experience doing hair and makeup for film, television, print and theatre. Her specialties include personal styling, period work and light special effects. She is also a certified skin care specialist and a stand up comic. *See Suzanne Wallace Whayne's shots taken by Mary Ann Halpin in the Photo section.*

Meredith Cross, 818/406-2735. Works with photographer Diana Lannes. Trained in doing hair and makeup for headshots, still shoots, commercials, television promos, music videos and films in Los Angeles and Colorado. Encourages a relaxed environment for enhancing an actor's natural beauty. *See Denise George's shots taken by Diana Lannes in the Photo section.*

Dawn Mattocks, 323/251-3305. makeupwithmattocks.com, festquest.com/dawn_m. Makeup and hair $85 (up to $150 for two looks). Graduate of Otis Parson School of Design with over 15 years experience as a makeup artist. Has worked on several projects and special events, including TV shows, music videos and commercials. *See Brittani Taylor's shots taken by Rich Hogan in the Photo section.*

Colette Taber, 818/749-8997. illuminatedbride.com. Works with photographer Mark Husmann. Prices start at $150. Has over 18 years of experience doing hair and makeup for headshots, celebrities and advertising work. A true professional with an emphasis on natural beauty. *See Denise George's shots taken by Mark Husmann in the Photo section.*

Victorio, 213/949-2534. Works at Sephora on Hollywood and Highland. 323/462-6898. Hair and makeup is $150-$450. Several years of experience in the business, working with celebrities and beginning actors alike. He says, "I hate the word 'client.' When I work with someone, I tell them I can be their brother or their sister. I work with them and make them comfortable." *See Caryn West's shots taken by Mark Bennington in the Photo section.*

MANICURISTS AND WAXING

Chinoiseri, 818/752-4347. 12246 Ventura Blvd., Studio City. Sharon Stone says, "Tammie Ly will create any nail color polish you want."

Esfir Tselner of Esther's Place, 310/274-4552. 9399 Wilshire, #205, at Canon Drive. Hair removal. Legs and bikini lines, $40. "My customers tell me I don't hurt them as much as other people do."

Yolanda Frye Skin Care, 310/275-3981. 632 ½ Doheny Dr., West Hollywood, 90069. She does manicures, pedicures and acrylics. Cathy Kerr and Chris Kerr love her manicures. Cathy often has a manicure and pedicure when returning from a long, exhausting business trip; it perks her right up. Waxing, men and women. Also offers facials and other skin care treatments.

WORKOUTS, EXERCISE AND DANCE

• **All actors need some type** of body movement class at least twice a week for body awareness, five times a week to change their bodies. The purpose of exercise is to become acquainted with every muscle and tendon. Acting is physical work, and if you don't know your body, you are denying a great many tools that could be available to you.

• **Working as an actor has a lot to do with how you look,** your weight, your health, discipline and stamina. There is no way to get around building your body and staying toned. If you don't have a steady, consistent work out program you will probably not be a working actor.

• **Glenn Close,** when talking about doing the stage play *Sunset Boulevard,* made these comments.

> • **It takes a great deal of stamina to do a play.** If I didn't do something physical every day, I wouldn't be able to make it through the show. You know those stairs you see me climbing? There are just as many stairs offstage that I climb to get to those stairs. I do a yoga class for forty-five minutes before each show. We do five shows each weekend. When working, I don't smoke or drink and eat very, very healthy. I have this policy that I can have two Oreos each performance. One of the things that gets me through the weekend is that I know I can have four Oreos on Saturday and four on Sunday.

• **Michael Richards,** who played Kramer on *Seinfeld,* introduced me to the practice of yoga. He is in such great shape, he can make his body do anything. In addition to his hour daily practice, he does a half hour of restorative yoga positions before each performance. Yoga enables him to do all of his physical comedy and not get hurt. He practices on his own, but when he takes a class it's at the B.K.S. Iyengar Yoga Institute.

• **Jerry Seinfeld** loves to exercise. Swimming, weights, treadmill, Nordic track and some yoga stretching before and after his workouts. During *Seinfeld,* he worked with a trainer at 6:30AM. Jerry had a very tough schedule. Along with writing, casting, acting, editing, and promoting *Seinfeld* (of course with a talented, accomplished staff) he still got in his meditation and exercise.

• **So dance, fence, run, lift weights, practice yoga,** anything that requires precision movements. Going to classes and the gym are good places to meet other actors and people in the biz who might have information about acting jobs. Your DVD player or VCR can help too. There are a lot of good exercise videos for sale or rent. You can also record workout television shows.

• **Personal trainer Rady Ouzounova answers the follow questions about getting and staying in shape.** DISCLAIMER: This information is not intended to replace the advice of health care professionals, nor is it intended to provide medical advice on personal health matters, which should be obtained directly from a physician.

Q: What is your background and qualifications for being a personal trainer?

> • Discovered by Neshka Robeva, one of the top gymnastic trainers in the world, I was on her exclusive team. Then accepted into the Bulgarian Olympic National Team, which led to my participation in international competitions. I am certified by the IFPA (International Fitness Professionals Association) as a personal trainer and gymnastics instructor.

Q: What is the best way to lose weight?

> • **To lose weight, we need to burn more calories than we consume.** A safe diet should **never** dip below 1,200 calories a day. It is most important to take into account your body type and size when determining your caloric intake. Consult with me or your health or fitness provider about what is best for you.

> • **An efficient program includes slow weight loss with diet** combined with regular exercise on a daily basis. This will help your body to adjust to your new weight more easily. Eat small, healthy meals, 4-5 times a day. This helps to speed up your metabolism and burn more calories. Most importantly, **DO NOT STARVE YOURSELF!** Waiting too long between meals can cause problems because the next time you eat, your body will hold on to more calories, believing that it needs them to sustain itself until your next meal.

> • **Centers for Disease Control** has charts that you can use to determine healthy levels for you. Body Mass Index: BMI for Adults: cdc.gov/nccdphp/dnpa/bmi/bmi-adult.htm. Your body type is individual to you. But BMI should factor into this so that you can be sure that you are within the healthy limits.

Q: What is a good eating plan for health and to build good muscles?

- **The best plan is one that includes the five food groups:** milk and dairy; meat, poultry, fish and alternative protein; vegetables; fruit; bread, cereal and grains. Depending on your specific health and diet needs, you should consume specific amounts of each group daily. Beware of fad diets that insist that you completely eliminate any of these groups, as you can do damage to your body, and defeat the purpose of the diet.

Q: What about when you are on location and the food offered may not be the healthiest or calorie conscious? What would be the best way to choose your food then?

- **One of the actor's biggest enemies on set** is the craft services table. The crew needs all those sweets, actors don't. Healthy options are a vegetable platter, fruit, granola and power bars—these are your best choices for snacking. For your main meals, a good choice is the salad buffet, but avoid the salad dressing; use lemon juice and olive oil. Lean meats, chicken, turkey and fish are great—stay away from pork and foods that are soaked in sauce. The best way to maintain healthy eating habits on set is to pack your own snacks. Almonds and walnuts are good; don't overdo it, as they are high in calories. A protein shake is a good choice.

Q: What about larger character actors who will never be thin; how can they look their best?

- **There are three main body types:** endomorph, mesomorph, and ectomorph. Ectomorphic bodies are the most slender of the three, followed by mesomorphs, who are more muscular and broad. The third is endomorph—a more full-bodied and stout build, where more weight is held around the midsection. If you happen to be endomorphic, you will not be able to reach an ectomorphic body shape but you can still be healthy and fit. In general, eat foods low in calories, avoid sugar and starchy foods, and foods loaded with sodium and saturated fat. Get your carbohydrates from fruits and vegetables. Regular physical activities are important; five to six times a week of a low-impact workout will improve your physical and mental well being, no matter what your body type.

Q: Can you suggest a general workout program actors can do on their own?

- **Most gyms are very affordable,** and offer seasonal discounts. If this is outside of your budget, there are alternatives, like fitness trails, swimming, biking—you don't need a fancy gym or a Nautilus machine to get fit, all you need is the will. You can get a good workout using your own body weight, with no equipment at all in your living room. Find ways to bring exercise into your daily activities. Rather than taking the elevator, take the stairs. Walk instead of drive.

Q: How can actors avoid getting injured when working out?

- **Two words: WARM UP!** If you are a beginner, get a medical evaluation from a doctor or licensed health professional, so you can be responsible about your training. A good warm up should include 10-15 minutes of cardio. Stretching is one of the most important things to include in your workout; it prevents muscle injury and helps your muscles to look long rather than bulky. Also important is the post-exercise cool down. 10-15 minutes of low impact cardio, like walking, is a good cool down.

- **Avoid working out with partners** who are more advanced than you— you can sustain serious injury by simply trying to keep up. Avoid taking stimulants, like the energy pills, before a workout. This can cause you to over-exert during your training, and may lead to injury.

Q: When hiring a personal trainer, how do you know if they are good or not?

- **Make sure that the trainer is certified.** Check their background, ask for references, ask the gym where they work about any issues in their employment history. Personality counts. Interview the trainer; make sure that it is a good match. A good partnership will make your workouts more enjoyable and keep you motivated and on track. It is good to check if the trainer is insured. Should you sustain an injury, it is important to know that you are protected.

- **I hope that this information has helped you,** and I wish you a happier, healthier body.

Resources

To download and print an updated version of this and all resource lists, go to actingiseverything.com.

Shelly's Discount Aerobic & Dance Wear, 310/475-1400. 2089 Westwood Blvd., Westwood, 90025. (Between Santa Monica Blvd. & Olympic) M-Sa 10-6, Su 11-4.

• NUTRITIONIST

Karen Cohen, CN, 310/444-9755. Learn2eatright@yahoo.com. Karen is a Certified Nutritionist. She is member of the National Association of Nutrition Professionals and is a Firstline Therapeutic Educator. She specializes in breaking the losing cycle of "yo-yo dieting" by recommending a personalized dietary plan based on habits and lifestyle along with nutritional supplements and exercise to help support optimal health and well-being. In her practice she uses a sophisticated computerized machine called Bioimpedance Analysis (BIA). It is a method of assessing your "body composition" – the measurement of body fat in relation to lean body mass. Initial consultation $185 for a 90 minute session plus a 45 minute follow-up session and Dietary Notebook that includes your personally designed food plan. My daughter, Chris Kerr, introduced me to Karen. On her plan I am never hungry, I'm going for health, weight loss and a new eating life style. Chris has been with Karen for about a year. She didn't need to lose weight but to learn how to eat for maximum strength and energy. She's now in maintenance and has never felt better.

• PERSONAL TRAINERS

Rady Ouzounova, 818/571-2697, superrady.us. World-class gymnast and private fitness trainer, Rady offers a wide range of fitness services, including elements from weight training, gymnastics, stretching, aerobic training, indoor/outdoor training, Pilates, martial arts. Personalized diet and nutrition programs tailored to fit the needs of her clients. No matter what you're looking for: weight loss, getting back in shape, or just training for a healthy lifestyle, she is able to create a custom fitness plan that suits your individual needs. My husband and I work out with her twice a week. She is always changing the routine and keeps us motivated. Fabulous!

Sean Barth, 310/872-8780. He is one of the top personal trainers around. His first session is free and he can train anywhere. He gives help with nutrition and concentrates on Core and Functional fitness. He is very creative with his workouts combining many styles of kickboxing, cardio, stretching, yoga, pilates, and weight lifting. He truly cares, has a great personality and is very motivational to help you achieve your goals.

David Brown, 323/957-9066, 213/321-4478. He is a great personal trainer, inexpensive, fun to be with and has a great looking body. He trains and teaches several spinning classes at Crunch, Equinox, or in-home.

Joey Kormier, 818/948-8108. KSSI.com. In-home training or at his private gym. Joey gives a free consultation. Rates and packages available upon request.

Javier at Hotte Bodies Technique, 818/508-4545. acufitnessplus.com. 11634 Ventura Blvd., Studio City, 91604. Training 3x a week is $60/session, 2x a week is $65/session, and once a week is $70/session. Nutritional evaluation and guidance for weight loss and weight gain, cardiovascular conditioning, flexibility training, physical rehabilitation and stress reduction.

Hayden Adams, C.P.T., 310/428-9280. Integratedfitness-la.com. He says, "You'll be pushed to go beyond what you might do on your own, but we'll always stay within the limits of your ability and safety. My training style is supportive and fun." Highly recommended by acting coach Caryn West who has been working out with him for years.

Carla Jones of Star Quality Fitness Training, 213/918-2906, Email: Starqly@aol.com. Certified personal trainer. One-on-one sessions; personalized program designs; fitness evaluations; nutritional evaluations. Single session in the gym, $60. In-home training, single session, $100. Body fat assessment, $30.

Tina Lynne, 323/939-9117. A specialist in the complete make-over. She does basic nutritional consulting. Instructs her clients in the proper exercises for posture lengthening and grace. Facial exercises for firming and toning. She teaches privately or in small classes. She also does facial and body work.

Pilates with Tawny Moyer, 323/650-0748. "With Pilates, we reshape the body for maximum strength and long, lean muscle." Specializing in women, focusing on muscle sculpting, strength training and flexibility. Recommended two to three times a week. Private sessions in her studio, $100.

AK Pilates, with Amber Krzys, 818/421-5282. Amber wants to share her experience, expertise and enthusiasm about Pilates with you. "Pilates has made a huge impact on my life. It has not only changed my body, but the person I am inside. My whole outlook on life is different. I am more confident, centered and happy." More details about AK Pilates are posted online at http://www.akpilates.com. Tell Amber I sent you and receive an additional discount. And, don't be intimidated by her last name, it is simply pronounced "Kris."

Align Beverly Hills Pilates, 310-854/0950, alignbhpilates.com. 8907 Wilshire Blvd., Suite 201, Beverly Hills, 90211. Re-design your body, redefine your muscles, re-align with pilates. Private, Semi-Private and reformer classes are the specialties here. My daughter Chris Kerr has changed her body shape around using their techniques. Julie is the owner and the other instructors are Dano and Keegan. Very highly recommended.

Absolution Pilates Studio, 310/657-7878, absolution-la.com. 8535 Santa Monica Blvd., West Hollywood 90069. No membership fee. Classes offered seven days a week; see website for schedule. Prices vary; for pilates, cost is $75 per class for solo session and $50 for a duet, Pilates class is $15. Also offer classes in aerial arts, bellydancing, capoeira, gymnastics, climbing and boxing. A favorite of actress Denise George.

Winsor West Pilates Studio, 310/442-1030, winsorfit.com. 12231 Wilshire Blvd., Santa Monica, 90025. Winsor Fitness Pilates Studio, 323/653-8767. 8204 Melrose Ave, West Hollywood, 90048. Both locations are fitted with shower and changing facilities. $70 an hour for a private class, utilizing the Cadillac and Reformer Pilates equipment. $15 for the group floor class with a trainer and maximum 15 people. Mats provided. Both types of classes can be bought in a series. Mari is well known for teaching the New York method of Pilates. She's written a book explaining the exercises and produced videos that can be used at home; sold on the website.

TAV Lifestyle Private Training, Teresa 323/605-4401, tavlifestyle.com. Fusion Group Training, outdoor sport conditioning workout. Single class $12, card of 10, $100. Teresa's Sport Conditioning program combines explosive training, balance, multi-directional movement, acceleration and velocity training. Private and home training available.

Michael Thurmond's Six-Week Body Makeover, 800/639-2639, bodymakeovers.com. He advertises in *LA Magazine*. I met a mature actress on the set of *Thea* who had lost 40 pounds. She said she looked better than she had in years. She was working out with weights and said Michael's program really motivated her. Free initial consultation.

Gyrotonic™ Instructor, Lisa Ebeyer, 818/892-0908. Lisa Ebeyer is a Level 1 Gyrotonic™ instructor working on the Gyrotonic Expansion System™ which stretches and strengthens the musculature while mobilizing and articulating the joints. Non-impact one-on-one.

Angel City Body Kinetics, 310/253-9500. labodyk.com. 4143 Glencoe Ave, Marina Del Rey, 90292. Many movement modalities, Pilates and Gyrotonic Expansion System™. Pilates group mat classes and Gyrokinesis™. Certification studio. Lisa Marie Goodwin is considered a Master Trainer of Gyrotonic™.

• PROFESSIONAL DANCE STUDIOS

Dance Arts Academy, 323/932-6230. danceartsacademy.com. 731 South La Brea Ave., Los Angeles, 90036. They offer professional quality dance training and performing opportunities, in all dance disciplines, to students of all ages and levels of experience. Founder/Director, Carla Luna has created beautiful quarters with over 10,000 square feet of space, state-of-the art sprung floors and ample dressing rooms. My friend, Catherane Skillen, takes ballet here every day; she's very devoted and disciplined.

Ballet with Lisa Ebeyer at Dance Arts Academy, Lisa's Direct Line: 818/368-8317 or cell 818/723-8327. 731 S. La Brea, Los Angeles. Lisa Ebeyer was a professional ballet dancer nationally and internationally before becoming a teacher. Teaching for more than ten years, her classes range from Intermediate to Professional level. Sundays 10-11:30. Class rates are $15 for one class, $65 for five classes, $120 for 10 classes. Catherane Skillen says, "Lisa brings both humor and a sense of joy to her classes. Not only does she understand how the body can affect and help movement, she also has the actors' understanding of how to communicate this knowledge to her student."

Edge Performing Arts Center, 323/962-7733. 1020 North Cole Ave., 4th Floor, Hollywood, 90038. All ages, beginning through professional; jazz, ballet hip-hop and tap. $11 a class; with SAG card, $10.

Debbie Reynolds Rehearsal Studios, 818/985-3193. 6514 Lankershim Blvd., North Hollywood, 91606. $10 a class, union $9. M-Th 9-9, Fri 9-8, Sat 9-6, Sun 9-4. Adult and children. Jazz, ballet and tap, hip-hop, musical theatre, specialty classes in turning.

Jennifer Nairn-Smith, 323/938-6836. outbackstudios.com. Master Ballet and Pilates Instructor: Associate of the Royal Academy of Dancing, London; former Ballerina with George Balanchine's New York City Ballet; original Fosse dancer in *Pippin* on Broadway, and the movie *All That Jazz;* trained with Jo Pilates, Carola Trier and Ron Fletcher. Pilates Reformer, Pilates mat work and ballet barre. Classes also available in ballet and Fosse jazz.

Moro Landis Millennium Dance Complex, 818/753-5081. 5113 Lankershim Blvd., North Hollywood, 91601. All ballet, jazz and hip-hop dance single classes are $13 and $12 for union. Dance coupons are 5 for $56 and 10 for $104.

Lauridsen Ballet Centre, 310/533-1247. southbayballet.org. 1261 Sartori Avenue, Torrance, 90501. For serious students. Dedicated to nurturing, developing, and guiding dancers through the world of ballet in a professional, caring and healthy environment. Live piano accompaniment. Teaching staff boasts professionals and guest artists from world-renowned ballet companies. Diane Lauridsen, Charles Maple, Colleen O'Callaghan and Alicia Head.

Pedro Montanez, 818/426-6895. Teaches privately. Ballroom, waltz, rumba, samba, salsa, fox-trot, hustle, hip hop, street dancing, ballet, jazz, and tap. He choreographs weddings and is hired to get people dancing at parties. He can be hired if you need to learn a dance step quickly for an audition. As an actor, you should know the usual dances for your resume.

• WORKOUT PLACES

Angel City Yoga Center, 818/762-8291, angelcityyoga.com. 12408 Ventura Blvd., Studio City, 91604. Multi-method Hatha yoga, Sivananda Hatha; Iyengar; Astanga; Kundalini. $15 per individual class. 10 class card, $130. Unlimited: $150 per month, $420 for 3 months.

Aquatic Masters Program, Southern California, 310/390-5700, swim.net. Clay Evans has designed this program to aid injury recovery, as well as overall fitness and swimming ability. You are videotaped during stroke-technique exercises. Has trained many celebrities in swimming roles.

B.K.S. Iyengar Yoga Institute of Los Angeles, 323/653-0357, 8233 West Third Street, Los Angeles, 90048. Individual 1½ hour class, $15; the noon one-hour classes, $12; series of 10, $120; monthly unlimited, $150. First class is free. I love this place, recommended to me by Michael Richards; the teachers are great. There are three levels so you don't have to worry if you are new. For your first class I would recommend Saturday morning 10:15 with Chris Stein. I love the 8:30AM and noon classes; they are small and the instructors really have the time and inclination to make sure you understand all the moves. All the teachers are very highly trained and are very aware of keeping you from injury. Marla, Larry and Herb are great too. Alice teaches a special class Saturday morning at 9 for people with scoliosis.

Bikram Yoga, bikramyoga.com. Popular in Los Angeles for many years. Check the website for the style and locations.

Yoga Works—Montana, 310/393-5150, yogaworks.com. 1426 Montana Ave., 2nd floor, Santa Monica 90405.

Yoga Works—Main, 310/393-5150, yogaworks.com. 2215 Main St., Santa Monica, 90405.

Yoga Works—West LA, 310/234-1200, yogaworks.com. 1256 Westwood Blvd., 2nd Floor, West LA 90024

Liberation Yoga, 323/964-5222, liberationyoga.com. 124 S. La Brea Ave, LA, 90036. SAG members 20% discount. All styles and levels of yoga.

Maha Yoga, 310/899-0047, mahayoga.com. 13050 San Vicente, #202. Corner of San Vicente and 26th, Brentwood. Meg Ryan, Goldie Hawn, Dennis Quaid, Elizabeth Berkley, Jim Belushi. High-energy power yoga classes as well as more meditative classes.

Train, 310/657-4140. 624 N. La Cienega, West Hollywood. This is not a membership gym; the trainers pay to belong and then charge you for the workout. Many trainers. They generally charge between $75 per hour and up.

Bally's Total Fitness, 323/461-0227, ballyfitness.com. 1628 N. El Centro, Hollywood, 90028. M-Th 5:00AM to Midnight, F 5AM –10PM, Sa-Su 6AM-10PM. Swimming pool, running track, many treadmills and bikes, TVs to watch. 818/760-7800. 11315 Ventura Blvd., Studio City, 91604. Open 7 days a week, 24 hours. I love Bally's because I can always find a gym in another city when traveling. Not as fancy as others but the price is right.

Body and Soul, 310/659-2211. BodyandSoulworkout.net. 8599 Santa Monica Blvd. It is a beautiful studio, very zen inside: wall to wall bamboo and candle lit. Morning classes are usually small. They have great spinning classes, yoga, ab and dance classes.

Bodies in Motion, 310/264-0777, bodiesinmotion.com. 12100 W. Olympic Blvd., Santa Monica, 90404. Kick boxing, boxing, yoga, aerobics, free weights, treadmills.

Crunch, 323/654-4550, crunch.com. 8000 Sunset Blvd. at Crescent Heights in Virgin Megastores complex. Hours: M-F 5AM–12AM, Sa-Su 7AM-10PM. This corner is where the old Schwabs Drugstore used to be. Madonna's trainer and Lordes' father Carlos Leon works there. Afro-Brazilian aerobics. Marisa Tomei, Julianna Margulies, Laura Dern, Brad Pitt, Jeff Goldblum, Julie Delpy, Jon Favreau, Debi Mazar and Ben Stiller have all been spotted here.

Dolly Mama, Dawnn Alane. 310/230-0390. Pacific Palisades. Dawnn also teaches privates for $75-$125 hour.

L.A. Fitness at Warner Center Club, 818/884-1100, lafitness.com. 6336 Canoga Ave., Woodland Hills. M-Th 5AM–11PM, F 5AM–10PM, Sa-Su 7AM–8PM.

Gold's Gym, 310/392-6004. 360 Hampton Drive, Venice. Also, 323/462-7012. 1016 N. Cole, Hollywood. Also 213/688-1441. 735 S. Figueroa St., Ste. 100, L.A. 90017. goldsgym.com. M-F 4AM–12PM; Sa-Su 5AM–11PM. The Venice gym is filled with every big name from the world of bodybuilding plus the likes of Janet Jackson, Lisa Bonet and Jodie Foster. The Figueroa Street gym is Brittani Taylor's favorite. "They have all the latest equipment, and it is a relatively new gym. Super clean and fun, laid-back environment; worth the drive from the valley!"

Gymnastics Center, 310/838-4228. 8476 Warner Drive, Culver City, 90232. santamonicagymnasticscenter.com Hours 9AM–10PM. Ask for adult gymnastic classes.

Carreiro's Gymnastics and Trapeze Arts, 310/652-3060. 722 N. La Cienega Blvd., L.A. 90069. 7:30-6:30PM. Package of 10 classes, $25/session. One class is $30, private is $80. Class size is 5 people or less. Bob Carreiro can turn even the most uptight body into one that is lithe, strong and obedient. The risk is higher; so are the rewards.

Easton Gym, 323/651-3636. 8053 Beverly Blvd. (near Crescent Heights.) 5AM to midnight. Cardio and strength training, personal training, complete locker facilities.

Karate, Simon Rhee, 818/224-3400, simonrhee.net. 22880 Ventura Blvd., Woodland Hills, 91364. Considered one of the best Karate studios, many celebrities have studied with Master Rhee. He is also a well-known action/stunt actor, Best of the Best I & II, and many others. Cathy Kerr is a Second Degree Black Belt—oh I hate to brag! Love my girls! See Master Rhee's interview in the Stunt-Action Acting section.

Karate, Jun Chong, 323/658-7570, junchongtkd.com. 6401 Wilshire Blvd. L.A. Also 818/769-9308. 5223 Lankershim Blvd., North Hollywood. Cathy and Cynthia Kerr trained with him when they were teenagers. Master Chong is an action actor. Third location: 310/449-1333. 11870 Santa Monica Blvd., Santa Monica, 90025 (two blocks east of Bundy).

24 Hour Fitness, 310/652-7440. 8612 Santa Monica Blvd., West Hollywood, 90069. 24hourfitness.com. Membership gym. Weight lifting; all types of exercise classes. M-Th 5:30AM-11PM, F 5:30-10, Sa-Su 7AM-8PM. Also 310/410-9909, Century City; 213/683-1400, downtown; 310/553-7600, West Los Angeles; 213/388-2700, Korea Town.

Sports Club L.A., 310/477-7799. 1835 Sepulveda Blvd., West Los Angeles. thesportsclubla.com. Very expensive, but in! This is the gym to get a day job at!

Stair Climbing on the 4th Street Stairs, at 4th and Adelaide Streets in Santa Monica, 189 steps.

Stairs, in Santa Monica. They ascend from the 400 block of North Mesa Road to Amalfi Drive, 201 steps. Less crowded than the 4th Street stairs and redwoods, wisteria and live oaks.

Swerve Studio, 323/782-0741 or 866/289-8939 swervestudio.com. 8250 West 3rd St. #206 Los Angeles, 90048. Private Training, fitness, dance and yoga. $15 single classes or membership packages.

Tim Weske's Swordplay Fencing Studio, 818/566-1777. swordplayla.com. timweske. com. 64 E. Magnolia Blvd. Burbank, 91502. Sir Ben Kingsley, Natalie Portman, Sandra Bullock, Brad Pitt are just a few of the names that have been trained by "Hollywood Premier Sword Master and Choreographer." Also a school of competition fencing. Mr. Weske is both an actor and a competitive fencer so he understands the needs of both. The art of fencing is a very valuable exercise for the actor.

Fitness Factory, 310/358-1838. fitnessfactoryla.com. 650 N. La Peer Drive, Los Angeles, 90069. Lots of celebrities. The gym's high tech resistance machines are known for flawless motion; Tectrix Bikemax stationary cycle gives a smooth ride. Great locker rooms, onsite massage therapist, rubdowns for a dollar a minute.

Working Actor's Guide lists many gyms and trainers.

AGE DEFYING AND
BEAUTY ENHANCING TECHNIQUES,
INCLUDING FACIALS AND MASSAGE

• **Your face is your billboard**; it's where the audience sees what you are feeling and thinking. The first time you see your face on a big screen, it is awe-inspiring.

• **When you are wearing makeup** and working in it for hours, you need a thorough cleansing. A facial every month or so is a wonderful way to relax and treat yourself well. Aging can be slowed down; our profession is so youth-oriented that it demands we look as young as we can for as long as we can. Surgery is a last resort because when they cut into the skin you never know how your body will heal.

• **Christie Brinkley** is known for her beautiful youthful skin; she has made a living with it. It is said that she never turns on her heat or air conditioner, as they dry out skin. I have an actress friend who has to be in her late forties, though she never tells her age, with the most flawless skin. She has never been in the sun and during the winter, layers her clothing so she doesn't use heat. She did this even while acting on soap operas in New York. It has paid off, she looks like she is in her thirties and is still being cast as that. Women have to stretch their young years as long as possible. Men need to stretch their mid-years.

• **Kim Basinger** is still a great beauty. Her skin is luminous without a wrinkle. She says she has avoided the sun with a "fanatical determination."

• **Bernadette Peters,** who is known for her flawless skin, is in her fifties but looks like she is in her thirties. "When I was thirteen and on a trip to Las Vegas, I got a slight tan—but no sun since. I use Coppertone WaterBabies Sunblock."

• **Rand Rusher, R.N., C.N.O.R.** randrusher.com. Botox, Collagen, Sculptra, Perlane and Restylane Injection Specialist at Leaf & Rusher Medical Skincare Clinic in Beverly Hills, shares the following information about suntans.

> • **I'm afraid there is no such thing as a safe suntan,** no matter how carefully you want to "get some sun." Tanning is still a defense mechanism of the skin. With sun exposure, the skin produces more pigment to provide protection against the sun. The presence of a tan indicates there has been some degree of damage. This damage is responsible for 85% of aging.

> • **If this is not going to stop you from getting a tan,** here are some tips that will help reduce the damage. Tan the hide, hide the face. Use a heavy SPF on your face, lower number on your body. Good face products are available, low oil to oil free, paba free. The FDA is changing the rules on SPF's, with SPF 35 being the highest possible. Always make sure that you use at least a 30 SPF on your face, and at least a 15 SPF on your body. Some of the better sunscreens are Ti-silc, Leaf&Rusher, leafandrusher.com, or Environ products. Avoid becoming sunburned at all costs. The damage may not show up for years, but it will. Always wear sunscreen even when it is cloudy, even if you have very dark skin. Lips need sunscreen too. Neostrata makes an excellent product for this. Fake tans are great; use self action tanners. The trick is to find one that complements your natural skin tone. Chanel smells great but is a bit greasy, California Tan has no smell and not greasy but can streak. You really have to try the products out on your own skin.

• **Sylvie Archenault, owner of Sylvie's Advanced European Skin & Body Care System,** has been doing facials for thirty years. She works with three chemists and two laboratories developing her cutting edge Sonage skin products, importing the raw materials from Europe, Japan and Australia. Sylvie talks about the results people can expect from facials:

> • **When you have a facial,** you should see a change right away; your skin will be glowing, energized, and cleansed. You are taking off all the makeup and grime, the skin is pure. If you have acne or a breakout, you should not be red when the treatment is over. A deep pore facial once a month is good for general cleaning and toning, but if there are skin difficulties or special occasions then you will need facials more often. The aesthetician can do things to make your skin beautiful for a photo shoot. Makeup responds beautifully when you have healthy skin underneath. The style now is very light makeup; you can't hide the imperfections so you must really clean your skin.

Q: How do you choose a skin care person?

- **Skin care is an art.** You will probably go to a facialist before the plastic surgeon and dermatologist. You want to choose a professional, first by their word of mouth reputation, then by the techniques they use and most importantly the results. Have a consultation or an over-the-phone interview. Finally, you must experience their facial. If it's too strong it can bruise the skin and leave you marked for a few days—that might interfere with your acting interviews. At Sylvie's we use the latest techniques and revolutionary ingredients; my goal is to fight aging.

Q: How can actors help their skin?

- **Drink a lot of water** because it provides energy, keeps the skin glowing and cleans up your system by drawing the toxins away from your body. Caffeine and smoking does a lot of damage. Exposure to the sun is damaging. It is easier to apply makeup on porcelain skin; you cannot take off the tan if you need a white skin.

• **Facialist and natural product developer Leah Ruiz** of The Vital Image gives some hints for skin care.

- **Don't touch your face,** unless you are going to be gentle. Don't rub your eyes if they itch. Use your middle fingers and pat to keep from stretching your skin. Use short, firm strokes to apply products.

- **In order to drink more water each day** make a pot of herb tea or add a splash of juice to your water and drink throughout the day.

- **Increase oxygen intake to relieve stress.** Oxygen bath: add a full 16 ounce bottle of common 3% Hydrogen Peroxide to a warm bath. Soak for 20 minutes. Oxygen break: make a point of taking ten deep breaths, ten times a day.

- **Acne skin is especially sugar intolerant.** Substitute a natural, sugar free sweetener such as stevia extract to sweeten drinks and food.

- **Be a fanatic** about your skin care routine at night before retiring. You will help your skin to rejuvenate itself by sticking to this good habit. Your skin is most actively regenerated between the hours of midnight and 4AM.

- **Don't sleep on your face.** Sleep on your back or side to avoid wrinkling and creasing your face while you sleep. It's easy for most people to train themselves into a favorable sleeping position. Satin pillow cases reduce friction that stretches and damages hair and skin. Look for pure silk rather than synthetic fabrics. To release tension around the eyes, put your head on the pillow, inhale deeply and with your thumbs, press upward toward the forehead on the eye socket—the sensitive area between the eyebrows. Exhale while applying pressure and relax the jaw, repeat three times. The results will amaze you.

- **Proper exfoliation can step up cell renewal.** You can use simple table sugar as an exceptional exfoliant. It has fine grains for gentle removal of dead surface cells, it is nondrying and rinses away completely. Wet your face and lather then add a half teaspoon or more of sugar to one lathered up hand. Dip the two middle fingers of your other hand into the sugar and gently wash your face using a circular motion. Rinse well and pat dry. Your face should look rosy but not irritated. After exfoliation, your skin will absorb more nutrients and moisture.

- **Perfume is okay but never directly on your skin.** It is best in your hair or on your clothes.

- **Tina Lynne, the creator of** *The Lynne Technique* answers the very important questions about how to look your best when you have overindulged.

  - **Our motto is: if you've had a "margarita and salty chips" night,** don't wear it on your face the next day; do the *Lynne Technique*. When you do the technique it helps to clean out the lymph system, which is a filtering system that removes toxic bloat in your body. Open your mouth into the "long O" which is like the men's shaving position, put on your cleanser then blot the face with a hot compress, working down towards the heart hitting some of the pressure points, press down, with your knuckles on your chest, two, three, pump. Then pushing the knuckles into the armpits, one, two, three, pumping. Next take some deep breaths; the breathing is really important to oxygenate the body.

  - **You can continue to reduce swelling and puffiness** by pressing accupressure points while you're applying your undereye concealer and makeup, just by rolling your finger on the inside corner of the eye, out the side to the temple, walking your fingers out. This technique will help reduce dark circles and puffiness. Make sure you're never stretching the skin on your face.

Q: How does your technique done professionally help to defy aging and enhance beauty?

- **What I do is called the body clearing treatment.** It is the best part of a facial or traditional massage, which brings up circulation and carries away toxins. I clean out the lymph system. If your lymph system is clogged up it becomes inefficient. The analogy is: how poorly your dryer works when you don't clean the lint screen. You clean out the lymph system so your body is removing it's waste efficiently and quickly. A lot of massages swish around the toxins, but they don't end up leaving the body, so people are still bloated afterwards. The treatment we do is to help dispose of the toxins though the kidneys, through both ends, so to speak. It's like a colonic without the machine.

• **Rand Rusher, R.N.**, describes products used for facial injections

   • **Botox softens or actually can erase certain wrinkles.** As an actor you should be careful not to completely get rid of wrinkles; softening certain wrinkles can help if you have more than you want due to genetics, sun damage, etc. Botox works by blocking the nerve to the tiny facial muscles that relate to expression lines. Botox relaxes muscles so they do not contract. After the treatment, the overlying skin remains smooth. Botox has been used for over 10 years to treat many other disorders and has recently been approved for the treatment of wrinkles by the FDA, so not to worry.

   • **Collagen is a natural occurring protein** found in both humans and animals. It provides structural support for bones, skin, tendons, and is the most abundant protein in the body. Collagen is injected into the wrinkle to fill in and soften lines, and also to define and plump up lips. Unlike Botox that stops the muscle from moving thereby softening the wrinkle, collagen fills out the wrinkle, while still allowing movement of the surrounding muscles. Today we have both animal-bovine (Zyplast) and human (Cosmoplast) options available. Bovine collagen (Zyplast) is an animal product, and requires a skin test to ensure that you do not have an allergy. After the test implant is done (usually on the inner right forearm), you will need to wait at least 30 days to insure there is no allergic reaction. Human collagen (Cosmoplast) is an excellent choice for beginners and it does not require a skin test. Both Human and Bovine collagen typically lasts about three months.

   • **Sculptra is one of the newer filler products** on the market. Like Hylauronic Acids and Collagens it is used to fill and soften lines on the face. It is composed of ploy-L-latic acid. It is a synthetic product that is not made from human or animal sources and therefore does not require a skin test. The effects of Sculptra are long lasting and in clinical studies have increased the thickness of the skin. It does require multiple treatments, usually spaced eight weeks apart. After the full course of treatment, Sculptra allows you to achieve the desired effect for up to two years. Please make sure you seek out an experienced injector, as Sculptra requires advanced injection knowledge. Visit sculptra.com for more information.

- **Hylauronic Acid.** There are many Hylauronic Acids out on the market. The most common today is Restylane. Restylane is a non-animal stabilized Hylauronic Acid. It is used, like collagen, to fill in and soften lines on the face. It is also an excellent product for defining and plumping up lips. Restylane lasts the longest of the hylauronic acids, typically 6-9 months There are other Hyluronic Acids such as Hylaform, Captique, and most recently approved Juvederm. Use of Hyluronic Acid requires advanced injection knowledge, so please research! Information on Hylaform, Captique and Juvederm can be located under Allerganandinamed.com (see information under facial aesthetics). Information on Restylane can be found on their website, restylaneusa.com.

- **Facialist Margaret Tomaszewicz,** who works at the Burke Williams Day Spa and Massage Center, talks about men's facials.

  - **Men can shave in the morning,** if they're having a facial in the evening, but should not shave right before; it makes the skin too sensitive. Men tend to have good facial skin, but they break out on their backs due to sports and exercises. If there are just a few spots, an exfoliation treatment will be enough with an occasional maintenance. When there are a lot of problems, the client would have to come in every couple of weeks. I would also advise a topical medication for them to use. We do full-body facials for swimsuit and body photo shoots. It polishes the skin.

Q: Why is a massage valuable for actors?

  - **Doctors in Europe** prescribe massages for health reasons. A massage gives oxygen to the muscles and the tissue, even more than exercise can provide. It gives life, circulation and relaxation as well. When directions on bottles of creams say to massage vigorously into the body, it's not the creams that are good, it's the actual massage that breaks up the toxins in your body. In short, it's great for relaxation

Resources

The Vital Image, 310/823-1996 or 800/414-4624. thevitalimage.com. Leah has a studio in Playa del Rey. $60 for an hour facial. Guaranteed quick results. She does minimal extractions so there is no marking at all. She believes the products will pull most of the toxins out. The facials, special Chinese lamp and all natural products heal skin damaged from age, sun and deep abrasion or laser work. I've had terrific healing with these facials. The three products, Face & Body Wash, Skin Renewal Complex and Phytohydrator (liquid moisturizer) are all you need to deliver fabulous skin. Among their many other products, they have a special under-eye bag cure, which removed my daughter Chris Kerr's inherited bags (from me, sorry Chris). Chris is thrilled with the results. I love their Shaving Miracle liquid; I've never gotten such a close shave. Men love it—no break outs. Newest is Lift & Firm, fights wrinkles and flaccid skin, eye lift, jaw-line and neck firming—it works! Sun Shield Moisturizer: amazing and 100% free of man-made chemicals, powerful nutrients. Call for their special product report.

Rand Rusher, R.N., C.N.O.R. Botox, Collagen, Sculptra, and Restylane Injection Specialist, 310/276-5558. randrusher.com Leaf & Rusher Medical Clinic, 436 N. Bedford Dr., #104, Beverly Hills. "Los Angeles's most sought out Botox and Collagen Specialist." He is a master with the needle. I love Botox, Collagen and the latest: sculptra, Restylane, and juvedrem; they do help defy the look of aging. A good technician will make all the difference; if they get too much botox in your forehead, your eyebrows can sag. Great for lines around the eyes and chin too, Rand leaves you with facial expression, which actors must have. The collagen fills in lines; especially chronic frown lines, and those pesky lines around the mouth. Sculptra and Restylane are for more extensive deep folds and depressions. Though Restylane and human collagen (cosmoderm) are both excellent for defining and fluffing up the lips. With Rand your lips look real not artificial and unattractive. Rand has a nursing and artistic background which is the best combination when working on the face. You want the artistic touch, he knows where and how much to inject for the best looking results. I've been going for years, always with great results, love my lips puffed a little! You need to make appointments in advance for Rand. He stays booked. He has been featured in many fashion magazines. Everyone in the office is very helpful. Appointments are mandatory.

August Denton, R.N. Botox, Collagen, Sculptra and Restylane Injection Specialist, 310/276-5558, leafskincare.com. Leaf & Rusher Medical Clinic, 436 N. Bedford Dr., #104, Beverly Hills. Three Baccalaureate's in Art, Physiology, and Nursing. August graduated with Honors from the top-rated University of Illinois at the Chicago College of Nursing in 2000, and began his clinical work at the University of Chicago Hospital. His talents in sculpture and physiology have enhanced his skills, giving his Botox and Collagen technique an artist's touch.

Leaf & Rusher Medical Clinic Inc. 310/276-5558. 436 N. Bedford Dr., Suite 104, Beverly Hills. leafskincare.com. They specialize in preventive maintenance, which can help reduce or forestall the need for restorative surgery. Lighter, non-invasive treatments can be adequate to bring back abused, over-stressed and over-exposed skin. They also excel in removing brown or red pigmentation, with some of the most advanced procedures available. Some of the treatments besides great facials are; light peels, micro dermabrasion, Cosmelan de-pigmentation mask, cover up make up, Photo-facial, laser hair removal and TITAN skin rejuvenation procedure. Renowned plastic surgeon Dr. Norman Leaf, "surgeon to the stars" is known for his undetectable facelifts, has designed Leaf & Rusher Medical Skincare Clinic to be a bridge between commercial skincare, beauty salons and the plastic surgeon's or dermatologist's office. Ask them to send you their brochure with descriptions of their many services. My special Esthetician is Maya—amazing.

Sylvie's Day Spa, 818/905-8815. sylviesskinandbodycare.com. 17071 Ventura Blvd., Encino, 91436. For men and women. Tu&F 9-5, W&Th 9-8, Sa 8-5. Deep pore cleansing facials start at $75. Micro-dermabrasion $125, vacupression body and face treatments $90, collagen treatment $130, seaweed facial $105, cell structure enhancement $85, enzyme $105. Other services at the Day spa include Eye Brow design, lash extensions, Safe Sun Tanning application, light therapy, Ultra sound, microdermabrasion and nutrition. One hour body massage $65. Varied prices for several types of massage including lymphatic drainage, reflexology, anti-stress detox, PMS treatment, exfoliation, cellulite, hair removal by electronic tweezers, electrolysis and European waxing. Aromatherapy. Manicures and pedicures. All of the aestheticians are trained by Sylvie using her techniques and methods. Her Sonage skin care products are healing, enhancing, concentrated, smell good; you see and feel a difference right away. Cathy Kerr's favorite. There is a discrete back entrance for clients who may not want to be seen. See below for the more treatments for the legs.

Magda of Sylvie's Day Spa, 818/905-8815. sylviesskinandbodycare.com. is Cathy Kerr's favorite because of her fabulous facials, her skin glows after Magda's treatment, and the perfect brow and lash tinting. Not to mention her consistently smiling face and her ability to make you feel completely relaxed.

Ruska of Institut De Beaute, 310/652-1414. 310/652-1414. 820 N. La Cienega Blvd. L.A. 90069. Ruska has a lovely little hideaway studio. She handles one client at a time so you feel very private and pampered. She was trained in France and only uses Guinot products. Using pressure points, ionization, oxygenation and facial massage you leave looking better and in the morning your face shows a pumped up improvement. The products are top quality. I find her treatments very thorough and you do look different the next morning.

Donald Huffman at Barneys, 310/276-4400 ext. 5598, reviveskincare.com, dhuffman@barneys.com. 9570 Wilshire Blvd., Beverly Hills 90212. Donald is the counter manager for ReVive, an incredible line of skin products. My friend Samantha Harper introduced me to these products; they are very high end and deliver results. Donald does a detailed skin analysis then advises what products will be to your best advantage. You then return for additional analysis, to make sure you receive the optimal results. Just a few of the devotees are Diane Lane, Sharon Osborne, Melanie Griffith and Marlo Thomas. You will be dazzled by the results.

The Lynne Technique **for Face and Body Care by Tina Lynne,** 323/939-9117. When actors overindulge, she can get them ready for their close-ups by taking the toxins and swelling out of their faces and body. Some of the symptoms her technique helps fight are puffiness, dark circles, facial lines, acne, headaches and jet lag. She combines a regimen of acupressure massage with a balance of minerals, herbs and emollients to firm muscles, clear sinuses and revitalize skin cells by inducing detoxification and faster metabolism of fats and other wastes and nutrients, thus stimulating cell renewal and growth. She works pre/post-op plastic surgery treatment to maintain and enhance surgical results. She brought me through a major detoxification in a short amount of time. Incorporating her own designed products and exercises, you can carry on the work at home. Many celebrity clients including international and Hollywood royalty.

Alex Khadavi, M.D., Encino Dermatology & Laser Center, 818/528-2500, lalasercenter. com. Botox, acne treatment, smoothbeam laser, scar augmentation, tattoo removal, hair removal, capillary removal, etc. Offers any and all procedures you could need as well as a number of skin care products. Offices in Encino, Thousand Oaks, Palmdale, Valencia, Ridgecrest, Glendale and Westwood. Dr. Khadavi works in Encino. Recommended by agent Bonnie Howard.

Doug Mest, M.D., Blue Pacific Aesthetics Group, 310/297-9111, bpacific.com, Hermosa Beach. Practices the latest in non-invasive, non-surgical cosmetics, including wrinkle treatment, radio-frequency skin tightening, skin rejuvenation and soft tissue augmentation. Also offers a number of skin care products. Recommended by casting director Stuart Stone. Normally charges a $75 consulting fee, but mention this book and he will waive the fee!

Jon Fong, MD, Laser Facials, 818/766-0110 and 877-LFACIAL. LaserFacials.com. 4605 Lankershim Blvd., North Hollywood, 91602. $375 for each treatment. Treating sun damaged skin is the goal. This is a laser process that treats the entire face, for men and women 20 to 60 including dark skin types. It treats fine lines, wrinkles, texture, tone, dark spots and sun damaged skin with no down or recovery time. I've had three over two years and will continue to do them. This is Dr. Fong's invention and is not like anything else others use. He is an emergency room doctor and is the on-set advisor for *E.R.* He also offers a lunch time Laser Facial that is cheaper and not as deep.

Yolanda Frye Skin Care, 310/275-3981. 632 1/2 N. Doheny Dr, West Hollywood, 90069. Her special beauty treatment is Oxiana, a European skin therapy, she calls "a fountain of youth for men and women's skin!" With Oxiana it is possible to apply highly concentrated oxygen and skin-enhancing nutrients where needed. Especially recommended after all laser resurfacing as soon as bandages are removed; all skin peel recipients; acne conditions; following electrolysis, waxing and permanent makeup procedures; and in combination with deep cleansing facials. Her facials start at $75 to $200. Cathy Kerr especially loves her back facials, great for when you are wearing a low back dress; men love this too. Yolanda does lash and brow tinting, skin and body waxing, full nail service and makeup.

The Arcona Studio Holistic Beauty Therapy For Face and Body, 818/506-5192. arcona. com. 12030 Riverside Dr., Valley Village, 91607. Men and women. $85 for non-surgical facelift and facial contouring with essential oils. This treatment is what attracts many people to them; you can tell the difference. Many other treatments including natural fruit enzymes treatment and oxygen facials and European deep-suction cleansing. Arcona is booked six months ahead by many celebrity clients including Sharon Stone; Nicki and Meagan are her trained assistants, but you need to book them two weeks in advance. Samantha Harper loves this place.

Beverly Hot Springs, 323/734-7000. beverlyhotsprings.com. 308 N. Oxford Ave., L. A., 90004. Everyday 9:30-9. This is not a fancy place but many celebrities go there. Built over a natural hot spring, they offer many services. Separate pools for men and women; everyone is naked. Admission M-Th. $40; F, Sa, Su $50 for a 90-minute visit.

Burke Williams Day Spa & Massage Center, 310/587-3366. burkewilliamsspa.com. 1358 4th St., Santa Monica, 90401 and 323/822-9007. 8000 Sunset Blvd., West Hollywood at Virgin Megastores complex at Crescent Heights, 90046. Have a facial with knowledgeable Margaret Tomaszewicz. Four-and-a-half-hour packages such as "Day of Beauty," and "Stress Therapy" cost from $420-635 plus a 15% gratuity or you can purchase services a la carte starting at $20. All sessions of $55 or more include free sauna and whirlpool.

Drew James, 310/395-1405. 733 10th St, Suite B, Santa Monica, 90402. Facials $100 and up. Glycolic and salicylic peels available. He's great at picking out your imperfections without marking you. Waxing and lash tinting. Large clientele of men and women.

Nina Bard, PME, 310/589-5385, on Pacific Coast Highway in Malibu. She does facials, waxing, scar camouflage and cosmetic tattooing including eyebrow enhancement and permanent eyeliner, plus her well-researched products. Tattooing is $250 for the first hour and $100 for each additional hour. Call for pricing on other services.

Spa Transcendental, Christina Marino 818/505-9511. christinamarino.com. 10645 Riverside Dr., Toluca Lake, 91602. At Christina Marino's spa, they have many specialized services and spa packages. Services include: acupuncture, herbs and nutrition and full service massage therapies; foot reflexology, 30 minutes, $40; deep tissue and sports massage, 60 minutes for $65. Body treatments and wraps. European Facial, 75 minutes for $65. Waxing, lash and brow tinting. Agent Bonnie Howard says, "You feel like you have been on vacation."

Mermaid Beauty Skin Care Products, mermaidbeautyskincare.com Grif Griffis introduced Samantha Harper to these seaweed based products, they find them to be outstandingly nourishing and considerably less expensive than department store brands.

• MASSAGE & BODY WORK ONLY

Sylvie's Day Spa, 818/905-8815. sylviesskinandbodycare.com. 17071 Ventura Blvd., Encino, 91436. They offer the Ultimate in Health and Wellness therapies with the Vacuodermie and Pressotherapy from France, the latest in face and body care in one treatment. Renown in France for dancers, actors and models to protect the shape and health of their legs. You can erase one to two inches immediately and feel lightness. The lymphatic system is the purifying system of the body's water and it is what women have trouble getting rid of. The treatment consists of regulating the temperature of the legs, promoting exchanges between the vascular and lymphatic channels resulting in thinner and energetic legs, deleting fatigue. Treatment of one hour and half hour includes refreshing or lifting of the visage, as well as the complete body enhancement. Averages $225 per session. Also Mesotherapy to treat unwanted Cellulite condition.

Spa-Go's, 818/249-7724, spa-gos.com. This is a mobile day spa. They come to you no matter where you are. My husband bought me one for a Valentine's gift and it was really wonderful. I chose the deep tissue massage; they offer several different types of massage. They give you instructions ahead of time of what to be wearing, how to prepare. They come in, set up with all of their own equipment and provide lovely music. You get the massage and they are off again. This is a great gift. They were featured on *Kathy Griffin's My Life on the D-List*.

Body Works by Myrna Moss, M.T., 805/526-1636 or pager 818/372-9474. She is a massage therapist to the stars and regular folks too. 13 years of experience. She brings her table to you. Deep tissue work; she is a healer. Massage lowers your blood sugar and enhances creativity and productivity. Many production offices and shows hire her to come in and give neck and shoulder massages to cast and crew. What a great Christmas gift or end of season present for a cast or crew member to give to their fellow workers.

See above for *The Lynne Technique*.

Health, Doctors, Dentists, Nutrition, Mental Health and Plastic Surgery

• **Choosing doctors, dentists, nutritionists, alternative treatments and therapists** are very personal decisions; what is perfect for one person may not work at all for someone else. I can only speak to you from my own experience and that of close friends.

• **I am inclined to investigate most everything**. I have received help and healings from many different types of traditional and nontraditional techniques.

• **As always, proceed with the utmost caution.** By investigating and following your own instincts, I believe you will be led to the paths that are best for your life.

PHYSICAL HEALTH

• **It is imperative to have your body in excellent condition** in order to be the best actor you can be; your body is your instrument. The following practitioners are all specialists in their fields. I hope you are never sick and only need to consult doctors in order to improve your life's condition. In my experience, holistic doctors allow me to take an active part in my recovery so I seek them out.

• **Dr. Cynthia Watson, Medical Doctor and Naturopath.**

Q: What are your recommendations for staying healthy?

    • **Maybe the most important factor is life style.** Make sure that you try to eat a healthy and balanced diet, lots of fresh fruits and vegetables. Stay away from the junk foods and sugar. Smoking, drugs, coffee and alcohol really rob your body of nutrients. Important to take a good vitamin program on a regular basis. Many of the congestion problems in Los Angeles are related to the pollution. Take antioxidant vitamins, A, C, and E. These vitamins help your immune system and handle some of the heavy toxins we're dealing with. One of the first things that I do with patients who have postnasal drip problems is take them off dairy products. Enzymes are a very important part of what the body does to help break down toxins, chemicals and food. As we age, we make fewer enzymes. I've found that taking enzymes between meals can help with some of the congestion problems like allergies and some of the digestive problems that I see in my practice.

Q: How do you keep healthy and keep the energy up when you are working the long hours our industry demands?

- **Again, antioxidant vitamins** like vitamin A, C, E and Zinc are important. B vitamins are essential for the nervous system, the adrenal glands and the liver. There are also herbs that can help give you energy and keep your immune system strong. Siberian Ginseng is an herb that really helps; it can be taken over long periods of time and it helps to support those glandular functions. Echinacea is an herb that helps to support the immune system. It shouldn't be taken over long periods of time, but on a short term basis like those three or four weeks that you're on a shoot, is fine. There are products on the market that have Echinacea and Golden Seal root together that help fight infection. Start these herbs in the beginning, as a preventative, and you'll have a much better effect in keeping illness away. Eat well. You can substitute coffee with Siberian Ginseng or American Ginseng for women, the Chinese Ginseng for men. Bee pollen, royal jelly or B vitamins will give you a little extra energy.

Q: What about traveling on locations, especially to foreign countries?

- **One of the things that helps my patients** is to take a form of acidophilus. That is a product that you can buy in your regular drugstore. It's a culture that's in yogurt and various milk products, and is available in capsule form that doesn't need to be refrigerated. When you take these capsules while traveling, you're continuing to fill your intestines with the healthy bacteria that your body is used to. It helps to prevent traveler's diarrhea and stomach problems. You want to be really careful about your water supply. If you're on a long air flight, take a bottle of water with you on the plane; don't rely on the plane water—it's generally not very good. Flying is extremely dehydrating. A little atomizer bottle helps to spray your skin. For motion sickness there is a homeopathic remedy called Cocculus. There are other drugs, but they tend to make you sleepy and give you dry mouth; the homeopathic won't.

- **Dr. Theresa Gormly, chiropractor and founder of the Los Angeles Center for Healing, offers additional information on staying healthy.**

  - **If people paid greater attention to their diet** they would not have as many physical complaints. I strongly recommend three meals a day consisting of 40% carbohydrates, 30% protein and 30% fat plus two small equally balanced snacks. The key is to eat high quality protein: lean red meat, turkey, chicken, fish and soy; low glycemic carbohydrates: vegetables, fruit, very little grain; and high quality fats such as raw nuts, cold pressed oils or avocado. For many people, it is also necessary to abstain from foods that they may be sensitive to, such as dairy and wheat.

  - **Nutrition is one side of the triad of health** that I assess when it comes to staying healthy. It is highly beneficial to care for the physical structure of the body. The spine and extremities house our central nervous system, the brain and spinal cord. Chiropractic care and plenty of exercise are great ways to care for the physical structure.

  - **Equally important is the emotional side of the triangle.** There are wonderful techniques that help clear the body of stored or toxic emotions such as Neuroemotional Technique (NET), Reiki and homeopathy. By paying attention to one's daily routine of nutrition, exercise, rest, work and play, it is easier to keep the triad of health in balance. EMOTION/CHEMISTRY/STRUCTURE.

Q: What do you recommend for delivering one's best performance when working long hours under a great deal of pressure?

  - **It is important to center one's mind** through meditation or attunement at the beginning of the day. The tool for long term *sustained* energy is blood sugar stabilization. This is done with the right choice and amount of food and no longer than four to five hours of time between balanced meals. This routine takes the stress off the adrenal glands and sustained energy and a clear mind will follow. A second 20 minutes of meditation or rest in the later part of the day will give the body a second wind for the evening hours. By combining rest or meditation with the appropriate food plan, you can't miss.

Q: What about air travel? Is it a concern when traveling to locations?

  - **Hobon Environs is a homeopathic remedy I recommend** for supporting the immune system during air travel and hotel lodging. This remedy helps prevent contracting airborne diseases that come through the ventilation systems. One capful per hour is recommended. It never fails. For jet lag, I recommend a Systemec Formula Gf to support the glandular system. It is to be taken at the beginning of the flight, mid-flight and every two hours on landing for about four to six hours. This helps the body handle the time zone changes.

Resources

To download and print an updated version of this and all resource lists, go to actingiseverything.com.

Working Actor's Guide lists doctors, dentists, alternative type treatments, nutritionists, mental health services, as well as medical insurance information.

MEDICAL DOCTORS, DERMATOLOGISTS

Free Clinics: Los Angeles Free Clinic, 323/653-1990. lafreeclinic.org. 8405 Beverly Blvd., Los Angeles, 90048. Valley Community Clinic, 818/763-8836. valleycommunityclinic.org. 6801 Coldwater Cyn, North Hollywood. They offer free pregnancy and HIV testing.

Low Cost Clinic: AIM Health Care Foundation, 818/981-5681. aim-med.org. 4630 Van Nuys Blvd, Sherman Oaks, 91403. Second location: 818/961-0291. 19720 Ventura Blvd., Woodland Hills, 91364. Tests for sexual transmitted diseases, no appointment needed. Exams and vaccines, by appointment only.

Cynthia Watson, M.D., Family Practice, 310/315-9101. watsonwellness.org, 3201 Wilshire Blvd., Ste 211, Santa Monica, 90403. Covered by SAG and AFTRA insurance; you file your own forms. A family practitioner treating men, women (obstetrics, gynecology included) and children, she combines conventional medical therapies with herbs, homeopathy, and nutrition. She is a nationally recognized authority in immune disorders and chemical toxicity. Her main interest is preventative medicine and longevity. Her book *Love Potions, A Guide To Aphrodisiacs and Sexual Pleasures* is a best-seller. She continues to write books on nutritional supplements that have healing capabilities.

Joan Osder, M.D., Dermatologist, 310/274-9954. 465 N. Roxbury Dr. #803, Beverly Hills, 90210. Wonderful; all the latest techniques. Samatha Harper told me about her—now we all go to her.

Emily Bloom, M.D., 310/278-8811. 436 N. Bedford Dr., Suite 202, Beverly Hills, 90210. Dermatologist. Highly recommended by our wonderful healer, Dr. Theresa Gormly. They give you a super bill and you file your own insurance forms.

Alex Khadavi, M.D., Encino Dermatology & Laser Center, 818/528-2500, lalasercenter. com. Botox, acne treatment, smoothbeam laser, scar augmentation, tattoo removal, hair removal, capillary removal, etc. Offers any and all procedures you could need as well as a number of skin care products. Offices in Encino, Thousand Oaks, Palmdale, Valencia, Ridgecrest, Glendale and Westwood. Dr. Khadavi works in Encino. Recommended by agent Bonnie Howard.

Doug Mest, M.D. Blue Pacific Aesthetics Group, 310/297-9111, bpacific.com, Hermosa Beach. Practices the latest in non-invasive, non-surgical cosmetics, including wrinkle treatment, radio-frequency skin tightening, skin rejuvenation and soft tissue augmentation. Also offers a number of skin care products. Recommended by casting director Stuart Stone. Normally charges a $75 consulting fee, but mention this book and he will waive the fee!

Harvey Abrams, M.D., Wilshire Aesthetics, *A Dermatology and Plastic Surgery Group*, 323/936-1245. wilshireaesthetics.com. 5757 Wilshire Blvd., Promenade 2, Los Angeles, 90036. Dr. Abrams and his associates are excellent. Laser dermabrasion, botox, collagen fills in lines, pumps up lips and smoothes out frowns. Nina Drucker-Bard's facials will not leave you marked but she gets everything out, $75 for cleansing and toning. They have vein and hair removal specialists and laser resurfacing.

Charles Schneider, M.D., Eyes, Ear, Nose and Throat, 310/201-0717. 2080 Century Park E, Century City, 90067. M-F 8–5 PM. Very highly recommended. He helped a singer friend of mine with chronic throat problems.

Uzzi Reiss, M.D., for women, 310/247-1300. uzzireissmd.com. Beverly Hills Anti-Aging Center, 414 N. Camden Dr. #750, Beverly Hills, 90210. They will file SAG and AFTRA insurance forms for you. Obstetrics, gynecology, infertility. He's delivered many babies of famous people. Although an M.D., he will prescribe homeopathic remedies. Very thorough, explains in great detail. A wonderful man and Julia Louis-Dreyfus' personal favorite.

DENTISTS

Vernon Erwin, D.D.S., Dentist, 818/246-1748. 620 E. Glenoaks, Glendale, 91207. Dr. Erwin uses all the latest technologies available. Ceramic fillings that last longer than metal ones; instant orthodontics, straightens teeth in weeks; implants replacing missing teeth; bleaching. He recently used a laser to correct my receding gums without surgery. They will file SAG and AFTRA forms for you. A homeopathic dentist, he will remove silver fillings and has all the equipment to test your body's reaction to what will be permanently put into your mouth. These types of dentists are hard to find. He does beautiful bleaching, repair and cosmetic work that looks like you have had nothing done, just beautiful teeth. He also treats TMJ. Theresa is the dental hygienist and she is excellent; very caring and gentle but thorough.

J. Alan Bloore, D.D.S., Orthodontist, 310/277-9700. 300 S. Beverly Drive, #101, Beverly Hills, 90212. M–Th 8:30–5:15, F 9–3:45; closed daily 1-2:15. My daughter, Cathy Kerr, had her teeth straightened as an adult. She just had to wear a retainer for several months and now they are beautiful. She says, "He is the best."

Conrad Sack, D.D.S., Orthodontist, 310/273-5775. 9201 Sunset Blvd., Suite 200, Los Angeles, 90069. He specializes in Crozat, a removable appliance to take the place of braces. He treats many actors.

Eric Donaty, D.M.D., 310/854-4999, 8920 Wilshire Blvd., Suite 625, Beverly Hills, 90211. killersmile.com. Brittani Taylor says, "He is such an artist in his field!! Does amazing dental work, and such a friendly office, your gonna love how gentle his hygentist is, and his assistants are great!"

William Dorfman, D.D.S., 310/277-5678. billdorfmandds.com. 2080 Century Park East, Ste 1601, Los Angeles, 90067. Cosmetic dentist. He is the inventor of Nite White, the country's most popular teeth whitener. He also does bleaching in the office. Used by the casts of *Friends, Melrose Place, Beverly Hills, 90210, ER, Seinfeld*.

Hal A. Huggins, D.D.S., Dentist, 866/948-4638. drhuggins.com. He is the author of the book *It's All In Your Head*. If you have some chronic medical problems that cannot be solved, you may be suffering from mercury poisoning which is caused from silver fillings in your mouth. This dentist is in Colorado. They will send you the book that lists all the symptoms.

Ron Sparks, D.D.S., 310/657-0674. 275 S. Robertson Blvd., Suite G Beverly Hills, 90211. Manager Steven Nash says, "He's great, very caring and good with both medical and cosmetic needs. Nice guy, easy to talk to, reliable. Good prices, despite his Beverly Hills location."

Raymond Ricci, D.D.S., 818/846-4271, 4405 Riverside Dr., Ste. 301, Toluca Lake 91505. From Anita Jesse, "I love my dentist and absolutely everyone who works in the office. Dr. Ricci specializes in cosmetic surgery and he and his superb technicians use state of the art equipment and technology. Procedures I had hated in the past are truly non-events with Dr. Ricci and his expert staff."

• **The following dentist is in Mexico.** Linda Small went to Dr. Morales. She took the train from Union Station to San Diego and then took a trolley, which is at the train station, to the border and the town of San Ysidro. You walk over the bridge and easily catch a taxi to take you to the dentist's office. A motel the dentists recommend is International Motor Inn, 190 E. Calle Primera, San Ysidro, 92173. Phone: 619/428-4486. Medical Clinic Discount rates, $50 per night. Free van service.

Javier Morales, D.D.S., Calle 6Ta. 1217 Esq. Mutualismo Zona Centro, C.P. 22000 (01152664). From the U.S. tel. 688-32-48 or 688-32-42. Fax: 685-34-57. Tijuana, B.C. Email: drmorales_tj@yahoo.com. He has a wonderful booklet that talks about silver fillings, root canals, generating toxins, diseases arising from mouth infections and nickel. Also includes a vitamin supplementation program and information on their detox programs. They have a D.M.P.S. chelation therapy as well as a Vitamin C therapy. Both in the form of IV drips. They have a variety of treatments for detox, including a masseuse that comes in several days a week.

EYE DOCTORS

Warren Reingold, M.D., of The Reingold Eye Center, 818/763-3937. reingoldeyecenter.com. 12139 Riverside Dr., Suite 101, Valley Village, 91607. Optometry, contact lenses, fashion eyewear, diseases of the eye. He is a very caring person and I find the office very friendly and helpful. Covered by SAG and Motion Picture Industry Health Insurance, they take care of the insurance for you. He also does all of the laser vision correction eye surgeries.

Caster Eye Center, Andrew I. Caster, M.D., F.A.C.S., 310/274-1221. castervision. com. 9100 Wilshire Blvd., Ste 265E, Beverly Hills, 90212. Laser vision correction. Frances Fisher says "I see the world through new eyes!" "Best Laser Eye Surgeon" in *Los Angeles Magazine*.

ALTERNATIVE DOCTORS AND TREATMENTS

Theresa Gormly, D.C., Los Angeles Center for Healing, 310/858-8886. center4healing. com. 1157 S. Robertson, Los Angeles, 90035. Covered by SAG and AFTRA insurance; you file your own forms. She is wonderful for relief of pain, stress, nutritional problems, candida, Epstein-Barr and general balancing. Networking and body integration. I cannot begin to explain the wonderful treatment I have received over the last twenty years from Dr. Gormly. Upon hearing my age, people are always surprised at how well I've held up—I owe the insides to her. Many, many celebrities and models go to her. Just a small percentage is covered by insurance but you can deduct the rest from your income taxes. She has cured me of the flu, sore throats, and a few cases of the "blahs" in a few hours with her homeopathic or flower remedies. For those of you into alternative medicine, she and her associates are a gold mine!

Noel S. Aguilar, PH.D., HMD, The DNA Health Institute, "The Power of Advanced Natural Medicine at Its Very Best." 310/858-8886. Los Angeles Center for Healing, 1157 S. Robertson Blvd., Los Angeles, 90035. Part of the Los Angeles Center for Healing. Dr. Aguilar uses many tests for diagnosis including electroacupuncture to screen the body. Using pen-shaped metal rods (microcurrent probes) that are hooked up to a computer, he touches the probes to different acupuncture points, or meridians, on the hands and feet that correspond to specific organs or body parts. The machine measures the small flow of electricity through each meridian, the numbers show on the computer and he can tell where your weak areas are. Two of my friends have been going to him for years with remarkable results. I'm very happy with the work I've done with him.

Mallory Fromm, PhD, and Therese Fromm of Sike Health Institute, 818/992-0713. sikehealth.com. Treatment facilities in the West Valley. $110 for initial diagnostic consultation, $80 for subsequent treatments. Mallory and Therese spent over 20 years in Japan learning a modern revision of classical Chinese medicine based on Qi Energy. To this they added Western movement and alignment techniques to create the SIKE Technique. The treatment is non-invasive, non-manipulative, and extremely effective. My husband has scoliosis, and Mallory has done wonders by straightening his spine, realigning his entire body's musculature, and completely removing his pain. Therese keeps me in excellent posture and quickly heals me when my structure falls out of alignment. They have helped many of my friends and family members. Mallory is the author of "The Book of Ki: The Healing Principles of Life Energy," and "Qi Energy for Healing and Health." Therese is a graduate of England's Royal Academy of Dramatic Art (RADA), is a certified instructor of Physio-Synthesis, has 25 years experience of Alexander Technique, and is also experienced in Feldenkrais Technique.

John W. Davis, 310/398-9196. 12036 West Washington Blvd., Suite #1, Los Angeles, 90066. Healer, body work, Reichian emotional release work, based on the body armor theories of Wilhelm Reich. John's work helps actors find the true depth and range of their feelings; a center inside from which they can make the transformation into the character. Sees a lot of actors, directors, writers and producers. My husband and I have both found great benefit from John's work.

Tawny Moyer–Reflexologist, 323/650-0748. For women only. $100, treatments are approximately an hour. Reflexology is an ancient healing technique used today which accelerates the body's own healing process by returning it to it's natural state of balance. It involves a steady, gentle pressure to specific reflex points on the feet that correspond to organs and glands throughout the body. Reflexology can provide relief for everything from minor aches and pains to chronic health conditions. It is also used for preventative health care and maintenance because it releases stress and tension through deep relaxation, as well as improving circulation, eliminating toxin, and revitalizing energy. It is a loving nurturing step toward better health and well-being. Tawny is a gifted reflexologist and very much in demand by actors and crew members when they have been working long hours on the set.

Health Within Holistic Center, 323/866-1808. healthwithincenter.com. 8370 Wilshire Blvd., Suite 230, Beverly Hills, 90211. "Health Within has established a reputation in the entertainment industry for offering the finest in holistic health care as well as a full service holistic facialist and massage therapist. We have an expert staff offering Acupuncture, Network Chiropractic, and Naturopathic care. By working with the body's energy, structure, matter and spirit, we create a level of health virtually unsurpassed in the healing arts." My friend Jonathan Levit loves this facility.

Murray Susser, M.D., a homeopathic doctor, 310/966-9194. 2211 Corinth Avenue, Suite 204, 5 blocks west of Sepulveda off Olympic in West Los Angeles. Also recommended by Sharon Stone, "He's created IV bags of vitamins and immune boosters, and when we were shooting *Casino* all night long, I was never tired. Also wonderful for jet lag; you take it the day before."

Eve Campanelli, Ph.D., 310/855-1111. evesherbs.com. 292 S. La Cienega, #307 Beverly Hills 90211. Remedies for healing, herbs, nutrition, minerals, acupressure. You can almost be healed from the website, you can certainly find out what's troubling you. Many celebrities including my friend Catherane Skillen.

Duong Huy Ha, C.A., Acupuncture. 310/394-9747. 1326 A 5th St., Santa Monica, 90401. M-F 8-5:30, Sat 8-3. First appointment is $130 for consultation and treatment and then it's $80 for each after that. Partially covered by SAG and AFTRA insurance. He started practicing in China at age nine. His phone number is unlisted; people come to him only through personal recommendation. He helped me quit smoking. Yeah!

Wing Hsieh, Acupuncture, 310/859-7618. 9400 Brighton Way, Suite 208, Beverly Hills, 90210. I have never been his patient but Lily Tomlin spoke of having a bad fall while doing a stage play; he helped her recover quickly and get back to work again.

Christina Marino, L.Ac., at Spa Transcendental, 818/505-9511. christinamarino.com. 10645 Riverside Dr., Toluca Lake, 91602. They have many spa packages and acupuncture for facial beauty. "When mind and body are in complete harmony, creating a perfect balance between the physical and the spiritual, the result is a state of well-being which is the most natural condition of mankind."

NUTRITIONISTS

Karen Cohen, CN, 310/444-9755. Learn2eatright@yahoo.com. Karen is a Certified Nutritionist. She is member of the National Association of Nutrition Professionals and is a Firstline Therapeutic Educator. She specializes in breaking the losing cycle of "yo-yo dieting" by recommending a personalized dietary plan based on habits and lifestyle along with nutritional supplements and exercise to help support optimal health and well-being. In her practice she uses a sophisticated computerized machine called Bioimpedance Analysis (BIA). It is a method of assessing your "body composition" – the measurement of body fat in relation to lean body mass. Initial consultation $185 for a 90 minute session plus a 45 minute follow-up session and Dietary Notebook that includes your personally designed food plan. My daughter Chris Kerr introduced me to Karen. On her plan I am never hungry, I'm going for health, weight loss and a new eating life style. Chris has been with Karen for about a year, she didn't need to lose weight but to learn how to eat for maximum strength and energy. She's now in maintenance and has never felt better.

Kristin Lundstrom, D.C., 310/858-8886. center4healing.com. Los Angeles Center for Healing, 1157 S. Robertson, Los Angeles, 90035. Covered by SAG and AFTRA insurance; you file your own forms. She is wonderful for relief of pain, stress and nutritional problems. She taught my husband and me about eating in The Zone. She tests different foods on you to make sure your body can tolerate your prescribed nutritional plan. She uses Contact Reflex Analysis (CRA) and Network Spinal Analysis to accurately determine the body's structural, physical, and nutritional needs. The root of the health problem is uncovered or it is used as a preventative technique to stop a problem from becoming a health issue. "Find it early and correct it."

The Vital Image, 310/823-1996 or 800/414-4624, in Playa del Rey. thevitalimage.com. Call for their special product report. Power O2 Tonic+ is a charged organic nutritional powder that gives you enhanced focus, concentration and willpower while fueling your energy reserves and stamina. Great for those early morning set calls and the long extended working hours. *Also see their listing under Age Defying Techniques for all of their valuable treatments and products.*

Weight Watchers, 800/651-6000, weightwatchers.com. They offer a very sound nutritional way of eating and motivational speakers. The "in" way of losing weight and keeping it off. Their program is all about health and eating education.

Susan Marque, susanmarque.com. Offers a food coaching service which not only teaches about good and bad foods, but also how certain foods affect people differently. Helps put together the right kinds of food for you and teaches how to cook or prepare your food to get the most out of it.

Elyse Resch, 310/551-1999. Nutritionist recommended by my friend and wonderful hair and makeup artist Rita Montanez. Elyse wrote a book called *Intuitive Eating: Feeding Your Body* in which she explores core issues surrounding particular foods by talking to people about their journeys in trying to eat better.

WEB SITES: FITNESS ONLINE
fitnessonline.com.
Rob Woods Home of Fitness Testing: topendsports.com/testing.
In Fitness and In Health Site: phys.com/
Nutritiously Gourmet Web Site: nutritiouslygourmet.com.

HOMEOPATHIC & HERBAL MEDICINES & REMEDIES
Dr. Richard Schulze, 877/TEACH-ME, herbdoc.com. Helps people help themselves through natural healing and herbal medicine. Sells a number of products, programs and books on his philosophies; all available on the website.
Santa Monica Homeopathic Pharmacy, 310/395-1131. smhomeopathic.com. 629 Broadway, Santa Monica, 90401. M-Sa 9:30 to 5:15; parking south of building.
Capitol Drugs, 310/289-1125. capitoldrugs.com. 8578 Santa Monica Blvd., West Hollywood, 90069. Nice coffee and juice bar. M-F 8:30-9, Sat 8:30-6, Sun 10-6.
Capitol Drugs, 818/905-8338. capitoldrugs.com. 4454 Van Nuys Blvd., Sherman Oaks, 91403. M-F 9-8, Sat 9-6, Sun 10-6.
Drug Stop 22 Pharmacy, 323/655-9761. 6753 Santa Monica Blvd, Los Angeles. M-F 10-6; Sa. 10-5.

MENTAL HEALTH

• **Knowing yourself can help you know the characters** you portray better; finding your own essence will help you find the essence of the character. As you learn to deal with your own anger, fears and anxieties, you will probably become a better actor. Working with a therapist or a self-help program can bring you to a deeper self-awareness.

• **Dr. Sherie Zander** gives the following advice on shopping for a therapist:

  • **Choosing the best psychotherapist** for your particular needs is of utmost importance. You will not only be spending time and money, but you will be talking about some very personal issues. The person you work with must be someone you believe you can trust. Base your trust on gathered information and an inner reaction or gut-level feeling about that person. If a therapist is recommended by someone whom you respect, that is a good place to start.

Q: What questions should you ask when interviewing a therapist?

  • **Are you licensed** by the State? How long have you been practicing? What type of therapy do you practice? Do you have experience with my particular issues? Have you had positive results? Would you do in-depth work to get to the root causes or would you have a more immediate behavioral approach? What is your fee? How often would I need to come in?

  • **As you gather information,** you will begin to get a feeling about the therapist and to form an opinion. It is important to trust that inner response you are having. If possible, interview at least three psycho-therapists and compare the information you get and the ways you respond to each one. Based upon all of this, make a choice.

  • **If, after several sessions,** you believe you have made the wrong choice, I would encourage you to tell your therapist that you are dissatisfied and then move on to someone else. It is far better to start over than to continue in a situation that is not working for you.

Q: What do you most enjoy about your work?

  • **It is a great source of encouragement** to me when I see someone move from a place of despair to a place of hope, when emotional pain is decreasing and wounds are healing, when someone begins to utilize new tools and techniques to handle old sets of problems and when life is being viewed from a new perspective.

Resources

To download and print an updated version of this and all resource lists, go to actingiseverything.com.

psychboard.ca.gov. The California Board of Psychology website has good consumer information as well as being able to verify whether a therapist is licensed by the state. **apa.org.** The American Psychological Association website has articles and can tell you if a therapist has been sued. They also have a referral system at 800/964-2000.

Sherie Zander, ph.d., 310/472-9736. drsheriezander.com. Psychotherapist—very supportive. Relationship Specialist—creator of *Can't Love Without It, Secret Strategies for Dating, Relating & Mating,* providing women's and men's classes. dating and flirt training. She has been a guest on my cable show several times, discussing how she helps actors learn to deal with their anger, fears and anxieties. Call her to request a free guide she uses with clients to help them deal with anger. Dr. Zander also treats depression, anxiety, obsessive/compulsive and addictive behaviors. Appearing weekly on *TV Bride,* Sunday, 2PM.

Jackie Jaye Brandt, m.a., mft, Corporate Communications and Psychotherapy, 818/505-1664. 3575 Cahuenga Blvd. West, #213, Los Angeles, 90068. Stress management, communications training, time management, group workshops, couples groups and individual counseling. Jackie has made a huge difference in my life. She works with people privately, usually for short periods of time; she wants you well in a timely manner. She is the co-author of *Finally Free,* a book that teaches people how to release their diet mentality, which then releases their excess weights. *See Jackie's list of Self-Esteem Builders in the Create Your Life chapter.*

Eve Brandstein, 310/499-4111, evebrandsteinproductions.com. Eve is a MFT psychotherapist, hypnotherapist and life coach. Her experiences in the entertainment industry—she was a casting director and is presently a producer/director/writer—gives her special insight in helping her industry based clients. One aspect of the therapy she does is called Narrative Therapy, she helps you rewrite your life's stories. Her motto is "what you believe is how you will live." Hypnotherapy, 2½ hours $295.

Pat Allen, Pd.D, 310/553-8248. drpatallen.com. Specializes in finding and keeping a mate. She gives private or telephone consultations and her books and lecture tapes are available. Monday evening seminars from 7-8:30pm are $10. The location and price are subject to change; call 310/557-2154 for the latest information. A great place to meet singles. Author of the book *Getting To I Do!*

Carol Woodliff, WMW Group, 626/737-1478, wmwgroup.com, San Marino. Hypnotherapist with background in the industry. Five Minute Stress Management is a product designed to help people quickly reduce stress in their daily lives, as opposed to an hour or so listening to a cd. She also offers private hypnotherapy coaching. Call or check out the website for prices.

The following clinics are available on an ability-to-pay basis.

Gay and Lesbian Center, Mental Health Services, 323/993-7500. laglc.org. 1625 N Schrader Blvd., L.A., 90028.
Maple Counseling Center, 310/271-9999. tmcc.org. 9107 Wilshire Blvd., Lower Level, Beverly Hills, 90210. Sliding payment scale for actors who live or work in Beverly Hills.
Open Paths, 310/398-7877. openpaths.org. 12655 W. Washington Blvd. #101, Los Angeles, 90066.
Southern California Counseling Center, 323/937-1344. sccc-la.org. 5615 W. Pico Blvd., Los Angeles, 90019. I've known people who have received good help here.
Thalians, 310/423-1040 at Cedars Sinai Hospital, thethalians.org. 8730 Alden Dr., Los Angeles, 90048.
AIPADA-AFTRA-**Industry Program for Alcohol & Drug Abuse** Hot Line: 800/756-HOPE Take 12 meets every Friday at 8:30 p.m. in the James Cagney Room at SAG. Closed meeting for union members only. Marijuana Anonymous, 323/964-2370 or 818/759-9194; Adult Children of Alcoholics (ACOA); Overeaters Anonymous; HOW/Overeaters Anonymous; Nicotine Anonymous; Narcotics Anonymous; Anger Anonymous; Co-dependents Anonymous (CODA); Debtors Anonymous; Gamblers Anonymous; Sex & Love Anonymous (SLA); and for people who deal with alcoholics or addicts in their life or addictions not listed here: ALANON 818/760-7122. Many meetings are held at the Crescent Heights Methodist Church, 1296 Fairfax Avenue, West Hollywood. Stop by and look at their posted schedules.
Alcoholics Anonymous (AA) Referral Service & Treatment: 800/711-6375.
24 hour hotline; can help you locate meetings in your area.

PLASTIC SURGERY, LIPOSUCTION, VEIN AND HAIR REMOVAL, SKIN RESURFACING

• **The most important thing you can do as an actor** is to stay out of the sun; it is what ages you. If you have already done the damage before you knew you wanted a long career in front of the camera as a leading actor. Unless you have fabulous genes you will need cosmetic corrections done. Check the *Age-Defying Techniques Section* for things to be done before the knife, including resurfacing, botox and collagen.

• **When considering breast implants,** understand that extremely large breasts will limit your casting possibilities. Yes, it will open up some roles but unless they call for nudity, you can do those parts with false breasts; even the nude ones can be done with body doubles. There is no way to make your breasts look smaller. Pamela Anderson removed her very large implants for just large ones. She still can't play a small-breasted woman. I think Demi Moore and Teri Hatcher have the best breasts because sometimes they look small and other times big. The most requested size for women getting implants is a full B or a C cup.

• **Liposuction, noses, eyes and breasts** seem to be the most popular procedures and I have found experts to discuss these and other procedures. Be conservative in your surgery decisions. I know it's tempting to have it all done at once because you save money, but it is wiser not to make plastic surgery decisions because of cost. Not all doctors are the same; they all have different views of the same surgeries. Choose carefully.

• **A new student of mine** came for a private class after having just been to a plastic surgeon. This girl is adorable, in her 20s, but looks like she's in her teens, ample breasts and lips, fashionably thin, attractive face, nice nose, cheeks. She went to a very notable plastic surgeon (a family friend) because she had a couple of small growths under her skin that needed to be removed. She was correct in seeing a plastic surgeon. But he met with her for an hour and showed her all the possibilities of improving her face and body. When she arrived at my house, she was feeling ugly and asked me for advice of what to do first. I said, "Leave yourself alone, you're unique and beautiful." Earlier that day I had been talking with an agent on the phone about meeting one of my very talented students. He said, "I hate her picture, looks like she's had her lips all pumped up." What could I say? She had. I relayed this to my new young student and told her to please let her good acting talent beam through her natural good looks.

• **Plastic surgeons are salespeople**, as are most doctors. Our goal should be to have as few surgeries as possible. Follow your instincts.

• **Your surgeon of choice is "a human being" not "God."** Ask questions, get clear answers and make sure costs, procedures and recovery are understood. Bring along a friend for moral support. Pay attention to the surgeon's attitude, temperament and responsiveness to questions. Ask for recommendations, photos or videos of befores and afters. Check the American Medical Association for negative reports. Remember that when getting a facelift, incisions will be made into the hairline. The skin removed in this area contains hair follicles and could mean a possible decrease in hair. Discuss each procedure.

• **Dr. Harvey Abrams, the founder of Wilshire Aesthetics,** A Dermatology and Plastic Surgery Group, talks about what liposuction can and cannot do.

  • **Thanks to recent technological developments**, especially the development of smaller, more refined instruments, liposuction is much improved. It can be offered to many more patients for whom I am able to remove larger amounts of fat safely and with minimal risk. In addition, the recovery process is much shorter and more comfortable.

Q: Who performs liposuction, how do you choose a surgeon, and how much does it cost?

- **Liposuction does not belong to any particular surgical specialty.** Board certified physicians, especially Dermatologists, Cosmetic and Plastic Surgeons who have performed many liposuctions and have an interest in liposuction, are the best choices.

- **Word of mouth is the best possible endorsement.** Get referrals from people who have had the procedure and are satisfied with the results and the care they received. It is important the physician is board certified in their area of specialization. It is best to find someone who has performed this type of surgery on a regular basis for many years.

- **Fees vary greatly** but generally range from about $4,500 to $9,000.

Q: Is this a good way to lose weight and does the fat come back?

- **Liposuction is not for weight loss.** It changes the shape of the body by removing unwanted fatty bulges. It is a very successful way of contouring for individuals who are within 10% of their ideal body weight.

- **Scientific evidence indicates** that removed fat cells do not grow back. If a person maintains a weight close to their normal body weight through proper diet and exercise, there is every reason to believe the body changes achieved will be permanent.

Q: Does laser hair removal work on everyone? Is it permanent?

- **The whole field of laser hair removal is very new.** It doesn't always work, that is why you have to go to someone who knows whether it will work for you or not. There are a lot of variables; it depends on the thickness and color of the hair and on the color of the skin. Not everybody is a good candidate. Go to a technician who has had a lot of experience and will level with you. In our office, Dana has had 23 years experience in hair removal. Hair can be removed from every part of the body and it can be expensive. There are many so-called bargains that turn out not to be bargains because the technicians can't deliver on their promises. New lasers are being developed all the time. It is an evolving field. You want to go to someone who keeps up with the latest research and owns the latest proven equipment.

Q: What can be accomplished with laser skin resurfacing?

• Lasers are used to eradicate many different flaws on the skin, including blood vessels, wrinkles, sun spots and other signs of aging. Wilshire
Aesthetics has a full range of laser services including tattoo removal.
The success rate depends on the tattoo. The ones that are a blue/black
are very successful. The ones that have many intricate colors, such as
blues, reds, yellows and greens, are much more difficult,and require
many more treatments. It doesn't usually leave a scar, but sometimes
you can't get out all the pigment, so don't start unless you are committed to finishing. It can take anywhere from eight to twenty treatments. A small tattoo could cost $1,000; a large one could be several
thousand dollars.

• **Dr. Guy Massry, specializes in reconstructive and cosmetic surgery
of the eye, eyebrows, forehead and mid-face lifting. I asked why some
doctors choose to specialize.**

  • I think when a doctor specializes in a specific area their experience
  will be greater, the surgical results superior and, most importantly,
  complications are minimized. For instance, in facial cosmetic surgery,
  a poorly done nose or eyes can cause significant disability to patients,
  as breathing and vision can be affected. It is vitally important that the
  surgeons performing these procedures are well versed and have vast
  experience in order to avoid post-operative problems.

  • The way I developed my practice is to combine the expertise of surgical subspecialists, thus creating a cosmetic team, in order to provide
  the best service and attain excellent results. A common example is
  the patient who desires a browlift, eyelid surgery and a rhinoplasty
  (nose job). I will evaluate the patient and perform the brow and lid
  surgery, while my associate who specializes in rhinoplasty will address that portion of the patients concerns. The patient gets the best
  of both worlds.

  • A significant part of my practice is revision surgery. This refers to
  patients who have had previous surgery who need further correction
  or are unhappy with the results. Typical problems are eyelids that
  won't completely close, lower lids that are pulled down or turned
  out, a "wide eyed" appearance, or residual puffiness of skin. These
  are complex problems that truly require the care of a specialist. For
  instance, when lower lids are pulled down, lifting the cheek to supply
  skin to the lower lids is often times necessary. Thus, to correct these
  problems, an understanding of mid-face surgery is essential.

Q: What about cheek implants?

- **You can lift the cheek without an implant**; the implant just brings the cheek out. Lifting the cheek is a procedure which brings the thicker cheek tissue higher and makes the cheek more prominent. If I can avoid putting foreign material in someone's face for life, I will. I'm very cautious about a foreign substance. When necessary, we will put it in.

- **Dr. Garth Fisher is a board certified Plastic and Reconstructive surgeon.** He specializes in aesthetic/cosmetic plastic surgery of the face and breasts. His practice has predominately included entertainers, celebrities and executives from around the world.

Q: When doing breast implants, do you make the incisions around the nipple for actresses that do not want any noticeable scars?

- **A large majority of the Playmates are my patients.** They often work with their clothes off, so I am very careful with the scars. I close the incisions carefully so that the scars are difficult to find. That is taken into account on a daily basis here.

Q: Is silicone still available?

- **For first-time patients, we primarily use saline implants,** unless there are mitigating circumstances, then we can use silicone. For reconstructive patients, I often use silicone.

- **There is an inclusion criteria set up by the FDA** and implant manufacturers. If the client fulfills the guidelines, then I use silicone. There are advantages and disadvantages to silicone implants. They are especially helpful for patients that have very thin skin.

- **There are different types of implants.** Teardrop shaped implants are mainly used on top of the muscle. Round implants can be used on top or below the muscle. The implant that is used depends on the person's body.

- **The important thing is having the implants look natural.** Small or large, you want to make them look like natural breasts. I find that is what most patients want. They don't like the hard, round, beachball look.

Q: I understand that you often have to do reconstructive surgery when a patient has had bad surgery elsewhere.

- **They are challenging cases and I've had a lot of experience with them.** I've done over 5,000 breast implants and associated reconstructive procedures. We try to convert people to a more natural look, a softer look. It depends on the particular problem they have.

Q: Is there any advice you would give people when interviewing doctors for breast implants?

- **Bring in pictures, show the doctor exactly what you want.** Communication is very important. Let the doctor know exactly what you are trying to achieve. Hopefully, he'll be honest enough to tell you whether he can deliver it or not. In our office, a patient will bring in a Playboy magazine. We know most of those girls, so we know what they are trying to accomplish. Look at before and after pictures, review some of the results of the doctor's work. Does he get the results that the patients are after?

Q: How can you try out breasts before having surgery?

- **They can fill Ziploc bags with saline or rice** and put them in their bra if they want to approximate sizes. It is not very reproducible or exact, but it may help.

- **Respected plastic surgeon Dr. Gregory Mueller** of Dr. Norman Leaf's office talks about facial surgeries.

Q: What kind of corrective facial surgeries are popular?

- **Eyelid lifts are the most common procedure** performed on patients in their thirties. Sometimes the upper lids will have excess skin; fat that can be easily removed under local anesthesia. The postoperative care consists of cool compresses to the eye area for 48 hours. The stitches are removed on the 6th day after surgery. Sometimes individuals also develop a creepiness under the lower eyelid—that too can be easily remedied with a mild chemical peel. For the individual with puffy bags under the eyes, lower lids can be improved by removing the bags and any excess skin. Both procedures result in a rested, refreshed look.

- **Another common surgery for younger patients** is called a platysmaplasty or neck muscle tightening and liposculpting of the neck. This procedure is done to improve and define the jaw line. Patents can usually return to work in just 4 to 5 days.

- **Cymetra is an amazing material** that requires zero down time and has immediate results. Injections of this soft tissue replacement material correct many defects, including repairing depressed scars, decreasing the appearance of facial creases, adding fullness to the cheeks and minimizing the laugh lines. Enlargement of lips. Like collagen, this treatment is not permanent and requires touch-up injections every 3 to 6 months.

- **Another procedure that is increasing in popularity** is male pectoral augmentation. The typical patient is physically fit, works out in the gym on a regular basis, but just cannot achieve the desired cuts and definition in the chest area. Other candidates include those born with a smaller muscle on one side, or someone who has injured the muscle. The surgery is performed on an out-patient basis, with the implants being inserted through a small incision in each armpit. The patient wears a compression vest for approximately 4 weeks. After this period, he may return to full physical activity.

Q: At what age should someone consider a face lift?

- **It really depends on your genetics and how you age.** When people notice they are beginning to get jowls around the jaw border area, or if they notice that skin is sagging under their neck, they may want to consider a facelift. This procedure can dramatically improve a person's appearance making them appear younger.

Q: How do you hide the scars?

- **The scars are very well concealed.** There is no way you can do surgery without scars, but putting them inside the ear can hide them. We actually pull the front part of the ear forward and we are able to make the incisions almost on the inside of the ear. And then we bring it right around the ear where the earlobe attaches to the head and then back behind the ear in the little crease where the ear meets the side of the head, and then along the hair line, or sometimes in women, we will go up in the hair. Done this way, it allows us to hide the scars within the natural contour of the ear. The scars are very hard to see after several months. It usually takes 6 months to a year for the scars to completely heal, but even after two weeks you can conceal the scars by putting on cover-up make-up.

Q: How do you keep from having a pulled artificial look?

- **When choosing a plastic surgeon**, ask to see photos of other patients. If you like the results, you will probably be satisfied with your result. If the look is "too pulled" or obviously surgical, I would choose another surgeon.

Q: What if you want to lift your forehead or raise your eyebrows?

- **There are a couple of different treatments for foreheads.** Probably the newest and the most popular is Botox. Botox helps people who have wrinkles on the forehead. It is a medicine that you inject, in an office procedure that takes about ten minutes. It basically relaxes the muscles so that they are unable to lift the eyebrows. What happens over a few weeks is it will lessen the wrinkles that run horizontally along your forehead. It will also improve frown lines and the crows feet around your eyes.

- **Some patients have very low eyebrows,** so they aren't candidates for botox, which could actually cause them to have a further drop of the eyelids. They would be a better candidate for a brow lift.

- **There are two types of forehead lifts.** There is one where the incision is made across the head from ear to ear. You basically take out a strip of scalp and then just pull everything up backwards and sew it together. That is the traditional brow lift. The new one is more popular, especially with men, because of receding hairlines. It is called an endoscopic brow lift. A series of five small incisions are made in the front of the scalp. A scope and digital camera system is used to visualize the operation with the skin still remaining on the forehead. We are able to release the eyebrows from underneath and then by using little anchors or screws, we are able to suspend the forehead. Fibrin glue is then applied to hold the forehead and brow in position.

Q: How long after a face procedure does it take to look presentable?

- **I recommend that my patients** have two to three weeks of down time if they don't want people to know. With makeup, you can pretty much conceal most of the scarring. You're still going to have swelling, but the majority of the swelling is usually gone. Usually the majority of the bruising is lower on the neck, so a high collar will conceal alot. After five to seven days, you can return to work if the appearance doesn't concern you.

Resources

To download and print an updated version of this and all resource lists, go to actingiseverything.com.

Cinema Secrets, 818/846-0579, cinemasecrets.com. 4400 Riverside Dr., Burbank, 91505. Face lifts without fear. Maurice Stein sells a nonsurgical face lift kit for $25 that purports to take 5 to 10 years off your face for four to six hours. Movie makeup experts have used these kits for years.

• *I give you the names of the following surgeons to start your research; rely on your own medical advisors before taking drastic surgical steps.*

LIPOSUCTION

Harvey Abrams, M.D. of Wilshire Aesthetics, a Dermatology and Plastic Surgery Group, 323/936-1245. wilshireaesthetics.com. 5757 Wilshire Blvd., Promenade 2, Los Angeles, 90036. Dr Abrams is the founder of the group and has been developing instruments and procedures for liposuction work for many years. He also teaches his procedures to other doctors. Dr. Abrams, in my mind, is "the artist of liposuction." The results depend on the artistry as well as the technique of the doctor.

American Society of Plastic and Reconstructive Surgeons, 847/228-9900. When you call they will refer you to their website for information, plasticsurgery.org. You can put in the name of the doctor and they will tell you whether or not they are certified. The website also has other links. If you are not online, call 888/475-2784, give them the names of the doctors and they will mail a printout with the information.

American Board of Plastic Surgeons, 215/587-9322. abplsurg.org. They will look up three doctors per phone call.

PLASTIC AND RECONSTRUCTIVE SURGEONS

Norman Leaf, M.D., F.A.C.S., 310/274-8001. Plastic and Reconstructive Surgery, 436 N. Bedford Dr., Suite 103, Beverly Hills. leafskincare.com. Practicing over 25 years. Specializes and is known for his beautiful facelifts. He was recommended to me as "the doctor for facelifts," by Dr. Theresa Gormly. Many, many celebrity clients. "W" magazine named him as one of the "World's Best Plastic Surgeons." Dr. Leaf has created Leaf and Rusher Medical Clinic, a ground-breaking facility in medical skin health and beauty. Teaming with Rand Rusher, R.N., to produce the Leaf&Rusher, www.leafandrusher.com, line of medical-grade skincare products. Dr. Leaf is my very special person and did my facelift a couple of years ago. It is very conservative and I certainly look in my age range, just tucked up a bit. I'm happy in every way. I recommend him from my own experience and from many I have sent to him, he is very talented.

Gregory Mueller, M.D. 310/273-9800. drgregmueller.com. 436 N. Bedford Drive, Suite 103, Beverly Hills, 90210. Dr. Mueller's practice is within Dr. Leaf's office, and involves all areas of plastic surgery, including plastic surgery for men. He is said to be "the brow lift king of Beverly Hills." Excellent bedside manner and aesthetic good sense. A famous retired plastic surgeon, when asked who would replace him, said, "Dr. Greg Mueller is the most talented up and coming surgeon in Los Angeles." Great, supportive staff. Dr. Mueller has pioneered several surgical techniques and has designed a pectoral implant for men. Dr. Mueller travels around the country teaching other surgeons his technique for pectoral augmentations, endoscopic brow lift technique and cymetra injection technique. He has been on several television shows including *Entertainment Tonight* demonstrating makeovers and surgical techniques. See his interview above.

Garth Fisher, M.D. 310/273-5995. garthfisher.com. 120 S. Spalding Drive, #222, Beverly Hills, 90212. Board certified. *Los Angeles Magazine* says "One of the best plastic surgeons in L.A." *Best Doctors in America Review* chose him as "One of the top facial cosmetic and breast surgeons." I am most personally impressed by his "tear drop" silicone breast implants. One of my students had implants that were too large, but Dr. Fisher replaced them. He went in through the nipple and performed a miracle, since this actress needed to have virtually invisible scars. I saw them after only three months —amazing results! International clientele. Very helpful staff. Laser skin resurfacing. Featured on television's *Extreme Makeovers*.

Guy G. Massry, M.D., 310/453-8474. ggmassrymd.com. 120 S. Spalding Drive, Suite 315, Beverly Hills, 90212. Dr. Massry specializes in reconstructive and cosmetic surgery of the eye, eyebrows, forehead, and mid-face lifting. He worked a miracle on my eyelids. They had already been through three surgeries; he cured my tearing problem, plus he brought back the natural shape that had been distorted. (yeah!) He also does laser skin resurfacing, treating skin that is sun damaged, wrinkled, pigmented and scarred. Dr. Massry performs a large amount of revisional work. I have accompanied close friends and relatives through their eyelifts—they all have been very happy. See his interview.

Dr. Gary Solomon, M.D., 562/424-7787, 1440 Atlantic Ave., Long Beach. About 30 years in the business. Recommended by agent Bonnie Howard. He is off the beaten path and his prices are much better than the Beverly Hills doctors. Chief of Surgery, Long Beach Memorial Hospital. Invokes great feeling of safety and confidence. Very natural looking facelifts, caring, sensitive. Terrific staff.

Harry Glassman, M.D., 310/550-0999. glassmanmd.com. 120 S. Spalding, Suite 205, Beverly Hills, 90212. Very large celebrity clientele.

George Glowacki, M.D., 310/540-0144. 4201 Torrance Boulevard, Suite 150, Torrance, 90504. Board certified. One of my students had implants that were too big for her body, saline double Ds. He replaced them with saline Ds and she was very happy with the outcome. Reasonably priced.

HAIR TRANSPLANTS

Dr. Lee Bosley, Bosley Hair Institute, 800/985-6405. Locations all over the country. bosley.com

Dr.Peter Goldman, 310/855-1160. 8631 W. 3rd St, #635. Los Angeles, 90048.

Dr. William Rassman, The New Hair Institute, 1-800-NEW-HAIR. newhair.com. 9911 W. Pico Blvd., Ste 301, Los Angeles, 90035. Considered the number one hair transplant surgeon in the United States.

SECTION SEVEN
ACTING IS EVERYTHING

LOVE OF YOUR CAREER AND SHOWBIZ

• **I decided I had to live my life as an actor**—that I could be nothing else—in January 1975, sitting in my car at the corner of Hollywood Blvd. and Vermont. That decision, ambition, drive, has guided my life every day since. If you can be anything else but an actor, be it. But if you can't, then forge ahead, and love your choice. It is great to learn to have fun in life, to find pleasure.

•**Tom Hanks said:**

   • **Acting is one cool gig.**

• **Kate Winslet said:**

   • **Because of the person I am, I won't be knocked down—ever.** They can do what they like. They can say I'm fat, I'm thin, I'm whatever, and I'll never stop. I just won't. I've got too much to do. I've too much to be happy about.

•**Timothy Hutton said the most important lesson he learned about acting** was from his actor father, Jim Hutton. When Jim was working and things were going well, he was happy; when things weren't going well, he was still happy because he had such a great appreciation for just being in the business.

• **James Woods said:**

   • **Acting per se has never been a struggle for me** because I enjoy it so much. I enjoy the other actors, being on the set, the excitement and the tension of going for the gold.

- **Janine Turner said, before she got Northern Exposure, the job that started her working career:**

  - **I was very depressed.** I had been auditioning for something like 11 years. I was wiped out. I couldn't even get a job as a waitress. So I went down to the jewelry district with the ring. (At one time she was engaged to Alec Baldwin.) I didn't know who to trust and I ended up walking away—I just couldn't do it. I had $8 in my checking account and wasn't able to make the rent. With nowhere to go but up, I tried for the part of Maggie.

- **Life can turn around on that phone call for an audition.**

- **We plant many seeds. It is important not to dig the seed up** to see if it is growing. We trust and have faith that it is indeed growing and it will manifest itself at the perfect time.

- **Ed Marinaro said:**

  - **If you can understand the reality of the business** and find a logical way of approaching it, your chances of being successful are going to be a lot better. There's nothing fair about the business. It's all about luck. The only thing you can count on is being prepared. You have to know what you're doing, train and become as good an actor as you can. What you can't count on is getting a break. But if you do get a break, you better be prepared; and that's true for every actor that's ever been successful. They got lucky. If you're really emotion-ally down and feel like the world's dumping on you, the next day you might get a shot and you're not going to be prepared. You're gonna blow it.

- **When we use acting tools, we cannot go for results.** We have to *make the effort* and then be willing for nothing to happen. The results will take care of themselves. It is hard to trust this, but by filling our hearts with love it is easier to trust.

- **When we read 12 plays to find one scene** that we want to do in class, when we audition for 20 plays and finally get a walk-on role, when we send out 200 pictures and get one response, when we have 10 different odd jobs just to support our career, when we go on 20 interviews before getting one line on a television show, when we have 50 commercial interviews before landing one, we are *making the effort* and we will reap the benefits. All of these endeavors are our careers. "Happiness is found along the way, not at the end of the road."

- **Naomi Watts said:**

  - **I was so broke I got kicked out of my rental apartment** and lost my health insurance. It was a very lonely time. I packed my bags to go back to Australia so many times.

- **Discouragement is a killer**—a heart killer—don't give it a chance to grab hold of you. Yes, there are the times of discouragement and depression, but we must emerge from those times with even more determination and faith that the efforts will bring forth the results.

- **William Hurt said:**

  - **There's nothing about being an actor that isn't silly.** That's one of the attractions. It is very important to focus on this side of the work or else life can become tedious. So much of the effort we put out does not seem to get immediate results. One of the important bonuses is that the work is fun.

- **Farrah Fawcett said:**

  - **No matter what the experience, good or bad,** I think in the long run it strengthens your character and furthers your career.

- **Never give up!** Think of Lisa Kudrow's story. She was originally cast to play Roz on Frasier before it was given to Peri Gilpin. The story goes that Kudrow simply didn't mesh on camera with the rest of the cast. She kept at it and not long after, became a multimillionaire star actor on *Friends*.

- **Be willing for the results to be different than you imagined.** Usually they will surpass your wildest dreams—that's why it is very important to dream big, bigger, biggest. Do not limit your dreams. Who do you know who is more worthy of their dreams coming true than you? I trust your answer is "no one." When your dreams come true, you can help others attain their dreams as others have helped you to attain yours.

- **Kevin Spacey said:**

  - **There is no prize out there.** The only prize is this one (pointing to himself), what you feel and what you want to accomplish. To want and to be ambitious is not enough. That is just desire. To know what you want, to understand why you are doing it, to dedicate every breath in your body to achieve it, if you feel you have something to give, if you feel that your particular talent is worth developing, is worth caring for. Then there is nothing that you can't achieve.

- **Matthew Broderick said:**

  - **Actors have this desperate need to get in front of people** and do something. I don't know where that comes from; I have it too. Sometimes I think about it and I find it totally embarrassing. It's some kind of exhibitionist quality that we all have.

• **Visualization is a valuable tool. See yourself driving to the studio,** saying hello to the guard and pulling into your parking place with your name on it. Hear those magic words on the phone, "You got the job." Watch yourself driving in your new car to your dream house with all the worldly goods that would represent your monetary success as an actor.

• **Most of us are daydreamers living in fantasy worlds.** Put your dreams to work for you; instead of dreaming negatively—worrying about future problems—dream positively. Guard and treasure your fantasy world; it is the key to your future. If you can picture yourself doing something, you can attain it. Your dreams will show you how to fulfill your desires.

• **Mary Steenburgen**, at a tribute for Jack Nicholson, told of working as a waitress in New York for five years while dreaming of an acting career. She heard of a casting call for *Going South* which Jack was directing. When she went by the office, the casting director told her, "We're only seeing well-known actresses or very beautiful models." Mary says, "Shy as I was, I did insist on seeing the script. Suddenly I hear this unmistakable voice, which said, "Are you waiting for me?" And I answered, "No, I don't have a script." After he gave me a script, he promised he'd see me for 10 minutes the next day." Several days later, Mary got the call to go to Hollywood for the screen test, and we know of the great career that audition fostered.

• **Julian Myers**, a Hollywood publicist, wrote a column years ago that I keep as an inspiration. Here are some of the ways he suggests to keep happy working in Hollywood.

  • **Be individualistic. Be different. Have outside interests.** Entertain, even if necessarily modestly. Master the Internet and use it. Attend many industry doings, including dinners and forums. Eat, drink and have your hair done where your colleagues do. Drive a more expensive car than you can afford, and keep it shiny. Keep in touch with prospective employers every few months, preferably by mail. Dress attractively. Work long hours if they are leading you upward. Set aside savings for when you are unemployed. You will be. Cheerfully fill special requests. Have time, interest and advice for those not yet up to your career level. Attend movies and observe what audiences react to. Try to see all important TV shows, and each series at least once. Average less than six hours sleep a night. You're in a tough race and you have to make each hour count. Read new books. Decide this is your industry and you'll always be a part of it, even when between jobs. Try to like almost everyone in the industry—and almost everyone will like you. Look for the good in Hollywood and defend it.

ACTORS WITH DISABILITIES

• **Otto Felix, an able-bodied actor, writer, director and photographer** is the founder of Handicapped Artists, Performers, Partners, Incorporated (HAPPI), the largest non-profit theatrical group for disabled performers in the country. Otto has written, produced and/or directed four films and 27 variety shows that have starred such big names as Billy Bob Thorton, Vince Vaughn and Bridget Fonda. He has done over 300 commercials, has been a regular on three TV series plus many guest-starring roles and worked in over 20 feature films.

Q: Tell me about HAPPI.

- • **I created HAPPI in 1986.** There are disabled actors, musicians, comedians and athletes looking for a break but finding it harder than the average able-bodied performer. HAPPI includes partners who are all able-bodied people that also have the same aspirations, and they work side by side with disabled performers. We have a 10-piece band made up of able-bodied and disabled people. We have acting and musical workshops every Tuesday and Thursday night. We haven't missed a night in 20 years.

- • **The honorary chairpersons** are Fred Dryer (Hunter) and Dwight Yoakam. The students elect their own president of HAPPI. Presently, it's Nanette Klatt, a visually impaired horse trainer and riding instructor. Vice-president is Marcy Lovett who was paralyzed from the waist down in an automobile accident when her car was blind-sided. The other VP is Lindsey Taylor, the original Jerry Lewis "March of Dimes" girl.

Q: How much does it cost to join the organization?

- • **There is no cost to join HAPPI.** Everybody pitches in and helps pay for the Film Actors Shop Theater, the space that I rent over in West L.A. which usually comes to $60 per person each month. It's a voluntary thing. We have just launched our new management agency The H.I.T. Agency, that's HAPPI International Talent. We represent both able-bodied and disabled actors, musicians, comedians, singers and performers. For any work we help establish for them, we only ask them to donate back 10 percent to HAPPI as they would do with any agency. It's not a big powerhouse management agency, but we are successful at training and jump starting careers.

Q: How do you get work for your people?

- **I get calls from producers, directors and casting directors**. I recently got a call for three blind guys that sing. We represent the best blind acappella singing group in the country, "OutASight." Needless to say, they got booked. More and more casting people are becoming aware of HAPPI and HIT. We represent about 180 people.

- **Twice a year, I produce a professional variety showcase** at the Film Actors Shop. These showcases are guest-hosted by celebrities from all walks of life. In the past, we've had the governor, the mayor, Keith Carradine, Elliot Gould, Johnny Rivers, Jon Voight, Bree Walker and Carl Weathers to name a few. I had celebrities give out little Ottos. Jon Voight calls them little Oscars. We give them out to handicapped people who did outstanding work in the previous year. The showcases are available to able-bodied as well as disabled and the performances weave the talent together…we show no discrimination at HAPPI. All the shows are professionally orchestrated and very entertaining.

- **My thanks to Terry Correll**, an actor/producer in a wheelchair, who told me about Otto and HAPPI. Terry is a wonderful, sensitive actor. He did a showcase scene on my cable TV show and had a leading role in a play I directed. His chair never made a difference. We didn't have to make any adjustments. He took care of everything.

Resources

To download and print an updated version of this and all resource lists, go to actingiseverything.com.

HAPPI, Handicapped Artists, Performers and Partners, Inc., The HIT Agency, 310/470-1939, The Film Actors Shop Theater/Studios, 10835 Santa Monica Blvd., Westwood, 90025. Workshops and classes to assist talented, disabled and able-bodied artists seeking careers in film, television, radio and other areas of show business. Interviews and auditions are held on a continuing basis. Free audits every Tu and Th nights, 7:30 p.m. at the Film Actors Shop.

Terre Worhach, manager, 310/670-5440. Terre represent actors with disabilities, very good at keeping up on what's available for the actors she represents. She is very helpful and will answer any questions you have.

Deaf West Theatre, 818/762-2998. Reservations: 818/762-2773. Voice: 818/762-2782 (TDD), deafwest.org. 5112 Lankershim Blvd., North Hollywood, CA 91601. Manager/artistic director is Ed Waterstreet. 99-Seat Equity Plan. Philosophy: to enrich the cultural lives of the two million deaf and hard-of-hearing Los Angeles residents, use of Sign Language Theatre (SLT), classics, contemporary and original works; other activities; professional summer school, children's workshops.

Down Syndrome Association of Los Angeles, Gail Williamson, 818/242-7871, dsala.org. Gail helps find employment for actors with disabilities. Lots of info on this site.

SAG Hollywood Affirmative Action/Diversity Department, 323/549-6645, sag.org. Performers with disabilities.

International Guild of Disabled Artists and Performers, igodap.org. Headquartered in New Zealand, but the website has a lot of helpful information and other links.

Writing and Directing
Workshops

WRITING

• **If you have a talent for writing**, it can indeed be one of your greatest career assets. You should certainly develop it. Final Draft is the industry standard scriptwriting software. Scriptware and Movie Magic Screenwriting are also popular.

• **We have all heard of Sylvester Stallone's** *Rocky* script. He was living penniless in New York but refused to sell his script unless he could act in it. It could happen to you.

• **Actors Matt Damon and Ben Affleck** decided, "If you want a good role, write it yourself." They sold *Good Will Hunting* to Castle Rock for well over a half a million dollars and both starred in it.

• **Copyrighting and/or registering your script is a must.** There are two ways to do it; some writers do both. The federal copyright office costs $30 and they keep the script for 75 years. Registering with the Writers Guild of America West costs $20, or $10 if you're a member. They keep the script for five years, which means you must re-register every five years.

To download and print an updated version of this and all resource lists, go to actingiseverything.com.

WRITING RESOURCES

An Abbreviated Screenplay Contest, aascreenplaycontest.com, 1483 N. Havenhurst Ave., Hollywood, 90046. Run by award-winning playwright Dan Roth and actors Biff Yeager and Barry Sigismondi, this contest costs $25-$45 to enter short film scripts. The organization than uses the money to film the winner's script under a SAG experimental contract. Very popular and successful!

Benderspink.com. Chris Bender and J.C. Spink are producers and managers of writers, known for their success with the American Pie franchise. You can submit scripts to their website and if they are interested they will give feedback and try and sell your project. Well respected. Also intern programs.

Scriptviking.com, 818/789-4032. John Winther is the founder of the script service, Script Viking. They have put together professionals with expertise to recognize script potential and financing. Visit the website for details and pricing.

Inkspot.com, many tips for writers.

Writing.com, a great resource for all kinds of writers, including screenwriters. Resources, message boards, job postings, etc.

Wordplayer.com. Run by successful screenwriters Terry Rossio and Ted Eliot, site has tons of helpful articles, message boards, etc.

The Writers Computer Store, 866/229-7483, writersstore.com. 2040 Westwood Blvd., Los Angeles, 90025. Anything and everything a writer needs. M-Sa 10-7.

For Copyrighting: Register of Copyrights, 202/707-3000, lcweb.loc.gov/copyright. Library of Congress, Washington, D.C. 20559. $30 fee. Find answers to questions regarding copyright and download copyright forms.

For Copyrighting: The Writers Guild of America West, 323/951-4000, wga.org. 7000 W. Third St., Los Angeles, CA, 90048. $20 fee, $10 if you're a member.

Alliance of Los Angeles Playwrights, 323/957-4752, laplaywrights.org. 7510 Sunset Blvd., No. 1050, Los Angeles 90046.

Beyond Baroque Literary/Arts Center, 310/822-3006, beyondbaroque.com. 681 Venice Blvd, Venice, 90291. Promotes reading, writing and publication of contemporary literature.

Broadway on Sunset, 818/508-9270. broadwayonsunset.org.

Dramatists Guild of America, Inc. 323/960-5115. dramaguild.com.

Mark Taper Forum New Work Festival, taperahmanson.com.

South Coast Repertory, scr.org.

Writers at Work, 323/661-5954, writersatwork.com.

Writer's Guild of America, West, 323/951-4000. wga.org.

SEMINARS

Beyond Structure, 310/394-6556; 866/239-2600, beyondstructure.com. Workshop comes with a full money-back guarantee. Emphasis on writing multi-dimensional characters and dialogue.

Truby's Writers Studio, 800/338-7829, truby.com. Classes, videos and tapes. Very popular among studio people.

Robert McKee's Story Seminar, mckeestory.com. Focuses on building a compelling story. Cost ranges from $325 to $545.

Syd Field, 310/656-8070, Ext. 17, sydfield.com. Characters workshops, general script help.

UCLA Extension courses, 310/825-9971, uclaextension.edu.

BOOKS ON SCREENWRITING

Story: Substance, Structure, Style, and the Principles of Screenwriting by Robert McKee. See him in Charlie Kaufman's movie, Adaptation.
Screenplay by Syd Field, an industry legend.
The Writer's Journey, Mythic Structure for Writers by Christopher Vogel. Based on the work of Joseph Campbell. Recommended by Maadison Krown. Jeff Arch says, "This book should come with a warning: You're going to learn about more than just writing movies, you are going to learn about life."
Fade In: The Screenwriting Process by Robert A. Berman.
From Script to Screen: The Collaborative Art of Filmmaking by Linda Seger and Edward Jay Whetmore.
Making A Good Script Great and others by Linda Seger. She's a premier "script doctor."
Making a Good Writer Great: A Creativity Workbook for Screenwriters by Linda Seger.
How To Write A Movie In 21 Days by Viki King.
Plots and Characters: A Screenwriter on Screenwriting by Millard Kaufman.
The Screenplay: A Blend of Film Form and Content by Margaret Mehring.
The TV Scriptwriter's Handbook; Dramatic Writing for Television and Film by Alfred Brenner.
The Script Is Finished, Now What Do I Do? The Scriptwriter's Resource Book and Agent Guide by K Callan.
Adventures in the Screen Trade by William Goldman.
Writing Screenplays That Sell by Michael Hauge.
The Complete Guide to Standard Script Formats, Part 1: The Screenplay by Hillis R. Cole, Jr., and Judith H. Haag. Also *Part 2: Taped Formats for Television.*
Dramatists Sourcebook and Writers Market

DIRECTING RESOURCES

Action/Cut Directed By: Industry Seminars, 800/815-5545. actioncut.com. In two days, gain first-hand career knowledge of the directing craft with a working director, Guy Magar, from page to film. Cost is $375. The only film learning workshop that offers a professional study of actual script scenes from the shooting process to viewing the final film. Step-by-step and shot-by-shot.
The Los Angeles Film School, 877/952-3456, lafilm.com. 6363 Sunset Blvd., Hollywood, 90028. 6-Week Digital Filmmaking Program plus many other workshops seven days a week. Daily tours at 11:30am Monday through Friday.
Sherwood Oaks Experimental College, 323/851-1769, sherwoodoakscollege.com. 7095 Hollywood Blvd., #876, Los Angeles, 90028. Many workshops for writers and directors.

BOOKS ON DIRECTING

Actors Turned Directors: On Eliciting the Best Performance from an Actor and Other Secrets of Successful Directing by Jon Stevens.
Directing the Film: Film Directors on Their Art by Eric Sherman.
The Director's Journey by Mark W. Travis
The Film Director's Team by Alain Silver and Elizabeth Ward.
On Directing Film by David Mamet.
On Film-making by Martin Scorsese.
Directing: Film Techniques and Aesthetics by Michael Rabiger.
Teach Yourself Film Making by Tom Holden.

Scams

• **In the years I have been writing this book** the number of scams has risen sharply. The first edition was published in 1985. I wrote it to help my students receive career services for good value.

• **If someone says they can make you a star or get you work** and you have no training and no experience, run! They want money or sex from you.

• **There is a scam going on where certain agents and casting directors** sell or make available to showcases or pseudo-acting schools the pictures that are submitted to them for employment. You will get a phone call from a salesperson who will say that you have come highly recommended from a casting director or agent. They won't know how they got your number but they want you to come in and audition for possible work. An actress told me she did a charity showcase with 80 people there from the industry. Each of the 20 actors received a call with this scam. One of the industry persons had sold or given away their folders that contained the actors' pictures and resumes.

• **Keep track of who you submit your pictures and resumes to.** Many producers receive thousands of submissions—they might throw them in the trash or they might pass them on to someone who has a scam going on. Actors are vulnerable because they want to act and are eager for the opportunity to do so.

• **There is a nonunion casting director** who has a showcase company. When you submit to the casting director for casting you may get a call from the showcase company asking you to come in and audition for the showcase. They usually say they don't know how they got your number; you will know how they got your number. It is fine if you contact the showcase yourself. I object to their practice of soliciting students in this way. I am not mentioning the showcase because they seem to present good showcasing opportunities and they are not a scam operation.

• **If anyone calls you out of the blue**, do not talk to them. If you have an agent or manager tell the caller to speak to them and get off the phone. I know it is tempting but there are no short cuts; you are not the exception. Do not trust anybody who has not come to you through your own thorough research or a personal introduction. Even then you have to be cautious.

• **Reported in** *Back Stage West,* a 17-year-old victim said he paid $25 to be given access to casting director Randy Callahan's casting "hotline" after being referred to him by photographer Bud Stansfield of Western Images Photography. When he called, the jobs were always for over 18. Nevertheless, Callahan did let the boy come in for a purported audition for a *Playgirl* video that would feature frontal nudity and simulated sex. The actor took a couple of friends to the casting director's house for the audition. Callahan told him he needed three nude pictures of him—one from the back and two from the front, with one depicting him in a state of arousal—to show the video's director. The friends waited outside near a window so they could hear everything.

• **The actor said the first two pictures** made him "very uncomfortable," but it was the third that made him most nervous. "Callahan took off his shorts and then he started playing with himself. He said, 'Look, you do it, too." The actor followed the casting director's instruction and let him take the third photo.

• **When the police came in to search,** they found the actor's pictures in a drawer along with a stack of similar pictures of other men. Callahan had never sent them to the so-called director. A spokesperson for *Playgirl* said that the magazine did not produce the videos that Callahan claimed to be casting for.

• **Video Scam: A pitch given to a** *Back Stage West* **reader** from a manager who somehow got her number to see if they could work together. The meeting took place in his apartment. He said he was putting 24 actors on video to be sent to selected agents and casting directors. Each actor got two minutes on the tape. The cost to each actor is $175 and $40 a month for the term of the contract. He talked for two and a half hours saying he needed a decision right away because he was shooting the next video in a few days. Look out for video scams!

• **Premier Casting, an extras' casting company** also known as Universal Casting, charges $89 for a registration fee. They say you will work within a few days. Thomas Mills, "Tombudsman," a former weekly columnist for *Back Stage West,* asked in his column for information. He was overwhelmed with complaints. After paying Premier, the actors had obtained no work or received a few post-midnight phone calls offering work early the following morning in faraway areas. They were promised a shot at small speaking roles if they signed up for $280 classes at Hollywood Way Pictures. The Better Business Bureau has logged 1,136 inquiries and 36 complaints against this company. Other names for the same company are Matthews Casting, Charles Matthews Casting and Take Five Casting.

Durkin Artists Agency, Debbie Durkin and On-Camera L.A. have been luring actors from out of state as well as in Los Angeles. She was a state licensed and SAG franchised agent. She insisted potential clients study at On-Camera, her company, and have pictures taken by a photographer she got kick-back from. It is illegal for an agent to charge anything or to insist you study at a particular place or have photographs from a certain photographer. She finally lost her SAG franchise when she negotiated a commercial reinstatement for a former client and failed to turn over his residuals earnings of $3,500 for more than a year. Debbie Durkin is now a personal manager and not under the watchdog of the state or SAG. You are holding a book in your hands that recommends plenty of legitimate photographers and teachers. Do not get ripped off by these type of promises. It takes a lot of violations and complaints for an agent to lose their SAG franchise. Don't even trust the list, investigate.

Kirk Owens was arrested for sexual battery of two actresses and probably more. He advertised for a 20-30 Caucasian, slender, blond, attractive actress for a one day nonunion shoot with pay. He used the name Tony Wilson, met one actress in a public place, then ask her to come to his apartment where the script was. He then ask her to take off her clothes down to her underwear because that would be how the scene would be shot. You are reading this and thinking, "Why would an actress do that?" but unfortunately they do. This is not the way to have a career—please hear me loud and clear.

• *Glamour Models* was reported to me by a reader of the 8th Edition. She said they bragged of all the careers they had developed. They wanted to represent her, and there would be a fee of $500 for color pictures. Actress Tiana Hynes, a reader of the 9th Edition, reported they wanted $750 for composite cards. She says, "Stay away from this company, it is a scam."

• **When auditioning for a "nudity required" role** you are never required to take your clothes off for the audition. You will have to do that after you have your contract which will spell out exactly what type of nudity will be expected.

• **West Coast Talent Ltd. Inc., Alexander Zafrin and David Leroy Harris** were convicted and sentenced to 30 days in jail for grand theft in connection with a scheme in which parents were enticed to pay thousands of dollars for promotional materials and acting classes for their children. These crooks are probably already operating again, look out!

• *Back Stage West* goes to extreme measures to make sure their notices are legitimate, but you still have to be extremely careful with independent, nonunion projects. There is no one to protect you. If you are the least bit suspicious, take someone with you to the audition location. If anything seems odd, leave. If you are asked for money for anything, even a $10 picture, leave. Report them immediately to *Back Stage West.*

• **Do not submit your picture and resume to any publications** other than the trades. The ads in other publications, such as free papers like *New Times* and *L.A. Weekly*, are paid ads and will come to no good.

• **Entertainment Studios** say they are a management company; they charge people $495 for a seminar.

• **John Robert Powers** advertises on Disney Radio. One of my readers wrote and told me of what happened when she took her son in to the office. "They tried to entice me to sign my son up to the exclusive invitation only John Robert Powers Club for $5,000." Her son said, "No Mom, let's go." A bright boy. Subsequently they sent in a snap shot to Ford Models and they now represent him without putting any money out. You will always have to buy pictures, but you choose the photographer. I've actually had several complaints about John Robert Powers. Investigate carefully when investing your money.

• **Stalkers and their Victims** (published by Screen Actors Guild.)

The Stalkers:

47% Simple obsession: Stalker, usually male, knows target as an ex-
    spouse, ex-lover, or former boss, and begins a campaign of harassment.

43% Love obsession: Stalker is a stranger to the target but is obsessed and
    mounts a campaign of harassment to make the target aware of the
    stalker's existence.

9.5% Erotomania: Stalker falsely believes that the target, usually some-
    one famous or rich, is in love with the stalker.

The Victims:

38% Ordinary citizens.

32% Lesser known entertainment figures.

17% Highly recognizable celebrities.

13% Former employee/employer; other professionals.

*To download and print an updated version of this and all resource lists, go to
actingiseverything.com.*

Gavin de Becker & Associates, 818/505-0177. gdbinc.com. 11684 Ventura Boulevard
#440 Studio City, 91604 A large staff of security people. Home-security systems, back-
ground checks. He is the author of *The Gift of Fear,* also an expert stalking consultant.

SAG, Affirmative Action, 323/549-6644, sag.org. **Legal Affairs,** 323/549-6627.

Bunko/Fraud Unit, LAPD, 213/485-3795 or 818/756-8323, lapdonline.org if you are
confronted by a dishonest operation.

Vice Squad, 213/485-2121. Deals with cases of immoral or lewd nature.

L.A. City Attorney's Office, 213/485-4515.

L.A. County Dept. of Consumer Affairs, 213/974-1452.

Actor Information Service @ Acting World Books, 818/905-1345. actingworldbooks.org

Back Stage West **Casting Line,** 323/525-2358. bswcasting@backstage.com If you have
any suspicious occurrences during the auditioning process, call immediately.

Section Eight
Becoming Geographically Desirable

the Right Time to Move to Los Angeles

and

the Scouting Trip

• **This section of the book was inspired** by an interview I had with Tony Shepherd. At the time he was Vice President of Talent for Aaron Spelling Productions, overseeing the casting of all of their television series such as *Beverly Hills 90210, Melrose Place, The Heights, The Love Boat, Colbys, Dynasty, Hotel, Family.*

Q: When do you think it's time for an actor to consider moving to Los Angeles?

• **If an actor** wants to earn a living in motion pictures or television other than doing commercials, they have to be in Los Angeles. It may be time to think of moving when you've outgrown the market you're in. That means if you're in Chicago and you're pulling 60-70% callbacks, booking 35-40% of the jobs, you're ready.

• **If you've never been to Los Angeles**, make a trial visit. It's a tough city to live in; it's expensive. When someone is moving to L.A., it's not the actor, it's the person. It's a question of whether you want to pick up stakes. To move to L.A., you need talent, marketability, desire, time, money and patience.

• **I agree with Tony. Make a trip to Los Angeles** and check out the town; see if you could live here before you move.

• **Don't even think of living "close" to L.A.** If you move to Orange, Ventura or San Bernardino Counties you have not moved to Los Angeles. Yes, the rent may be cheaper but there is a reason. You can't drive into Los Angeles for an audition, interview, class or networking in less than two hours most times of the day. You must be close enough to be a part of the show biz community. If you are making the move here, give yourself as many advantages as possible by living where the action is. Be sure you have a Los Angeles cell phone number too, it is smart to get one before you move: 213, 323, 310 or 818. No excuses; do it.

• **When you do move to Los Angeles,** it is in your best interest to be debt free, computer/on-line savvy with your own up-to-date computer and a paid-for reliable car. You'll need money to set up a place to live, which is usually first and last month, a security deposit and for sanity, a two month cushion; this could total $5,000 or more. Money for pictures and picture reproductions—figure $1,000 and it will take about a month to have them ready to go. It would be wonderful to know you have enough money to take two classes a week plus a networking group for at least six months. Conservatively, that would be $450 a month, so $2700. Keep in mind you are moving here to be an actor; it is most important to be acting. Next will be your spending money for three months. What is your life style? How much money do you need each week? This could be another $3,000. While you are preparing to move, keep track of your daily expenses. Most things in Los Angeles cost more than where you live, unless you're moving from NYC, and there are so many more things you will want to take advantage of here. Don't plan on being a different person when you move; it just doesn't happen.

• **When you arrive here with this kind of financial backing** it will still be a jolt—moving is one of the most stress-causing events a human can experience. With your above basic needs taken care of, you will be more likely to have a successful move. You will be more at ease while you are finding that survival job to eventually pay for these expenses after your hometown savings have been exhausted. You will be living your dream of being an actor in Los Angeles.

• **Many move here without financial backing** and make a go of it as well. You can work and earn money here, so if you want to move, move. Will it be harder? Yes. But you will be here and at least learning what it is like to be here. Some people have more courage than others and some are more willing to live on the edge than others. You decide for yourself. You don't want to end up at 50 years old and say, "Gee, I never took the chance."

• **Do not count on a public transportation system** to get around; you will be sorry. In your home town, buy a Sunday *Los Angeles Times* newspaper or get it online. Also check online: *Craig's List* (Los Angeles.) You will find lots of information, possible survival jobs available and the costs of rents. When you get here, pick up the *L.A. Weekly* newspaper and the *Recycler*. They're free and can be found at most 7-11s, liquor stores, music stores, newsstands, theaters, restaurants and other locations.

• **Carry this book with you** and purchase *The Thomas Guide* (street map book). Many rentals will expect a six month or one year lease. There are bulletin boards and rental services where you can look for a roommate. Be careful, don't trust too easily.

• **Jay Bernstein, manager, writer, producer**, taught a course called *Stardom, the Management of, the Public Relations for, and the Survival and Maintenance In.*

Q: What is your advice for actors who are moving here from out of town?

> • **They should be studying the town.** It's very tricky with a lot of roads and some of them look like freeways. You have to be very careful where you're going. I tell people to spend a year like you were in college. If your parents paid for your college, they may pay for a year here. If you worked your way through college, then work a year here. Get a feeling of what's going on. Weigh every decision. There's plenty of time. Get that career team together.

• **If you are new, visit or call the local Police,** crime prevention section, and ask if where you are planning to stay is a safe area.

• **Always be on the lookout** for film and television personalities. You will see them.

• **Actor/writer Jim Martyka moved here from Minnesota** and has become a resident tour guide for his family and friends who come to visit. He has added some great cool spots to this section.

Losangelesalmanac.com. All the L.A. neighborhoods.

To download and print an updated version of this and all resource lists, go to actingiseverything.com.

• HOTELS & MOTELS

• **There are many hotels and motels here.** You can probably pick up a guide book at your local bookstore or over the internet. Those below are mentioned to give you an idea of some acceptable areas.

Grove Guesthouse, Bed and Breakfast, 888-LA-Grove or 323/876-7778. groveguesthouse.com. Located in a safe, celebrity-filled West Hollywood neighborhood, it is central to everything you will want to see. This is a fabulous value and one of my special secrets. For under $200 a night you are the only guests in your own private luxury villa with separate bedroom, and eat in kitchen, beside a wonderful pool/spa and delightfully landscaped yard. Parking, high speed internet access, and domestic phone calls are free and you'll save money preparing your own meals. Your hosts are very savvy entertainment industry folks. Major movie stars stay there because it is very special! **Mention** *Acting Is Everything* **for best rate.**

Extended Stay America, 818/567-0952. extendedstay.com. 2200 Empire Ave., Burbank 91504. A very good area. Walk to a big outdoor mall; many eating places. Stay a week or more for big savings. Two miles from Burbank airport. A good place to stay while looking for an apartment.

Banana Bungalow Hollywood at The Orbit Hotel and Hostel. 800/446-7835 bananabungalow.com. 7950 Melrose Ave., West Hollywood. Dorm rooms $20 to $22. Weekly Dorm rates: $133 to $147 private rooms are: 1-2 people $69 to $76 three people $79.00 to $88, four people $89 to $100.

Best Western Farmer's Daughter Motor Hotel, 323/937-3930. farmersdaughterhotel. com. 115 S. Fairfax Ave., L.A. $149.00 to $189.00 single or double. Across the street from Farmer's Market and CBS Studio City, where shows are taped. Also the greatest little hip shopping center—The Grove.

Beverly Garland's Holiday Inn Hotel, 818/980-8000. beverlygarland.com. 4222 Vineland, North Hollywood. Right off the 101 Freeway. Moderately priced. $149 to $179. Special rates for AAA, entertainment cards. Paradise Cafe is a favorite.

Beverly Laurel Motor Hotel, 323/651-2441. 8018 Beverly Blvd., Los Angeles. Near the Beverly Center Shopping Mall. $90 single, $94 double. Adjacent to Swinger's Coffee shop.

Beverly Terrace Hotel, 310/274-8141. beverlyterracehotel.com. 469 N. Doheny, Beverly Hills, 90210. Basic but in a safe, central spot across from a great little market. Single $159.95 a night or $550 weekly. Double $194.95 a night. Weekly rate depends on date.

El Patio Motel, 818/980-2176. 11466 Ventura Blvd., Studio City, 91604. Near Universal and CBS Studios. AAA recommended. $55 single, $59 double.

Holiday Lodge, 818/843-1121. 3901 Riverside Dr., Burbank, between Hollywood Way and Pass Ave. off the 134 Freeway. Very near Warner Bros., NBC, Disney and Universal Studios. $75 single, $85 double.

Holloway Motel, 213/654-2454. hollowaymotel.com. 8465 Santa Monica Blvd., West Hollywood. $85 to $95 a night. Weekly rates are less. Jim Morrison stayed here many times in the old days.

Hollywood Roosevelt Hotel, 323/466-7000. hollywoodroosevelt.com. 7000 Hollywood Blvd. Hollywood, 90028. Great old hotel in the heart of Hollywood. Not a great neighborhood but safe enough and very handy for getting anywhere. Rates are $199 to $5,000 in tower, $500 to $5,000 for cabana rooms overlooking pool.

Olive Manor Motel, 818/842-5215. 924 W. Olive, Burbank, at Victory and Olive. Close to Burbank; not too far from Hollywood and freeways. Average is $66 for single and $77 for double.

Ramada West Hollywood, 800/845-8585. ramada.com. 8585 Santa Monica Blvd., West Hollywood. Great location. $90 a day includes breakfast. To get a corporate rate, sign up for their free RBC club when you arrive to check in.

The Graciela, 818/842-8887. thegraciela.com. 322 North Pass Ave., Burbank, 91505. The Graciela Burbank is a first-class hotel located two miles from Burbank/Glendale/Pasadena Airport. Rates are from $270 to $475.

Sportsman's Lodge, 818/769-4700. slhotel.com. Ventura Blvd. and Coldwater in Studio City. $139 to $154. AAA rate. Restaurants and shopping. Great place, great location.

The Standard Hotel, 323/650-9090. standardhotel.com. 8300 Sunset Blvd., West Hollywood. $195 to $225, weekend $275 to $450 (two-day min) On the strip. Very much one of the "in" places to stay!

• CAR RENTALS

Very valuable web site: **lawa.org**. *LAX airport parking lots, rates and locations, car rental agencies, hotels, busses and shuttle vans, a map of the airport and nearby streets.*

All the national companies are here in Los Angeles. You generally get a better deal renting at either LAX airport (Century and Sepulveda) or at the Burbank airport (Hollywood Way, between Victory and San Fernando.)

Both of the companies below have many locations. They will pick you up if you are in the vicinity of their location. Good standby rates for the weekends.

Avon, 323/850-0826. avonrent.com. 7080 Santa Monica Blvd., Hollywood. Open every day. Rates are $29.99 to $39.99

Enterprise, 323/654-4222. enterprise.com. 8367 Sunset Blvd., West Hollywood. Rates are $27.99 to $89.99. LAX

• THINGS TO SEE

Universal Studios, 1-800-864-8377. universalstudios.com. Go on a weekday. It is an actual studio lot with an amusement park-like tour for $56. Stay all day; take the tram out to the back lot where you may see working productions. I've worked on many shows produced here and I still get excited driving on the lot. Don't miss City Walk; if you can't afford the tour, at least check out the movie theater and night life. You can park on Cahuenga Blvd. West and walk over the bridge and save the $10 parking fee. You can also take the Metro Line and get off at Universal. Take the tram up the hill.

Warner Bros. VIP Studio Tour, 818/954-1744. warnerbrothers.com. 9-3 weekdays, $32. Reservations and photo ID are required. One of the staff will lead you on a two-hour informal drive-and-walk jaunt around the studio. You will even get to go on some working sound stages and see the faux streets. You will most likely see famous faces.

NBC Television Studio Tour, 818/840-3537. nbc.com. 3000 West Alameda Ave., Burbank. A 70-minute walking tour of the TV production complex departs at regular intervals, weekdays from 9-3. $7.

NBC's Tonight Show with Jay Leno: Get in line before 8AM on the day of the show. Box office: Look for a small sign, "Guest Service, Audience and Gift Shop." Two tickets per person. Then line up around 3PM to get the best seats. Watch the show the night before to see who the guests will be.

Disneyland, 714/781-4565. disneyland.com. Open M-F 9AM-11:00PM Sa & Su 9AM-midnight.

See tapings of TV shows. It doesn't cost anything and you will see the actors working. For a half-hour sitcom, plan at least three hours. Eat first because you'll have a long evening of sitting.

Audiences Unlimited, 818/753-3470. tvtickets.com. The ticket office is located on the Van Ness Street side of the Fox Television Center Building, 5746 Sunset Blvd. between Gower and the 101 Freeway. M-F 8:30-6. There is recorded information for all the shows they have tickets for. Write for their monthly newsletter of current shows. Send a stamped, self-addressed envelope to Audiences Unlimited, 100 Universal City Plaza, Bldg. 153, Universal City, CA 91608. Tickets are available for more than 40 sitcoms, game and talk shows.

Fox Television Center, 310/584-2000. foxla.com. 5746 Sunset Blvd., Hollywood. M-F 8:30-6 and Sa Su 11-6. Tickets are offered on a first-come basis starting on Wednesdays for most shows scheduled for the following week. Tickets are sometimes available the day of the show, but early arrival is advised.

Paramount Visitors Center, 323/956-1777. 860 N. Gower St., Hollywood. Weekdays 8-4.

Beverly Center Shopping Mall, 310/854-0071. beverlycenter.com. 8500 Beverly Blvd., Los Angeles corner of La Cienega between Beverly Blvd. and Third St. This is really state-of-the-art cool. See-and-be-seen MTV generation.

The J. Paul Getty Museum, 310/440-7300. getty.edu. 1200 Getty Center Drive, Los Angeles. T-Th, Su 10-6, F, Sa 10-9, closed Monday, $7 parking, museum is free.

Griffith Park Observatory. 323/664-1181. griffithobservatory.org. Take Hollywood Blvd. east to Western Avenue then go north or toward the mountains. Just past the American Film Institute (on your left) will be a curve in the road where Western turns into Los Feliz Blvd. The next street is Ferndale; turn left and follow the signs. Great hiking and picnicking there too.

The Grove, 888/315-8883, 323/900-8080. thegrovela.com. 189 The Grove Drive, off Fairfax by CBS Studios. Outdoor shopping, dining and a great movie theater. Adjacent to the Farmer's Market, The Grove also features a dancing fountain and a trolley. A must-see for its decorations during the holidays.

Hollywood Bowl, 323/850-2000. hollywoodbowl.com. 2301 N. Highland Ave., Hollywood, near the 101 freeway. Gift shop. One of the best places in L.A. to see a show, especially on a clear night under the stars.

Hollywood Fantasy Tours, 800/STAR-BUS, 323/469-8184. hollywoodfantasytours. com. 6231 Hollywood Blvd., Hollywood, 90028. Tour prices are $20 and up. Tours are every day from 10--4 every hour.

Hollywood Sign. From the 101 Freeway or Hollywood Blvd., go north on Gower, right on Franklin and left at the next street: Beachwood. As you drive up Beachwood, look up and there you are. There is no public access to the sign but this is one of the best views.

Beachwood Canyon is a lovely area. There is a small cafe where many locals eat. There's a great bulletin board outside for rentals, roommates and other stuff.

Lake Hollywood, where earthquakes and floods are filmed. From the 101 Freeway, take Barham Blvd. north. Turn right at Lake Hollywood Drive. Follow around until you see the lake. It's about 3½ miles to walk around it. Drive past the lake, continue on Canyon Lake and you will get a real close-up of the Hollywood sign. Continue down to the Beachwood area.

Los Angeles Sports Teams, Angels, Dodgers, Bruins, Trojans, Kings, Mighty Ducks, Galaxy, Clippers and of course, the Lakers (star spotting at the Lakers Games).

Main Street, Santa Monica and Venice Beaches. Shopping and eating. Take the 10 West/Santa Monica Freeway, exit Fourth Street, turn left to Pico, then right to Main St., then left and that's it.

Montana Avenue in Santa Monica between 17th and 9th streets. Celebrities!

Third Street Promenade in Santa Monica, begins at the 4th Street Mall and runs north for several blocks of shopping, eating and people watching.

Rose Bowl Flea Market, 323/560-7469. rgcshows.com. 1001 Rose Bowl Dr., Pasadena. Miles and miles of junk or treasure, depending upon your tastes. Truly a spectacle. Once a month.

Grauman's Chinese Theater on Hollywood Blvd. between Highland and La Brea. Go and put your feet in the foot prints of the stars!

Kodak Theater, Hollywood Blvd. and Highlind, opened in 2001, is the first permanent home of the Academy Awards show. The very first Oscar night was held across the street at the Roosevelt Hotel. Also at this location is a six-screen extension of Grauman's Chinese Theater, 70 shops and the Renaissance Hollywood Hotel.

Tackiest souvenirs are on Hollywood Blvd. around the Grauman's Chinese Theater.

RESTAURANTS & HANGOUTS
See the L.A. Scene / Hangouts Section

• **Now we begin your scouting trip.** Refer to this section and the L.A. Scene section for locations. Plan to arrive in L.A. on a Thursday.

• **If I were planning your trip for you,** I would say bring your best friend, at least $2,000 plus money for car rental and accommodations. Drive in to your hotel or motel on Thursday afternoon. If you are flying, rent a car at the airport. Pick up a Thursday *L.A. Times* at the airport newsstand. The Thursday *Calendar* section has everything that is happening during the weekend.

Day One - Friday

Three-mile walk around Hollywood Lake. From Barham Blvd., find your way through the hills with the help of the Thomas Guide. You will drive very close to the Hollywood Sign.

Breakfast at the Village Cafe in Beachwood Canyon below the Hollywood Sign, 323/467-5398. 2695 Beachwood, Hollywood. After breakfast, drive down Beachwood to Franklin, right to Gower then left to Santa Monica Blvd. Turn left then right into Hollywood Cemetery, drive slowly; lots of stars buried here. Come out, turn left and left again on Gower past Paramount Studios, right on Melrose, then an immediate left on Larchmont for two blocks, cross Beverly Blvd. and park.

Coffee at Starbucks and shopping in Larchmont Village. Back to Melrose, left for several blocks past La Brea; park and walk both sides of Melrose Ave. Shop for designer clothing at Attitudes, animal bones at Necromance and everything in between.

Lunch. Plenty of places to eat here. If you want something quick, check out Pink's, 709 N. La Brea, just north of Melrose, a local hotspot with a wide variety of exotic hot dogs. Drive east on Melrose, turn left on Cahuenga, following it all the way over the hill to Barham, and turn right. Barham turns into Olive and the gate to Warner Bros. will be on your right.

Take the Warner Bros. Tour, the most informative, behind-the-scenes tour in town, Fridays are good days as many of the shows are filming and chances are you'll see celebs walking about. Tours run continuously until 4PM.

Hotel/motel/friend's or relative's. Rest and get ready for a movie or play in Westwood, Century City, Santa Monica, The Grove, The Hollywood Arclight or Burbank, depending on where you are staying.

Movie or a play.

Coffee or drinks at a local place.

Day Two - Saturday

Breakfast at Patrick's Roadhouse in Santa Monica, then walk the beach from there to the Santa Monica Pier, then past the pier south to Venice Beach for shopping, watching street performers and incredible homemade ice cream at Charlie Temmel's. At the end of the merchants on the boardwalk, turn left and walk a few blocks inland to:

Main Street in Venice and walk back to Santa Monica along Main Street. When sights thin out, turn left to Ocean Blvd. Walk past the pier and turn right to the Third Street Promenade.

Lunch on the Third Street Promenade. Blocks of shopping and people watching. Then the long walk back to the car.

Rest, recoup a little and get ready for the evening.

See a play in a little theater. Pick up the early edition of Sunday's *L.A. Times* or the *LA Weekly* at any newsstand, 7/11 store or Starbucks. The *L.A. Times Calendar* section will have a complete listing of plays in little theaters. Choose a play that is recommended; see *Pick of the Week*. There are also plays listed in *Back Stage West*.

Day Three - Sunday

Disneyland all day and evening, till it closes. Get there early. When you have breakfast at the Disneyland Hotel, you get into the park an hour earlier. If Disneyland isn't of interest then spend the day hanging out in Malibu at the beach. If you do go to the beach take the 101 West to Topanga Canyon heading west to the Pacific Coast Highway — you will wind through mountains, hills and stunning views before hitting the beach. Turn right to go to Malibu.

Day Four - Monday

Breakfast at Good Neighbor Restaurant on Cahuenga Blvd West.
Universal Studios, till it closes. Go on a week day; you will see some shooting on the back lot.
Dinner at Universal's City Walk. Check out B.B. King's Blues Club, 818/622-5464, for great Southern cooking and music, Café Tu Tu Tango, 818/769-2222 for international cuisine or the popular Hard Rock Café, 818/622-7625.

Day Five - Tuesday

Jerry's Deli on Beverly Blvd. for Breakfast.
Farmer's Market at Third Street and Fairfax, and The Grove for shopping.
See a television show taping or filming. Check with Audiences Unlimited for shows that are shooting. If you are going to a show at CBS at Radford, go to a late lunch/early dinner at Dupar's coffee shop or Midori Sushi right down the road, all you can eat for just over $20 and well worth it. If you are seeing a show at Paramount, go for an early or late Mexican dinner at Lucy's El Adobe on Melrose. Sometimes you can find free tickets for shows being handed out on Hollywood Blvd., outside the Kodak Theatre, especially for the late night talk shows.

Day Six - Wednesday

Breakfast at Duke's or at The Griddle, both on Sunset Blvd.
Research (during breakfast) areas where you might want to live and map out a plan for looking at as many as you can tomorrow. Head east on Sunset to Stanley, turn left then turn right in the first driveway to park in the Samuel French Bookstore parking lot.
Samuel French Theatrical Bookstore at 10AM. Plan two hours to hang out and look at all the information.
Coffee or lunch at Urth Cafe, 8565 Melrose, just west of LaCienega. Many young celebs.
Free afternoon. If you're in the mood, check out The **J. Paul Getty art museum,** 1200 Getty Center Drive just off the 405 freeway, getty.edu. Besides classic works of art and a beautiful garden with lawns, The Getty also has one of the best views of the city, from the mountains to the ocean. $7 parking and free admission.
Dinner at Yamishiro Restaurant, 323/466-5125. Overlooking the city, above the Magic Castle on Franklin Ave. between Highland and LaBrea Ave.

Day Seven – Thursday

Start with breakfast at The Aroma Café, 818/508-6505. 4360 Tujunga Blvd., Studio City right across the street from Vitello's, where actor Robert Blake left his gun in the booth.

Map your route at breakfast and look all day at areas you think you may like to live; start Valley side to the Westside.

Grauman's Chinese theater on Hollywood Blvd. Hollywood Chamber of Commerce has a free book, "Walk the Walk" with the locations of all the stars on Hollywood Blvd.

Kodak Theater complex, in the same block.

Dinner at Hamburger Hamlet across the street. Shop for souvenirs.

After dinner, head back down to Melrose and check out an improv or sketch show at **The Groundlings**, where many top comedians trained. Sometimes, they come back for surprise shows. 7307 Melrose Ave., 323/934-4747, groundlings.com.

Day Eight - Friday

Breakfast at Hugo's in West Hollywood, Santa Monica Blvd.

Griffith Park Observatory. Right on Los Felix to Hollywood Blvd. and lunch.

Lunch at Musso & Franks, 323/467-7788. 6667 Hollywood Blvd. Then take Cahuenga Blvd. over the hill, turn right on Barham, go past Warner Bros. Studio. When the street splits into Olive and Alameda, stay to the right for Alameda. 3000 W. Alameda Ave., Burbank. NBC is on your right. If you want to eat some place closer to the studio, check out the original **Bob's Big Boy** down the road, 4211 Riverside Dr., 818/843-9334.

NBC Television Studio Tour, a 70-minute walking tour of the TV production complex. Departures at regular intervals weekdays from 9-3. 818/840-3537. nbc. com. 3000 West Alameda Ave., Burbank. When you leave, return on Olive to Hollywood Way, turn right to Magnolia, then right.

Visit "It's a Wrap." 3315 W. Magnolia. Used clothes from films and current tv shows.

Vitellos Restaurant, 818/769-0905. vitellosrestaurant.com. 4349 Tujunga Ave., Studio City. Robert Blake's booth is the back booth on the left. You can request that booth. He always sat where he could see who was coming in.

Night spots you think you'll enjoy. If you want to go to Burbank, take Tujunga north to Magnolia and turn right, heading east into Burbank. Turn right on San Fernando and hit **The Blue Room**, 916 S. San Fernando Blvd. where charming old ladies serve you drinks with hip hop blasting in the background. Then take the 5 south for a few miles, get off on Los Feliz Blvd. and check out **The Derby**, 4500 Los Feliz Blvd. for swing dancing and the nearby **Dresden Room**, 1760 N. Vermont Ave. for Marty & Elayne's lounge act. Both places featured in the movie *Swingers*.

Day Nine - Saturday

Walking tour of Beverly Hills. Park south of Wilshire around Bedford, Canon or Beverly. Make sure you walk Rodeo Drive to window shop and celebrity watch.

Lunch at Barney's department store on Wilshire, or for a less expensive lunch drive east on Wilshire to La Cienega, turn left to the Beverly Center.

Spend afternoon at the Beverly Center.

Play at a little theater, and nightclubbing. Hit the **Sunset Strip,** an eclectic mix of Hollywood bars. Within a block you can get karaoke and sushi at Miyagi's, mingle with Hollywood's elite and pay way too much for drinks at The Standard and then get some cheap beer and ride a mechanical bull at The Saddle Ranch. And that's just the start! If you want music, further up Sunset is the legendary **Viper Room** and **Whiskey a Go-Go,** where tons of rock bands have got their start.

Late, late night. Canter's Deli, 419 N. Fairfax, after 2am or Roscoe's House of Chicken & Waffles, 1518 N. Gower St. all night.

Day Ten - Sunday

Breakfast with Hollywood hipsters at the retro-chic 101 Coffee Shop, 6145 Franklin Ave. in Hollywood, the same coffee shop where they shot most of *Swingers.* Review your trip and spend the rest of the day doing whatever you have been dying to do.

Day Eleven - Monday

Return home.

NICE THINGS TO FIT IN:

La Conversation, 310/858-0950. 638 N. Doheny Dr., West Hollywood, 90069, near Santa Monica Blvd. Lovely food, sit outside. Have a facial at Yolanda's next door. This is the way to live!

Beverly Hills Hotel's poolside Cabana Club Cafe, 800/283-8885. 9641 Sunset Blvd. Beverly Hills. Expensive—pay cash so you don't have to explain you aren't staying there.

Book Soup and Tower Records on the Sunset Strip.

Starbucks and other coffee places like Priscillas in Toluca Lake, that are located close to studios. Hang out.

• **This is not a vacation for relaxing;** this is the type of pace it takes to work and live here. If you follow this plan, you will cover many of the areas that are part of a Los Angeles actor's life. When you arrive be prepared to go; you can relax when you get home. Meet people, talk to everyone; ask them about living in Los Angeles. Your time is very precious here.

L.A. Scene / Local Hangouts

• **You have moved here to seek your fame and fortune.** Here are places you may wish to check out that will put you in the neighborhoods where some of the action is. I've picked spots that are known to be hangouts for people in show-biz. Places of business have a way of disappearing, but find your own. Have fun finding your favorite hangouts. *L.A. Magazine* and the Sunday and Thursday editions of the *L.A. Times* Calendar Section will help you keep up on the latest happenings. A special "thank you" to actress Carol Hernandez for rechecking all the businesses and to actor/writer Jim Martyka for adding the latest cool spots.

The L.A. Weekly *is the free local newspaper and comes out on Thursdays. Pick it up at newsstands, 7-11s, liquor stores and businesses.*

To download and print an updated version of this and all resource lists, go to actingiseverything.com.

• WEBSITES FOR MORE L.A. HOTSPOTS

citysearch.com
groovenow2000.com
worldsbestbars.com
hipguide.com
laweekly.com
la.com
cooljunkie.com
guidemag.com
clubplanet.com
thelamusicscene.com
eyespyla.com

• COFFEE HOUSES

The Abbey, 310/289-8410. abbeyfoodandbar.com. 692 N. Robertson Blvd., West Hollywood. Cappuccino and dreams of Tuscany midst all the fountains.

The Aroma Café, 818/508-6505. 4360 Tujunga Blvd., Studio City. Very peaceful, great place to write and study. Also, incredible cappuccino. Many celebrities in this low-key outdoor spot. Great little bookstore here too.

Coffee Bean & Tea Leaf, 1-800-tealeaf coffeebean.com. Ice-blended mocha drink, no fat, no calories, but fabulous.

Cyber Java, 323/466-5600. cyberjava.com. 7080 Hollywood Blvd. L.A.'s first online coffeehouse.

Lu Lu's Beehive, 818/986-cafe. 13203 Ventura Blvd., Studio City. Wednesday open mike night. Los Angeles Magazine says, "Best coffee scene in the Valley."

Highland Grounds, 323/466-1507. highlandgrounds.com. 742 N. Highland Ave., Los Angeles. Live comedy, avant-garde music and readings every night.

King's Road, 323/655-9044. 8361 Beverly Blvd., West Hollywood. Always packed. I love to meet people here for lunch. Near the Beverly Center.

Library, A Coffee House, 562/433-2393. 3418 E. Broadway Blvd., Long Beach. Carries thousands of titles on metaphysics, psychology, etc. More than cappuccino. Ted Danson and Mary Steenburgen stop in for the chili.

Newsroom Cafe, 310/319-9100. 530 Wilshire Blvd., Santa Monica. Great coffee, sweets, sugar-free desserts. Many celebs.

Newsroom Cafe, 310/652-4444. 120 N. Robertson. Healthy menu selections. Spotted: Sharon Stone, Ellen DeGeneres, Chris Rock.

Peet's Coffee & Tea Incorporated, 310/979-7892. peets.com. 11750 San Vicente Blvd. Voted as one of L.A.'s best on CitySearch.

Urth Cafe, 310/659-0628. urthcaffe.com. 8565 Melrose Ave., West Hollywood, just west of La Cienega. Indoors/outdoors. Many young celebs stop for coffee, snacks and lunch.

• RESTAURANTS—UPSCALE

Bistro Garden, 818/501-0202. bistrogarden.com. 12950 Ventura Blvd., Studio City.

BOA Steakhouse, 323/650-8383. boasteak.com. 8462 W. Sunset Blvd., Hollywood. Cool atmosphere and great bar.

Cabana Club Cafe, 800/283-8885. beverlyhillshotel.com. 9641 Sunset Blvd., Beverly Hills. Poolside dining at the Beverly Hills Hotel. Live large and pretend you are staying at a $700 per night bungalow.

Ca' Del Sol, 818/985-4669. cadelsole.com. 4100 Cahuenga, Toluca Lake, near Universal.

Cafe de Paris, 310/358-0908. 650 North Robertson, West Hollywood. Another Sharon Stone favorite.

Cafe Med, 310/652-0445. 8615 Sunset Blvd., West Hollywood. Keanu Reeves favors the spaghetti Bolognese and James Woods enjoys the pasta with olive oil and garlic.

Dan Tana's, 310/275-9444. dantanasrestaurant.com. 9071 Santa Monica Blvd., West Hollywood. Italian food in a busy restaurant. Celeb hangout. Great New York steak. A place to be seen.

Divino, 310/472-0886. 11714 Barrington Court, Brentwood. Clientele ranging from Diana Ross to Billy Crystal.

Dolce Enoteca e Ristorante, 323/852-7174. 8284 Melrose Ave., Los Angeles. Great layout with black leather couches and marble structure. Partially owned by past and current members of the *That 70's Show* cast, including Ashton Kutcher.

Eat. on sunset, 323/461-8800, patinagroup.com. 1448 N. Gower St., Los Angeles, 90028. One of the newer places to be seen. Pricey, but slick design and great outdoor patio. Many celebrities who are shooting next door at Sunset Gower Studios.

Geoffrey's Malibu, 310/457-1519. gmalibu.com 27400 Pacific Coast Highway, Malibu, 90265. Power place in Robert Altman's *The Player*.

Il Tiramisu, 818/986-2640. il-tiramisu.com. 13705 Ventura Blvd., Sherman Oaks. Small space, but incredible lunches and dinners and charming servers and hosts. Hint; tell the owner it's your first time there.

The Ivy, 310/274-8303. 113 N. Robertson, L.A., south of Beverly. Minimum $25 for lunch. If you can afford it, eat here at least once. The place to be seen!

Ivy at the Shore, 310/393-3113. 1541 Ocean Ave., Santa Monica.

Joss, 310/276-1886. 9255 Sunset Blvd., Los Angeles. Very classy Chinese place that can be expensive. But thrifty diners can make a meal out of the delicious appetizers.

Koi, 310/659-9449. koirestaurant.com. 730 N. La Cienega Blvd., West Hollywood. THE sushi place to see and be seen. Featured in the must-see show *Entourage*.

La Fondue, 818/788-8680. 13359 Ventura Blvd., Sherman Oaks. Pricey but a fun experience. The chocolate fondue with fresh fruit is to die for.

La Loggia, 818/985-9222. 11814 Ventura Blvd., Studio City. Power dinners.

La Pergola, 818/905-8402. 15005 Ventura Blvd., Sherman Oaks, Marlon Brando came in often for the pastas and Italian cuisine.

Lavande, 310/576-3180. loewshotels.com. 1700 Ocean Avenue, Santa Monica. A favorite place of Goldie Hawn, Steven Bochco and Sharon Lawrence.

Le Dome, 310/659-6919. ledomerestaurant.com. 8720 Sunset Blvd., Sunset Plaza, West Hollywood. Big music business hangout. See and be seen.

Kate Mantilini, 310/278-3699. 9101 Wilshire Blvd. at Doheny Drive, Beverly Hills. Many celebrities. Great for power breakfast; also open late at night. Jerry Seinfeld sightings when he is in town.

Mastro's Steakhouse, 310/888-8782. mastrossteakhouse.com. 246 N. Canon Dr., Beverly Hills. Celebrity sightings every night, from athletes to movie stars. Great steaks, hip servers.

Max, 818/784-2915. maxrestaurant.com. 13355 Ventura Blvd., Sherman Oaks. Cal-Asian eatery is a pioneer in Valley dining revival.

Mr. Chow, 310/278-9911. mrchow.com 344 N. Camden Drive, Beverly Hills. Prices are high, cooking is good and celebs go there.

Ocean Front, 310/581-7714. hotelcasadelmar.com. 1910 Ocean Way, Santa Monica.

Orso's, 310/274-7144. 8706 W. Third St., West Hollywood. Power patio dining, hidden from the street; used to be Joe Allen's.

Pinot Bistro, 818/990-0500. patinagroup.com. 12969 Ventura Blvd., Studio City. Near CBS/Radford and Universal. Even Warner Bros. people go there for lunch and dinner. Decorated beautifully during the holidays.

Pinot Hollywood, 323/461-8800. patinagroup.com. 1448 N. Gower St., Hollywood. Close to Paramount lot; many celebs and executives at lunch and dinner.

Polo Lounge, Beverly Hills Hotel, 310/276-2251. beverlyhillshotel.com. 9641 Sunset Blvd., Beverly Hills. Have breakfast in the coffee shop and look around.

Smoke House, 818/845-3731. smokehouserestaurant.com 4420 Lakeside Drive, Burbank, very near Toluca Lake. The best garlic-cheese bread in the world.

Spago, 310/385-0880. wolfgangpuck.com 176 N. Canon Drive, Beverly Hills. Los Angeles legend.

The Spanish Kitchen, 310/659-4794. spanishkitchen.com. 826 North La Cienega Blvd., between Melrose Ave. and Santa Monica Blvd. All dishes are authentic and all ingredients are imported from Mexico.

Sushi Nozawa, 818/508-7017. 11288 Ventura Blvd., Studio City. When you sit at the counter, don't dare ask for what you want—you get what they are serving. People love it, including my daughters. Go figure.

Sushi Roku, 323/655-6767. sushiroku.com. 8445 W. 3rd Street, near LaCienega. Very popular, many celebrities.

The Grill, 310/276-0615. thegrill.com. 9560 Dayton Way, Beverly Hills. Power lunch for agents.

The Palm, 310/550-8811. thepalm.com. 9001 Santa Monica Blvd., Los Angeles. Spotted: Courtney Cox Arquette, Adam Sandler, George Clooney, Leonardo DiCaprio, Denzel Washington, Madonna and Guy Ritchie. A favorite for years.

Trattoria Amici, 310/858-0271. tamici.com. 469 S. Doheny Dr., Beverly Hills. "Friends" buddies Jennifer Aniston, Courteney Cox and Lisa Kudrow are served delicious pastas.

Tropicana Bar, 323/769-7260. 7000 Hollywood Blvd., Hollywood. Located in the legendary Roosevelt Hotel. Decades-old charm. Lots of celebs, some dead (Roosevelt said to be haunted).

Typhoon, 310/390-6565. typhoon.biz. 3221 Donald Douglas Loop South (off Centinela). View of the airfield at Santa Monica Airport. Lauren Bacall orders the salmon with ginger poached in banana leaves. Robert De Niro, Al Pacino and Harrison Ford dine here.

• RESTAURANTS—MEDIUM TO LOWER PRICES

The Apple Pan, 310/475-3585. 10801 W. Pico Blvd., West Los Angeles. Open Friday and Saturday until 1AM, other days except Monday until midnight. Great burgers and apple pie. All counters; people stand behind you and wait. Great after a late movie at Westside Pavilion. Love these hamburgers!

Amazon, 818/382-6080. amazonbarandgrill.com 14649 Ventura Blvd., Sherman Oaks. The atmosphere is not to be missed.

Art's Delicatessen, 818/762-1221. 12224 Ventura Blvd., Studio City. Favorite of the Hollywood community that resides in the Valley, also the television stars working at the CBS lot. Best Black & White cookies!

Aunt Kizzy's Back Porch, 310/578-1005. 4325 Glencoe Ave., Marina Del Rey. Southern cooking. Actors and athletes love the fried chicken and baked ribs.

A Votre Sante, 310/451-1813. 13016 San Vicente Blvd., Brentwood. Gourmet Vegetarian.

Barney Greengrass, 310/777-5877. 9570 Wilshire Blvd., Beverly Hills, in Barney's Dept. Store. Great fish straight from Barney's in New York.

Barney's Beanery, 323/654-2287. barneysbeanery.com. 8447 Santa Monica Blvd., Hollywood. One of the oldest restaurants in L.A., built in 1920. Was a favorite of some rock greats like Janis Joplin, Jim Morrison and Jimi Hendrix. Menu has hundreds of items … anything you want. Great atmosphere.

Belevedere at the Peninsula Hotel, 310/788-2306. peninsula.com. 9882 Santa Monica Blvd., Beverly Hills, near CAA.

Birds, 323/465-0175. 5925 Franklin Ave., Hollywood. Perched in the shadow of the Hollywood sign.

Bob's Big Boy, 818/843-9334. 4211 Riverside Dr., Toluca Lake. bigboy.com. The original Big Boy in L.A. Still has car-hop service on weekend nights.

Broadway Deli, 310/451-0616. foodcowest.com. 1457 Third Street Promenade, Santa Monica.

Bristol Cafe, 310/248-2804. bristolfarms.com. 9039 Beverly Blvd., West Hollywood. Located in the market. Home of the original Chasen's restaurant. Original Chasen's booth; order the famous Chasen's chili.

Bungalow Club, 323/964-9494. thebungalowclub.com. 7174 Melrose Ave., Daily, it's almost like being poolside at a fancy hotel, dining in an outdoor cabana on a private patio with fluttering bamboo in the middle of Hollywood.

Cafe Brasil, 310/837-8957. café-brasil.com. 10831 Venice Blvd., Culver City. Excellent food, also vegetarian.

Caffe Capri, 323/644-7906. 2547 Hyperion Ave., L.A. Lunch and dinner, Wednesday through Monday. Italian food served in a cute, diminutive restaurant.

Canter's Fairfax Restaurant, 323/651-2030. cantersdeli.com, 419 North Fairfax, L.A. Open 24 hours. Folksy by day; underground by night. In the old Jewish neighborhood. Great for the middle of night after play rehearsal. Bakery open all the time.

Carney's Restaurant, 323/654-8300. carneytrain.com. 8351 Sunset Blvd., West Hollywood. Restaurant is in an authentic railroad car. Also on Ventura Blvd. in Studio City.

Casa Vega, 818/788-4868. casavega.com. 13301 Ventura Blvd., Sherman Oaks. Red vinyl and Tiffany lamps make up this hip Mexican joint that hosts celebs and struggling actors alike. Open very late at night.

Castaways Restaurant, 818/848-6691. 1250 Harvard, Burbank. Great place for cocktails and weekend brunch.

Chez Nous, 818/760-0288. 10550 Riverside Dr., Toluca Lake. Breakfast meetings.

Chin Chin, 310/652-1818. chinchin.com. 8618 Sunset Blvd., Hollywood. Indoor and outdoor seating; watch the crowd go by! Other locations. I love the light chicken salad.

Dimples, 818/842-2336. dimplesshowcase.com 3413 W. Olive Ave., Burbank. Lunch and dinner, continuous karaoke, 6pm-1:30am. Cheap, fun.

Duke's, 310/652-9411. dukescoffeeshop.com. 8909 Sunset Blvd. Big breakfast place, served all day, parking in rear.

DuPar's, 818/766-4437. dupars.com 12036 Ventura Blvd. in Studio City; also 3rd & Fairfax at Farmers' Market, close to CBS lot. Great pancakes.

El Coyote, 323/939-7766. elcoyotecafe.com. 7312 Beverly Blvd, Hollywood. Popular with the twenty-something crowd. Great margaritas.

Formosa Café, 323/850-9050. 7156 Santa Monica Blvd. Long time old movie star hangout.

Four Seasons Hotel, 310/273-2222. fourseasons.com. 300 S. Doheny Dr., Beverly Hills border. Self park under the hotel. Many celebrities stay here, especially at award times.

Full O' Life Restaurant, 818/845-8343. fullolife.com. 2515 W. Magnolia, Burbank. Total nutrition center next to a grocery store specializing in organic foods. Hot spot for those on the health kick. Brittani Taylor's favorite!

Good Neighbor, 818/761-4627. 3701 Cahuenga Blvd. West, Studio City. Great place, near Universal. Breakfast & lunch only; closes at 4PM.

Gladstone's 4 Fish, 310/454-3474. gladstones.com. 17300 PCH, where Sunset Blvd. ends at the beach. Fun place!

Greenblatt's, 323/656-0606. 8017 W. Sunset Blvd. Parking in rear. Next to the Laugh Factory. The best deli in town. Open till 2 am.

Home, 323/665-HOME. Homelosfeliz.com. 1760 Hillhurst Ave. Breakfast, lunch and dinner daily. Homey dining room with a jukebox, romantic patio.

Hugo's, 323/654-3993. 8401 Santa Monica Blvd., just east of La Cienega, West Hollywood. Power breakfasts, many celebs. Also a location at 12851 Riverside Dr. in Studio City.

Jerry's Deli, 818/980-4245. jerrysfamousdeli.com. 12655 Ventura Blvd, Studio City, 91604; 24 hrs. Huge menu. A favorite of many celebs, including, when the show was shooting, the writers and cast of Seinfeld.

Jerry's Deli, 310/289-1811. jerrysfamousdeli.com. 8701 Beverly Blvd., West Hollywood. Very "in," especially late at night. Celebs spotted: Billy Crystal, Garth Brooks, Jon Voight, and Paula Abdul.

Killer Shrimp, 818/508-1750. 4000 Colfax, Studio City. The name says it all. They serve three shrimp dishes, all bubbling in a delicious spicy broth and that's it.

Light House, 310/451-2076. lighthousebuffet.com. 201 Arizona Ave. Santa Monica. All you can eat Sushi, under $10 at lunch time.

La Conversation, 310/858-0950. 638 N. Doheny Dr., West Hollywood. Adorable; open weekdays for late breakfast and lunch. My daughters love the soups and great pastries.

Lucy's El Adobe, 323/462-9421. 5536 Melrose Ave., Hollywood. Across from Paramount Studios. Lots of celebs. Very casual and old Hollywood!

Magnolia Grille, 818/766-8698. 10530 Magnolia Blvd. (at Cahuenga), North Hollywood, 91601. 6AM-10PM daily. Very homey place, lots of regulars, including my husband and me.

Mel's Drive In, 310/854-7200. Melsdrive-in.com. 8585 Sunset Blvd., West Hollywood. 24 hours. Great outdoors and in, good people-watching. Second smaller location: 323/465-3111. 1650 N. Highland Ave., Hollywood. Close to the Kodak Theater at Hollywood and Highland. Also: 818/990-6357. 14846 Ventura Blvd., Sherman Oaks.

Mexicali, 818/985-1744. 12161 Ventura Blvd., Studio City. Some of the Valley's best Mexican food with great ownership. Big spots for local celebs like Jessica Simpson and Jaime Pressly. Great Tortilla Soup.

Midori Sushi, 818/623-7888. 11622 Ventura Blvd., Studio City. Friendly staff, incredible rolls and all you can eat lunches for less than $25. Often overhear studio execs from nearby CBS Radford talking shop.

Musso & Frank Grill, 323/467-7788. 6667 Hollywood Blvd., Hollywood. Old time hangout. You must check this place out!

Nate 'n Al's, 310/274-0101. natenal.com. 414 N. Beverly Dr., Beverly Hills, 90210. When you're in Beverly Hills, this is the deli! This is a power breakfast spot for the film industry. You must check this out!

Off Vine, 323/962-1900. offvine.com. 6263 Leland Way, Hollywood. Romantic spot with great home cooking.

Original Pantry, 213/972-9279. 877 S. Figueroa, Los Angeles. Figueroa & 9th Streets, downtown L.A. 24 hrs. Known for their breakfasts and long-time waiters.

Patrick's Roadhouse, 310/459-4544. patricksroadhouse.com. 106 Entrada Dr., Santa Monica. Lots of celebrities for breakfast. Patrick was a legend; he is gone now but his son is carrying on the tradition.

Pig'n Whistle, 323/463-0000. pignwhistle.com. 6714 Hollywood Blvd., Hollywood, 90028. Old Hollywood eatery rebuilt.

Pink's Hot-Dog Stand, 323/931-4223. pinkshollywood.com. 709 N. La Brea, just north of Melrose. Sean Penn proposed to Madonna there.

Roscoe's House of Chicken & Waffles, 323/466-7453. roscoeschickenandwaffles.com. 1514 N. Gower, Hollywood. Also 323/934-4405, 5006 W. Pico, one block west of LaBrea. Best in the middle of the night; down home food. Another Sharon Stone favorite.

Russia, 323/464-2216. russiarestaurant.net. 1714 N. Ivar Avenue, Hollywood. A Hollywood version of a Russian style restaurant. Within walking distance of the Pantages and Doolittle theaters. Live music and dancing on the weekends.

Saddle Ranch Chop House, 323/656-2007. srrestaurants.com. 8371 Sunset Blvd., West Hollywood. Rowdy steak-and-suds hangout. Gas "campfires" for self-serve s'mores and a mechanical bull for urban cowboys with something to prove. Also a location at Universal City Walk.

Senor Fred, 818/789-3200. senorfred.com. 13730 Ventura Blvd., Sherman Oaks. Quality food and reasonable prices, cool booths and décor.

Silver Spoons, 323/650-4890. silverspoonrestaurant.net. 8171 W. Santa Monica Blvd., Hollywood. Usual crowd is breakfast and lunch. Big hangout. There's the swapping of Hollywood gossip, stories of pending deals, recent auditions and past glories.

Sittons Coffee Shop, 818/761-3341. 11329 Magnolia, N. Hollywood. 24-hour coffee shop. Good food and prices.

Swinger's, 323/653-5888. swingersrestaurant.com. 8020 Beverly Blvd. Very "in" hangout for actors and other entertainment people; good prices plus many healthy and vegetarian selections.

The Griddle Café, 323/874-0377. griddlecafe.com. 7916 Sunset Blvd. Huge portions, incredible pancakes. Saturday and Sunday can bring huge waits so get there early.

The Rose Cafe, 310/399-0711. rosecafe.com. 220 Rose Ave., Venice. Simple cafe and patio where the locals do breakfast and lunch.

The Standard Diner, For Reservations 323/650-9090 standardhotel.com 8300 Sunset Blvd. 24-hour, modern take on a coffee shop.

Toast Bakery Cafe, 323/655-5018. 8221 W. Third Street, between Crescent Heights and LaCienega. All breakfasts 'til 11AM. Great atmosphere. The best cupcakes!

Village Cafe in Beachwood Canyon, 323/467-5398. 2695 North Beachwood Dr., about one mile north of Franklin Avenue in Hollywood. Look up and see the Hollywood sign. Great hidden neighborhood and memo board outside.

Village Pizzeria, 323/465-5566. villagepizzeria.net. 131 N. Larchmont Blvd., Los Angeles. If you crave New York-style pizza, this is where to go and many young celebs do.

Vitello's, 818/769-0905. vitellosrestaurant.com. 4349 Tujunga Ave., Studio City. This is where Robert Blake was eating and had to return to pick up the gun he left in the booth. His wife was killed on the adjacent street. Great food!

Yamishiro Restaurant, 323/466-5125. yamishirorestaurant.com. 1999 N. Sycamore Ave., Los Angeles. Great view of the city.

• HANGOUTS

Bar Marmont, 323/650-0575. committedinc.com. 8171 Sunset Blvd., Los Angeles. No cover. At this moment, it is the place to be.

The Belmont, 310/659-8871. thebelmontcafe.com. 747 N. La Cienega, Los Angeles. Cool blue atmosphere, great place to grab a quiet drink, though it can get packed on weekends.

The Blue Room, 323/849-2779. 916 S. San Fernando Blvd., Burbank. Charming old ladies serve you reasonably-priced drinks while hip hop blares in the background.

Club A.D., 323/467-3000. 836 N. Highland Ave., Hollywood. Dancing ala Studio 54.

Daddy's, 323/463-7777. 1610 N. Vine Street, Hollywood.

Diane Bennett's Personal Introductions, Hotline: 310/859-6929. dianne3562@yahoo. com She plans parties at hotels for singles.

Doug Weston's Troubadour, 310/276-1158. troubadour.com. 9081 Santa Monica Blvd., West Hollywood. Singer/songwriter-based shows. Cover.

The Downtown Standard, 213/892-8080. hotelstandard.com. 550 S. Flower St., L.A. Space-age party center. Also a location at 8300 Sunset Blvd., 323/822-3111.

Dragonfly, 323/466-6111. dragonfly.com. 6510 Santa Monica Blvd. Hollywood club with a different type of music each night.

The Dresden Room, 323/665-4294. thedresden.com. 1760 N. Vermont Ave., Los Feliz. An L.A. classic celebrated in the movie *Swingers*. Marty & Elayne still do their lounge act and the bartenders serve up some great classic drinks. Great vibe here.

Falcon, 323/850-5350. falconslair.com. 7213 Sunset Blvd., Hollywood. Chic eatery. Star sightings.

Fantasia Billiards, 818/848-6718. 131 N. San Fernando Blvd., Burbank. Lots of tables, cheap drinks but very crowded on the weekends.

Father's Office, 310/393-Beer. 1018 Montana Ave., Santa Monica. Excellent foreign draft beer.

Firefly, 818/762-1833. 11720 Ventura Blvd., Studio City. One of the valley's new, hot clubs.

Forty Deuce, 323/465-4242. fortydeuce.com. 5574 Melrose Ave., Hollywood. Live music comes from a bump-and-grind combo. Dancers who strip down to pasties and skivvies. Nicole Kidman, Sandra Bullock, Naomi Watts, George Clooney, Matthew Perry, Vince Vaughn have been spotted here.

4100 Bar, 323/666-4460. 4100 Sunset Blvd., Silverlake. Late-night entertainment.

Geisha House, 323/460-6300. 6633 Hollywood Blvd., Los Angeles. Top club and restaurant owners teamed up to open this very trendy Pan-Asian place. Great place to get an expensive drink and people watch.

Harvelle's, 310/395-1676. harvelles.com. 1432 Fourth Street in Santa Monica. Smokey blues bar.

H.M.S. Bounty, 213/385-7275. hmsbounty.net. 3357 Wilshire Blvd., Los Angeles. Across the street from the Ambassador Hotel. Free jukebox.

Hollywood Athletic Club, 323/462-6262. 6525 Sunset Boulevard, Hollywood. Young industry types.

Hollywood Billiards, 323/465-0115. hollywoodbilliards.com. 5750 Hollywood Blvd., Hollywood. 35 tables, video games, snacks, open all night.

House of Blues, 323/848-5136. houseofblues.com. 8430 Sunset Blvd., West Hollywood.

Ivar, 323/465-4827. 6365 Hollywood Blvd., Los Angeles. Very chic, New York City vibe.

Key Club, 310/274-5800. keyclub.com. 9039 Sunset Blvd., West Hollywood. This is the site of the old very famous Gazzarri's and Billboard Live. Cover varies. Call for bookings.

Miceli's, 323-466-3438. micelisrestaurant.com. 1646 N. Las Palmas Ave, Hollywood. Singing waiters, fun.

Molly Malone's, 323/935-1577. mollymalonesla.com. 575 South Fairfax, Los Angeles. High spirited bar, band.

Maloney's Sports Bar, 310/208-1942. 1000 Gayley Ave., Westwood. 14 TVs and drink specials. Near UCLA but all ages go there.

The Mint, 323/954-9400. themintla.com. 6010 Pico Blvd., Los Angeles. Great place for music of all kinds any night of the week. Lots of rock stars have been seen there, from Mick Jagger to Ben Harper.

Nacional, 323/962-7712. nacional.cc. 645 Wilcox Ave., Hollywood. Havana-style supper club.

NoBar, 818/753-0545. 10622 Magnolia Blvd., North Hollywood. One of North Hollywood's best kept secrets. Unassuming front opens up to hip lounge bar with couches and one of the city's best juke boxes.

The Sapphire, 818/506-0777. 11938 Ventura Blvd., Studio City. Cool, high-class lounge close to CBS Radford. Cast members from Scrubs have been seen in there.

Sky Bar, 323/848-6025. 8440 Sunset Blvd., Los Angeles. One of the hottest spots on the Sunset Strip. Great view of the city from back patio. Has played host to a number of celebrity parties and Oscar parties. Leonardo DiCaprio hangs out there.

Sunset Marquis Hotel Bar, 310/657-1333. sunsetmarquishotel.com. 1200 N. Alta Loma Rd., West Hollywood. Young, hip, celebs and music industry folk.

Standard Lounge, 323/822-3111. standardhotel.com. 8300 Sunset Blvd., Hollywood. This hip hotel bar has a retro feel thanks to Ultrasuede hammocks and go-go-booted waitresses. Spotted: Keanu Reeves, Tobey Maguire, Sofia Coppola.

The Parlour Club, 323/650-7968. parlourclub.com. 7702 Santa Monica Blvd., West Hollywood. Wild and eclectic.

The Roxy, 310/276-2222. theroxyonsunset.com. 9009 Sunset Blvd., West Hollywood. L.A.'s major showcase for rock, pop and jazz artists. Call for bookings.

The Scene, 818/241-7029. 806 Colorado Blvd., Glendale. thescenebar.com. Deejays, live rock, country, alternative, depending on the night of the week.

Viper Room, 310/358-1880 viperroom.com 8852 W. Sunset Blvd., West Hollywood. Used to be owned by Johnny Depp; where River Phoenix died. Still THE place to play if you're an up and coming rock band.

Whiskey a Go Go, 310/652-4205. whiskeyagogo.com 8901 Sunset Blvd., West Hollywood. Loud; world famous in the '60s and '70s … where The Doors broke out.

Whist at the Viceroy, 310/260-7500. viceroysantamonica.com. 1819 Ocean Ave., Santa Monica. Elegant resturant and bar.

White Lotus, 323/463-0060. 1743 N. Cahuenga Blvd., Hollywood. Asian-inspired place with great cocktails. Becoming a hot spot for young celebs.

Yankee Doodle's, 310/394-4632. yankeedoodles.com. 1410 Third Street Promenade, Santa Monica. 29-table billiard parlor.

• JAZZ

Baked Potato, 818/980-1615. thebakedpotato.com. 3787 Cahuenga Blvd. West, Studio City. 7pm-2am.

Catalina Bar & Grill, 323/466-2210. catalinajazzclub.com. 6725 W. Sunset Blvd. Hollywood.

Charlie O's Saloon, 818/994-3058. charlieos.com. 13725 Victory Blvd., Van Nuys.

Jax Bar and Grill, 818/500-1604. jaxbarandgrill.com 339 N. Brand Blvd., Glendale.

Jazz Bakery, 310/271-9039. jazzbakery.org 3233 Helms Ave., Los Angeles, off Venice Blvd. Tickets $10-$20; call for bookings. Concert style listening room.

LaVe Lee, 818/980-8158. laveleejazzclub.com 12514Ventura Blvd., Studio City. Tu-Su 8pm-1am. Specializes in Lebanese dishes. Latin jazz and R&B.

Lunaria, 310/282-8870. lunariajazzscene.com. 10351 Santa Monica Blvd., West L.A. Happening jazz scene in Westwood.

Spazio, 818/728-8400. spazio.la. 14755 Ventura Blvd., Sherman Oaks. Good food; good jazz.

• PLACES TO DANCE

Salsa dancing, salsaweb.com. Do a city search for clubs in Los Angeles.

Swing dancing, nocturne.com and theswingthing.com. This is for Los Angeles clubs.

Cava, 323/658-8898. 8384 West Third Street, West Hollywood.

Coconut Club at the Beverly Hilton, 310/285-1358. 9876 Wilshire Blvd., Beverly Hills. Open Fridays and Saturdays. Full dinner menu. A supper club with dining, dancing and a cigar lounge. Visitors include Victoria Principal, Loni Anderson, Esther Williams and Mickey Rooney. Private booths, 900 square foot dance floor. A special place for a special occasion.

Conga Room, 323/938-1696. congaroom.com. 5370 Wilshire Blvd., Los Angeles. Co-owners are Jennifer Lopez and Jimmy Smits. Liva Salsa music and dancing.

Crush Bar Continental, 323/461-9017. 7230 Topanga Canyon Blvd., Canoga Park. Big dance floor.

The Derby, 323/663-8979. the-derby.com. 4500 Los Feliz Blvd., Los Angeles. Swing dancing , cool place. Featured in *Swingers*.

El Centro, 323/871-2462. 1069 N. El Centro Ave., Los Angeles. Good place to dance with Paris Hilton and other celebs, though they're often in the VIP section. Hard to see if you don't know exactly where it is.

Good Bar, 310/271-8355. 9229 Sunset Blvd., West Hollywood.

Harvelle's, 310/395-1676. harvelles.com. 1432 Fourth Street, Santa Monica. Oldest blues club.

The Hollywood Dance Center, 323/467-0825. hollywooddancecenter.com. 817 N. Highland Ave., Hollywood. Pedro Montanez tells me Pam is the owner, "a wonderful, sweet spirit!"

LAX, formerly Las Palmas, 323/464-0171. 1714 Las Palmas, Los Angeles. Owned by the renowned DJ AM, who has worked parties for a number of celebrities, including Leonard DiCaprio. Great club with airport-inspired décor.

Prey, 310/652-2012. 643 N. La Cienega, Los Angeles. Cool, swanky hell-inspired décor. Big place for fashion shows, dancing and other events. Usually lines to get in.

Sportsmen's Lodge, 818/755-5000. sportsmenslodge.com. 12825 Ventura Blvd., Studio City. Call for info. Disco, House Music, Jazz, Salsa, Swing.

Swing Dancing, The best place to find out what's happening now is to log on to nocturne.com, Southern California's most comprehensive swing site.

The Brig, 310/399-7537. 1515 Abbot Kinney Blvd. A casual Venice Beach vibe. Celebs have been spied strutting their stuff.

The Nacional, 323/962-7712. nacional.cc. 1645 Wilcox Ave. Glamorous 30's Havana-style cocktail lounge in the former space of Fuel.

• GAY AND LESBIAN SCENE

Big scene in West Hollywood on Santa Monica Blvd. between Fairfax and Doheny Blvds. Many street festivals. Bars, clubs, restaurants, coffee houses and shops. Most welcome everyone, straight or gay. The dance clubs are also popular with straight young women, who want to dance and have fun without getting "hit on." Be sure to park legally; they tow-away fast.

Gay and Lesbian Community Services, 323/993-7400. lagaycenter.org.

Celebration Theatre, 323/957-1884. celebrationtheatre.com. 7051 Santa Monica Blvd., West Hollywood. Gay/lesbian theatre company; quality work in a beautiful small theatre.

• COMEDY CLUBS

Acme Comedy Theater, 323/525-0202. acmecomedy.com. 135 N. La Brea Ave., Hollywood. Call for times and reservation.

Laugh Factory, 323/656-1336. laughfactory.com. 8001 W. Sunset Blvd., Hollywood. Thanksgiving and Christmas dinner free to people in the biz.

The Improvisation, 323/651-2583. improvclubs.com. 8162 Melrose Ave., L.A. Top comedy acts. Talent nights and open mike nights.

The Original Comedy Store, 323/656-6225. thecomedystore.com. 8433 Sunset Blvd. Many actors have been discovered here. Open mike nights.

Groundlings Theatre, 323/934-9700. groundlings.com. 7307 Melrose Ave., Hollywood. Improvisational group doing consistently good work.

Second City, 323/658-8190, 888/873-9285. secondcity.com. 8156 Melrose Ave., Hollywood. Another troupe that has introduced some of today's top comedians.

• ACTIVITIES

Backbone Trail. Three-mile hike in Malibu Creek State Park, which takes you to the old M*A*S*H set.

Barbara Streisand's former Malibu estate, 310/589-2850. smmc.ca.gov. 5750 Ramirez Canyon Rd. Now part of the Santa Monica Mountains Conservancy, the two-hour tour offers a thorough look at the estate, including three of the five houses. $30.

Book Soup, 310/659-3110. booksoup.com. 8818 Sunset Blvd., You may never go back to a chain book store. Especially strong film section.

All Star Lanes, 323/254-2579. highoctane1.com. 4459 Eagle Rock Blvd., Eagle Rock. Home of Bowl-A-Rama on alternate Saturdays. A blend of rockabilly, punk fashion and bowling.

Canoga Park Bowling, 818/340-5190. canogaparkbowl.com. 20122 Vanowen Street, Winnetka. Open 24 hours. 32 lanes, billiards and video arcade.

Casablanca Tours, 323/461-0156 or 1-800/498-6871. casablancatours.com. A four-hour van tour includes stops at the Hollywood bowl, Grauman's Chinese Theatre, Sunset Strip, Rodeo Drive and a look at 25 to 30 celebrities homes.

Coldwater Canyon Park. Treepeople.org. Just east of the intersection of Coldwater Canyon and Mulholland Drive. Five miles of marked trails.

Culver City Western Hemisphere Marathon, 310/253-6650. culvercity.org. Early registration, $25; race day, $35. Expansive views of the Pacific Ocean above Dockweiler Beach.

Dodgers Adult Baseball Camp, 800/334-7529. hihardl.com/lad/dtnhmpgl.htmlfantasycamp. $4,195.

Equestrian Center, 818/840-9063. la-Equestriancenter.com. On Riverside Drive in Burbank. This is our horse country. Many stables, restaurants, ice skating rink.

Gaona's Trapeze School, 818/710-8191. flytrapeze.com 5702 Lubao Ave., Woodland Hills. Students at Richie Gaona's Trapeze School must check any fears at the door. Within 30 minutes they're strapped into the safety harnesses, ready to ascend the 24-foot ladder and reach out to clutch a trapeze bar.

Glendale Batting Cages, 818/243-2363. 620 East Colorado Blvd., Glendale. Softball or hardball batting cages.

Hiking: Mount Hollywood Trail, Griffith Park. Latrails.com. Enter Griffith Park from Los Feliz Blvd. and turn onto Griffith Park Drive. Parking lot next to the carousel. 800-foot uphill trek from the carousel to the planetarium. There are also easier trails. Griffith Park also has some great golf courses, horseback riding, the Los Angeles Zoo and a number of other activities.

Hollywood Bowl Rehearsals, 323/850-2000. hollywoodbowl.com. 2301 N. Highland Ave., Hollywood. During the Hollywood Bowl season from June to September, mostly Tuesdays, Thursdays and Fridays, you can see the program scheduled for that evening for free.

Hollywood Boxing Gym, 323/845-1420. hollywoodgym.com. 1551 La Brea Ave., Hollywood.

Hollywood Fantasy Tours, 1-800-starbus hollywoodfantasytours.com.

Los Angeles County Museum of Art, 323/857-6110. lacma.org. 5905 Wilshire Blvd., L.A.

Los Angeles Downtown Walking Tour, 213/623-2489. laconservancy.org. All downtown walking tours begin at 10AM and last approximately 2-1/2 hours (except the Biltmore Hotel tour which begins at 11AM and is 1-1/2 hours long and the City Hall tour which begins at both 10AM and 11AM and is 1-1/2 hours long). Tours are free to Los Angeles Conservancy members and $8 for the general public (Angelino Heights is $5 for members and $10 for the general public). No strollers or young children. Advance Reservations required.

Indoor Climbing at Rockreation, 714/556-ROCK. rockreation.com. 1300 Logan Ave., Costa Mesa. 10,000 sq. ft. of sculpted artificial rock.

J. Paul Getty Museum, 310/440-7300. getty.edu. 1200 Getty Center Drive. Parking is $7, the museum is free. The other museum, in Malibu, is devoted to ancient Greek and Roman art. 310/458-2003. 17985 Pacific Coast Hwy. Spectacular! Both museums are a "must see."

Laser Storm, 310/373-8470. gablehousebowl.com. 22535 Hawthorne Blvd., Torrance or 818/999-3150. 20929 Ventura Blvd., Woodland Hills. Laser tag venue lets you shoot at one another or at electronic objects in an arena filled with black and neon lights. Everything glows in the dark.

Mar Vista Bowl, 310/391-5288. amf.com/marvistalanes/centerhomepage.htm. 12125 Venice Blvd., Mar Vista. Call for open bowling times. Also has a great coffee shop for an inexpensive breakfast.

Melrose News, 323/655-2866. 647 N. Martel Ave., L.A. Celeb newsstand. Eddie Murphy allegedly stopped by the night of his infamous adventure with a transvestite.

Merchant of Tennis, 310/855-1946. 1118 S. La Cienega Blvd., Beverly Hills. 9-6. $15 per hour, per group. Lessons 6:30am-1pm, $45 an hour.

Moore-N-Moore Sporting Clays, 818/890-4788. moorenmoore.com. 12651 N. Little Tujunga Canyon Road, San Fernando. Practice your marksmanship skills with clay pigeons. Celebs John Milius and Charlton Heston have been spotted here.

NBC Television Studio Tour, a 70-minute walking tour of the tv production complex. Departures at regular intervals, weekdays from 9-3. $7. 818/840-3537. nbc.com.

Poetry Readings, Beyond Baroque, 310/822-3006. 681 Venice Blvd., West Los Angeles.

Natural History Museum, 213/763-3466. nhm.org. 900 Exposition Blvd., Exposition Park, Los Angeles, near USC.

Paramount Ranch, 805/370-2301. nps.gov/samo/. Hit "In Depth" button. 401 W. Hillcrest Drive., Thousand Oaks. Free. This location has played the role of colonial Massachusetts, ancient China and countless Wild West towns. Take 101 Frwy. west to Kanan Road, south on Kanan half a mile to Cornell Way. Follow Cornell three miles to Paramount Ranch Road and turn right into parking lot.

Power Pools. Swim in the pools if you buy lunch at The Mondrian, Chateau Marmont, Regent Beverly Wilshire, Hollywood Roosevelt, or Sunset Marquis hotels. Takes a great body and nerve.

Romantic Rides/Hermosa Cyclery, 310/374-7816. hermosacyclery.com. 20 13th St., Hermosa Beach.

Runyon Canyon Park. Runyon-canyon.com. Franklin Ave., 1 blk. east of La Brea, on Fuller. Past old Errol Flynn estate; foundations, old swimming pool still visible. At top, a bench and a view.

Santa Monica Pier, santamonicapier.org. At the end of Colorado Blvd., in Santa Monica. Historical carousel and a whole amusement park, rides open on weekends, but plenty to do during the week. Bands play on the pier early evenings during the summer.

Shatto 39 Bowling Lanes, 213/385-9475. shatto39.com. 3255 W. 4th Street, L.A. 19 pool tables, bar and coffee shop.

Silent Movie Theater, 323/655-2510. silentmovietheatre.com. 611 N. Fairfax, Hollywood. Shows nothing but classic silent films, complete with a working organ to provoe backing music. Very cool experience seeing Chaplin films as they were meant to be seen.

Sports Center Bowl, 818/769-7600. pinzbowlingcenter.com. 12655 Ventura Blvd., Studio City. 32 lanes. Lots of industry clientele.

Stair Climbing, 4th Street Stairs, 4th and Adelaide streets in Santa Monica (189 steps).

Stairs in Santa Monica. They ascend from the 400 block of North Mesa Road to Amalfi Drive (201 steps). Less crowded than the 4th street stairs. Redwoods, wisteria and live oaks.

Sunset Beach, one of the best surfing spots. Take Sunset Blvd. west and park on Pacific Coast Highway, just south of Gladstone's 4 Fish.

Sunset Ranch Hollywood Stables, 323/464-9612. sunsetranchhollywood.com. 3400 N. Beachwood Dr., Hollywood. Friday night rides on horseback in the Griffith Park Hills.

• AREAS

Beverly Hills, between Santa Monica and Wilshire Blvd., Canon on the east and where Santa Monica and Wilshire cross on the west.

Farmers Market, 323/933-9211. farmersmarketla.com. On Third and Fairfax, Los Angeles. M-S 9-7. Su 10-6. Great shopping and eating. The Grove, L.A.'s new and beautiful outdoor mall.

Hollywood Farmers Market, Ivar Avenue between Sunset and Hollywood Boulevards, Sundays, 8:30AM to 1PM. Attracts a lot of Hollywood types.

Chinatown, in downtown Los Angeles, Hill and Broadway. Experience a dim sum tea breakfast for an unusual treat.

Fairfax Avenue, from Melrose to Sixth Street. The heart of the old Jewish district.

Koreatown, Olympic Blvd. from Vermont to Western. The Korea Plaza mall on Western features designer clothing, housewares, a bakery and large Korean grocery store.

Larchmont Blvd., between Melrose and Beverly Blvd. and Rossmore (Vine) and Gower. Old world village shopping and dining district.

Little Tokyo, 1st and 2nd streets between Los Angeles Street and Alameda in downtown L.A. Check out the new National Japanese American Museum. The Japanese Village features shops and restaurants. Also visit Yaohan Plaza at 4th and Alameda to see an incredible Japanese super grocery store, restaurants and an extensive Japanese bookstore. There's also a karaoke lounge where you can book private karaoke rooms by the hour.

Melrose Avenue, between La Brea and Fairfax. Underground chic shopping, eating and looking.

Montana Avenue, at 16th St. in Santa Monica. Great place for shopping and eating. A small town environment; lots of celebs live close.

Mulholland Drive. Enter from Cahuenga Blvd West (off Barham and the 101 Freeway.) On a clear day you can see the ocean, downtown L.A., and Century City Towers. 20-minute drive to the 405 freeway. Take in the Valley and the City. If it is not a clear day, you'll be above the smog.

Old Olvera Street, by Union Train Station in downtown L.A., off the 101 Freeway at Alameda. Permanent Mexican street festival.

Old Pasadena, 134 Freeway east, exit at Colorado. Check out Green Street and Fair Oaks. Antiques, dining, hot night scene, very in!

Santa Monica, Malibu, Zuma, Laguna, Newport Beaches!

Sunset Strip, starts around Crescent Heights and continues west for a couple miles. Legendary rock clubs, high-priced celebrity hangouts and some of the best tourist bars in town.

Third Street Promenade, 3rd Street between Colorado and Wilshire Blvd. in Santa Monica. Pedestrian mall with restaurants, movie theater and live street performers. A fun evening of strolling and browsing.

Venice Beach Boardwalk, great shopping, walking, looking. Take Venice Blvd. west. Funky and crowded.

Walk By Moonlight, 626/398-5420. ecnca.org. On Friday nights closest to the full moon, walkers gather at 190-acre Eaton Canyon Natural Area in northeast Pasadena, at the base of the San Gabriel Mountains, for docent-led moonlight hikes.

Day trips: Don't forget that Los Angeles is located near many other fun cities to explore, for a day or a weekend. Drive a couple hours south to **San Diego** to check out the legendary San Diego Zoo or Wild Kingdom. If you feel like going a little further, you'll hit **Tijuana**. Drive north about an hour to **Santa Barbara** and tour a bit of wine country. Drive east a couple hours and spend some time day-tripping in **Palm Springs**. 90 miles northeast to Lake Arrowhead and Big Bear. And let's not forget **VEGAS!!!!!**

• BOOKS

City Tripping Los Angeles by Tom Dolby. Great guide for singles.
Curbside L.A.: From the Pages of the Los Angeles Times by Cecilia Rasmussen.
Frommer's Irreverent Guide to Los Angeles by Jeff Spurrier and Chrissy Coleman
Lonely Planet Los Angeles by Andrea Schulte-Peevers and David Peevers
Pocket Guide to the Best of Los Angeles by Gary McBroom & Charlotte McBroom
The Ultimate Hollywood Tour Book by William A. Gordon. Fantastic!
The Underground Guide to Los Angeles by Pleasant Gehman, Editor.
This is Hollywood by Ken Schlesslers.

• NOVELS ABOUT L.A.

The Big Sleep by Raymond Chandler.
What Makes Sammy Run by Budd Schulberg.
Ask the Dust by John Fante.
The Day of the Locust by Nathanial West.
City of Quartz by Mike Davis.
A Red Death by Walter Mosley.
Maps to Anywhere by Bernard Cooper.
Golden Days by Carolyn See.
I Should Have Stayed Home by Horace McCoy.
Sad Movies by Mark Lindquist.
Armed Response by Ann Rower
Los Angeles Without a Map by Richard Rayner.
L.A. Is the Capital of Kansas by Richard Meltzer.
Series of novels featuring Harry Bosch by Michael Connelly

• MOVIES ABOUT L.A.

Adaptation	*The Bad And The Beautiful*
Barton Fink	*Beyond The Valley Of The Dolls*
The Big Sleep	*Blade Runner*
Boogie Nights	*Bowfinger*
Boyz N The Hood	*Chinatown*
Crash	*Day of the Locust*
Detour	*Devil In A Blue Dress*
Dogtown And Z-Boys	*The Doors*
Double Indemnity	*Echo Park*
Ed Wood	*Get Shorty*
Heat	*In A Lonely Place*
Jackie Brown	*Killing Of A Chinese Bookie*
Kiss Me Deadly	*L.A. Confidential*
Laurel Canyon	*The Long Goodbye*
Lost Highway	*Magnolia*
Mulholland Dr.	*The Party*
The Player	*Pulp Fiction*
Short Cuts	*Singin' In The Rain*
S1mOne (Simone)	*Sunset Boulevard*
Swimming With The Sharks	*Swingers*

Section Nine

Child Actors

• **If your child really wants to act—really wants to work**—it can happen with your help. This is the consensus of all the experts I have interviewed. Children, as well as adults, need dedication, talent and luck to make it.

• **In the writing of this Eleventh Edition, Austin Tovar,** my 18-year-old grandson, is in the 12th grade and has retired from acting for the time being. He worked on several long running Jack-In-The-Box commercials playing Jack Jr.—yes, he was wearing the big head. He loved working and being on the set but then he didn't like being pulled away from his activities for the hour drive to an audition. His parents opened a bank account for him as well as the mandatory trust fund. He pays for special things he wants to participate in from his own earnings. He gets to spend $5 to $20 from each paycheck he receives, depending on the amount of the check. He still receives residual checks and holding fees. *(See Austin's pictures in the Photo section.)*

• **Austin's younger brother, Jackson Tovar,** from age seven to nine also took acting classes and had an agent. He auditioned for a couple of years getting a few small jobs, but as he got more active in sports he also got tired of the long drives to audition. *(See Jackson's pictures in the Photo section.)*

• **Scams abound in the children's field.** We all think our children are fabulous. We can get swept away by the praise for our children and the promise of stardom. I have heard horror stories of families losing thousands of dollars after paying money up-front to illegitimate talent companies or acting schools for services that were promised but never provided. Throughout this section, I have quoted respected professionals in the business. Please read it carefully. Do not get ripped off.

- **Tracy Martin, acting coach, warns:**

  - **Stay away from studios that offer pictures and lifetime classes** and more for an outrageous amount of money. Call around. Compare class fees and photographer fees. Again, see if these people are "in the know" with current agents and casting directors. Ask questions. Find out if they have students who are working. Often a snapshot and good cover letter is enough to submit to an agent. If the agent is interested, they will recommend several photographers.

- **There are expenses involved in getting any business started.** Your child will need classes, pictures and a working wardrobe, but you only pay for these at the time of service, not before. Agents and managers get paid commissions only after the child gets paid for working. At the end of this section I list teachers, photographers, agents and managers that I know personally or who were recommended by friends in the business. Check these resources out, do your own research, find out what you are paying for and follow your intuition.

- **Carlyne Grager of Dramatic Artists Agency Inc.** in Seattle is a mother of child actors and for the past 15 years has been an agent and co-owner of an agency that represents many children in the Northwest. I asked for her views of child actors as a parent and agent.

  - **I think every parent's level of investment** grows beyond what they originally intended and they all get caught up in the industry more than expected, but some parents nearly imprison their children within the Hollywood cycle of networking, classes, showcases, auditions, etc.

  - **It is far better for a parent** to think that a career should be developed in much the same manner that they would develop their child athletically or scholastically. In those areas they start small and invest as their child's interest grows, skills develop and passion increases. Sports and academics can affect children's lives in many of the same ways that acting for film and television can. Good or bad, it all depends on the attitudes and character of parents, coaches and professional guides such as agents/managers. How will the child's self-esteem and cultural enrichment be developed?

  - **In my opinion, acting has been a saving grace** with my children when school wasn't going well or athletics were too political and competitive. It gave them another "arena" in which to shine or excel. Their acting friends always remained a separate entity outside of the social politics at school and in sports, giving them a "port" in the storm.

- **Acting can enhance the natural skills** and alter the course of a child's life in a very positive manner. I've had actors with "issues" that were overcome with the artistic expression found in acting. My own son overcame a high functioning form of autism because of acting for the camera. I've had several A.D.D. and Dyslexic children excel at acting when they were struggling in school. I've had a few kids who were dealing with substance abuse issues that found acting to be their survival and reason to stay recovered. It's my personal belief that acting has prevented many of its disciples from ever straying in the first place toward drugs, alcohol or delinquency. Mainly, because it provides calculated risk and the type of "highs" or peer support that can never be maintained through drugs or alcohol.

- **The enrichment and exposure** that a child receives in acting teaches tolerance, acceptance, discipline and camaraderie. It gives the child a venue to explore and dream that it is seldom found elsewhere. Where can a child live the moments of being crowned homecoming queen or being an international spy or even becoming a cartoon character when clearly "real life" doesn't always allow that? When do they get to be Peter Pan or Harry Potter other than in their imagination? The answer is that they get to be those types of characters and live different life scenarios every time they step into a casting office, or acting class. My oldest son, a sports enthusiast, got to spend a day talking to Olympic Medal Athletes on the set of *Prefontaine*. My daughter, got to bowl for free all day while doing a photo shoot at a bowling alley. Some experiences are great, some are simple, but often the experiences are unique.

- **The very behaviors** that young actors are trained to develop and display—social manners, memorization skills, character insight, action and reaction (scientifically referred to as "cause and effects")—are all the behaviors that contribute to academic or athletic success.

- **T.J. Stein of Stein Entertainment Group was a child actor** himself and then evolved into management representation.

Q: What is the first step to get your child into the business?

- **I think the first step would be enrolling your child in an acting class.** Basically to get in front of the camera, get an idea of where the camera is and what to do, following directions and to see themselves on TV. They will learn about being creative and using their imagination.

- **Most children really have no idea what to do** when they first walk into a room to interview with an agent or to audition. In class they get the experience of what is going to be asked of them. Class for kids is really a training and a practice ground for them to go into the audition.

• **When the child gets to know how to work with the camera,** feels comfortable and wants to pursue acting professionally, it would be time to look for an agent. A licensed and/or franchised agent makes 10% of any fee your child is paid on a union job. There are never any up-front charges for you to pay to the agent.

• **Manager Diane Hardin of Hardin/Eckstein Management,** along with her partner, Nora Eckstein, manages careers of some of the top working young actors in town. Diane owns and teaches at the Young Actor's Space in Van Nuys, California. She also teaches three times a year in New York.

Q: What is the best way to find an agent for your child?

   • **If the parent doesn't know any agents** they can go to the Screen Actor's Guild or Association of Talent Managers and get a copy of the SAG franchised agents. It will say which agents handle children. Take some good color snapshots of the child, close-ups and full body shots. The children should look like real kids wearing play clothes, like they've just come from school or the playground. Get 3x5 or 4x6 copies made and send them with a cover letter listing their birthday, interests and skills to all the agents.

   • **Have a meeting with the agents** who call you. Look at their track record, at the other clients they represent. What sort of reputation does the agent have? You should sign with the agent who shows the most enthusiasm for your child.

• **Hettie Lynne Hurtes, actress, newscaster and manager** of her children's careers responds to the question: "On the child's interview with the agent, what will they talk about?"

   • **It is important to know the child will be going into the agent's office alone.** The parents will be waiting in the front office. The agents want to find out if the child is open to talking to strangers, to people they are not familiar with. This can be a difficult situation for young actors because they are used to their parents telling them not to talk to strangers. The parents will have to tell the child, "This is an atmosphere where your mom is right outside the door and you can feel safe talking to these business people."

   • **The best thing a child can do is to be real** and talk about anything they want to. Sometimes they will have specific questions like, "How old are you? What school do you go to? What grade you are in? What is your favorite subject?"—things that they know you know. The way they find out about your personality is to ask questions about your everyday life. They want to see if you are an outgoing kid. That is very important in a child actor. The kids who are gregarious and precocious are the ones who usually work. If they are shy and quiet they will not be interesting to the agent.

• **Tracy Martin, acting coach for kids and teens,** has coached many actors for their auditions and their roles. Her actors are currently working on series, in films and commercials.

Q: How would you advise a parent to help their child on an audition?

• **It is the "trend" now in Hollywood** for young actors to be real and natural. Gone are the days of overacting and super cute smiles. Casting directors want to hire kids that look like "kids" and act like "kids." For that reason, some agents are discouraging their clients from being coached. I had a young girl come to me from a very reputable Hollywood agency. Her mom told me that the agent told her not to get coaching because they wanted the girl to remain "natural." The young girl arrived and actually read the stage directions out loud! She also "yelled" all of her lines as she did in her last "school play." Again, be a smart shopper. My students train hard with me and remain real and natural because that is how I train them. Find the coach or teacher that will help your child to book the job.

• **If you must coach your child yourself,** here is what to look for. No acting. Have them read the lines to you as though they were really the character, having a real conversation. Encourage them to be themselves!

• **Understand the material.** You cannot play something you do not understand.

• **In comedy, it's about beats and timing.** If you do not have a good comedy coach to work with, watch classic sitcoms like *I Love Lucy* and *All In The Family*. You can actually count out the beats in a joke and between the jokes.

• **Agent Judy Savage of the well-respected Judy Savage Agency,** represents children and very young adults. She started with her own three children, then opened the agency when her youngest son was 14. The children she represents work in commercials, movies, television and stage.

Q: When you get a picture in the mail and you are interested in that child, will you call?

• **I look at all the pictures that come in.** One Saturday a month, we set up a time where the children come in and do a monologue for me if they're old enough, or I have them read something. I spend about 15 or 20 minutes with them and also with the parents. Out of 15 or 20 kids that I see on a Saturday, I'll find maybe three or four new ones. You always have to build from the bottom up in an agency. You've got to get new little ones.

Q: At what age do you start them?

• **In California, the legal age to work is six.** I do start interviewing at three years old, but I prefer not taking them until they're old enough. When producers hire children under six, they usually want twins or they want a six year old to play four so they can work them more. It's a business. If they can save money, then that's what they're going to do.

Q: How would you advise parents?

• **Make sure that they're with an agent who cares about children.** There are some agents and acting classes that make the kids cry. Protect them. Make sure the team around them supports, loves and nurtures them. When they go on an interview, it's a really special time for a mother and a child. They should play games in the car or whatever they can think of to make it fun. If you make it fun, they're going to do better. When my children were little, I used to take all kinds of toys. When you get to the interview, take them aside, teach them the dialogue, make sure that they know it, and then relax and have a good time. Don't hound them to death by combing their hair, etc. When they come out of the interview, don't insist on knowing everything that goes on. The kids hate that.

Q: How do you get children and parents started?

• **We talk to them about the business,** the good and bad points. This business is very good for children, especially those who are extremely intelligent or have a lot of energy, even children who have a bad time in school. Some wanted to be in this business so badly they have gone from F's to straight A's, because in order to get and keep a work permit, they have to maintain a C average. The parents are astounded.

• **When you have interviewed and signed with an agent,** you will need your career tools. T.J. Stein talks about pictures, resumes and work permits.

• **The picture is the calling card for the child.** It is important to research the photographers you are thinking of using. Agents and managers have photographers that they will recommend. The Screen Actors Guild requires that an agency recommend at least three different photographers. The parents can base their choice on which photographer's work they like and how the photographer works with the child.

Pictures cost $100-$250, depending on the photographer and how many shots you will get. I would not pay anything over $250 for a child getting a headshot. The pictures should be taken after you have signed with an agent so that the agent and/or manager can help you choose which picture to blow up into an 8x10. The commercial shot will tend to be a smiling shot because commercials are always happy. The theatrical shot shows a more serious side of the actor.

- **Resumes are attached to the back of the 8x10.** On the resume you have the child's name, birth date, unions, a list of the projects the child has worked on, name of the show, the part played. List the child's special skills and the acting classes they have taken.

- **It is necessary to have a work permit for the child.** It allows them to work in the entertainment industry. Go to the Department of Labor Standards—there is one in Van Nuys at 6150 Van Nuys Blvd. Fill out the application; if the child is of school age there is a section for the child's teacher to complete. During the summer, a current report card will take the place of the teacher's signature. The parent can do all of this without the child being present. Each time they work, the permit will be stamped. The child must maintain a C average in order to be eligible and the permit must be renewed every six months. It can be renewed through the mail and must be kept current or the child can lose a job.

- **When your child is on an audition** they are not covered by the state's strict laws because they apply only when your child is actually employed. So you must be on guard that there is never a situation where your child is in danger. If you have any misgivings, remove your child immediately.

• **Doreen Stone, known for her photography of children,** recommends when having your child's pictures taken to keep it simple. Bring simple Gap-looking clothes, no logos. What they wear everyday is perfect for the pictures. When she shoots she actually plays with them, gets down on the floor, makes it fun.

Q: How does a parent prepare a child for a photo shoot?

- **Photographer David LaPorte answers:** The best way way to prepare a child for a photo session is to encourage the child to have fun, relax and be natural. Other than organizing the clothes for the various looks (which should be clothes that they normally wear that are not too distracting) there should not be any preparation. If a child receives too many ideas of how they should behave, then the spontaneity, which is the essential ingredient, will suffer.

• **More from Diane Hardin:**

Q: What is required of the parent?

- **Constant vigilance.** The parent has to be ready at a moment's notice to run on interviews or to sit on a set. A parent, grandparent or somebody who is really connected to that child should be with them. Children have to attend three hours of school every day and maintain a high grade average in order to keep their work permit. There are a lot of wonderful experiences and nice people involved, but it's also a lot of pressure.

Q: How old do you think a child should be before they start?

- **I wouldn't do it before six.** Children may be asked to be in uncomfortable situations and they don't understand the difference between an angry scene on the set and an angry scene in real life.

Q: When is it time to put your child in the business?

- **Only when your child is constantly begging you** to be in the business. It should come from the child's saying, "Oh, I can do that. I want to do that." And if the child wants to try out for all the school plays and really seems to have a need to do it, then I think that they should have every encouragement in the world, just like you would encourage someone who wanted to play Little League or the violin.

Q: How do the young actors take rejection?

- **My main suggestion is to make it about the work**, about doing the best acting job every time they go out and not about getting the job. When they land the job it's a nice surprise.

Q: How should a parent interview acting schools?

- **There's only one reason for a child to take acting classes**, and that's because it's fun. I don't think it should be too psychological or too critical. I am very strongly based on positive reinforcement, rather than the negative. I will be quick to tell them what I believed in their work, rather than what I didn't believe. You can't build your confidence if you're constantly being torn down. If it's a chore and it makes them feel bad about themselves because somebody is tearing them down, then that's not the right place to study acting.

- **You can't really teach someone to act.** You can just give them a way to discover how to be real in the moment—how to listen and react. They have to learn to make very quick decisions and strong choices.

- **At the Young Actor's Space,** we help these young people discover what it feels like after they've made strong choices about who they are, where they are and what they want in the scene. They read it, make those choices, relax, listen and react within the given situation.

- **Every class at the Young Actor's Space** is based on improvisation. The first hour is improv warm-ups, improv scenes of different kinds. They have scenes to do every week. I tell them the scenes have to look like an improvisation, like this is happening for the first time, every time they do it.

- **Kids and teens coach Tracy Martin's students** are now appearing on television in series regular, recurring and guest-starring roles. In films, they appear in lead and supporting roles. Numerous students are working consistently in the commercial world.

Q: What does it take for a child to land jobs, luck?

- **Luck? No one will deny the magic of luck and timing.** But to really make it these days as a child actor in Hollywood, it takes more; it demands more. They will need passion, a good attitude and the ability to work hard. They will also need self-discipline, intelligence, talent, energy and a loving and supportive family.

- **Why passion? A working child actor** may miss sporting events, class trips, birthday parties and family vacations. They may have their heart broken when the part they "really wanted" goes to a "name actor" at the last minute. They may have the sniffles and want to stay in bed, but they have a callback they need to be at in one hour. They may be tired after a long day at school and have to learn seven pages of dialogue for a TV audition that very afternoon. The family may miss presenting a united front at one sibling's school play because "Johnny" has to be on the set late one night.

- **My working students all have one thing in common.** They love to act. They love to act more then they love anything else and they are fortunate that their families support them. A family life may be turned inside out and upside down to support such a "passion."

• Q: What kind of training does a child need?

- **There are many different classes,** depending on the direction you are taking with your child's career. As a general rule, I discourage school plays for the simple reason that most of this kind of acting is over the top. Most film and TV acting is more understated and real.

- **A good improv class is invaluable.** It will help build confidence in the child, help them to think on their feet and will help them greatly if they get into commercials.

- **Scene study is very helpful when first starting out.** Make sure the class provides feedback. Just reading lines with a scene partner will not provide the skills that are necessary for successful auditions.

- **There are some good on-camera commercial classes** out there. Try to get referrals.

- **Audition technique.** Depending on where you live, you may not be able to find this kind of class. I teach the students how to break down the scenes, (make notes) and then they read against me as though I were the casting director. I try to duplicate the audition process for them so that they feel prepared and empowered when they walk into the casting directors office. I also hold "mock" producers' callbacks so they can get a sense of that as well.

- **Agent Judy Savage:**

Q: How do the kids turn out as adults?

- **I think I've known every child actor since Jodie Foster and Ron Howard** when my kids were working. It is absolutely, positively the family structure that makes the difference. If they have a good family, ethics, morals, some sort of spiritual background and the work is treated like a hobby they get paid for, they turn out just great.

Q: What about scripts with violence or sexual abuse? How do you deal with that?

- **We are alerted by the casting directors.** They'll call us, or they'll have on the breakdowns, "This is really sensitive material; make sure you alert the parents." We get the material ahead of time. We let the parents look at it and decide if they think their child is able to handle it. Some do and some don't. I've had people turn down major work. I believe these children have to have a life first because show business can come and go but they have to have a life afterwards.

Q: Anything you think parents should know?

- **It is very, very competitive in this business,** and there are many, many, many rejections. You may go on a hundred interviews before you get something. People are almost never discovered overnight. Some people think that they can come to Hollywood and get work in three months. My experience in working with really talented kids who are in training every week has been it takes about three years to get somebody started. There are twice as many parts for boys than there are for girls, yet there are probably 10 times as many girls in the business. If you're a 6-year-old, there are maybe 10 other kids, and by the time you are 14, there are 400, and by the time you are 18, there are 2,000.

- **It's a myth that child actors make all this money** that their parents spend. When a child works, 15% of their money goes into a Coogan Account trust fund, 10% goes to the agent, 15% goes to the manager, if they have one. Because they are making a high amount of money each week, they are in a 40% tax bracket. When a child actor works, their check is about 10% of their salary but they do have a nice trust fund when they turn 18. Usually their mother has to give up a job and work full-time as a driver. By the time you're on a series for eight years, you may be making $30,000 an episode, so even if you take home 10%, that's $3,000 an episode. Actors making their first movie usually earn scale plus 10% for the agent, even for adults. By the second movie, they make $40-$50,000; by the fourth movie, $100-$125,000. They may make $200,000 if it's a lead part, unless they luck out and it's a hit movie, like Macaulay Culkin did. Macaulay is the only child since Shirley Temple that's received a million dollars a film. Everybody thinks, "I want to do movies so I can make money like Macaulay." *Home Alone* was Macaulay's third or fourth movie. He made $100,000.

- **Manager Diane Hardin:**

Q: What are the manager's duties?

- **My partner and I are, perhaps, a little different than some managers;** we meet our clients on every single audition and give them hands-on coaching. We also coach them when they get the job. If they get a series, we coach them on their weekly scripts. Nora and I feel our main job as managers is to nurture their talent through coaching, exposing them to theater, recommending books for them to read, such as Uta Hagen's *Respect for Acting,* insisting that they take acting classes and that they stay in class. We do offer our clients as many acting classes as they care to take at the Young Actor's Space. It's all part of the management fee.

Q: What is the manager's fee?

- **We take 15% of their salary.** We take 5% of commercials, because we don't go with them on commercial auditions. But we do know that the good training does affect their commercial potential.

• **Manager T.J. Stein:**

Q: When is the right time to look for management?

- **I think that you really need the guidance and support right away.**
  Some people say, "Well, what do you have to manage if you are
  brand new?" You have a lot to manage. You need to get to the right
  people, you need to make sure that I, in my position, open the right
  doors. A child is a child for a very short period of time. There is a lot
  of competition.

• **Brigitte Burdine is a working actress,** casting director and commercial
and theatrical teacher for children and teens. The commercials she teaches
in her classes are those she has followed from the beginning of casting
through the production. She knows who the advertising clients wanted
to see and why the children were picked for the spots.

**Q: How should young actors get experience before they move to
Los Angeles?**

- **I started acting and modeling** when I was 14 years old in the Washington D.C. area. I think it is a good idea to get as much experience
  as you can in a small market. There aren't as many opportunities, but
  there isn't as much competition either. Expect that there will be some
  traveling involved. I had to commute to NY from time to time.

- **If you are outside the LA or NY area,** the best place to start is by
  checking with your local SAG office for reputable representation (sag.
  org). The same rules apply in a small market that apply here. Never
  pay for representation. Agents get 10% of your earnings when you
  work union jobs.

**Q: When does a parent know it is time for their child to study? Should
they try to get an agent first?**

- **Generally speaking, a child is ready to start training at 5.** It is fine to
  seek representation by an agent before you begin to study. Usually the
  agent will want the child to take a class before they send the child out on
  auditions. Children are able to be themselves morre easily if they are in a
  comfortable situation. A class will help with that. Think of it this way: we
  tell our children not to talk to strangers. Then we proceed to send them
  into a room on an audition with a bunch of people they aren't familiar
  with and expect them to feel safe and be their wonderful, uninhibited
  selves. From casting for more than 14 years, I can tell right away when a
  child enters the casting room whether or not they have had a class. They
  will have a confidence about them that other children don't have.

Q: How can the parents help their children at the auditions?

- The best way is to explain to them what they are going to do and make sure they understand what it means. Do not try to give them line readings. (Don't tell the child, "Say it like this.") Once you have directed them into a line reading, it is very hard for the director to change what you have told them to do. The more prepared and relaxed you are, the more prepared and relaxed your child will be. Have you ever noticed how your mood and state of mind directly affects your child's? Treat auditioning like a fun after school activity like baseball or dancing. It is important to take it seriously, but it isn't the cure for cancer.

- **Will Estes (willestes.com) has appeared in 40-plus commercials** and as a regular on eight series, including: *The New Lassie, It Had To Be You, Kirk, Kelly Kelly, American Dreams* and *Reunion* plus guest-starring television and supporting film roles. As a young adult, he has four starring roles in the films, *Terror Tract, U571, Blue Ridge Fall* and *The Road Home. (See his resume in the Resume section)*

Q: What about rejection?

- **I've never really had a problem with rejection**, it never bothers me. There are other things I have a lot of fun doing. I go to an audition and then head on down to gym class. I'll get in the car and it'll just leave my mind; I don't even think about it.

Q: What is it that your mother does that helps you in your career?

- **Well, before I could drive, she took me to all my auditions.** She would sit in the waiting room and I would go into the actual audition by myself. She would read the other characters lines in the script to help me memorize my lines. Sometimes she gives me suggestions; that's cool. I like having her opinion.

Q: What do you do on auditions?

- **If there are lines, I'll look over those.** If I have my lines down or there are no lines, as the case with some commercials, sometimes there will be people there I know, I can talk to them and hang out.

Q: What about young actors getting on drugs?

- **I don't see that acting relates to drugs.** I've never even come across it.

Q: Do you have any advice for kids?

- **If you really want to do it, then give it a try.** Don't take it too seriously, when it comes to an audition. What's the big deal if you don't get the job? It's not worth being stressed over.

Mary Lu Chasteen is the mother of actor Will Estes and was his manager for many years.

Q: How old was Will when he got into the business?

- **He started when he was nine.** Friends of ours referred us to the Kelman/Arletta Agency who had been in the business for years representing all but one of the kids on *The Brady Bunch.*

- **Arletta said, "Yeah, we'd like to sign him."** He has an All-American look they liked. Within the first month, he booked a print ad for Lee jeans. Then he got his first commercial, Fruit of the Loom. It was real exciting for us. From that point on it just kind of snowballed.

Q: How did you know what to do?

- **Well, the agent tells you but it's learn as you go.** The agent would call and give us the interview, the time, what he should wear, what he should take with him like a skateboard, skates or anything, and then we'd go on the audition. In a few days if they were interested they'd call him back. Then sometimes he'd book the commercial.

- **Within the first year,** Arletta started sending him out for theatrical auditions. He tried out for a part on *The New Lassie.* There were eight callbacks over a few months period.

Q: How long did he work on that series?

- **It turned out to be one of the greatest experiences we've had.** We did 48 shows. He was there nine-and-a-half hours a day, five days a week. To this day he still keeps in touch with some of the friends he made on the set, people he worked with and the owners of *Lassie;* it was really like a family situation for him. I think that's hard for kids as they get older; when the show stops, the family stops. Will did tell me, not too long ago, that he was glad he was old enough to have his own self-identity before he started this business.

Q: What about his schooling, grades and outside activities?

- **Some of the money Will made went for his private schooling.** It was a half day, straight academic school. When he worked, they prepared his lessons for the set. If he missed, they would tutor him to catch him up. Because of the concentrated studies he skipped a grade and graduated one year early with honors.

- **All the things he's interested in** seem to stem from things he did on jobs. He's really into gymnastics, and that came from a job he did on a commercial where he had to use a trampoline. They had a coach from UCLA work with them. He got the bug for gymnastics and is still taking classes. When he worked on *Lassie,* the guys on their lunch hour would ride bikes; they took him and now he's into mountain biking. Karate is something he initiated on his own. But the agent said parts come up that call for karate. So he has enhanced his ability to get jobs.

- **I made sure the teachers on the set** were accredited and able to teach him what he needed. The thing I was always most concerned with was that his educational needs were met. I don't want to jeopardize his education with the business. I don't want to compromise anything for him. That's why parents really have to watch out for the kids.

Q: How did you pass the time on the set?

- **When you are on the set there is observing to do.** For instance, one time when Will was younger, he was inside an airplane prop where I couldn't hear him so I was listening to him on the headset. I heard him say to the guest actress that she had a mustache. I knew I had to tell him that you aren't supposed to say that to women.

Q: How are the finances and show-biz life style for you?

- **You put a percentage of the child's earnings away.** When he works we usually let him buy something like a skateboard, video game or something to reward him but not all the time. The busier he got, the less I could work. My job is pretty much taking care of Will; getting to auditions, taking care of his finances, going with him when he works on the set. We've had to travel to different areas. So we have to be ready at a moment's notice to go wherever.

- **I loved spending time with my kid**, being with him, going places; we did a lot together. It's been exciting, to say the least. I'm really proud of him. It's changed my life because it enables us to do things we would probably never do. When we went to Miami, we saw the Everglades. We've been to Hawaii twice, Vancouver, New York, Texas, Chicago, Italy.

- **If children want to work**, I think it's important that the parents are supportive and helpful. Having the support of their families helps them get through the tough times.

• **Al Burton, executive producer for Al Burton Productions:**

Q: **What are some of the shows you've done?**

• My list of shows that children worked on would include *One Day at a Time,* which introduced McKenzie Phillips and Valerie Bertinelli, *Diff'rent Strokes* with Gary Coleman, Todd Bridges and Dana Plato, *Silver Spoons* with Ricky Schroeder. In that show, we introduced Jason Bateman when he was 12. I worked with Michael J. Fox in *Palmerstown, U.S.A.,* a Norman Lear show that predated anything Michael had done in the U.S. The cast of *Square Pegs* was Sarah Jessica Parker, Jamie Gertz, Tracy Nelson, all teenagers, varying in ages from 15-19. Molly Ringwald started at age 12 in *Facts of Life.* She was a regular in the first year, then she got *The Tempest* with Mazursky, which shot her into a movie career.

• Then *Charles in Charge* and *The New Lassie.* In *Charles in Charge* we had Josie Davis, Nicole Eggert, Alexander Polinsky and Christina Applegate, very early in her career; Erika Eleniak who went on to become Ellie May in *Beverly Hillbillies* and starred in *Baywatch,* and Pamela Anderson who played the girlfriend of Charles for several weeks. I recommended both Nicole and Pamela to the *Baywatch* people and they became *Baywatch* stars. *The New Lassie* starred Will Estes, who is now starring on *American Dreams.*

Q: **When you were casting *Facts of Life* and *Diff'rent Strokes,* you saw a lot of kids, didn't you?**

• Yes. I was not satisfied until I felt I had cast the very best actors in the United States. We sent casting people to New York, Atlanta, Dallas, Denver and Boston to look for kids.

Q: **How would they find kids in other states?**

• They start with little theater people. If they had cast six kids in the previous year, we would see every one of them. We would put many on tape. I remember a casting director who went to Chicago, was told by somebody he ought to see a little kid in Zion, Illinois. He went up to Zion and found Gary Coleman. I got the tape when it came back and I looked at this little pair of eyes and this little nose peering over the desk. I ran and showed the tape to Norman Lear, he agreed and we brought Gary out and signed him to a contract from just the first meeting. He was perfect. His delivery was fabulous from day one.

Q: You seem to understand working children.

- **I feel very protective about children.** I have conversations with my directors and writers where my argument is, "Protect the kid." Don't ever say, "the kid can't act" or "the kid is bad." Your material needs to be fixed or your directing needs to be fixed. I often show a documentary on Steven Spielberg directing a 13-year-old boy in *Empire of the Sun* to directors. Spielberg gives direction that shows he unconsciously cares for, works with and has respect for the kid. I admire him a lot.

Q: If a child has that desire, what should they do to be discovered?

- **There are ways to get exposure** in Sheboygan, Dallas, Atlanta, etc. Acting is acting, whether it's in school, community theater or church, and I think experience in acting gives you the where-with-all to begin having a career. I began my career in Columbus, Ohio. By the time I was 15, I had engineered every opportunity I could find, which included producing shows for the Boy Scouts and local radio shows, just to give myself a part. It turned out that I liked the producing better than the acting, but it didn't start out that way. I created my own opportunities every step of the way.

- **In my heart of hearts,** I always want to say that if you're a parent and you see your child wants to be in the entertainment world, encourage it, and then get them close to a production center.

Q: How did you cast Will Estes on *The New Lassie* series?

- **Will was just a terrific 10-year-old.** We made him come back, I think, seven or eight times to audition because we weren't quite sure. He was littler and younger than we wanted in that part and, other than Lassie, it was the starring role. He kept having something that we didn't want to let go of. He never lost his cool or got disgusted. He just came and was the same sunny Will he always was. I've known him for 12 years now and we remain friends.

Q: What is it that makes you pick the kids that you pick?

- **I'll use Will Estes as an example.** His engine in the office worked very well. He's a dynamo, and yet he's not hyper. He had something in him that was very, very good, and it looked to me very promising. When it was Jami Gertz or Sarah Jessica Parker or Tracy Nelson, they had a package that was great. It wasn't just a voice or just acting or timing. It was everything: great eyes, great presence. They were interesting and had a totality. Norman Lear used to say, "They have to have television eyes." I think everybody I have liked did have eyes that could give a great close-up.

• **Agent/mother Carlyne Grager talks about relocating to Los Angeles from an outside market.**

• **The reason most parents come to Hollywood with their children** is because they love them and believe in their ability to succeed. They saw an opportunity where their child could pursue a dream and didn't want to keep them from it. Childhood is the most opportune time in one's life to pursue a film and television career. If you hadn't helped your child when you were asked, you might later regret it.

• **The first move to L.A. is usually a temporary one.** One parent and child/children generally show up for a pilot or episodic season. They are usually guided to enroll in acting classes, secure talent representation and pursue auditions. The other parent generally stays behind to hold down the fort and is usually working full time shelling out big bucks for this opportunity. If the family is very traditional or tightly bonded, bringing their child to Hollywood in pursuit of a film/television career can be the weirdest and most expensive venture of their life.

• **If you're really lucky**, you might be fortunate enough to have a relative living here who doesn't mind "extended staying/non-paying guests." If you're not so fortunate, you will likely be staying at a corporate apartment complex such as the Oakwoods. Leases are generally done on a month to month basis and cost around $2000 per month. Acting classes and industry showcases will probably add another $500-$700 per month for at least the first 3-4 month stay. New headshot photos will probably "ring in" at $400-500. There will be gas and groceries and extra curricular activities.

• **When you first arrive in L.A.** you are starting from ground zero as far as marketing goes. Every door has to be opened by someone for you. Every step you advance happens because somebody believed enough in you. When I think of all the agents, managers, acting coaches and casting directors who have given a "break" to a new talent thousands of times over, it's amazing they have the strength or desire to continue giving.

• **I encourage you to be the parent** of the actor who makes sure every good action is reciprocated or appreciated. Say, "thank-you." You cannot say "thank you" enough times throughout the day. Encourage your child to be the one having "fun" while auditioning, while working on the set and while participating in acting classes.

• **If you do return home** without your child starring in television and films, remember you gave it your best effort. The only thing under your control as a parent, from the beginning, is the opportunity to provide your child with the thrilling experience of pursuing a dream. The educational and character building process that comes with it counts for everything.

Resources

To download and print an updated version of this and all resource lists, go to actingiseverything.com.

• PHOTOGRAPHERS

David Carlson, 323/660-0028, davidcarlsonphoto.com. Basic package is $350 and includes 3-4 looks, CD of shots, online proofs and about 700-800 images. David charges $300 for children under the age of 12. He specializes in natural light, but does offer studio lighting. He also offers group discounts. David is terrific to shoot with, very laid back but makes sure he gets all the shots needed. He shoots in a neighborhood that provides great backdrops. I love the look that he got in my photos. *See his shots of children Melodie Gorow and Aaron Gorow and shots of Judy Kerr in the Photo section.*

David LaPorte, 310/452-4053, davidlaporte.com. Two rolls for $275, $95 for makeup. Includes proofs and negative. Also shoots digital and includes CD. You order your own 4x6s and 8x10s. Unconditional guarantee means you and your agents have to love the photos or he will re-shoot. He helps people to just be themselves; that's why agents and managers love his work. "Bringing out the personality helps market the actor." Very likeable, open and truthful. Shoots just two to three people a day. Several of my students have used David and I loved their photos. They said he was great to work with. *See shots of children Melodie Gorow and Aaron Gorow and shots of Suzanne Wallace Whayne in the Photo section.*

Kevin McIntyre Photography, 818/293-9200. kevinmcphotograph.com. Email: kevin mcphotograph@comcast.net. Specializing in beautiful natural light photos of children and adults. Prices range from $235 for two looks to $365 for six looks. Disk included with each package. Negatives or a CD of shots are always included. Kevin believes that by putting a child into the natural light, it encourages openness and confidence. Kevin is comfortable photographing kids of all ages. Work is guaranteed. He is recommended by many top agents and managers. *See shots of young actors Austin Tovar and Jackson Tovar and shots of Judy in the Photo section.*

Rich Hogan, 323/467-2628, richhoganphotography.com. Digital rates start at $395 for three looks and 180 shots. He says his clients can choose "digital or film, black & white or color, headshots or body shots, commercial or theatrical, creative and edgy or clean and captivating." The new photographic techniques Rich uses are getting incredible reviews from the people in the business. It took him two years to perfect this technique but the results are amazing. No children under three years old. He's fun and the kids love working with him. He took Austin's very first picture when he was seven and got great results. *See shots of Brittani Taylor and Kevin Anthony in the Photo section.*

Diana Lannes Photography, Voice Mail: 213/427-8096, Studio: 323/465-3232, dianalannes.com. $250-$350, depending on the package. Diana has been taking pictures for 12 years in New York and Los Angeles. She works out of the Hollywood Raleigh Studios office that she shares with her husband, photographer Randall Michelson. She shoots for children's fashion catalogues as well. She really enjoys the kids. She shoots with natural or studio light and they do all their own printing and retouching with gorgeous, flawless results. Clients are able to view their photos during the shoot and they can take home the whole photo shoot plus finals on a CD for $25. Professional Makeup available, $125. *See shots of Denise George in the Photo section.*

Wayne Rutledge, 206/550-1820, rutledgephoto.com. Shoots on film, then scans images in photo shop on to CD disk, 3 looks, 4x6 proofs. Wayne works in Orange County, Los Angeles and Seattle. Very highly recommended by agent Carlyne Grager. *See shots of Kevin Anthony in the Photo section.*

Doreen Stone, 323/876-2636. Ages 3 to 21, $180. Highly recommended by agents, managers and coaches; many say, "She is 'the' photographer for children." T.J. Stein of Stein Entertainment Group says, "She catches the child's personality and energy in the way that really sells the child; triple A rating!" Doreen tells parents, "Keep it simple; simple clothes. And don't worry, a child can't do it wrong."

Marina Rice Bader, 310/859-4687, marinarice.com. Her digital studio sessions are $325 and cover multiple looks. She approaches each session as a fun publicity shoot, making each client feel like they are already an established working actor. Her comfortable studio is located in Burbank. She is the mother of three young ones herself and truly understands the dynamics of children.

Gayle Garnett, 310/712-3911, photographybygayle.com. Gayle shoots both digital and film, black and white or color. Time is spent discussing how you will market your child. Keep clothing simple. The key is focusing on your child's energy and personality! Babies and children under four years are also very welcome; the fee may be slightly higher depending on what is needed.

• CHILDREN'S ACTING CLASSES

Hiller Academy, 818/385-1800, HillerAcademy.com. Winnie Hiller, artistic director, has been training top professionals in Hollywood for the past 20 years. Frequent industry showcases. This is the only fully accredited private Performing Arts Academy in Los Angeles. Teaching acting, dancing, singing and academics in an artistic ways.

Young Actor's Space, 818/785-7979, youngactorsspace.com. 5918 Van Nuys Blvd., Van Nuys, 91401. $450 for a 10 week session. Several types of classes are offered. You can audit a class for free but they encourage people to take one class to see how they like it. Diane Hill Hardin developed these supportive classes. She was a student of Joan Darling and her husband and daughter are actors. She and her partner Nora Eckstein also manage a few lucky young actors. At the end of each session they have a demonstration class where agents, managers, friends and parents are invited to watch the actors perform. I have attended several of their demonstrations and was very impressed with the talent I see in their classes.

Tracy Martin is Koaching Kids & Teens, 818/752-8487, email: mstracyco@aol.com. $325 for 8-week Audition Technique Class. Ages 5 and up. Breaking down sides, listening, reacting, call backs and booking the job are part of what the classes contain. Tracy earned a BFA from NYU's Tisch School of the Arts. Highly recommended by agents and parents. She works with each child individually at whatever level they are at and helps them to be confident when they walk into the audition room. "We have fun every week in class and the students show great growth in their work." Classes held in Toluca Lake. "My students work and are real and natural." Audition coaching $60 an hour. Private lessons; rates depend on how many lessons booked. Free career coaching for parents who have children in her classes. Many working students.

Stanzi's Kidz Acting Studio, 818/762-8448, stanziskidz.com, Stanzi Stokes. On-going; off during summer months. $140 for ages 7 and up, $100 for ages 4-6; complimentary class available before signing up. Improv, cold reading, on-camera, audition techniques and intensive cold reading for the older students. The studio also has two summer musical theatre workshops. See website for past and upcoming shows. She also offers private coaching for $60 an hour; coaching sessions are taped so students can watch their session.

Class Act: The Young Actor's Studio, 310/281-7545, youngactorsstudio.com, Noho Actors Studio. Full conservatory based on the work of Stanislavski. Jeff Alan-Lee heads the very experienced staff. $135 for 12 weeks; classes are only an hour long. Kids and teens 4-18. They also produce new original plays for the kids. I love Jeff and have had so many wonderful reports about his classes. Their website lists all their classes.

Kimberly Crandall, 310/463/7136, kimberlycrandallactingcoach.com. $175/four weeks and many Free classes for Actorsite.com members. She has taught and privately coached hundreds of child actors of all ages. Her well-rounded and comprehensive classes focus on audition technique and acting fundamentals, helping kids cultivate the skills needed to have the best chance possible to book the part! Classes include: cold reading, scene study, on-camera technique, script analysis, mock auditions, interview skills, commercial techniques and much more all with a major focus on "audition technique." Kimberly can help increase the effectiveness of your child's auditions with private coaching. Kimberly has a real gift with kids, an ability to pull their best acting out of them while making it a fun and encouraging experience. She focuses on guiding kids to strive to reach their full potential by instilling the tools and confidence necessary for them to persevere and always do their best.

Brigitte Burdine's Kids and Teens On-Camera Commercial and Theatrical Workshops, 818-377-9538, bbcasting.com. BBCasting, 520 Washington Blvd., Ste. 468, Marina del Rey, 90292. $275 for six-weeks. For commercials: learn how to audition, improv, short and long dialogue, voiceovers and great advice to the parents who watch the playback at the end of class. Plus she brings in an agent for the last session so the kids and teens get a real audition. In the theatrical class: $275 for eight-week on camera workshop. Kids and teens learn how to audition for TV and film. She emphasizes the child actor getting out there working while having fun.

Jorge Pallo of the Scott Sedita Acting Studios, 323/465-6152, scottseditaacting.com. 526 N. Larchmont Blvd., Los Angeles, 90004 $330 per 8-week cycle. This Comprehensive On-Camera class is designed to provide young actors (ages 14-21) with an understanding of the craft, coupled with "On The Set" knowledge. Students will learn Scott Sedita's script analysis techniques, W.O.F.A.I.M. and THE PRIVATE EYE METHOD. These two tools are specially designed to provide actors with a clear and effective approach for uncovering, examining and breaking down the facts of any audition material in ten minutes. By utilizing the techniques, actors learn to quickly identify the story of a scene, create multidimensional characters and make strong choices for their auditions. Each class begins with a movement, voice & speech or improvisational exercise. Within each eight-week cycle, class assignments alternate between: audition drills, monologues, cold reading, dramatic improv and prepared scenes.

Actorsite.com, run by Jack Turnbolt, 818/762-2800, 5856 Cahuenga, North Hollywood, 91601. This is a great membership site. $40 a month or $299 a year. Lots of helpful information and actor chat rooms. Free to members: monthly headshot sessions, agent workshops, several acting classes a week, and getting great advice from Jack who is always around. Wonderful supportive group of actors. Also, great information and resources for kids looking to break into the business, including classes, audition and event notices and answers to many questions parents might have. They run "The Angry Children Improv" group on Saturdays in which they write and prepare for a show for agents, managers and casting directors. Great reputation, good investment. Free daily newsletter filled with uplifting information and encouragement, always focused on education. Extra fees: headshot dropoffs to casting directors, Casting Director Showcases.

Edgemar Center for the Arts, 310/399-3666, edgemar.org. Holds occasional seminars, workshops and classes for children, including a month-long summer acting and writing camp for ages 7-13 for $850, improv story-telling for ages 3-5 for $375 and on-camera cold reading for ages 7-14 for $430.

Academy Training Center, 818/771-8687, 4942 Vineland Ave., North Hollywood, 91601. Classes are $265 for new students and $220 for ongoing students, starting at age five. "Our workshops encourage the young actor to develop the skills and confidence needed to perform in film and television. New students may try the first class for free. Our Saturday sessions are six weeks long and on the last week we have TJ Stein, President, Stein Entertainment Group and other industry guests." Academy Training's director is Dawnnie Mercado, a New York-trained professional actress.

Laura Lasky of Quit Acting! 818/623-8830. 5044 1/4 Colfax Ave., Valley Village, 91602. Ages 4-17, $175 for four weeks of group class. The Quit Acting! Acting Workshop is on-camera for children pursuing a professional career in TV, film and theater. Skills necessary for the pre-read to the screen-test; geared to the individual needs of each student; a safe self-esteem building environment. Laura says, "An actor's ability comes from a strong foundation and trust of him/herself. Find out what's holding you back—and quit it! You are never acting a role; you are the role. Understand the difference between acting and pretending. The audition is the job." Private coaching available, $45 an hour.

Kevin McDermott's The Actors Circle, 310/837-4536, centerstagela.com. He is also an on-set children's coach. "Acting classes provide the young actor with an opportunity to practice their craft in a safe and creative environment." They offer theatrical workshops for ages five to 18, scene study, cold reading, improv, character development and interview techniques.

Hines & Hunt Entertainment, 818/557-7516. $235 for six classes. A children's and teen class is taught by staff teachers. In addition to acting and improvisation, they cover the pilot season, the audition, the interview and dealing with rejection. Terrance is a very highly respected personal manager along with his partner, Justine Hunt. Terrance is also the author of *An Actor Succeeds*.

TotaLook Young Actor Classes, 818/364-9947. Email: TotaLookCares@aol.com. $25 a class or $100 a month for ages five thru teens plus a one-time $25 family registration fee which includes the required workbook and the optional weekly parent workshop/discussion group. Maximum six students per class, grouped by age and experience. Extensive on-camera work with commercials, scenes and monologues. Weekend classes are taught by professional teachers who each have over 20 years of active experience in the Industry. Parents select the dates they can attend and receive evaluations weekly. Discounts for siblings. The workbook: *How to Get In & Stay In Show Biz*, plus *101 Ways to Avoid Being a Stage Parent* is filled with "tricks of the trade." Private pre-audition coaching, $35 an hour. Family Workshops & coaching at your location or at studio. "There's only one chance to make a good *first* impression! Classes give the students the necessary tools as well as valuable life skills."

Kids Improving Inc., 818/422-1414, kidsimproving.com, 4348 Tujunga Ave., Studio City, 91604. $140 per four-week cycle. Classes for ages 5-18 are on-going. Lisa Gerber uses improv techniques to build confidence in scenes and auditions. She keeps the environment supportive and fun, helping kids learn to trust their instincts and approach the work with a sense of contagious joy. The teachings of Sanford Meisner and Uta Hagen are also utilized to get kids "off the page." Also included; audition technique, camera work, guest speakers and teachers. Linda has over 15 years of entertainment experience.

Improv Class and Performing Group, 818/784-1868, laconnectioncomedy.com, 13442 Ventura Blvd. Sherman Oaks. Ages 5-14. Class meets every Sunday. Performances every Sunday. $300 for 10 sessions.

Margie Haber Studios, 310/854-0870, margiehaber.com. Reel Teens and Kids program features a weekend intensive followed by a four-week ongoing class that uses both cold reading and scene study with some of the studio's top teachers. Cost for kids ages 7-12 is $200 for the intensive and $200 for the class; for kids 13-17, the cost is $300 for each. They teach the young actors to use their imagination to "live the life" of the character.

South Coast Repertory Professional Conservatory, 714/708-5549, scr.org, 655 Town Center Dr., Costa Mesa, 92628. Offers ongoing youth and teen programs throughout the year and a summer theatre workshop for kids from 3rd through 12th grade. Cost is $275 and includes movement, dramatic acting, play-making and character development.

A very good training ground is right on-the-set. If you have the time and your child really wants to see what it is like to be on a set, why not get their work permit and do some extra work? Your child will not make much money but they will gain the experience of being on-the-set and they will get to watch professional actors acting! Maybe they can earn enough to pay for acting classes.

Kids! Background Talent, 661/964-0131, kidsmanagement.com, 207 S. Flower, 2nd Floor, Burbank, 91502. $30 registration and they take a 20% commission when the children work. Parents and children can get a good feel of what the business really is by working at least a few days as an extra. If you want your children to work background jobs, you will pay 15% to 20% commission on the $40 a day pay scale. Adults wouldn't stand for this but I guess they figure the kids don't need to earn a living and they get the parent along to take care of the child for free.

• VOICE AND DANCE TEACHERS

Rosemary Butler, 310/572-6338, rosemarybutler.com. Works with teen singers.

Claire Corff, 323/851-9042, corffvoice.com. $45 and up. Speaking, singing and accent reduction. She's fun and easy to be with. She is an associate of the very famous Bob Corff, specializing in children and young adults, beginners through advanced. Singing, speaking and accent reduction. My grandson Austin Tovar loved working with her; he learned how to slow down and to be easily understood. He loves the exercises she gave him.

Dance Arts Academy, 323/932-6230, danceartsacademy.com, 731 South La Brea Ave., Los Angeles, 90036. Carla Luna, director. They have classes for children from age six and up in ballet, tap, jazz, funk jazz, flamenco and hip-hop. See their website for the extensive schedule or call for brochure.

Dance at the Outback Studio with Jennifer Nairn-Smith, 323/938-6836, outbackstudios.com. $15 for a single class, $135 for 10 classes.

Lauridsen Ballet Centre, 310/533-1247, southbayballet.org, 1261 Sartori Avenue, Torrance, 90501. Starting at age three. The faculty is dedicated to nurturing, developing, and guiding dancers through the world of ballet in a professional, caring and healthy environment. The students are privileged to study in a traditional ballet atmosphere with live piano accompaniment.

• MANAGERS

2 Reel Blondes Management, Owner Jared Grager, 818/842-2008, 250 S. San Fernando Blvd., # 301, Burbank, 91502. Children and young adult actors. Represents comedians interested in acting and will consider writers and select athletes.

T.E.G. Management, Stanzi Stokes and Kelly Heffernan, 310/902-9469, trioentertainment.com. Clients range in age from 4-60 but a majority are kids, teens and young adults. T.E.G. helps build careers. Stanzi also provides coaching for auditions.

Hines & Hunt Entertainment, 818/557-7516. Terrance Hines and his partner, Justine Hunt are highly regarded. Terrance is also the author of *An Actor Succeeds*.

Stein Entertainment Group, T.J. Stein personal manager. 323/822-1400. SteinEntertainment.com. 1351 N. Crescent Heights Blvd., #312, West Hollywood, 90046. Children and young adults.

The West Coast Performer's Complete Personal Managers Directory of Personal Managers for All Performing and Creative Talents, an Acting World Books Publication. At theatrical bookstores and actingworldbooks.org. This is much more than a directory—it has the information you need to shop for and land a personal manager.

• AGENTS

• **A few children's agents out of the many listed by** SAG **and the Association of Talent Managers.**

Screen Actors Guild—SAG **Young Performers Committee,** 323/549-6420 or 323/549-6419, sag.org. 5757 Wilshire Blvd., Los Angeles, 90036 M-F 9-5.
SAG **Child Actor Hotline,** 323/549-6420
SAG **Franchised Agents List,** 323/549-6733.
The AFTRA-SAG **Young Performers Handbook** is downloadable on the website.

Dramatic Artists Agency, 818/566-1421, 103 W. Alameda Ave., Ste. 139, Burbank, 91502. Carlyne Grager has only been an agent for a short time in Los Angeles, but already has had several of her clients in major blockbuster films. Carlyne heads the theatrical division and longtime L.A. agent, Carolyn Mace, handles the commercial division.

The Savage Agency, 323/461-8316. 6212 Banner Ave., L.A., 90038. Ages 3 to mid-20s.

Buchwald Talent Group, (TGI), Youth Division, 323/852-9555. buchwald.com. 6500 Wilshire Blvd., 22nd Floor, L.A., 90048. Ages 3 to early 20s.

Acme Talent & Literary Agency, 323/954-2263. acmetalentagents.com. 4727 Wilshire Blvd., Ste. 333, L.A., 90010. Ages 4-25.

Alvarado Rey Agency, 323/655-7978. alvaradorey.com. 8455 Beverly Blvd., Ste. 410, L.A. 90048. Ages 5 and older. Especially Latinos and diverse ethnicities.

Howard Talent West Agency, 818/766-5300. 10657 Riverside Dr., Toluca Lake, 91602. Ages 5 and older.

Innovative Artists, 310/656-0400. 1505 10th St., Santa Monica, 90401. Ages 8 and older.

In Orange County: Baby Talent Agency, babytalent.com. This is the best in Orange County; they place their clients with Los Angeles agents.

• *Consult your State Film Advisory Board for agents in your area.*

• HELPFUL ORGANIZATIONS AND WEBSITES

Lacasting.com, 323/462-8000, 6671 Sunset Blvd., Hollywood, 90028. Site has a section devoted to providing information for child actors and their parents.

Startips.com. Updated material about childt actors.

Moviesbykids.com. Animation and movie making summer camps. For kids 7 to 16. A creative program taught by industry professionals.

Create Now!, 213/484-8500, createnow.org. Nonprofit organization that offers troubled, abandoned and neglected children a creative outlet, in the form of acting, etc.

Cynthia Turner's Cynposis Kids!, cynopsis.com, CynEzine@aol.com. The latest showbiz news everyday, from new shows to ratings to casting calls to job opportunities. Separate information for kids.

• BOOKS AND TAPES

How to Get In & Stay In Show Biz, plus 101 Ways to Avoid Being a Stage Parent by Coral Leigh. Cost is $25 payable to TotalLook to Book Publishers Ent., 15455 Glenoaks Blvd. #271, Sylmar, CA 91342. Email: TotalLookCares@aol.com. Coral Leigh shares insider information from her past years as an agent, personal manager, casting associate and a stage mom. This guidebook is filled with "tricks of the trade" to help the child actor as well as showing parents what to do to help and to understand how the Industry works. I highly recommend it for all parents who want to help make their children's dreams of being an actor come true. This workbook has exercises for the actors and instructions, everything you need to know for the babies up through the young adults. *See above for information about the classes with the TotalLook group.*

By Kids, For Kids: A Collection of Original Monologues for Kids and Teenagers 6 to 18 Years Old, edited by Catherine Gaffigan. $7.95

Acting for Young Actors: The Ultimate Teen Guide by Mary Lou Belli and Dinah Lenney. Book focuses not just on acting techniques, but also age-specific tips for teenagers looking to break into and succeed in the business.

Launching Your Child in Show Business: A Complete Step-By-Step Guide by Dick Van Patten. He should know how, having started on Broadway at age seven, as did his sister Joyce. "My mother was a real stage mother. On the other hand, it's terrible if a stage mother pushes a child into the business. People berate stage mothers—but how about mothers who push their kids to become doctors or lawyers?"

Your Kid Ought To Be In Pictures: A How-To Guide For Would-Be Child Actors and Their Parent by Kelly Ford Kidwell and Ruth Devorin.

• **The trade papers put out annual special issues** for Show Business Kids with many agencies, managers, photographers and teachers listed.

Mail Order Tape: *Lights, Camera, Kids! How to Get Your Child in TV Commercials, by Carolyne Barry*, 323/654-2212, carolynebarry.com. $39.95. Actress/commercial coach Barry produced this very informative tape and booklet.

• SCAMS

West Coast Talent Ltd., Inc., WCT, Screen Artist Talent, Alexander Zafrin and David Leroy Harris illegally operate an employment counseling service enticing parents to pay thousands of dollars for promotional materials and acting classes for children. They've been charged with many crimes, including making false and misleading statements and making false and deceptive representations. By the time you read this, these two men have probably changed the name of their business and continue to steal from parents. Be your child's watchdog!

A photographer tells me of a current scam. A person approaches you in a public place, like a shopping mall and tells you your child is great looking. They say they are a casting director, gives you a business card and asks you to make an appointment. That person gets $100 for everyone who makes an appointment. If you do meet with the promoters, they give many promises, and if you believe them and enroll in their "program," you pay a lot for nothing.

Section 10

Cities Outside of Los Angeles

• **Many of you reading this book** are outside of Los Angeles and wondering how you will make the leap into the Industry.

• **Al Burton gives an excellent interview** in The *Child Actor section* about the work you can do in your hometown. Throughout the book the information can be found to gain training and experience to help you achieve a satisfactory artistic life where you live. If you can become a big fish in a little pond, you can achieve a great sense of accomplishment.

• **My daughter, Cynthia Kerr's,** husband was transferred to Dallas, Texas. She had been an accomplished actress as a teenager. After marriage, motherhood and a successful real estate career, she wanted to return to her first love, acting. This move was her opportunity. The first week, I visited and we checked out the town. I had asked actors from Dallas who studied with me, where to look. KD Studio was mentioned by several. We met with the director and knew we had found a home. Cynthia enrolled in KD Studio Actors Conservatory of the Southwest. She thrived on going to classes every day, the voice and body work, the rehearsals, the camera, acting classes and the friendships. She had her pictures taken and interviewed with four agents; one offered to take her on the spot. Because of the excellent schooling and networking at KD Studio she was in two plays, three industrials and a McDonalds' national commercial during her first year. At the time of her graduation, she had paid for her education and expenses from her acting work, and the residual payments continued. She had another baby and then, at last, they were transferred home to Los Angeles.

• **Order books** on acting in your city through Samuel French Bookstore, samuelfrench.com and contact your state's Film Advisory Board for agents, films and extra casting agencies that will be casting in your area. Also, look for film and acting schools in your area; they are usually full of useful information and industry people.

• *This is by no means a complete listing of acting related resources. These are some that I've worked with or that were recommended to me. They should be used to get you started, but always explore your market for more opportunities and resources.*

CALIFORNIA (ORANGE COUNTY, SAN DIEGO, SAN FRANCISCO)
• **Obviously this market is dominated by Los Angeles.** However there are some opportunities in the surrounding Orange County region, all the way down to San Diego. And up north, San Francisco has one of the most vibrant theatre scenes in the country. Here are some listings for you Californians that aren't living in Los Angeles.
• **Thanks to** San Diego-based actress **Carolyn Bishop** and actor/writer **Jim Martyka** for their research and contributions to the Orange County and San Diego sections and **Carl Miller**, actor and co-founder of The Bridge SF, for providing San Francisco resources.

• ORANGE COUNTY
TALENT AGENCIES
South Coast Rep, 714/708-5500, scr.org. Box 2197, Costa Mesa, 92628-2197. Casting director: Joanne DeNaut.
Artist Management Agency, 949/261-7557, 1800 E. Garry St., Suite 101, Santa Ana 92705.
Berzon, Marian Talent Agency, 949/631-5936, 336 East 17th St., Costa Mesa 92627.
Brand Model and Talent, 714/850-1158, 1520 Brookhollow Dr., Suite 39, Santa Ana 92705.
UNION OFFICES/ASSOCIATIONS
Orange County Film Commission, Janice Arrington is commissioner, 714/278-7569.
CLASSES, COACHES, STUDIOS
South Coast Repertory Professional Conservatory. 714/708-5549. scr.org. 655 Town Center Dr., Costa Mesa, 92628.
THEATRES
Laguna Playhouse, 949/497-2787. lagunaplayhouse.com. P.O Box 1747, Laguna Beach, 92652. Casting director: Wally Ziegler.
HEADSHOT REPRODUCTION
Photomation, 800/439-6363, 714/236-2121, photomation.com, 2551 West La Palma Ave., Anaheim. The work I've seen has been very good quality. Lab and reproduction. At last, a resource for people living in Orange County. However, make the trip to L.A. for the best quality.

• SAN DIEGO
CASTING OFFICES
Samuel Warren & Assoc. International Casting Service, CSA, 619/264-4135.
Tina Real Casting, 619/298-0544. tinarealcasting.com. Specializes in extras casting.
Background San Diego, 858/974-8970. backgroundsandiego.com. The exclusive extras casting agency for Stu Segall Productions. They also cast for *Veronica Mars*, and *Desire Table for Three.*
Stu Segall Productions, stusegall.com. From Stu's website: "Stu Segall Productions is the only Motion Picture and Television Studio located in San Diego County. The studio was created in 1991 when San Diego was chosen as the location for the hit television series *Silk Stalkings*. Since that time the studio has grown to encompass over 11 acres.

Over 500 hours of prime time, network quality television series, 6 feature films and 30 two hour telefilms have been produced at the studio."

Four Square Productions, foursq.com. Commercials and industrials.

Harris Goldman Productions, 619/299-7051, harrisgoldman.com.

Iris Hampton Casting, 619/582-4632. actors rave about Iris.

TALENT AGENCIES

Artist Management Agency, 619/233-6655. 835 Fifth Ave., #411 San Diego, 92101.

Elegance Talent Agency, 760/434-3397. eletalent.com. 2763 State St., Carlsbad, 92008.

Jet Set Talent Agency, 858/551-9393. 2160 Avenida De La Playa, La Jolla 92037.

Nouveau Model & Talent Agency, 858/456-1400. 909 Prospect Pl. #230, La Jolla, 92037.

San Diego Model Mgmt. Talent Agency, 619/296-1018. electriciti.com/sdmm. 438 Camino Del Rio South, San Diego, 92101.

Shamon Freitas Talent Agency, 858/549-3955. shamonfreitas.com. 9606 Tierra Grande St., #204 San Diego, 92126.

UNION OFFICES, ASSOCIATIONS

Actors Alliance of San Diego, 619/640-3900, 619/640-3333, actorsalliance.com. Very helpful organization. Website has everything a local actor needs to know about acting in San Diego, including resources and audition opportunities. A very valuable resource.

San Diego Film Commission, Sdfilm.com.

CLASSES, COACHES, STUDIOS

Billy Cowart, WCI Studios. wcistudios.com. Teaches in San Diego and Los Angeles; recommended by Bonnie Gillespie.

Lara Dolinski-Mazour, 760/479-0186, larasstudio.com. Taught acting and auditioning for film and television in Las Vegas and now in San Diego. She introduces her students to casting directors, agents and producers through showcases and personal introductions.

THEATRES

The Old Globe Theatres, 619/231-1941. oldglobe.org. Box 122171, San Diego, 92112.

San Diego Repertory Theatre, 619/231-3586. sandiegorep.com. 79 Horton Plaza, San Diego, 92101. Casting director: Delicia Turner.

La Jolla Playhouse, 858/550-1070. lajollaplayhouse.com. P.O Box 12039, La Jolla, 92039. Los Angeles locals submit to Sharon Bialy @ Sherry Thomas Casting, 1149 N. Gower #103 D, LA, 90038. NY locals submit to Tara Reuben Casting. 212/445-0088.

Mo'Olelo Performing Arts Company, 858/761-3871, moolelo.net.

The Theatre in Old Town, 619/688-2494, theatreinoldtown.com, 4040 Twiggs St., San Diego 92110.

Welk Resort Theatre, 760/749-3448, welkresort.com, 8860 Lawrence Welk Dr., Escondido 92029.

HEADSHOT PHOTOGRAPHERS

Kathy Sharpe Digital Photography, sharpedigitalphotography.com. Specializes in headshots, also shoots children. Prices on website.

Michael Graham Photography, michaelgrahamphoto.com. Headshots for actors and models.

WEBSITES, PUBLICATIONS

Sandiegoforum.com, Chat board for San Diego actors, models and production crew.

Sandiegoplaybill.com, What's playing, auditions, classes/workshops.

Sdtheaterscene.com, Similar format to San Diego Playbill.

Sdresource.com, general acting resource site.

• SAN FRANCISCO
CASTING OFFICES
San Jose Rep, 408/367-7255. sjrep.com. 101 Paseo de San Antonio, San Jose, 95113. Casting director: Bruce Elsperger.

Beau Bonneau Casting, 415/346-2278. beaubonneaucasting.com. 84 First St., San Francisco, 94105.

Nancy Hays Casting, 415/558-1675. hayescasting.com. 400 Treat Ave., #E, San Francisco, 94110.

UNION OFFICES, ASSOCIATIONS
Theatre Bay Area, 415/430-1140, theatrebayarea.org. TBA is a nonprofit organization whose mission is to unite, strengthen and promote theatre in the Bay Area by providing communications networks and opportunities, creating resources for theatre companies, theatre-makers and theatre-goers.

The Bridge SF, 415/236-1783, thebridgesf.com. Cooperative network of professional actors focused on helping each other advance their careers. They provide industry workshops including casting directors, directors and producers that come from Los Angeles and provide helpful insight to the San Francisco actor.

CLASSES, COACHES, STUDIOS
Richard Seyd, 415/354-1762, seydways.com. The Richard Seyd Acting Studio is a comprehensive lab committed to the art and craft of professional acting. Recommended for all actors interested in serious training.

SF School of Digital Filmmaking, 415/522-1200, afdigifilm.com. On-camera film acting classes at all levels taught by experienced teachers and industry professionals. These classes provide the students an additional benefit of working on films created by the students in the school's filmmaking program.

BATS Improv, 415/474-6776, improv.org. Whether you're an actor working to enhance your performance skills or someone who thinks that improve just looks like fun, BATS Improv has a class for you.

Actors Theatre of San Francisco (ATSF), 415/345-9582, actorstheatrefest.org. ATSF Performance Workshops feature traditional method training. The workshops are held in a scene/monologue performance format.

Joie Sheldon, 510/434-9552. joiesheldon.com. Oakland. Joie Seldon teaches a very unique class called Accessing Emotional Truth at San Francisco Acting Academy and other locations. "Can you cry on cue? Express fear or anger without being cliched? And after you've done it once, can you do it again? One of the most challenging aspects of an actor's job is to be able to access a wide range of genuine emotions on demand, whether shooting a scene over and over, or performing night after night on stage. This class will help you develop the emotional 'muscles' you need for even the most difficult roles." *This explanation makes me want to fly up to S.F. and take it.* Joie also does private sessions working with acting blocks, and career blocks. In addition to twenty years as an acting teacher, she holds a Master's degree in Somatic Counseling Psychology.

Academy of Art University, San Fransisco. 800/544-ARTS. Academyart.edu. 79 New Montgomery St., San Francisco, 94105. Offers an incredible acting program headed up by wonderful actors like Diane Baker and Mala Powers. Also have incredible classes for directing, cinematography, writing, special effects, etc. Many of the school's projects go to festivals. Has a huge number of graduates working in the biz.

San Francisco Acting Academy, 415/777-1163, sfactingacademy.com. The San Francisco Acting Academy provides a variety of on-camera acting classes to actors of all levels. SFAA was established by Beau Bonneau Casting to provide quality education to actors in the Bay Area through industry experts. The teachers are professional actors whose goal is to share their knowledge and talent with other actors in the Bay Area.

Jean Shelton Actors Lab 415/433-1226. San Francisco. Union Square in the theater district. The studio teaches Method acting.

Marin Theater Company, San Francisco. Artistic Director, Lee Sankowich, 415/388-5208. Lee is great. He also has other instructors come in to teach classes. The Theater Company is excellent; high caliber performances.

The Burton Group, 916/428-7827. theburtongrouponline.com. 5660 Freeport Blvd., Suite 200, Sacramento, 95822. Nonprofit educational and training facility dedicated to the advancement of the arts.

Robert Weinapple, 510/559-1029, Oakland. Native New Yorker with years of theatre experience on both coasts. Trains actors for the stage.

THEATRES

• **San Francisco has an extensive and well-respected theatre market**, considered one of the best in the country. These recommended theatres are but a fraction of what San Francisco has to offer. Check out the websites below for more listings.

SF Playhouse, 415/677-9596, sfplayhouse.org. One of the most well-known. Casting: submit headshot and resume. Internships in theatre production and administration.

American Conservatory Theatre (ACT). 415/834-3200. act-sfbay.org. 30 Grant Avenue, San Francisco, 94108. Casting: annual general auditions for AEA actors. Internships in theatre production and administration. MFA program in acting. Contact Heather Kitchen, managing director.

American Musical Theatre of San Jose. amtsj.org. 1717 Technology Drive, San Jose, CA 95110. Casting: auditions held in San Jose, NY and Los Angeles, both AEA and non-union. Limited internships available.

Berkeley Rep, 510/647-2900. berkeleyrep.org. 2025 Addison Street, Berkeley, 94704. Casting director: Amy Potozkin. Berkeley Rep is top notch. I didn't take classes there but talked with others who did and they gave it rave reviews. The theater company is excellent. Went to many of their productions.

California Shakespeare Festival, 510/548-3422. calshakes.org. 701 Heinz Ave., Berkeley, 94710.

Foothill Theatre Company, 530/265-9320. foothilltheatre.org. P.O Box 1812 Nevada City, 95959. Casting director: Carolyn Howart.

Ross Valley Players, 415/456-9555. Marin County. Community theater that is highly professional. They have a great following, usually sold out and well-respected. They are located in The President. Ken Rowland, played the father role in *Heiress*.

Sacramento Theatre Company, 916/446-7501. sactheatre.org. 1419 H St., Sacramento, 95814.

HEADSHOT PHOTOGRAPHERS

J. Michael Tucker, 415/601-0622. jmichaeltucker.com. Has shot celebrities. Recommended by Bonnie Howard.

Sasha Gulish, 415/455-9343, sashagulish.com. Good photographer for commercial or theatrical.

WEBSITES, PUBLICATIONS

Reel Directory, reeldirectory.com.

Beau Bonneau Casting, sfcasting.com

Bay Area Casting News, bayareacasting.com.

Casting Connection, castingconnection.com.

THE NORTHWEST (Portland, Seattle)

• **Thanks to:** Carlyne Grager of Seattle and Los Angeles-based Dramatic Artists Agency, Inc., for an interview and providing the following information for the Northwest market.

• **The Northwest is primarily a commercial market** and well over 50% of the projects are nonunion. Unlike Los Angeles, joining SAG or AFTRA will knock actors out of contention for many film and video projects.

• **Breaking in to the Northwest Film and Television Industry** is easier than in Los Angeles or New York. However, hundreds of actors are competing for a relatively small slice of pie.

• **The "Indie" market** is starting to flourish and that means more opportunities. Even if the pay isn't high, the experience is rewarding.

• **There are approximately 30-40 talent and modeling agencies** of varying sizes. Nine are franchised by at least one of the unions.

• **The "Big 4" Northwest talent agencies** are Actors Group, Dramatic Artists Agency and Topo Swope, in the Seattle market and Ryan Artists in Portland. They are the oldest and most well established agencies, franchised by both SAG and AFTRA. The top three modeling and print agencies are Seattle Models Guild, Heffner Management of Seattle and Cusicks in Portland.

• **Contact the SAG or AFTRA office** or website and get the list of franchised agents. They may also venture an opinion on a nonunion agency that operates in an ethical fashion.

• **Many Northwest agencies** do not wish to adhere to the rules of the actor unions. Commissions or fees for processing modeling and headshots packages, fees for acting classes and industry seminars are often a significant source of income to these agencies. They stock their files full of hopeful talent willing to spend several hundred or even thousands of dollars to get their chance at auditions and bookings. Children's agencies have been particularly notorious for preying on parents wishing to help their children. If ever an agent says that it is customary to charge fees or commissions other than for securing employment, move on. If a union agent pressures you to pay for picture packages or in-house seminars or classes, report them to the local union office.

• **I always recommend an on-camera class** with one of the local casting offices that offers beginning workshops. The classes are usually under $100 for the day and will put the student through the paces of the "on-camera" fundamentals. The casting director will quickly see how advanced the student's skills are and make adjustments in their curriculum to accommodate them. The casting directors also know who the local agents are and can give a reference on behalf of their student if they deem them ready for representation. In addition, casting directors are usually very well versed on who the best acting coaches are and can steer a student in that direction as well.

• **If you have an extensive theater background** it's likely you will have skills for a successful career in film and television. However, casting directors will be cautious about calling in an actor who doesn't list some type of camera training on their resume.

• **Before seeking agency representation**, get a professional headshot taken, but choose a high quality photographer. Print about 50 headshots. Once you secure an agent they will likely choose a different headshot for marketing purposes. Don't print a modeling zed card until you have agency representation. Fashion and commercial print agents can determine their level of interest based on the talent's physical statistics and a few snapshots or Polaroids. Once a talent is offered representation the print agent will make a recommendation of a photographer that will best capture a particular "look."

• **If you are interested in voiceover work**, start with training. Voiceover is very technical and without proper instruction you will not present your voice in a competitive

Also, the good trainers are often producers and can help you prepare a demo CD or MP3 file (tapes are rarely used anymore.) You have to have a voiceover demo in order to be professionally marketed by an agent. Everything is produced onto computer and auditions are submitted in the same fashion. You will need an understanding of the market you're entering and classes are the best way of getting that information.

• **Is it necessary for Northwest actors to have the level of professional training,** headshots and other marketing tools that the Los Angeles actors have. The local casting directors and producers have to market you to industry professionals from other markets such as Los Angeles or New York. Though remember, no marketing tool will override lack of ability or novice skills. You are presenting yourself as a total package of talent.

• PORTLAND
CASTING OFFICES
Lana Veenker Casting, 503/221-3090. 2580 NW Upshur Portland, OR. 97210.
Megann Ratzow Casting, 503/251-9050.Email:catsratso@comcast.net 8902 NE Milton St., Portland, Oregon 97222. She also has an "Extras" Casting Division.
FASHION AGENCIES
Cusick's Talent Management, 503/274-8555. Q6talent.com. 800 E. Burnside Studio #2 Portland, OR 97214.
UNION OFFICES, ASSOCIATIONS
AFTRA, 503/279-9600. 1125 SE Madison St. Ste. #204 ,Portland, OR 97214.
SAG, 206/270-0493. Dena Beatty. Executive Director for Seattle and Portland. sag.org.
CLASSES, COACHES, STUDIOS
The Voice Project, Mary Beth Felker, 503/284-9488. Mary Beth is the Northwest associate to Seth Riggs, LA voice/singing coach. Her prices are reasonable relative to the Northwest market (much less than her mentor Seth Riggs, whose clients include many Grammy award winners.)
Sandra Peabody, 503/245-8525. Children's Acting coach.
The Cast Group, 503/692-8926. Audition fundamentals, actor development.
Jessica Stuart, CSA, 503/246-4111. Drama coach with excellent credentials.
Gloria Manon, 503/972-8117. Voice-over coach.
Actor's Avenue, 503/234-2399. theactorsavenue.com. Portland Owner/Laurel Smith. Private coaching, scene study, Meisner and audition technique.
Theatres
Oregon Shakespeare Festival, 541/482-2111. ossashland.org. Box 158, Ashland, 97520. Casting directors: Libby Appel, David Dreyfoos, Penny Metropulos, Timothy Bond. Portland Center Stage, 503/248-6309. pcs.org. 1111 SW Broadway, Portland, 97205. Casting Director: Rose Riordan
HEADSHOT PHOTOGRAPHERS
Dave Ross 503/329-4178, davidrossstudios.com.
HAIR AND MAKEUP
Mr. Thom, 541/779-8406. 59 S. Stage Road, Medford, OR 97501. Full service day spa and hair salon performing all services including hair extensions. Mr. Thom travels to Portland and Seattle; call for his travel times.

• **SEATTLE**
CASTING OFFICES
Big Pants Casting, 206/448-0927. 1600 Dexter Avenue N. Ste. A, Seattle, 98109. Jodi Rothfield and Heidi Walker.

Stephen Salamunovich, 206/903-6500. completecasting.com. 1415 Western Ave. Ste. 503 Seattle, 98101.

Kalles/Levine Casting, 206/522-2660. Kalleslevineauditions@yahoo.com. Patti Kalles and Laurie Levine.

Spokane Casting & Production North By Northwest, 509/324-2949, nxnw.net. 903 W. Broadway Ave., Spokane, 99201. Boise: 208/345-7870.

TALENT AGENCIES
Actors Group, 206/624-9465. theactorsgroup.com. Adult Talent. Tish and Jamie Lopez, 3400 Beacon Ave. S. Seattle, 98144. Full service agency.

Dramatic Artists Agency, Inc. Adult and Youth Division, 425/827-4147. Business cell 818/288-1859. dramaticartists.com. 50 16th Avenue Kirkland, 98033 Full Service agency, Carlyne Grager and Nancy Fox.

Topo Swope Talent, 206/443-2021. toposwopetalent.com. Adult Talent. 2540 1st Ave. W., Seattle, 98119. Full service agency.

Emerald City Model & Talent, 206/329-7768. emeraldcitymodelandtalent.com. 1980 Harvard Ave. E. Seattle, 98102. Full service agency, adult and youth.

FASHION AGENCIES
Heffner Model Management, 206/622-2211. heffnermanagement.com. 1601 Fifth Avenue Suite #1802, Seattle, 98101.

Seattle Models Guild, 206/622-1406. smgmodels.com. 1809 Seventh Avenue Suite #608 Seattle, 98101. Open calls on Monday, Wednesday and Friday at 3 p.m. every week.

UNION OFFICES, ASSOCIATIONS
SAG, 206/270-0493, sag.org. Dena Beatty. Executive Director for Seattle and Portland.

AFTRA, John Sandifer Executive Director, 206/282-2506, aftra.org. 4000 Aurora Avenue N. Ste. #102, Seattle, 98103.

CLASSES, COACHES, STUDIOS
The Northwest Connection. 425/823-8491, Husband and wife team, Kirk and Jenny Posey. Email: nw.connection@verizon.net The Northwest Connection regularly features drama coaches, casting directors and other industry professionals from Los Angeles, New York and Chicago. The partners in the Northwest Connection do not collect commissions or salaries for themselves and they operate with a very small overhead budget, marketing mostly by word of mouth and student referrals from the Northwest Talent Agencies and Casting Offices. Because they operate more like a non-profit than a commercial business, they provide outstanding instruction at a very low cost to actors. Their list of industry guests is prestigious and highly regarded by the Film and Television Industry

Gary Austin, 206/781-4279; Seattle 818/753-9000. Founder of Los Angeles' Groundlings Theater and acting coach to Helen Hunt, Jennifer Grey, Lindsay Crouse, Qorianka Kilcher, (Disney kids) Danielle and Kay Pannebaker, the late Phil Hartman and many other celebrity talents, makes his way to Seattle approximately every 4-6 weeks. Gary's classes are hard to top at the low cost of only $65 for a 4-hour workshop. Northwest actors who work with Gary swear he is the reason for their remarkable acting success in such a lean market.

Steven Anderson, 310/284-8282. sanderson@actorswork.com. Steven travels from Los Angeles to the Seattle market a few times each year to conduct an excellent intensive weekend workshop. Through the weekend's teaching he will get his actors to trust that they are "always ready" to perform and how to keep their power in the room. He demonstrates how to integrate nervous energy and how to prepare audition material to get the job!

Richard Liedle, 206/367-2313. Drama coach (Richard teaches in both Los Angeles & Seattle).

Terry Edward Moore, 206/729-7985. Drama coach.

John Jacobsen, 206/325-4915. Drama coach.

Valerie Mamches, 206/524-9231. Theatrical and Voice-over coach. Full service acting studio. Valarts@cnet.com

Patti Kalles, CSA and Laurie Levine, 206/522-2660. On-camera audition.

Jodi Rothfield, CSA 206/448-0927. worldperc.com. On-camera audition technique.

Kathryn Luster, 425/378-0223. Voice-over coach.

Veronica Weikel & Steven Mitchell Productions, 360/863-6297. Voice-over classes and demos.

SAG, AFTRA & Equity Conservatory, 206/270-0493.

Freehold, 206/323-7499. Freeholdtheatre.org (Robin Lynn Smith-Artistic Director) Drama.

Northwest Actors Studio, 206/324-6328. info@nwactorsstudio.org.

Taproot Theater, 206/781-9705. taproottheatre.org. Adult & children.

Professional Actors Studio, Valerie Raymer, 425/829-5908.

Seattle Children's Theater (Children), 206/443-0807. sct.org.

Village Theater (Children), 206/392-1942

Youth Theater Northwest (Children), 206/232-4145.

BOOKSTORES

Cinema Books, 206/547-7667. 4753 Roosevelt Way NE Seattle, 98105.

THEATRES

A Contemporary Theatre (ACT), 206/292-7660. acttheatre.org. 700 Union, Seattle, 98101-2330. Casting director: Margaret Layne

Intiman Theatre, 206/269-1901. intiman.org. P.O. Box 19760, Seattle, 98109. Casting director: Kate Godman.

Seattle Repertory Theatre, 206/443-2210. seattlerep.org 155 Mercer Street, Seattle, 98109. Casting director: Jerry Manning.

HEADSHOT PHOTOGRAPHERS

Wayne Rutledge, 206/550-1820.

David Hiller, 206/325-0525, davidhiller.com.

Anita Russell, 425/746-6506.

Susan Rothschild, 425/335-3277.

HAIR AND MAKEUP STYLISTS

Bocz Salon, Karen Bocz owner, 206/624-9134. boczsalon.com. 1523 6th Ave. Masters with color and styling, will do consulting. All of the agencies send their models here.

Hair Lounge, Mike Hall, 253/941-3680. hair-lounge.om. 1626 S. 310th Street, Suite A, Federal Way, 98003. Mike is a master. He does all the high end jobs at fashion shows (Halston, Hilfiger, Versace etc.) Film set styling and fundraisers. Respected throughout the Northwest.

Seattle Models Guild, 206/622-1406. smgmodels.com. 1809 Seventh Avenue Suite #608 Seattle, 98101. They also represent stylists. Here are some that were recommended; Tom Pollock, Brandee Slosar, Glynn Davies, Vanessa Philipp and Amie Lynn.

WEBSITES, PUBLICATIONS

Actorspost.com, general information on the acting community.

Tpsonline.org, for theatre professionals.

Seattleactingschool.com, listings for all sorts of resources.

THE SOUTHWEST (LAS VEGAS, PHOENIX)

• **This market obviously is dominated by Los Angeles,** but there is a lot of work for actors in a number of other Southwestern cities.

• **Thanks to:** **Christopher Buzzell**, owner of Buzzell Films and Vegas Background for his Las Vegas contributions, actor **John Janezic** on Phoenix.

• LAS VEGAS

• **Note from Christopher:** Las Vegas is unique in the sense that you don't have to get just one agent exclusively. All of the agents in town act as casting directors as well. So I went into the Yellow Pages under talent agents and called every single one of them and said, "Hello, I am a new actor in town, how do I register with your agency?" They will tell you. A couple of them will try to represent you exclusively but I don't recommend it. You will not work as much. No matter what they tell you, you will not work as much. Keep each agency stocked with plenty of headshots and resumes and keep them updated. Some agencies will email you auditions and others will call you directly. You will receive multiple calls and emails for the same auditions. Just go with the agency that contacts you first. Or go with the agency that offers the most money. In Las Vegas, agents generally take 20 to 40 percent for nonunion work, sometimes more, so try to get as much as you can.

• **Las Vegas is 90 percent nonunion work**, so stay nonunion as long as you can; you will work more. Do some background work in this town to get agents to trust you for principal work as well as a chance to get the three union vouchers that you need to join SAG. Join AFTRA as soon as you can because there is no AFTRA talent here at all. Most of my guest star appearances on national TV are AFTRA and I did them right here in Vegas. You can also work as a stand-in on the award shows that come to town because they are AFTRA. Just make sure that you get some teleprompter experience before you try the award shows.

CASTING OFFICES

Casting director, Marilee Lear, CSA. 41 N. Mojave Road, Las Vegas, 89101.
Vegas Casting, vegas-casting.com. A principal casting company.
Vegas Background, vegasbackground.com. A background casting company.

TALENT AGENCIES

Here are some agency websites: gacasting.com, acesofacts.com, creativeimageagency.com, spectrumtalent.com, langetalent.com, t-tymeproductions.com, netvisiontalent.com, steveaugust.com, baskow.com, best-agencies.com, donnawauhobagency.com, esilasvegas.com, envymodeltalent.com, Impact-Models.com, lenztalent.com, mccartytalent.com, premieremodelsinc.com, rbcepiphany.info, wildstreaktalent.com, redmodelslv.com.

UNION OFFICES, ASSOCIATIONS

SAG Las Vegas, 702/737-8818.
Nevada Film Office. 702/486-2727.
SAG Conservatory. 702/226-5620.

CLASSES, COACHES, STUDIOS

Rose Heeter. 702/594-4198, rosewrap@aol.com.
Gerald Gordan. 702/648-8716, gge13@aol.com.

HEADSHOT PHOTOGRAPHERS

Kelly Garni. 702/433-8873, kellygarni.com. Perfect for starter photos when you don't want to invest a lot of money at first.

Michael Helms. 818/353-5855. active-media.com/helms/ L.A.-based photographer who comes to Las Vegas often to shoot.

PHOTO DUPLICATION

abcpictures.com. For black and white photos.

Silk Impressions. 702/592-6944. silkimpressions.us. Excellent color work. Christopher highly recommends him.

DEMO REELS

Wild Dog Arts & Entertainment. 702/339-1078 wilddogarts.com

WEBSITES, PUBLICATIONS

callbacknews.com, yoursingingcenter.com, reviewjournal.com, casting-entertainment.com, lvlbreakdown.com, vegasauditions.com, hollywoodvegasstyle.com, wiflassvegas.org, 48hourfilm.com, talkinbroadway.com, uvf.bataluer.com, nevadafilm.com, redsquarefilms.com, actornews.com, buzzellfilms.com.

HOTLINES

Wild Streak Talent. 702/252-4695.

Casting Entertainment. 702/940-7779.

Baskow Talent Hotline. 702/391-9309.

• PHOENIX

TALENT AGENCIES

Dani's Agency, 602/263-1918. danisagency.com. One E. Camelback Rd. #550, Phoenix, 85012. Recorded information line for submissions: 480/929-1382.

Ford/Robert Black Agency, 480/966-2537; Info: 480/966-2537 Ext. 150. fordmodels.com. 4300 N. Miller Rd. Ste 202, Scottsdale, 85251.

Leighton Agency Inc. Phone: 602/224-9255; Info: 602/468-6880. leightonagency.com. 8707 East Vista Bonita Dr. Ste.240, Scottsdale, 85255.

Signature Models & Talent Phone: 480/966-1102; 480/902-0186. signaturemodelsandtalent.com. 2600 N. 44 St., #209, Phoenix, 85008.

CLASSES, COACHES, STUDIOS

Elayne Stein, 602/266-3498. For commercials, on-camera work.

D & D Company, 602/956-8604. For beginners to advanced.

Faith Hibbs-Clark 602/385-9228 Coach turned Casting Director.

Good Faith Casting CSA. faith@goodfaithcasting.com.

Ramona Richards, 602/274-2881.

Marla Finn, 480/922-9267, 480/239-3286 for voiceover.

Scottsdale Community College has a film making dept.

There are many theaters in Phoenix and they have their auditions on the Durantcom.com service.

THEATRES

Arizona Theatre Company, 520/884-8210. arizonatheatre.org. P.O Box 1631, Tucson, 85702. Accepts head shots and resumes. Also has musical theatre program.

HEADSHOT PHOTOGRAPHERS

Still n' Motion, 602/253-1035. near112.com.

Richard Petrillo, 480/921-8366. richardpetrillo.com.

WEBSITES, PUBLICATIONS

Azproduction.com. This is a website for auditions. Hit the "Valley Auditions."

Durantcom.com. This site is great to submit your email to for a listing of auditions both professional and non-professional. When you get to her site you give her your email and she emails you with any listing for auditions.

THE UPPER MIDWEST
(CHICAGO, MINNEAPOLIS / ST. PAUL)

• **Long ignored, the Midwest has gained a reputation as a strong stepping stone for actors to both New York and Los Angeles.** This market is really dominated by two cities in two very different ways. Chicago has grown as a commercial, television and film market with some great comedy schools on the side. Meanwhile, the Twin Cities of Minnesota has one of the most vibrant theatre markets in the country mixed with some big business commercial work and a ton of independent films. Studios used to flock to the Midwest, but cheaper rates in Canada have recently taken some of the action away. Nevertheless, the Midwest remains a strong community for artists.

• **Missouri has a couple of gems for actors.** In St. Louis, check out **theatrgroup.com.** In Springfield, look up acting coach **Scott-Arthur Allen** at 417/725-8267, creativeactorsworkshop.com. A well-respected Hollywood coach who has taught Heather Locklear, Sela Ward and Tea Leoni among others, he has returned to teach in his hometown.

• **There are some occasional acting jobs in Cleveland.** If you're an actor there, look for representation with **Doherty Talent Agency,** 216/522-1300, dohertyagency.com. Also, check out **North Coast Stunts and Movie Extras,** 216/651-5441, worldeonline.com.

• **In Milwaukee, all of you writers** should look up **redbirdstudio.com.** Group does a lot more than just write.

• **Thanks to:** Actress **Lexi Livengood** for her Chicago contributions and actor/writer and co-founder of the Twin Cities Actor's Forum, **Jim Martyka,** for providing information on the Twin Cities.

• CHICAGO
CASTING OFFICES
Simon Casting, 312/202-0124, simoncasting.com. Casting for all genres, but most known work is film, including *High Fidelity, Save the Last Dance, Hardball* and *At Home at the End of the World.*
Tenner Paskal & Rudnicke Casting, 312/527-0665, tprcasting.com. THE casting leader in Chicago for commercials, film, television, etc. More popular films they've cast are *Ice Harvest, The Weather Man, Road to Perdition* and *Mr. 3000.* Also does some reality TV casting.
David O'Connor Casting, 312/226-9112, oconnorcasting.tv. Lots of commercials.
Casting by McLean/ For Extras, PO Box #10569, Chcicago, 60610.
TALENT AGENCIES
• *For extensive list of agencies, check out the Chicago Creative Directory at creativedir.com.*
Baker & Rowley Talent Agency, 312/850-4700, bakerandrowleytalent.com. Both union and nonunion.
Lily's Talent Agency, 312/601-2345, lilystalent.com. Union and nonunion; the most reputable in the city.

BMG Model and Talent, 312/829-9100, bmgmodels.com. Also offices in Chicago, Orlando and Phoenix.
FASHION AGENCIES
Ford Models, 312/243-9400, fordmodels.com. Representing children and adult models for Commercial and Fashion print, as well as Runway and Artists.
CLASSES, COACHES, STUDIOS
Ed Hooks, edhooks.com. Well-known teacher and writer.
Steppenwolf Theatre Company, steppenwolf.org.
Piven Theatre Workshop, 847/866-6597. piventheatre.org.
The Second City Training Center, secondcity.com.
The Audition Studio, 312/527-4566. actingstudiochicago.com.
Victory Gardens Theatre, victorygardens.org.
Act One Studio, actone.com.
THEATRE
League of Chicago Theatres, chicagoplays.com.
HEADSHOT PHOTOGRAPHERS
Suzanne Plunkett, 773/477-3775. suzanneplunkettphotographs.com.
Rick Mitchell, 312/829-1700. rickmitchellphoto.com.
Michael Brosilow, headshots@brosilow.com.
Larry Lapidus, 773/235-3333. lapidusphoto.com.
PHOTO DUPLICATION
National Photo Service, 312/644-5211.
BOOKSTORES
Act 1 Bookstore, act1books.com. The city's leading acting bookstore.
WEBSITES, PUBLICATIONS
PerformInk Newspaper is where most all auditions are posted. performink.com.
The Book, *An Actor's Guide to Chicago.* Everything you need, including all agents.

• MINNEAPOLIS / ST. PAUL

• **From Jim Martyka:** This is a great market for theatre in that the Twin Cities not only has some of the most prestigious in the country, they also have a ton of well-respected community theatres. With a number of agencies, casting offices and production houses, this region also is booming with independent filmmakers. The Twin Cities is a great place for any actor to get started in their career or to build a career. Lots of nonunion work. One of the first resources you should check out is the **Twin Cities Actor's Forum,** a group of actors, writers and directors dedicated to success in the industry, mntalent.com. The Forum meets once a week to practice, work on projects or listen to incredible guest speakers. It is a supportive and well-connected local group with a ton of resources.
CASTING OFFICES
Lynn Blumenthal Casting, 612/338-0369. Union and nonunion casting for all mediums.
JR Casting, 612/396-9043. Mainly commercials. Jean Rohn also teaches a phenomenal commercial class.
Bab's Casting, 612/332-6858. "Womb to Tomb" casting as they call it. Very cool, laid back casting office; does a lot of nonunion.
Akerlind & Associates Casting, 612/339-6141. This is the big one in town. Lots of commercials (many a lucky actor has gotten their SAG card here) and some film.
Joyce Lynne Lacey, 651/969-1916, jllproductins@hotmail.com. Extras casting.

PRODUCTION COMPANIES
• **While there are a number of production houses** that do shows for cable television (Home and Garden, Discovery, etc.), there are many more independent production companies putting out some good shows and films. Here are some of the more reputable ones; great places for actors to submit their headshots.

The WaZoo! Show, wazoo.tv. Sketch comedy, original programming.

YNG TURK Productions, yngturkfilm.com. Run by filmmaker Ryan Wood, this company is probably the best independent film company in the area. Recent projects have generated Hollywood buzz, if you get a chance, work with Ryan.

Winterprises Inc., 651/646-8382, winterprises.com. Original projects, short and feature films.

Cricket Films, cricketfilms.com. Jon Springer puts together some unique films, also has over 700 commercial credits. Great writer.

Reel Cinema, reelcinema.net. Solid film company.

Bluestream Films, 612/486-5850. A lot of spec TV commercials, great opportunities for new actors.

TALENT AGENCIES
Talent Poole, 612/843-4294, talentpoole.com. Nonunion, very friendly staff.

Richter Casting, 952/975-9305. Raulla Mitchell is a sweet woman who will work hard for you. Represents actors, models and dancers.

NUTS, 763/529-0330, nutsltd.com. The biggest and best of nonunion talent agencies. If you land some roles they send you for, they will keep you busy.

Agency Models and Talent, 612/664-1174, agencymodelsandtalent.com. Another good nonunion firm.

Moore Creative Talent, 612/827-3823, mooretalent.com. One of the two big union agencies in town.

Caryn Model & Talent Agency, 612/349-3600.

The Wehmann Agency, 612/333-6393, wehmann.com. THE big union agency in town. Your goal should be to get representation from them. Handle the best local actors and models.

UNION OFFICES, ASSOCIATIONS
The Minnesota Film Board, 651/645-3600, mnfilmandtv.org.

CLASSES, COACHES, STUDIOS
Stevie Ray's Improv, 612/825-1832, stevierays.org. More than just staged improv, also does corporate training.

The Brave New Workshop, 612/332-6620, bravenewworkshop.com. Longest running satirical comedy theatre in the country and one of the most respected. This is where locals study comedy.

Lev Mailer, 952/930-0636. One of the best acting coaches in town. He's studied with Meisner and Strasberg among others and did some work in Hollywood. He's great at getting you to make your scene work real.

Sandra K. Horner, 818/997-6740. Teaches and puts on showcases in both Minneapolis and LA. Great teacher, especially in Meisner.

Cheryl Moore Brinkley, chermoorebrinkley@juno.com. Vocal and performance training. Also a great commercial coach.

The University of Minnesota, umn.edu.

Minneapolis College of Art and Design, mcad.edu.

Minneapolis Community and Technical College, mctc.mnscu.edu.

THEATRES

Theatre de la Jeune Lune, 612/332-3968, jeunelune.org. Has won many awards as one of the best independent theatres in the country. Very progressive, brings in a lot of big names.

Red Eye Theatre, 612/870-0309, theredeye.org. Small, but one of the more progressive theatres in town.

Bloomington Civic Theater, 952/881-4300, bloomingtoncivictheater.com. You standard community theatre, but does great productions and has some ex-Broadway people involved.

Chanhassen Dinner Theatre, 952/934-1525, chanhassentheatre.com. If you want to do dinner theatre, this is the place to play. Very tough to get cast in their high-quality shows.

Mixed Blood Theatre, 612/338-6131, mixedblood.com. Provides a number of multi-cultural shows.

The Guthrie Theater, 612/377-2224, guthrietheater.com. This is the big theatre in town with a tremendous national reputation. Puts on expensive shows with talent from all over the world. Also has the Guthrie Lab, which provides opportunities for newer actors and writer and lesser known or original works.

Theatre In The Round, 612/333-3010, theatreintheround.com. The ultimate local community theatre, everything they do gets local attention.

The Jungle Theater, 612/822-4002, jungletheater.com. Edgy classic and contemporary shows in a great space.

*Other Theatres worth looking into:
Theatre Unbound, In The Basement Productions, Gremlin Theatre, Fifty Foot Penguin Theatre, The Children's Theatre Company, Starting Gate Productions, Eye of the Storm, Old Log Theatre, Pigs Eye Theatre, Lakeshore Players, The Historic Mounds Theatre, Hey City Theatre, Stage Theatre Company, Park Square Theatre.

HEADSHOT PHOTOGRAPHERS

Dani Werner, 651/776-7614, daniphoto.com. Recommended by many actors, very relaxing environment.

Ann Marsden, 612/374-1000. Probably the area's leading photographer. Prices are a little up there, but the results are phenomenal.

James Gross, 612/788-8830, jgstudios.com. Highly recommended. $150 for digital session and will let you play with different ideas.

WEBSITES, PUBLICATIONS

Mntalent.com. The official website of the Twin Cities Actor's Forum. Check out the Resources section for lots of great information on the local acting community.

MID-AMERICA (AUSTIN & DALLAS, TEXAS)

• **Actors in this part of the country flock to Texas,** more specifically Austin, which has not just a vibrant film, television and theatre scene, but also a great music community. While industry people say Houston has fallen off the map, Dallas still provides a number of opportunities for actors.

• **Though limited, Oklahoma, Kansas and Colorado** also have some theatre. In Denver, check out the **Denver Center Theatre Company** at 303/893-4000, dcpa.org. They hold open calls.

• **Thanks to:** Actress and coach **Juli Erickson** for providing information on Dallas and **Peter Blackwell** from Austin Soundmine for contributions to the Austin section.

• AUSTIN
WEBSITES, PUBLICATIONS
Austin Actors net, austinactors.net.

Groups.yahoo.com/group/AustinFilm Casting, While in the groups section, also check out casting notices for Houston, Lubbock and South Texas as well. This is the newsletter for all of Austin's news for actors, they post daily notices for everything going on in Austin.

CASTING OFFICES
Beth Sepko, 512/472-5385. bethsepkocasting.com.

Donise L. Hardy, CSA/Casting Works LA, 512/485-3113. castingworksla.com.

TALENT AGENCIES
CIAO! Talents, 512/930-9301. ciaotalents.com.

Collier Talent, 512/236-0500. colliertalent.com.

Acclaim Talent, 512/416-9222. acclaimtalent.com.

Actors Clearinghouse, 512/476-3412. actorsclearinghouse.com.

Lee Peterson and Associates, 512/912-9918. LeePeterson.com. Talent manager.

UNION OFFICES, ASSOCIATIONS
Texas Film Commission, governor.state.tx.us/divisions/film/hot;ine.

Austin Film Society, austinfilm.org.

CLASSES, COACHES, STUDIOS
C.K. McFarland, 512/441-3738, ckmcfarland.com. Great acting coach, she owns and teaches at Alleywood Studios, home of Me Jane Movies. C.K. teaches on-camera acting, nuts and bolts of film work and a wonderful creativity class for actors. The studio space is very comfortable for taking risks, this is where I like to teach when I come to Austin.

Lee Peterson, 512/912-9918. LeePeterson.com. Acting for Film.

Mona Lee, 512/323-2090. thebizonline.com/britelites.

Andy Crouch, 512/443-3688. Heroes of Comedy, improv.

Keene Studios, keenestudios.com. Email: KeeneStudios@gvtc.com.

Peter Blackwell, 512/423-3680. ciaotalents.com.

University of Texas, 512/471-5793. utexas.edu/cofa/theatre.

Austin Community College, austincc.edu.

THEATRES
Hyde Park Theatre, Hydeparktheatre.com.
ONSTAGE Theatre Company, Onstagetheatreco.com
PHOTOGRAPHERS
Fabrizio Photography, 512/453-8000. actorsphoto.com.
Caroline Mowry Photography, 512/589-7412. CarolineMowry.com.
Kenneth Gall Photography, 512/736-2851. kennethgall.com.
Andrew Shapter, Andrewshapter.com
VOICEOVER REELS
Austin Soundmine, 512/291-0214. AustinSoundmine.com.

• DALLAS
CASTING OFFICES
Abrams-O'Conner Casting, abramscasting.com.
Atomic Casting, atomic.casting@mac.com.
Toni Brock Cobb, brockandco@sbcglobal.com.
Buffalo Casting, 214/220-9991, tisha@buffalocasting.com.
Fincannon Casting, mffincannon@aol.com. Does a lot of casting in Louisiana using Texas talent.
TALENT AGENCIES
The Campbell Agency, 214/522-8991, campbellagency.com.
The Clutts Agency, thecluttsagency.com.
The Mary Collins Agency, 214/871-8900, marycollins.com.
The Kim Dawson Agency, 214/630-5161, kimdawsonagency.com.
The Horne Agency, 214/350-9220, the horneagency.com.
UNION OFFICES, ASSOCIATIONS
Society for Theatrical Artists Guidance and Enhancement, stage-online.org.
Texas Association of Film/Tape Professionals, taftp.com.
Women in Film, Dallas, wifdallas.org.
COACHES, CLASSES, STUDIOS
Juli Erickson and Grant James, 972/238-7703, ladyactsalot@yahoo.com. Small groups and private coaching.
Hartt & Soul, harttandsoul.com.
REACT, reactactors.com.
KD Studio Actors Conservatory of the Southwest, 214/638-0484, kdstudio.com. They have a four-semester program where you can earn an AA degree. Includes every phase of actors' development including opportunities for gaining actual working experience. Evening and weekend classes for actors not involved in the Conservatory program. My daughter Cynthia got her degree here and just loved every moment.
THEATRES
Dallas Theater Center, dallastheatercenter.org.
Theatre Three, 214/871-3300, theatre3dallas.com.
HEADSHOT PHOTOGRAPHERS
Bryan Chatlien, 469/363-1604, chatlienphotography.com.
Charlie Freeman, 214/920-9311.
Tyler Mason, 214/827-2784.

THE NORTHEAST (BOSTON, NEW YORK)

• **New York City defines the acting community in this region.** New York tends to attract more theatre actors...for obvious reasons. Besides the opportunity to possibly see their name on billboards on Broadway, New York offers so much with its Off and even Off-Off Broadway theatre scene, acting classes and quick-moving pace. Plus, the city grows in the television, feature and independent film markets each and every year. And let's not forget all the soap operas shot there. It is an entirely different market than Los Angeles and it runs at a different speed, a different rhythm, but actors of all experience levels know that if they can make it there, they'll make it anywhere.

• **But the Big Apple does have a steadily growing rival in Boston.** A vibrant theatre scene and some great acting coaches are leading actors to Bean Town, as well as some other Northeastern markets.

• **If you're in New Jersey,** two theatre companies you should try to work with include **Two River Theatre Company**, 732/345-1400, 21 Bridge Ave, Red Bank, 07701 and **Paper Mill: The State Theatre Of New Jersey**. 973/379-3636. Brookside Drive, Milburn, 07041.

• **If in Pittsburgh,** try to get on stage at the **Bristol Riverside Theatre**, 215/785-6664, brtstage.org. Actors should also seek out representation with the **Docherty Talent Agency**, 412/765-1400, dochertyagency.com.

• **For resources in other Northeastern states** check out: **Connecticut Film Division**, ctfilm.com, **Maine Film Office**, filminmaine.com, **New Hampshire Film & TV Office**, filmnh.org, **Rhode Island Film Office**, Rifilm.com and **Vermont Film Office**, Vermontfilm.com.

• **Thanks to:** Actor and consultant **Lori Frankian** for her contributions to the Boston market entry and acting coach **Caryn West** for her New York recommendations.

• **BOSTON**

• **Boston is wildly rich with talented performers,** hundreds of professional resources and surrounded by culture and diversity. The Boston arts community is thriving, passionate and recognized for it's award-winning theatre, film, talent and powerful unified voices. Whether you are interested in stage, television or radio, you may travel or relocate to Boston and find endless performance, technical, artistic and administrative opportunities.

• **There are over 140 theatres** that produce dramatic, classical, comedic, experimental and musical theatre. The theatre community is highly regarded, tight knit, proactive and extremely supportive of one another's initiatives. Boston is well known for its open door policy for the works of local playwrights. Original works are produced, greatly supported and shine brightly under the Boston spotlight!

• **Clint Eastwood's Academy Award-winning** *Mystic River* was shot in Boston. Thirty local actors were cast in principal roles. *Mona Lisa Smile* and *Alex and Emma* were also shot in Boston recently. As for television production, *Boston Legal*, *Trading Spaces* and *Sabrina The Teenage Witch* worked their way into Boston. From 2001 to 2005, approximately 130 features, indies and television projects were produced in New England. This does not include student films or nonunion work. Commercials, industrials, trade shows, print advertising and voiceovers also keep the talent hustling. At present, there are roughly 130 signatory companies signed to AFTRA or SAG contracts within New England and 2200 union members residing and working in the busy region. Boston has a wealth of opportunities and resource organizations.

CASTING OFFICES
Boston Casting, 617/254-1001, bostoncasting.com.
CP Casting, Inc., 617/451-0996, cpcasting.com.
LDI Casting, 401/364-9701, ldicasting.com.
Maura Tighe Casting, 617/424-6805, mauratighe.com.
TALENT AGENCIES
Maggie Inc., 617/536-2639, 35 Newbury St., Boston, 02116.
Prestige Model & Talent, 978/688-3000, 236 Pleasant, Methuen, 01844.
FASHION AGENCIES
Candy Ford Group, 617/266-6939, candyford.com.
Click Models, 617/266-1100, clickmodel.com.
Image Makers, 617/254-3622, imagemakersmodels.com.
Model Club, Inc., 617/247-9020, modelclubinc.com.
UNION OFFICES, ASSOCIATIONS
Massachusetts Sports & Entertainment Commission, Masportsandfilm.org.
Arts and Business Council of Greater Boston, artsandbusinesscouncil.org.
Arts/Boston, artsboston.org.
Boston Association of Cabaret Artists, BostonCabaret.org.
Boston Dance Alliance, bostondancealliance.org.
Boston Office of Cultural Affairs, cityofboston.gov/arts.
Center for Independent Documentary, documentaries.org.
Cultural Access Consortium, culturalaccess.org.
Filmmakers Collaborative, filmmakerscollab.org.
Massachusetts Advocates for the Arts, Sciences and Humanities, maash.org.
Massachusetts Cultural Council, massculturalcouncil.org.
Massachusetts Foundation for the Humanities, mfh.org.
Massachusetts Office on Disability, state.ma.us/mod/.
Massachusetts Production Coalition, Massprodcoalition.com.
New England Foundation for the Arts, nefa.org.
New England Theatre Conference, netconline.org.
Volunteer Lawyers for the Arts of Massachusetts, vlama.org.
VSA arts of Massachusetts, vsamass.org.
Women in Film and Video/New England, wifvne.org.
AFTRA/SAG, 617/742-2688, aftra.com. sag.com, 535 Boylston Street, Boston.

CLASSES, COACHES, STUDIOS

Boston Casting, 617/254-1001, BostonCasting.com.

Lori Frankian, Business Consultant for Actors, 617/437-0334, lorifrankian.com.

Improv Asylum, 617/263-1221, improvasylum.com.

Southwick Studio, 978/266-1165, southwickstudio.com.

The Studio at CP Casting, 617/423-2221, cpcasting.com.

John O'Neil, vocal coaching, 617/247-6787, cabaretfest.com.

Dossy Peabody, 617/547-6977, dossypeabody.com/actors

Paula Plum, 781/393-5495, paulaplum.com.

Jordan Rich, Chart Productions, V/O Training and Production, 617/542-8251, chartproductions.com.

Wren Ross, V/O Training, 617/924-7464, wrenross.com.

Jeannie Lindheim's Hospital Clown Troupe, 617/277-2488, hospital-clowns.org.

ART, Institute for Advanced Theatre Training, 617/496-2000, amrep.org.

Boston College, 617/552-0823, bc.edu.

The Boston Conservatory, 617/912-9153, bostonconservatory.edu.

Boston University, 617/266-7900 Ext. 1657, bu.edu/cfa/theatre.

Brandeis University, 781/736-3340, brandeis.edu/theatre

Brown University/Trinity Repertory Theatre, 401/863-3283, brown.edu/Departments/Theatre_Speech_Dance/

Emerson College, 617/824-8780, emerson.edu.

Northeastern University, 617/373-2244, dac.neu.edu/theatre.

Suffolk University/C. Walsh Theatre, 617/573-8282, cas.suffolk.edu/theatre/

Tufts University, 617/627-3524, ase.tufts.edu/drama-dance.

Wellesley College, 781/283-2029, wellesley.edu/Theatre/thst.html

THEATRES

The Lyric Stage, 617/437-7172, Lyricstage.com.

New Repertory Theatre, 617/332-7058, newrep.org.

Shakespeare & Company, 413/637-1199 Ext. 114, shakespeare.org.

Williamstown Theatre Festival, 413/597-3388, wtfestival.org.

Theatre Directories, 802-867-2223, theatredirectories.com.

HEADSHOT PHOTOGRAPHERS

Claire Folger, 781/799-8954, clairephoto.com.

Linda Holt, lindaholtphoto.com.

Lynn Wayne, 617/451-1223, lynewayne.com.

HEADSHOT REPRODUCTION

Pro Black & White, 800/932-9354, probw.com.

WEBSITES, PUBLICATIONS

Betweengigs. Casting & Boston Auditions.

VSA Arts Massachusetts, 617/350-7713, vsamass.org.

New England Access Expressed! Directory

Boston Pheonix, 617/536-5390, bostonpheonix.com. A comprehensive arts and entertainment newspaper that also lists auditions of all kinds. Tip: This newspaper does not discriminate with advertisers, which means some auditions call for, let's say, an open mind. Be careful and use your gut.

Imagine News Magazine, 617/576-0773, imaginenews.com. A print and online resource that highlights production news and stories within the Film, TV, Video industries.

New England Entertainment Digest, 781/272-2066, jacneed.com. A trade newspaper/online resource that lists theatre, music, dance, film and video auditions, news, classified ads and reviews. It covers the New England and New York markets.
NewEnglandFilm.com. A diverse, intelligent online production resource that provides endless information from Pre-Post Production, Contact information for: Casting agencies, Producers, Talent, Crew, Equipment Rentals, Sales and Marketing and much more. Get on their mailing list!
New England Theatre 411, netheater411.com. An online site that lists production opportunities for actors, technicians, directors and audience members.
The Source/The Greater Boston Theatre Resource Guide, stagesource.org. A thorough directory that lists hundreds of resources within the areas of theatre, film, casting, audio/film/video and training. A must!
Theater Mirror, theatermirror.com. An online resource that posts theatre news, company information, production and announcements.

• NEW YORK
• To try and cover the resources offered in New York would require another whole book. If you're living in New York or planning to move there, you should check out *Making It in New York City: An Actor's Guide* by Glenn Alterman, glennalterman.com. Both the book and the website provide tons of information on this acting hotbed.
• Other books to check out include, *The Actor's Guide to Qualified Acting Coaches* and *Act New York 2005*, both by Larry Silverberg and *The New York Agent Book* by K. Callan.
• For acting coaches, Caryn West recommends Michael Howard Studios, 212/645-1525, michaelhowardstudios.com, 152 W. 25th St, NY, 10001. Beginners and the very advanced actors study here. Also check out The School for Film and Television, 212/645-0030, filmandtelevision.com, 39 West 19th St, 12th Floor, NY, 10011. Caryn West used to teach Commercial audition technique there, has great admiration for owner Joan See. Camera based school. The New Actors Workshop, 212/947-1310, newactorsworkshop.com, 259 W. 30th Street, 2nd Floor, NY. Two year conservatory program, created and designed by founders Mike Nichols, George Morrison and Paul Sills. Great for beginning actors, teaches a hybrid of methods from Stanislavski to Viola Spolin.

THE SOUTHEAST

(ATLANTA, NORTH CAROLINA, SOUTH FLORIDA, NASHVILLE, NEW ORLEANS)

• There's a lot more happening in this region of the country than people think, and not just in North Carolina. In fact, Atlanta and several cities in Tennessee and Florida are quickly becoming hot markets for television, film and especially theatre. It's still no Los Angeles or New York, but the Southeast has a lot to offer to actors at any point in their career.

• The Southeast is primarily "right-to-work" states, which means there are many opportunities for both union and nonunion actors.

• There are some good general resources for acting in this market. Check out backtoholding.com/castinghotlines.htm for castings in the area, Southeastern Players Directory at seplayersdirectory.com and the Southern Screen Report (like Variety but for the Southeast) at screenreport.com.

• In South Carolina the top talent agency is Coastal Talent, 843/886-8898, coastaltalent.com. They also have a kids division. Also call Z-1 Models and Talent, Donna Ehrlich at 803/581-2278, zlmodelsandtalent.com. Also check out Professional Actors' Association at caan.biz and the South Carolina Film Commission at scfilmoffice.com.

• In Alabama a top agency is Real People/Kiddin' Around, realpeople.com.

• In Virginia call the Virginia Film Hotline at 800/641-0810. Also good to perform with Mill Mountain Theatre, 540/342-5730. millmountain.org. One Market Square, SE Roanoke, 24011. Casting: Auditions held locally Fall and Spring. Contact Doug Patterson, production manager. Opportunities for interns.

• Thanks to: Bonnie Gillespie for providing most of the following information on the Southeast market, especially Atlanta and Tennessee. An author and casting director, Bonnie has taught seminars to working actors in Atlanta, New York and Los Angeles. Her weekly column The Actor's Voice is available at showfax.com. Also, thanks to Beverly Brock of The Brock Agency, an agent in North Carolina for the last 15 years, for contributing to the North Carolina section. Most of the information on South Florida comes from Marc Durso and Actors Info Booth.

• ATLANTA

• Atlanta is where most of the action takes place in Georgia. However, there are some good acting resources for other cities. In Augusta, check out the Augusta Film Commission at freewebs.com/augustafilm and Augusta Filmmakers at augustafilmmakers.com. In Athens, Film Athens at filmathens.net. And in Savannah, look up the Savannah Film Commission at savannahfilm.org.

Allure Image Management, Amelia Keith, 770-256-0880, allureimagemgmt. com. An Image Consulting Company that specialize in developing the complete image of entertainment professionals. Make sure that you are always prepared to make that positive first impression!

CASTING OFFICES

Annette Stilwell, 404/233-2278, stilwellcasting.com, PO Box 53017, Atlanta, 30305.

Don Slaton, 404/371-0299, 770/316-5122, Decatur.

JoAnn Smith and Kimberly Smith Holt, Atlanta Casting, Inc., 770/968-5500, atlantacasting.com, Jonesboro.

Kris Redding, 770/329-0404.

Shay Griffin, Chez Casting, 404/603-8755, chezgroup.com 2221 Peachtree St. NE, Ste. X-14, Atlanta, 30309.

TALENT AGENCIES

Agency for Performing Arts/Atlanta Models and Talent, Kathy Hardegree, 404/261-9627, 3091 Maple Dr., Ste. 201, Atlanta, 30305, SAG/AFTRA franchised.

Houghton Agency, Gail Houghton, Mystie Buice, 404/603-9454, houghtontalent.com, 919 Collier Rd. NW, Atlanta, 30318. Submission guidelines on website; great agency with lots of heart.

The People Store, Rebecca Shrager, 404/874-6448, 770/986-9600, peoplestore.net, 2004 Rockledge Rd. NE, Ste. 60, Atlanta, 30324. An excellent agency that Bonnie says she was proud to call home for several years.

Other agencies to check out:

About Faces Models and Talent, aboutfacemt.com.

Amsel, Eisenstadt, and Frazier/Elite Model Management

Arlene Wilson, arlenewilson.com.

Atlanta's Young Faces, atlantasyoungfaces.com.

Babes 'n' Beaus, babesnbeaus.homestead.com.

Dance 411 Entertainment, dance411.com.

Donna Summers

Glyn Kennedy Models and Talent

Hot Shot Kids, hotshotkids.net.

Kiddin' Around, kiddinaroundmodels.com.

Madison Agency, madisonagency.net.

Real People, realpeoplemodels.net.

Talent Network Atlanta, talnetatlanta.com.

Ted Borden and Associates

The Burns Agency, theburnsagencyonline.com.

TMA Talent.

UNION OFFICES, ASSOCIATIONS

SAG/AFTRA, 404/239-0131, sag.org and aftra.org.

Georgia Big Picture Conference, gabpc.com.

Georgia Film, Video, and Music Office, provides monthly newsletter about what's being shot where and by whom, casting status, etc. georgia.org.

Georgia Production Partnership, georgiaproduction.org.

Atlanta Coalition of Performing Arts, atlantaperforms.com.

Atlanta Films, calendar of events, production schedule, message board, atlantafilms.com.

CLASSES, COACHES, STUDIOS

Alliance Theatre School, 404/733-4700, alliancetheatre.org/education/education_classes.asp, 1280 Peachtree St. NE, Atlanta, GA 30309, biggest and most prestigious acting school in Atlanta.

Atlanta Workshop Players, Lynn Ellis-Stallings, Don Stallings, Michael Monroe, 770/998-8111, atlantaworkshopplayers.com. Great for kids, summer camp, touring company for extremely advanced students, trips to Los Angeles for industry workshops.

Dorsey Studios, Sandra Ellenburg-Dorsey, 404/633-3256, dorseystudios.com, 3593 Clairmont Rd., Atlanta, 30319.

Image Film and Video, Steve Coulter, 404/352-4225, 678/469-5882, 770/419-1259, imagefv.org. Also a media resource center with courses in film and video production, a film festival, and on-camera acting classes at all levels.

Laughing Matters, Tommy Futch, 404/225-5000, laughingmatters.com.

Martha Burgess, 770/206-4002, martha-burgess.com, 195 Brandon Pl. NE, Atlanta, 30328, film and stage classes for all levels.

Professional Actors Studio, Nick Conti, Michael Cole, John Tillapaugh, 404/943-1873, proactorsstudio.com, 2849 Piedmont Rd. NE, Atlanta, 30305, on-camera classes for all ages and all levels.

Shannon Eubanks, 770/518-9885. Private coaching for film auditions.

The Actor's Scene, 770/904-6646, theactorsscene.com.

The Celebrity Actors Studio, 770/997-1574, celebrityactorsstudio.com.

The Company Acting Studio, Lissina Longo, 404/607-1626, thecompanyactingstudio. com. Classes for all ages and levels including audition prep and improvisation.

Theatre 4, 678/984-6837, theatre4.org.

YourACT, Bob Harter and Della Cole, plus guest instructors from Los Angeles including Margie Haber and Bonnie Gillespie, 404/377-5552, youract.tv, 1434 Scott Blvd., Ste. 1, Decatur, 30030. Classes for kids and adults at all levels, website has a great list of local acting resources and links.

THEATRES

14th Street Playhouse, 404/733-4754, 173 14th St., Atlanta, 30309.

7 Stages, 404/523-7647, 404/522-0911, 7stages.org, 1105 Euclid Ave., Atlanta, 30307.

Alliance Theatre at the Woodruff, 404/733-4650, 404/733-5000, alliancetheatre.org, 1280 Peachtree St. NE, Atlanta, 30309.

OnStage Atlanta, 404/897-1802, onstageatlanta.com.

Theatrical Outfit, 678/528-1500, theatritcaloutfit.org.

Other theatres worth looking into: Academy Theatre, Actor's Express, Ansley Park Playhouse, Atlanta Dance World, Centre Stage, Expressions Theatre, Kudzu Playhouse, Off-Off Peachtree, Southside Theatre Guild, Stage Door Players, The Punchline Comedy Club, Theatre Decatur, Theatre Gael, Theatre in the Square

HEADSHOT PHOTOGRAPHERS

Atlanta's Young Faces, 404/255-3080, atlantasyoungfaces.com/photo.

Bob Mahoney, 404/949-9431, bobmahoney.com.

Brian Doughtery, 404/294-4739, 404/299-0174, doughertyphoto.com.

Carolyn Buttram, 404/405-2586, carolynbuttram.com.

David Rams, highly recommended photographer: davidrams.com.

Derek Blanks, 678/457-5332, dblanks.com.

Eric Beach, 404/791-2018, ericbeach.com.

J. Reneé Colquit, 678/481-4609, jreneephotography.com.

Kelsey Edwards, 323/936-6106, kelseyedwardsphoto.com. Los Angeles-based, but makes frequent trips to Atlanta to shoot headshots.

Kyle Egan, 404/642-8295, 770/460-1315.

Michael Wray, 678/777-8373.

Paul Amodio, 770/423-1654, paulamodio.com.

Raquel Riley, 404/545-1878, 404/454-1378, photographybyraquel.com.

Richard Mellinger, 404/222-9599, 404/641-9277, rmellinger.com.

Teryl Jackson, 770/218-6138, terylphoto.com.

Tricia McCannon, 404/355-2211, triciamccannon.com.
PHOTO DUPLICATION
Atlantic Color, 770/931-3054.
Full Image, 404/678-9126.
Hodgson, 404/872-3686.
KO Comp Cards, Paula Giannes, 678/523-8805.
Kwik Comps, 770/968-9819.
Photo Retouching by Melody Knighton, 770/966-1661.
Photobition, 404/892-1688.
Prima Atlanta, 404/355-7200, primaatlanta.com.
Spit Fire Imaging, 404/872-0046.
The Pixel Pusher, 404/781-1111, thepixelpusher.biz.
Digi Card, Dave Male digi.card@verizon.net (215) 836-0166
Photoscan, info@ggphotoscan.com
DEMO REELS
Chris Paul, 404/663-6920.
Joey Willis, 404/808-5140.
Justice Leak, 404/441-2573.
Paul Ryden, 678/777-7825.
Randall Sims, 404/314-2715.
WEBSITES, PUBLICATIONS
Arts in Atlanta, master list of resources, artsinatlanta.org.
Atlanta Theatre Mailing List, groups.yahoo.com/group/atlantatheatre.
Women In Film/Atlanta, wifa.org.
CinemATL, regional film and video magazine includes production listings and a blog
with updates, cinematl.com.
Creative Loafing, Newsstands, audition listings, atlanta.creativeloafing.com.
The Actor's Guide for Kids by Jen Kelley and Brenda Krochmal, 404/784-7970,
theactorsguide.com.
The Actor's Guide Online Industry Directory, theactorsguide.com.
The Actor's Guide: Southeast, 404/784-7970, theactorsguide.com.
Weekend Leisure Guide in Atlanta Journal & Constitution, Saturday edition, ajc.com.

• NORTH CAROLINA
CASTING OFFICES
Corrigan & Johnston Casting, Mitzi Corrigan, Paige Johnston and Gigi Wasiak,
704/374-9400. cjcasting.com. 3006 North Davidson Street, Charlotte, 28205. See
their site on how to submit to them.
Marty Cherrix, 828/230-6692. 217 Paragon Pkwy, #116 Clyde, 28721.
Craig, Mark, and Lisa Fincannon, CSA, Fincannon and Associates Casting, 910/251-
1500, 910/262-2003, fincannoncasting.com, 1235 N. 23rd St., Wilmington, 28405.
TALENT AGENCIES
The Brock Agency, Inc., Beverly Brock, 828/322-8553. thebrockagency.com. Email:
beverly@thebrockagency.com. 329 13th Ave NW Hickory, 28601. Beverly's website
thebrockagency.com has information on how to purchase the very important Southeast
Actor's Guide. Actors living in this area are lucky to have this most valuable guide! There
is also other interesting information and links on the site.
JTA Talent, Inc., Linda Newcomb and Kecia Michelle, 704/377-5987. jta-talent.com.
Email: janoneill@jta-talent.com. 820 East Blvd., Charlotte, 28203.
Capital Artists of NC, 919/458-6839. Email: caiofnc@aol.com. 1405 Bloomingdale
Drive, Cary, 27511.

Marilyn's, Inc., Kathy Moore, Agent, 336/292-5950. marilyn-s.com. Email: models@marilyn-s.com. 601 Norwalk St., Greensboro, 27407.

Talent One, Anne Greene, 919/872-4828. Talentone.net. Email: tlntone@aol.com. 1305 E. Millbrook Rd. Ste. C32 Raleigh, 27609.

William Pettit Agency, Bill Pettit, 704/643-8880. futuregloryracing.com. Email: billpettit@aol.com. P.O. Box 11798, Charlotte, 28220.

Talent Link, Inc., Vince Paul and Rosa Paul, 704/333-0027. talent-link.com. Email: director@talent-link.com. P.O. Box 480035, Charlotte, 28269.

Artists Resource Agency, 336/349-6167, artistsresourceagency.com.

Talent Trek, 828/251-0173, talenttrek.com/main/index.cfm.

UNION OFFICES, ASSOCIATIONS

North Carolina Film Commissions, awnc.org. Email: 121webb@bellsouth.net.

The Charlotte Regional Film Office, Beth Petty, Director, charlotteusa.com.

Winston Salem Piedmont Triad Film Commission, piedmontfilm.com.

Research Triangle Partnership, Charles Hayes, Executive Director, researchtriangle.org.

Durham Film Office, Carolyn Carney, durham-nc.com.

Wilmington Regional Film Commission, Johnny Griffin, Director, wilmingtonfilm.com.

North Carolina Eastern Region, Leonard D. Kulik, Project Manager, nceast.org.

Charlotte Film and Video Association, cfvonline.com.

Professional Actors' Association, caan.biz.

CLASSES, COACHES, STUDIOS

• Acting coaches are not as easily found here as in New York or Los Angeles. Some Talent Agents and Casting Agents teach their own classes locally or bring in coaches from major markets for acting seminars.

Joan Darling, 919/928-8088. Emmy award-winning actress and acting coach. Teaches acting for both the stage and screen in classes and privately. She often travels and teaches in seminars. If you get a chance, study with her. She is the best.

The Film School at North Carolina School of the Arts in Winston-Salem holds semiannual open casting calls. Directors will be casting for their film projects. For further information call Janice Wellerstein in the Production Office, 336/770-1322. This is an extremely impressive school and student filmmakers have won the top prize at the prestigious 2000 Angelus Award. One of their senior thesis films won Showtime's Black Filmmaker Showcase.

Piedmont Community College, 336/694-5707. piedmont.cc.nc.us. 331 Piedmont Drive, Box 1150, Yanceyville, 27379. Sarah Costello, Co-coordinator, Michael Corbett, Director.

Lees-McRae College is known for its great stage company and musicals. Auditions are held, usually in February, for students who are interested in being a part of Lees-McRae Summer Theatre. Professional auditions in order to hire the best possible performers for the company.

East Carolina University in Greenville is also a great theatre school and a great beginning for new actors. Diversity in the theatre offerings as well as apprenticeships. Timothy O'Keefe, timothy@timothyokeefe.net.

HEADSHOT PHOTOGRAPHERS

Taylormacy Photography, Inc., Kristin Vining, 704/258-3117. taylormacy.com. 118 E. Kingston Ave., Suite 34, Charlotte, 28203.

WEBSITES, PUBLICATIONS

Actors' Grapevine, auditions and resources, actorsgrapevine.com.

Tar Heel Films, auditions, production, and resources, tarheelfilms.com.

• SOUTH FLORIDA

• **Most of the acting opportunities are in South Florida.** However, there are the occasional jobs in the northern part of the state. Actors in Orlando should contact Brevard Talent, 407/841-7775, brevardtalentgroup.com for representation.

WEBSITES, PUBLICATIONS

Actors Info Booth, actorsinfobooth.com. A tremendous resource for actors with information on how the business works in Florida as well as resource lists, industry news workshops and castings.

Film in Florida, like Variety but for Florida, filminflorida.com.

Florida Actors, message board of film jobs and castings, florida-actors.com.

Florida Film Directory, filmfla.com/index.cfm.

Green Room (resources and discussion forums), greenroomorlando.com.

Florida Acting, floridaacting.com.

Actor websites, actorsgetawebsitehere.com. Specializing in actor websites.

CLASSES, COACHES, STUDIOS

Marc Durso, 954/647-7569. acttrue.com. Classes in Hagen Process, Linklater voice and Imagery Tech throughout US and Europe. Past clients can be seen in blockbuster films, TV shows, commercials, etc. Proven technique that reveals truthful human behavior. No tricks, no gimmicks, no shortcuts, no attitudes!

Workshops, 954/731.4888. LA and NY industry professionals teaching in Florida, actorsinfobooth.com/workshops

Norene Bini, 305/891-0047. Dialogue and dialect coach, specializes in Spanish, French , Italian.

CASTING OFFICES

Dee Miller Casting, 305/757-6055, 7300 NE 4th Ct., Miami, 33138.

Lori Wyman Casting, 305/354-3901, 16499 NE 19th Ave., Miami, 33162.

Di Prima Casting, 305/672-9232, (3 locations) diprimacasting.com

Ellen Jacoby Casting, 305/531-5300, 300 Biscayne Blvd., No. 1150, Miami, 33131.

Protocol Models on the Gulf—Casting, 239/417-1200, 5017 Tamiami Trail East, Naples, 34113.

The Extras Group, 305/981-7580, theextrasgroup.com.

• **More casting directors** can be found at actrosinfobooth.com.

TALENT AGENCIES

• There are a number of both union and nonunion agencies in South Florida. For a complete listing, check out Actors Info Booth Inc. at actorsinfobooth.com.

UNION OFFICES, ASSOCIATIONS

Florida Film Commission, filmflorida.org.

THEATRES

Red Barn Theatre. 305/293-3035. Box 707, Key West, 33401. Casting: Open call for AEA actors in October. managing director, Mimi McDonald. Opportunities for interns.

Riverside Theatre, Inc. 772/231-5860. riversidetheatre.com. 3250 Riverside Park Drive, Vero Beach, 32963. Casting: auditions through Florida Professional Theatre Assoc..

Florida Stage, 561/585-3404. floridastage.org. 262 South Ocean Blvd, Manalapan, 33462. Casting: open calls during the summer months, send pix to Nancy Barnett, managing director.

HEADSHOT PHOTOGRAPHERS
Bob Lasky, 305/891-0550. boblasky.com. North Miami. You can use pictures taken by him in Los Angeles.
Paul Greco, paulgrecophotography.com.
Lynn Parks, lynnparks.com.
PHOTO DUPLICATION
G.N.A. Professional Photo Lab, 305/893-3500, gnaphoto@msn.com. 12460 NE 13th Place North, Miami, 33161.

• NASHVILLE
CASTING OFFICES
Jo Doster, CSA, 615/463-9883.
Regina Moore, Talent Connection Casting, 615/831-0039, moorecasting.com, 417 Welshwood Dr., Ste. 109, Nashville, 37211.
Suzzane Skinner, Image Casting, 615/251-1400, imagecasting.com, 118 16th Ave. S., Music Row 200, Nashville, 37203.
TALENT AGENCIES
Advantage Models and Talent, Carol Lahrman, 615/790-5001, advantagemodel.com, Nashville.
Agency for the Performing Arts, Brad Sugarman, 615/297-0100, apa-agency.com.
Dan Agency Models and Talent, 615/244-3266, danagency.com, 1104 16th Ave. S., Nashville, 37212.
DS Entertainment, Darlene Studie-McDowell, 615/331-6264, dsentertainment.com, 4741 Trousdale Dr., Ste. 2, Nashville, 37220.
Opry Link Modeling and Talent, 615/320-9501, 50 Music Square West, Nashville, 37203.
Sharon Smith Talent, 615/742-4277, sharonsmithtalent.com.
Talent Trek, Evelyn Foster, 615/279-0010, talenttrek.com/main/index.cfm, 2021 21st Ave. S., Ste. 102, Nashville, 37212. Website also has a great resource list with links.
The Cannon Group, Ms. Jimmi McCarter, 615/297-0608.
TML Talent Agency, Betty Clark, 615/321-5596, PO Box 40763, Nashville, 37204.
UNION OFFICES, ASSOCIATIONS
Film Nashville, filmnashville.com.
Tennessee Film, Entertainment, and Music Commission, state.tn.us/film.
THEATRE
Clarence Brown Theatre at the University of Tennessee. 865/974-6011. 206 McClung Tower, Knoxville, 37996. MFA program in Acting.
Playhouse on the Square, 901/725-0776. 51 South Cooper, Memphis, 38104.
WEBSITES, PUBLICATIONS
Nashville Rage, audition listings, nashvillerage.com.
Nashville Scene, free paper with audition listings.
The Tennessean, audition listings in the Sunday edition, tennessean.com.

• NEW ORLEANS
1st Step Consulting, 985/649-0561, 1stsca.com. Training, pictures and booking for models and actors.

ACTORS IMMIGRATING TO THE USA

INFORMATION AND WORK VISAS

• **There are hundreds of foreign actors who have found success** in American film and television. Jackie Chan, Nicole Kidman, Antonio Banderas, Charlize Theron, Hugh Grant, Penelope Cruz, Mike Myers, Juliette Binoche, etc. That's just a very short list of some of the most successful; that doesn't include all the actors whose names we may not know, who are routinely working here in films, television shows and theatre.

• **Because of the efforts to encourage diversity in casting** by the unions and other associations, there are more opportunities today for foreign actors. According to the U.S. Department of State, there were 32,040 performer visas issued in 2004. That should be encouraging; why shouldn't you be one of those people out of the thousands? You must be a well-trained, committed, dedicated, lucky actor to become eligible to work here.

• **There are rules and regulations** to be followed if you are a foreign performer wanting to work in the United States. The most important is that you need to obtain a **work visa!** I can't stress this enough. A tourist visa works fine for scouting, but only lasts for a few months. And people that continually try to keep coming back on a tourist visa are a red flag for immigration officials. And remember, if you don't have a work permit, immigration officials can send you back to your country essentially at any time. Plus, most talent agents, casting directors and producers simply won't hire you without a work visa as it poses a huge risk for them.

• **Getting a work visa can be difficult.** It is often tedious and expensive. For more information on what is required, go to the U.S. Department of State at travel.state.gov and U.S. Citizenship and Immigration Services at uscis.gov. You also need to get a Social Security number. If you are having difficulty with the process, there are a number of Los Angeles attorneys who specialize in this field.

• **Actor Michael Cohen** provided this information on moving here from Canada to work.

   • **In order to work in the U.S.,** Canadians either need a visa or a green card. Visa's are expensive and hard to come by, but green cards are even more difficult. So I'll focus on the visa. The visa for actors is the 0-1 visa which is the "extraordinary ability" visa. It is also for athletes, singers, dancers, comedians etc. You can only work in the area for which you apply. So if you're a comedian, you can only do comedy. If you're a dancer, you can only dance. They are granted for a period of up to three years and then have to be renewed annually. In order to get the visa, you have to prove your "extraordinary ability." Proof is provided via letters of recommendation from producers, directors, casting directors, etc. that you've worked with.

   • **You have to also include copies** of any press, playbills, etc. In addition, you must provide a letter from a management organization in the U.S., letter from a peer group (union), a petitioning organization in the U.S. (a production company, a talent agent, a manager...) Actor's applying for the visa also have to supply a proposed itinerary of work for their next three years. Of course, they have to make it up because no one knows what they will be doing. It's not hard to put together and an immigration lawyer working on the actor's behalf should be able to provide a sample (as well as sample reference letters).

   • **The legal costs run** $5,000 (Canadian) plus tax. The application fee is $195 plus $1,000 to expedite the application. Actors will also have to join one of the unions (SAG or AFTRA) in order to get a letter from them, so you should budget in another $1,500 for initiation fees.

• **An attorney who asked that his name not be used** says he has seen actors get work on just a tourist visa and work for many years, essentially cheating the system. But he doesn't recommend it. He does recommend obtaining a work permit well ahead of your move here.

• **Actress Gloria Carmona recommends:**

   • **The most effective way to get a visa** is to enroll in a Los Angeles acting school, something you can do online. With the registration form an embassy will give you a student visa so you can come here to study. Of course while you are here you can decide if this city is for you.

An EST (English as a Second Language) class at UCLA is always an instant student visa for the length of the course, which will provide enough time to find other solutions once you're here.

• **Another way to become eligible to work here** is to marry a USA citizen. From a friend:

- **My immigration process started** in 2002 when my husband and I got married by a judge in Van Nuys. The next step was to fill out processing sheet form I-485 and send it to the immigration office downtown. In a couple of months, I received an "alien number" and authorization for work in the U.S. Then I was able to get my Social Security number.

- **In about a year and a half**, my husband and I were called for an interview where we had to present the documentation that proved that we've been living together as a husband and wife. That's how I received my green card, good for two years.

- **About six months before my green card expired**, my lawyers prepared my documents and once again I needed to show everything that proved that my marriage was legitimate, pictures together, tax returns, etc. Fortunately, they did not request another interview, so I just showed up in the immigration office downtown with two photos, filled out an application in front of the officer and gave a fingerprint. They said I should receive my permanent green card in about six months. After that, I will qualify for American citizenship. I consider myself very lucky because I went through all this in a very short period of time.

• **Another way is to land a leading role** in a film shooting in your country and make a name for yourself. If you become "in demand" as an actor, the producers will move mountains and the immigration service to get you a work visa. Another option is to open a business here. Of course that takes a great amount of money, but if you are in a family business you may talk the family into expanding it to Los Angeles. Be creative.

• **My advice is to make a scouting trip to Los Angeles**, see how the industry works, talk with everybody you can and make the decision on whether you would like to live here. If it looks promising, follow the guidelines and get the process rolling as quickly as possible.

• **For American actors wanting to work in other countries,** look up local government websites for rules and regulations pertaining to working in a particular country.

• **When moving to Los Angeles**, one of the most valuable skills you can have to broaden your casting range is the ability to speak with a Standard American dialect.

Resources

To download and print an updated version of this and all resource lists, go to actingiseverything.com.

U.S. Citizenship and Immigration Services, uscis.gov. The place to go to find out about living and working in the U.S.

U.S. Department of State, travel.state.gov. Where to get all the information you need on different types of visas and work permits.

U.S. Immigration Support, usimmigrationsupport.org. An independent agency set up to help foreigners obtain the necessary permits to work in the U.S.

Screen Actors Guild, sag.org. The acting union does provide a little information on the website for foreign actors. The union also has a branch dedicated to encouraging diversity in casting.

Carl Shusterman, 213/623-4592, shusterman.com, 600 Wilshire Blvd., Ste. 1550, Los Angeles, 90017. Considered by many industry professionals to be one of the best who works specifically on immigration law. Featured in the Martindale Hubbell Legal Directory, which is a listing on the top U.S. attorneys as decided by their peers.

Fragomen, Del Rey, Bernsen and Loewy, 310/820-3322, fragomen.com, 12121 Wilshire Blvd, Suite 1001, L.A., 90025. An international firm; immigration is their specialty. Margaret David is the attorney my friend used.

Lawyers.com. A website designed by Martindale Hubbell to help you find the best attorneys no matter what your legal issue or where you're located. Very easy to use. A search for immigration attorneys in Los Angeles pulled up dozens.

In Canada:
Borden, Ladner, Gervais, 416/367-6127, blgcanada.com. A number of attorneys throughout Canada, they work on a number of legal issues, including immigration.

Guberman, Garson and Bush, 416/363-1234, gubermangarson.com. Specializes solely in immigration. Heather Segal is a lawyer there that specializes in actor's immigration. Recommended by actor Michael Cohen.

Latino Organization:
Nosotros, 323/465-4167, nosotros.org. They hold networking brunches every three months. "An event for the entertainment industry professional as well as the Hollywood hopeful. It is 'a place where we aspire to inspire' and honor special guest speakers from every aspect of the entertainment business." You do not have to be a member to attend. Membership is $50 a year and meetings are the first Wednesday of each month. Online membership is available for $40 a year. If you are Spanish-speaking, I would think you would want to be a part of this long established group.

See the Voice and Voice Teachers Section for coaches who can help you lose or refine your accent.

INDEX

ABOUT THE AUTHOR

Accomplished acting coach, actress and director, Judy Kerr brings over 25 years of experience to this 11th edition of *Acting Is Everything*.

Photo by Kevyn Major Howard
kevynmajorhoward.com

Judy is recognized in Hollywood for her unique gift of nurturing talent and helping actors succeed. Coaching one-on-one with some of the top names in the business, Judy works to enhance the artistry and technical skills of actors while building their confidence so they deliver their best performance.

As dialogue coach on the hit series *Seinfeld*, she worked with the series regulars Jerry Seinfeld, Julia Louis-Dreyfus, Michael Richards and Jason Alexander as well as the show's many guest stars including Teri Hatcher, Janeane Garofalo, Raquel Welch and Bette Midler.

Other television coaching credits include: *It's All Relative, All About The Andersons, Bob Patterson, The Ellen Show, The Michael Richards Show, It's like, you know..., The Single Guy, Alright Already*.

Her cable television show in Los Angeles, *Judy Kerr's Acting Is Everything*, is in its 18th season. She is the bestselling author of ten previous editions of *Acting Is Everything*, contributing to the success of thousands of readers.

With this 11th Gold Edition, Judy opens the doors of Hollywood to a new generation of acting hopefuls and professionals with a straight-forward road map for building their careers. Judy Kerr takes special pleasure helping young talent and veterans grow as she continues to coach both privately and on sets, and to teach workshops and seminars worldwide.

Email: Judy@JudyKerr.com